# Learn to Program Databases with Visual Basic 6

John Smiley

Active Path Ltd. ®

# Learn to Program Databases with Visual Basic 6



First published August 1999

activepath

Published by Active Path Ltd, Arden House, 1102 Warwick Road, Acocks Green, Birmingham, B27 6BH, United Kingdom

Printed in USA

ISBN 1-902745-03-5.

## Trademark Acknowledgements



## Credits

**Author**
John Smiley

**Development Editor**
Andy Corsham

**Technical Editors**
Andy Corsham
Donna Covey
Devin Lunsford
Liz Toy

**Layout and Production Team**
Tom Bartlett
David 'Dave' Boyce
Mark Burdett
Jonathan Jones
John McNulty
Hubert St. Gerard

**Technical Reviewers**
Humberto Abreu
Monica Atkinson
Dr. Zoë M Backman
Eddie Correia
Antoine Giusti
Emma Morgan
Marc Simkin

**Index**
Martin Brooks
Andrew Criddle

**Cover**
Chris Morris

## About the Author

John Smiley, a Microsoft Certified Professional in Visual Basic, is the President of John Smiley and Associates, a computer consulting firm located in South Jersey that serves clients large and small in the Philadelphia Metropolitan area. John is also an adjunct professor of computer science at Penn State University, the Philadelphia College of Textiles and Science, and Holy Family College, and has been teaching computer programming courses for nearly 20 years. He also teaches a number of very popular online courses for Ziff Davis University (ZDU).

On the writing front, John is the author of *Learn to Program with Visual Basic 6* and *Learn to Program with Visual Basic Examples*, both published by ActivePath, and has done technical editing on a number of Wrox Press and Que Visual Basic titles. You can find a case study he wrote in *Beginning Visual Basic 6* by Wrox Press. He is also the author of 4 ZDU Workbooks.

Feel free to visit John's Web Site at

`http://www.johnsmiley.com`

or contact him via email at `johnsmiley@johnsmiley.com`. He religiously answers all of his emails, although not necessarily instantaneously!

## Dedication

This book is dedicated to my wife Linda.


## Acknowledgments

First and foremost, I want to thank my wife Linda for her love and support.

My thanks also go to my three wonderful children, Tom, Kevin and Melissa. A third book is no easier on the family of the author than the first two – there are still pleas for quiet, which can be almost impossible to be had with three children. Each one of my children contributed in a way to this book. Tom and Kevin, as budding Visual Basic programmers, provided me with ideas for questions that beginning Visual Basic programmers might need answered. Melissa, who at the time I wrote my first book spent time on my lap asking me to read Snow White to her, is now a 3 year old who once again kept me company while writing this book. Snow White is still her favorite story!

Many thanks go to the great People at Active Path/Wrox Press. Once again, I want to thank Dave Maclean for giving me the opportunity to pursue my dream of writing innovative books on computer programming. I want to thank Andy Corsham, Donna Covey and Devin Lunsford, my editors at Active Path, for their dedicated hard work in getting this book ready for publication. Many thanks to all of my other friends at Wrox and Active Path for their kind words and encouragement.

Books aren't produced in a vacuum. Behind the scenes there are reviewers, technical editors, artists, layout specialists, copy editors, indexers, and a group of marketing experts all working towards the goal of making the book a success. My thanks to all of you.

Many thanks also go to the thousands of students I've taught over the years for your tireless dedication to learning the art and science of computer programming. Your great questions and demanding persistence in getting the most out of your learning experience truly inspired me, and has contributed greatly to my books. Many of you dragged yourself to class after a long hard day of work, or rose early on your Saturday day off to learn Visual Basic and the other programming languages I have taught. You have my greatest respect and admiration.

I want to thank the many readers of my first two books, *Learn to Program with Visual Basic 6*, and *Learn to Program with Visual Basic Examples*, who took the time to write to me about those books. I truly appreciate hearing from you, and I want you to know that I read and respond to each email I receive.

I want to thank all the members of my family for their belief in and support of me over the years, in particular my mother, who continues to say several hundred novenas for the success of my books. Special thanks to Bob and Pat for giving my books priority placement in bookstore windows whenever you can!

Finally, I want to acknowledge my father who, although not physically here to see this book, is surely flipping through the pages of it right now. It's been nearly twenty five years since I last saw you – and your role in the writing of this and my first two books can never be understated –you and mother have been a great inspiration and role models for me. As I've said before, I know that the God who made us all will someday permit us to be together again.

isual Basic Learn to Program Databas
ith Visual Basic Learn to Progra
atabases with Visual Basic Learn
rogram Databases with Visual Basic Lea
o Program Databases with Visual Bas
earn to Program Databases with Visu
asic Learn to Program Databases wi
isual Basic Learn to Program Databas
ith Visual Basic Learn to Progra
atabases with Visual Basic Learn
rogram Databases with Visual Basic Lea
o Program Databases with Visual Bas
earn to Program Databases with Visu
asic Learn to Program Databases wi
isual Basic Learn to Program Databas
ith Visual Basic Learn to Progra
atabases with Visual Basic Learn

# Table of Contents

isual Basic Learn to Program Databas
vith Visual Basic Learn to Progra
atabases with Visual Basic Learn
rogram Databases with Visual Basic Lea
o Program Databases with Visual Bas
earn to Program Databases with Visu
asic Learn to Program Databases wi
isual Basic Learn to Program Databas
vith Visual Basic Learn to Progra
atabases with Visual Basic Learn
rogram Databases with Visual Basic Lea
o Program Databases with Visual Bas
earn to Program Databases with Visu
asic Learn to Program Databases wi
isual Basic Learn to Program Databas
vith Visual Basic Learn to Progra
atabases with Visual Basic Learn

# Introduction

Most programs that really have something useful to say will use a database in some way. Whether it's a customer and inventory program for a store, or a program that helps you find exactly the right video for your current mood, you'll find that 9 times out of 10, there'll be a database behind it. And if you want to really get serious with data storage, you'll probably want to go beyond using text files to store your data.

But databases are *difficult*, aren't they? Well yes, they are, but with a little work you'll be up and running with the best of them. I warn you, it's not like falling off a log, but you *can* do it. Just like anything else, if you can break it down and see it working, all will become clear. And that's what we'll do in this book.

But don't you need to know a lot of database theory? Well, kind of, and we'll be tackling it as and when we need to. We'll be putting it into context, too, so that you can see what it means in relation to a real project. I think you'll find it a challenging and rewarding experience. By the end of this book, you'll have a grasp of the fundamentals, and a firm foundation to build on as your experience and knowledge grows.

## Who is this Book for?

You've already taken your first steps into Visual Basic programming. In fact, you've probably written a program or two yourself. Anyway, you know your way around, and you can probably work out what's going by looking at a section of code. But you've come to realize that a program without data is like a car without gas. If you can build one, it's quite impressive-looking, but it won't go anywhere in a hurry. Now you want to know how you can use databases in your programs to really unleash their potential. That's what we're going to do here.

You need to be comfortable discussing core VB terminology and code. If you've read John Smiley's previous books and understand pretty much everything you've learned (I don't mean that you need to *remember* everything, but that if you looked it up, you'd still understand it), then you should find this book useful. Or if you've come up the VB tree a different way, by reading another text or taking a course, and you can work your way through a VB problem without having to ask too many questions, you should also be comfortable with this book. It's a hard climb, but we've supplied the ropes, tools, and handholds that you'll need to make it to the top. And, of course, you have the best guide there is, right by your side, talking you through the climb.

If you aren't confident about your VB skills, consider working through John's previous books, *Learn to Program with Visual Basic 6* and *Learn to Program with Visual Basic Examples*. And practise!

## What will you Need?

Well, you'll need to be running some edition of Visual Basic 6. If you don't already have Visual Basic, consider purchasing *Learn to Program with Visual Basic 6*, which actually includes the Visual Basic **Working Model Edition**. Everything in this book works fine with this stripped-down version of VB, and that way you can get a working copy of VB to try out for under $30!

If you have Microsoft Access, that'll also help, as you'll be creating a database as part of the project. If you don't have Access on your machine, don't worry, because you can use the database we've supplied on the CD, pre-built and ready to talk to Visual Basic (you'll find the database file in the For Chapter 4 folder on the CD).

## What's Covered?

This book teaches you the basics of using a database with Visual Basic. As in the previous *Learn to Program with Visual Basic* titles, we aim to give you depth rather than breadth. So, what we cover, we cover in detail, so that you'll absorb and understand it.

Essentially, what we teach you in this book is this:

- How to approach database design and implementation tasks
- Basic database theory
- How to design and build a database using Microsoft Access
- How to communicate with the database using Visual Basic
- How to create a solid user interface so that your program's users get the most out of the database
- How to integrate the database and the Visual Basic program

## How's the Book Structured?

I'd like to make the distinction between 'hard' and 'too hard'. A lot of people think that if something's hard, they can't do it. That's just not true. It just needs a little more work. Hopefully this book takes DB programming from the realms of 'too hard' back down into being 'hard'.

Structurally, this means that we want to give you a consistent project to relate your learning to. Here, we use an existing program – the China Shop program – which John Smiley and his students built in a previous book. But don't worry if you haven't got that book – we supply the base project on the CD in the back of *this* book, so you're ready to pick it straight up and run with it. If you *did* build the China Shop project already, you can continue working with your own version.

**For instructions on getting the China Shop project up on your PC, please refer to Appendix B**

The China Shop program was designed and built to cater for the computing needs of a small store.

We'll talk you through the China shop program as it stood at the end of the previous book (Chapter 1). Next, we'll teach you the basics of database theory and how they relate to the China Shop (Chapter 2), and then we'll design and build the database itself (Chapter 3). The rest of the book (Chapters 4 through 10) focuses on applying this database knowledge and expanding it as we enhance the China Shop project.

## What's on the CD?

The CD in the back of this book contains all of the code to get the China Shop installed on your machine as it stood at the end of the previous *Learn to Program with Visual Basic 6* book.

**If you didn't read our previous title, you'll need to copy across the China Shop program before you can get started on this book – see Appendix B for how to do this properly.**

The CD also has folders containing the project at various stages as we add to it in *this* book. We've supplied this pre-built code so that you have a backup version if your own code gets lost, destroyed, or corrupted.

However, we really do recommend that you create your own enhanced, database-enabled version of the China Shop program by keying all the code yourself rather than copying the 'built in stages' versions that we've supplied on the CD. The whole point of the *Learn to Program* series is that you *learn by doing*, building your skills and expertise through practice. You owe it to yourself to build the code in this book for yourself.

## Do I Get any Support?

What do you do if you get stuck in a book?

You're not alone, OK? Just remember that. The Active Path website on **`www.activepath.com`** is there as a resource for you to use. There'll be the opportunity to ask the book's editors questions and give us feedback (positive or negative – we can take it). Just email us at **`feedback@activepath.com`** if you have a question or suggestion about the book. Please don't ask us about general VB questions, though, unless they're really related to the books – we'd love to be able to help you out individually but there just isn't enough time in the day to do that *and* bring out the great books you want to see from Active Path.

## What is Active Path?

Active Path is a reasonably new publishing house with a fresh attitude to learning about computer programming. As a publisher, we understand your need to have the most up-to-date, cutting edge information about the computing world around you. We also understand that the computing world is full of jargon, and awash with unhelpful books that either treat you like an idiot or talk over your head, making no attempt to help you *learn* and build your skills.

So what makes Active Path different? Books from Active Path start at your level. There will always be an entry-level book, for which there's no previous experience required – guaranteed. We're not going to blindly show you everything about a subject in one massive brain-dump; we'll present the concepts when they become relevant to the problem. We don't believe anything is too complicated to learn; but we do believe that if you can imagine the problem, we should be able to illustrate the solution in terms you can understand.

We like detailed examples, and giving you the chance to work out your own solutions to problems designed to get you thinking and applying your knowledge. Most books try to cover everything, but end up leaving you baffled. We think that if you can pick it up and use it yourself, you're well on the way to thinking it's not so hard after all.
Basically, we believe that you should be able to learn what you want, how you want, when you want, and at a pace you feel comfortable with. All we do is write books to let you do that.

## What about Text Styles?

To help you pick out important pieces of information and distinguish a piece of code in a paragraph of text, we've used certain fonts and styles throughout the book. We've kept it simple, so we don't distract you from the content, which we believe is the key here. Here are examples of each kind of style we use:

Since this book is about programming, there are quite a few times when we need to point out pieces of code. There are three ways of doing it, but they all look similar, so you can easily pick them out of a crowd. Sometimes we'll use `this style` to refer to a `procedure` or `code-related thing` in the middle of the text.

```
When we describe new code, it'll be displayed on gray like this

If you see this twisted arrow symbol,
↳ it means that you should type all the code on one line,
↳ leaving out the twisted arrow.
↳ Don't try to find this symbol on your keyboard -
↳ it's not there!
```

```
Code that has already been explained won't have the gray background.

↳ Quite often it will be a chunk of code you've seen before, but we've
↳ changed one line of it, or added something. So the new part looks
↳ like this.
```

Important **terms** and **new phrases** will be bolded like this.

Text from a Menu or on buttons appears like this, much as it does on the screen.

> **If we want to point out something important that you need to know, it will stand out like this.**

**And if John's scribbling merrily away on his whiteboard, it'll show up like this.**

OK – let's *Learn to Program Databases with Visual Basic 6.*

isual Basic Learn to Program Databas
vith Visual Basic Learn to Progra
atabases with Visual Basic Learn
rogram Databases with Visual Basic Lea
o Program Databases with Visual Bas
earn to Program Databases with Visu
asic Learn to Program Databases wi
isual Basic Learn to Program Databas
vith Visual Basic Learn to Progra
atabases with Visual Basic Learn
rogram Databases with Visual Basic Lea
o Program Databases with Visual Bas
earn to Program Databases with Visu
asic Learn to Program Databases wi
isual Basic Learn to Program Databas
vith Visual Basic Learn to Progra
atabases with Visual Basic Learn

# Chapter 1
# The China Shop Revisited

In this chapter, we'll begin our examination of database programming in Visual Basic by looking at the real-world based program called the China Shop project, which was developed and written in my first book, *Learn to Program with Visual Basic*. Don't worry if you haven't read that book; it doesn't really matter where your knowledge of Visual Basic came from as long as you understand a little about it – and if there's anything important from the original book that you need to know then I'll explain it here. If you *have* read my first book then please be patient during these explanations – I need to make sure that everyone is keeping up!

During the course of this chapter and the remainder of this book, we'll modify the China Shop project to utilize Visual Basic's database capabilities to store and retrieve information using a Microsoft Access database. Quite naturally, along the way, we'll learn a bit about database theory and design as well.

## Why Databases are important in Visual Basic Programming

As you develop your programming skills, it will become important for you to be able to maintain data or information after a program ends. You will often want this information to be available again when the program restarts. This characteristic – maintaining data and making it available again – is called **data persistence**. In my first book we looked at two ways of implementing data persistence – through the use of disk data files, and through the use of the Windows Registry.

The Windows Registry is great for maintaining snippets of information such as the user's preferred color settings, or whether or not they wish to see the date and time displayed. However, it's not an ideal way to maintain more voluminous data such as a list of customers' names or telephone numbers, or prices of inventory in your China Shop. That's the type of information that we maintained in a disk data file in the Bullina China Shop project in *Learn to Program with Visual Basic*.

There's nothing wrong with maintaining this type of information in the registry or in a disk file. However, in this book we'll be learning a third way, which is both more elegant and more efficient. You'll see how a modern database management program such as Microsoft Access provides the programmer with features – such as data validation, and quick, powerful search capabilities – that simply aren't available by using disk data files.

For those of you unfamiliar with the learning paradigm in *Learn to Program with Visual Basic*, this chapter (and the rest of the book) will place you in a classroom setting as my university class and I modify the China Shop project for database interaction. Follow along with us, and have fun at the same time!

# The China Shop Revisited

For those of you unfamiliar with our story, during the course of my fall semester **Introduction to Visual Basic** course at Penn State University, my students and I had designed and programmed a price quotation program for Joe Bullina, the owner of the Bullina China Shop. It was with quite a bit of celebration and fanfare that we had delivered the final working version of the program to Joe at the end of the fall semester class. As part of our agreement with Joe, a number of the students from the class had agreed to check in with him from time to time to see how the program was operating. All of the reports I had received indicated that the program was operating very well and that Joe was delighted with it.

Shortly after the Christmas holidays, however, I was surprised to receive a frantic telephone call from Joe. From the sound of his voice, you would have thought that the world was ending. Midge – probably his most valued employee – had just told him that she was retiring as of March 1$^{st}$. Midge was the only person in the China Shop with any real computer experience. It was Midge who, each week, updated the inventory prices for the China Shop program, using Microsoft Notepad to edit the `Prices.txt` disk file stored on the PC's hard disk drive.

"I don't know what I'll do without her," Joe told me in a panic. "There's no-one else here who understands how the china inventory prices are updated. What am I going to do if I need to change prices?"

I did my best to try to calm Joe. I recalled that we had designed the China Shop program to read inventory prices from a disk file for one reason only – disk file access was part of the introductory Visual Basic course curriculum. I had a brainwave: why not use Joe's problem to drive forward my next course, too? After all, I would be meeting with my Visual Basic Database Programming class in just a few weeks.

"You know, Joe," I said, "I think there are some changes we can make to the program to make it a great deal friendlier for you and the rest of the office staff. The method we chose to update inventory prices was chosen mainly because it was simpler for my class to program."

I explained to Joe that in a few weeks – two weeks, to be precise – many of those same students would be returning to the university as members of my Visual Basic database class.

"By using database processing," I said, "we can make the updating of your inventory prices a seamless part of the program itself. That means no more Microsoft Notepad to update your prices."

"I don't know what a database is," Joe said, "but if you can make updating inventory prices as easy to use as the rest of the program, I'll be a very happy man!"

I offered to run this idea by my Visual Basic database class during our first class meeting – I had no real doubt that they would readily agree to work on another real world application, and I asked Joe if he would mind meeting with us on that first day of class. He accepted enthusiastically.

## I Meet with my Database Programming Class

Two weeks later, on a cold and windy Saturday morning, I met with my Visual Basic Database Programming class for the first time. The database class is a popular follow-on class after my introductory course, and runs for ten weeks instead of fifteen.

Joe Bullina and I had agreed that he would arrive about an hour into the first class and that I would introduce him. The first day of a follow-on class like this one is almost like a reunion day, as so many of the students already know one another and, of course, me!

As I entered the teaching lab, I noticed immediately that some changes had occurred since the end of the previous semester. There was new carpeting on the floor, and the PCs had been upgraded; we now had eighteen new Gateway computers. I should tell you that my university classroom is about 40 feet by 20 feet, with a double set of three rows of long tables, each one holding 3 PCs. Each student has use of their own PC, and in the front of the room I have my own PC, cabled to a projector that enables me to show the contents of my video display on a large screen at the front of the room.

Having spent fifteen Saturday mornings together the previous semester, many of the students were talking comfortably with one another. Just about all of the faces were familiar. I exchanged greetings with several of the students and asked how everyone was. At nine o'clock I formally welcomed everyone to the Penn State Visual Basic Database Programming class.

I began by distributing a catalog from the university bookstore listing the academic software titles in stock (there were a bunch), and then distributed my two-page class syllabus. This semester I had gone high-tech – I used the classroom projector to display an HTML version of the class syllabus residing on my Web site.

As I opened up my roll book, I asked each one of my eighteen students to write a brief biography of themselves explaining why they were in the class and what, if any, special questions they needed answering. I had been putting students through this ritual for a number of years. The written biography gives me a chance to get to know the students a little bit, without the pressure of forcing them to "open themselves up" via an oral introduction to a room full of strangers. It's helpful if I know something about the abilities of my students before I start.

I gave the class about five minutes to compose their biographies, and when they were done, I collected them and placed them in a pile in front of me.

I then began to formally call the roll. As usual, I called out only first names – I like to keep the class as informal as possible. Calling the roll took a bit longer than usual – it always does in a follow-on class like this. During the fall semester, I had grown to know many of them very well. Spending sixteen weeks with a group of people will do that – and that familiarity was amplified since we had all shared such a great experience building the original China Shop Project.

Alphabetically (by last name), I called out the roll in the following order:

**Valerie**, **Peter** and **Kate** – they had all been members of the Introductory Visual Basic class. I was also glad to see that **Rhonda** was back. In the introductory class, even though we basically developed the China Shop program as a team, each student in the class had been encouraged to complete their own version of the program. Although I personally don't like the idea of competition in my classes, we really had no choice but to hold a little 'contest' on the last day of class to see whose program would be the one installed and run in the China Shop. The consensus of the members of the class had been to use Rhonda's version of the program in the Bullina China Shop. To say that she had been elated that day would be a gross understatement. Rhonda – by her own admission – had been the student who asked the most questions – questions that other computer instructors might have considered 'dumb'. But I had welcomed Rhonda's questions. She asked questions that probably were in the minds of other students as well – questions that might have gone unasked and unanswered without her.

Everyone at the university knew that in my classroom there was no such thing as a dumb question: as far as I'm concerned, nothing is obvious in the world of computers. And of course, for Rhonda, her continual questioning had paid off with a project that was just about perfect.

Continuing on with the roll...

**Kevin**, **Tom**, **Melissa** and **Rachel** were new students to the university, and seemed a bit uneasy. I knew though, that they would feel comfortable in no time.

**Steve, Kathy, Dave, Ward, Blaine, Linda, Mary, Chuck, Lou** and **Bob** were all returnees from the introductory class.

All in all, there were fourteen repeat students in the class, and four new students. I did my best to make everyone, particularly our new class members, feel welcome: I certainly didn't want them to feel 'left out' because they hadn't been present for the development of the China Shop Project in the introductory class.

"Has anyone heard from Joe?" Bob asked.

"Yes," I replied, "Joe sent me an e-mail. He was always a bit of a free spirit, and he told me that he was offered a Visual Basic programmer job in San Diego – with a big raise – in part due to the Visual Basic he learned in this class. It also helped that he took and passed the Visual Basic Certification test."

"What about Rose and Jack?" Valerie asked. "Are they still honeymooning somewhere?"

For those of you unfamiliar with the story – we had a classroom romance the previous semester. Rose and Jack, two students who worked for the same engineering firm, left on an adventurous business trip to stress-test a new ocean liner they had helped design, and wound up married right there on the bridge of their ship.

"They e-mailed me too," I said. "They said that after the hectic pace of their lives the last few weeks, they decided to sit out a semester. They will either take this database course the next time it's offered, or possibly the Visual Basic Objects course I'm teaching next semester."

"A course on Visual Basic Objects?" Lou asked. "That should be interesting. What about Barbara?"

Dave answered that question. He explained that Barbara's worst fears had been realized – she'd been laid off from her job as a COBOL programmer shortly after the last class of the Introductory Visual Basic course. Fortunately though, she'd quickly obtained a position with another company as an entry-level Visual Basic programmer.

"She's putting in a lot of overtime right now, on a project with a tight deadline," Dave said, "and regrettably she'll have to wait until this course is offered again to take it."

We had accounted for the four missing students. It remained for me to get to know the eighteen students a little better. I began to read the biographies I had collected silently – once in a while remarking on something they had written. I then put them aside; I would read them in more detail at home.

You'll find the detailed student biographies documented in Appendix A

At this point, normally I would distribute the course syllabus and discuss it for a few minutes before taking a short break, after which I would start my lecture on Visual Basic and databases. Most likely we would then have looked at a Visual Basic database application – probably one of the commercial ones I had recently written. After about an hour or so of demonstrating the program, I would then have spent the remainder of the class on an introductory lesson dealing with database theory and – time permitting – distribute the semester project before dismissing class for the day.

This time, things would be different, and I could hardly wait to tell everyone. I was sure that the students from the introductory class had no inkling that we would be continuing to work with Joe Bullina's China Shop project. Everyone in the class was aware of how much he loved the program – but they were also very much aware that he thought it was so perfect, that there was no need to modify or enhance it in any way. Wouldn't they be surprised! As far as the four new students were concerned, I was sure that they believed they were in for a typically dry computer class.

"I have a little announcement to make," I said as I put the student biographies into my briefcase.

"Let me guess," Rhonda said. "You found another client willing to let us work on a real project?"

"You mean this course isn't going to be the usual read-the-textbook-and-code-the-examples course?" Rachel interjected.

"That's exactly what I said last semester, Rachel," Linda said, laughing. "Instead of just reading the book, and coding up some exercises and problems, we spent the semester writing a real-world Visual Basic application, and did we have a great time! Do you mean you found someone willing to let us develop a Visual Basic database project?"

"Better than that," I said, "I didn't just find someone – Joe Bullina found *us* again. He wants us to modify the program we wrote for him last semester – and in order to meet his needs, it makes perfect sense to add database processing to the program."

The four new members of the class appeared confused, and so I explained that in last semester's introductory class we had developed a real-world application built around Joe's China Shop. We had written the program in Visual Basic using the **Systems Development Life Cycle (SDLC)** as a guide. I also explained for the benefit of the new students that the SDLC was a series of steps that aided the development of a software package from its inception right through to implementation and maintenance. The SDLC helps to ensure that we don't leave out any important stages in the development.

> If you're unfamiliar with the SDLC, you'll find a summary of its stages in Appendix C of this book.

"So there's already a program written – and we're going to take that program and do what to it?" Melissa asked.

"We're going to **database-enable** it," I said, "by modifying the program to interact with a Microsoft Access database."

"That sounds great," Tom said, "that's what I'm here to learn – how to develop Visual Basic database programs. And what could be better than a real-world application?"

"That sounds great to me too," Kevin said, "but for those of us who weren't here for the introductory class, could you give us a run-through of the China Shop program?"

"I think that would be a good idea for everyone. I have the requirements statement for the original China Shop project right here," I said, as I displayed it on the classroom projector. "These slides also show snapshots of the Visual Basic controls that we added to the program's user interface to satisfy these requirements."

# A Review of the China Shop Project

## <u>Requirements Statement</u>
## Bullina China Shop
## General Description

1. The program will consist of a main form, on which there will be:

   a. A list box containing brands of china:

   b. 6 check boxes for china piece components:

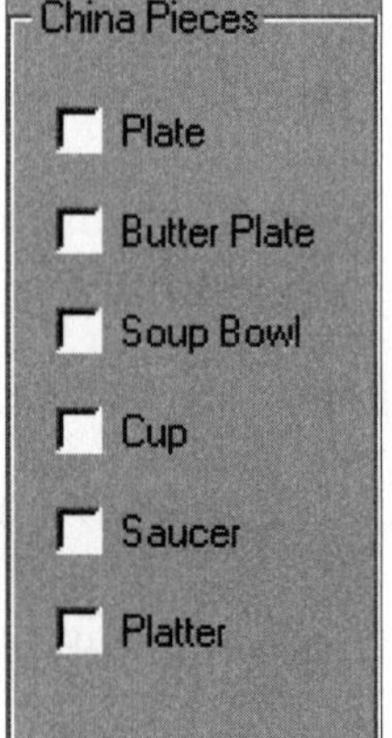

**c.** A single check box to permit the customer to select a "Complete Place Setting":

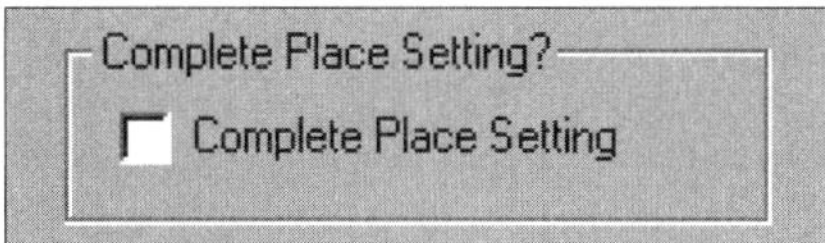


**d.** 4 option buttons representing quantities:

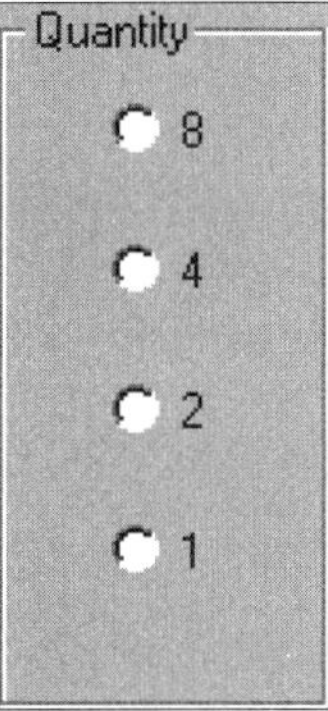


**e.** A button which, when clicked, will perform the price calculation:

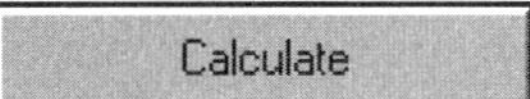


**f.** A button captioned "Reset" which, when clicked, will clear the selections in the list box, check boxes, and option buttons:

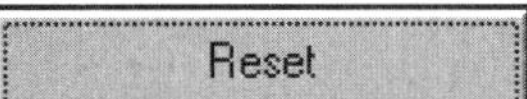


**g.** Menu items for File and Preferences:

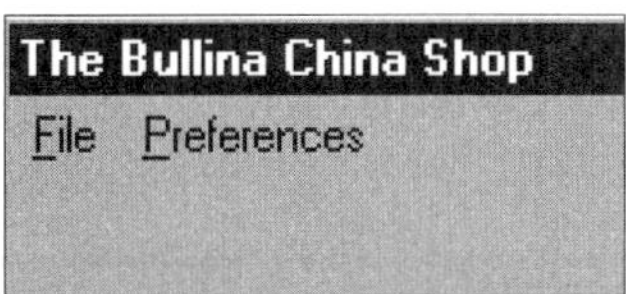

2. The File menu will display only an Exit command. The File menu will be alternatively accessible by pressing the *Alt+F* combination. The Exit command will be alternatively accessible by pressing the *Alt+X* combination:

3. The Preferences menu will display a submenu called Colors and commands to set a Date and Time display:

4. The Colors submenu will consist of two commands called "Custom" and "Default". The Custom command will permit the customer to set the color of the main form to any color they desire through the use of a color dialog box. The Default command will set the color of the main form back to a predetermined color:

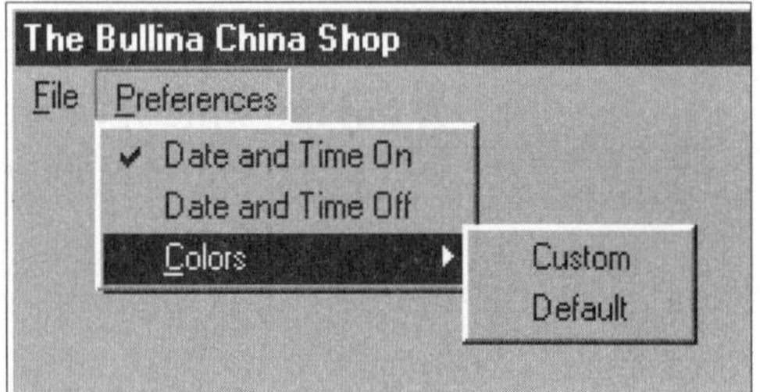


5. The Date and Time command will permit the user to switch the displayed date and time off and on.

6. A password will be required to exit the system from the Exit command of the File menu.

# Output from the System

1. A price quotation contained in a label displayed on the main form:

The price of your order is $32.00

2. Current Date and Time displayed prominently on the form:

# Input to the System

The customer will specify:

1. A single china brand (to be selected from a list box).
2. One or more component pieces (to be selected using check boxes).
3. A quantity for the component pieces (to be selected using an option button).

The following is not customer input, but:

1. The program will read china brands and prices from a text file. The inventory and prices can be updated by the sales clerk when necessary using Microsoft Notepad.
2. Any changes made to the user's color preferences will be saved to the Windows Registry and read by the program at startup.
3. Any changes made to the user's preference for Date and Time display will be saved to the Windows Registry and read by the program at startup.

## Business Rules

1. No more than one platter may be selected.
2. Quantities may not be mixed and matched in an order. Only one quantity selection per order.
3. Brands may not be mixed and matched in an order. Only one brand per order.

## Definitions

1. Complete Place Setting: A user's selection composed of a plate, butter plate, soup bowl, cup and saucer of the same brand.

## Other

1. The program will read china brands and prices from a text file, which can be updated when necessary by the sales force.
2. Any changes made to the user's preferences (colors, date and time display) will be saved and read by the program at startup. Therefore, both the color settings and the date and time display will be the same as they were when the program ended previously.

I could see from the looks on the faces of my new students that they had a bit of a learning curve to negotiate. From their biographies, I knew that they were familiar with Visual Basic, but they didn't know the China Shop, and they didn't know Joe Bullina.

"I think it might be useful for the new members of the class to see the China Shop program," Rhonda said.

"That's a great idea," I replied. I started Visual Basic, found the China Shop program on my PC's hard disk drive, and loaded up the project. "Rhonda, would you mind running us through a typical purchase scenario?"

## The China Shop Program in Action

Rhonda came up to the front of the classroom, sat down in front of my PC, and spent the next few minutes running through this purchase scenario. Two prospective customers – Rita and Gil – enter the China Shop, and approach the PC-based "kiosk" in the middle of the store.

> Remember that if you didn't build the China Shop Program following the instructions in my Learn to Program with Visual Basic book, you'll need to load the application onto your PC so that you can try it out for yourself and database-enable it. The instructions for installing the original China Shop application on your PC can be found in Appendix B of this book.

**1.** Rita stands before the China Shop kiosk PC, and this is what she sees:

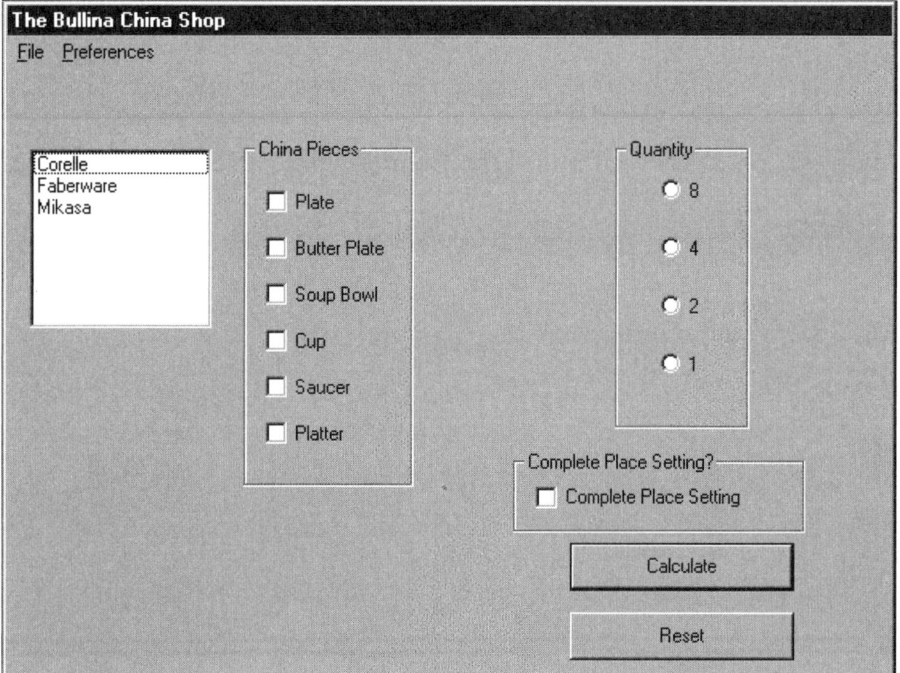

2. Rita wants Mikasa china, so she uses the mouse to click on Mikasa in the list box. The Mikasa pattern appears in the image control on the form:

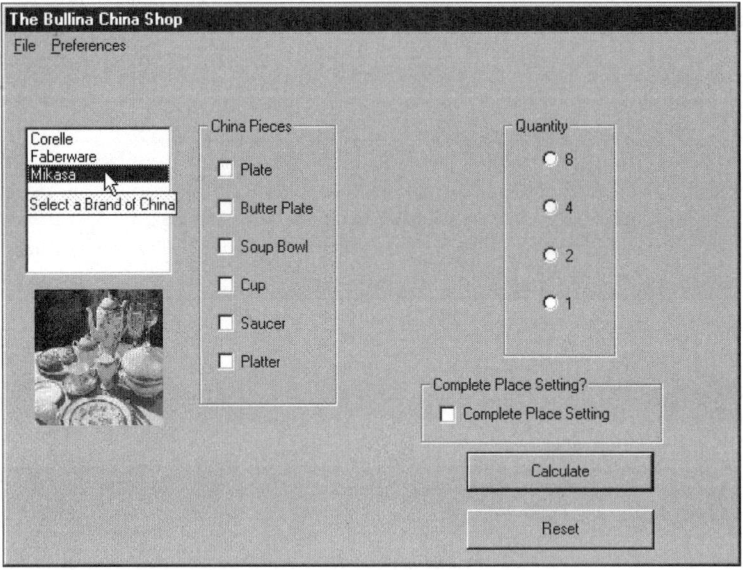


3. Rita wants a complete place setting, so she clicks on the complete place setting check box. Five check marks appear for the china items comprising a complete place setting:

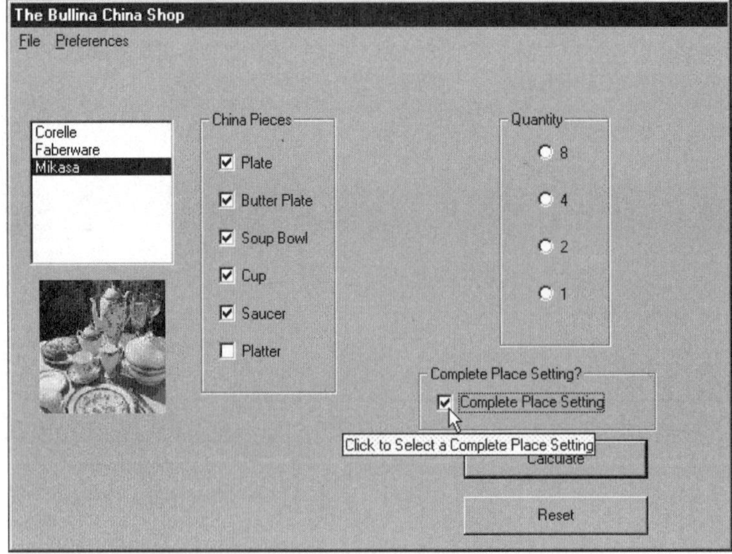

4. Rita clicks on the Calculate command button. A message box displays a warning that she has not yet picked a quantity:

The bell that sounds when the message box displays startles her!

5. Rita clicks on the OK button to make the message box go away. Rita selects a quantity of 8 by using the mouse to click on the option button labeled "8":

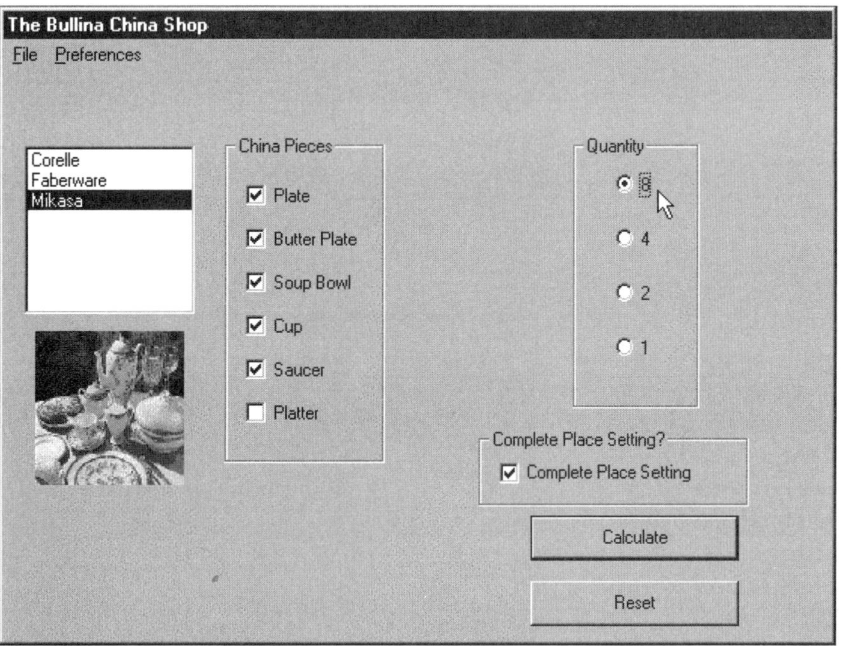


6. Rita again clicks on the Calculate command button.

7. A message box pops up. This indicates that the calculated price reflects a discount for a complete place setting:

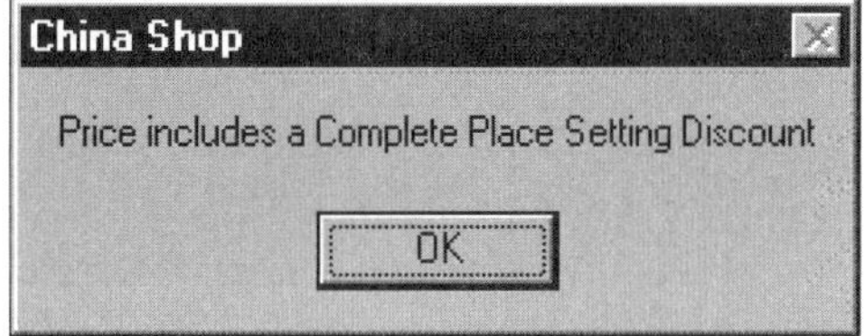

8. Both Rita and Gil are puzzled as to what this message means. Rita clicks on the OK button to make the message box go away.

9. The quotation price of $400 is displayed in the lower left-hand corner of the form as the caption of a label control:

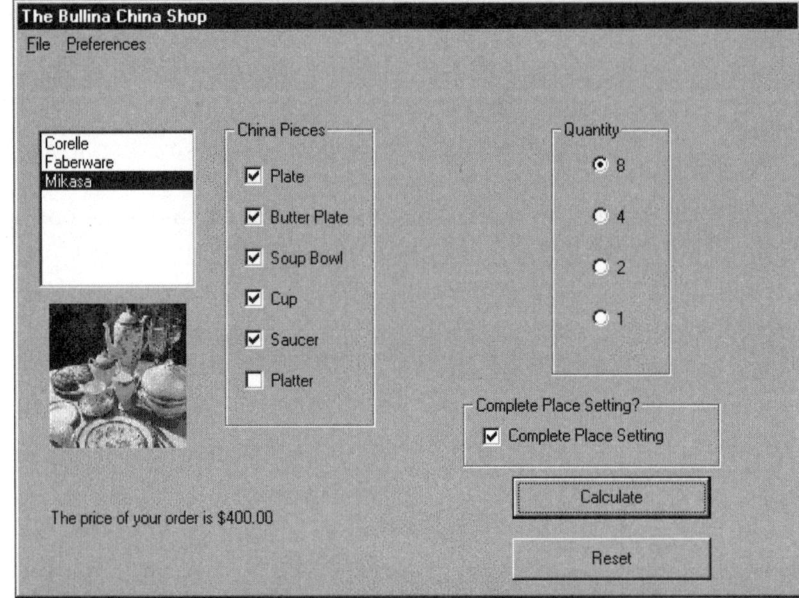


10. Gil takes over now and uses the mouse to click on the Reset command button. All of the other controls (i.e. label price, check boxes, option buttons, list box selection) are reset:

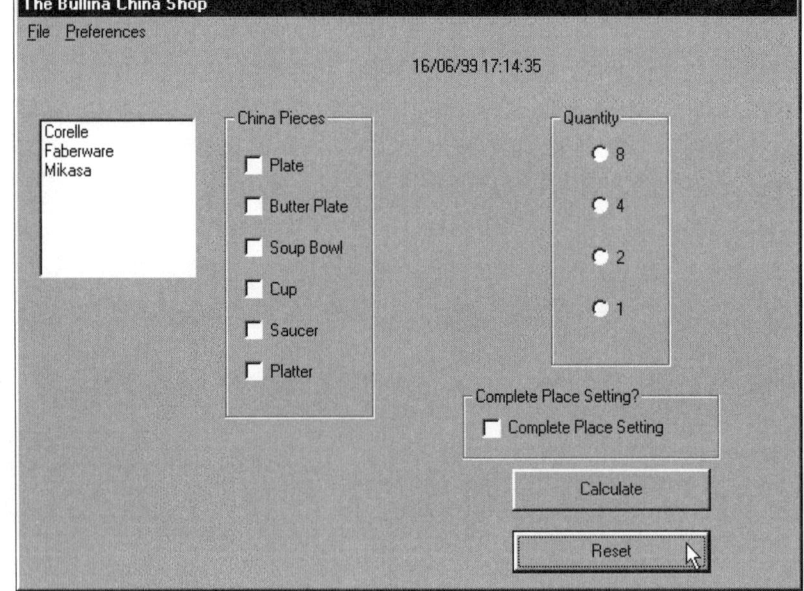

11. Gil is having trouble seeing the display, so he changes the color of the form from the default gray to cyan by using the main menu of the form. He remarks that he wishes the font were larger:

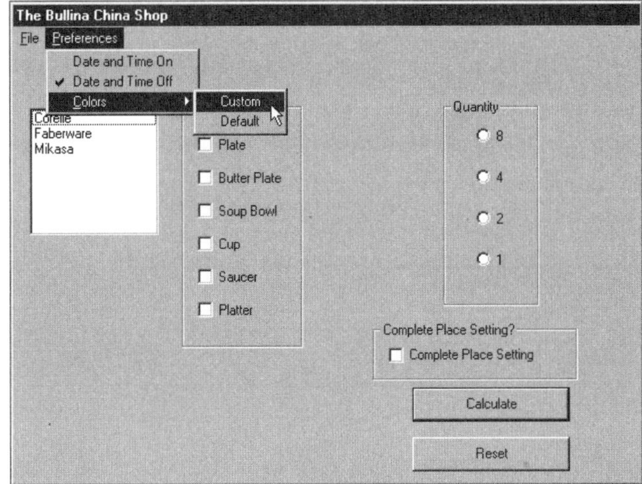


12. Gil believes that he and Rita are running late for a movie that they want to see. He turns the display of the date and time 'on' using the main menu of the form:

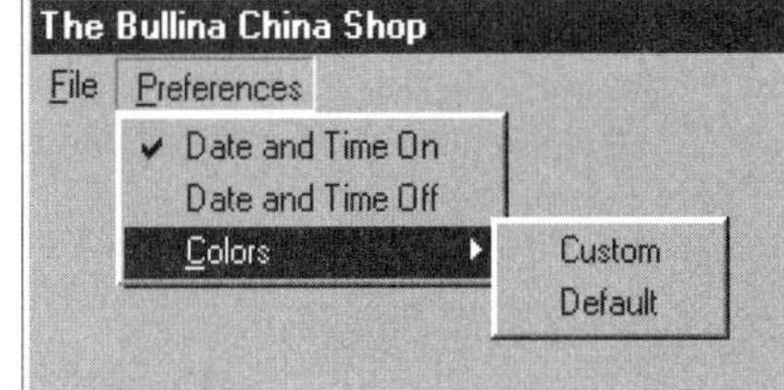


13. The time display appears on the form:

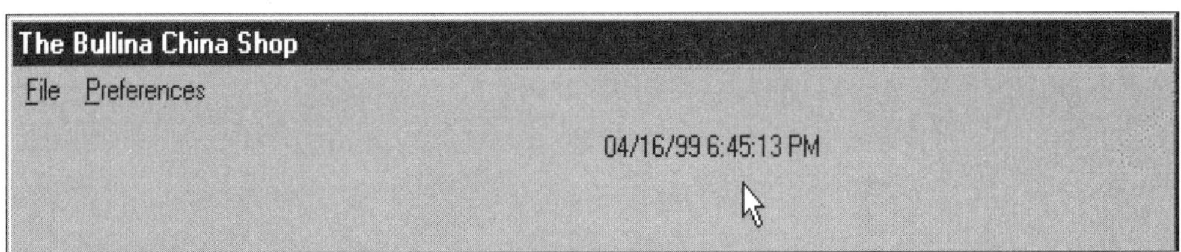


Now he knows they really are late!

14. Gil thinks the price of Mikasa is too expensive and clicks on Faberware in the list box:

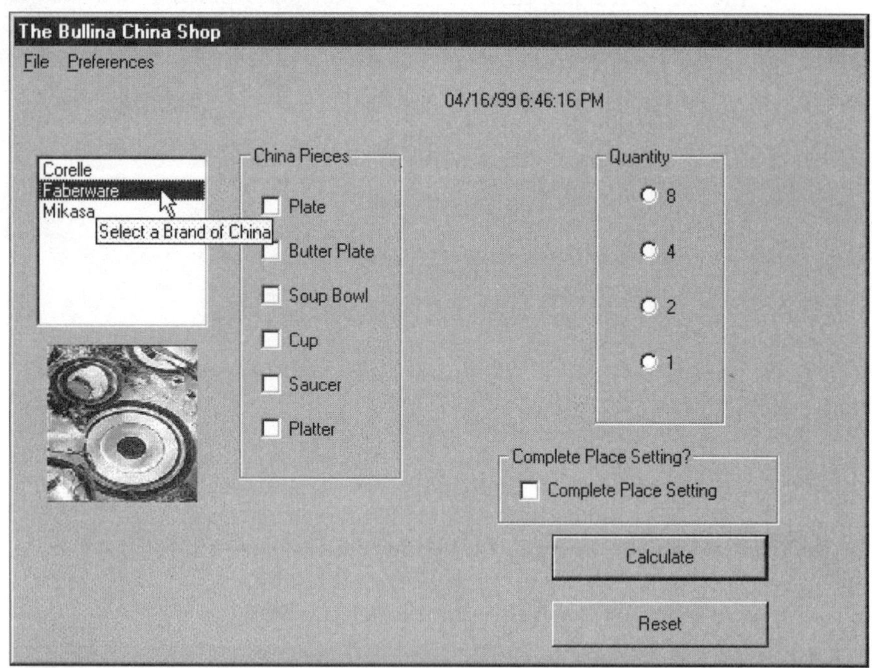


15. Gil doesn't think they need a complete place setting. Instead, he selects plate, cup, saucer and a platter from the items displayed:

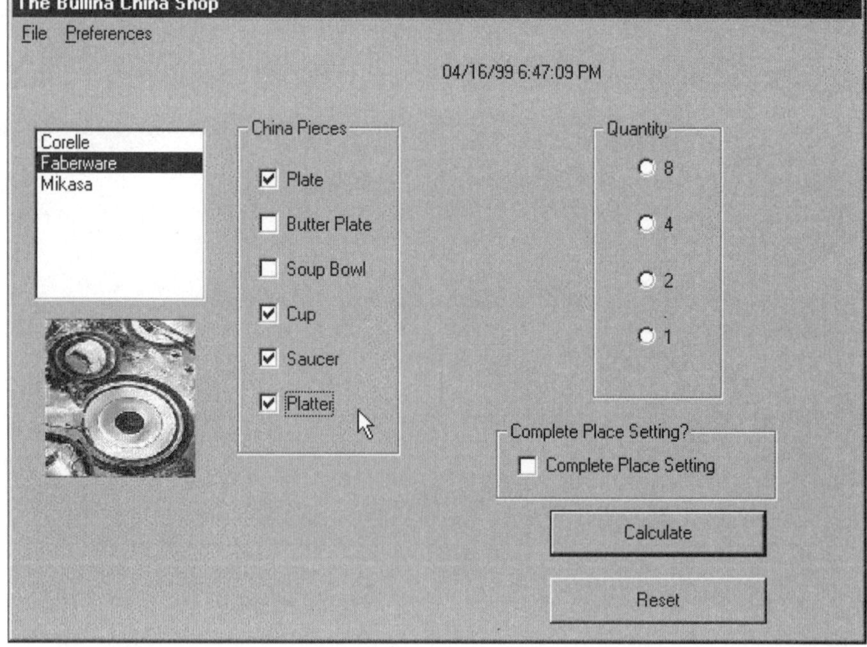

**16.** Gil thinks they only need 4 of each item, and so he clicks on the option button labeled "4":

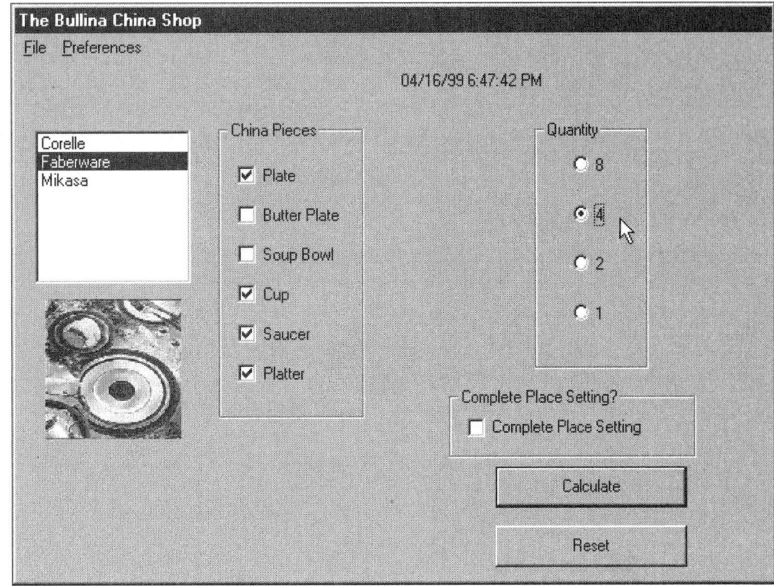


**17.** Gil only wants one platter, but is confused because there is no place to specify a quantity for the platter.

**18.** Gil clicks on the Calculate command button.

A message box is displayed saying that he is limited to a quantity of one platter:

**19.** He clicks on the OK button to make the message box go away.

20. The quotation price of $77 is displayed in the lower left-hand corner of the form as the caption of a label control:

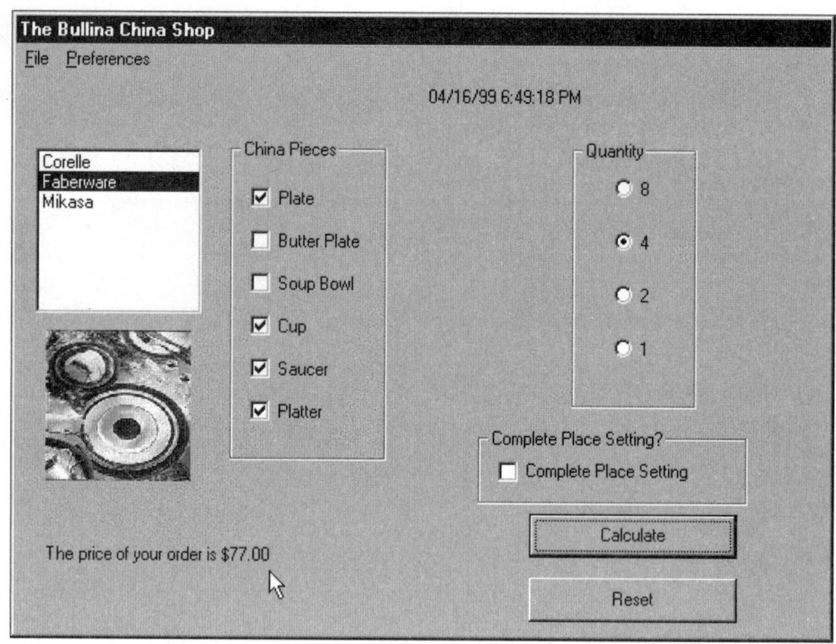


21. Apparently pleased with the price, Rita and Gil head towards the counter to make their purchase.

It took Rhonda about 10 minutes to run through the demonstration of the China Shop program. There were a few questions from the new members of the class: for instance, Melissa had anticipated Gil's confusion about the platter quantity – but overall, the demonstration really seemed to solidify their understanding of the program.

I thanked Rhonda for her excellent demonstration. After she had taken her normal seat, she asked the million-dollar question: "What enhancements is Joe Bullina looking for in the program?"

## Enhancing the China Shop

"Before you answer that, John," Dave interjected, "am I right to assume that we'll be developing a requirements statement for the enhancements to the China Shop program the same way that we developed the original requirements statement in the introductory course?"

"That's right," I said, "we'll need to develop requirements statements for the modifications."

"But how can we do that without Joe Bullina?" Melissa said.

Linda answered her: "Well, Melissa, for the original program, Professor Smiley interviewed Joe Bullina himself to gather preliminary requirements. Then I made a second trip to perform a more detailed analysis." Then, directing her question to me, she asked, "Have you already been to see him?"

"No, I haven't interviewed him yet," I said, "you'll be doing that yourself today!"

As if on cue, the door opened and Joe Bullina made his grand entrance into the classroom.

"Am I on time, John?" Joe asked.

"Perfect timing, Joe," I said, "as ever!"

"Hi, everyone," Joe said. "I see a bunch of familiar faces! For those of you who don't know me, I'm Joe Bullina, proud owner of the Bullina China Shop, and of course, the Bullina China Shop program. John said that he would be pitching the idea of having you enhance the program you wrote for me last semester. I hope you agree to do it. The China Shop program has saved me so much money, I may even be able to pay you double what I paid for the first program!"

"Pay us?" Kevin asked.

"That's right," Joe said. "I paid the class $450 to develop the original China Shop program. At the time I was really running the business on a shoestring."

"Yes, Kevin," I said, "Joe's program gave everyone in the class the chance to become professional programmers in their first Visual Basic class. You can't beat that! Joe, I'm sure I speak for the class when I say let's keep the arrangement as it is: another $450 for the enhancements."

Everyone seemed in agreement with that. The payment would permit everyone to honestly indicate that they had a paying Visual Basic job under their belt – but the experience of writing a real world application was the really important thing.

"If you're sure..." Joe said hesitantly, "then that's fine with me. $450 it is. At any rate, John asked me to stop by today and help you in developing the requirements statement for the modified program. We all know how important it is to have a requirements statement documenting the needs that the program is satisfying!"

"Joe," I said, "Rhonda was just asking what kinds of enhancements you are looking for in the program – can you tell us what types of changes you think the program needs?"

"Before I start," he began, "let me tell you how much I and the rest of the China Shop staff appreciate the China Shop program. As you remember, my primary purpose in asking you to write the original program was to relieve my sales clerks from the burden of giving price quotations to customers who would then immediately turn and leave the shop. The program has certainly done that – now my sales clerks are profitably engaged in helping customers who actually want to make purchases. That's good for them, and good for me. Customers who only want to come in and browse can use the program to produce a quotation, and then leave to check prices somewhere else. So from that perspective, everything is fabulous."

"Displaying prices for comparison shopping sounds like a great web application," Kevin said enthusiastically, sparking an idea for a possible future course in my mind.

"Maybe down the road," Joe said. "I'm not sure that I'm ready to offer my services on the World Wide Web just yet."

"Maybe we can do that in Professor Smiley's Web course?" Kevin replied.

"But obviously," Dave said, bringing us back on track, "there's something that needs to be changed, or you wouldn't be here this morning. Is there a problem?"

"You're right, Dave," Joe Bullina said, "there is a problem – but not with the program. It's a personnel problem. Midge, who is the one person I simply can't afford to lose, is retiring soon, and quite frankly, I'm a little worried. You probably know that Midge takes care of updating the China Shop's inventory prices. I just don't think anyone else can do that. As an example of how crucial she is to our operations, this weekend we're having a huge sale and Midge needed to make price changes to the system last night. I know it only took her a minute or two to make the changes...but I'm just not sure anyone else will be able to do it after she leaves."

"As I recall from the Requirements Statement you displayed on the projector," Tom said, "the inventory prices are stored in a disk file. How are they updated?"

Joe Bullina looked at me, and I answered.

"Midge uses Microsoft Notepad to update a disk file called '`Prices.txt`' on the hard drive of the China Shop PC," I said.

"Why didn't you store the prices in a database when you wrote the original program?" Melissa asked.

"The primary reason," Dave explained in his usual confident manner, "is that we decided up-front to develop the program using only with the skill-set developed out of the introductory Visual Basic class. Database-enabling the program at that point simply wasn't an option, as database programming wasn't a topic covered in the introductory class. Isn't that right, Professor Smiley?"

"That's right, Dave," I said. "When Joe called me last week, quite understandably upset at the prospect of losing Midge, I told him that if ease of use in updating the inventory prices was a concern, it would be easy to modify the program to update inventory prices from within the program, rather than outside of it using Notepad, as happens now. And while we could achieve that using disk files, this is a perfect opportunity to use a Microsoft Access database to store the inventory prices. Using a database, we can combine efficient data storage with a friendly interface for Joe's staff to use when updating prices."

"Using a database to store this information sounds like a great idea to me!" Kathy said, obviously pleased that her background in Microsoft Access would come in handy in the development of this project.

"I guessed you would all think that modifying the China Shop program for database access would be a great practical project for the class," I said. "While we're at it, Joe, is there anything else we can do for you in addition to updating inventory prices?"

With that, Joe quickly pulled out a piece of paper from his shirt pocket.

"Well, since you asked, I do have a wish list", he said, half-embarrassed.

## Joe Bullina's new Requirements

"Go on," I said, smiling. "As long as we're going to modify the program, we might as well go all the way. What else can we do for you?"

"I do have a few things I've been thinking about since we last talked on the phone," Joe said. "For instance, I'd love to have information about the people using the program."

"Do you mean," Valerie said, "the customers who leave the store after obtaining a quotation, or those who actually buy something?"

"For the moment, I'm really only interested in maintaining information about the customers who make a purchase. The way the program works right now," Joe continued, "after the customer receives a sales quotation, they approach the sales counter if they want to make a purchase, and a sales clerk waits on them.

For the last few years, my sales clerks have been gathering information about the customer – their name and address – so that I can keep in touch with them in the future. For instance, on occasion – like this weekend - we have sales, and I use this information to notify my customers by mail."

"So you'd like the program to get this information directly from the customer?" Kate asked.

"That's right," said Joe. "Nearly all of you have been to the China Shop. On a busy day, we may have customers lined up at the sales counter two- and three-deep. My sales clerks are great, don't get me wrong, but the last thing they want to do is to bypass a potential sale by taking the time to ask customers for their name, address and phone number. Also, some customers don't feel comfortable giving this information aloud to a sales clerk in front of a line of other customers – they might feel more comfortable providing that information to the program."

"How do you envisage that working?" Peter asked.

"Well, at present," Joe continued, "after the customers receive a quotation they approach the sales counter if they want to make a purchase. I'd like the customers to tell the program that they want to purchase the quoted china, and have the program respond by asking them for their name, address and phone number."

"That shouldn't be a problem, should it?" Ward said, directing the question to me.

"No, not at all," I replied. "We can do this in a number of ways. But we'll have to give the actual process some thought. For instance, we only need to capture the customer's information one time. There's really no sense in asking the customer to re-enter their address and phone number every time they make a purchase."

"You're right," Joe said. "My customers definitely wouldn't appreciate having to key in that information more than once. But how will the program know if we already have the customer's information stored somewhere?"

"That's a good question," I said. "The program needs to know who it's dealing with – which means that the customers will need to enter some piece of identifying information, such as a customer ID, whenever they use the program."

"You mean whenever the customers announce their firm intention to make a purchase?" Rachel asked, "as opposed to when they use the program?"

"I think that's right," Joe said, "I don't think we want to prompt the users for their customer information unless they actually want to make a purchase."

"One way to do that," Dave said, "is to modify the current program to include another button: when it's clicked it could tell the program that the customer wants to make a purchase. At that point, we can then prompt the customer for something – perhaps a customer ID – to identify them."

"A customer ID," Kate said. "That's a good idea. At my video store, I was given a membership card with a customer ID printed on it. I received the card, and the customer ID, when I signed up for a membership at the store."

"That's one method," I agreed. "Assign each customer a customer ID, and then have them enter it into the program when they want to make the purchase."

"At my video store," Chuck said, "my customer ID is my Mom and Dad's phone number."

"That's another method," I said. "In fact, using a telephone number is a pretty common way of assigning a customer ID to a customer. Everyone knows their telephone number, and the telephone company ensures that the number is unique."

Joe offered another idea: "Why do we need a customer ID at all?" he said. "Can't we just have the customer enter their name, and have the program recognize them that way?"

"The answer to that question involves some database theory," I replied. "Simply speaking, the problem is duplicate names. Each customer's stored information must be tracked by a **unique** bit of information in the database – and there's no guarantee that you won't have two customers with the same name purchase china from your store."

"I see the problem," Joe said. "In that case, if we need to use customer IDs, I'd rather not pre-assign them. And I really don't want to be printing customer cards either. That's too much of an administrative hassle. I'm also a bit worried about using a telephone number as a customer ID. I had a major problem a few years ago when I gave out my telephone number. I want to make this as simple a process as possible."

"Joe's point about the telephone number is a good one," Mary agreed. "I don't think every customer is going to want to supply the program with their phone number. I know I wouldn't."

"My preference," Joe said, "would be to have the program ask the customer if they have a customer ID, and, if they don't, then prompt them for their customer information and record it in the database. As far as a customer ID goes, is there any way to automatically assign a customer ID to a new customer and display it for them on the PC?"

"Yes, there is," I said. "We can do that – automatically assign a customer ID after we obtain the customer's information for the first time."

"I think we'll need to add a second form in the project," Dave said.

"There goes Dave, reading ahead again," Rhonda joked. "I don't know how to add a second form to a Visual Basic project. And why will we need one?"

"A second form will allow us to display a series of text boxes for the customer to input their details," I said. "But don't worry about that; it's really no big deal. I can show you how to do this in just a few minutes in a later lesson."

"That sounds great," Joe said. "And after the customer enters their information, perhaps at that point we can display their newly assigned customer ID number?"

"Definitely," I said. "We can do that."

"Joe, I know you said you didn't want to print customer cards," Kevin remarked, "and I understand your reluctance to do that. However, I think the chance of a customer remembering their customer ID the next time they come into the China Shop is pretty remote. Why not have some customer cards pre-printed and placed next to the PC, along with a laundry marker or pen?"

"Then, when the program assigns a customer ID and displays it on the PC, the customer can write the number on one of the pre-printed cards and take it with them."

"That's not a bad idea," I said. "It's either that or have the program print a customer card itself. But I can see that being a big hassle. I like the idea of having the customer jot down their number on a preprinted card."

"I like that idea too," Joe said. "It's simple – and you know that's what I like."

"I think I'm OK with all of this," Steve said, "but I see one potential problem. Let's say that the customer decides they like the sales quotation. They click on a button, and the program then prompts them for a customer ID. If they know it, that's fine. If they're a first time customer, they indicate that in some way. We can then prompt them for some basic customer information, automatically generate a customer ID for them, and ask them to jot it down on a pre-printed customer card. So far, so good. But suppose the customer is not a first time customer; suppose they already have a customer ID, but they don't know it. They might have misplaced their card or left it home. Then what?"

"That's a good question," I said. "If the customer has purchased something before, their information is already recorded in the database. We don't want them re-entering their customer information, do we?"

"Definitely not," Rhonda said, "that would generate duplicate customer information. I suppose we could always have the customer come up to the sales counter, and ask a sales clerk for help?"

Dave disagreed: "The program is supposed to streamline operations," he said. "If we have the customers come up to the sales counter for help with their customer ID, aren't we imposing more work on the sales staff? I don't think Joe would be very happy with that, would you Joe?"

"No, I wouldn't," Joe replied. "Besides, if the customer doesn't know their ID number, how would a sales clerk? Unless there was some kind of master list of customers and their ID numbers."

"Aren't we losing sight of the forest for the trees here?" Valerie asked. "All Joe is really interested in doing is collecting customer information to use in the production of mailing labels. If the customer can't remember their customer ID number, or left their customer card at home, why don't we just display a list of customer names already stored in the database, along with their customer ID numbers, and have the customer select their name from a list?"

"That's a great idea," Joe said. "If the customer doesn't know their customer ID, display all of the names in a list, and let them choose the correct one. This is similar to the way we display a list of brands in the program right now."

"That will work," I said, "and we can implement it pretty easily."

## Documenting the new Requirements

We spent the next few minutes discussing particulars of the process – information to be requested from the customer, Visual Basic controls to be used, captions for the controls, and the general flow of the customer entry process. As he did in our introductory class, Dave volunteered to record our discussions in a Word document, and then shared his notes with us via the classroom projector:

1. The China Shop program will be modified to collect customer information (name, address, city, state, zip code, and optionally a phone number) from the customer and store it in a Microsoft Access database. Collection of customer information will take place in this way: when the sales quotation is displayed, a new command button labeled "I'll Take It" will become visible. When the customer clicks on this command button, a new Visual Basic form captioned "Do you have a Customer ID?" will be displayed, containing three command buttons - one labeled 'Yes', one labeled 'No - New Customer' and the other reading 'Yes, but I can't remember'.

2. If the customer selects 'Yes' then an input box will be displayed, prompting the customer for their customer ID. The customer ID they enter will then be located in the database. If the customer ID does not exist, a message will be displayed, informing the customer that they have entered an incorrect customer ID, and they will be returned to the previous form to re-enter the number.

3. If the customer selects 'No - New Customer' then a form captioned "Welcome New Customer!" will be displayed, containing a series of text boxes to be used for them to enter their customer information, which will then be stored in the database. A message box will be displayed with their newly assigned Customer ID, along with a reminder to write it down on a pre-printed customer card stacked near the PC.

4. If the customer selects 'Yes, but I can't remember', then a form captioned "Let me help you" will be displayed with a list box containing every customer name and customer ID in the database. The customer will then be able to select a customer ID from the list.

At this point, I sensed that everyone seemed content with this process. There were still some particulars that we would need to work out, but we would be doing that in the coming weeks. At this point, there simply was no benefit in discussing them – the students had much to learn about database processing before we could get into details.

"Anything else, Joe?" I asked, turning to Joe. "We might as well give you everything you need at one time. This is a 10 week class – you want to keep us busy!"

"Well," Joe said smiling, "I was wondering if there is any way we that we can keep track of the items that the customer has purchased? In addition to the customer's name and address?"

"That's not a problem at all," I said. "We can easily record the sales transaction information in the same database that we use to store the customer's information. In fact, as soon as the customer enters a valid customer ID, or enters their customer information for the first time, we can immediately record all of the items that they have purchased."

"Along with the inventory prices that we mentioned earlier," he added.

"Along with the prices," I said. "No problem!"

Dave was busy taking notes about this new requirement when Joe spoke again: "Is there any way," he said, "that we can place a printer at the PC and have the customer's sales quotation printed there? That way, they can then take it with them to the sales counter"

"Printing the transaction is no more difficult than storing it in a database," I said. "Of course, Joe, it does mean that you'll need to purchase a printer."

"I don't mind buying the printer," he said. "And I love the idea that the customer can just bring the sales quotation to the counter, hand it to one of my sales clerks, and get their merchandise."

I looked at Joe and asked him if there were any other modifications he needed in the program.

"No," he said, "I think that just about covers it. My wish list consists of: gathering customer information, recording sales transactions, and printing the sales quotations. Of course, we can't forget the main reason I called you – the need for a more staff-friendly way of updating inventory prices."

I thought it would be a good idea at this point to have Dave display for us a formal requirements statement based on the notes he had taken. I asked the class to have a ten-minute breather and a coffee while Dave and I worked together on the requirements statement. When the class reconvened, Dave displayed the following amendments to the requirements statement on the classroom projector:

5. After the customer has supplied a valid Customer ID, the program will write a transaction record to the database for each item of china purchased.

6. A sales quotation will then be printed on a printer attached to the PC. The customer can then pick it up and carry it to the sales clerk at the front of the store.

"Is there anything missing from the requirements statement?" I asked the class, knowing full well that there was.

Initially, no one said anything. But then Joe volunteered this: "I think the requirements statement fails to mention the primary reason that I'm here today. That is, to modify the program so that inventory prices can be updated in a more user friendly fashion."

"Of course," Rhonda laughed. "How could we forget that?"

"I think it's that forest for the trees syndrome," Steve offered. "We spent so much time reviewing the customer information process that we forgot about the inventory processing."

"That's why we follow the systems development life cycle," I said. "The SDLC helps us to avoid making mistakes like that. Of course, it helps to have the ultimate user of the program intimately involved in the process. That's why Joe is here today."

"I suppose," Rhonda said, "that we'll need to add another form to the project for inventory update?"

"That's right," I confirmed. "We'll need a form to allow a member of the China Shop sales staff to view, update, and perhaps even add records to an inventory table in our database."

"I must admit, I've been reading a bit ahead," Dave said. "Are the terms **database** and **table** used interchangeably?"

"They are different," I said. "In Microsoft Access, a table stores information of the same type: so, in an overall database that held information about the University, we'd store information about courses in a `Courses` table, information about students in a `Students` table, and so on. A database is the name given to the entire collection of these tables."

"I'm still a little unsure about some of these terms that we're using here," Mary said. "Are these terms – database, table, transactions – something that we'll be learning about during this course?"

"Yes, they are," I said. "We'll be discussing these terms in much more detail next week."

I asked Dave to add a requirement to view and edit inventory records to the requirements statement.

"Anything else?" I continued.

"Well, it seems to me," Rachel said, "that if we're providing a means for the sales staff to view and edit inventory information, we should also provide a way for them to view and edit customer and transaction data. What do you think?"

"I don't think I understand," Rhonda interjected. "I thought that the customer would be entering their own information, and that the program would be creating transaction records on its own. Why would the sales staff need to view or edit this information?"

"Primarily," I said, "it gives the sales staff a way to correct any data that is incorrect. For instance, if the customer enters an incorrect address, or if they change their telephone number."

"I like the idea of a form to view and edit customer information," Joe said, "but I would prefer that the program didn't permit anyone to edit the transaction data."

"That's a good point," Kate said. "Transaction records are automatically created by the program – they should be correct, shouldn't they?"

"That's right," I said. "Transaction records can't be wrong, so it's probably not a good idea to allow members of the sales staff to modify them."

"But I definitely want to be able to view them," Joe said. "Those records will be valuable for future decision-making."

I asked Dave to add the requirements to view and edit customer records, and to view transaction records. In just a minute or so, he nodded that he had done that, and he then showed the latest additions to the requirements statement for everyone to see:

7. The China Shop program will be modified to store inventory data (china brands, items, and prices) in the database. As part of this modification, a new Visual Basic form will be designed to permit the China Shop staff to view inventory, edit existing inventory, or add new inventory records.

8. A new Visual Basic form will be designed to permit the China Shop staff to view, edit or add Customer records.

9. A new Visual Basic form will be designed to permit the China Shop staff to view Transaction records.

After a few minutes of silence, as the class reviewed the requirements statement, Ward spoke up.

"I think the requirements statement we've developed so far lacks some of the detail that we had in the original. Do you think we need to be more specific?"

"Can you give us an example, Ward?" I asked him.

"Sure," Ward continued, "for instance, we haven't specified names for any of the tables in the database, nor any of the field names or their data types in the database yet."

"Ward, I have absolutely no idea what you're talking about," Rhonda smiled.

"Don't worry," I said to Rhonda, "We'll be covering those topics next week."

Turning to Ward, I said, "Ward, I think it's safe to say that we'll have one database – most likely called China – containing three tables called **Customers**, **Inventory**, and **Transactions**. As far as the field names, we'll get there eventually – but I wouldn't advise getting that detailed in our requirements statement."

"Anything else, now?" I asked again.

"I think we may have forgotten something," Peter said. "What about the list box containing the names of the china brands on the China Shop form? Right now, the items in that list box are read from records contained in the `Prices.txt` disk file. If we eliminate the disk file in favor of a database, the code to load up the entries in the list box will need to be changed too."

"Good point, Peter," I affirmed. "You're right. The items in the list box will have to come from the Access database. I think you'll find that introducing the database into the program will require some other changes as well."

"Such as the way we get the china prices into the program?" Valerie asked.

"That's right," I agreed. "Both the names of the china brands in the list box and the china prices used in the calculation of the sales quotation will now be coming from the Access database – not the `Prices.txt` disk file on the PC."

"I just thought of something," Joe Bullina suddenly said. "You mentioned that the sales staff will be able to view or update customer and inventory records, and also be able to view transaction records. If that functionality exists for the sales staff, how do we keep the customer from getting at it? Will we have some kind of password, the way we do when we exit the program?"

Joe had brought up an excellent point – viewing this kind of 'behind the scenes' information (or worse yet, editing it!) was the last thing we wanted a customer in the China Shop to be able to do. But how could we stop them?

"There are a number of ways we can handle this," I said. "I think the easiest way is to create a table called **Users** in our database, and then to create a Login form as a new startup form for the China Shop program. We can add two records to the user table – one for administrative work, and one for regular customer access. Then, when the China Shop program is started up, the sales staff can login with the administrative user ID that tells the program to make these administrative functions available via hidden menu items.

If no administrative work is required, then the sales staff member can log in with a user ID that tells the program to hide these functions. How does that sound?"

"That sounds great to me," Joe said.

I began to say that I believed we might be through with the requirements statement when I was interrupted by Valerie, who said that she thought we needed to modify the program in one final, subtle way.

"I was thinking," Valerie said. "With the introduction of all of these new forms – the procedure that currently changes the color of our form was designed to work only with the single form in the original China Shop project. Since we are adding several new forms to the project, we'll also need to modify that procedure, won't we?"

"Right you are, Valerie!" I said.

I saw Dave dutifully make this change to his copy of the requirements statement.

"I have only one question," Lou said. "Do we need to provide a means to add or edit the passwords in the **Users** table from within the program?"

"I don't think so," I said. "That might be more trouble than it's worth. It's my intention to only have two valid login IDs anyway. We'll just add two records to this table directly through Microsoft Access, with unique user IDs and passwords. If for some reason Joe has a desire to change either the user ID or password, he can always do that directly through Microsoft Access."

"Asking Joe to use Access to update the user records," Kathy said, "seems to me to be introducing the same type of problem he now has with Midge and Notepad. Shouldn't he be able to update the user records from within the program – even though he might never need to do so?"

I thought about Kathy's comment for a minute or so, and told her and the class she was right – we should provide that functionality. Of course, we would still need to use Access to add the initial user records.

"Dave, would you add a view and update capability to the requirements statement?" I asked.

I gave everyone a moment to think about any other changes to the program they might want to make. There were none, and after a minute, I asked Dave to display the requirements statement in its entirety on the classroom projector:

# Requirements Statement
## Bullina China Shop Modifications

The China Shop program will be modified in this way:

1. A Microsoft Access database called China will be created. This database will contain four tables called Customer, Inventory, Transaction and Users.

2. The China Shop program will be modified to collect customer information (name, address, city, state, zip code, and optionally a phone number) from the customer and store it in the Customer table of a Microsoft Access database. Collection of customer information will take place in this way. When the Sales Quotation is displayed, a new command button labeled "I'll Take It" will become visible. When the customer clicks on this command button, a new Visual Basic form captioned "Do you have a Customer ID" will be displayed containing three command buttons - one labeled 'Yes', one labeled 'No - New Customer' and the other reading 'Yes, but I can't remember'.

3. If the customer selects 'Yes' then an input box will be displayed prompting the customer for their customer ID. The customer ID they enter will then be located in the database. If the customer ID does not exist, a message will be displayed informing the customer that they have entered an incorrect customer ID, and they will be returned to the previous form to re-enter the number.

4. If the customer selects 'No - New Customer' then a form captioned "Welcome New Customer!" will be displayed, containing a series of text boxes to be used for them to enter their customer information, which will then be stored in the database. A message box will be displayed with their newly assigned Customer ID, along with a reminder to write it down on a pre-printed customer card stacked near the PC.

5. If the customer selects 'Yes, but I can't remember' then a form captioned "Let me help you" will be displayed with a list box containing every customer name and customer ID in the database. The customer will then be able to select from a customer ID from the list.

6. After the customer has supplied a valid Customer ID, then the program will write a transaction record for each item of china purchased to the database.

7. A sales quotation will then be printed on a printer attached to the PC for the customer to pick up and carry to the sales clerk at the front of the store.

8. The China Shop program will be modified to store inventory data (china brands, items, and prices) in the database. As part of this modification, a new Visual Basic form will be designed to permit the China Shop staff to view inventory, edit existing inventory, or add new inventory records.

9. A new Visual Basic form will be designed to permit the China Shop staff to view, edit or add Customer records.

10. A new Visual Basic form will be designed to permit the China Shop staff to view Transaction records.

11. A new Visual Basic form will be designed to permit the sales staff to login with a special administrative password, allowing them to perform administrative functions identified in numbers 8, 9 and 10 above. Because of this, a new table will be created in the database containing a user ID and a password.

12. A new Visual Basic form will be designed to permit the China Shop staff to view, edit or add User records.

13. The program will be modified to include a Staff function menu with submenu items for Customer, Inventory and Transactions. This menu will be accessible when the user logs in successfully with the administrative password - otherwise, they will remain invisible to the customer.

14. Because the China Shop program will now consist of multiple forms, the Colors submenu items "Customize" and "Default" must be modified to change the colors of all forms within the program.

I looked around the classroom. It had been a long first day of class, and I could see that in the faces of the students. Joe Bullina looked happy, though, and that's what mattered most.

"I know everyone is probably anxious to get started on these modifications," I said, "but we need to learn something about database theory and Microsoft Access before we even make the first change – it will probably be a few weeks before we begin modifying the China Shop program. Next week, we'll look at database theory, and try to solidify in your minds some of the terms you heard today. Then, the following week, we'll build our China Shop Access database."

I turned to Joe, thanked him for coming, and told him that in 9 weeks he would have his modified China Shop program. With that, I dismissed the class for the day.

## Chapter Summary

In this chapter we reviewed the status of the real world China Shop Program, and met with Joe Bullina who assisted us in discussing the modifications to the China Shop program that he wants us to implement.

During the course of our first class together, we developed the detailed requirements statement for the modified China Shop program. The requirements statement will form the basis of the actions we will take during the remainder of the class to database-enable the China Shop.

In essence, the new requirements cater for the following enhancements to the original program:

- Allowing staff to update inventory price information from within the China Shop program
- Gathering and storing information about customers
- Creating and storing information about purchases made by customers over time
- Giving the China Shop staff the ability to update information about who can use the system

In the next chapter, we'll follow the second class in my database programming course, during which I'll introduce my students to the theory and practice of databases, and start thinking about how to implement these new requirements.

Learn to Program Databases with Visual Basic

## Chapter 2
# Database Primer

In the last chapter, we reviewed the China Shop Project and discussed the new requirements that Joe Bullina had for the system. In this chapter, we'll follow my Visual Basic Database class as we discuss database theory using Microsoft Access as our database tool of choice. In doing so, we'll introduce the terminology that's used to describe databases, and concentrate on the features of databases that will let us enhance the functionality of the China Shop application.

The key topics I'll cover in this week's class are:

- What a database is
- The components of an Access database
- How Access stores information
- How Access links together data from different sources

By covering these topics, we'll enable the students in my class to understand how to implement the China Shop project's new features using an Access database. Let's rejoin my class as they assemble for the second week's session. We'll start off by briefly talking about what a database *is*.

## What is a Database?

"OK, everyone," I said as I welcomed the students back to our second class, "today we'll be discussing databases. In general terms, 'database' is just a word to describe a collection of information. These days, though, the term 'database' usually refers to an **electronic store of related information**."

"Related?" queried Rhonda. "What does that mean?"

"Simply," I replied, "that the information that's stored there all has something in common – it's related to a particular subject or activity. So, all the information in the China Shop's database will relate in some way to the shop's activities – we won't, for example, be storing information about Joe Bullina's favorite films in there."

"OK," said Rhonda, "that sounds sensible – 'related' means that everything in the database is connected with the same thing."

I decided to get back to my introductory theme.

"Specifically," I continued, "we'll be looking at **Access** databases. I'll be taking you through some material on database theory to give you some background that'll help you understand how Visual Basic talks to databases when we come to that later in the course."

"Database theory sounds pretty deep," Mary said, "I hope I can follow along with this. I took a course on database management theory last year, and I found it to be pretty tough."

"I know what you mean," Rhonda said. "I took that same course, and when it came to discussing some of the technical material, I was completely lost."

"Don't worry," I said. "We'll discuss some database theory today, but we won't be getting into theory nearly as much as you would in a course on database management. Today, you'll learn enough theory to make you comfortable working with databases in Visual Basic."

"So," I asked, "what would we want to use a database for?"

"Um...to store information?" ventured Chuck.

"Yes, that's right," I confirmed, "but information about what?"

"Well," answered Dave, "it could be about anything."

"Yes," I agreed, "and the emphasis is on the word **thing**. Databases store information about things: people, places, or objects – for example."

"That sounds very much like the definition of a noun," Rachel ventured.

"You're right, Rachel," I replied, "in the sense that a noun is a name for a tangible object like a person or a place. And if you think about it, the type of information that we decided we wanted to keep track of in the China Shop database last week was just like that – Customers, Inventory (i.e. the china pieces we have in the store), Transactions, and Users. All of those are nouns."

I paused for a moment, letting this sink in, before continuing:

"In database terminology, anything that we store information about is called an **entity**. An entity is a **thing**. So it's really information about entities that we're storing in our database."

I drew a quick sketch on the board:

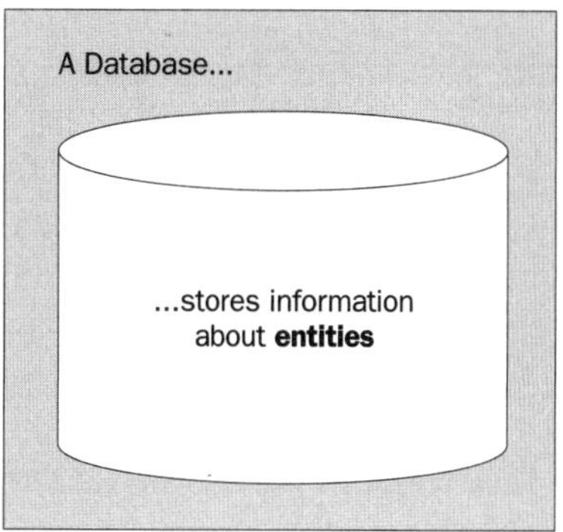


"This drum-shape is the one I'll use whenever I draw a database," I said. "I think it's a good way of showing that a database is really a repository for storing information about entities."

"Can you clarify this a little for me?" Ward chimed in. "You've already given us an example of some of the things that a database keeps track of in the China Shop – customers, inventory, transactions and users. These are all entities, because they're the real things in the China Shop we need to store data about. Is that right?"

"That's right," I said

"Can you give us another example of some entities that a database might keep track of?" Rhonda asked.

"Sure thing," I answered. "How about our own university? I can tell you there's a big database here that the university uses to keep track of students, instructors, courses, and rooms – to name just a few. Again, these are all things – entities – that we can put a name to."

I thought for a moment and then said, "Let me make this easier to visualize. Since it won't be until next week that we actually create our own China Shop database, we don't yet have a database of our own to look at with Microsoft Access. However, there's a sample Access database supplied with Access and Visual Basic. It's called **Biblio**, and it can be a great learning tool. Let's look at it now..."

> You should find the Biblio database in the same directory that your Visual Basic program files are stored in. On my machine, this is `C:\Program Files\Microsoft Visual Studio\VB98`. If you can't find this database immediately, you can open up Windows Explorer and use the **Tools | Find | Files or Folders** menu options to locate it. To explore Biblio for yourself, you'll need Microsoft Access installed on your machine. Otherwise, just follow along with the text.

"Umm – what does **Biblio** store information about?" asked Dave.

"**Biblio** is packed full of information about books – titles, authors, publishers and so on. It was designed to demonstrate the features of Access databases, and it's pre-filled with thousands of lines of information so that we can do some realistic data manipulation. Let's take a peek..."

I started up Access on my classroom PC, and navigated via the File | Open Database menu option to the **Biblio** database file – **Biblio.mdb**:

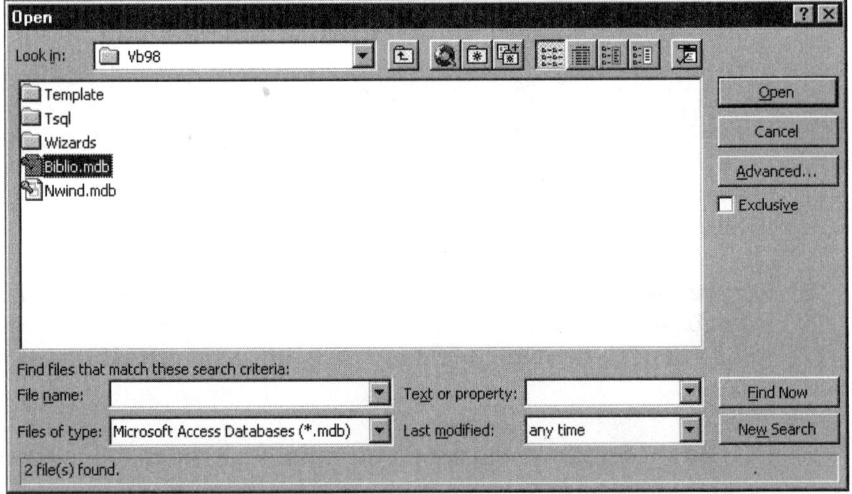


"Notice," I said, "that this file has the extension **.mdb**. This indicates that this file is an Access database. In Access, this **.mdb** database file is the overall container that holds all of our data, and it's this **.mdb** file that physically sits on your computer's hard drive or networked file server. The way that the detailed data in the database is *physically* stored is hidden from us – thankfully! The Access program acts as a **database management system** and looks after all the physical data storage and retrieval for us. This means that we don't have to worry about how to write the data to the disk – we just tell Access to do it for us, and Access handles all of the details."

"So," said Dave, "we don't need to know how the input and output processing works on the database file?"

"No," I answered, "all of that can remain invisible to us. What we're really interested in is how we can get at the database and use it via our Visual Basic program."

"Sounds good to me," said Blaine, "anything for an easy life!"

"Just a minute," said Ward, "what would happen if Joe Bullina didn't have Access on his store's PC? How would the China Shop program be able to get at the database?"

"That really is an excellent question, Ward," I replied, "and the answer is that so long as you have Visual Basic on your machine, you can store and retrieve data from any Access database; that is, a database with a `.mdb` extension that was created using the Access application. The reason for this is that Visual Basic has the facilities built into it to allow it to communicate directly with Access databases – even without the Access program there to act as intermediary."

"That's good," said Ward approvingly. " It sounds a bit magical to me."

"Not really," I said, "just some cleverness built into Visual Basic's armory of DLLs!"

"DLLs?" Rachel queried.

"I know what they are!" exclaimed Rhonda. "We covered this in the introductory class. It means **Dynamic Link Library**."

"That's right, Rhonda." I said. "A DLL is a file which is used to store pre-written and pre-tested program instructions. We can incorporate a DLL into our own programs by including a reference to it. This gives us access to the functionality of the DLL without having to physically include the code in our own programs. So DLLs are, essentially, shared programs whose functionality we can use when we run our own programs."

Moving along, I double-clicked on the file to open the `Biblio` database in the `VB98` directory of my PC. When I did, the following screen appeared on the classroom projector:

"This is the Access **Database Window**," I said. "When you first open up a database file in Access, this is the window that you see. I should also say that the *exact* window that's displayed will vary depending on which version of Access you're using – but the overall content will be similar. Notice that there are six tabs in the database window – Tables, Queries, Forms, Reports, Macros and Modules:"

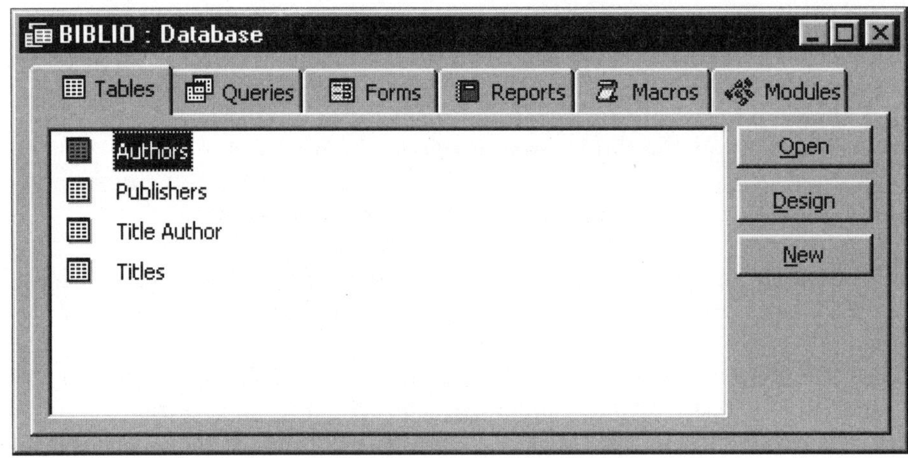


"Each tab," I continued, "gives us access to a collection of different Access components: these are the different types of **objects** that can make up a Access database. In our course, we're really only going to be concerned with the first tab – the Tables tab. The objects in the other tabs are used for manipulating and displaying database data within Access, but the tables shown on the Tables tab are where our data is actually stored. We'll be using our Visual Basic program to display and manipulate the data, rather than the Access program itself. This is because Visual Basic is a more powerful programming tool than Access, although Access databases are a great way to store information. So we get the best of both worlds."

Nobody seemed to have a problem with this, so I continued, "OK then, let's see how the tables on the Tables tab relate to the `.mdb` database file."

## Databases and Tables

"The Tables tab is almost like a filing cabinet, with each one of the icons representing a different file drawer in the cabinet. In this sense, our filing cabinet as a whole contains 'information about books', and the individual drawers contain that information broken down into subdivisions. These subdivisions are the **entities** that we mentioned earlier."

"Right..." began Ward, "those four icons labeled `Authors`, `Publishers`, `Title Author`, and `Titles` – they represent the entities?"

"That's right," I said. "Each one of those icons represents one of the entities that makes up the `Biblio` database. In Microsoft Access, each entity is stored in a structure called a **table** – so there is a separate table for each entity. Our `Biblio` database has four tables, one for each type of thing that we want to store information about – for instance, authors or publishers."

"In summary, a database is made up of one or more tables that hold information – or **data** – about entities. Everybody OK with this so far?" I asked.

Most people nodded, but a few avoided my eyes, so I decided to reiterate a little.

"Let me just recap where we've got to," I said. "The `Biblio` database stores information about books..."

Looking a little frustrated, Dave interrupted me: "Books is a pretty fluffy concept, isn't it? There are loads of things that could be connected with books."

"Yes indeed," I replied. "The information we need to tell us about the global idea of 'books' can be broken up into chunks: information about individual books, information about who writes them, information about who publishes them, and so on. These types of information – all related to books - are the entities we discussed earlier. Let me show you."

I quickly sketched out another diagram on the board:

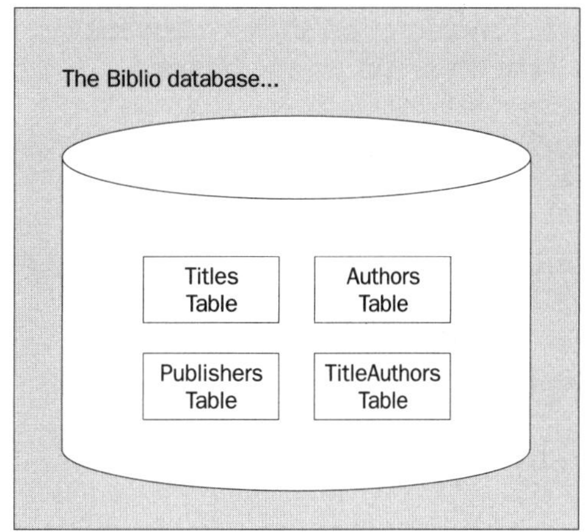


"Yes, I can see that," said Dave.

"I guess," Kate said, "that our China database will be made up of several tables in the same way?"

"You're right. Are you sure you haven't done this before, Kate?" I said, jokingly. "We'll look in detail at the Customers, Inventory, Transactions and Users tables that make up the China database later. These tables will store all the information that we need to keep about the China Shop. But for the moment, let's stick with the `Biblio` database so that we can get a clearer idea of how Access databases fit together and function."

Taking a breath, I carried on.

"We've seen so far that an Access database is a file that contains data stored in tables, and that these tables represent the global information subdivided into entities. What we need to do now is look at how that information is further broken down and stored so that we can view it and manipulate it."

"Wow," said Rhonda, "that was a mouthful!"

"Yes," I agreed, "it will all become clear shortly – just bear with me for a while. Let's think about the data stored about 'books' in bit more detail, by looking at just *one* of the Biblio entities: in this instance we'll take a look at the **Authors** entity, the information about which is stored in the `Authors` table of the `Biblio` database. Earlier, I likened the **database** to a filing cabinet, and the **table** to a drawer in the filing cabinet. The next thing we're going to do is open up one of those drawers and take a closer look at the information inside."

"OK," I continued, "the Authors table contains information about the entity - the thing - called Authors. If we're talking about a real instance of an author, what might be the kind of information that we'd want to store about them? You call your ideas out, and I'll write them up on the board."

After a few moments of pencil-tapping and brow-furrowing, the students started to come up with some suggestions:

"Well, we'd need to know their name, I guess," ventured Bob.

"Yes," agreed Lou, "you'd want their first name, surname, and maybe their middle initials."

"Uh-huh," I said, "maybe. What else?

"Um," began Tom "how about their address and telephone number?"

Writing these up, I said: "Yes, these are good ideas too. Anyone else?"

Rhonda raised her hand and said "What about their age?"

"Sure," I agreed, "that could be useful. Any more?"

I let the silence last a few seconds, then said, "OK, that's enough for the moment. Let's see what we've got..."

On the board, I'd scribbled the following:

Name
First Name
Surname
Middle Initials
Age
Address
Telephone Number

I already knew how the `Authors` table was constructed, so I needed to try and shape this brainstormed material a little.

"Let me simplify this information some," I said. "Here's what I suggest we store about each author we want data about," I continued, and drew another sketch on the board:

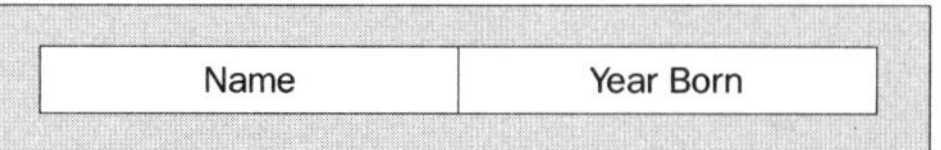


"I've changed 'age' to 'year born' so that the information can be calculated instead of needing to be physically updated when the author's age changes after every birthday."

"What about the telephone number and address?" queried Tom, "where have they gone?"

"Ah, yes," I replied. "The point about the `Biblio` database is that it's more suited to use in libraries and bookshops: they're more likely to contact the publisher rather than the author direct – that's why I've left that information out."

"OK," said Tom, maybe a *little* reluctant to let his idea go.

"We'll look at how `Biblio` stores information about Publishers later," I added. OK, now just suppose that there are two authors with the same name – how could we choose between them?"

"Easy," said Dave, "you can tell them apart by the year that they were born."

"Probably true," I agreed. "But what if they were born in the same year?"

There was a silence that lasted a few seconds, which I broke by saying:

"What we need is a bit of information that **uniquely identifies** each author. So I'll add another element to the data that we'll need to store:"

| Au_ID | Name | Year Born |
|---|---|---|

"Now, Au_ID stands for 'Author Identifier', which is a bit of information – say, a number – that lets us uniquely identify each individual author. Now, in my opinion, we have the core information that we'll need to store about each and every author."

"That makes sense to me," said Dave.

Rhonda put up her hand again: "John, can I ask you something?"

"Sure," I answered, "ask away."

"My question is this: how does this relate to the table structure?"

"That's a great question – it takes me on to what I want to cover next! Say we were going to store the Name, Year Born and Au_ID data in a **spreadsheet**: we could use these as headings for three columns in the spreadsheet:"

| Au_ID | Name | Year Born |
|---|---|---|

"Then, for each author, we'd add the data in successive rows:"

| Au_ID | Name | Year Born |
|---|---|---|
| 1 | Jane Doe | 1967 |
| 2 | John Doe | 1965 |
| 3 | Gillian Doe | 1984 |
| 4 | Jim Doe | 1986 |

"That's clear'" said Ward, "this isn't as difficult as I thought it might be!"

"Thank you," I replied. "So," I went on, "we've got our columns, with headings that describe the nature of the information in the column. Remember, each of these headings/columns is going to store data that will tell us something about the entity called **Author**. We've also got our rows, which contain the data for individual authors, who are real-world instances of the Author entity. This 'spreadsheet' format is exactly how Access shows us the data in each table. The rows of information in our spreadsheet example each describe an individual instance of an author, and in database terminology, each row is called a **record**. All the information in a particular row relates to a specific instance of an author."

## Tables and Records

"Tables contain records, and each record in a table represents a particular instance of a thing – or entity. I mentioned that here at the university we have a database table called Students. Within the Student table, there are records, and each record in the Student table represents a single real world instance of a student."

"Almost like a folder in a filing cabinet drawer labeled 'Students'?" Melissa put in.

"Precisely," I said. "And next week, when we design and build the China Shop database, you'll see that each record in the Inventory table will represent a single real world piece of china, with a name and a selling price."

"So there's something in the record that describes the entity, is that right?" Rhonda asked.

"Exactly," I replied. "The descriptive data is in the rows of the spreadsheet I drew earlier. Each **cell** of descriptive data in the spreadsheet is known as a **field** in database terms."

"I'm beginning to see now," Lou said. "A single table called Inventory will contain many records, with each record describing a piece of china."

"You have it, Lou," I replied, "each field in the row would give us a part of that description, and all of the fields in the row put together would be the complete description of that piece of China. That might look something like this:"

| China Brand | China Item Name | Price | Item Identifier |
|---|---|---|---|
| Mikasa | Plate | $4 | 1 |
| Corelle | Plate | $5 | 2 |

I continued by explaining that **ordinarily** a table should **not** contain information about any other entities – if it does, that's usually an indication that there's a problem with the design of the database. For example, the China shop's Inventory table shouldn't contain information about customers, and `Biblio's Authors` table shouldn't contain information about titles of books that the author had written.

"That means that the Customer table in the China Shop database we discussed last week should contain information **only** about customers, and nothing else, is that right?" Peter asked.

"That's right," I agreed.

"And not transactions!" Dave interjected.

"Right again," I said.

There were a few seconds of silence and then...

"But," Linda asked, "if we don't store information about the items of china that the customer purchased in the Customer table along with the Customer's record, how will we ever know what the customer purchased?"

"Good question," I said, "and this is where the Transaction table comes into play. The Transaction table will store information about customers, the china items that they have purchased, and the date that they purchased them."

"I'm confused," Ward said, frowning. "If the Transaction table contains information about Customers *and* Inventory, then isn't that a contradiction of what you just said – that a table should contain information about only one entity?"

"I used the word **ordinarily**," I said, smiling. "**Most** tables will contain data about only one entity, but there are special tables – called **bridge tables** - which we'll learn about in more detail next week. Bridge tables, by design, contain data about more than one entity. These tables are designed to link together information about entities from different tables."

"I'm starting to get a little bit lost," said Rachel, "can we see some of this for ourselves in Access, please?" inquired Rachel.

"Of course," I answered, "let's start by taking a look at the `Authors` table in the `Biblio` database."

I selected the Authors table on the Tables tab, and clicked on the Open button:

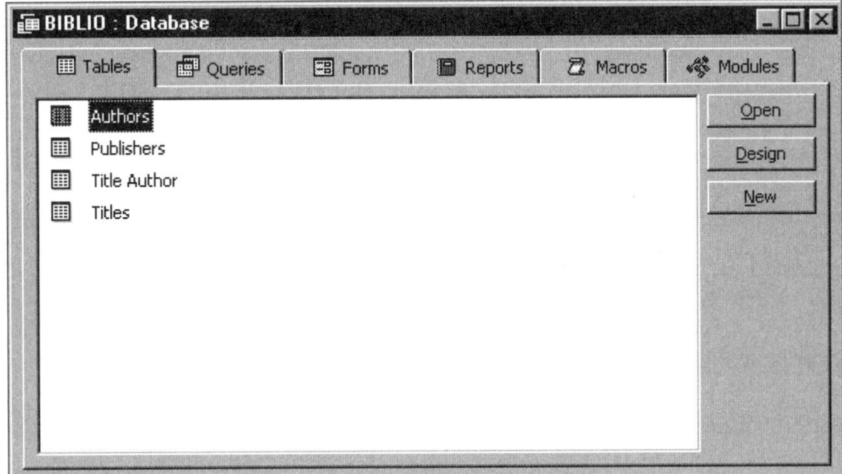


This is the screen that appeared once the table opened up:

Authors : Table

| Au_ID | Author | Year Born |
|---|---|---|
| 1 | Jacobs, Russell | |
| 2 | Metzger, Philip W. | |
| 3 | Boddie, John | |
| 4 | Sydow, Dan Parks | |
| 6 | Lloyd, John | |
| 8 | Thiel, James R. | |
| 10 | Ingham, Kenneth | |
| 12 | Wellin, Paul | |
| 13 | Kamin, Sam | |
| 14 | Gaylord, Richard | |
| 15 | Curry, Dave | |
| 17 | Gardner, Juanita Mercado | |
| 19 | Knuth, Donald E. | |
| 21 | Hakim, Jack | |
| 22 | Winchell, Jeff | |
| 24 | Clark, Claudia | |

Record: 1 of 6246

"This is a view of the Authors table," I said, "known in Access as the **Datasheet View**. You can see that it's very similar in appearance to a spreadsheet. In database terminology, the columns are referred to as **fields**, and the rows are called **records**. Now, this view shows us that the `Authors` table contains three fields: **Au_ID**, **Author** and **Year Born**. Obviously, the `Author` field is the same as the Name heading that I used in the earlier example. If you look at the bottom of datasheet view window, you'll see that the table contains 6,246 records and that our record pointer – the triangle in the first column of the datasheet – is positioned on record number 1."

## Records and Fields

"So these are the actual records in the table?" Rhonda asked. " It really helps to be able to see what you are talking about. How would you define what a record is, again?"

"I can answer that," Melissa said. "A **record** is a collection of attributes that describe a particular instance of an entity."

"And a field?" asked Rhonda.

"A **field**," continued Melissa, "is just an attribute or a characteristic of a record, such as the Author's Id, Name, or year of birth."

"Great work," Kevin interjected.

"Absolutely right," I agreed, "but here's another question: can anyone tell me how I know that the `Authors` table contains only three fields?"

"May I?" said Melissa. "We know that the `Author's` table contains three fields, Au_ID, Author and Year Born, because their names appear in bold at the top of each column in the datasheet view window. We also know that the `Authors` table has only three fields because, if there were more fields, we would see a horizontal scroll bar at the bottom of the datasheet view window. This would allow us to scroll to the right to see the rest of the rest of the fields in the table."

"Yes, that's a good explanation," I said, realizing that Melissa had more Access experience than the other students in the class.

"Let me sum that up with this diagram," I said, while displaying the following slide:

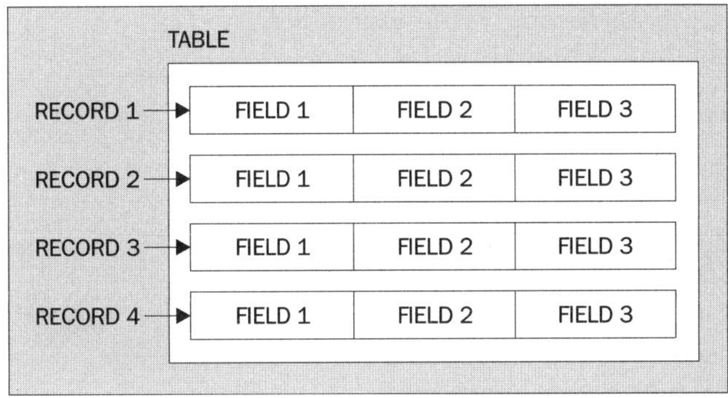


"So a database **field**," Rhonda said, "is just a characteristic of the record in which it appears?"

"That's right," I said. "Remember, a record is a representation of a particular real world thing (such as an individual author) – and database fields contain data or information used to describe that thing. Tables are made up of records, and records are made up of fields. Quite naturally, the more fields in a record, the more descriptive the record."

"What about that number at the bottom of the datasheet view window?" Rhonda asked. "I believe you said that was the record count. And you also mentioned something called a record pointer?"

"Actually, there are two numbers that appear at the bottom of the datasheet view window," I said. "The last number, in this case 6246, is the total number of records in the table. The first number represents the current record, which is the record on which the record pointer is currently positioned:"

"And the record pointer is that arrow pointing to the right in the left margin of the window?" Kathy asked.

"That's right," I said, "although technically speaking, we say that the record pointer is in the first column of the datasheet view window."

"What does the record pointer do?" Chuck asked.

"The record pointer," I answered, "is much like the insertion point in a Word document – in Access, the record pointer tells us what the current record is."

"Current record?" Rhonda asked.

"You'll see later on," I continued, "that in Access, in addition to adding records to a table, you can also edit and delete existing records. It's important to know which record in the datasheet view is the current record, prior to editing or deleting the record."

"Can you show us how to change which is the current record?" Valerie asked.

"Sure, Valerie," I said, and I used my mouse to change the current record simply by clicking in that left-hand column:

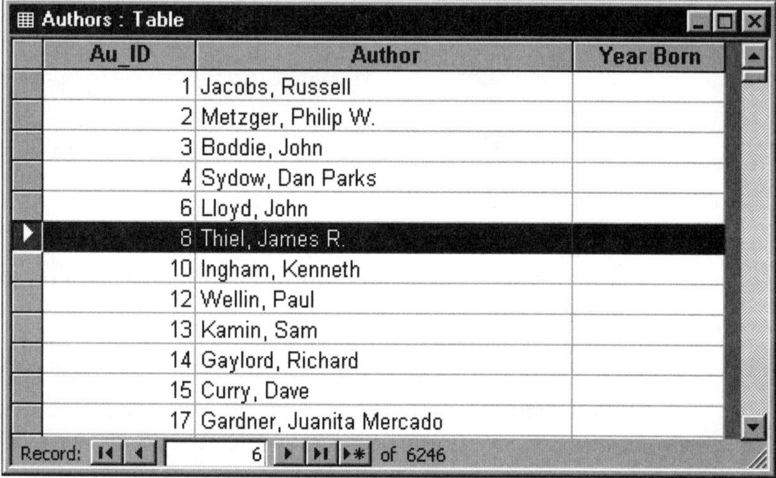

Authors : Table

| Au_ID | Author | Year Born |
|---|---|---|
| 1 | Jacobs, Russell | |
| 2 | Metzger, Philip W. | |
| 3 | Boddie, John | |
| 4 | Sydow, Dan Parks | |
| 6 | Lloyd, John | |
| 8 | Thiel, James R. | |
| 10 | Ingham, Kenneth | |
| 12 | Wellin, Paul | |
| 13 | Kamin, Sam | |
| 14 | Gaylord, Richard | |
| 15 | Curry, Dave | |
| 17 | Gardner, Juanita Mercado | |

Record: 6 of 6246

"Notice," I said, "that if you click your mouse anywhere on the record, that action makes that record the current record. You can also use the vertical scrollbar to quickly scroll through the records in the table – although you still need to click on a record to make it current."

I then used the vertical scroll bar to scroll several hundred records down into the table, and then again to move back to my original position.

"What are those buttons at the bottom of the Table window for?" Bob asked. "There are five buttons and one textbox."

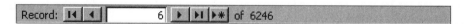

"Those are called VCR buttons," I said, "and they provide us with a quick way of moving the record pointer through the table. For instance, if you click on the left-most button, it moves your record pointer to the first row or record in the table. The button to the right of that one, the one with the arrow pointing to the left, moves your record pointer up one record in the datasheet view."

"In other words," Dave said, "that button moves the record pointer to the previous record in relation?"

"That's right," I agreed. "That's a more technical way of putting it, Dave."

"I've noticed," Rachel said, "that you've used the term 'row' several times when talking about records. Can those terms be used interchangeably?"

"Yes," I answered, "you will see the terms used interchangeably."

I continued my demonstration of the datasheet view window by explaining that the textbox appearing after the Previous button allows you to move to a specific record in the table by entering its record number into the textbox.

"How practical is that?" Ward asked. "Do you often know the record number of the record you want to move to?"

"Your point is a good one, Ward," I replied. "Record numbers aren't all that useful when moving through the records of a table. But if you had a table with a million records in it, entering 500000 into this text box to get you to the mid-point of the records would be a lot faster than trying to scroll there."

I waited a moment for questions, but there were none.

"The third button," I continued, "the first one to right of the textbox, with the arrow pointing to the right, advances your record pointer to the next record in the table. The fourth button, with an arrow pointing to the right followed by a vertical line, moves the record pointer to the very last record in the table."

"What's that button with the asterisk?" Rhonda asked, just as I was about to explain it.

"That button," I said, "tells Access that you want to add a new record to the table. Clicking on it actually opens up a new, 'empty row' for you to fill in values for the fields comprising the new record. We'll take a closer look at that next week."

To summarize, I displayed a slide showing the different components of a Access table seen via the datasheet view:

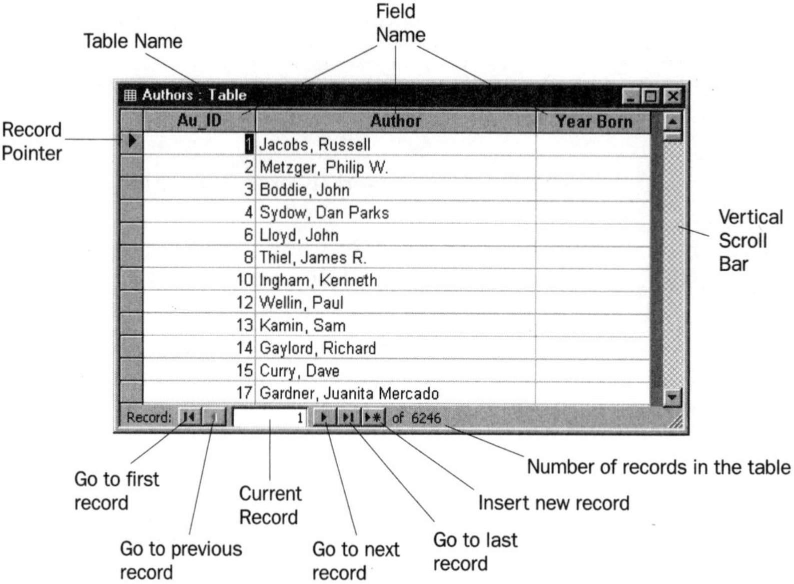


"In many ways," Blaine said, "an Access table really *does* remind me of an Excel spreadsheet."

"I agree, as I said earlier," I replied, "and that's a good way to think about Access databases: in the datasheet view, a database table is laid out much like a spreadsheet, consisting of rows and columns. Each column represents a field, and each row represents a record."

I waited a moment before continuing:

"While we're inside Access, let me talk a little about the different types of data that we can store in Access fields. That way, we can see how the nitty-gritty of data storage relates to the table, record and field structures that we've already talked about."

## Access Field Types

"In Visual Basic," I began, "we have different types of variables, and we saw in the last lesson that we have different types of fields in the disk file we use in the China Shop project. Access has different types of fields for us to use as well. In Access, there are a variety of field types that you can specify for the fields in your table when you design it. I just happen to have a chart here."

I then displayed this chart on the classroom projector:

| **Access Field Type** | **VB Comparable Data Type** | **Description** |
|---|---|---|
| Text | String | Text or combinations of text and numbers, as well as numbers that don't require calculations, such as phone numbers. Up to 255 characters. |
| Memo | String | Lengthy text or combinations of text and numbers. Up to 65,535 characters. |
| Number | Integer, Long, Single, Double | Numeric data used in mathematical calculations. |
| Date/Time | Date | Date and time values for the years 100 through 9999. |
| Currency | Currency | Currency values and numeric data used in mathematical calculations involving data with one to four decimal places. Accurate to 15 digits on the left side of the decimal separator and to 4 digits on the right side. |
| AutoNumber | | A unique sequential (incremented by 1) number or random number assigned by Access whenever a new record is added to a table. AutoNumber fields can't be manually updated. |
| Yes/No | Boolean | Yes and No values and fields that contain only one of two values (Yes/No, True/False, or On/Off) |

"These aren't all of the them," I said, "but these are the field types that we'll be concerned with in our course. Remember, my goal here is not to turn you into Access experts – I want to give you enough information to be able to create your own databases and tables, and interface them with your Visual Basic programs."

"These field types seem pretty similar to the Visual Basic data types we use for variable declarations," Bob observed.

"That's true," I said, "and I think that you'll find that the rules for their use are just about the same as well."

"I think Bob spoke too soon," Linda said. "What is the AutoNumber field type used for? We don't have that in Visual Basic."

"You're right, Linda," I replied, "AutoNumber is not a data type in Visual Basic. Do you remember our discussion last week with Joe Bullina, when we said we could automatically generate a **unique** Customer ID when a new customer registered with the China Shop? Well, the AutoNumber field type is how we'll do that. By specifying a field as AutoNumber, whenever a new record is added to the table, Access will take the value in this field for the previous record in the table, add 1 to it, and make that result the value for the field in the new record. So, if there are 39 records in a table, and we add a new record, it will automatically be given the value 40 in the relevant AutoNumber field. Furthermore, there's an option to generate a random number in the field, as well as the more regular 'increment by 1' option."

"That sounds incredibly powerful," Tom said.

"It is," I agreed. "We could do the same thing with some processing logic in Visual Basic – but by using AutoNumber as the field type, we don't need to worry about this in our program – the database will do it for us."

I noticed that Ward had been studying the field types chart intently.

"It seems to me," he said, "that in Access you seem to have fewer choices for numeric data types than you do in Visual Basic. Visual Basic has four numeric data types; Access seems to have just the one type – **Number**."

"From the chart I displayed," I answered, "that would seem to be the case. However, my chart is showing you a list of the possible values for the field type in the Access **Table Design** window. It's only one piece of the puzzle when it comes to designing tables in Access – there's a wider range of options available to you when you're in the Access design window. Let me close the datasheet view window and open up the design window for the Authors table. The design window is where we design (of course!) and create our Access databases, and where we can change the properties of existing databases. You'll see that there are some additional parameters that can be specified in the design window besides field type."

I closed the datasheet view window and opened up the design view window for the `Authors` table by selecting Authors on the Tables tab and clicking on the Design Button:

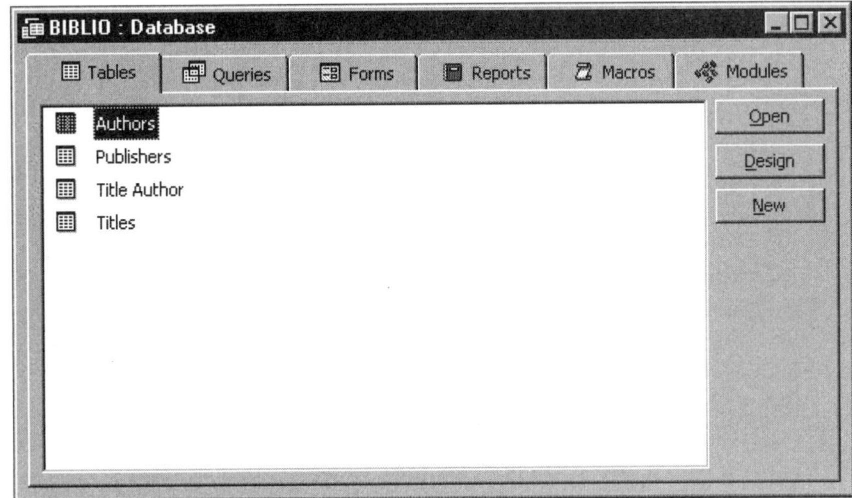


As a result, the following screen shot was displayed on the classroom projector:

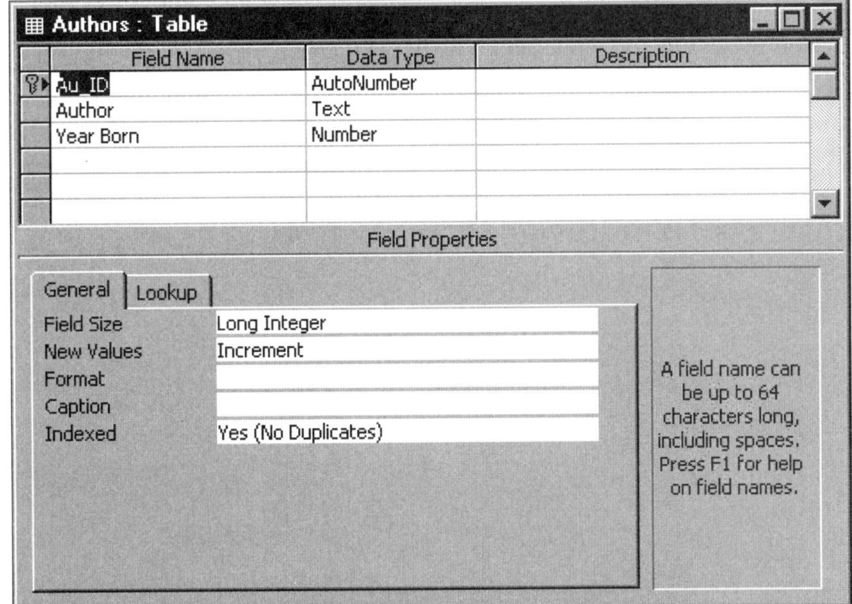


"This is the Access Table Design view window," I said, "and it is here that we specify the design of the `Authors` table."

"I'm surprised that we can get to the design view window for this table – the `Authors` table already exists, and we didn't create it, after all." Kevin said.

"Yes, that's right, we can," I confirmed. "In Access, we can change the design and structure of our database anytime, even if the table already has records in it. As you can see, there are a lot of similarities between the datasheet view window and the design view window," I said. "Both have rows and columns. The difference is that whereas the datasheet view has columns of fields and rows of records, the design view window's columns represent **field definition characteristics**. So, Field Name, Data Type, and Description are what Access needs us to supply details of for each of the fields that we want to define in our table. In design view, the rows are where we enter the specific information about the fields themselves: the information in each row describes a distinct field in the table."

I saw some confusion in the faces of my students, and so I gave them a moment or two to absorb this. I continued by pointing out that the structure of the Authors table in the design view window matched up perfectly with what we had seen in the datasheet view window.

"The design view window." I continued, "contains the definitions of the three fields that we saw in the datasheet view window. But in the design view window, we get to see so much more than just the data in the fields – we get to see the actual definition for the field in the table. Notice that the Au_ID field is defined as an AutoNumber field, Author is defined as a Text field, and Year Born as a Number field."

"Getting back to your point, Ward – about the single Number Data type," I said, "if you look at the Field Properties window in the bottom half of the design view window, there's a property there called Field Size..."

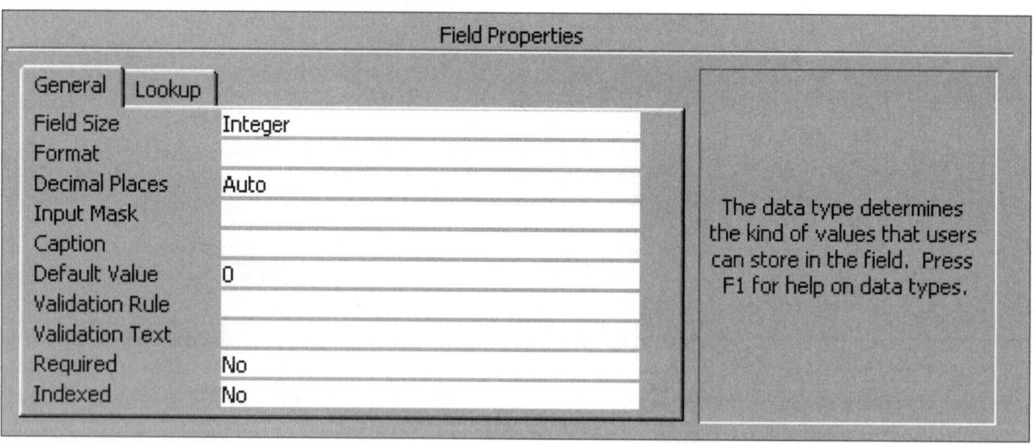


"...notice that it currently reads **Integer**. That's the default value. However, there are other possible values for Field Size."

I then clicked on the Field Size property, and a list box appeared:

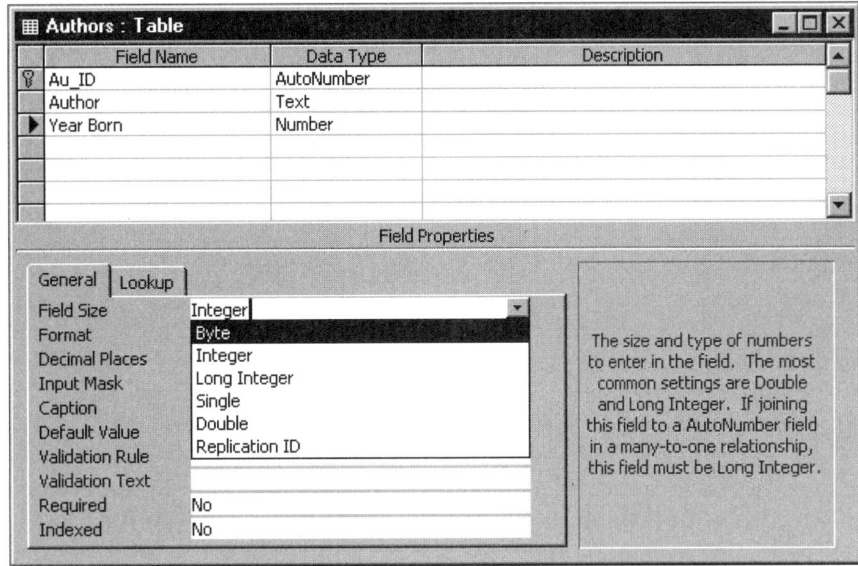


"Now I see," said Ward, "there *is* more than just one kind of numeric data type."

"Exactly," I said, "and you'll find that these Access numeric data types are identical to their corresponding Visual Basic data types."

"That's good," Kate said. "Are we going to cover what the other properties in the Field Properties window mean?"

"For the most part, no," I said. "Next week, when we create our China Shop database, we'll work with a few of them – but remember, I just want to show you enough Access to enable you to create a working database that you can then interact with from within Visual Basic. Those other properties can provide you with a great deal of control over the way your database looks and behaves in Access itself. But for our purposes, working with them is not really necessary. So, if you need to know any more information than that, you're on your own."

We had been working for quite some time, and so I suggested that we take a fifteen-minute break.

After our break, we resumed class with a question from Dave.

"When you were talking about the design view window before the break," Dave said, "I noticed that there was a little symbol next to one of the fields, like a little key. What does that mean?"

"It is a key," I replied, and it's a symbol that represents an important database concept that we should talk about next."

## Keys

"In database terms, a **key** is a device that lets us ensure that records are unique. This is important, because if we have duplicate records in a database where we don't want them, then they can cause confusion for users and wreak havoc on any programs that use the database. In Access, a **Primary Key** consists of a field (or combination of fields) in a record that **uniquely identify** that record. That means there can be no duplication of this field or combination of fields in other records, ensuring that each and every record is unique in some way. For instance, when we design the China Shop database next week, for the `Customer` table, the primary key will be the `Customer ID` field. For the `Users` table, most likely it will be the `User ID` field. In the world of databases, it's vitally important that each record be uniquely identified in this way, otherwise confusion and chaos may reign! One of the steps in designing an Access table is to specify what field or fields comprise the primary key."

"You keep saying field or fields," Melissa said, "the primary key is not always just a single field then?"

"That's right," I replied. "Sometimes a single field is not sufficient to uniquely identify a record in a table. Let me show you why. Let's take a look at the `Author` table:"

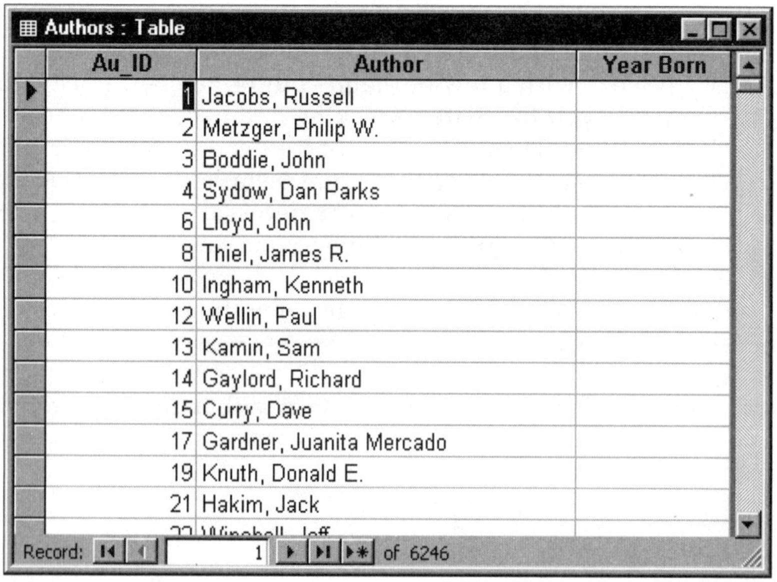

Authors : Table

| Au_ID | Author | Year Born |
|---|---|---|
| 1 | Jacobs, Russell | |
| 2 | Metzger, Philip W. | |
| 3 | Boddie, John | |
| 4 | Sydow, Dan Parks | |
| 6 | Lloyd, John | |
| 8 | Thiel, James R. | |
| 10 | Ingham, Kenneth | |
| 12 | Wellin, Paul | |
| 13 | Kamin, Sam | |
| 14 | Gaylord, Richard | |
| 15 | Curry, Dave | |
| 17 | Gardner, Juanita Mercado | |
| 19 | Knuth, Donald E. | |
| 21 | Hakim, Jack | |

Record: 1 of 6246

"Can anyone tell me which field or fields in this table would be a good choice for the primary key?"

"Would it be the author's name – the Author field?" Rhonda suggested tentatively.

"Depending on the number of records in the table," I said, "that may or may not be good choice. The more records we have in the table, the more likely it is that we will have duplicate author names – which would make the choice of using the Author's name as the primary key a bad one. Remember, the field or fields designated as the primary key must be unique – there can be no duplicates."

"Do we have duplicate author names?" Rhonda asked.

"As I recall, we do have three records where the author's name is James Smith, " I said "See if you can verify that for yourself."

I expected the class to take a few minutes to verify this – the records in the table were not in author name order, but by default, were displayed in Au_ID order. However, Kevin answered in a heartbeat.

"Yes," Kevin agreed, "but they have different middle initials."

"Wait a minute, Kevin," Rhonda said, "how did you find that out so fast? I haven't found the first Smith yet. These records aren't in Author name order!"

"I sorted them," Kevin said.

"My apologies, Rhonda," I said to her, "I forgot to tell you and the rest of the class that you can sort the records in datasheet view by clicking on the name of the field at the top of its column, then clicking on the button on the toolbar labeled AZ:"

"That sorts the datasheet alphabetically based on the selected field."

"You can also select the column header using your mouse, then right-click and select Sort-Ascending or Sort-Descending," Ward added.

"Good point, Ward," I said, and I did exactly that myself. This is the screenshot that the class saw on the classroom projector:

| Au_ID | Author |
|---|---|
| 1 | Jacobs, Russell |
| 2 | Metzger, Philip W. |
| 3 | Boddie, John |
| 4 | Sydow, Dan Parks |
| 6 | Lloyd, John |
| 8 | Thiel, James R. |
| 10 | Ingham, Kenneth |
| 12 | Wellin, Paul |
| 13 | Kamin, Sam |
| 14 | Gaylord, Richard |
| 15 | Curry, Dave |
| 17 | Gardner, Juanita Mercado |
| 19 | Knuth, Donald E. |
| 21 | Hakim, Jack |
| 22 | Winchell, Jeff |
| 24 | Clark, Claudia |
| 25 | Scott, Jack |
| 27 | Coolbaugh, James |

Sort Ascending
Sort Descending
Copy
Paste
Column Width...
Hide Columns
Freeze Columns
Insert Column
Lookup Column...
Delete Column
Rename Column

"That's much easier," Rhonda said, after taking a minute to sort the records herself using this new technique. "Now I see. There are three records whose author name is 'Smith, James'. But as Kevin pointed out, their middle initials do make them unique."

"That's true in this case," I agreed. "In this case, the Author field would be acceptable as a primary key. But still, it's possible that as the `Authors` table grows, somewhere, somehow, we'll wind up with an author name that totally duplicates a record already in the table."

"What would happen then?" Peter asked.

"In that case," I said, "we wouldn't be able to add the record."

"That would be problematic, wouldn't it?" Rhonda said. "But what can we do? Suppose we just don't have a field or fields in the record that make it unique?"

"In this instance," I said, "we can do one of two things. When it comes to people, there are two agencies that have gone to a lot of trouble to assign people something unique. The government assigns you a Social Security Number at birth, and the telephone company assigns you a phone number. Both of these are unique, and some database designers use them as the primary key to tables that keep track of people."

"Doesn't the use of a Social Security Number create a potential privacy issue?" Dave asked.

"That's right, it is a privacy concern, Dave," I agreed. "That's why my advice – unless you have a very good reason to store a Social Security Number in your database - is not to use it."

"What about a telephone number as the Primary key then?" Chuck asked.

"The telephone number is unique," I replied, "but unlike a Social Security Number, it's not yours for life. If you move, you'll receive a new telephone number, and sooner or later your old telephone number will be assigned to someone else. For that reason, it's not the best of choices."

"Not to mention the fact that – for the China Shop database anyway – Joe Bullina didn't want to force the customer to give their telephone number," Bob reminded us.

"That's true," I said. "The telephone number can also be a privacy concern for many people."

"You mentioned we could do one of two things," Mary said. "Since you're advising against using either a Social Security Number or a telephone number as the primary key, what's the other option?"

"The second choice is to create a special identifier field – an 'artificial field', so to speak – that we know is unique, and assign it to the record. This technique is one that is used all the time. For instance, I believe everyone here at the university is assigned a Student ID when they enroll?"

"That's right," Melissa said. "It's on my student ID card, and I needed it when I purchased a copy of Visual Basic in the campus bookstore. I was a little surprised that the school didn't ask me my Social Security Number when I registered for this class – instead they asked me for my Student ID. I didn't know it off the top of my head, and so I had find it on my Student ID card."

"The university chose not to use the Social Security Number as the primary key to the Student table in its database," I said, "exactly for the privacy reasons I cited earlier. Assigning a Student ID number is much safer for all parties."

"I would imagine then," Melissa said, "that's why we've chosen to create a Customer ID field in the China Shop database. Will that be the primary key to the Customers table?"

"That's exactly right," I said. "We'll do that next week."

"And I would guess," Dave said, "that the primary key of the **Authors** table is really the **Au_ID** field, not the **Author** field. Is that why the table is sorted by **Au_ID**?"

"You're right on both counts," I said. "The primary key of th **Authors** table is the **Au_ID** field. The designer of the database chose to create a special identifier field to ensure the uniqueness of each record in the table. By default, in Access, the records are sorted by the primary key in the datasheet view window."

"Is there any way," asked Rhonda, "to determine which field or fields comprise the primary key, by looking in the design view window?"

"Yes, Rhonda," I replied, catching Dave's eye, "and it's actually very easy. Let's go back to the design view window for the **Authors** table, and I'll show you."

I closed the datasheet view window, selected the **Authors** table in the Tables tab, and clicked on the Design button. The following screen shot was displayed on the classroom projector:

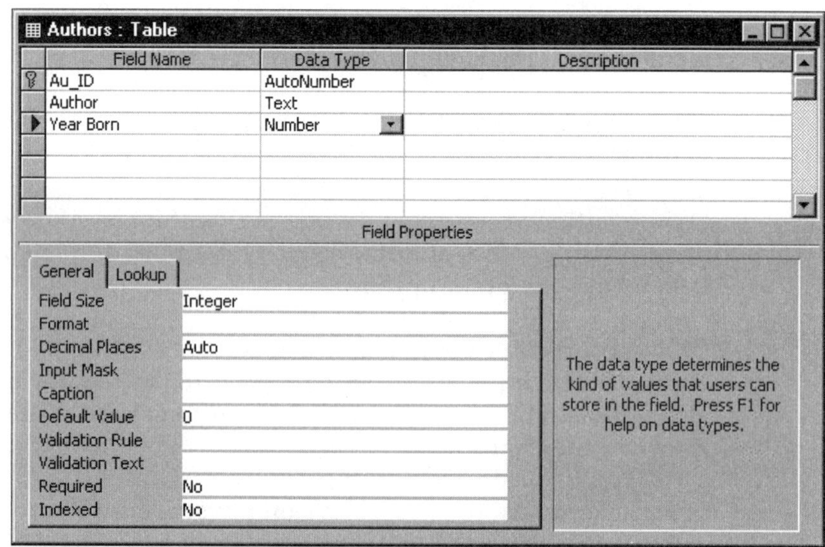


As soon as the rest of the class saw this screenshot, I knew they realized...

"I bet I know!" Rhonda said excitedly. "That key in the column next to the **Au_ID** field name – that icon indicates the field that is the primary key?"

"That's right, Rhonda," I said, "and if a combination of more than one field comprised the primary key, all the fields that made up that 'compound key' would have the key icon next to them."

"When we design the China Shop database next week," Tom asked, "will we need to have primary keys for all of the tables? And will they all be this special type of artificial field we see here?"

"Well, Tom," I answered, "each and every table needs a field or fields to be identified as the primary key. So next week, when we discuss our `China` database design in depth, we'll need to give that some thought. It's quite possible that each one of the four tables we create will have one of these artificial fields defined for it."

"What about assigning values to this special identifier field?" Rhonda said, "Isn't that going to be a big pain? Does it mean that our Visual Basic program will need to assign unique values to these fields when we start adding records to the tables?"

"That's really an excellent question, Rhonda," I said. "I mentioned a little bit before our break that there's a special data type in Access called AutoNumber, which will automatically increment a field value by 1 over the value in the previous record. This can come in quite handy with these identifier fields. In fact, if you check the data type for the `Au_ID` in the `Authors` table, you'll see that's the data type for that field. As I also mentioned earlier, that means that if the last record in the `Authors` table has an `Au_ID` value of, say, 555, then when we add a new record to the `Authors` table, its `Au_ID` value will automatically be set to 556."

"I see," Rhonda said. "That's great – I bet that can save us some coding in our program. Will each one of the primary keys in our China Shop tables be the AutoNumber data type?"

"`Customers`, `Inventory` and `Transactions`, for sure," I said. "`Users`, no."

"Why not `Users`?" Kate asked.

"The primary key of the `Users` table will probably be the `UserID`," I said, "which will be a text field – it's easier for people to remember a text-based User ID rather than a string of numbers. AutoNumber only applies to numeric fields. We'll look at the ins and outs of all of the tables in the `China` database next week."

I paused for a moment before moving on to the next topic.

"While we're talking about keys, I want to introduce you to the concept of **planned redundancy**," I resumed.

## Planned Redundancy

"Planned *what*?" interjected Rhonda.

"Redundancy," I repeated. "**Planned redundancy** is something we need to think about whenever we design a database. Allow me to explain – I'll start with the term redundancy. In database terms, redundancy means that the same piece of data appears in more than one table. And planned redundancy means that it's not an accident. In fact, for reasons that we'll discuss later, it's often a necessity."

"Let me make sure I understand this," Rhonda said. "I know that a database is a collection of tables that store data about related entities, and that tables should contain information about only one entity. Now, you're saying that the same bit of data can be in more than one table, which must mean that sometimes it's OK to have a table that contains information about more than one entity? Is that right?"

"That's perfectly correct." I said

"Saying it and understanding it," she replied, "are two different things."

"Redundancy," I went on, "helps us to establish special relationships between tables, so that we can store our data as efficiently as possible. For example, in the China Shop, we'll want to store information about customers and the items that they've purchased – purchases that possibly constitute a number of transactions. For reasons that I'll explain in detail next week, it would be inefficient to store all of that information in a single table. This means that we need to store the customer's details, the transaction details, and the details of the china items themselves, in three separate tables."

"So," Dave queried, "how can we join up all the different sets of information and see which customers bought which items, and when?"

"What we'll do," I explained, "is create some fields in the `Transactions` table that help us tie together the information about customers, transactions, and items purchased. In doing so, we'll duplicate a couple of fields from other tables, but this duplication will link the tables together usefully and provide us with benefits that outweigh the cost of having duplicate fields. A little planned redundancy will buy us a lot of flexibility and power. Don't worry, we'll work through this in a lot more detail next week."

"So what you're saying," said Dave, "is that the duplicated fields link the tables together in some kind of enriching relationship?"

"That's exactly right," I agreed.

"Is there any planned redundancy in the **Biblio** database?" asked Ward. "I may be wrong, but it seems to me that the **Authors** table only contains information about authors – so there's no redundancy there, is there?"

"That's right," I said. "The **Authors** table contains fields pertaining only to authors – **Au_ID**, **Author**, and **Year Born**. In the same way, the **Publishers** table contains fields pertaining only to publishers. But it's the remaining two tables in the **Biblio** database, **Titles** and **Title Author**, that contain fields that are also found in the other tables. The **Titles** table contains a field, **Pub_ID**, that matches the primary key in the **Publishers** table. In database theory, we give a primary key field that's duplicated in another table a special name. It's called a **Foreign Key**."

"What's that again?" Rhonda said. "Can you give us the definition of a foreign key again?"

"Sure thing," I said. "When a table contains a field whose contents duplicate the primary key values of another table, we call that field a foreign key field. We'll see next week that foreign keys make obtaining information from the multiple tables in a database easier."

"So a foreign key is an example of the planned redundancy you spoke about earlier?" said Kate.

"Well," I replied, "most, but not *all* instances of planned redundancy involve the use of foreign keys."

"The **Title Author** table", Peter observed, "seems to have taken planned redundancy to an extreme. All the fields in that table appears to be a foreign key – that is, all the fields are themselves primary keys in other tables."

I took a moment to bring up the **Title Author** table in datasheet view on the classroom projector:

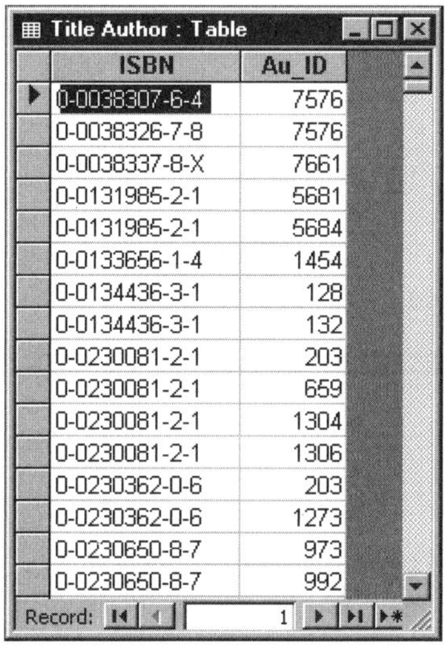

Title Author : Table

| ISBN | Au_ID |
|---|---|
| 0-0038307-6-4 | 7576 |
| 0-0038326-7-8 | 7576 |
| 0-0038337-8-X | 7661 |
| 0-0131985-2-1 | 5681 |
| 0-0131985-2-1 | 5684 |
| 0-0133656-1-4 | 1454 |
| 0-0134436-3-1 | 128 |
| 0-0134436-3-1 | 132 |
| 0-0230081-2-1 | 203 |
| 0-0230081-2-1 | 659 |
| 0-0230081-2-1 | 1304 |
| 0-0230081-2-1 | 1306 |
| 0-0230362-0-6 | 203 |
| 0-0230362-0-6 | 1273 |
| 0-0230650-8-7 | 973 |
| 0-0230650-8-7 | 992 |

Record: 1

"You're quite right, Peter," I affirmed. "The `Title Author` table, a type that I alluded to earlier today. It's called a **Bridge Table** (sometimes called a **Bridge Entity**), and it's used to establish and implement a relationship between two tables. As you can see, the `Title Author` table has only two fields – `ISBN`, which is the primary key of the `Titles` table, and `Au_ID`, which is the primary key of the `Authors` table. There is obviously a direct relationship between an author and the books that they have written. In the `Authors` table, the `Au_ID` uniquely identifies an author, and in the `Titles` table, the `ISBN` uniquely identifies a book."

"ISBN?" enquired Blaine.

"Yes," I answered, "in the publishing industry, the ISBN (International Standard Book Number) is the unique number that's assigned to every book that is published – no two titles in the world have the same ISBN. So the `Title Author` table allows us to use to primary keys from separate tables to link up an author's details with details of all of the books that they have written: "

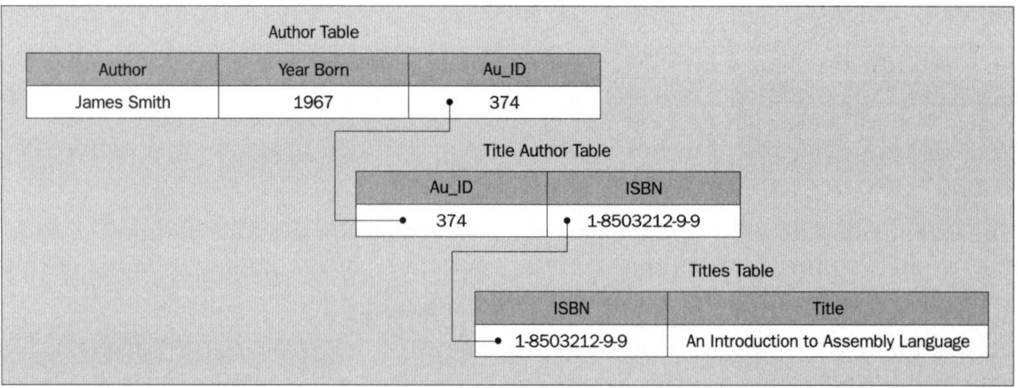


"That's how planned redundancy helps us to establish relationships between tables." I concluded.

"You've mentioned relationships a couple of times today," Rhonda said. "What exactly *is* a relationship in the database context?"

"It may be easier to answer your question by asking another one," I said.

## Table Relationships

"Let's take a look at the first record in the `Titles` table:"

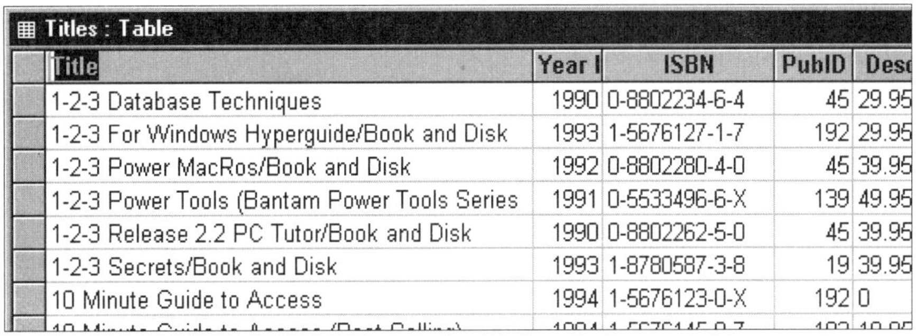

Titles : Table

| Title | Year I | ISBN | PubID | Desc |
|---|---|---|---|---|
| 1-2-3 Database Techniques | 1990 | 0-8802234-6-4 | 45 | 29.95 |
| 1-2-3 For Windows Hyperguide/Book and Disk | 1993 | 1-5676127-1-7 | 192 | 29.95 |
| 1-2-3 Power MacRos/Book and Disk | 1992 | 0-8802280-4-0 | 45 | 39.95 |
| 1-2-3 Power Tools (Bantam Power Tools Series | 1991 | 0-5533496-6-X | 139 | 49.95 |
| 1-2-3 Release 2.2 PC Tutor/Book and Disk | 1990 | 0-8802262-5-0 | 45 | 39.95 |
| 1-2-3 Secrets/Book and Disk | 1993 | 1-8780587-3-8 | 19 | 39.95 |
| 10 Minute Guide to Access | 1994 | 1-5676123-0-X | 192 | 0 |

"Can you tell me the publisher's name and address for the book 1-2-3 Database Techniques?"

There was a period of silence interspersed with keyboard activity and then, "No – they're not there," Steve said.

"So where are the publishers' details, then?" asked Rachel.

There were a few moments of mouse-clicking, then Dave said:

"They're in the `Publishers` table."

"That's right," I agreed, bringing up the relevant screen on my PC/projector:

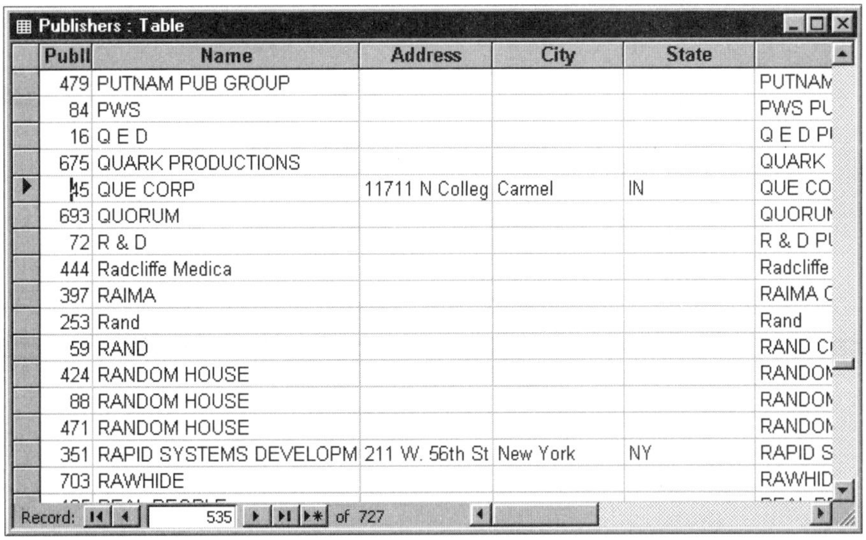

Publishers : Table

| PubI | Name | Address | City | State | |
|---|---|---|---|---|---|
| 479 | PUTNAM PUB GROUP | | | | PUTNAM |
| 84 | PWS | | | | PWS PU |
| 16 | Q E D | | | | Q E D PI |
| 675 | QUARK PRODUCTIONS | | | | QUARK |
| 45 | QUE CORP | 11711 N Colleg | Carmel | IN | QUE CO |
| 693 | QUORUM | | | | QUORUI |
| 72 | R & D | | | | R & D PU |
| 444 | Radcliffe Medica | | | | Radcliffe |
| 397 | RAIMA | | | | RAIMA C |
| 253 | Rand | | | | Rand |
| 59 | RAND | | | | RAND C |
| 424 | RANDOM HOUSE | | | | RANDOI |
| 88 | RANDOM HOUSE | | | | RANDOI |
| 471 | RANDOM HOUSE | | | | RANDOI |
| 351 | RAPID SYSTEMS DEVELOPM | 211 W. 56th St | New York | NY | RAPID S |
| 703 | RAWHIDE | | | | RAWHID |

Record: 535 of 727

"Now," I continued, "supposing we wanted to look at – or print out – the title of a book and the name and address of the publisher?"

"Well," said Dave, "you'd need to get some information from both tables: the `Titles` table and the `Publishers` table."

"Bang on," I said. "Now, in th `Titles` table, we *do* have a reference to the identity of the publisher – in the `PubID` field for each book title. And each record in the `Publishers` tables also has a unique `PubID` field..."

"So," interjected Rhonda, "we can tie together `Titles` and `Publishers`!"

"Absolutely right," I confirmed. "We can use this little bit of planned redundancy to link a book title up with its publisher. Remember, in the `Publishers` table the `PubID` is the primary key, and in the `Titles` table, the `PubID` is the foreign key of the `Publishers` table. And since we know that the `PubID` field is a foreign key to the `Publishers` table, we can open up the `Publishers` table and determine the `name` and `address` for that `Publisher.`"

I displayed the `Publishers` table on the classroom projector, clicked on the `PubID` column header, sorted the datasheet by `PubID`, and scrolled down to the record with a `PubID` value equal to 45 (the `PubID` for the title that we looked at earlier):

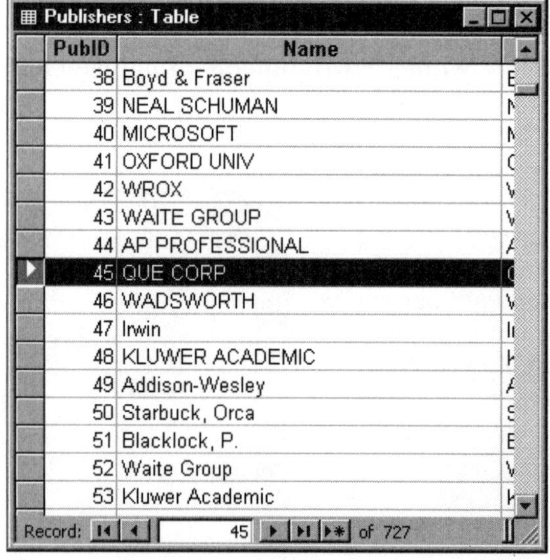

Publishers : Table

| PubID | Name |
|---|---|
| 38 | Boyd & Fraser |
| 39 | NEAL SCHUMAN |
| 40 | MICROSOFT |
| 41 | OXFORD UNIV |
| 42 | WROX |
| 43 | WAITE GROUP |
| 44 | AP PROFESSIONAL |
| 45 | QUE CORP |
| 46 | WADSWORTH |
| 47 | Irwin |
| 48 | KLUWER ACADEMIC |
| 49 | Addison-Wesley |
| 50 | Starbuck, Orca |
| 51 | Blacklock, P. |
| 52 | Waite Group |
| 53 | Kluwer Academic |

Record: 45 of 727

"There it is," I said. "The Que Corporation is the Publisher's Name, and they're located in Carmel, Indiana. Again, we're using key values to encode the relationship between different pieces of information in the database. In this case, because **one** publisher can publish **many** titles, we're dealing with what's known as a **one-to-many** relationship."

"This seems like an awful lot of trouble to me," Peter said. "Why not just maintain the publisher's name and address information in the `Titles` table? Wouldn't that be easier than having to use the `PubID` field to look up the information in another table? In fact, we could eliminate the `Publishers` table altogether, couldn't we?"

"That's true," I said, "but do you remember what I said earlier this morning? Each table should ideally contain information about one entity, and one entity only. Publisher information doesn't really belong in a table with book titles – otherwise, we'd have a lot of duplicate information, which would result in extra unnecessary typing and possible inconsistencies. For each book title, we'd have to duplicate **all** of the publisher information. Separate tables for each is the way to go – and it's the foreign key that allows us to **relate** the two tables together as if all of the information was in a single table."

"I just noticed something," Mary said, "there seems to be a problem with the `Titles` table. The book's author isn't there. How would we determine the author of a book by looking in the `Titles` table?"

"The answer," I said, "is that you can't. That's what the `Title Author` bridge table is for. Using the `ISBN` of the book, which is a field contained in the `Titles` table, we can go to the `Title Author` table and use the `ISBN` to obtain the `Au_ID` for the book. Once we have that, we can then look up the author's information in the `Authors` table."

I saw a number of confused faces in the classroom.

"Let me give you an example," I said. "A friend of mine wrote a book called Access for Windows 95 for Busy People. If I asked you to tell me his or her name, could you do it?"

There was a minute or two of silence, and then Dave said:

"First go to the `Titles` table, look up the `Title`, then obtain the corresponding `ISBN`."

I did as Dave had instructed, first sorting the `Titles` datasheet by the `Title` field, and then scrolling through the records until I found the correct title:

Titles : Table

| Title | Year P | ISBN | Pub |
|---|---|---|---|
| Access for Smart Beginners/Book and D | 1994 | 1-5668615-6-X | 1 |
| Access for Windows 95 (Teach Yourself/ | 1995 | 1-5582844-1-9 | |
| Access for Windows 95 : The Visual Lea | 1995 | 0-7615023-8-6 | 1 |
| Access for Windows 95 for Busy People | 1995 | 0-0788211-2-6 | |
| Access for Windows 95 for Dummies | 1995 | 1-5688492-9-X | |
| Access for Windows 95 for Dummies Qu | 1995 | 1-5688498-2-6 | |
| Access for Windows 95 Secrets | 1996 | 1-5688472-5-4 | |
| Access for Windows by Example/Book& | 1995 | 1-8639800-3-2 | 1 |
| Access for Windows Hot Tips | 1993 | 1-5652923-4-0 | |
| Access for Windows Power Programmin | 1993 | 1-5652919-4-8 | |
| Access for Windows Quick Reference (Q | 1993 | 1-5652923-3-2 | |
| Access for Windows Suresteps | 1993 | 1-5652953-4-X | |
| Access from the Ground Up | 1994 | 1-5595851-1-0 | 1 |
| Access from the Ground Up (Windows M | 1993 | 1-5595830-3-7 | 1 |
| Access Insider (The Wiley Insider | 1993 | 0-4713043-0-1 | |
| Access Nippon 1996 : How to Succeed i | 1996 | 9-9954618-7-0 | 4 |
| Access Programming for Dummies (--For | 1994 | 1-5688409-1-8 | |
| Access the Internet | 1995 | 0-7821174-4-9 | 7 |
| Access the Internet!/Book and Disk | 1994 | 0-7821152-9-2 | 7 |
| Access to Air Travel for People With Red | 1995 | 9-2821120-0-4 | 2 |

Record: 221 of 8569

"There it is," I said.

"By the way," Ward interrupted gently, "you might want to mention that if you click on the **Title** column, then select Edit | Find from the Access menu bar, you'll be prompted for search criteria, and Access will take you right to that record."

"Good point, Ward," I said. "That's a really useful tip!"

"OK," Tom said, "we now have the **ISBN** – but that still doesn't give us the name of the author. At this point, we need to take the **ISBN**, open up the **Title Author** table, and find the relevant **ISBN** in the table."

I opened up the **Title Author** table as Tom had directed, and using Ward's technique, selected the **ISBN** column, selected Edit | Find on the Access menu bar, and typed the **ISBN** of the book into the Find What dialog text box.

"This is a great shortcut Ward pointed out," I reiterated. "Just make sure that you have selected the column representing the field you wish to search through (or at least that you have clicked in the relevant column). The Find dialog has some parameters you may want to experiment with on your own."

I then clicked on the Find First button, and the following screen shot was displayed:

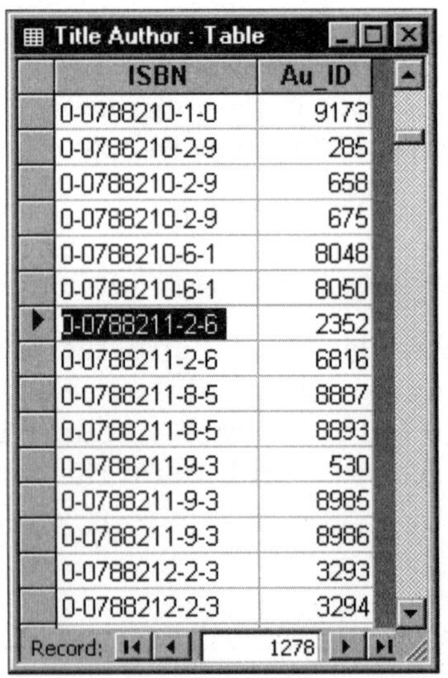

Title Author : Table

| ISBN | Au_ID |
|---|---|
| 0-0788210-1-0 | 9173 |
| 0-0788210-2-9 | 285 |
| 0-0788210-2-9 | 658 |
| 0-0788210-2-9 | 675 |
| 0-0788210-6-1 | 8048 |
| 0-0788210-6-1 | 8050 |
| 0-0788211-2-6 | 2352 |
| 0-0788211-2-6 | 6816 |
| 0-0788211-8-5 | 8887 |
| 0-0788211-8-5 | 8893 |
| 0-0788211-9-3 | 530 |
| 0-0788211-9-3 | 8985 |
| 0-0788211-9-3 | 8986 |
| 0-0788212-2-3 | 3293 |
| 0-0788212-2-3 | 3294 |

Record: 1278

"Now we have the author's ID corresponding to the book we're looking for," I said. "A this point, if we open up the **Authors** table and look for the author whose **Au_ID** is 2352, we should know the name of my friend who wrote this book."

"I don't know whether you noticed," Kate said, "but there are two author records with that same **ISBN** - 2352 and 6816. Is that a mistake?"

"I would suspect that means the book was co-authored," I said.

"It wasn't you, was it Professor Smiley?" Ward joked.

"No, it wasn't me," I said smiling. "Maybe next year! Let's look them both up."

I then opened up the **Authors** table and navigated to the record containing an **Au_ID** of 2352. The following screen shot was displayed on the classroom projector:

Authors : Table

| Au_ID | Author | Year I |
|---|---|---|
| 2331 | Schroeder, Al | |
| 2333 | Ueberhuber, Christoph W. | |
| 2334 | Tomas, Gerald | |
| 2336 | Rustagi, Jagdish S. | |
| 2338 | Waggoner, Glroia | |
| 2339 | Cashman, Thomas J. | |
| 2340 | Shelly, Gary B. | |
| 2344 | Van Berkel, Kees | |
| 2348 | Desberg, Peter | |
| 2350 | Levy, Steven | |
| 2352 | Neibauer, Alan | |
| 2355 | Cilwa, Paul | |
| 2357 | Infanger, Gerd | |
| 2359 | Collopy, David M. | |
| 2363 | Dzeroski, Saso | |
| 2364 | Lavrac, Nada | |
| 2366 | Obin, Raymond | |

Record: 1175 of 6246

"That's my friend Alan," I said. "At one time we taught together – now he writes computer books full time."

"I don't mean to interrupt," Mary said, "but I just checked that other author ID, and that author's name is 'Neibauer, Alan R.' It looks like there may have been some data entry problems when the records in this table were entered – these two records really represent the same person."

"Those things can happen," I said. "I see that all the time. You're right – those two records really are the same person."

Rhonda looked very perplexed.

"What's wrong, Rhonda?" I asked.

"I just can't believe," she said, "that someone actually designed a database like this. From my point of view, there are four tables when there easily could be just a single table. I'm afraid that I just don't see the advantages of having information all over the place – it seems so cumbersome. I don't see how we're ever going to be able to write a Visual Basic program that interacts with a database like this!"

"Rhonda, it's not nearly so bad as you think," I said. "If you remember, you said the same thing last semester about the China Shop project – but you did fine, and you'll do well here as well. Let me take your questions one at a time, starting with the last one. Yes, by the end of this course, you'll be able to write your own Visual Basic programs that interact with a database just like this one consisting of multiple tables. We'll take it a step at a time, and everything will be fine. In fact, next week, we'll begin by designing, creating, and populating the China Shop database – with multiple tables just like this one."

"What about the advantages of having multiple tables," Lou said, "what are they? As Rhonda said, surely we could implement this database with a single table, couldn't we? Wouldn't that be easier to learn?"

"It might be easier to learn, but you'd be learning really bad habits!" I argued. "Using a single large table poses problems that using multiple, smaller tables does not. A single large table would have large amounts of duplicated data. For instance, suppose that we created a single table called `Books` with a record containing every field in the `Biblio` database's four tables. If we did that, we'd have a single table containing 18 fields, with a size of 909 characters (not including the `Memo` fields that can range from 0 to 65,535 characters). Here's what the single table would look like."

I displayed the following chart:

| Original Table | Field Name | Field Size |
|---|---|---|
| Title | Title | 255 |
| | Year Published | Integer (2 Characters) |
| | ISBN | 20 |
| | Description | 50 |
| | Notes | 50 |
| | Subject | 50 |
| | Comments | Memo (Up to 65,535 characters) |

*Table continued on following page*

| Original Table | Field Name | Field Size |
|---|---|---|
| Author | Author | 50 |
| | Year Born | Integer (2 Characters) |
| Publishers | Name | 50 |
| | Company Name | 255 |
| | Address | 50 |
| | City | 20 |
| | State | 10 |
| | Zip | 15 |
| | Telephone | 15 |
| | Fax | 15 |
| | Comments | Memo (Up to 65,535 characters) |

"I don't see anything wrong with this," Rhonda said. "We've eliminated those duplicated, redundant fields, haven't we? Is that bad?"

"You're right, Rhonda," I said, "because all of the data is in a single table, we no longer have a need for the foreign keys that we had before."

"I would think this would make finding information much easier," Peter said. "Everything's in a single table."

"That may be true," I agreed, "but now we have a bloated database."

"What do you mean?" Steve asked.

"Since each record contains full information on both the author *and* the publisher," I said, "all of that **`Name`**, **`Year Born`**, **`Address`**, and **`Telephone`** information is repeated for each and every record. That information is always the same for a particular publisher – repeating it in each record is not necessary. For example, if an author has written five books, all of the author details and all of the publisher details will appear in all five of those records. Just in the case of the publisher, we're repeating 430 characters of information we don't need to repeat. It may be true that multiple tables are a bit more cumbersome to navigate, but the multiple table approach cuts down on the 'bloat' of the database by substituting a bunch of repeating information with a foreign key."

"Say that again?" Melissa asked.

"In the original `Titles` table," I said, "that 430 characters of publisher information was represented by a single foreign key – a four character `PubID` field."

"I think I see what you're saying now," Dave said proudly. "The foreign key replaces a bunch of repetitive data with a small key field."

"You're right on the mark, Dave," I said. "Ultimately, having more than one table in a database may be a little more cumbersome in terms of finding all the pieces of the information you may need to answer a question or display results to the user, but the *overall* size of the database is smaller. Furthermore, that translates into faster processing speed. By the way, the process of taking one big table and breaking it down into several smaller tables is called **Database Normalization**."

"That term sounds familiar from my database class," Rhonda said. "But is processing speed the only advantage?"

"There is one other important issue," I said. "And that's the issue of what is known as a **data anomaly**."

"Sounds like a contagious disease!" Kate said, smiling.

"That's not far from the truth," I said. "Data anomalies occur more frequently in unnormalized tables – that is, one big table."

"What exactly is a data anomaly?" Rhonda asked.

"Let me give you an example that I think will illustrate it," I said. "Suppose Wrox Press moves their offices, and we need to change their address. Wrox Press is listed as the publisher of 16 records in the current `Titles` table. With the database normalized as it is, changing the address is no big deal – we just go to the single record representing Wrox Press in the `Publishers` table – `PubID` equal to `42` – and change their address information one time. However, if we had all of the data in one large table – `Books`, for instance – we would need to change 16 records in the large table. If this were being done manually – by someone sitting in front of a PC using Access, for instance – the chance of missing one of those 16 records is much higher than the chance of missing the update to a single record. Not only that, but it's a lot of extra work that can be avoided through efficient database design. And if the `Publisher` was someone like M & T Books – which has 189 records in the `Titles` table – the chances of missing one manually is almost a foregone conclusion."

"So a data anomaly is a missed update or an inconsistent one?" Kevin asked.

"That's right," I said. "Does everyone see how this situation can be avoided by having several smaller tables?"

"I guess I still don't fully understand," Rhonda said. "How is the single table scenario different than the multiple table database when it comes to changing the address for M & T Books?"

"Well," I answered, "with our four-table database, the publisher's ID number is stored in the `Titles` table as a foreign key to the `Publishers` table. However, the address for M & T Books is stored in just one record in the `Publishers` table. Therefore, if we need to change the address of M & T books, we only need to change that single record. We don't need to modify the records in the Titles table at all."

"I think I'm beginning to see now," Rhonda said. "But I can see that this will take some practice. Maybe working on the China Shop program will help?"

"I'm sure that will help quite a bit," I said.

"Is it the job of the programmer," Kate said, "to design databases?"

"That all depends," I said, "on how and where you're working. If you're working in a large Information Technology Department, then the job of designing a database will be in the hands of a database designer or database administrator. But if you're an independent developer like me, most likely you'll be doing the design yourself."

"I really don't know how I'll ever feel comfortable doing a database design of my own," Lou said.

"Like anything, Lou," I replied, "it takes practice. Once you get one or two under your belt, it won't be a problem. Believe me."

I looked for signs of confusion in the class, but I didn't see any.

"Now let me recap a little," I continued. "I said earlier that a database is made up of related tables. But to be even more correct, a database is a collection of related **records**."

"Related how, again?" Rachel asked.

"Related by their subject matter." Dave said.

"That's right, Dave," I agreed. "Databases contain tables of related information stored as records. For instance, in the `Biblio` database, we could easily add a table to keep track of professional baseball players' salaries, but it wouldn't make much sense to keep track of that information in a table within the `Biblio` database. In the same way, Joe Bullina could use the China Shop database to keep track of his son's baseball card collection, but it wouldn't make any sense to do that either."

"Getting back to the China Shop project, then," Melissa said, "now I can see that the China Shop database will consist of related tables named `Customers`, `Inventory`, `Users`, and `Transactions`."

"That's right," I said, "and as we stated earlier, all four of those tables collectively represent everything that Joe Bullina, from an information point of view, considers to be the China Shop."

"Getting back to those four tables," Peter said. "Personally, I'm OK with `Customers`, `Inventory`, and `Users`, since these are 'entities' that I can see and touch. But the `Transactions` table? I don't know, but every time I think of that entity, I become more confused – it's not as if you can *touch* a transaction, or pick it up."

"You make a good point, Peter," I said. "Sometimes the entities that we track in a database – and therefore the tables that we create – are not necessarily things that appear to be tangible at first glance. I can think of some other examples of seemingly non-tangible entities I've worked with in the past year or so. For instance, if you take a course at school, you receive a grade. Is a grade something that is really tangible? If you create a database table called grades, are you really keeping track of something you can touch and feel? Here's another example. A few months ago, I worked on a personnel management system for a large corporation. Part of the system involved maintaining records of employee rules infractions, and that was the name of the Access table that I created. Are infractions a tangible or an intangible entity?"

"Definitely intangible," Peter said. "Thanks for that explanation – that really helps."

"In the China Shop," I continued, "when a customer – who is very real – purchases an item of china – which is also very real – a transaction is generated. This transaction, although somewhat abstract, *is* very real to Joe Bullina, and is crucial to Joe's accountant being able to calculate his bottom line at the end of his fiscal year. I'm sure if you think about it, you can think of many other examples of intangible entities that concern us each day.For example, your children's school bus schedule, or the amount of interest your retirement account earned last month, or the number of visits to your web page – all of these are less than tangible, but important nonetheless. And as we'll see in the next few weeks, they can easily be tracked in a database."

We were coming towards the end of the class, and I asked if anyone had any further questions they wanted clearing up.

"You mentioned a one-to-many relationship a little earlier," Linda said, "are there any other kinds of relationships?"

"That's a good question," I answered.

## Types of Relationships

"There are three kinds of relationships in database theory: **one-to-one**, **one-to-many**, and **many-to-many**. As a byproduct of normalization which, remember, means breaking one large table into several smaller tables, you will most commonly establish **one-to-many** relationships between the records in your different tables."

"Can you give us an example of a one-to-one relationship?" Chuck asked.

"Sure, Chuck," I said. "The classic example of a one-to-one relationship is marriage – at least, in most Western cultures. One man marries one woman, and one woman marries one man – traditionally, at least."

"In other words," Dave said, "Mary Smith is related to John Smith, and vice versa."

"That's exactly right, Dave," I said.

"What about a one-to-many relationship?" Rhonda asked.

"How about this one," I said. "One instructor – me – teaches many classes here at the university. In database terms, there is a one-to-many relationship between an instructor and their scheduled classes."

"That makes sense," Melissa said. "I don't think I can quite fathom a many-to-many relationship."

"Well," I said, "there's a many-to-many relationship between the **`Authors`** and **`Titles`** tables. Remember how I said earlier that it's possible for more than one author to have written a title, and for an author to have written more than one title? Well, as far as the table relationships are concerned, there's the potential for a many-to-many relationship between the **`Titles`** and **`Authors`** tables. Many-to-many relationships are just too complex to represent in databases, and so when we detect that we have a many-to-many relationship between two tables, here's what we do: create another table that duplicates the primary keys from both tables – that's the bridge table or bridge entity I mentioned earlier."

"And that's why," Dave said, " the **`Title Author`** table contains only two fields – **`ISBN`** and **`Au_ID`**?"

"That's why," I agreed. "Creating that third table allows us to get rid of the problematic many-to-many relationship between the original tables."

"Do you envisage any many-to-many relationships in the China Shop database?" Valerie asked.

"No, I don't," I answered. "Actually, many-to-many relationships are pretty rare."

"Thank goodness!" Rhonda exclaimed.

"Do we need to do anything special to implement relationships in Access?" Valerie asked.

"In some database packages," I said, "relationships may be implied by the foreign key in the tables. In Access (and some other databases) you need to explicitly specify the relationships in order to gain any benefits from them."

"What benefits would those be?" Ward asked.

"The benefits are the enforcement of **Referential Integrity**," I answered.

## Referential Integrity

"Let me give you an example of **Referential Integrity**. For instance, I can tell Access that I want to establish a one-to-many relationship between the `Publishers` table and the `Titles` table, and that I want to enforce referential integrity. That tells Access that a record cannot be added to the `Titles` table if it has a `PubID` that does **not** exist in the `Publishers` table."

"I can see that's a valuable feature," Valerie said. "That will prevent invalid values from being entered into the `PubID` field – very important, considering the fact that codes are being entered into that field and not the actual name of a publisher."

"That's a good point," I agreed. "Because we are using a code to represent the Publisher, it's critically important to have some way of ensuring the integrity of the value entered into the `PubID` field – and specifying the enforcement of referential integrity when we establish the relationship is vital."

"I believe that the enforcement of referential integrity works both ways, doesn't it?" Dave asked. "That is, if we try to delete a record in the `Publishers` table, and there are records in the `Titles` table with that `PubID`, Access will stop us from erasing the `Publishers` record?"

"That's excellent, Dave," I answered. "You're right about that."

"Is there any way that we can see the relationships that exist in the `Biblio` database?" Blaine asked.

"Yes, there is." I said. "If you select Tools | Relationships from the Access menu bar, the **Relationships Window** will be displayed. Here, take a look at this:"

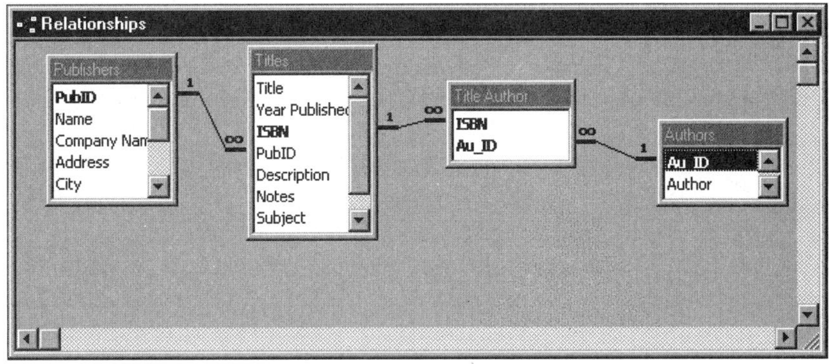


I explained that the relationships window revealed that there were three relationships in effect between the tables in the `Biblio` database.

"Each line that you see drawn between two tables," I said, "represents a table relationship."

"What's that symbol that looks like an infinity character?" Chuck asked.

"That symbol," I said, "is the character that Access uses to indicate the **many** part of a relationship. Access uses a **1** to indicate the **one** part of a relationship. As you can see, we have three one-to-many relationships in the `Biblio` database."

"How do we set up a relationship?" Tom asked. "And where do we specify that we want referential integrity?"

"We'll be setting up relationships next week when we design, create and populate the China Shop database." I answered. "If you don't mind, I'm going to wait until next week to show you how to set up relationships and define their referential integrity. It's been a long class, and I want to give you some time to absorb this. Next week, we'll take the theory of what we've learned here today and use it create our China Shop database. Just before we finish, let me show you a quick summary slide – this is reminder of the way that all the different database components hang together. I call this slide the **data hierarchy**."

With that, I displayed the following slide:

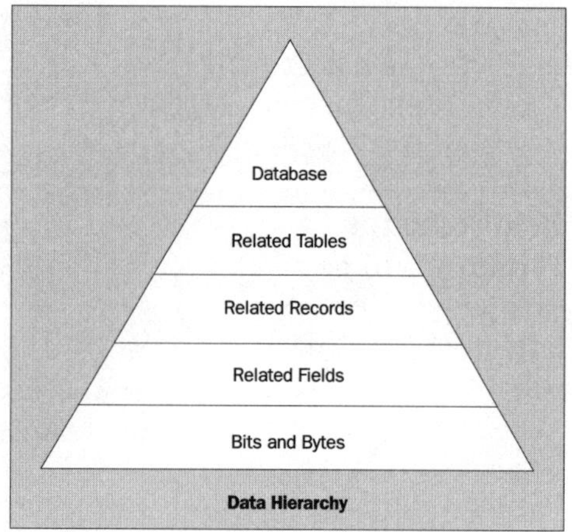


"So, this is what I call the **Data Hierarchy**," I said. "At the top of the pyramid, we have the database. The database is made up of related tables. A table is made up of related records. And a record is made up of related fields. And fields, ultimately, are made up of bits and bytes – but the Access database management system hides the really low-level bits and bytes processing from us."

With that, I dismissed class for the day.

# Chapter Summary

This chapter presented a survey of database theory, as we'll apply it to the China Shop database. This theory session has prepared us for the third lesson, where we'll design and create the China Shop database itself, based on the requirements that we agreed with Joe Bullina in the first lesson of the course. During the class, we discussed the following topics:

- Databases
- Tables
- Records
- Fields
- Primary Keys
- Foreign Keys
- Database Normalization
- Relationships
- Referential Integrity

At the end of the class, I also distributed a handout with reminders of the most important concepts that we had covered:

**A Database is a repository for data or information.**

**Databases contain information about entities – persons, places, or things.**

**Database is made up of one or more tables.**

**A Table is a collection of records.**

**A record in a table is a representation of a real world object.**

**Records are made up of fields, and a field is a characteristic of a real world entity.**

**Tables ordinarily contain information about a single entity.**

**Each record in a table must be uniquely identified by a field or fields called the Primary Key.**

**A field in a table that is itself the Primary Key of another table is called a Foreign Key.**

**To represent a many-to-many relationship between two tables, create a third table whose only fields are the primary keys of both tables. This is called a bridge table.**

**The process of taking one big table and breaking it down into several smaller tables is called Database Normalization.**

Join my class again next week as we start to create the China Shop database in earnest.

Learn to Program Databases with Visual Basic

# Chapter 3
# Database Design

In the previous chapter, you followed along with me as my university class and I explored database theory. In this chapter, we'll get started on creating the structures that will let us upgrade the China Shop project to meet Joe Bullina's new requirements. These are the areas that we'll cover in this chapter:

- Designing the China Shop's **`China`** database: to do this, I'll walk you through my universal seven-stage database design process
- Creating the database's **`.mdb`** file using Microsoft Access
- Creating the four tables that make up the database
- Creating the relationships between the tables that will let us store, retrieve and manipulate data efficiently
- Adding data to the tables about the system's users and the china items that Joe stocks

Remember that if you *don't* have Access installed on your machine you can find a completed version of the **`China.mdb`** database on the CD supplied with this book. You'll still be able to read and manipulate the database with VB when we start enhancing the China Shop project in Chapter 4, even if you don't have Access. In the meantime, you can follow along with the creation process that we'll cover shortly.

**The completed `China` database is in the `For Chapter 4` folder on the CD.**

Let's begin – the class is waiting…

## Designing the China Shop Database

Where do we begin? That's a question we answered in the first few chapters of *Learn to Program with Visual Basic*. The starting point for a database design is the same as that for a computer program. We must create a logical description of what the program should do to accomplish its goals.

# Database Design

I began our third class by letting everyone know that we would be joined once again by Joe Bullina, who would be assisting us in the design of the China Shop database.

"I'm expecting him any minute," I said. "It could be that he's been tied up in traffic – I heard that there was an accident on the expressway this morning. I don't think Joe would mind if we start off our discussion of database design without him."

I continued by explaining that there are two distinct phases in designing a database – the **Logical Database Design**, followed by the **Physical Database Design**.

"Why two phases?" Rhonda asked.

"The **Logical Design** phase," I said, "results in a design that is not database product specific. In other words, we produce a schematic design that can then be used to physically implement our database using any number of different database software packages – such as Access, Oracle or SQLServer."

"A schematic?" Steve asked.

"Yes, a schematic," I repeated. "A **schematic** is like a drawing or a model of the database. We'll be developing one ourselves during the course of today's class."

"I thought we'd already decided that we were using Access for the China Shop database?" Ward said.

"We are, Ward," I confirmed, "but the logical design phase presupposes that no particular database product has been settled on. At the end of it we will have a model of the database that can be implemented using any package."

Dave said, "I would think that would give us a great deal of flexibility in the ultimate choice of a database package."

"That's absolutely right," I said. "Remember, we use the logical design stage to make sure we don't miss out any of the steps in the database design and creation. At the end of the logical design phase we've drawn up a model of the database that we can then map onto any database management package that fits our needs."

"What do you mean by 'database management package'?" asked Rachel. "Are you talking about the software we'll be using, or also about the computer it will be running on?"

"The **software**," I replied. "And Dave is right. Even though we know in our class that we will be using Access to implement the China Shop database, in large-scale application developments, the ultimate decision about which database management software to use as the repository for our data may be months away."

"How is the **Physical Database Design** different from the logical design then?" Steve asked.

"The physical design stage is where we decide how our sketch – or schematic – is going to be physically implemented; that is, how we'll actually build the database. Each database management package," I went on, "has different characteristics and capabilities. For instance, during the logical design phase we might identify a field to be used in a record – such as the customer's last name – as a **string** data type. As we saw last week, a string data type in an Access database would be implemented as a **text** field. In Oracle, that same field would be implemented as a **VARCHAR** data type."

"VAR what?" Rhonda asked.

"V-A-R-C-H-A-R," I said. "VARCHAR is one of the data types used in the Oracle database management package – but it doesn't exist in Access."

"So database-specific issues such as this," Dave suggested, "are handled in the physical design phase?"

"That's right, Dave," I said. "The physical design phase takes the model of the database that comes out of the logical design phase and customizes it for the database management package in which the data will ultimately reside."

"Will we need to know Oracle or SQLServer for this class?" Melissa asked, a little anxiously.

"Don't worry", I said, "we'll only be using Access – and after today's class, we'll never use Access *directly* again. Once the database has been built, we won't need Access again."

"Are we using Access because other databases are more complicated?" Linda asked.

"That's right," I said," Access is well-suited to small-scale applications like Joe's shop. Databases other than Access are designed, implemented and maintained by specially trained computer professionals called database administrators, who spend all of their time working with those types of databases. If you wanted to write a database for a large corporation you probably wouldn't use Access. It's perfect for us, though, and our small-scale project."

"That's a relief," Kate said.

"What did you mean," Rhonda chipped in, "when you said that after today's class, we'll never use Access directly again?"

"In today's class," I replied, "we'll design and create the China Shop database. After that, all of the data entry and retrieval that we perform will be done using our Visual Basic China Shop program."

"That's great!" Kevin said.

Just then, Joe Bullina walked into the classroom.

"Sorry I'm late," he said. "There was a little 'coming together' on the expressway."

"We thought you might have been caught in that," I said. "Thanks for coming in to help us out with this. We were just discussing logical and physical database design, and I was just about to display a chart I've prepared on the classroom projector. Here it is:"

**John Smiley's Steps for Logical Database Design**

Determine the information that you need to maintain
Break that information into individual pieces of data
Translate these into database fields
Categorize the fields by table
Identify fields with unique values in order to assign primary keys
Specify data types for fields
Identify relationships between tables

I gave the class a chance to absorb this.

"I notice," Dave said, "that your list of steps is a little different from the recommendations I read in my Microsoft Access manual last night."

"That's right," I said. "The Microsoft recommendations are a little too 'surgical' for me. I think you will find my steps a little easier to follow."

## Step 1. Determine the Information that you Need to Maintain

We began by displaying the requirements statement that we'd developed in our first week of class. I should mention that although the requirements statement had identified the information that would eventually become database fields, we decided to follow my 7 step process to the letter. This would give us a clear and systematic approach to database design. So we continued by examining Joe Bullina's overall information needs, as defined in the requirements statement. I asked Dave to record our observations in the form of a table, and, after a few minutes of discussion, this is what was displayed on the classroom projector:

**Information Joe Bullina wants to maintain:**

| Customer Information |
|---|
| Inventory Information |
| Transaction Information |
| User Information |

## Step 2. Break that Information into individual Pieces of Data

At a global level, everyone agreed this was fine – these four categories of information represented exactly what Joe Bullina wanted to maintain in the China Shop database.

"We already know what we want to maintain about inventory," I said. "It's the same information that is currently being maintained in the `Prices.txt` file – brand, item and price. Unless you can think of anything else, Joe?"

"No, that's fine," Joe responded.

User information was equally easy to determine – just two fields, one for a User ID, and one for a password.

"I know we discussed this in our first week," Rhonda said. "But what's the purpose of that `Users` information again?"

I reminded Rhonda and the rest of the class that when the modified China Shop program first starts up, it will now prompt the user of the program to login with a User ID and password. The China Shop staff will be the people who start up the program, not the customers.

"The **`Users`** table," I said, "will allow us to identify whether the user of the program is going to be used for sales staff functions, or whether it's being switched on so that customers can use it to get price quotations. If the China Shop staff want to use the program to display menu items permitting them to view Customer records, transaction records, and Inventory records, then they'll log in using the staff User ID. If they want to start up the program for the customers to use, they'll enter the customer User ID when they login: this means that program will allow the customer to get price quotations, but they won't see the extra menu options that the sales staff need."

"I see," Rhonda said. "And as I recall, we'll have two records in that table – one for the sales staff functions, and one to identify the customer. So the customer never uses this login facility – it's always the sales staff who set the program up for the customer to use?"

"You're on the mark, Rhonda," I confirmed.

I explained that, from our requirements statement, it appeared that the **`Users`** table would have only two records in it. One would designate a Customer and the other would designate a Staff Member or Administrator. The simplest way to do this would be to have **`CUSTOMER`** as the **`UserID`** for the customer price quotation function, and **`ADMINISTRATOR`** to designate a sales staff member or administrator.

We then began to discuss the Customer and Transaction requirements. I asked Joe to further define what he meant by Customer and transaction information.

"For the **Customer**," Joe said, "I'd like Name, Address and optionally a Phone Number. For **Transactions**, I'd like China Brand, Item and the Quantity of the purchase, along with the Total Purchase Price and the Date Of Purchase."

I asked Dave to make those changes, and to display the updated table of information:

**Information Joe Bullina wants to maintain:**

| |
|---|
| Customer's Name |
| Customer's Address |
| Customer's Phone Number |
| Total Purchase Price |
| Item, Quantity, Brand and Price of each item purchased |
| Date of Purchase |

| Inventory Brand Name |
| --- |
| Inventory Item |
| Inventory Price |
| UserID |
| Password |

"This is great for a first attempt at this," I said. "I think we've identified the information that Joe is interested in maintaining. Now we need to start thinking about translating this information into fields in our `China` database. Can anyone think of anything else that we can add or modify?"

### *Step 3. Translate the Individual Pieces of Data into Database Fields*

Almost immediately, Dave suggested that the customer's address needed to be refined.

"I think Address is too broad," he said, "that could be broken down even further."

"That's a good point, Dave", I concurred. "We should probably break Address into Street, City, State and Zip Code."

"Some programs I've used," Dave added, "also have fields for Apartment, Room and Suite Numbers."

"That's another good point," I agreed. "In the databases I've designed, I typically create database fields called Address1 and Address2 for just that purpose."

"If the idea is break this information into its smallest components," Ward said, "should we also break the Quantity and Brand of each item purchased into separate fields as well?"

"Right you are, Ward," I agreed, "those really are two distinct pieces of information."

"What about Name?" Rachel asked. "Should we break that field into two pieces – First Name and Last Name?"

"That's a question that's debated quite a bit," I said. "Some database designers consider it a toss up. If we store the customer's name in a single database field, will there ever be a need to work only with pieces of it – such as the Last Name portion – and if so, how hard will that be to access? On the other hand, if we break the field up into more than one field, how easy will it be to join them together if we need to present them as a single field?"

"Is there likely to be a problem with that?" asked Rachel.

"We saw how easy or difficult it is to break strings apart last semester," Peter observed, "when Professor Smiley had us doing exercises in string manipulation. I don't know about anyone else, but I thought breaking a string into pieces was pretty difficult. Personally, I agree with Rachel. I think we should break the Name into two fields – First Name and Last Name."

"That's true," Melissa said, "but I don't think I understand why we would want to join First and Last Name?"

Joe Bullina interjected at this point.

"I must say I'm learning quite a bit myself here," he said, smiling. "Let me take a shot at that one. If we have separate fields for First Name and Last Name, we might want to join them together to generate those mailing labels we mentioned earlier?"

"Great job, Joe," I said, "that's one reason. Any time we wanted to present the First and Last Name fields to the user of the China Shop program as single entity would require us to write code to 'join' them together. However, I also think that joining two or more fields together is infinitely easier than trying to take one field and extract information from it."

"So, will we use two fields?" Rhonda asked.

"Not to throw a monkey wrench into this," I responded, "but what about the customer's middle initial?"

"I happen to know," Joe Bullina interjected, "that I have two customers with the same first and last names. A middle initial would prevent confusion over the two of them."

"Some database designers," I said, "would include the middle initial as part of the First Name field. Some would create a separate Middle Initial Field. And don't forget, Microsoft's own sample table in the `Biblio` database created a single Name field."

"What's your advice, John?" Joe Bullina asked.

"I would prefer to separate the Middle Initial into a separate field," I said.

"Let's do that then," Dave said.

Dave had been updating his table during our discussion, and took this opportunity to display it on the classroom projector:

**China Shop Database Fields:**

| Customer's First Name |
|---|
| Customer's Middle Initial |
| Customer's Last Name |
| Customer's Address1 |
| Customer's Address2 |
| Customer's City |
| Customer's State |
| Customer's Zip Code |
| Customer's Phone Number |
| Total Purchase Price |
| Brand of item purchased |
| Item purchased |
| Quantity of item purchased |
| Price of item purchased |
| Date of Purchase |
| Inventory Brand Name |
| Inventory Item |
| Inventory Price |
| UserID |
| Password |

"I think the database is really beginning to shape up," I said. "How's it look to everyone?"

"It looks pretty good to me," Mary said. "I can't think of anything else. I suppose if we forget something, we can always come back and modify our design later."

"Yes, that's right," I agreed.

"I have a question concerning the Total Purchase Price," Blaine said. "I thought I had read in my Microsoft Access manual that it isn't a good idea to have a field in the database that is a calculated field. Isn't that what the Total Purchase Price is?"

"That's a good point, Blaine", I said.

"What's that about a calculated field?" Rhonda asked.

"Blaine was pointing out," I said, "that Total Purchase Price is a field that can be calculated by adding the individual prices of each item – which we are tentatively also storing in each record. Database designers generally don't store fields in a record that can be calculated by a program, such as Visual Basic."

"Why not?" asked Valerie.

"Because alterations in other parts of the program could render data in this field invalid." I responded. "For example, if the price of a particular brand changed, then the Total Purchase Price would also have to be amended. Otherwise the data in your database would become inconsistent – this is the data anomaly problem we talked about last week. If this can happen to your database then it hasn't been very well designed."

I asked Dave to remove the Total Order Price field from his schematic.

"I'm content," I said, "that we have now identified all of the database fields that we need."

"Are these going to be the names of the database fields?" Tom asked.

"Not necessarily," I said. "Field names, like variable and control names in Visual Basic, should be as descriptive as possible, using with as few characters as possible. These names are just a bit on the long side, and you'll see that we'll shorten these names in a few minutes."

I waited a moment to see if anyone else had any questions.

"Who can tell me what our next step should be?" I asked.

### *Step 4. Categorize the Fields by Table*

"Well," Ward said, " I think we've completed steps 1, 2 and 3. So our next step is to categorize the fields we've identified by table."

"Yes, Ward," I said. "You're right. By categorizing the fields by table, in essence we are defining the records in our database. And who can tell me what a table is?"

"A table," Peter said, "is a collection of data or information about a specific entity."

"Right you are," I said.

"Are you saying," Mary said, "that all we need to do is to go through the schematic, and categorize the fields as belonging to one entity or another? That sounds too easy."

"That's exactly what I'm saying, Mary," I said, "but don't be fooled – this process can be harder to perform than it sounds. You'd be amazed how many beginners place a field in the wrong table!"

Together, we spent the next twenty minutes attempting to categorize our fields into one of four tables. At the end of the process, I dismissed the class for a well-deserved fifteen-minute break. When we returned, I asked Dave to display his schematic on the classroom projector. This is how it looked:

**China Shop Database Fields:**

| Table | Field |
|---|---|
| Customers | Customer's First Name |
| Customers | Customer's Middle Initial |
| Customers | Customer's Last Name |
| Customers | Customer's Address1 |
| Customers | Customer's Address2 |
| Customers | Customer's City |
| Customers | Customer's State |
| Customers | Customer's Zip Code |
| Customers | Customer's Phone Number |
| Transactions | Brand of item purchased |
| Transactions | Item purchased |

*Table continued on following page*

| Table | Field |
| --- | --- |
| Transactions | Quantity of item purchased |
| Transactions | Price of item purchased |
| Transactions | Date of Purchase |
| Inventory | Inventory Brand Name |
| Inventory | Inventory Item |
| Inventory | Inventory Price |
| Users | UserID |
| Users | Password |

"I notice," Joe Bullina said, "that we don't seem to be recording the name of the customer."

"That's a good point," I agreed. "We'll need to add that."

"Does that mean," Bob said "that *each* record in the `Transactions` table is going to contain *all* of the Customer information? Won't that lead to the data redundancy problem you spoke about last week?"

"Excellent, Bob!" I exclaimed. " You're absolutely right. If we include the customer's First Name, Middle Initial and Last Name, plus all of the customer's address information for each china item that they purchase, we're going to end up with quite a bloated table."

"Not to mention the data anomaly potential if they need to change their address," Lou said.

"I hate to say this," Rhonda confessed, "but this is confusing me all over again. Is there any way that you can draw a diagram describing what you're talking about?"

"That's no problem, Rhonda," I said. "I'm sure you're not the only person who's confused. Let's examine a hypothetical sale, where a customer, John D. Smith, purchases four Mikasa plates, four Mikasa saucers and one Mikasa platter. That should generate three separate transaction records – one transaction record each for the plates, the saucers, and the platter. Here's what the transaction records for that purchase would look like if we included all of John Smith's customer information in the Transaction record (we've had to split the transaction record into two parts to fit it on the page):"

| First Name | Middle Initial | Last Name | Address1 | Address2 | City | State | Zip |
|---|---|---|---|---|---|---|---|
| John | D | Smith | 22 Twain Dr | | Fresno | CA | 93612 |
| John | D | Smith | 22 Twain Dr | | Fresno | CA | 93612 |
| John | D | Smith | 22 Twain Dr | | Fresno | CA | 93612 |

| Phone | Brand | Item | Qty | Price | Date |
|---|---|---|---|---|---|
| 555-1111 | Mikasa | Plate | 4 | 10 | 12/31/1998 |
| 555-1111 | Mikasa | Saucer | 4 | 10 | 12/31/1998 |
| 555-1111 | Mikasa | Platter | 1 | 40 | 12/31/1998 |

"Each transaction record," I explained, "shows what John Smith purchased, how much it cost at the time of the purchase, and *when* it was purchased. Unfortunately, each transaction record also shows John Smith's complete customer information."

"That's right," Rhonda said. "Now I remember. That's the bloat you referred to last week, and that's why we need to substitute all of that extra information with something like a CustomerID."

"That's perfect, Rhonda," I answered. "Do you also see the problem now if John Smith moves?"

"Yes, I think so," she said. "If he moves from 22 Twain Drive in Fresno, to somewhere in Philadelphia, then either someone or a program we write would have to ensure that we updated every transaction record with his new address."

"Right again," I agreed, "and that can be a real pain, especially if there are many records involved."

"Now what's the alternative to this bloat?" Melissa asked. "Using the CustomerID in the transaction record?"

"That's correct," I said. "First, we need to establish a record for John Smith in the `Customers` table with a unique `CustID`, like so:"

| Cust ID | First Name | Middle Initial | Last Name | Address 1 | Address 2 | City | State | Zip | Phone |
|---|---|---|---|---|---|---|---|---|---|
| 1 | John | D | Smith | 22 Twain Dr | | Fresno | CA | 93612 | 555-1111 |

"Now that we have a customer record established for John Smith," I continued, "we then simply use the `CustID` field for John Smith in the transaction record instead of all of those other customer fields like we had before. Look at this..."

| CustID | Brand | Item | Qty | Price | Date |
|---|---|---|---|---|---|
| 1 | Mikasa | Plate | 4 | 10 | 12/31/1998 |
| 1 | Mikasa | Saucer | 4 | 10 | 12/31/1998 |
| 1 | Mikasa | Platter | 1 | 40 | 12/31/1998 |

"Do you see how the size of the transaction record is much smaller?" I asked. "Plus, if any of John Smith's customer information changes, there's absolutely no need to update any of the records in the `Transactions` table. This takes care of any potential data anomalies."

"So the number `1` in the `CustID` field, "Lou said, "relates back to the record in the `Customers` table with a `CustID` of `1`?"

"That's right, Lou," I said. "And that's what enables us to know who purchased the Mikasa plate on December 31, 1998."

"That's great," Mary said. "Can we take this a stage further by not including the actual description of the china items in the `Transactions` table? Couldn't we use some kind of inventory code instead?"

"Are you sure you haven't done this before, Mary?" I agreed. "That's exactly what we should do. That will eliminate more bloat in the transaction record, and reduce the chance of data anomalies even more. Of course, we would first need to create an `Inventory` record for each of these china items – like this:"

| ItemID | Brand | Item Name | Price |
|---|---|---|---|
| 1 | Corelle | Plate | 4 |
| 2 | Corelle | ButterPlate | 1 |
| 3 | Corelle | Bowl | 2 |
| 4 | Corelle | Cup | 1 |
| 5 | Corelle | Saucer | 1 |
| 6 | Corelle | Platter | 5 |
| 7 | Corelle | Complete | 8 |
| 8 | Faberware | Plate | 10 |
| 9 | Faberware | ButterPlate | 3 |
| 10 | Faberware | Bowl | 5 |
| 11 | Faberware | Cup | 3 |
| 12 | Faberware | Saucer | 3 |
| 13 | Faberware | Platter | 13 |
| 14 | Faberware | Complete | 21 |
| 15 | Mikasa | Plate | 25 |
| 16 | Mikasa | ButterPlate | 10 |
| 17 | Mikasa | Bowl | 10 |
| 18 | Mikasa | Cup | 5 |
| 19 | Mikasa | Saucer | 5 |
| 20 | Mikasa | Platter | 50 |
| 21 | Mikasa | Complete | 50 |

I then displayed this illustration of the **Transactions** table, replacing the names of the china items with the appropriate **ItemID** from the **Inventory** table:

| CustID | ItemID | Qty | Price | Date |
|---|---|---|---|---|
| 1 | 15 | 4 | 10 | 12/31/1998 |
| 1 | 19 | 4 | 10 | 12/31/1998 |
| 1 | 20 | 1 | 40 | 12/31/1998 |

"This is beginning to make more sense to me now," Valerie said. "We've really streamlined the size of that transaction record."

"Is this typical of the database design process," Chuck asked, "that, wherever possible, you replace descriptions with IDs and codes?"

"It's not so much that," I said. "What we are doing is removing fields from tables in which they don't belong in the first place. The **Transactions** table is not really where the customer's **Address** and **Phone number** belong, is it? They really should be in the **Customers** table."

"That transaction record," Rhonda said, "is starting to look more and more cryptic each time we change it. Not only don't we know who the customer is, but also which china item that was purchased."

"That's not quite true," I said. "With the **CustID** and the **ItemID** present in the transaction record, we can determine both the item that was purchased, *and* the customer who purchased it. We just need to use other tables to determine the details."

"And we do that," Rachel said, "by using the **CustID** to look up the customer in the **Customers** table, and by using the **ItemID** to look up the inventory record in the **Inventory** table?"

"That's perfect," I replied.

I then looked down at Dave, and saw that he had been updating his schematic of the China Shop database. I asked him to display it on the classroom projector:

**China Shop Database Fields:**

| Table | Field |
|---|---|
| Customers | Customer's ID Number |
| Customers | Customer's First Name |
| Customers | Customer's Middle Initial |
| Customers | Customer's Last Name |
| Customers | Customer's Address1 |
| Customers | Customer's Address2 |
| Customers | Customer's City |
| Customers | Customer's State |
| Customers | Customer's Zip Code |
| Customers | Customer's Phone Number |
| Transactions | Transaction ID Number |
| Transactions | Customer ID Number |
| Transactions | Inventory ID Number |
| Transactions | Quantity of item purchased |
| Transactions | Price of item purchased |
| Transactions | Date of Purchase |
| Inventory | Inventory ID Number |
| Inventory | Inventory Brand Name |
| Inventory | Inventory Item |
| Inventory | Inventory Price |
| Users | UserID |
| Users | Password |

## Step 5. Identify Fields with Unique Values in order to Assign Primary Keys

"Where did that Transaction ID Number in the `Transactions` table come from?" Rhonda asked. "I don't remember discussing that. Did I miss something?"

Dave replied by saying that he had anticipated the `Transactions` table would be needing this, since both the `Customers` and `Inventory` table each had a unique ID of their own.

"That's a good point," I agreed. "Step five of my methodology says that we need to identify a field or fields that will uniquely identify each record. These fields become the **primary key** of the table. Adding a Transaction ID field in the `Transactions` table makes perfect sense to me."

"Couldn't the primary key of the Transactions table," Blaine asked, "be the combination of the CustomerID, ItemID, Quantity and Date fields? That way we wouldn't have to assign a Transaction ID when the record is added to the table."

"At first glance that seems fine, Blaine," I said, "however, suppose our customer, John Smith, returns the same day and purchases another Mikasa Plate. We would then have a transaction record with the same Customer ID, Item ID, Quantity and Date. As Access prevents us from adding records to a table where the primary key is duplicated, we'd then have a situation where we couldn't add the record to the `Transactions` table, and that would be a big problem."

"That's right," I said, "and please don't be concerned about the need to assign a unique number to this field. As you'll see in just a little while, if we define this field as an AutoNumber field, Access will take care of that for us."

"What about the `Users` table?" Rhonda asked. "What will be the primary key to that table?"

"`UserID`," I said, "makes perfect sense there. That field value alone will make the record unique."

I then asked Dave if he would mind modifying his schematic by marking each primary key field with an asterisk. In no time, Dave had the following schematic displayed on the classroom projector:

**China Shop Database Fields:**

| Table | Field |
|---|---|
| Customers | **Customer's CustID*** |
| Customers | Customer's First Name |
| Customers | Customer's Middle Initial |
| Customers | Customer's Last Name |
| Customers | Customer's Address1 |
| Customers | Customer's Address2 |
| Customers | Customer's City |
| Customers | Customer's State |
| Customers | Customer's Zip Code |
| Customers | Customer's Phone Number |
| Transactions | **Transaction ID Number*** |
| Transactions | Customer ID Number |
| Transactions | Inventory ID Number |
| Transactions | Quantity of item purchased |
| Transactions | Price of item purchased |
| Transactions | Date of Purchase |
| Inventory | **Inventory ID Number*** |
| Inventory | Inventory Brand Name |
| Inventory | Inventory Item |
| Inventory | Inventory Price |
| Users | **UserID*** |
| Users | Password |

I asked the class if there were any questions about the logical design of our China Shop database. There were none.

"That just about wraps up the logical design of our `China` shop database," I said. "For the rest of today's class, we'll be dealing with Access-specific issues – which means that any fine tuning we do from this point forward really encompasses **physical database design**."

I could detect a sense of excitement in the class.

"We really should look at the names of the fields now," I said. "Remember, we want to make the names as short as possible, yet still descriptive."

"Are there any special rules for naming the fields?" Steve asked.

"That's a good question," I said. "Different database management packages may have different rules about naming fields in a table. In general, Access is the most lenient in terms of naming fields – something that at first glance seems great, but could come back to haunt us."

"Why is that?" Linda asked.

"For instance," I replied, "Access allows us to create field names with spaces in them – but other databases, such as Oracle, would flag a field named like this as an error. If we name our fields with spaces, and in the future, move our database to an Oracle database platform, for instance, we would have to rename the fields without spaces to adhere to Oracle's naming rules. Even more importantly, we'd have to change any Visual Basic programs that might have referenced the old field names. Additionally, having field names with spaces in will cause you extra work when it comes to coding in VB."

"So the bottom line then," Kevin said, "is **never** name your fields with a space in the name."

"Right you are, Kevin," I said. "That will save you a lot of potential grief in the future."

We spent a minute or two discussing field names for the tables. This didn't take too long, as we already knew what the fields were – it was just a matter of deciding on a formal name. There was some disagreement over the name of the Quantity field in the `Transactions` table. Some students felt that we should abbreviate Quantity to *Qty*. My vote was to use the full spelling of Quantity rather than the abbreviation. Just a personal preference on clarity – nothing more.

"Doesn't using the full word `Quantity` bloat the `Transactions` table?" Rhonda asked.

"No, Rhonda," I said. "The size of the name of the field has no material impact on the number of characters stored in the database – after all, we only store the field name once, as the heading for the field."

In a few minutes, we came to an agreement on the field names, and Dave displayed this updated schematic on the classroom projector:

**China Shop Database Fields:**

| Table | Field Name | Description |
|---|---|---|
| Customers | **CustID*** | Customer ID |
| Customers | FirstName | Customer's First Name |
| Customers | MI | Customer's Middle Initial |
| Customers | LastName | Customer's Last Name |
| Customers | Address1 | Customer's Address1 |
| Customers | Address2 | Customer's Address2 |
| Customers | City | Customer's City |
| Customers | State | Customer's State |
| Customers | Zip | Customer's Zip Code |
| Customers | Phone | Customer's Phone Number |
| Transactions | **TransID*** | Transaction ID Number |
| Transactions | CustID | Customer ID Number |
| Transactions | ItemID | Inventory ID Number |
| Transactions | Quantity | Quantity of item purchased |
| Transactions | Price | Price of item purchased |
| Transactions | DateOfPurchase | Date of Purchase |
| Inventory | **ItemID*** | Inventory ID Number |
| Inventory | Brand | Inventory Brand Name |
| Inventory | ItemName | Inventory Item |
| Inventory | Price | Inventory Price |
| Users | **UserID*** | UserID |
| Users | Password | Password |

"At what point do we need to concern ourselves with determining the data types for these fields?" Steve asked.

"Steve, your timing is perfect," I said. "The answer is, right about now."

## Step 6. Specify Data Types for Fields

"Does everyone remember our discussion concerning data types from last week's class?" I asked.

Everyone nodded that they did remember.

I then suggested that everyone try to determine, on their own, the data types for each of the database fields we had identified. I also asked them to specify the field size for any text data fields they identified. I gave the class about 10 minutes to complete this little exercise, and then we began to discuss what they had done.

There were no big problems with the solutions that the class came up with – just lots of little nagging ones.

One area of difficulty we had right up front was with what I call 'pseudo-numeric' fields. These fields contain numbers, and at first glance appear to be numeric data that can have mathematical operations performed against it. However, sometimes they are *really* just string-type data: for example, a phone number looks like it could be multiplied by two, but it wouldn't really be helpful to do that, would it? Pseudo-numeric fields like this should *not* be defined as numeric fields, but rather as text fields instead.

"You mean that the **`Zip`** field should really be declared as a text field then?" Rhonda asked.

"That's right," I said. "We won't be performing any mathematical operations on the Zip code, will we?"

"I suppose not," Rhonda agreed. "It's not like we would sum zip codes or average them or anything."

"The same rationale applies to the **`Customers`** table's **`Phone`** field," Pete said. "Even though the **`Phone`** field contains all numbers, we should also define it as a text field."

"That's excellent, Pete," I affirmed. "You've got it now."

We then spent the next ten minutes or so in a debate over the length of the text fields in the records of the database. This is always a tricky issue for beginners, and I told the class that there's really no magic formula that we can use to determine the optimal length for a database field.

"I've changed my mind about ten times over the field size for the **LastName** field," Valerie said.

"You said there's no magic formula," Rachel said, "but there must be some guidelines."

I suggested that they should begin by sampling any existing data that they may be able to find.

"For instance," I said, "if there is an existing customer list, go through it and determine what the longest last name in the list is. If it's 20 characters in length, you could take that number and add 5 to it, just to be safe."

"I believe Access automatically creates a text field with a width of 50?" Dave said. "I suppose we could just accept that default – but of course, we might be introducing some wasted space in the database."

"That's right, Dave," I agreed, "but I think that 50 is a bit too much for a default – as you say, that would introduce a fair amount of wasted space in the database. Also, look at the State field in the **Customers** table – it will never be more than two characters, so accepting the default is really a bad idea."

"I can help you out with the Customer names and addresses," Joe Bullina said. "I just happen to have my Customer list with me."

"That's great, Joe," I said, "nothing beats sampling real data!"

We spent a few minutes examining Joe Bullina's customer list to determine the longest existing occurrence of a first name, last name, and address field. After a few minutes of discussion, we came to the following consensus: 30 characters for the customer's **LastName**, and 20 characters for the **FirstName** field. We agreed that the **Address1**, **Address2**, and **City** fields would all be defined as 30 characters in length.

"Do we have to get these field names and definitions perfect right up front?" Rhonda asked, "Before we start building the database in Access?"

"That's a good question, Rhonda," I said, "and the answer is 'no'. Changing the structure or definition of the database is pretty easy in Access, even after you've already added records to it."

"That's good news," she replied. "I'd hate to have to start all over again if I made a mistake, or left something out."

We then discussed the **State** field in the Customers table. This was an easy choice – since there is a standard two-character designation for every state in the United States, we just settled on a two-character text filed for State.

Rachel had suggested that the **Zip** field should be five characters. Then Joe Bullina reminded us that by using the nine character format for the Zip code (5 numbers, plus a dash, plus 4 numbers) on his mailing labels, he could receive a discount from the Postal Service when it came to mailing his circulars or advertisements.

"What about the dash in the zip code?" Steve asked. "Will we also be storing the dash in the database? If we do, shouldn't we make the field size 10?"

"That's another good question," I said.

I then explained that with the **Zip** field, we were faced with the same kind of dilemma we faced when we were trying to decide whether to define the customer's name as a single field, or to break it up the way we did into three separate fields.

"I think you've already seen," I said, "that in database design, there are 'gray' areas where one designer may go in one direction, and another designer in another. The issue of breaking the name field into three pieces – **First Name**, **Middle Initial** and **Last Name** – is a perfect example. The **Zip** field is another."

"You mean we could define the **Zip** field as two separate fields?" Linda asked.

"Yes we could," I said, "and some database designers might do exactly that, by creating a field called **Zip-5** and another called **Zip-4** to separate the two parts of the **Zip**. My rule of thumb is to break the fields into their smallest logical pieces. In my mind, there was a good reason to break the name field into first name, middle initial and last name, since those are distinct pieces of a person's name, used and referenced all the time. My feeling here is that we should define **Zip** as a single text field 9 characters in length. I don't see the need to break it up any further."

"What about the dash, though?" Steve repeated.

"If you think about it," I replied, "the dash is really a **constant**: it *always* appears between the fifth and sixth characters of the zip code. Here again, you might find some disagreement among database designers, but in my mind, there's no need to waste a character of data storage by including the dash in the **Zip** field of every record. We'll just need to be aware of this format whenever we output the zip code information."

"Output?" Rhonda said, obviously puzzled.

"What I mean, Rhonda," I said, "is that whenever we display or print the contents of the **Zip** field, we need to remember to include the dash."

"We can do that," she replied, "even though the dash isn't in the database?"

"Sure, no problem," I answered. "Although we'll need to use a little string manipulation in the process!"

Rhonda seemed content with that explanation. I continued by explaining that there are some other common fields of this type – fields containing constant dashes – that we might encounter in the future.

"The customer's phone number is another example of the use of a constant in a field, isn't it? Rachel said. "We usually display phone numbers with a dash between the third and fourth characters."

"And we also usually have parentheses around the area code." Valerie interjected.

"You're both right," I nodded. "The customer's phone number requires only ten characters – three for the area code, and seven for the number – although, as is the case with the **Zip** field, we'll need to bear in mind the need to format the phone number whenever we display or print it."

"You mean," Melissa said, "that we'll need to place parentheses around the area code, and a dash between the third and fourth characters whenever we display or print the contents of the **Phone** field somewhere."

"That's right," I said.

"Will we use string manipulation to do that as well?" Ward asked.

"Yes, on the output side of things," I said.

"What about the input side?" Tom said. "Will the customer be entering information into text boxes on a form?"

"Exactly right, Tom," I said. "However, in the case of these two fields – **Zip** and **Phone** – we'll place a special kind of text box on the form. Don't worry about that for the moment – we'll be discussing this next week.

"Can I ask something?" Dave asked. "Will the dashes and parentheses automatically appear as the customer enters their Zip code and phone number? I've seen that effect in some other programs I've used."

"That's just what will happen, Dave," I said, "the China Shop program will display the parentheses and dash in the **Phone** field, and the dash in the **Zip** field. All they'll need to do is just enter the numbers."

With the discussion of the **Phone** and **Zip** fields out of the way, we quickly came to an agreement on the format and field length for the remainder of the fields in the database.

"Before we move onto the final step in our design process, **Specifying Relationships**," I said "we should also determine which of the fields in the database are **required**, and which are **optional**."

"Shouldn't they *all* be required?" Rhonda asked.

"Not all of them," Steve said. "For instance, not every customer will have something to enter into the **Address2** field."

"Good point, Steve," Valerie said. "And there are some people who don't have middle initials either."

"And don't forget," Joe Bullina said, "I don't want to force my customers to enter their phone number if they don't feel comfortable doing so."

"So it looks as though we have three optional fields," Dave said, "**MI**, **Address2**, and **Phone**."

"I think that's about it," I replied.

Dave displayed his schematic on the classroom projector:

| **Table** | **Field Name** | **Field Type** | **Field Size** | **Required?** | **Description** |
|---|---|---|---|---|---|
| Customers | **CustID*** | AutoNumber | | | Customer ID |
| Customers | FirstName | Text | 20 | Yes | Customer's First Name |
| Customers | MI | Text | 1 | **No** | Customer's Middle Initial |
| Customers | LastName | Text | 30 | Yes | Customer's Last Name |
| Customers | Address1 | Text | 30 | Yes | Customer's Address1 |

| Table | Field Name | Field Type | Field Size | Required? | Description |
|---|---|---|---|---|---|
| Customers | Address2 | Text | 30 | **No** | Customer's Address2 |
| Customers | City | Text | 30 | Yes | Customer's City |
| Customers | State | Text | 2 | Yes | Customer's State |
| Customers | Zip | Text | 9 | Yes | Customer's Zip Code |
| Customers | Phone | Text | 10 | **No** | Customer's Phone Number |
| Transactions | **TransID*** | AutoNumber | | | Transaction ID Number |
| Transactions | CustID | Number | | Yes | Customer ID Number |
| Transactions | ItemID | Number | | Yes | Inventory ID Number |
| Transactions | Quantity | Number | | Yes | Quantity of item purchased |
| Transactions | Price | Currency | | Yes | Price of item purchased |
| Transactions | DateOfPurchase | Date/Time | | Yes | Date of Purchase |
| Inventory | **ItemID*** | AutoNumber | | | Inventory ID Number |
| Inventory | Brand | Text | 20 | Yes | Inventory Brand |
| Inventory | ItemName | Text | 20 | Yes | Inventory Item |
| Inventory | Price | Currency | | Yes | Inventory Price |
| Users | **UserID*** | Text | 13 | Yes | UserID |
| Users | Password | Text | 8 | Yes | Password |

The class took a few minutes to look at Dave's schematic.

"This schematic is important," I said, "as it will form the basis of our China Shop database. Anything we forget to include here can have a significant impact on the China Shop program. The last thing we want to do weeks from now is to try to add information to our database, and find that we don't have a field for it!"

"But you did say we can always change the database after the fact, didn't you?" Rhonda asked.

"That's right, Rhonda," I agreed. "We can always change the database later – but it's much easier for us to get everything correct up front."

"I keep forgetting about our `Users` table," Steve said. "How did you decide on a field size of 13 for that, Dave?"

"`ADMINISTRATOR` has thirteen characters," Dave said, "so that seemed reasonable."

"And as you've pointed out, Professor," Melissa interjected, "if we need to make the field larger, we can easily do that, even after the database has records in it."

## *Step 7. Identify Relationships Between Tables*

There were no other questions or comments concerning Dave's schematic, and so I explained that the final step in our database design was to identify any relationships that might exist between the tables in the database.

"I know we discussed relationships last week," Peter said. "But I'm still a bit confused by them. Can you tell me again, why do we specify relationships?"

"Relationships," I said, "help to prevent invalid data from being entered into our database. For instance, when we enter a record into the `Transactions` table, we want to ensure that the customer ID and the inventory ID exist in the `Customers` and `Inventory` tables respectively. By specifying a relationship between the `Transactions` table and the `Customers` table on the `CustID` field, and between the `Transactions` table and the `Inventory` table on the `ItemID` field, we can enforce that requirement."

"That doesn't sound all that bad," Rachel said. "But what about those one-to-one, one-to-many, and many-to-many relationships you talked about last week?"

"The database design process," I said, "works toward an ultimate design where all of the relationships are one-to-many. And that's exactly what we have here."

"What about the `Users` table?" Dave asked. "That doesn't appear to be related to any other table. Is that OK?"

"Yes, Dave," I replied. "It's perfectly fine to have stand alone tables that have no relationships to other tables."

"So it looks like we have just two relationships then," Kathy said. "A one-to-many relationship between `Customers` and `Transactions`, and a one-to-many relationship between `Inventory` and `Transactions`."

"That's right, Kathy," I said. "When we start using Access we'll be able so see how these relationships look. We'll do this by drawing the connections between them on-screen. This will help to clarify the subject if any of you are confused at all."

There were no further questions, and I announced that the design of our China Shop database was complete.

"All that remains now," I said, "is for us to implement it."

"What about the physical design of the database?" Mary asked. "Don't we still have to do that?"

"Physical database design," I reiterated, "involves taking the logical design that we created after Step 5 and enhancing that design for use in a particular database management software package – in our case, Access. Because it's relatively easy to define and implement a database using Access, we really started and completed that process in Step 6, where we named our fields and specified Access data types."

At this point, I suggested that we take a fifteen-minute break before we started to implement our design. I wanted everyone well-rested for that process!

## Creating the China Shop Database in Access

When the class returned from break, I distributed the following exercise for them to complete. This would begin the process of creating the China Shop database.

### Exercise – Creating the China Shop Database

In this exercise you will use Access to create the China Shop database. All screen shots show Access 97, but you can follow along with any version of Access. If you don't have Access installed on your machine, just follow along with the text.

1. Start up Microsoft Access.
2. Select the Blank Database option button :

If you are not using Access 97, this procedure may vary, but will be similar. For instance, in Access 2.0, you will need to select File | New Database from the Access menu bar. If you are unsure how to proceed, check your Access documentation.

3. You now need to give Access both a name and a location for the database. We'll call it China.mdb (naturally), and save it in the same directory (folder) where the China Shop Visual Basic project should already exist: in the C:\VBFILES\CHINA directory:

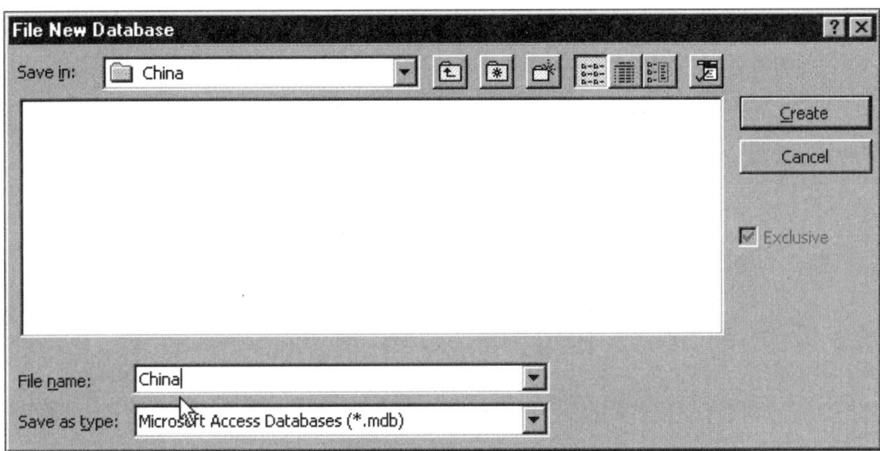


4. Click on the Create button, and the China database will be created for you. You'll then see this Database window. At this point, all we've done so far is create the database. It does not yet consist of any objects:

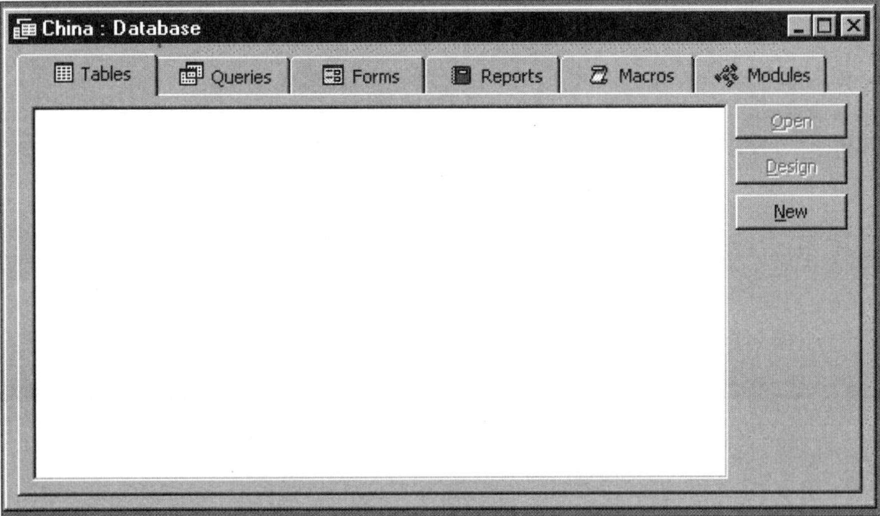

### Discussion

I took a quick tour around the classroom to see if anyone was having any problems – but everyone seemed to be doing fine.

"So at this point then," Kevin said, "all we have is an empty `China` database?"

"That's right," I agreed, taking the opportunity to remind everyone in the class that a database is a collection of tables, and that as yet we had not created any.

"That's our next step," I said, "to create the four tables that will comprise the China Shop database."

I then distributed the following exercise:

## Creating the China Shop Tables

### Exercise – Creating the Customers Table

In this exercise you'll use Access to create the `Customers` table in the China Shop database. Once again, all screen shots show Access 97, but you can follow along with *any* version of Access.

1. I'm presuming you still have Access running, and that the China database window is still open.
2. In the Database window, make sure that the Tables tab is selected, then select the New button. The following screen shot will appear:

3. Select Design View and the following screen shot will appear:

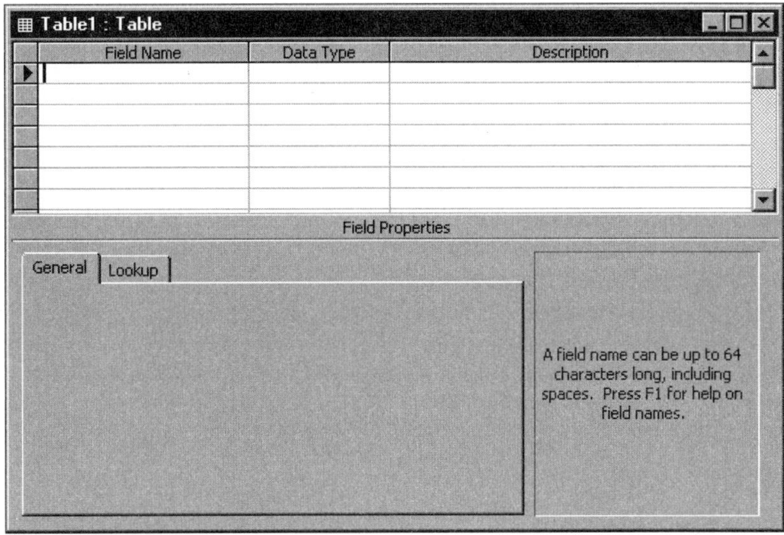


This is the Design View window. Notice that it contains a column for Field Name, Data Type, and Description. Don't worry about naming the table yet – we'll do that shortly:

4. Now we need to tell Access the field names for the **Customers** table. We'll start by entering CustID into the Field Name column. Remember not to type the asterisk – that was for our guidance only! Then either press *Enter*, or tab to the Data Type column. For the moment, ignore the Field Properties pane at the bottom of the window – we'll come to that later:

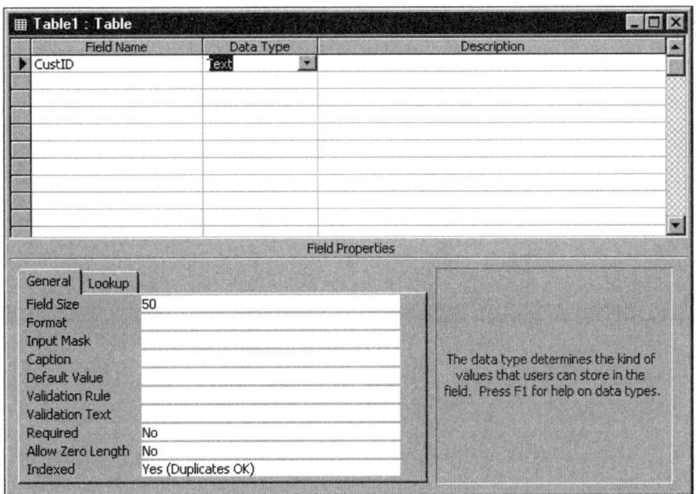

5. Notice that Access presumes that CustID will be a Text field. We need to change the Data Type from Text to AutoNumber. Do that now by clicking on the drop-down list box in the Data Type column, and selecting AutoNumber from the list:

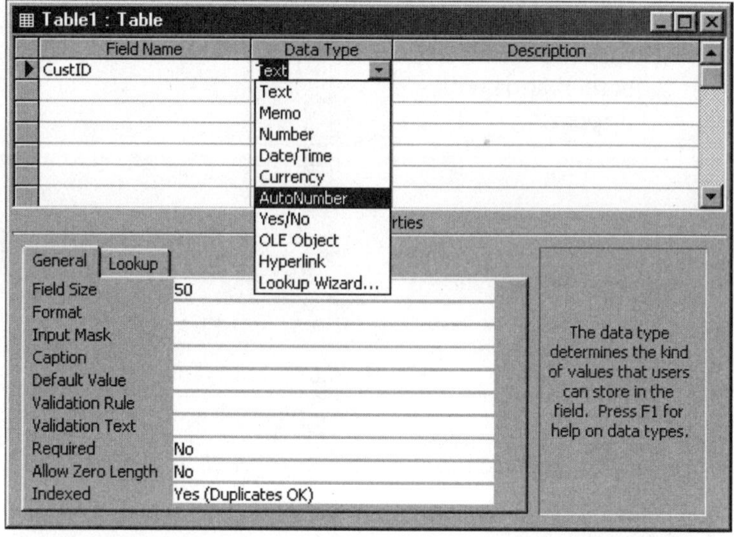


6. Once you have selected AutoNumber for the Data Type, tab to the Description column and enter CustID. Your screen should look like this:

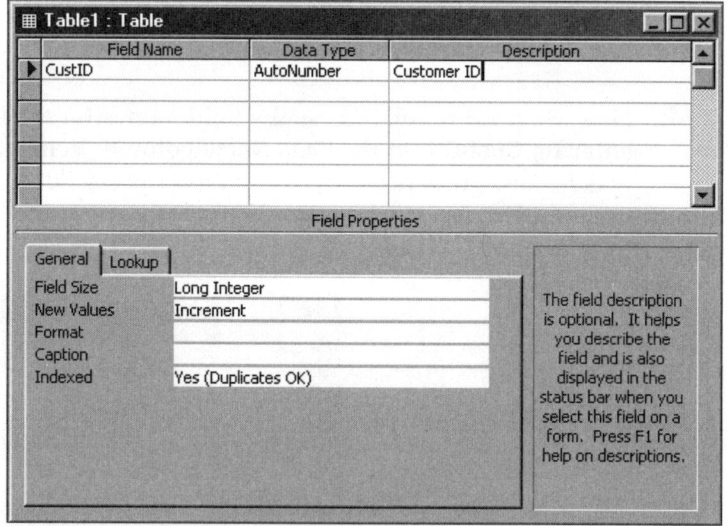


Notice how Access has completed the Field Properties section for you, and has also automatically created an index on this field (indexes help Access find the data that it's looking for more quickly). Furthermore, notice that Access has specified in the Indexed property that Duplicates are OK (i.e. that there can be more than one record with exactly the same value in this field). That's about to change, as we will now designate CustID as the primary key for the Customers table, and primary keys, as we learned earlier, may **not** be duplicated.

7. Right click your mouse anywhere on the CustID row, and this shortcut menu will appear:

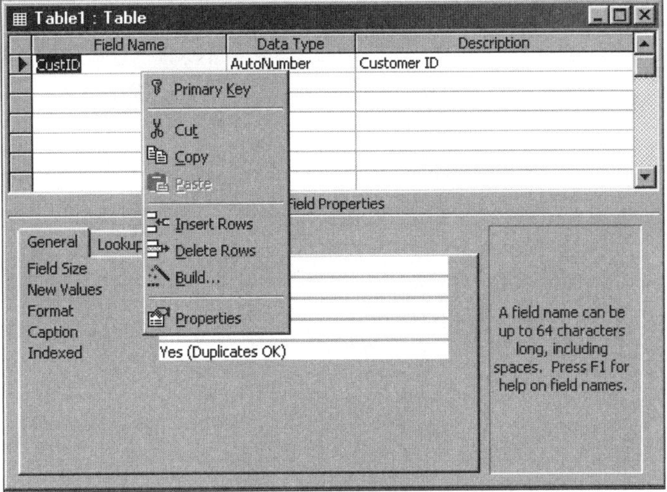


8. Click on Primary Key, and CustID will be designated as the primary key for the Customers table. Notice that a 'key' icon appears to the left of the word CustID, designating this field as the primary key to the table, and that the Field Properties' Indexed property now reads No Duplicates:

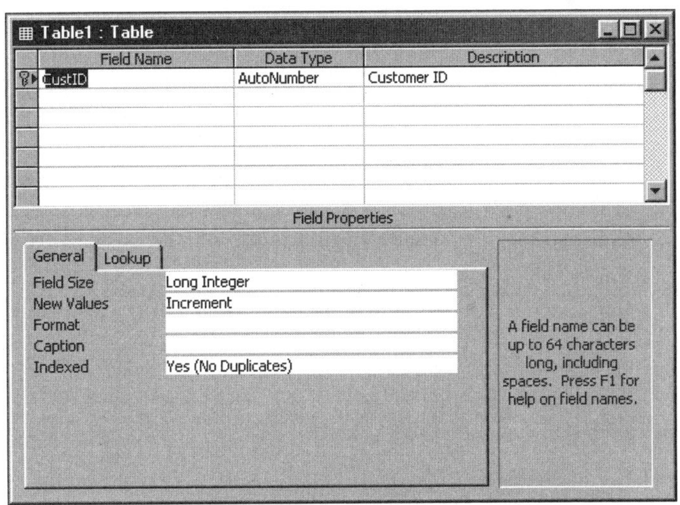


9. We now want to add the second field, FirstName, to the `Customers` table. Just click your mouse on the Field Name column of the second row, and enter FirstName (be careful **not** to insert spaces in the field name). Accept the default Data Type of Text, and enter a description of Customer's First Name into the Description column. Before adding the next field, click on the Field Size property in the Field Properties section, and change it from its default value of 50 to 30. Also, change the Required property from No to Yes. You can do this by double-clicking on this row. (Note that you can use *F6* to get to the Field Properties section of the table design form):

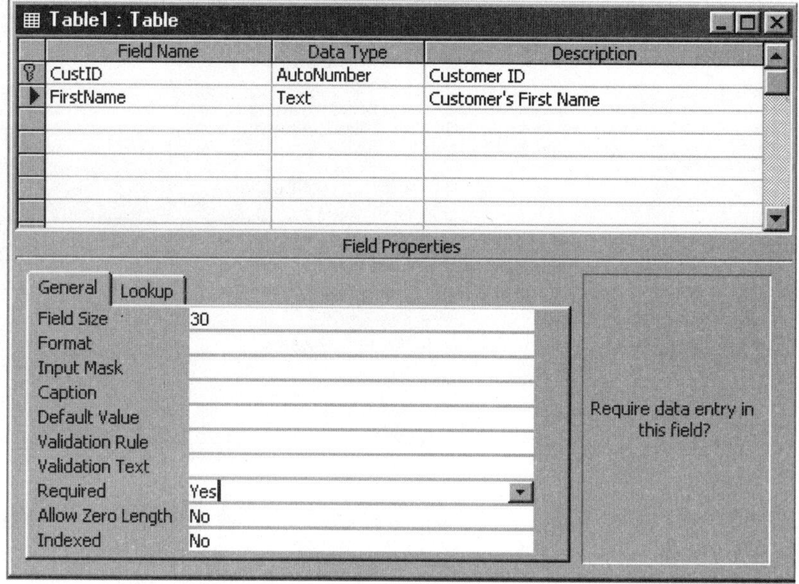


10. Continue adding the rest of the fields in the **Customers** table following the same process you used before. Use this table as your guide:

| Field Name | Field Type | Field Size | Required? | Description |
|---|---|---|---|---|
| CustID* | AutoNumber | | | Customer ID |
| FirstName | Text | 20 | Yes | Customer's First Name |
| MI | Text | 1 | **No** | Customer's Middle Initial |
| LastName | Text | 30 | Yes | Customer's Last Name |
| Address1 | Text | 30 | Yes | Customer's Address1 |
| Address2 | Text | 30 | **No** | Customer's Address2 |
| City | Text | 30 | Yes | Customer's City |
| State | Text | 2 | Yes | Customer's State |
| Zip | Text | 9 | Yes | Customer's Zip Code |
| Phone | Text | 10 | **No** | Customer's Phone Number |

When you have entered the final field, Phone, your screen should look like this:

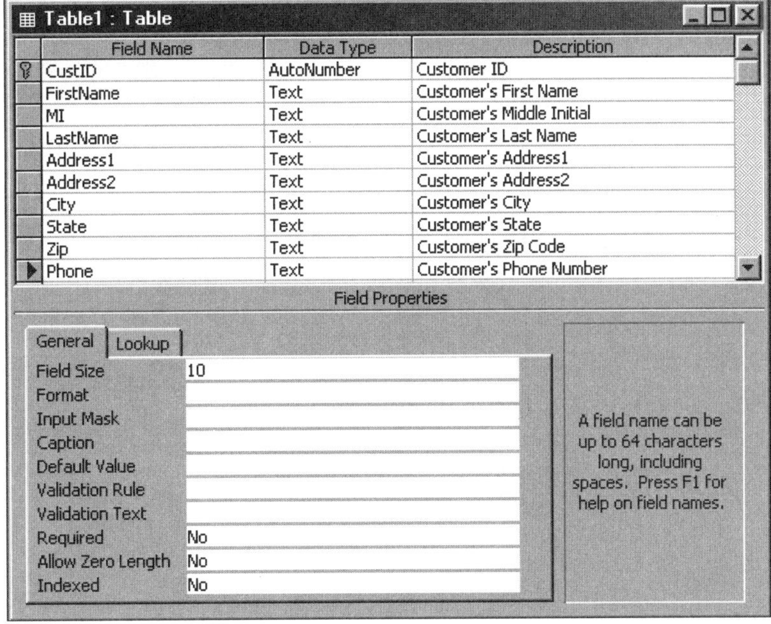


**11.** Now what? You've entered the final field, Phone. Now we need to save the table, and name it `Customers`. To do that, just close the Table window by clicking on the 'close' button in the upper right hand portion of the Table window (the big X at the top-right of the screen). When you do, you'll see the following message:

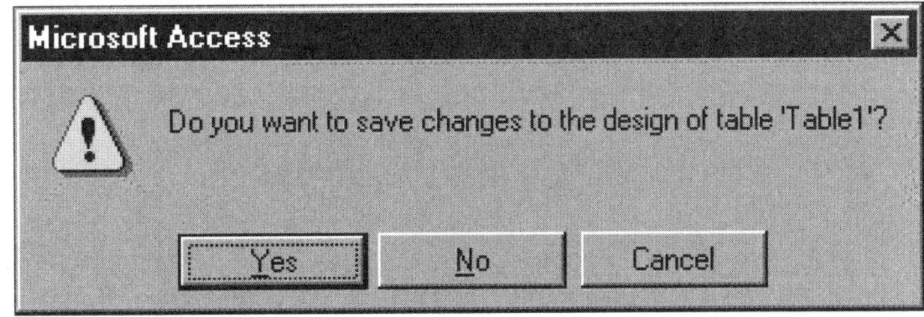


**12.** Click on the Yes button, and you will then see this message, prompting you to name the table:

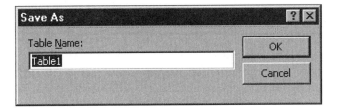

13. **Warning!** Many students at this point immediately click on the OK button. If you do that, you'll name your table Table1, something you don't want to do! Instead, enter Customers as the Table Name, then click on the OK button:

14. The Table window will close and you should then see the Customers table listed as an object in the Database window:

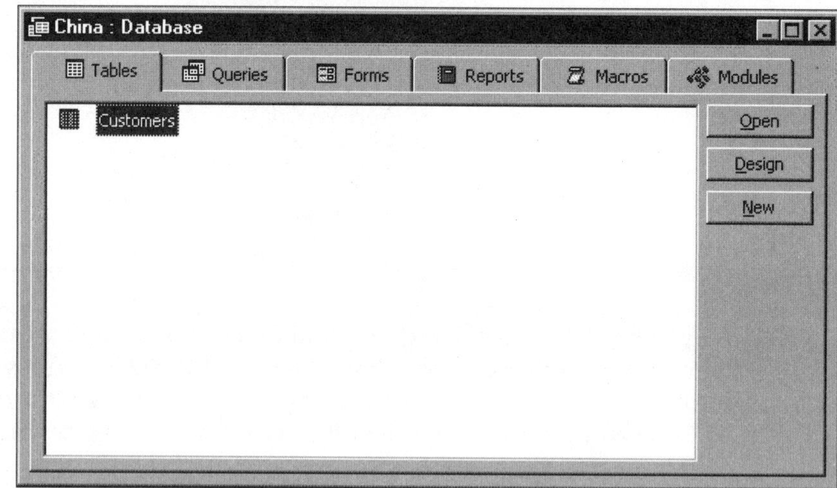


Congratulations! You've done it. You've created your first China Shop table – the `Customers` table.

***Discussion***

As was the case with the previous exercise, there weren't a lot of problems with this one, although since there were a number of steps required to complete the exercise, there were a number of typos.

As I wandered through the classroom while the students were completing the exercise, I reminded everyone that if they made a mistake while completing the exercise, they could immediately correct it right then and there.

As there were no questions, I distributed the next exercise.

## Exercise – Creating the Inventory Table

In this exercise you'll create the second of our four tables, the **`Inventory`** table.

1. As you did when you created the **`Customers`** table in the previous exercise, make sure that the Table tab is selected in the Database window, then select the New button.

2. As you did before, select Design View in the New Table window.

3. Use the following table to design the **`Inventory`** table. Don't forget to specify ItemID as the primary key for the table by right clicking your mouse on that row, and selecting Primary Key from the pop up menu. Note that **`ItemID`** will not have an option for Required because of its field type:

| Field Name | Field Type | Field Size | Required? | Description |
|---|---|---|---|---|
| ItemId | AutoNumber | | | Inventory ID Number |
| Brand | Text | 20 | Yes | Inventory Brand |
| ItemName | Text | 20 | Yes | Inventory Item |
| Price | Currency | | Yes | Inventory Price |

4. When you have entered the final field, Price, your screen should look like this:

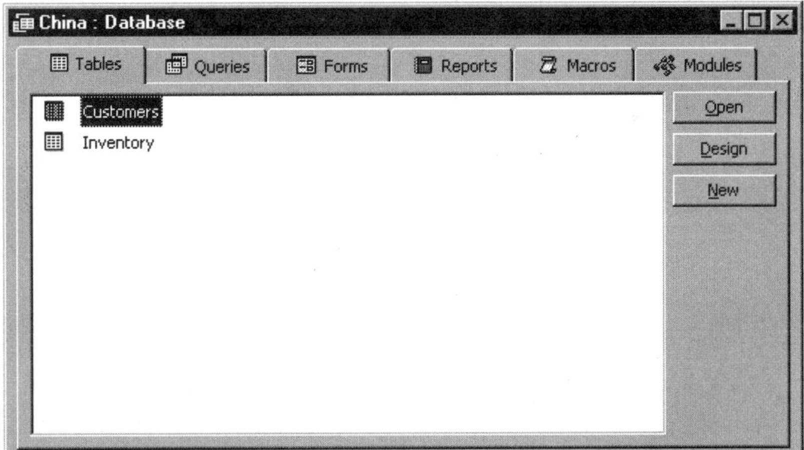


5. We now want to create a second index in addition to the primary key index we have just specified. With the Design window still open, select View | Indexes from the Access menu bar:

This screen shot will appear. Notice that the **`Inventory`** table currently has just a single index, called PrimaryKey:

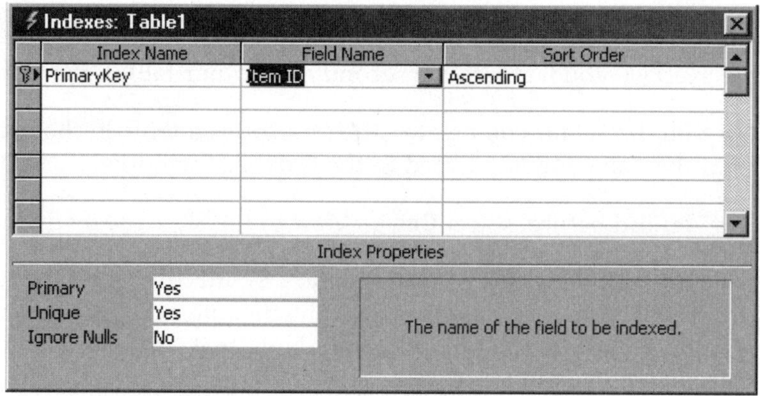


6. Add an index to the **`Inventory`** table by typing BrandItemName in the Index Name column, and selecting both Brand and ItemName as the field names that the index will act upon from the drop-down list box. This will create an index based on the two fields, and will permit us to seek a record in the **`Inventory`** table based on Brand and ItemName:

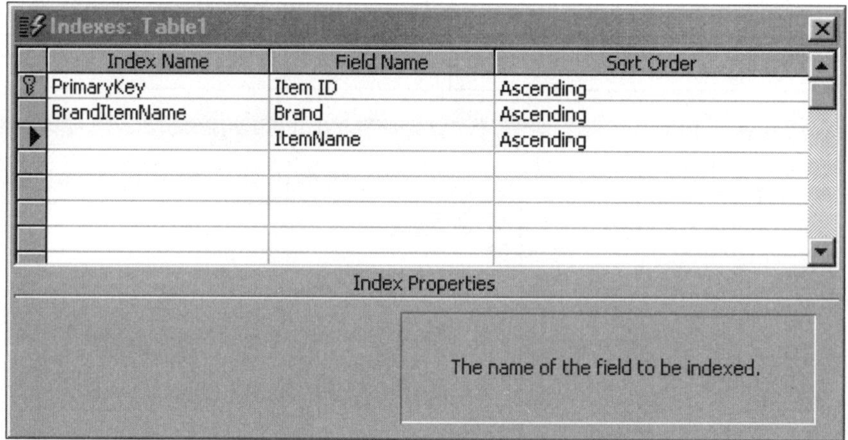


7. Close the Indexes window, then close the **Table** window, and, when prompted, name this table **`Inventory`**.

You should now see two tables in the Database window:

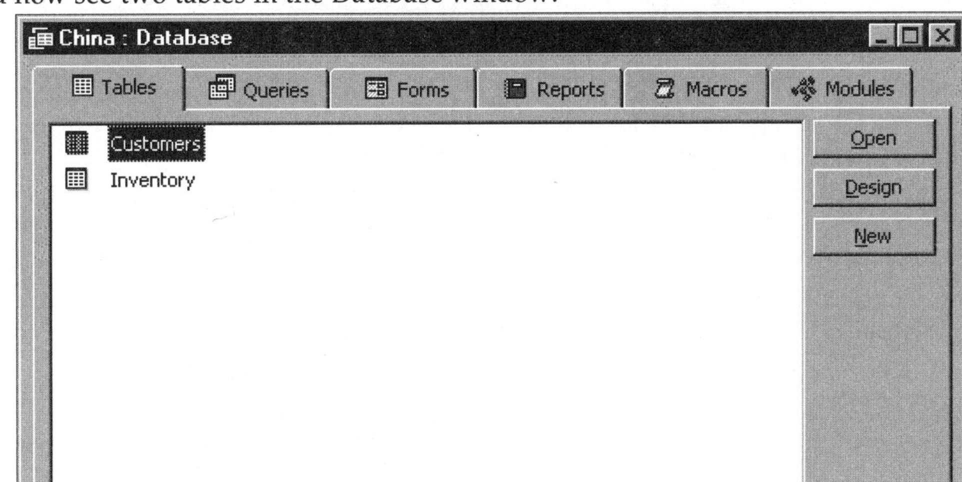


***Discussion***

After everyone had completed the exercise, there was only one question.

"I may have missed this somewhere along the line," Rhonda said, "but why did we chose the Currency data type for the `Price` field?"

"I thought we had discussed this already," I said. "The currency type is identical to the currency type in Visual Basic, and is recommend by Microsoft as the data type to use for monetary values."

"Oh yes!" said Rhonda, "I guess it just slipped by me..."

"Why the second index?" Tom asked.

"This index will come in very handy later on in the program," I said. "We'll use it to quickly locate china items in the `Inventory` table".

There were no more questions, and so I distributed the next exercise.

## Exercise - Creating the Transactions Table

In this exercise you'll create the third of our four tables, the `Transactions` table.

1. As you did when you created the Inventory table in the previous exercise, make sure that the Table tab is selected in the Database window, then select the New Button.
2. As you did before, select Design View in the New Table window.
3. Use the following chart to design the `Transactions` table. Don't forget to specify TransID as the primary key for the table by right clicking your mouse on that row, and selecting Primary Key from the pop up menu:

| Field Name | Field Type | Required? | Description |
|---|---|---|---|
| TransID* | AutoNumber | | Transaction ID Number |
| CustID | Number | Yes | Customer ID Number |
| ItemID | Number | Yes | Inventory ID Number |
| Quantity | Number | Yes | Quantity of item purchased |
| Price | Currency | Yes | Price of item purchased |
| DateOfPurchase | Date/Time | Yes | Date of Purchase |

4. When you have completed the final field, DateOfPurchase, your design view window should look like this:

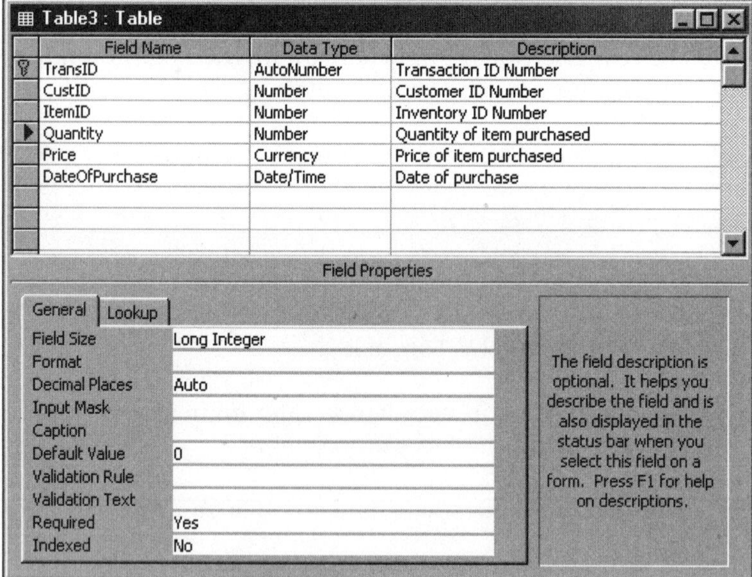

5. Close the Table window and, when prompted, name the table **Transactions**. You should now see three tables in the Database window:

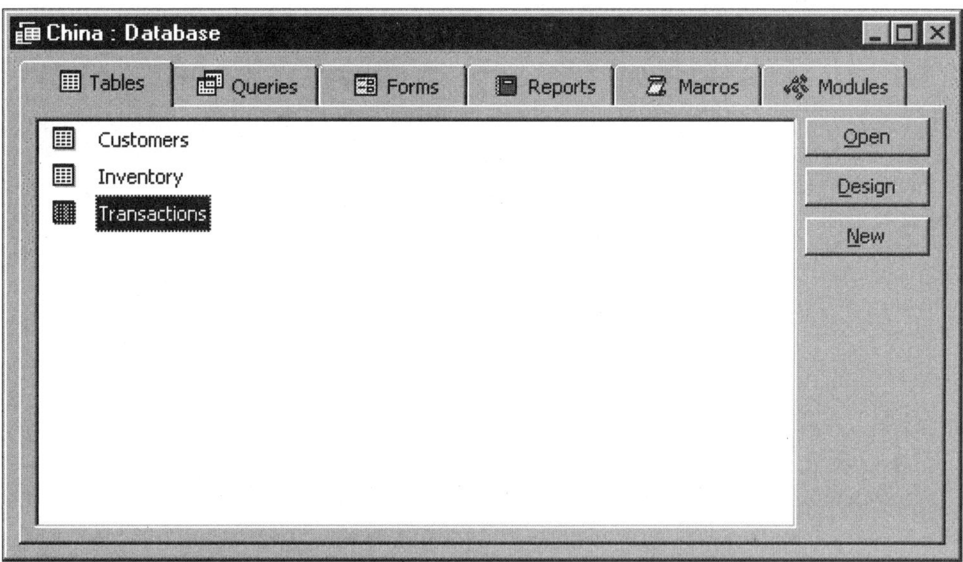


***Discussion***

Once again, there were no major problems in completing the exercise, so I distributed the following exercise, which completes the design for the final table in the database, the `Users` table:

## Exercise – Creating the Users Table

1. Create a new table in the same way as before and select Design View.

2. Use the following chart to design the `Users` table. Don't forget to specify UserID as the primary key for the table by right clicking your mouse on that row, and selecting Primary Key from the pop-up menu:

| Field Name | Field Type | Field Size | Required? | Description |
|---|---|---|---|---|
| UserID | Text | 13 | Yes | UserID |
| Password | Text | 8 | Yes | Password |

3. When you have completed the final field, Password, your design view window should look like this:

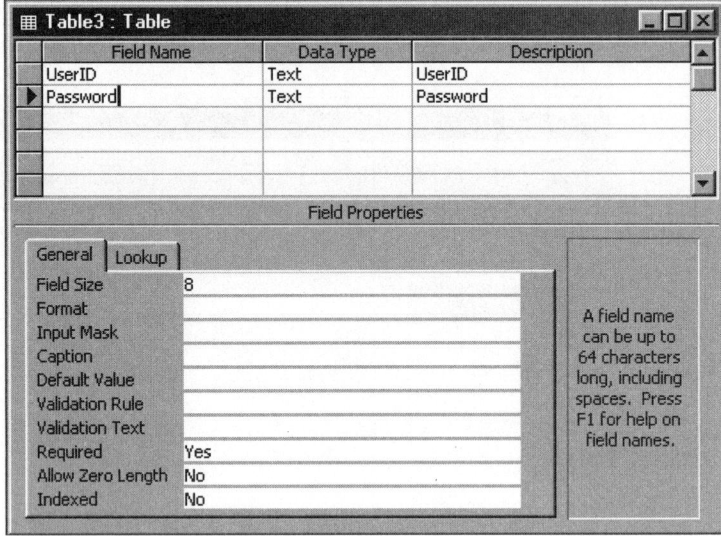


4. Close the Table window, and when prompted, name this table **`Users`**. You should now see all four tables in the Database window:

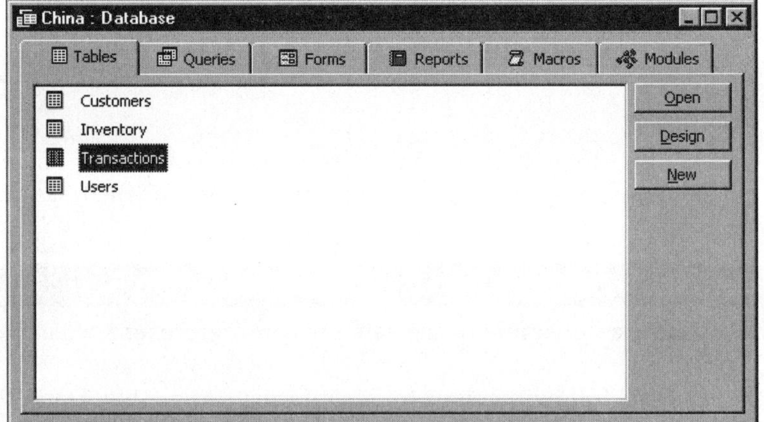


***Discussion***

As I walked around the classroom, it became apparent that my students were pretty pleased with themselves. Even Joe Bullina was getting excited about this. He watched along with me, as each of the students completed work on the China Shop Database's four tables. Finally, when everyone was finished, I said:

"Great work! You've all just completed creating the four tables in the China Shop Database. We're just about done creating the database now."

"I've been wondering about some of those other properties I see in the Field Properties section," Rhonda said. "Should we be doing anything with those?"

"Most of those properties," I said, "affect the way that the fields appear within Access itself, and will have no impact on our Visual Basic program. Others, such as Input Mask and Default, can impact our Visual Basic program – but I'm pretty pleased with what we have in place right now."

## Creating Relationships in the China Shop Database

There were no more questions about the creation of the China Shop database or tables themselves, so I moved on to the next exercise.

### Exercise – Creating Relationships in the China Shop Database

In this exercise you'll use Access to specify relationships between the **`Customers`** table and the **`Transactions`** table, and between the **`Inventory`** table and the **`Transactions`** table. Remember, establishing these relationships will let us link together data from multiple tables and help guarantee the integrity of the information that we're storing in the **`China`** database.

1. With the Database window open, select Tools | Relationships from the Access main menu:

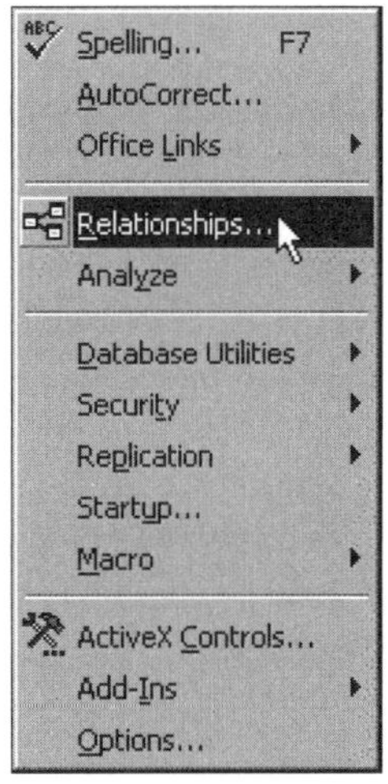

2. You should see the Show Table window. (If you don't, right click your mouse and select Show Table from the pop up menu). You'll now see the following screen:

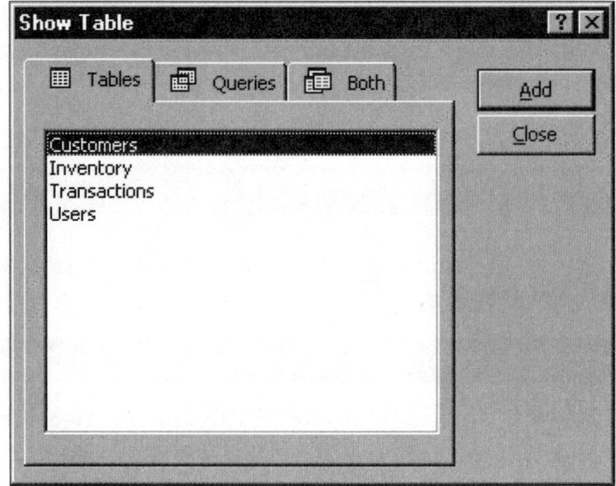


3. Select Customers, then click the Add button. After you do, you should see the Customers table added to the Relationships window:

4. Select Transactions, then click the Add button. The Transactions table will be added to the Relationships window:

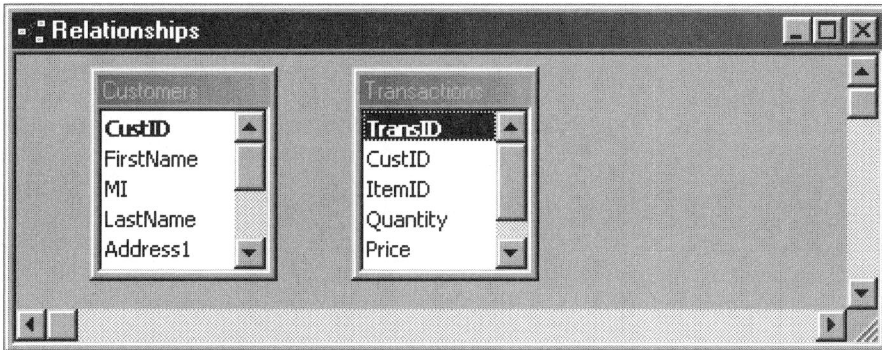


5. Select Inventory, then click the Add button. In case you're wondering why we didn't add these in the order they appear in the list, it's because we need the Transactions table in the middle. In order to see the Relationships window properly you will now have to close the Show Table box:

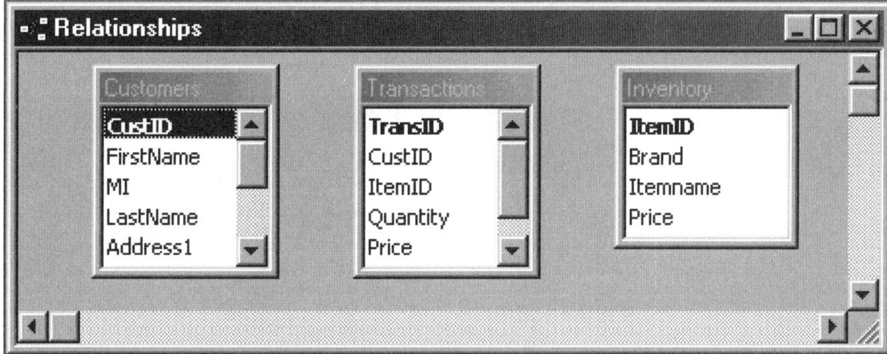

6. You may want to resize the tables in the Relationships window so that you can see all of their fields:

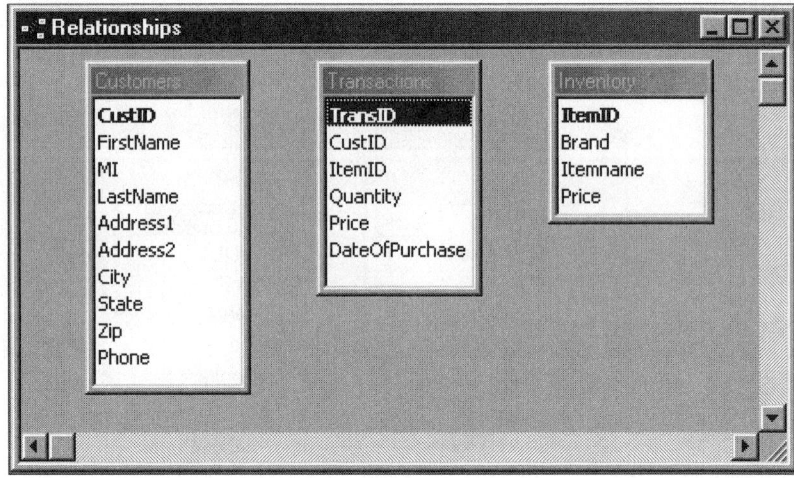


7. We will now establish a relationship between the CustID of the Customers table and the CustID of the Transactions table. Doing this will ensure that a transaction record cannot be created with a CustID that does not first exist in the Customers table – **this is extremely important!** Select the CustID field of the Customers table in the Relationships window with your mouse, then drag your mouse to the CustID field in the Transactions table – this dialog box should appear:

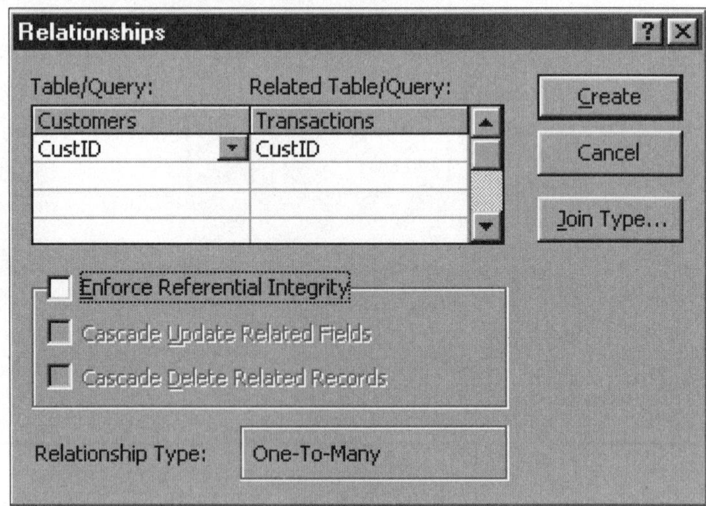

8. Microsoft Access has already inferred the relationship between the two fields in `Customers` and `Transactions` as a **one-to-many** relationship (one `CustID` from the `Customers` table may appear as the `CustID` in many records in the `Transactions` table). All that we need to do now is to check the Enforce Referential Integrity check box, and select the OK button. The Relationships window will change to reflect the relationship between `Customers` and `Transactions`:

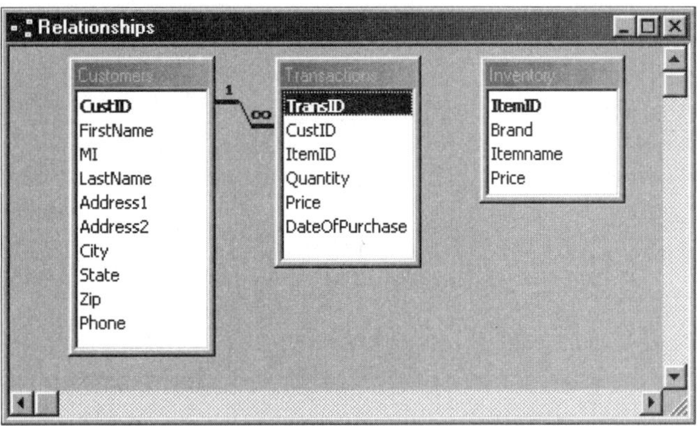


9. Now we need to establish a relationship between the `ItemID` of the `Inventory` table, and the `ItemID` of the `Transactions` table. Doing this will ensure that a transactions record cannot be created with an `ItemID` that does not already exist in the `Inventory` table. To do this, select the `ItemID` field in the `Inventory` table by clicking on it with the left-hand mouse button, then (still holding down the left mouse button, drag your mouse pointer across to the `ItemID` field in the `Transactions` table, and release the button. When you do so, this dialog box will appear:

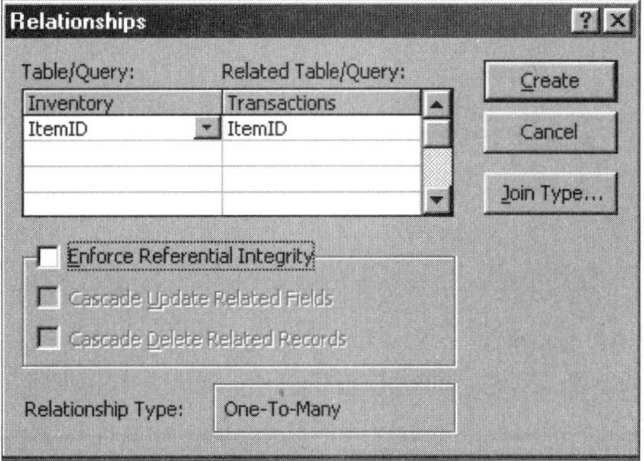

As was the case with the relationship between the **Customers** and **Transactions** tables, Access has already inferred the relationship between **Transactions** and **Inventory**: this time as a one-to-many relationship (one ItemID in **Inventory** may appear as the ItemID in many records in **Transactions**).

**10.** All that we need to do now is to check the Enforce Referential Integrity checkbox, and select the Create button. The Relationships window will change to reflect the relationship between **Inventory** and **Transactions**:

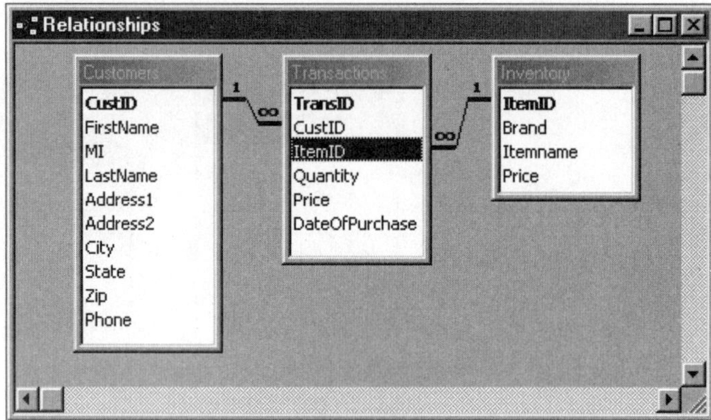


Enforcing referential integrity will make it impossible to create records that violate the relationship rules that we have specified: the database will not allow these rules to be broken.

Now close the Relationships window either by double-clicking on the control menu icon, or use the close button at the upper right-hand portion of the Relationships window. When you do, you'll see this message:

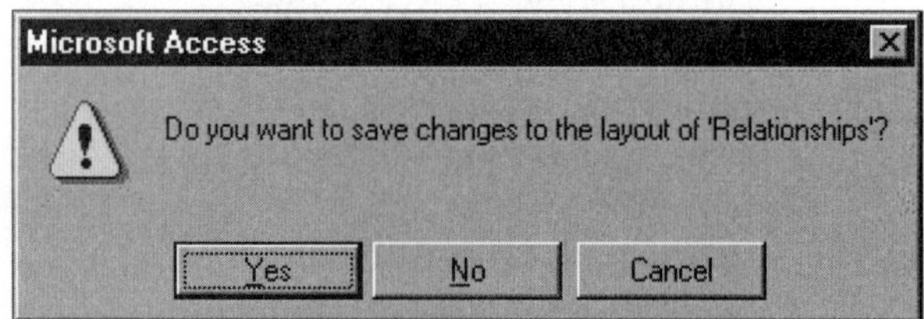


Click on the Yes button and, once again, you'll see the Database window.

### *Discussion*

I had expected some confusion with this exercise, but surprisingly, there wasn't much. Once the students had displayed the tables in the Relationships window, they quickly and easily established the relationships between the tables.

Of course, establishing relationships between tables by clicking and dragging fields from one table to another is tricky the first time you do it – and I did notice that students were repeating the process over again. But all in all, no one seemed to have any serious problems with the exercise.

"I noticed," Rachel said, "that we did nothing with the `Users` table in these exercises. Does that mean that there's absolutely no relationship between the `Users` table and any other table in the database?"

"That's right," I agreed. "No relationship."

"What will happen," Rhonda said, "if someone tries to add a record to the `Transactions` table with a `Customer ID` that doesn't exist in the `Customers` table?"

"The answer to that question," I said, "depends on whether the record is being added to the `Transactions` table within Access, or from within our program. If a user attempts to add a record to the `Transactions` table in Access, they'll receive an Access error that looks like this..."

I then attempted to do add a record to the `Transactions` table from within Access. Since there were currently no `Customers` or `Inventory` records, neither the `CustID` or `ItemID` number I entered was found in those tables, and the following error was displayed:

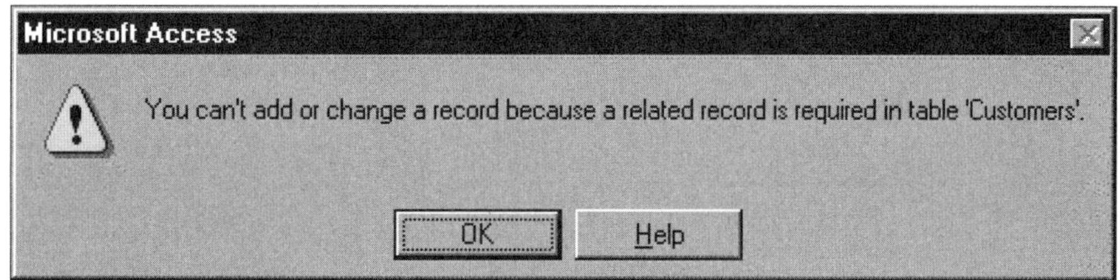


"If we were to attempt to add this same invalid transaction record through Visual Basic," I said, "our Visual Basic program could conceivably bomb – unless we had some error-handling code in our procedure."

I saw a look of confusion come over the class.

"Don't worry," I reassured them, "we'll be looking at this later on in the course. For now, let's complete our work for today by adding some data to the Database."

I then distributed the following exercise for the class to complete.

## Adding Data to the China Shop Tables

### Exercise – Adding a Record to the Customers Table

In this exercise you'll use Access to add a single record to the **Customers** table.

1. With the Database window open, select the **Customers** table in the Tables tab, and then select the Open button.
2. You will then see this Table grid, where you will be able to add a record to the **Customers** table:

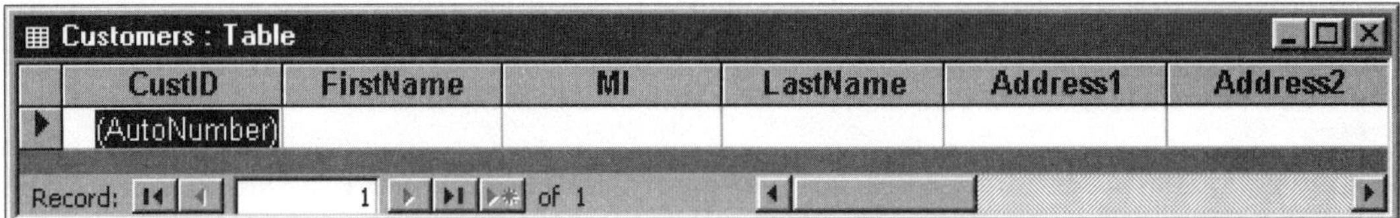


3. Use the following chart to add a single record to the **Customers** table, by tabbing to the appropriate field and entering the data. Because the **CustID** field is an AutoNumber field, you won't need to make an entry in that field – Access will automatically create the field value for you. In fact, as soon as you tab past the CustID field, Access will automatically update the **CustID** field:

| Field Name | Entry |
|---|---|
| FirstName | Marion |
| MI | H |
| LastName | Hobson |
| Address1 | 22 Oak Drive |
| Address2 | |
| City | Lansdowne |
| State | PA |
| Zip | 190501111 |
| Phone | 2155551111 |

4. When you have finished entering the data, there are a variety of ways that you can save the record. One technique is to move your record pointer to the next row in the grid. Whenever you move the record pointer in Access, any changes you have made to the current row are automatically saved. However, when you are working on a row and the pointer is displayed as a pencil, then your data-entry work has not yet been saved. You can also save the record by closing the Table window, either by double-clicking on the control menu bar or by clicking on the 'close' icon in the upper right hand portion of the window. Choose one of these two methods to save your record.

### *Discussion*

Most of the class had no problem in adding the single record to the `Customers` table.

"I don't understand," Chuck said, "why we are adding a record to the `Customers` table?"

"This record," I said, "is a record that we'll use to test our program in the coming weeks. It's a good idea to have a few test records already in the database when you start to write your Visual Basic database programs."

"I have a problem," Steve said. "I added the record to the `Customers` table, but then I realized I had made a mistake. So I selected the row containing the record with the mistake in it, and instead of just correcting the field value, I pressed the *Delete* key. The record was deleted, but then when I tried adding the record again, Access added it with a `CustID` of `2`, not `1`. And when I try to change the `CustID` from `2` to `1`, Access won't let me."

"Yes, that is a slight problem," I agreed. "Access demands complete control over the assignment of values in `AutoNumber` fields, and it just won't allow you to change it. In most cases, this isn't really a big deal, since the `AutoNumber` is a value that doesn't mean anything anyway. But I can understand that you'd like the first customer in the `Customers` table to have a `CustID` of `1`."

"Is there anything I can do?" Steve asked.

I explained to the class that we have two choices here.

"First," I said, "you can just accept the value that Access has assigned for you. But if you absolutely **must** change the value, there is a way – but it's a bit cumbersome."

"What is it?" Rhonda asked.

"You can delete all the records in the `Customers` table," I replied, "close the window, select the `Customers` table in the Database window, and then select the Design window. Once you have the `Customers` table opened in design view, change the Field Type from AutoNumber to Number, then save the table and close the design window. Now go back into Table Design again, and change the Field Type from Number back to AutoNumber. **Now** if you add a record to the `Customers` table, the first record added will have a `CustID` of `1`."

"That does sound a bit of a go round," Rhonda said.

"I should also warn you," I said, "that you must perform this process in two distinct steps. First, you must open the Design window, change the Field Type from AutoNumber to Number, and then **close** the design window. Then open the design window *again*, and change the Field Type back to AutoNumber. I've seen some students change the Field Type from AutoNumber to Number, then go right back to AutoNumber without closing the Design window. That won't work."

A minute later Steve reported:

"Well it may be cumbersome, but it **did** work."

There were no further questions about adding records to the `Customers` table, so I distributed the following exercise to the class.

## Exercise – Adding Records to the Inventory Table

In this exercise, you'll add all of the China Shop's inventory records to the `Inventory` table.

1. With the Database window open, select the `Inventory` table in the Tables tab, and then select the Open button.
2. As in the previous exercise, you'll see a Table grid, in which you will be able to add records to the `Inventory` table.
3. Use the following chart to add records to the **Inventory** table. Tab to the appropriate field, and make the correct entry. As was the case with the **AutoNumber CustID** field in the **Customers** table, you won't need to make an entry in the **ItemID** field either:

| **ItemID** | **Brand** | **Item Name** | **Price** |
|---|---|---|---|
| 1 | Corelle | Plate | 4 |
| 2 | Corelle | ButterPlate | 1 |

| ItemID | Brand | Item Name | Price |
|---|---|---|---|
| 3 | Corelle | Bowl | 2 |
| 4 | Corelle | Cup | 1 |
| 5 | Corelle | Saucer | 1 |
| 6 | Corelle | Platter | 5 |
| 7 | Corelle | Complete | 8 |
| 8 | Faberware | Plate | 10 |
| 9 | Faberware | ButterPlate | 3 |
| 10 | Faberware | Bowl | 5 |
| 11 | Faberware | Cup | 3 |
| 12 | Faberware | Saucer | 3 |
| 13 | Faberware | Platter | 13 |
| 14 | Faberware | Complete | 21 |
| 15 | Mikasa | Plate | 25 |
| 16 | Mikasa | ButterPlate | 10 |
| 17 | Mikasa | Bowl | 10 |
| 18 | Mikasa | Cup | 5 |
| 19 | Mikasa | Saucer | 5 |
| 20 | Mikasa | Platter | 50 |
| 21 | Mikasa | Complete | 50 |

4. When you have finished entering the data, your datasheet window should look like this:

Inventory : Table

| ItemID | Brand | Itemname | Price |
|---|---|---|---|
| 1 | Corelle | Plate | $4.00 |
| 2 | Corelle | ButterPlate | $1.00 |
| 3 | Corelle | Bowl | $2.00 |
| 4 | Corelle | Cup | $1.00 |
| 5 | Corelle | Saucer | $1.00 |
| 6 | Corelle | Platter | $5.00 |
| 7 | Corelle | Complete | $8.00 |
| 8 | Faberware | Plate | $10.00 |
| 9 | Faberware | ButterPlate | $3.00 |
| 10 | Faberware | Bowl | $5.00 |
| 11 | Faberware | Cup | $3.00 |
| 12 | Faberware | Saucer | $3.00 |
| 13 | Faberware | Platter | $13.00 |
| 14 | Faberware | Complete | $21.00 |
| 15 | Mikasa | Plate | $25.00 |
| 16 | Mikasa | ButterPlate | $10.00 |
| 17 | Mikasa | Bowl | $10.00 |
| 18 | Mikasa | Cup | $5.00 |
| 19 | Mikasa | Saucer | $5.00 |
| 20 | Mikasa | Platter | $50.00 |
| 21 | Mikasa | Complete | $50.00 |
| (AutoNumber) | | | $0.00 |

Record: 1 of 21

5. Save the records using one of the techniques we discussed in the earlier exercise.

***Discussion***

I gave the class about ten minutes to complete this exercise – it was pretty tedious, but extremely important, as these records represented all of the china pieces and their price information that were essential to the China Shop database.

"This table, then," Joe Bullina said, "really takes the place of **`Prices.txt`**, is that right?"

"That's right, Joe," I said.

"I can see where I could even use Access to update these records if I needed to," Joe said.

"You could," I agreed, "but don't worry – we'll build you a very user-friendly form to simplify the process."

I then distributed the following exercise to the class.

## Exercise – Adding Records to the Users Table

In this exercise you'll use Microsoft Access to add all two records to the `Users` table.

1. With the Database window open, select the `Users` table in the Tables tab, and then select the Open button.
2. As in the previous exercise, you will see a Table grid, where you will be able to add records to the `Users` table.
3. Use the following chart to add records to `Users`. Tab to the appropriate field, and make the correct entry. Unlike the other tables we've populated with records, this table does not have an AutoNumber field – so you will need to manually make an entry in each field:

| UserID | Password |
|---|---|
| ADMINISTRATOR | 061883 |
| CUSTOMER | 030655 |

4. Save the records using one of the techniques we discussed in the previous exercise.

***Discussion***

Everyone completed this exercise successfully – two user records, one to log in to the China Shop program to access Administrator functions, and the other to login if all we wanted, was to have available Customer type functions.

"Will we be adding any records to the `Transactions` table?" Dave asked. "You said it's a good idea to have records in the tables for testing."

"I agree, I think it would be a good idea to add a record to the `Transactions` table," I said, as I distributed the last exercise of the day.

## Exercise – Adding a Test Record to the Transactions Table

In this exercise you will use Microsoft Access to add a single test record to the **Transactions** table.

1. With the Database window open, select the **Transactions** table in the Tables tab, and then select the Open button.
2. As in the previous exercise, you will see a Table grid, where you will be able to add records to the **Transactions** table.
3. Use the following chart to add records to the **Inventory** table. Tab to the appropriate field and make the correct entry. As was the case with the AutoNumber **CustID** field in the **Customers** table, you won't need to make an entry in the **TransID** field either. The transaction record we're creating here means, in English, that Marion Hobson (Customer #1) bought one Corelle Plate (Item #1) for $4 on 4/23/98:

| TransID | CustId | ItemID | Quantity | Price | DateOfPurchase |
|---|---|---|---|---|---|
| 1 | 1 | 1 | 1 | 4 | 04/23/98 |

4. Save the record using one of the techniques we discussed in the previous exercise.

***Discussion***

This completed the design and population of the tables for the China Shop project. To say that the students were pleased with themselves would be an understatement.

Mary had a question: "I hate to bring this up now," she said, "but don't we have redundancy here with the **Price** field in the transactions record? We already have that information in the **Inventory** table."

"That's a good point," I said. "But the **Price** field in the **Transaction** table is not really the same as the **Price** field in the **Inventory** table. The **Transaction** table's **Price** field represents the price that the customer paid for the item *at the time they purchased it*– the **Price** field in the **Inventory** table is the *current* selling price of the item. Since the **Inventory** price will change from time to time, we need to maintain the **Price** in the **Transaction** table also in order to know what the customer actually paid for it."

"That gives us some historical pricing information, doesn't it?" Dave said.

"That's right," I said. "We can look at the **Transaction** table and know how much the price of an inventory item was at any given point in time."

"I think I have a problem," Rhonda said. "I just added a record to the **Transaction** table, but I made a mistake. Instead of entering a **CustID** value of **1**, I entered a **2**. I shouldn't have been able to do that, because Customer **2** doesn't exist yet, but I could do it anyway. Something must be wrong somewhere."

"You're right, Rhonda," I said, "you shouldn't have been able to do that – sounds like **Referential Integrity** isn't being enforced between the **Customer** and **Transaction** tables."

I took a quick look at Rhonda's **China** database. Just about everything was perfect, but when I checked the Relationships window, I discovered that she had not checked the Enforce Referential Integrity checkbox when she had established a relationship between the **Customers** and **Transactions** tables. As a result, she was able to add a record to the **Transactions** table even though the CustID of the transaction record did not exist in the **Customers** table.

"Will that be hard to fix?" Rhonda asked.

"It's not a big deal," I said, "here's how."

I first deleted the transaction record that Rhonda had added to the **Transactions** table, then went to the Relationships Window:

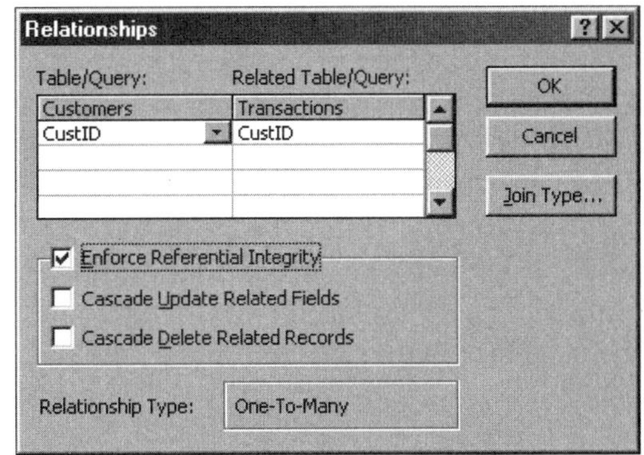


"At this point," I said, "all we need to do check the Enforce Referential Integrity checkbox and everything will be fine."

I asked if there were any other problems or questions.

It had been a long, productive class. There were no more questions, so I dismissed class for the day, thanking Joe Bullina for his help, and reminding everyone that next week we would be accessing some of the data in our database through the China Shop Visual Basic program.

## Chapter Summary

This was an exciting class for my students: we planned and implemented the design of the `China` database from start to finish. We now have a fully functional database to support the enhanced China Shop project.

Here are a few reminders of the key things that we did in this chapter as we walked through the stages of my database design methodology:

- We saw how it's important to decide which pieces of information we need to store, and how to organize this data logically
- We continued the database's **logical design** by translating that data into **fields** and categorizing the fields by **table**
- The next stages in the logical design were to assign primary keys and specify the data types for the fields
- We then took this logical design and implemented it physically using our database management system of choice – Microsoft Access. Here, we took the results of the logical design and used it to create the `China.mdb` database and its four tables: `Customers`, `Inventory`, `Transactions`, and `Users`. These tables will store all of the data that we use in the enhanced China Shop program

We now have the database foundation for expanding the functionality of the China Shop program. In the next chapter, we'll start looking in detail at the data-access features that will let our program satisfy Joe Bullina's new requirements.

# Database Design

isual Basic Learn to Program Databas
vith Visual Basic Learn to Progra
atabases with Visual Basic Learn
rogram Databases with Visual Basic Lea
o Program Databases with Visual Bas
earn to Program Databases with Visu
asic Learn to Program Databases wi
isual Basic Learn to Program Databas
vith Visual Basic Learn to Progra
atabases with Visual Basic Learn
rogram Databases with Visual Basic Lea
o Program Databases with Visual Bas
earn to Program Databases with Visu
asic Learn to Program Databases wi
isual Basic Learn to Program Databas
vith Visual Basic Learn to Progra
atabases with Visual Basic Learn

Chapter 4

# Basic Data Access with the Data Control

Having designed the China Shop database in Chapter 3, you'll now rejoin my university class as we learn how to connect to, open, read and update a Microsoft Access database from within Visual Basic. This chapter is all about looking at the tools that we'll need so that our Visual Basic program can communicate with the `China` database and display the information it contains in the context of the existing China Shop program.

Opening a database and viewing its contents using the Microsoft Access application was easy. All we needed to do was start up the application, click on a few icons, and there was the data, laid out neatly for us in the datasheet view. When we communicate with an Access database from a Visual Basic program, things are a little more complicated. However, there is nothing to fear – all the techniques of database access rely on using standard Visual Basic controls, and on manipulating their properties, methods, and events in the same way that you'll already be familiar with from the programming that you've done with Visual Basic. Once we've established the basic techniques of database access using Visual Basic, you'll find that you can use these simple techniques to use data powerfully and flexibly from within your Visual Basic programs.

In this chapter we'll cover a lot of ground and introduce some new terms and concepts. Specifically, we'll look at:

- How Visual Basic and the database fit together
- The Visual Basic **Data Control**, which lets us link our Visual Basic project to the data in a database
- **Bound** controls, which allow us to display the data on our Visual Basic forms
- How to **read** data from a Microsoft Access database using the data control
- How to **update** data in a Microsoft Access database using the data control
- The properties, methods and events of the data control

For the moment, don't worry about these new terms – I'll explain them all shortly. Although there is a lot to get through in this chapter, it will all feed into the detailed work that we do later on when we get into heavy-duty data manipulation in the enhanced China Shop program. Let's join my class.

## Connecting to a Microsoft Access Database

I began our fourth class by telling my students that this would be a momentous day for us all – today we would actually read from, and write to, a Microsoft Access database from within Visual Basic.

"The simplest way to do that," I said, "is to use a Visual Basic control called the **Data Control**. The Visual Basic data control acts as a portal or doorway to a variety of different databases, the most common of which is the Microsoft Access database."

"Having created our China Shop database last week," I continued, "the first inclination you may have is to immediately try to open the China Shop database, and start working with it. However, knowing me, you know I like to make sure you *understand* what you're doing as well as know the mechanics. For that reason, I want to take a good, thorough look at the Visual Basic data control. This lesson will concentrate on the theory and practice of the data control – we'll talk about what the data control does, and I'll tell you what you need to know to be able to use it effectively. Before we talk about the details of using the data control, let me a paint a quick contextual sketch of where the data control fits in the database access scheme of things."

I saw a few approving nods, so I set about painting that 'big picture'.

"OK," I began, "we already know that we've got our Visual Basic application – the China Shop program itself - and that we've just created the **China** database (with its four tables) that the program will read from and write to. Take a look at this slide:"

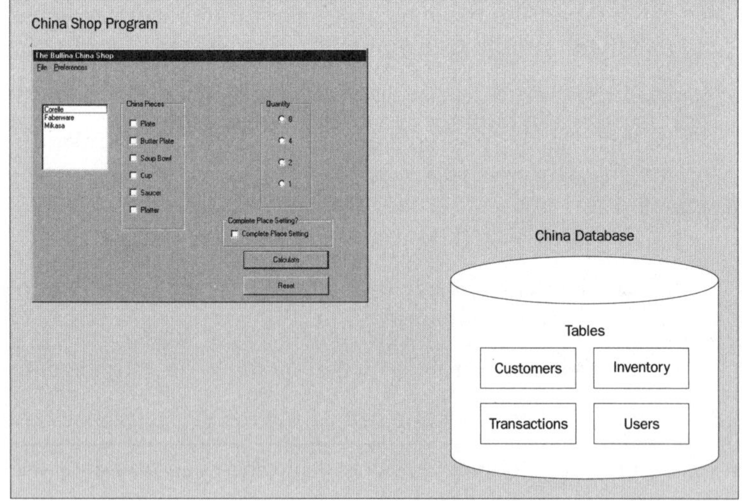

"We already know that we can use the Microsoft Access program to design and create our database as well as add, amend, and delete data in that database. Our task in this course is to build the functionality into our China Shop program that will let us manipulate the data in the database programmatically. We want our China Shop users to be able to interact with the database, and we want this interaction to be integrated with the existing functions of the China Shop program."

I paused for a moment, letting this sink in before continuing.

"There are a number of key Visual Basic components that will let us to achieve this aim, and I'm going to introduce them briefly here so that you have a basis for understanding them when we talk about them in detail later. I'll start with the **data control**, since the data control provides the foundation for all of the other data access techniques that we're going to look at. By placing a data control on our Visual Basic form, we give our VB program the capability of connecting to an Access database and communicating with it, and making the data in the database available to our program:"

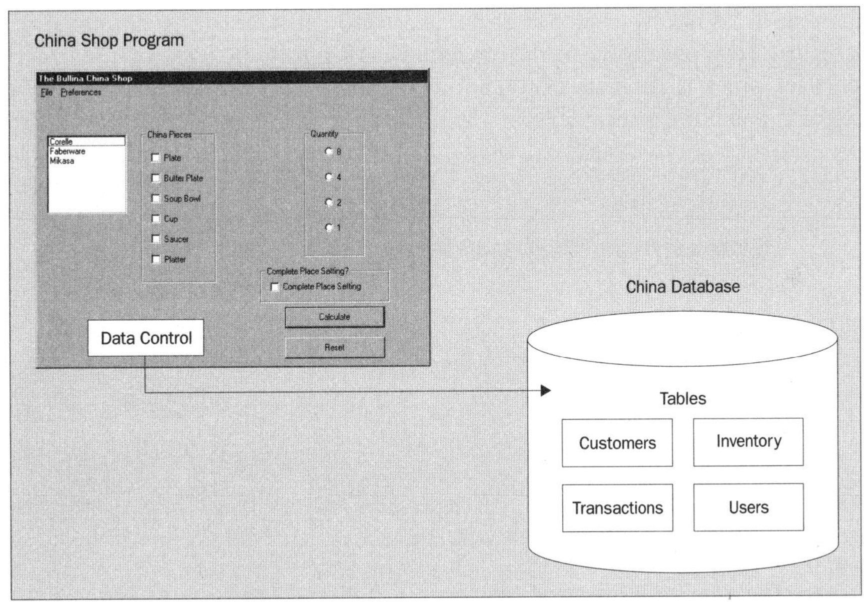


"Once we've established a connection from our program to the database, the DLLs that Visual Basic uses to mimic the database management functions of Access start to weave their magic. At the heart of the Access application is a **database engine** called **Jet**. A database engine is the part of a database management system that actually does the work of managing the physical input and output of the data to and from the database – in Access, the code to handle these operations is embedded in the Jet engine."

"Just a minute," said Ward, "I thought we weren't going to use Access to get at the database once we'd created it? How can we do that if this Jet database engine controls the way that the information in the database is read and written?"

"You raise a good point, Ward", I replied, "but it's true that we won't be using the Access application again. Fortunately, the DLLs that Visual Basic uses encapsulate the Jet functions, meaning that our Visual Basic database is independent of the Access program: all we need is our Visual Basic program, the Visual Basic DLLs, and a database to connect to. We don't even need to know how the technical aspects work – for our purposes, all we need to know is that Visual Basic has functionality built into it to let our Visual Basic programs communicate directly with Access databases."

"And that's all in the DLLs, right?" checked Rhonda.

"That's correct," I said, "once we've created our database, we're independent from the Access program – it's just us, our Visual Basic program, and the database."

I paused, then said: "When we use the data control to connect to the database, Visual Basic creates a 'working copy' of the underlying data that we're working on. This working copy is called a **recordset**, since it consists of the set of records from the underlying physical database that our program has connected to:"

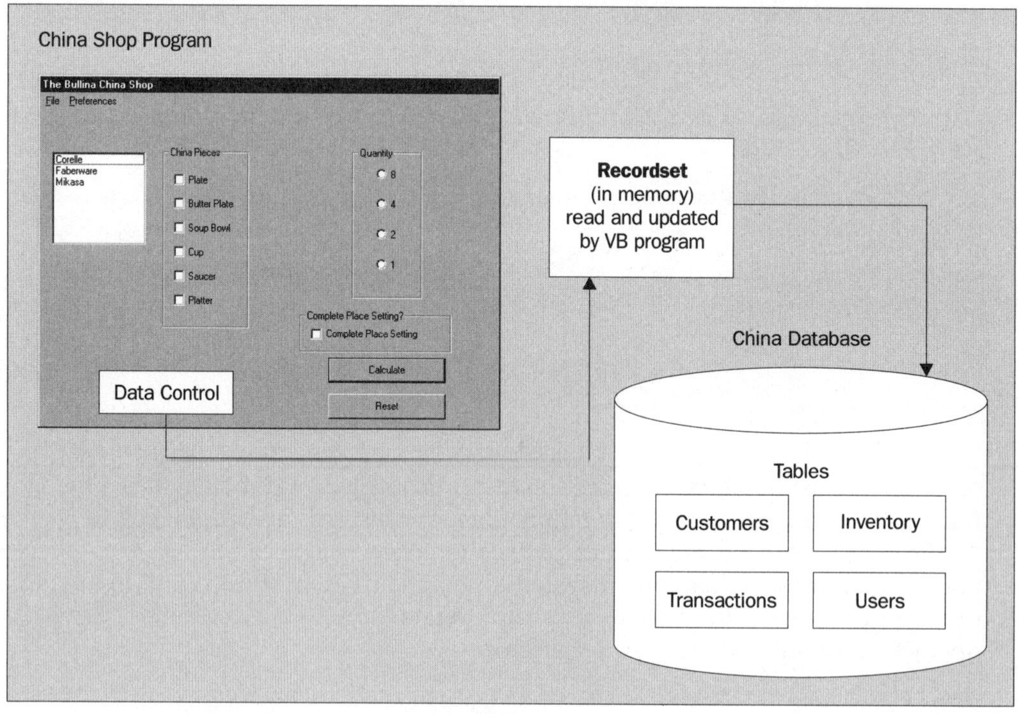

Rhonda looked perplexed: "So are you saying that our program doesn't actually talk directly to the database?"

"As far as our program is concerned," I explained, "it interacts programmatically with the **recordset**. We need to understand this so that we can see why we code up our program the way we do. To all intents and purposes, though, when we make a change to the recordset, that change is made to the database. The recordset acts as a kind of buffer in memory, ensuring that any changes we make are properly processed and applied to the underlying database at the right time."

I also explained that we'd look at how our program worked with the recordset in much more detail later, and said: "For the moment, just remember that when the data control connects to the database, it creates a temporary recordset based on the records in underlying database. Any changes that we make to the records via our Visual Basic program are initially made to the in-memory recordset, and applied to the underlying database at the relevant time."

Rhonda, still looking puzzled, said: "Do we have to understand how this all works in detail?"

"No," I reassured her, "all we need to do is tell the controls in the Visual Basic program what we want them to do, and the database management functionality built into Visual Basic handles all of the details for us. Once again, Visual Basic insulates us from all that nitty-gritty input and output processing."

"That sounds less scary," said Rhonda.

"Let's continue our discussion of the big picture," I said. "Having made our connection and created a recordset to work with, we next need to consider how to display the contents of the recordset on our Visual Basic form."

"Doesn't the data control display the data for us automatically?" asked Dave.

"No, it doesn't," I replied. "The data control only acts as our connection and intermediary – we still need to do some extra work to make the records in the recordset visible on our form. Once we've opened up the connection and the data control has created the recordset for us to work with, we need to add some controls that will actually display the data on the form. These controls could be text boxes, label controls, or a host of others that let us achieve different effects on the form."

"How does that work?" asked Ward, "Do those display controls need to connect to the database as well?"

"Not quite," I answered, "they use the existing recordset that the data control creates when it connects to the database. All we need to do is tell these controls to use the data control's associated recordset, and they can 'piggy-back' on the work that the data control has already done. What we do is link these controls to the underlying data using the recordset as the binding agent: we bind them to the data control, which in turn is connected to the database – so controls that we use in this way are called **bound controls**:"

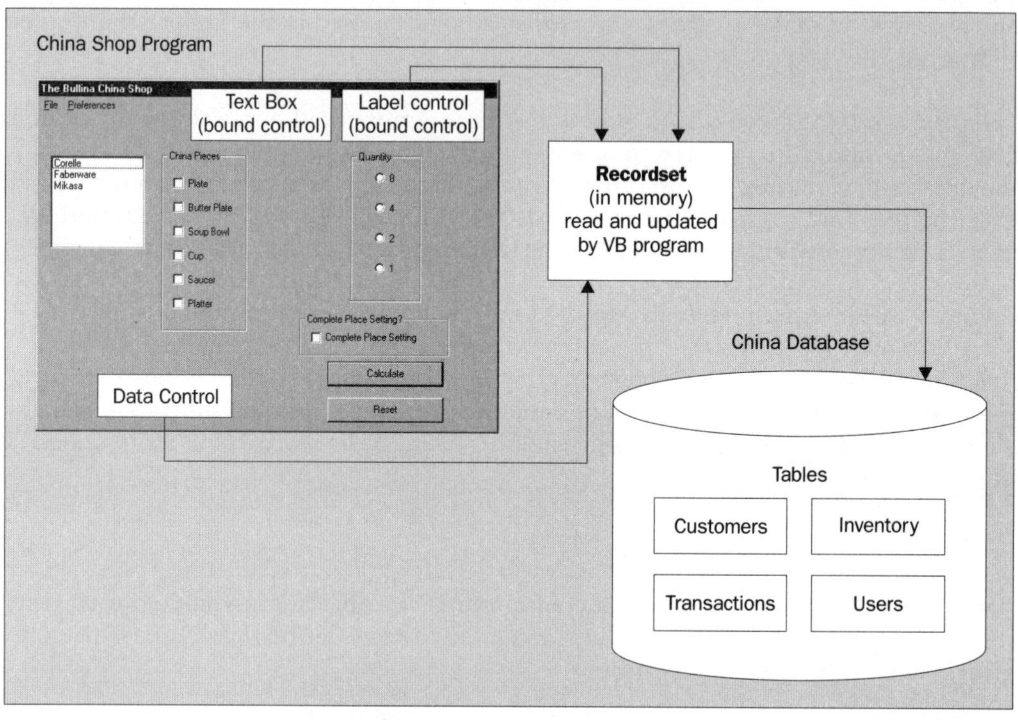


"So let me get this straight," said Lou, "the data control sets up the recordset in the computer's memory, based on information in the database we connect to?"

"That's right," I confirmed, "the recordset is like a 'virtual copy' of the physical database."

"And our Visual Basic program communicates with the recordset, and through that, with the database?" Lou went on.

"Right again," I averred.

"And," interjected Rhonda, "we can display the records from the recordset on the form using standard Visual Basic controls?"

"It's gratifying that you're all listening so closely," I said, "you're right again! These controls can be bound to the underlying database through the recordset generated by the data control – they take advantage of the bridge that the data control builds between the Visual Basic program and the database. With that bridge in place, data can be passed backwards and forwards between the bound controls and the database."

"So," said, Dave, "the data control is pretty central to all the work that we're going to do with the `China` database, isn't it?"

"Yes indeed," I replied. "The data control is at the heart of everything that we'll do with the database – without it, we can't talk to the database."

I looked around the room and saw a miniature sea of attentive faces looking back at me.

"OK," I continued, "let's put some flesh on those theoretical bones. It's about time we saw what the data control looks like on-screen."

## The Data Control in Action

I opened up Visual Basic and, starting a new `Standard.EXE` project, proceeded to look for the data control in the Visual Basic toolbox.

"In previous versions of Visual Basic," I said, "there was just a single data control available for our use – this was known as the **DAO** data control. DAO stands for **Data Access Objects**, and DAO was (and is) a collection of Visual Basic objects dedicated to providing VB with data access. However, with the release of Visual Basic 6, there are now two data controls that we can use – DAO and **ADO**. The DAO data control is the older of the two, and is currently more widely used than the ADO version. The DAO data control is also a little simpler to work with and therefore easier to learn – especially for beginners. For these reasons, plus the fact that once you learn how to use the DAO data control you can pretty quickly pick up the ADO data control, we're going to be dealing with the DAO data control exclusively in this class."

"What does ADO stand for?" Dave asked.

"Sorry – I forgot to mention that, Dave," I replied. "ADO stands for **ActiveX Data Objects**."

"You say we can also use the ADO data control in our Visual Basic projects?" Dave asked.

"Yes you can," I answered, "the DAO data control is located in the Visual Basic toolbox, whereas the ADO data control is not. However, you can select it by selecting **Projects | Components** from the Visual Basic menu bar. Just remember, in this class, we'll only be discussing the DAO data control. Let me show you where you can find the DAO data control in the toolbox."

With that, I pointed to the DAO data control in the Visual Basic toolbox, and this screenshot was displayed on the classroom projector:

"This icon represents the DAO data control," I said. "Remember, if you don't know which control is which in the toolbox, just hold your mouse pointer over a control until `ToolTips` appear."

"It may be my imagination," Rhonda said, "but the icon for the data control looks a little bit like the navigation buttons at the bottom of the datasheet window in the Access application."

"I think you're right, Rhonda," I replied, "and I don't believe that's an accident. The data control, in conjunction with certain types of bound control, can provide your program with the same kind of functionality that you get with the datasheet window in Access. But before I get into the details of that, I'd like to give you a little tour of the data control."

Next, I double-clicked the data control in the Visual Basic toolbox, and it was placed right in the middle of my form:

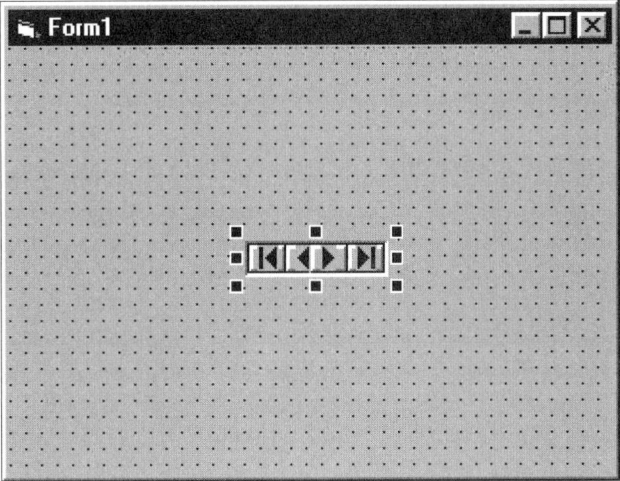


"The data control isn't very useful to us like this," I said, "so let's resize it a little bit."

I resized the data control so that it looked like this:

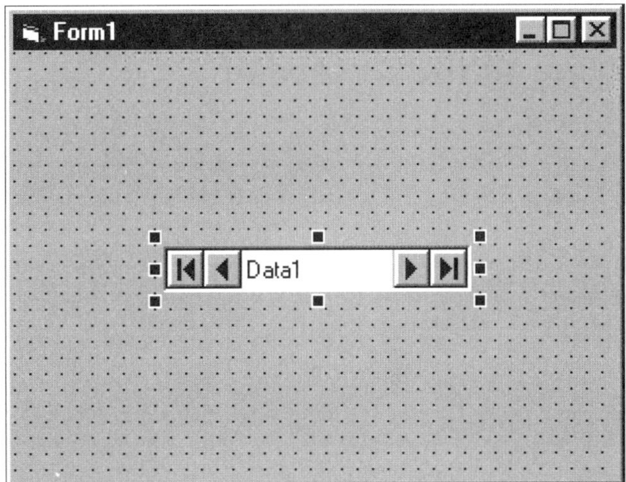


"That's better," I said, "but the data control by itself isn't very helpful to us. While it is an extremely powerful tool that provides a portal to the data in a database, it can't display that data. For this, we need to use other Visual Basic controls – some of which you are already familiar with, such as the label or text box controls. These controls can be 'bound' to the data control by referencing the name of the data control in their `DataSource` property. Once bound, these controls are then used to display or edit the data in the underlying database. Next, I'd like to spend a few minutes discussing the properties, methods and events of the data control."

There was a look of disappointment in the faces of several students, most noticeably Rhonda and Ward.

"What's wrong, Ward?" I asked.

"I think," Ward replied, "that most of us are pretty anxious to see the data in the China Shop database from within Visual Basic. For many of us, accessing data in a database is something that we've been waiting to do for a long time. Can you at least give us a quick demonstration before you start lecturing about the data control?"

I chuckled to myself, and agreed with him. Just about everyone is anxious, at this point in the class, to do 'something' with the database. The theory of data control, and its properties, methods and events, could wait a minute or two.

"I think I can do that," I said. "Let me give everyone a quick demonstration of the data control, using it to connect to the `Users` table of the China Shop database we built last week."

I paused for a moment to see if everyone was happy. All the students looked keen to see the data control in action.

## Connecting to the Database

"We can easily use the data control to display the two records in the `Users` table of the `China` database," I said. "To do this, we need to set three properties of the data control – the `DatabaseName` property, the `RecordsetType` property, and the `RecordSource` property."

First, we'd look at the `DatabaseName` property. Not surprisingly, this property is where we specify the name of the database that we want to connect to.

I brought up the Properties window for the data control that I'd previously added to my form, and clicked on the ellipsis in the **DatabaseName** property:

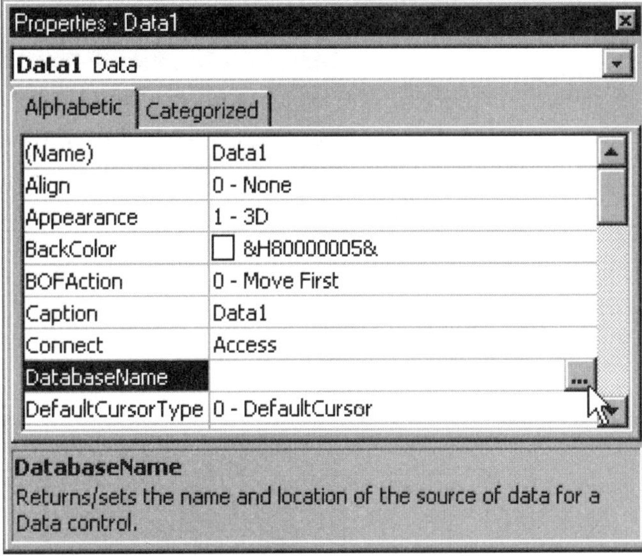


That brought up this DatabaseName dialog box:

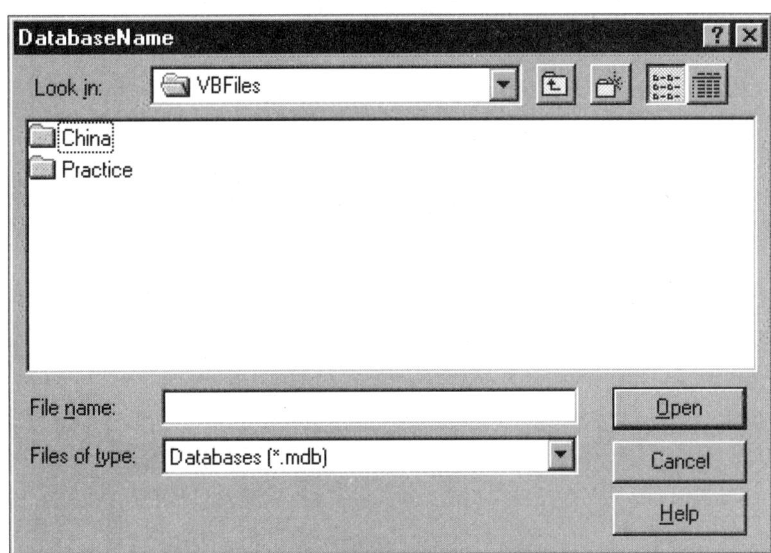


"At this point," I said, "it's just a matter of using the dialog box to navigate to the database that we want to connect to."

I then opened the **China** folder:

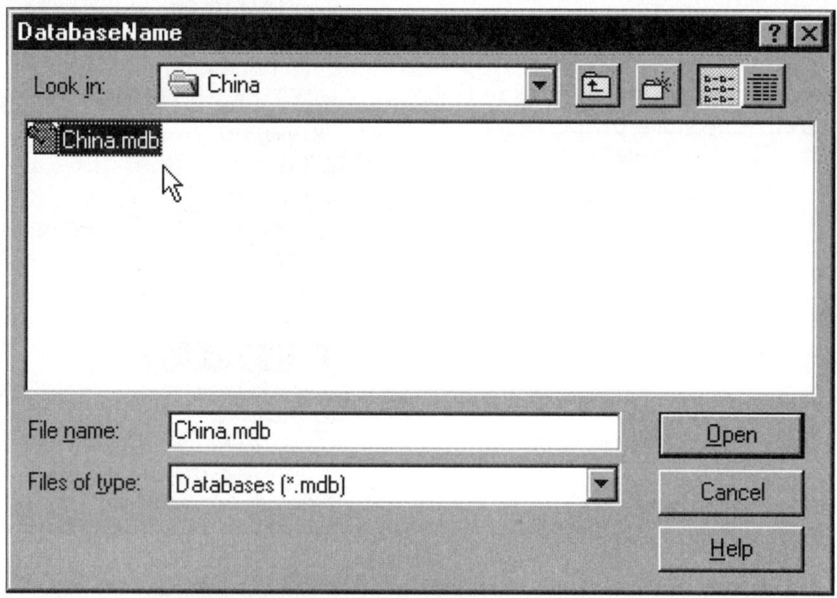


... and selected the **China.mdb** file. The database name was entered into the property box:

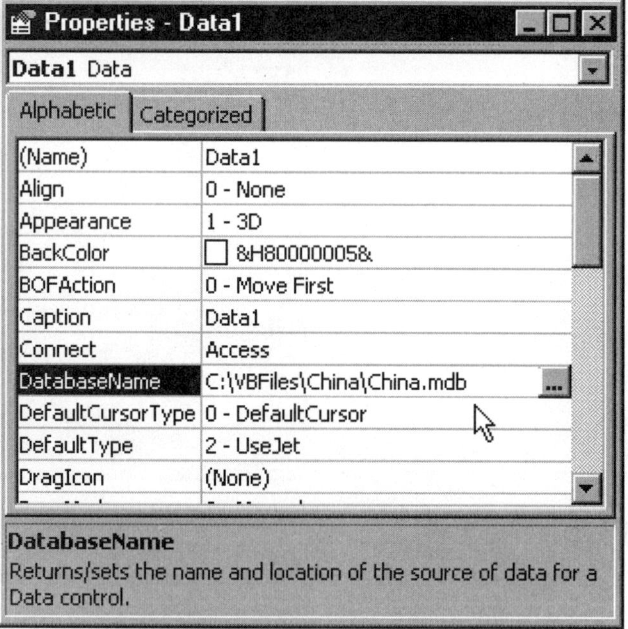


"Is that all there is to it?" Melissa asked. "Are we connected now?"

"Not quite," I said. "We need to set three properties of the data control. All we've done so far is tell Visual Basic which database we wish to open, by specifying a value for the **DatabaseName** property. Don't forget what we've learned about databases in our previous classes – the physical database file is just the tip of the iceberg when it comes to working with the objects (that is, the tables) that the database contains. Now we need to tell Visual Basic the individual **table** in the database that we want to work with."

### *Choosing a Table to Work with*

I selected the **RecordSource** property, and a drop-down list box appeared, containing the names of the tables in the **China** database:

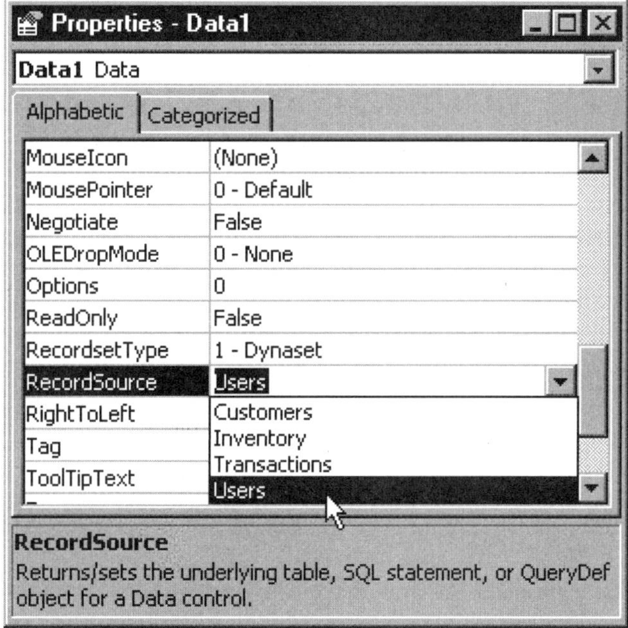


"Because we want to display records from the **Users** table," I said, "I'll select Users from the RecordSource property's list box."

"That's pretty easy," Chuck said. "Are those *all* of the tables in the **China** database that we're seeing there?"

"Yes, Chuck," I said. "Provided you have first specified a database in the DatabaseName property, the RecordSource property displays a drop-down list box of every table in the database. I should also mention that if there are any Access **saved queries** stored in the database, they would appear in this drop-down list box as well."

"Saved queries?" Rhonda asked.

"That's right," I said. "In a few weeks I'll show you how to create and save a query in Access. You'll then see that it's possible to ask Access a question about the data in the database and have it display the results of your question as records in a datasheet window. Rather than reformulate that question again the next time you need to ask it, you can save that question away as an Access query for future use."

"And if I've already saved a query on that database in Access," Dave asked, "then it will appear in the drop-down list box of the `RecordSource` property?"

"That's right, Dave," I said. "Visual Basic allows us to specify an Access query as the `RecordSource` property for the data control."

"Can you give us an example of a query?" Blaine asked. "What type of question could we ask?"

After thinking for a moment, I said, "Here's an example of a question we might pose in an Access query. We know that Joe Bullina has requested the ability to see the `Transaction` records representing customer purchases at the China Shop. It's conceivable that in the future Joe might ask us to give him the capability of seeing only the transactions for the last 30 days. Returning a list of `Transaction` records that are 30 days old or less is something that we could easily do in Access using its query creation ability. We could then save and name this query, perhaps as `QTrans30`."

"So," Bob said, "we'd then see `QTrans30` in the drop-down list box of the `RecordSource` property?"

"Exactly," I replied.

"Did you say we won't be using queries for the China Shop project?" Mary asked.

"I don't envision creating queries for the China Shop project," I replied. "But you never know – Joe Bullina could always call me one evening and ask us for exactly that capability."

"You said that there are three properties of the data control that need to be set," Rachel said. "We've looked at the `DatabaseName` and the `RecordSource`. What's the third again?"

"The third property is the **`RecordsetType`**. When you connect to a database in Visual Basic, the act of making that connection creates a **recordset**. As I explained earlier, this is where the records from the named database are stored in memeory for our program to work on. The **`RecordsetType`** property allows you to specify which of the different available *types* of recordset you wish to create. The different types have slightly different characteristics, which we'll discuss in a moment. There are three possible values for the **`RecordsetType`** property – **`Dynaset`**, **`Snapshot`** and **`Table`**. The default value is **`Dynaset`**, and we'll just accept that for this demonstration:"

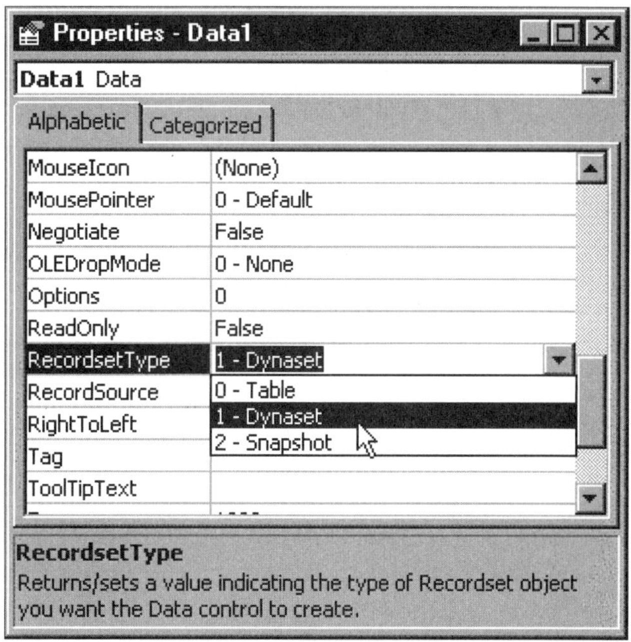


With all three properties of the data control set and verified, I then ran the program, with this result:

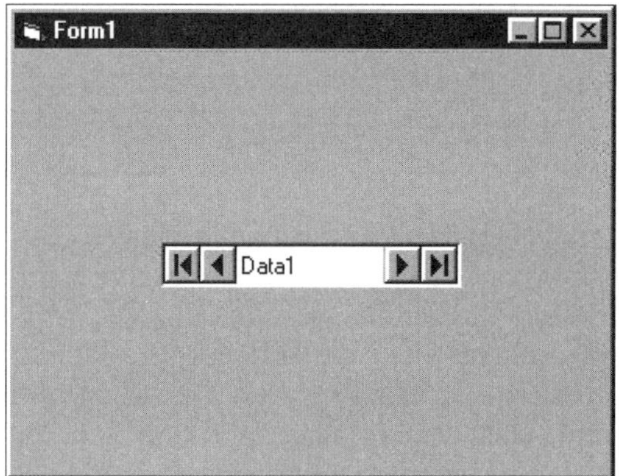


"Nothing happened," Rhonda said, "well, not much. The form shows up, and the data control's on it, but there's no data."

"Exactly," I responded. "As I mentioned earlier, all the data control does is open up a portal to a database, and builds a bridge to it. By itself, the data control has no capacity to display or edit records. In order to see the records in the recordset returned by the database connection, we need to place one or more **bound controls** on our form. Remember, we link these controls to the data control, thus giving them access to the recordset."

### *Displaying Data with Bound Controls*

I then placed two label controls on the form, just above the data control, and stretched them both a little horizontally so that all of the data would show up in them:

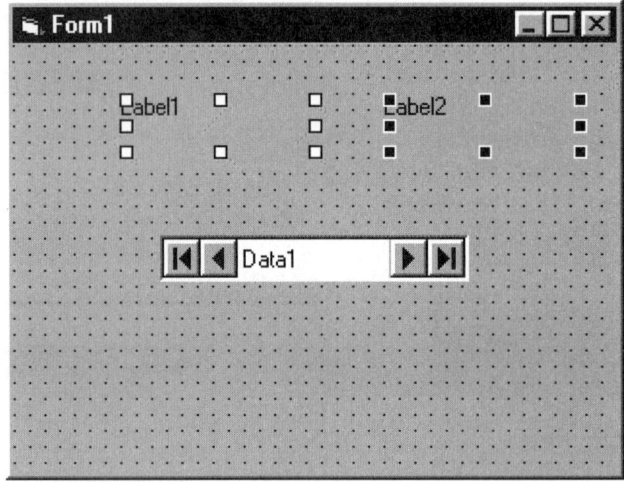


"Label controls and text box controls are commonly used as bound controls," I said, "although since the label control can't receive focus, data presented in this can't be updated – which makes the label control ideal if you want to protect the data in the underlying database. When you designate a control such as a label or a text box control to bind to a data control, you need to set two properties – the `DataSource` and the `DataField` properties. For a label control, data from the database will populate the `Caption` property. For a text box control, data will populate the `Text` property."

"So the data from a field in the database will actually be displayed in the label control's `Caption`?" Valerie asked.

"That's right," I said, "and that's why, out of habit more than anything else, I clear the caption of the label control in the properties window."

To demonstrate, I cleared the caption properties of each label by selecting the **`Caption`** property and pressing the *Delete* key:

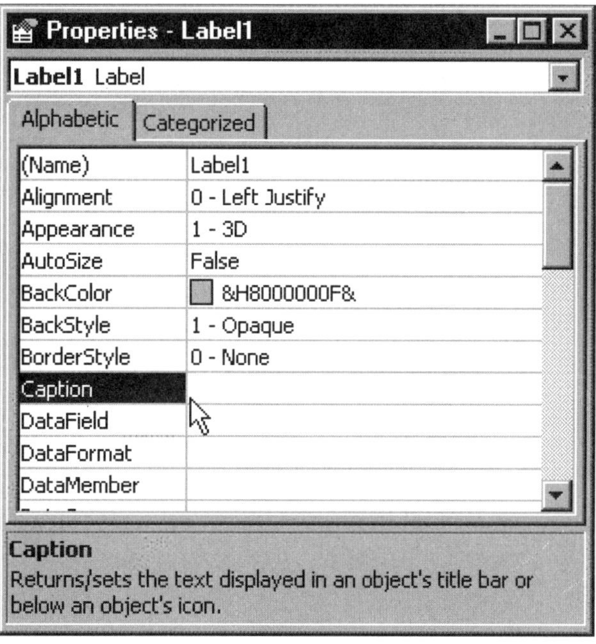


"Are you saying it's not absolutely necessary to clear the **`Caption`** property?" Dave asked.

"That's right," I said. "Data from the database field we specify in the **`DataField`** property will appear as the label's caption anyway. But as I say, I always do this out of habit, and a passion for neatness!"

I waited to see if there were any questions.

"As I mentioned before, to bind a control to the database, we need to set two properties. Firstly, the **`DataSource`** property, which tells the bound control which data control it should get its data from; and secondly the **`DataField`** property, which specifies the particular field from the recordset that this bound control should display. By the way, these same two properties are present in the label control, the text box control, and other controls in the toolbox such as the check box and option button."

"Can the check box and option button be bound to a database too?" Ward asked.

"Yes," I confirmed. "Any control containing a **`DataSource`** and **`DataField`** property can be bound to a database."

I then selected the DataSource property of the first label control in the properties window, and a drop-down list box appeared:

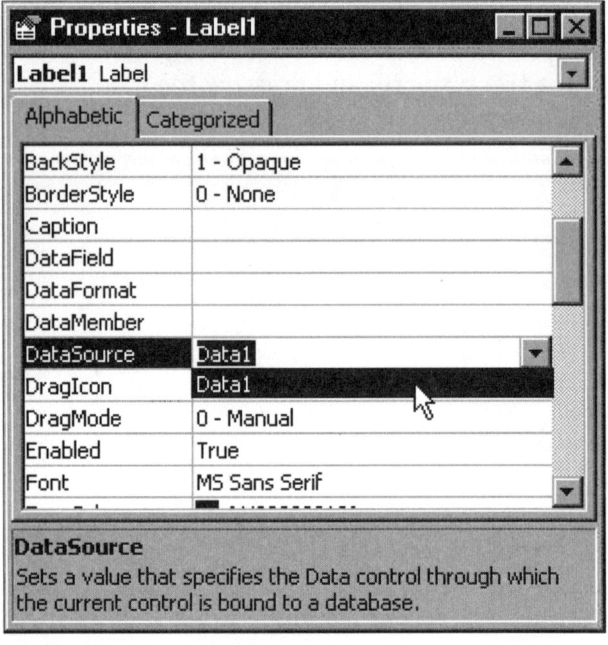


"The **DataSource** property will display the name of every data control that's present on the form," I said, "since it's through the data control that the control will actually be bound to a database field. Notice that the default name of this form's sole data control – **Data1** – appears as the one and only item in the drop down list box."

"So it's possible to have more than one data control on a form?" Kathy asked.

"Yes it is," I said. "You may have a form that needs to display information from more than one table – perhaps more than one database. In that case you would need to have more than one data control on the form. For now, we'll just select **Data1**."

"I was just experimenting on my own," Kevin said, "and I noticed that I was able to type **Data1** into the **DataSource** property value. Is that OK?"

"I don't recommend it, Kevin" I said. "My rule of thumb in the Visual Basic properties window is that if a drop-down list box appears, specify the property's value by selecting an item from the list. Even if you can type an entry into the property's value, fight the temptation – it's not a good idea, as it's prone to infuriating errors like typos that you'll have to track down later."

I then clicked on the **DataField** property, and again a drop-down list box appeared. I selected **UserID** in the list box:

"Does anyone recognize the two items in this **DataField**'s drop-down list box?" I asked.

"Yes, I do," Linda said. "Those are the two fields in the **Users** table of the **China** database."

"Good, Linda," I said.

"How does the label control know about them?" Rhonda asked.

"It's because of the data control," I said. "The label control uses the reference to the data control in its **DataSource** property to point to the **Data1** data control, and the **DataField** property to point to the underlying **UserID** field in the **Users** table. And because we told the data control – via its **DatabaseName** and **RecordSource** properties – that we wanted to create a recordset based on the **Users** table in the **China** database, the data control automatically makes all of the fields in the **Users** table available to any bound control:"

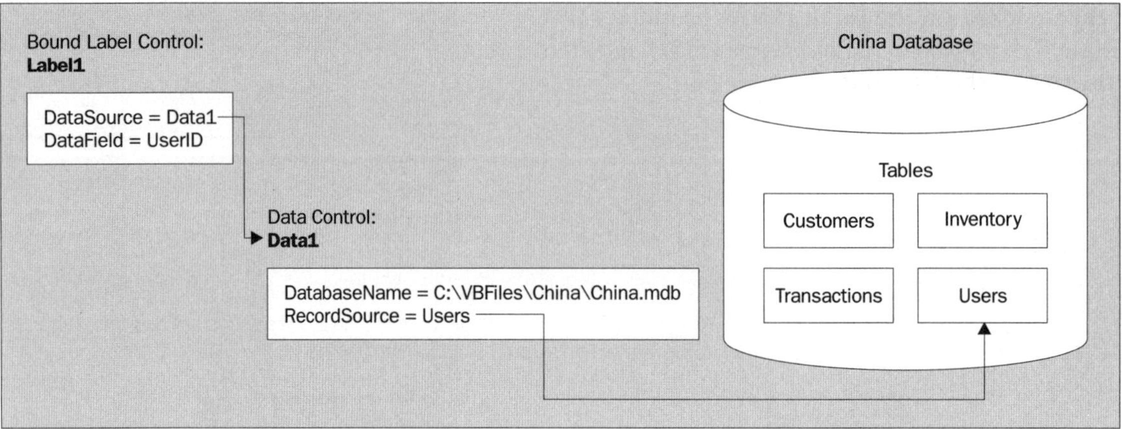


"I think that makes sense," Rhonda said, "although it does seem a little indirect – can I assume we need to do the same thing for the second label control?"

"That's right," I said. "As we did with the first label control, we need to set the **`DataSource`** property to **`Data1`**, and in this instance, specify the **`DataField`** property as **`Password`** – making sure to select it from the drop-down list box:"

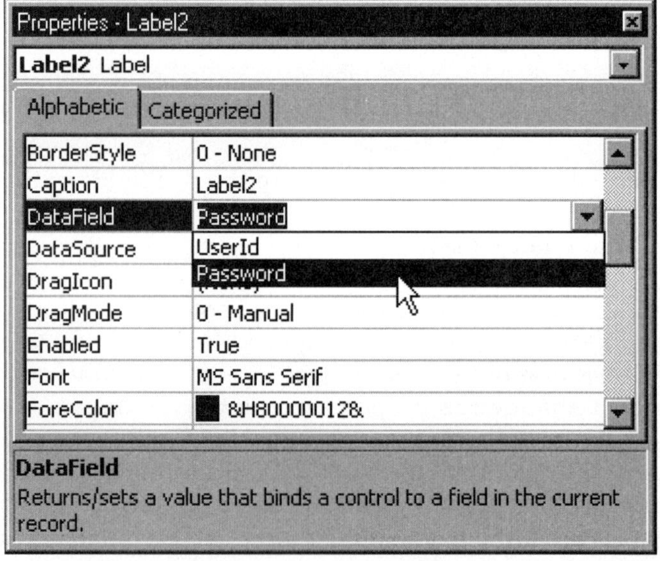

I did that, and then ran the program. This is what the class saw on the classroom projector:

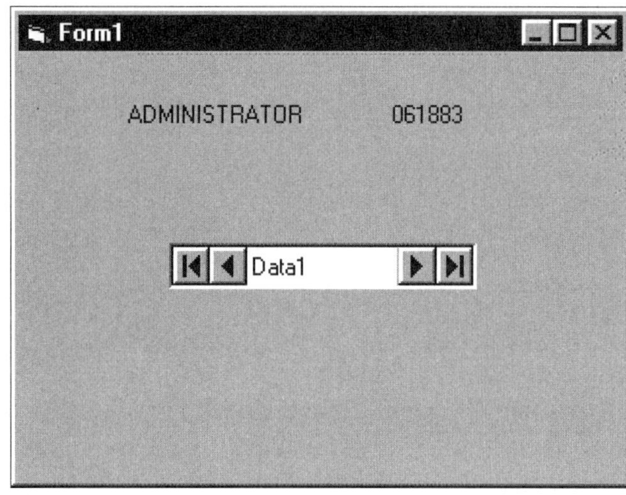


"That's the first record in the **Users** table, isn't it?" Kate asked. "This is really impressive."

"That's right, Kate," I said. "That is the first record in the **Users** table. What's happened is that **Label1**'s **Caption** property has been set to the value of **UserID** in the first record's in the **Users** table, and **Label2**'s **Caption** has been set to the **Password** value of the first record."

"Is there any way to see the next record?" Blaine asked.

"Yes there is," I said.

### *Browsing through Data with the Data Control*

"I believe it was Rhonda who remarked that the data control icon in the Visual Basic toolbox looks a little like the datasheet view navigation buttons in Access. If we wish to move to the next record in the recordset, all we need to do is click on the 'next' button on the data control, which is the second button from the right."

I did that, and the following screen shot was displayed:

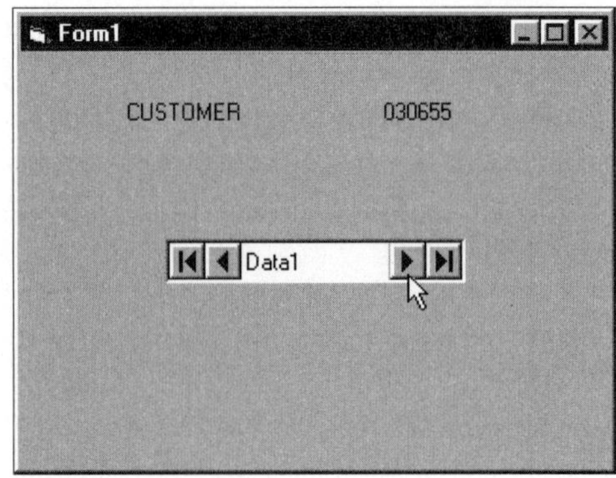


"These are the fields from the second record in the **`Users`** table," I said.

"Accessing information in a database doesn't seem all that bad to me," Ward said. "Is that all there is to this – placing a data control on the form, and then some bound controls?"

"Basic database access is pretty quick and easy, as you've seen here," I said, "but there are many nuances involved, which is why we'll spend the next three weeks just talking about the basics."

"What are those other buttons on the data control?" Rachel asked.

"Those are the Visual Basic data control navigation buttons," I said, "and they're functionally equivalent to the buttons that we saw in the Access datasheet window a couple of weeks ago. Here, take a look at a chart I've prepared:"

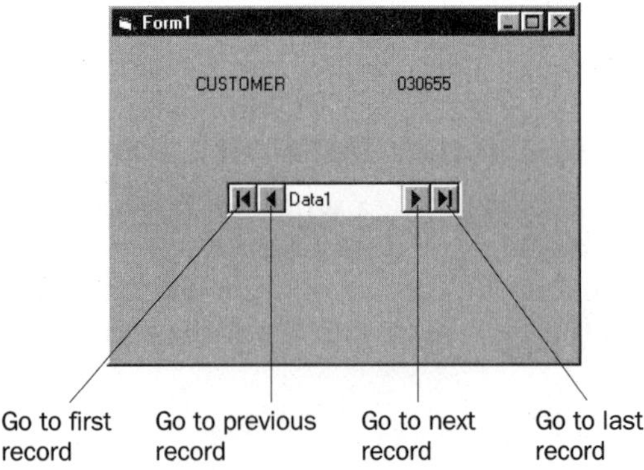


"As was the case with the datasheet view in Access," I said, "if you click on the left-most button, the data control moves your 'record pointer' (which indicates which is the current record) to the first record in the recordset. The button to the right of that one, the one with the arrow pointing to the left, moves your record pointer to the previous record in the recordset. The third button, the one with the arrow pointing to the right, advances your record pointer to the next record in the recordset. Finally, the fourth button, with an arrow pointing to the right followed by a vertical line, moves the record pointer to the very last record in the table."

"I have a question," Ward said. "I notice that you seem to be using the term recordset in your descriptions, not table. Is there a difference?"

"That's a good observation, Ward," I said. "Technically, what we are viewing here are records in the data control's recordset – although because the **`RecordSource`** value of the data control is the **`Users`** table, there is no difference. However, as we'll see later in the course, it's possible to build a recordset made up of fields from more than one table."

"These navigation buttons are nearly identical to the datasheet view in Access," Mary said. "It looks like the only difference is that there is no button to add a new record."

"Plus, there's no display of the current record number, or of the total number of records in the table," she added.

"That's right on both points, Mary," I replied. "There is no 'add' button on the data control, or displays of the current record number or total number of records".

"With no 'add' button," Valerie said, "is there a way for the user to add a new record to the **`Users`** table? For that matter, can the records in this recordset be updated?"

"Yes, there is a way to add a record," I said, "and if we hadn't bound the fields in the **`Users`** table to a label control (which can't receive focus, and is therefore non-updateable), we could update these records very easily. However, label controls like we've used here can only display values in the underlying database – not update them."

"So," Rhonda asked, "what can we do that will let us to update the existing records in the **`Users`** table, or allow us to add new records?"

"All we need to do," I said, "is replace the bound label controls with any other control that's capable of receiving focus and which contains **`DataSource`** and **`DataField`** Properties – such as the text box control. There's also a special control, called the **DBGrid** control, which lets us display multiple records and fields in a single bound control (as compared to the solitary field per control that we can display with simple bound controls like the label or text box). Let's replace the two label controls with a single **`DBGrid`** control and demonstrate what it can do."

## The DBGrid Control

I stopped the program, deleted the two label controls from the form, and selected Project | Components from the Visual Basic menu bar.

"The **DBGrid** control is not included in the Visual Basic toolbox," I said, "so we'll have to select it from the Components menu."

I did that by selecting Microsoft Data Bound Grid Control 5.0 (SP3) from the Components menu:

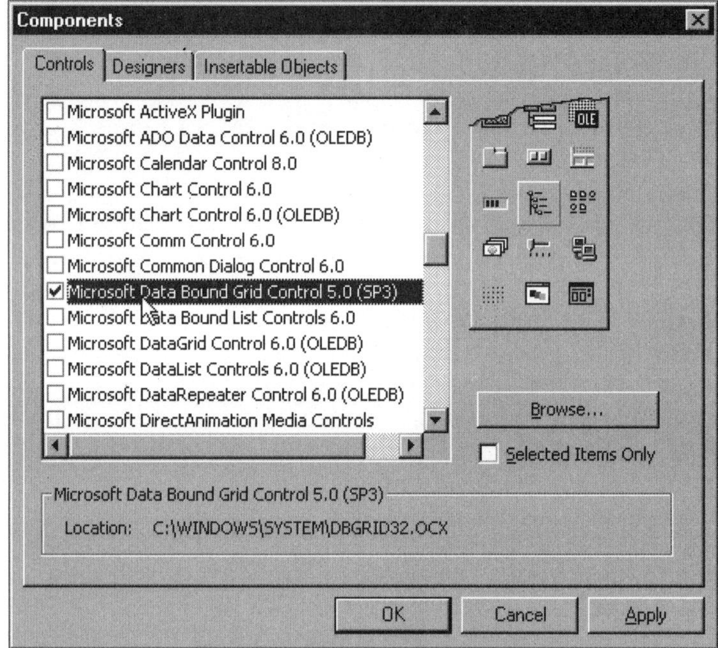


> **Please note that this control is not supplied as an integral part of the Working Model and Learning Editions of Visual Basic, so it's possible that you won't be able to work your own way through all of this demonstration, depending on which version of VB you're running. Rest assured, however, that you don't need this control to successfully enhance the China Shop project. Also, the DBGrid allows us to demonstrate more graphically some of the important features of data access in VB.**

After clicking on the OK button in the dialog box, the **Data Bound Grid Control** (**DBGrid**) appeared in my Visual Basic toolbox:.

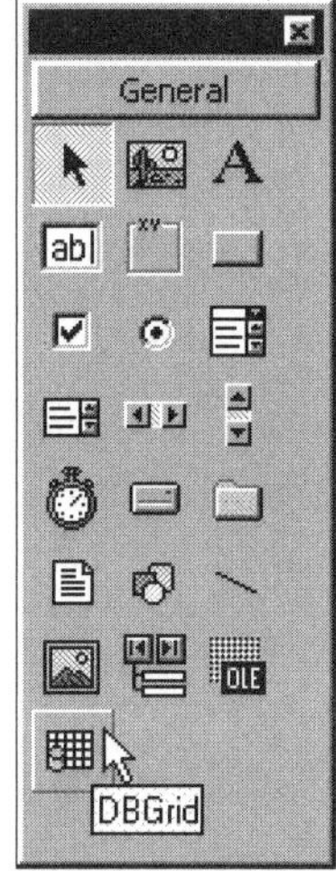


"Let me now move the data control to one side and place a `DBGrid` control in the middle of my form," I continued:

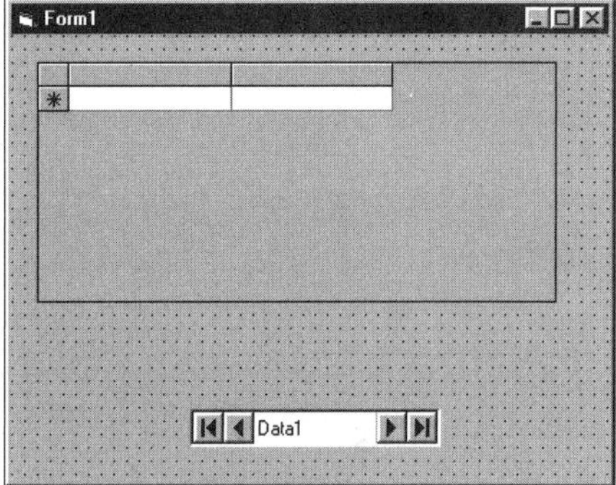


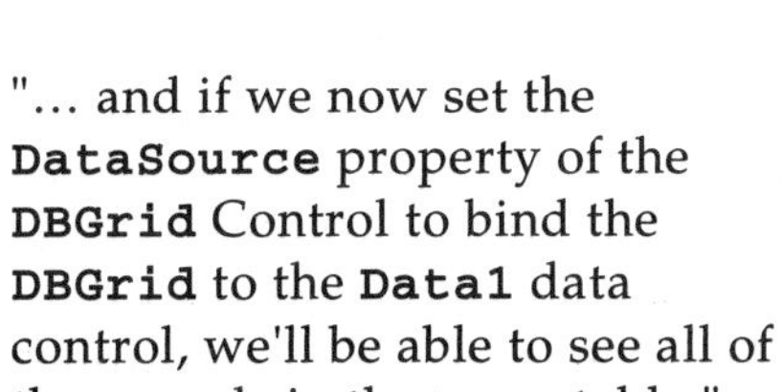

"... and if we now set the `DataSource` property of the `DBGrid` Control to bind the `DBGrid` to the `Data1` data control, we'll be able to see all of the records in the `User` table:"

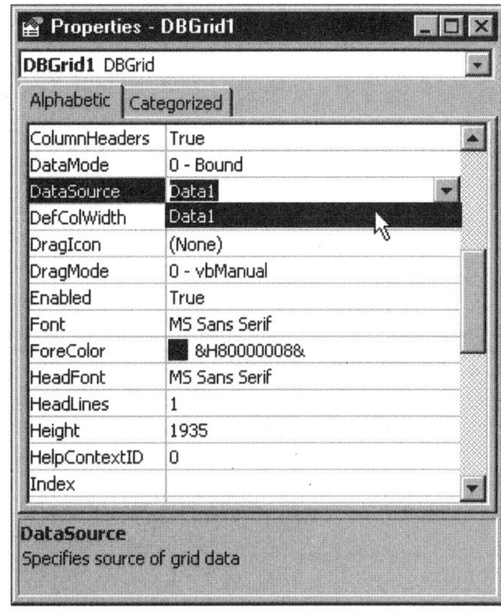

"There's no **DataField** property in the DBGrid to set?" Mary asked.

"No," I said, "By default, every field in the recordset is displayed in the DBGrid. We'll see later on in the course that we can specify the fields to be displayed in the DBGrid, but we need to do that through the **Custom** property tab."

I then ran the program, and the following screen shot was displayed on the classroom projector:

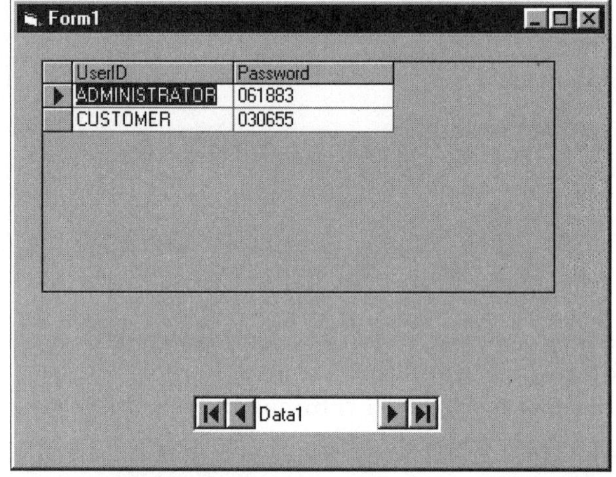


"This is what is known the **Grid View** of the **Users** table within Visual Basic," I said. "As you can see, it's very similar to the datasheet view in Access, in that you can see all of the fields and all of the records in the underlying recordset simultaneously. If there were more fields and more records in this recordset, horizontal and vertical scrollbars would appear on the DBGrid. The important thing to note here is that the data control and the DBGrid did all of the hard work for us. After deleting the two label controls, all I needed to do was add the DBGrid control to the form, and set one property – the **DataSource** property – to point to the data control. We didn't specify anything other than that in the properties of the DBGrid."

"This is impressive," Ward said. "It makes the task of connecting to, and viewing records in a database much less daunting. Now suppose we want to update one of those records – can we do that using the DBGrid?"

"Yes we can," I said. "Let's change the value of the **UserID** field for the second record from CUSTOMER to WARD."

> **If you are following along with this demonstration at home, make sure that the value of** Options **property of the data control is set to 0, and that its** ReadOnly **property is set to** False**. And if you change the value of CUSTOMER in the** Users **table to WARD, don't forget to change it back again!**

I then moved my mouse pointer to the **`UserID`** field of the second record, and changed the **`UserID`** from CUSTOMER to WARD. I ended the program by closing the form, and then started the program again by clicking on the Run button on the toolbar. When I did, the following screenshot was displayed on the classroom projector:

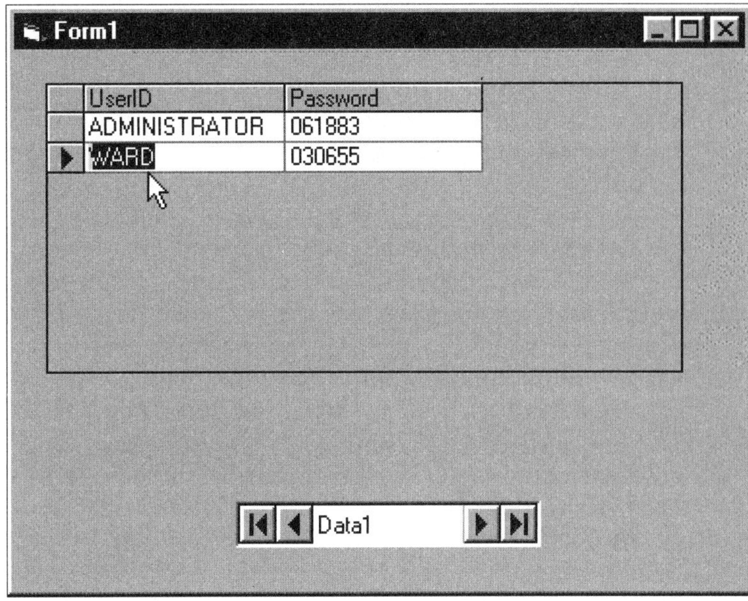


"That's great," Ward said. "That's all it takes to modify a record in the **`DBGrid`** – just type over it."

"That's right," I said. "And by stopping and restarting the project I proved that the change had been made to the underlying database, since it got picked up when a new connection was established with the database. Let me change that value back to CUSTOMER, before I forget."

I did so.

"What about adding a new record to the **`Users`** table," Linda asked, "you did say that could also be done, didn't you?"

"Yes I did," I said, "but before we can do that, there are a number of default property values that we would need to change on the DBGrid and the data control. If it's OK with you, I'd like to show you how to do that a little later."

No one had any major objections to demonstrating that capability later, so I asked everyone to take a fifteen-minute break prior to beginning a discussion of the properties of the data control.

## Data Control Properties

After fifteen minutes, we resumed class with a discussion on the data control's properties.

"Just like any control," I said, "the data control has a number of properties that affect its appearance and behavior."

"Are we going to discuss *all* of the properties of the data control?" Rhonda asked. "During break time I was looking at the data control's properties in the properties window, and quite a few of them are properties that we've already seen with some of the other controls."

"You're right, Rhonda," I said. "Many of the properties of the data control are shared by other controls. Properties such as `Left`, `Top`, Height and `Width`, which we discussed in our Intro class, and really need no further explanation here with the data control. In answer to your question, today we'll be concentrating on the unique properties of the data control that allow it to connect to a database – specifically its `Data` properties."

I then displayed the properties window for the data control on the classroom projector, and clicked on the Categorized tab:

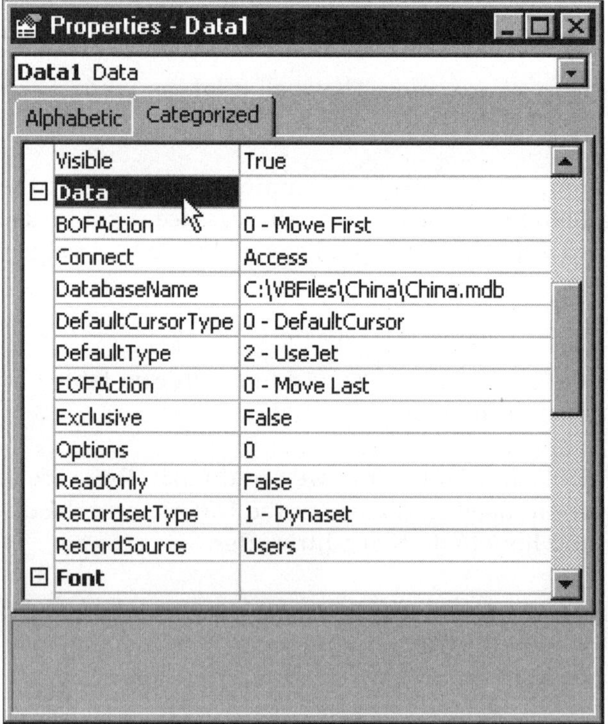

I suggested that we go through each one of the properties in the `Data` category step by step.

"Let's start with the first property we set for our demo," I said, "the `DatabaseName` property:"

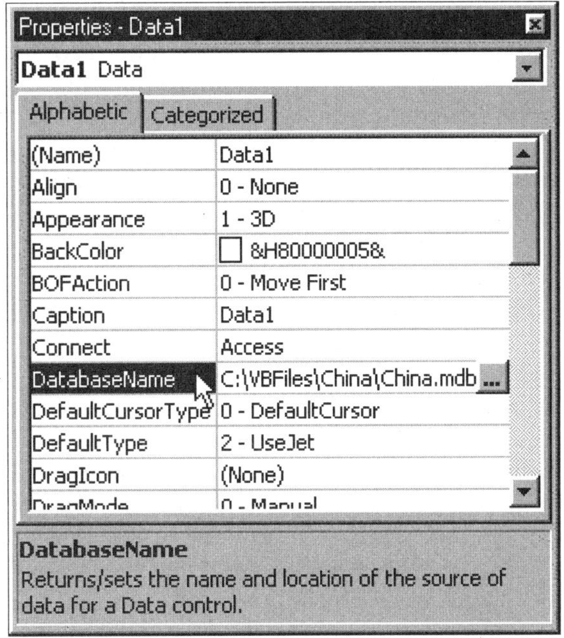


### *The DatabaseName Property*

"This one's easy," Kathy said, "the DatabaseName property is just the full path and name of the Access database."

"That's true," I said, "provided that the database to which we are connecting is an Access database."

"Can we connect to other types of databases besides Microsoft Access?" Chuck asked.

"Yes, we can Chuck," I said. "The native database of Visual Basic is Microsoft Access – but it's possible to connect to a whole load of other databases as well."

"What do you mean by the phrase Visual Basic's '**native** database'?" Linda asked.

"What I mean," I said, "is that you can easily connect to an Access database just by setting three properties of the data control; you can think of Access as being the 'default' database type for Visual Basic. While it's not really technically more difficult to connect to any other type of database, doing so requires us to set a few more properties of the data control."

"What other kinds of databases can we connect to?" Rachel asked.

"There are two broad categories of databases we can connect to," I said. "**ISAM** databases such as dBase, FoxPro, and Paradox (to name a few) – and **ODBC** databases, such as Oracle and SQLServer.

"ISAM and ODBC?" queried Rhonda, "what does that mean?"

"ISAM stands for Indexed Sequential Access Method," I said, "which describes the way that database engines get hold of the data in them. When these types of databases – such as FoxPro or Paradox – are installed on the user's PC, they make an entry in the Windows Registry that points to a database 'driver' on that PC. This database driver then provides Visual Basic with information that it needs to open that particular type of database. This information will include the database type, and details on how to read from it and write to it."

"So what does ODBC stand for?" Lou asked.

"ODBC stands for Open Database Connectivity," I replied. "ODBC databases are designed to be accessed in a more sophisticated manner than ISAM databases (which tend to be older). Open Database Connectivity is a technology that allows different types of programs to access a range of database more easily."

"I had no idea you could connect to a database other than Access," Tom said. "I guess that I presumed you could only connect to Microsoft databases such as Access and FoxPro. Being able to connect to other databases will come in very handy at work, where we have a lot of old data in Paradox databases."

"And we have a lot of data in Oracle tables where I work," Linda said. "Will we learn how to connect to those types of databases in this class?"

"No, not in detail – we'll be concentrating on connecting to Access databases in this class," I said. "However, I think you'll find that once you're comfortable with that, connecting to other databases is not that big a deal. Essentially, connecting to any other type of database other than Access requires us to change the `Connect` property from its default value of `Access`."

### *The Connect Property*

"I just mentioned that Access is considered the native database of Visual Basic," I said. "A that means is that by default, Visual Basic assumes that you are connecting to an Access database. It's the `Connect` property of the data control that specifies the database type to which you wish to connect."

I brought up the `Connect` property of the data control in the properties Window, and displayed the drop-down list box containing the other types of databases that can be selected for the `Connect` property:

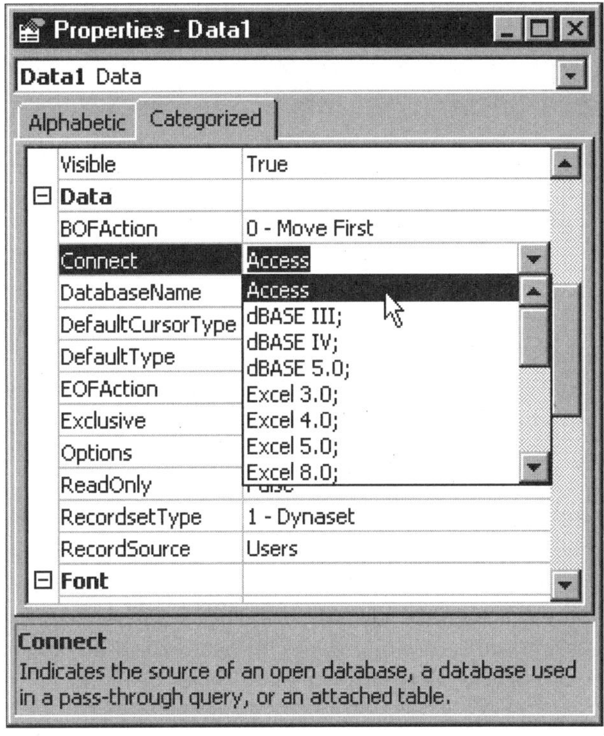


"As you can see," I said, "the default value for the Connect property of the data control is Access. But there are others – a variety of dBase database versions, Excel, and – if you scroll further down the list, you'll see FoxPro, Lotus, and Paradox – among others."

"These are the ISAM databases that you mentioned earlier," Dave commented.

"So the list that we see in the `Connect` property of the data control," Kevin said, "is a list of all of the ISAM databases registered on the user's PC?"

"That's right," I said. "Visual Basic has nothing to do with what appears as an ISAM database in this list – these are the databases that have been installed on the user's PC, and registered as ISAM databases in the Windows Registry."

"That makes Visual Basic pretty flexible, doesn't it?" Peter said. "Basically what you are saying is that if the user installs a database package on their PC, provided the installation program makes an entry in the Windows Registry, Visual Basic will be able to connect to it. I really had no idea that Visual Basic could read and write so many different types of databases."

"What about Oracle or SQLServer?" Valerie said. "Those are the types of databases I need to connect to at work – and neither one appears in the `Connect` property's drop-down list box."

"That's because Oracle and SQLServer are not ISAM databases," I said. "Of the two technologies, ISAM is the older one: Oracle and SQLServer are newer, ODBC-type databases."

"Does that mean that Visual Basic can't connect to Oracle or SQLServer?" Valerie asked.

"On the contrary, Valerie, Visual Basic *can* connect to both Oracle and SQLServer," I said smiling. "In fact, Visual Basic can connect to *any* ODBC database. It's just that ODBC connectivity in Visual Basic requires a little bit more work. As you saw earlier, ISAM databases only require you to select from the drop-down list box in the `Connect` property of the data control – although some may require an additional parameter or two beyond the name of the ISAM database. With an ODBC database, you'll need to enter something called a **Connect String** into the `Connect` property. The connect string can be pretty cryptic, and may require four or five arguments in order to properly connect to an ODBC database."

"That sounds complicated," Linda said. "How do we know the proper format of the connect string for a particular database?"

"Since Oracle and SQLServer are high powered databases," I said, "they almost always have a person or persons in charge of them called a **Database Administrator** (DBA). Your Database Administrator can help you with your connect string."

"I don't know about anyone else," Rhonda said, "but I'm glad we're sticking with Access in this class."

"Using Access does make database connectivity pretty easy," I said, "but believe me, after this class, connecting to another database won't be much of a problem. Just about all the key ideas that you learn in this class concerning databases will essentially be the same in most applications – regardless of whether you are connecting to a small Access database or a huge Oracle database."

"That's good news," Kate said. "Just to double check then – if we are connecting to an Access database, then we should accept the default value for the `Connect` property – Access."

"That's perfect, Kate," I said. "For the duration of this class, you'll never need to change the `Connect` property – just leave it alone."

"As I mentioned earlier, when we use Visual Basic to connect to a database," I said, "we create a recordset. Recordsets are such an important topic that we'll be talking about them both next week and the week after. Remember, you can think of a recordset as a 'virtual table' of records maintained in the computer's memory or RAM, and based on the underlying physical database. In Visual Basic, using the standard DAO data control, you can specify the three types of recordsets – **Snapshots**, **Dynasets**, and **Tables**. Each type has its own advantages and disadvantages. Let's take a look at these types in a little more detail."

## *The RecordsetType Property*

I opened up the properties window for the `Data1` data control and clicked on the down arrow of the `RecordsetType` property's drop-down list box:

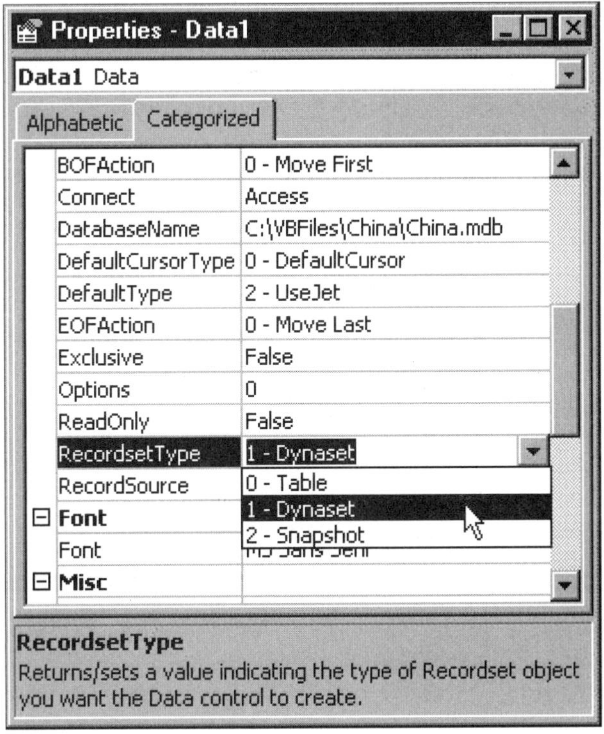

"Isn't everything we look at a `Table`?" Steve asked. "After all, that's what we created last week in Access."

"That's true in Access," I said, "but not necessarily true in Visual Basic. It's easy to get the concept of an Access table confused with a `Table` type `recordset`, but they are different animals. You're right, Steve –Access opens everything up as a `Table` – but Visual Basic is more powerful in that it gives us three types of recordsets to choose from when we connect to a database – and it's the value of the `RecordsetType` property that allows us to make that choice."

"Three types of recordsets?" Dave asked. "Why?"

"Each `RecordsetType` has different characteristics," I said, "and there are advantages and disadvantages to each..."

#### *Table Type Recordsets*

"For instance," I continued, "let's start with the `Table` type recordset. With the `Table` type, you can add, change or delete records in the recordset. However, a `Table` type recordset in Visual Basic can only show you the contents of a single table."

"You say 'single table' as if it were possible to retrieve data from more than one table simultaneously," Rhonda said. "Can you?"

"Actually, you *can* retrieve data from more than one table," I replied, "and you can do that with both `Dynaset` and `Snapshot` recordset types."

There was a look of confusion on the faces of several of my students.

"Do you remember our discussion of **foreign keys** last week?" I said.

"Yes," Melissa said, "I believe you said that foreign keys enable us to relate one table to another."

She thought a moment and then added: "So what you're suggesting is...that by specifying a recordset type of `Dynaset` or `Snapshot`, and by using the primary and foreign keys that relate tables to each other, we can retrieve data from more than one table at the same time?"

"That's excellent, Melissa," I said. "That's exactly what I'm saying. I'll be showing you how to do this in two weeks, but let me give you an example. In the China Shop database, we have a `Transactions` table that contains a field called `CustID`, but there's no way, just looking at the `Transactions` table alone, to determine the customer's name."

"That's right," Ward interjected, "the customer's name and address are in the **Customers** table – not in the **Transactions** table."

"That's right," I agreed, "With a recordset type of **Dynaset** or **Snapshot**, we can tell Visual Basic to retrieve the records from the **Transaction** table, and in the process 'look up' the customer's name in the **Customers** table based on the **CustID** found in the **Transactions** table:"

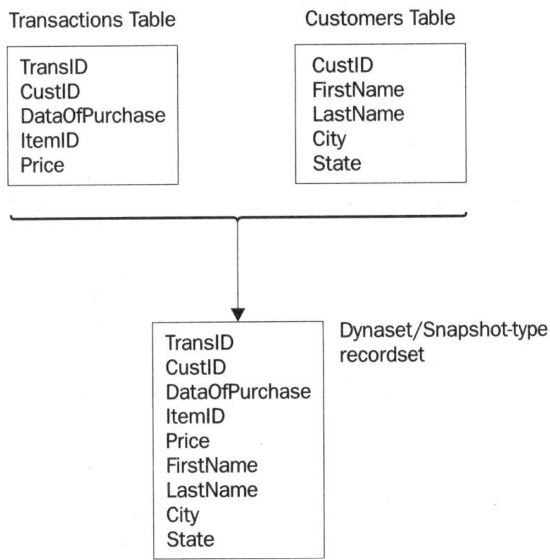


"So it is possible then," Rhonda said, "to retrieve data from more than one table – but *not* if we specify a recordset type of **Table**?"

"Right," I replied. "If we specify a **Table** type recordset, we can only retrieve data from a single table. And remember, we can only retrieve data from multiple tables in this way if there is a pre-existing relationship defined between the tables."

"I'm a little confused by this discussion of multiple tables," Lou said. "If we specify a recordset type of **Dynaset** or **Snapshot**, and we want Visual Basic to retrieve data from more than one table, what do we put into the **RecordSource** property? In the demonstration you gave us before break, you selected the **Users** table in the drop-down list box of the **RecordSource** property. Is it possible to select more than one table in the **RecordSource** property?"

"That's a great question, Lou," I said. "The answer is 'no', you can't specify more than one table in the **RecordSource** property's drop-down list box. In order to retrieve data from more than one table you need to code a special type of statement, called a **SQL statement**, in the **RecordSource** property. You use this method for data retrieval, instead of selecting a table name from the drop-down list box."

"A what kind of statement?" Rhonda asked, obviously befuddled.

"An S-Q-L statement, usually pronounced like the word 'sequel'." I replied. "SQL stands for **Structured Query Language**, and it's a standard language developed for accessing data in database tables. We'll discuss it in more detail in a few weeks, and you'll see that we can easily use it to retrieve data from more than one table, and the resulting recordset will appear as though the data all came from a single table."

"When you say 'language'," Peter said, "do you mean that we'll need to learn a new language, like Visual Basic?"

"SQL has a very limited vocabulary," I said, "and although parts of it can be tedious to write, it has nowhere near the number of commands and statements that Visual Basic has. I can teach you the basics of SQL very quickly. In no time at all, you can be using SQL to retrieve data from database tables, and the great thing is that the core part of SQL – known as ANSI Standard SQL – is implemented identically in every major database there is."

"So if we know the core part of SQL for Access," Linda said, "we can use those same SQL statements in an Oracle database?"

"That's correct," I replied, "although Oracle and the other major database packages frequently implement additional SQL features – called **extensions** – of their own. These extensions allow you to perform more complex and more database-specific functions. However, ANSI Standard SQL is ANSI standard SQL. The SQL you will learn in the coming weeks you will be able to use on any database platform."

I waited a few seconds, and then Rhonda asked a question: "Getting back to those recordset types," she said, "let me make sure I understand this. A `RecordsetType` of `Table` permits you to retrieve data from one table and one table only."

"You seem to understand perfectly, Rhonda," I said.

"Is there anything else we should know about the `Table` type recordset?" Dave asked.

"As I mentioned," I answered, "each one of the recordset types has advantages and disadvantages. From the point of view of some programmers, the fact that the `Table` type recordset can retrieve data from only one table would be considered a big disadvantage. On the other hand, the primary advantage of the `Table` type recordset is its ability to quickly retrieve a single record in the recordset using the recordset's `Seek` method."

"The word 'seek' sounds fast," Peter said.

"You're right, Peter," I agreed. "The **`Seek`** method of the recordset gives us very rapid retrieval of records. The **`Seek`** method uses an Access table's **index** to quickly locate a record in a **`Table`** type recordset."

"Is an index the same thing as a primary key, then?" Dave asked.

"Well spotted, Dave," I said. "A primary key is one kind of index, and in Access you can define other indexes as well. A database index is very much like the index in the back of a book. It's stored internally in the database and acts as a set of directions to exactly where the indexed data can be found – using it, Visual Basic can quickly locate a record in a table. When we write code for our login form, we'll use an index to quickly locate a user in the **`Users`** table at login time."

"You said that you can only use the **`Seek`** method of the data control against a **`Table`** type recordset," Chuck said. "Is there anything comparable to locate a record in a **`Dynaset`** or **`Snapshot`** type recordset?"

"Be careful, Chuck," I said, "there is no **`Seek`** method of the *data control*. The **`Seek`** method belongs to the *recordset*. The distinction is subtle, but important. We'll discuss recordset properties and methods starting next week."

"That's right," Chuck laughed. "I remember now that you drew a distinction between the data control and the underlying recordset that it generates."

"That's an good way of putting it, Chuck," I said. "Effectively, we're dealing with two separate objects when our program is running and the data control has connected to the database: the first object is the data control itself, and the second object is the recordset associated with that data control. Now, getting back to your question concerning an alternative to the **`Seek`** method – yes, there is an alternative. With either the **`Dynaset`** or **`Snapshot`** type recordsets, we can use the recordset's family of **`Find`** methods to locate records. However, the **`Find`** methods are much slower than the **`Seek`** method, since they start at the beginning of the recordset, and work their way to the end, record by record."

"Comparing the **`Seek`** method to the **`Find`** methods then," Dave said, "if the **`Seek`** method is like locating a topic in a book by using the Index in the back to find the page number, the **`Find`** methods are like thumbing through the book page by page until you find what you are looking for."

"That's perfect, Dave," I said, "if I ever get around to writing that book I'm always talking about, maybe I'll use that analogy myself."

"Would I be correct in saying that the **`Table`** type recordset is the best choice," Kate said, "unless you need to retrieve data from more than one table?"

"Yes, that's accurate, Kate," I said. "**Table** type recordsets are the hands down choice for data retrieval from a single table. Not only do they allow us to use the **Seek** method for quick record retrieval, but they are also the fastest to work with, and consume the least amount of memory of all three recordset types."
"So that leaves us with a choice of either using a **Dynaset** or a **Snapshot** recordset for data retrievals involving multiple tables," Dave said. "Which is preferable?"

"From a functional point of view," I answered, "**Dynasets** and **Snapshots** are identical – with one big exception: a **Snapshot** recordset is **read-only** – it can't be updated, whereas a **Dynaset** *can* be updated."

"When you say read-only," Rhonda asked, "you mean that the underlying records can't be changed."

### *Snapshot Type Recordsets*

"That's right," I said, "neither can you add records to the **Snapshot** recordset."

"Granted, that's a significant difference," Ward said, "but is that the only difference between the two?"

"From a functional point of view, that's the only difference," I said. "Although you'll find that because Visual Basic does not need to worry about updating the underlying recordset of a **Snapshot**, **Snapshot** recordsets tend to be a little faster than **Dynasets**."

"I don't understand why anyone would want to use a **Snapshot** then." Rachel said, frustrated. "Wouldn't you want to update the records in *every* recordset you create?"

"Not necessarily," I said. "I've created some recordsets where I had no intention of updating the underlying records. For instance, in a few weeks, we'll use data that we retrieve from the **Inventory** table of the **China** database to load china brands into the list box of our main form. The recordset that we'll create when we connect to the **Inventory** table won't need to be updated in any way. What type of recordset do you think we should choose when we connect to the **China** database to access the **Inventory** records?"

"I see what you mean now," Rachel answered. "A **Snapshot** would make perfect sense there, since we're just *reading* data in the **Inventory** table to load up items in a list box. There's no need to create a recordset which can be updated."

"Now you're getting the idea!" I said. "That's exactly when you use a **Snapshot** – to retrieve data that doesn't need to be updated."

"Didn't you say earlier," Rhonda said, "that we can't locate a record in **Snapshot** or a **Dynaset** type recordsets?"

"Not quite," I answered, "I said that you can't use the **Seek** method of the recordset to quickly locate a record in a **Snapshot** or a **Dynaset** type recordset. You can still locate a record – you just have to use the slower family of recordset **Find** methods."

### *Dynaset Type Recordsets*

"Can we talk about the **Dynaset** type recordset?" Kevin asked. "You said that a **Dynaset** recordset is identical to a **Snapshot** – except that the **Dynaset** recordset is updateable?"

"That's right, Kevin," I said. "And don't forget, because the **Dynaset** is updateable, it is a bit slower to work with than the **Snapshot** type."

I then displayed this chart on the classroom projector to summarize the differences between the different types of recordset:

| Recordset Type | RAM Usage | Speed | Methods to Locate Records | More than one Table? | Updateable? |
|---|---|---|---|---|---|
| Dynaset | | Slowest | Find (Slow) | Yes | Yes |
| Snapshot | Most | | Find (Slow) | Yes | No |
| Table | Least | Fastest | Seek (Fast) | No | Yes |

"As you can see from the chart," I said, "the **Table** type recordset is the fastest of all three recordsets to work with – however, it can only retrieve data from a single table, which is a decided disadvantage in the eyes of many programmers. Both the **Snapshot** and **Dynaset** type recordsets can retrieve data from more than one table – however, the **Snapshot** is read-only, whereas the Dynaset is updateable. Of the two, the Snapshot is the fastest – but also consumes the most amount of RAM."

"Can you clear something up for me that is still confusing me?" Steve said. "We're in the midst of discussing data control properties – but a minute ago, you mentioned a method of the *recordset*. Did you mean to say a method of the data control?"

"I'm sorry for the confusion," I said, "and it's certainly understandable. When we talk abou database Access using the data control, we tend to think *only* in terms of the data control. But what you must remember is that when we initialize the form that the data control is placed upon, the data control makes a connection to the database specified in the **DatabaseName** property, and this connection then spawns a recordset. It's this recordset, by and large, that our bound controls then work with. When the user clicks on the 'next' record button on the data control, that action triggers a method of the underlying recordset – *not* a method of the data control. As a result, during our learning process, we'll be discussing methods and properties of both the data control *and* the recordset created by the data control. In the beginning, you're bound to be confused – but it's like anything in Visual Basic – with a little demonstration on my part, and a little practice on your own, it will all make sense soon. We just need to work through the theory and the practice a few times and it will start to slot into place."

"I'm still a little confused," Mary said, "but I know from my experience with the introductory class that you're right – a little practice will go a long way!"

"You're right, Mary. Just to recap, today we'll discuss the methods and properties of the **data control**. Starting next week, we'll begin to discuss the properties and methods of the **recordset**."

"I'll now talk you through some of the properties that it's most important to learn early on," I said. "First, let's take a look at the data control's `RecordSource` property."

### *The RecordSource Property*

"A little earlier, we saw that for a `Table` type recordset, the `RecordSource` property is simply the name of a table in the database. Even for a `Dynaset` or `Snapshot RecordsetType`, the `RecordSource` property may still be the name of a single table selected in the drop-down list box:"

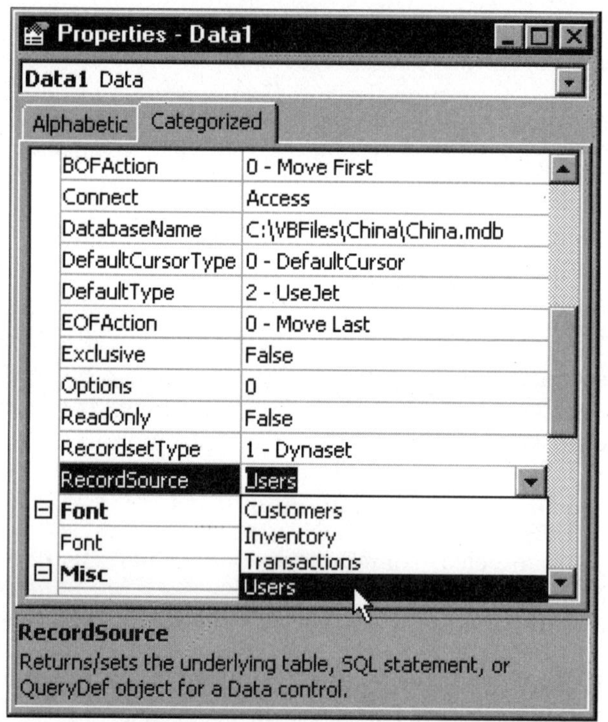


"It isn't until we decide that we need to access data from more than one table," I said, "that the `RecordSource` property will be anything but a table name. Remember, I said earlier that when we want to retrieve data from more than one table, we need a means other than selecting a single table in the list box. Next week, or possibly the week after, you'll see that we can type a SQL statement directly into the `RecordSource` property – and through that SQL statement, create a recordset that contains data from more than one table. Another method is to create a saved Access query that queries more than one table – remember that any saved Access queries will also show up in the list box."

### *The DefaultType and DefaultCursorType Properties*

"The next two properties," I said, "the **`DefaultType`** and **`DefaultCursorType`** properties should be left at their default states of **`2-Use Jet`**:"

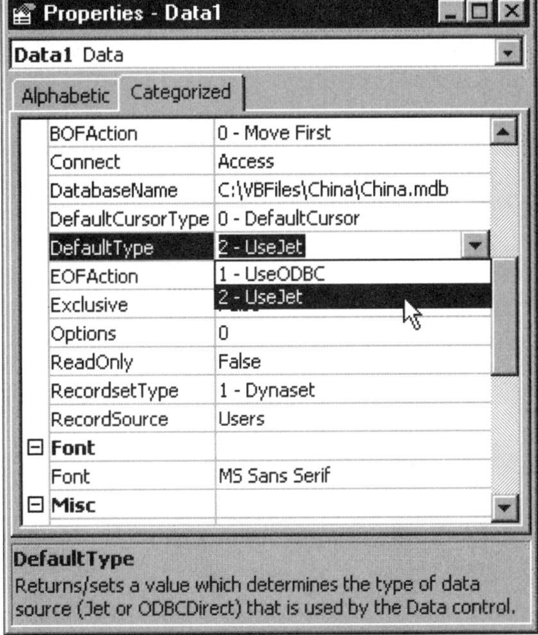


"...and **`0-DefaultCursor`** respectively:"

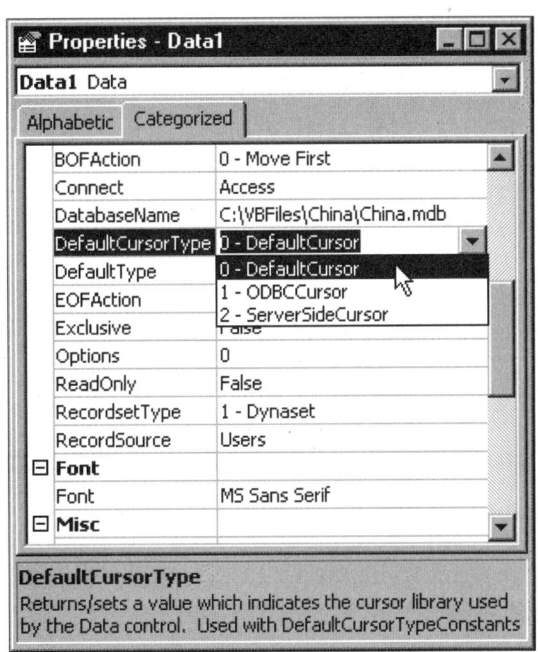

"The **DefaultType** refers to the database types we've already discussed: since Visual Basic uses the Jet database engine functionality to connect to Access databases, this is the type we'll be using throughout."

"I can see that," said Dave, "but what's the **DefaultCursor** property for?"

"This is a tricky one," I said, "and you're just going to have to trust me on it. A **cursor** is used by the database management system (or by our Visual Basic program that's mimicking the DBMS) to navigate around the recordset and present us with the data that we ask for. Cursors are really beyond the scope of this course, so we'll just have to take it as read that they are there in the background, helping us to retrieve and process that data that we're interested in."

I looked around, and nobody seemed eager to examine the inner workings of the cursor.

"OK," I continued, "let's get back to the **DefaultCursor** and **DefaultType** properties. These default values," I said, "are the property values to connect to an Access database. In the event that you need to connect to another type of database such as Oracle or SQLServer, then these properties would need to be changed to something other than their default values. But, as I've mentioned a few times already, in this course we'll only be looking at connecting to an Access database."

"Whenever you open a database, either in Microsoft Access or in Visual Basic," I said, "you have the choice of opening the database exclusively – that is, in **exclusive mode**."

### *The Exclusive Property*

"What does that mean?" Steve asked.

"Simply speaking," I said, "when you open a database for exclusive use, that means that only one user can have the database open at a time. Setting the **Exclusive** property of the data control to **True** will prevent another user – perhaps another Visual Basic user, or even someone trying to open the database directly in Access – from being able to open the database at the same time."

"I guess I don't understand why more than one user would have a database open at the same time?" Blaine asked.

"There are databases installed on networks," I said, "that are intended to be used by more than one user at the same time."

"That's right," Blaine said, "I've got to get out of my single PC mindset, and join the network revolution!"

"Having said that," I continued, "if we set the **`Exclusive`** property of the data control to **`True`**, we can prevent that from happening. Can anyone venture a guess as to why we would want to open the database so that only one user could have it opened at one time?"

"I think I can answer that one," Kathy said. "At work, we have several Access databases on a network drive that are accessed by several hundred people. There are some operations that we perform against the database – such as a long running update query I run once a week where a field in one of our tables is recalculated – where I don't want users updating the data in the table while this operation is going on. In that case, I open the database in **exclusive** mode in Access. This prevents other users from opening the database."

"Thank you, Kathy," I said, "that's an excellent real-world example. I couldn't have said it better myself. If you need to keep others from opening the database while you are working with it, then set the **`Exclusive`** property of the data control to **`True`**:"

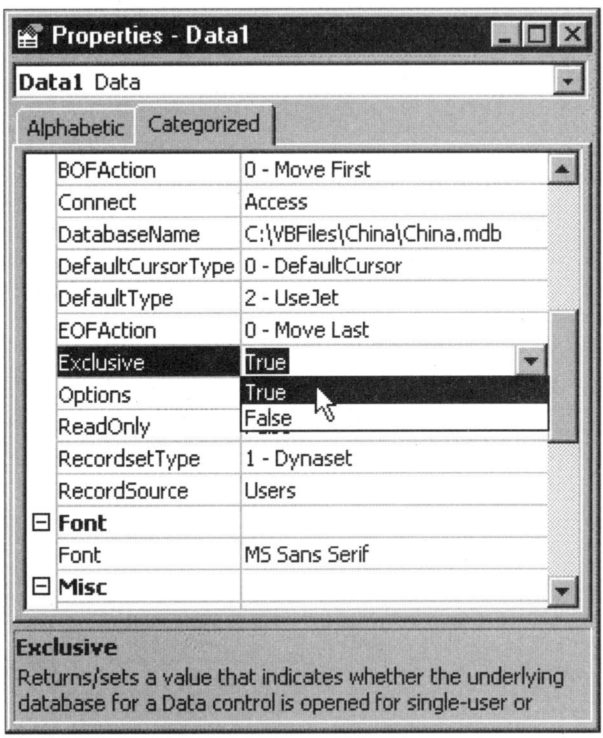


"Will others still be able to open it to view the records?" Kathy asked.

"No," I said, "setting the **`Exclusive`** property to **`True`** prevents the database from being opened – period. By the way, the default value for the **`Exclusive`** property is **`False`** – meaning that more than one user can open the database at the same time."

### The Options Property

"The **Options** property," I continued, "is one of the more interesting data control properties. What's particularly interesting is that although we're setting its value in the data control's Properties window, the values apply to the *recordset* that's created by the data control – remember, these are two separate objects in programming terms. Anyway, the **Options** property's default value is 0:"

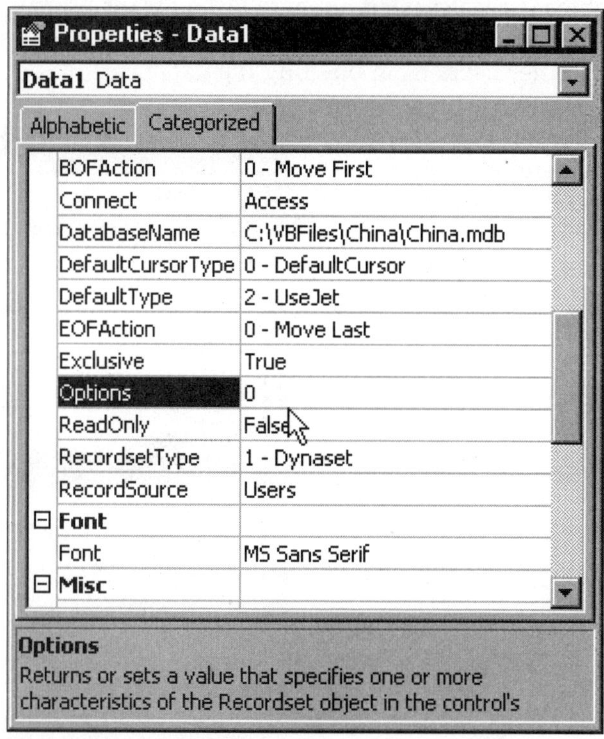


"The **Options** property," I continued, "gives us a tremendous amount of flexibility over the characteristics of the recordset created by the data control. For instance, if we set the **Options** property to a value of 8, that means that the user of our program can add new records to the recordset, but *can't* see any existing records."

"OK," Dave said, "I can see that particular setting could be very useful. For instance, maybe in a program where security issues dictate that a particular user shouldn't see existing records – but should still be able to add data to a table or tables. What are the other values for the **Options** property?"

I then displayed the following chart on the classroom projector, and also distributed a copy:

| Constant | Value | Setting |
|---|---|---|
| | 0 | None |
| **dbDenyWrite** | 1 | In a multi-user environment, other users can't make changes to records in the recordset |
| **dbDenyRead** | 2 | In a multi-user environment, other users can't read records (`Table`-type recordset only) |
| **dbReadOnly** | 4 | You can't make changes to records in the recordset. |
| **dbAppendOnly** | 8 | You can add new records to the recordset, but you can't read existing records. |
| **dbInconsistent** | 16 | Updates can apply to all fields of the recordset, even if they violate the join condition. |
| **dbConsistent** | 32 | Updates apply only to those fields that don't violate the join condition. |
| **dbSQLPassThrough** | 64 | When using data controls with an SQL statement in the `RecordSource` property, this sends the SQL statement to an ODBC database, such as a SQL Server or Oracle database, for processing. |
| **dbForwardOnly** | 256 | The recordset object supports forward-only scrolling. The only move method allowed is `MoveNext`. This option cannot be used on recordset objects manipulated with the data control. |
| **dbSeeChanges** | 512 | Generate a trappable error if another user is changing data you are editing. |

"I've given you this chart for reference purposes, but I won't be going through all of these possible values here today. Instead, I'll just concentrate on the most important ones as far as we're concerned at this stage of our learning."

"As you can see," I continued, "specifying a value of `1` for the **`Options`** property prevents other users from making changes to the records in your recordset. Specifying a value of `8`, as I mentioned earlier, allows the user of your program to add new records to the recordset, but prevents them from reading existing records. The interesting thing is that specifying a value of `9` does *both* – prevents other users from changing the records in your recordset, and prevents the user of the program from being able to see existing records – but permits them to add new records."

"So the **`Options`** property is **additive**?" Dave asked.

"Yes, " I replied.

"*Additive*?" Rhonda asked, "what's that?"

"Additive," I said, "means that you can add these values together to achieve a cumulative effect. If you want to set more than one characteristic as specified in the chart I distributed, all you need to do is add up the values and place the result in the **`Options`** property."

I waited a moment to see if there were any questions.

"I should mention," I added, "that in addition to specifying a value for this property in the **`Properties`** window at design time, you can also set the **`Options`** property at run time. However, if you do, you'll need to execute the **`Refresh`** method of the data control: this will rebuild the recordset and your reset **`Options`** value will take effect."

"The **`Refresh`** method?" Chuck asked. "Is that a recordset or data control method?"

"The **`Refresh`** method is a data control method," I said. "It's used to rebuild a recordset from scratch. It's really the same process that occurs when a form is first loaded, and the data control connects to the database. Here, let me give you an example..."

I displayed this code on the classroom projector:

```
Data1.Recordset.Options = 9
Data1.Refresh
```

"Confusing, isn't it?" I asked. "Here I'm setting the property of the recordset, and executing the **method** of a data control."

"I think I'm OK with the `Options` property," Linda said, "although I must admit that some of these settings are a bit over my head."

"Remember," I said, "some of these `Options` values won't make much sense to you until you actually start working with the data control and recordsets. All of this will become clearer when we start working on our code in detail in later lessons."

Next, we turned our attention to the `ReadOnly` property.

### *The ReadOnly Property*

"I bet I know what this property means!" Rhonda said. "Setting this value to `True`:"

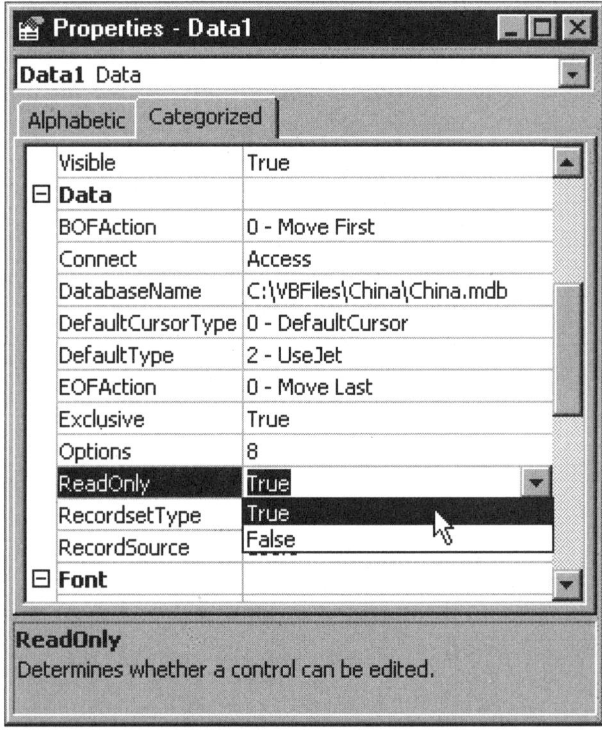


"... means that the resultant recordset is read-only, and therefore cannot be updated."

"Right you are, Rhonda," I said, "good job!"

"A read-only recordset," Peter said, "isn't that in essence a `Snapshot`?"

"You're right, Peter," I said, "that certainly does sound like a `Snapshot`."

I took a breath and prepared to talk about some very important properties: discussing these would teach us a lot about how our Visual Basic program interacts with the recordset.

### *The BOFAction and EOFAction Properties*

"I've been waiting to get to these properties," Ward said. "What exactly do these mean?"

"Let me give you an example," I said, "suppose we have a recordset – any type, it doesn't matter – that contains eight records."

I then displayed this drawing on the classroom projector:

| BOF |
|---|
| Record 1 |
| Record 2 |
| Record 3 |
| Record 4 |
| Record 5 |
| Record 6 |
| Record 7 |
| Record 8 |
| EOF |

BOF and EOF are buffers at the top and bottom of a Recordset

"In the drawing, records 1 to 8 are the records in the recordset that contain the data that we've read from the database tables. At the very top of the recordset," I continued, "is a special, invisible record called the **BOF** – which stands for the **Beginning Of File**. At the very bottom of the recordset is a special, invisible record called the **EOF** – which stands for **End Of File**."

"Isn't the BOF the first record in the file then?" Rhonda asked.

"No, it's not – but that is an excellent question, Rhonda," I answered. "It's important that we all understand the distinction between the BOF and the first record proper. The BOF is the record **before** the first (data) record in the recordset. The EOF is the record **after** the last record in the recordset."

"What about these properties though," Ward asked, "`BOFAction` and `EOFAction` – what do they do?"

"These properties," I said, "determine what happens if your record pointer somehow moves onto the special BOF or EOF records."

"Is it possible for that to happen?" Kate asked.

"Yes it is," I said. "For instance, if your record pointer is positioned on the first record in the recordset, and you click on the 'previous' button on the data control, your record pointer will actually move to the BOF. The same principle applies to the EOF: if your record pointer is on the last record in a recordset, and you click on the 'next' button on the data control, your record pointer will move to the EOF. It's the value of both of these properties that determines what action to take when this happens."

"What do you mean by that?" Steve asked.

"Let's take a look at the possible values for the **BOFAction**, Steve," I said, "and I'll try to explain. By default, the BOFAction property is **0-MoveFirst**:"

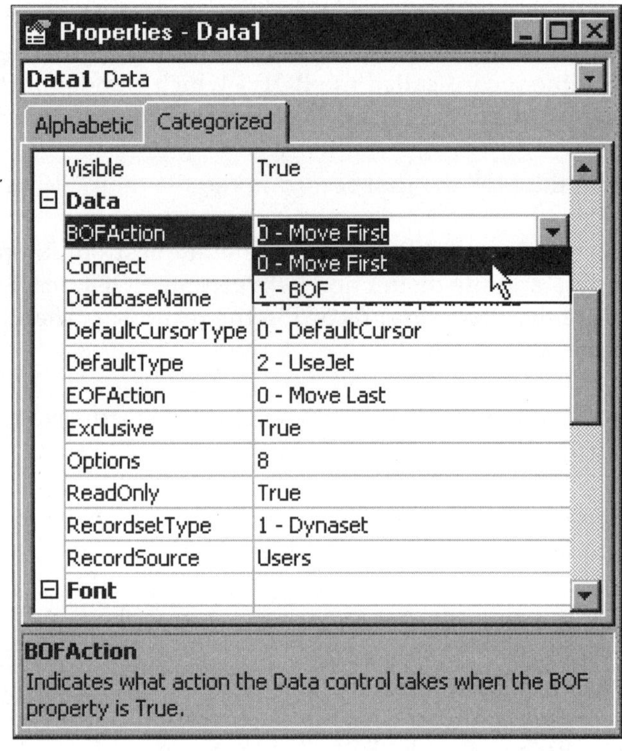


"...what that means is that if the record pointer somehow moves to the BOF, the data control will move the record pointer right back to the first proper record in the recordset – that is, the first record that contains real data."

"So the user will never know they actually moved the record pointer to the BOF?" Tom asked.

"That's right," I said. "Again, if the user's record pointer is currently positioned on record number 1 in the recordset and they click on the 'previous' button on the data control, then – behind the scenes – the data control will move the record pointer to the BOF. Then the **BOFAction** property will kick in, and move the record pointer right back to the first record in the recordset."

"And the alternative?" Ward said.

"The alternative," I said, "is to keep the record pointer at the BOF."

"That's like being in no-man's land," Steve said. "Why would you ever want to keep the record pointer positioned there?"

"I can't think of a good reason," I said, "which is why I never change the default value of **BOFAction**. I always leave it set at **MoveFirst**."

"I understand the **BOFAction**," Rhonda said. "So the **EOFAction** property work in a similar way does it?"

"Yes it does," I said, "except that the EOFAction has three possible values for us to choose among – **MoveLast**, **EOF**, and **Add New**:"

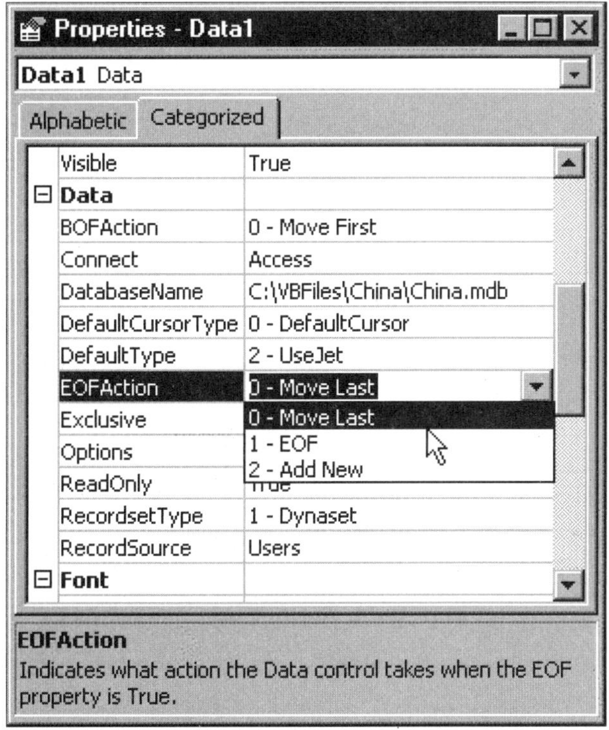


"By the way, **0-Move Last** is the default value."

"I'm betting," Valerie said, "that last value, **2-Add New**, needs to be set to enable you to add a new record to the recordset – is that the property you alluded to earlier when you were discussing adding records to a recordset via the DBGrid?"

"That's right," I said. "By default, if the user moves the record pointer to the EOF of a recordset, the record pointer will be moved right back to the last data record in the recordset. However, if we set the **EOFAction** property to **2-Add New**, and the user moves the record pointer to the EOF of the recordset, they can then add a new record to the underlying recordset."

"Can we can see this property in action?" Melissa asked.

"Sure thing," I said. "Let me modify the demonstration program we've been working on...and we'll also need to change a property of the **DBGrid** called **AllowAddNew** from its default value of **False** to **True**:"

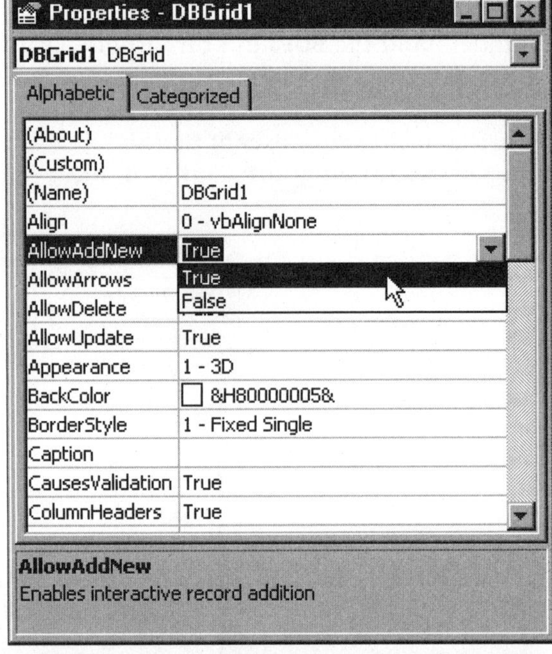


"... otherwise the **DBGrid** itself will prevent us from adding new records. Now if we change the data control's **EOFAction** from its default value of **LastRecord** to **Add New:**"

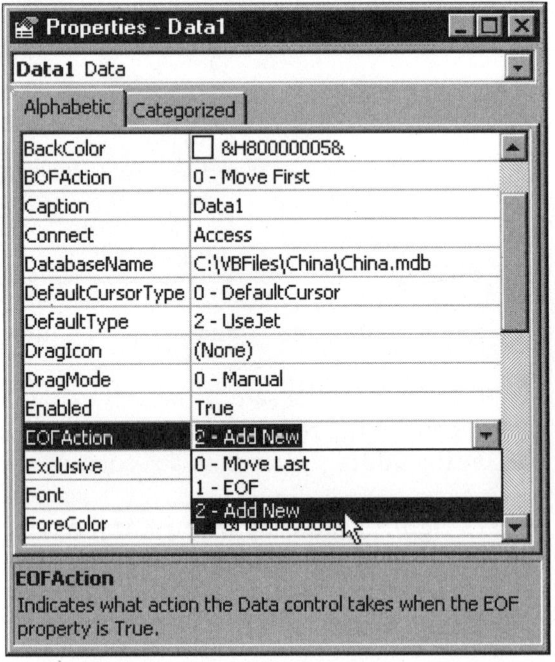

"... and run the program, we should see a slightly different look to the DBGrid:"

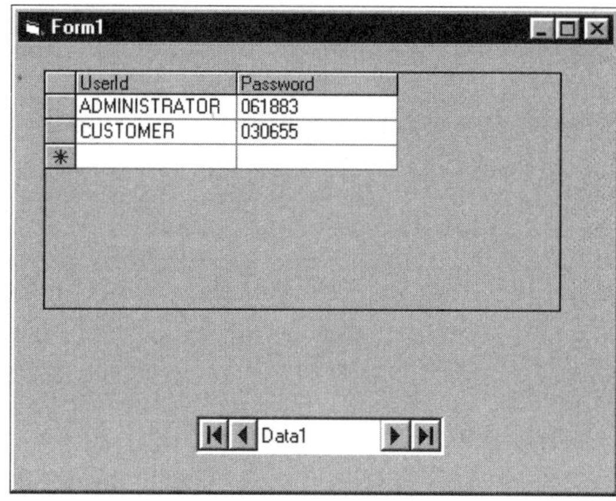


"Does anyone see the difference," I said, "between this view of the DBGrid and the view that we saw before we changed the `EOFAction` property of the data control and the `AllowAddNew` property of the DBGrid?"

"I think I do," Melissa answered. "Instead of two rows of data from the `Users` table, we now have a third empty row, and the third row's first column contains an asterisk."

"Well observed, Melissa," I answered, "and you're absolutely right, the row containing an asterisk is the 'new record' row. To add a new record to this recordset, all we need to do is to click our mouse on that row to move the record pointer to it, and fill in the data for the fields. If we then move the record pointer off the new record, the record will be added to the `Users` table."

I then entered values for a new `UserID` and `Password`, and clicked on the 'first record' navigation button on the data control:

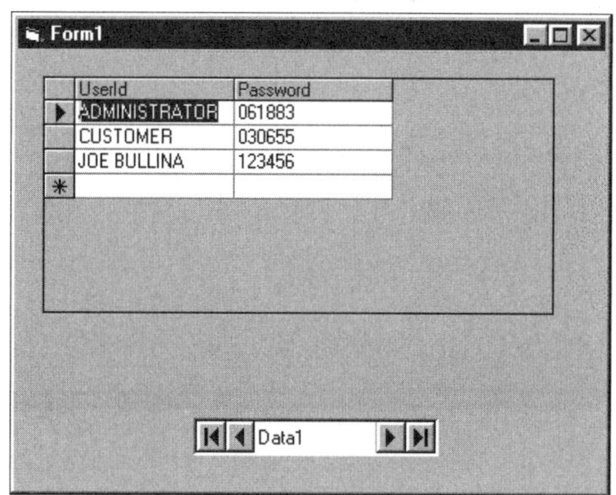


For the skeptics in the class, I then ended the program by closing the form, and re-started it to prove that the record had indeed been added to the `Users` table.

"That's neat," Chuck said, "and it's pretty easy."

"Just to review," I said, "this morning I've shown you how easy it is to modify existing records in a database, and also to add new records. What's left?"

"Shouldn't we delete Joe Bullina's record?" Mary asked.

"That's right, Mary," I replied. "There are four main operations performed on records in database tables – **`View`**, **`Add`**, **`Edit`**, and the one you've just mentioned – **`Delete`**."

I began to demonstrate just how easy it is to delete a record using the data control and the DBGrid, when I realized that I first needed to change a property of the DBGrid.

"Before we're able to delete a record using the DBGrid," I said, "we need to change the **`AllowDelete`** property of the DBGrid from its default value of **`False`** to **`True`**."

"The DBGrid seems to be pretty flexible and very powerful," Dave said, "in terms of restricting the types of operations that can be performed on it."

"That's right, Dave," I said. "The properties of the DBGrid that restrict user actions – **`AllowAddNew`**, **`AllowDelete`**, and **`AllowUpdate`** – let you restrict the actions which users can perform. You can also update these properties at run-time based on the user who is working with your program – very flexible. That's why the DBGrid is great for demonstrating the capabilities of the data control and the things that we can do with Access databases."

I then brought up the properties window for the DBGrid, and changed the **`AllowDelete`** property to **`True`**:

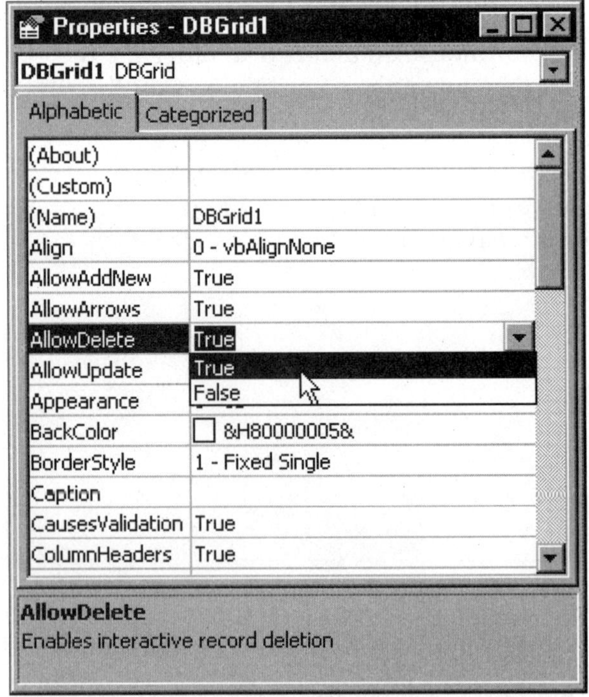

"That's better," I said, as I ran the program. "Now, in order to delete Joe Bullina's record in the **`Users`** table, all we need to do is select the row on the DBGrid that we wish to delete by clicking on his row's record selector:"

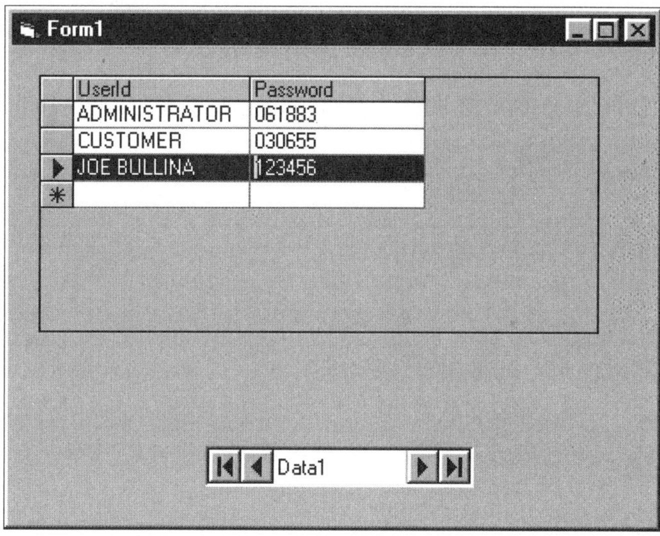


"...and press the *Delete* key. The record will then be deleted."

I did that, and Joe Bullina's record was deleted:

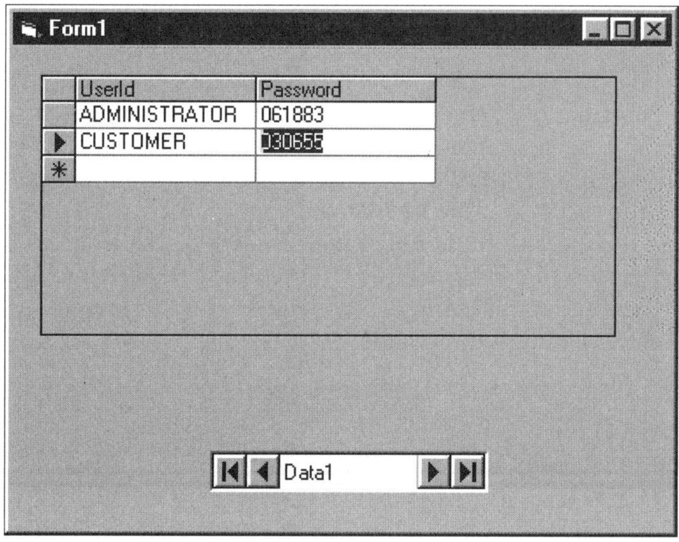

"Wow, that was fast," Ward said. "I noticed there was no confirmation warning of any kind. Is there a property we can set to give us one?"

"Good question, Ward," I said, "but no, there is no property we can set to give us an 'Are you sure?' dialog box. However, the action of deleting Joe Bullina's record did trigger a DBGrid event that we can use to create one of our own. We'll look at DBGrid properties, methods and events in more detail in a few weeks."

"That's about it for data control properties," I said. "Now I want to discuss the events of the data control."

## Data Control Events

"I guess I never really considered events for the data control," Melissa said. "So there are events that the data control reacts to?"

"Yes there are," I replied, "Most of them are standard events, which you're already familiar with – such as the **`MouseDown`**, **`MouseUp`**, and **`Resize`** events. However, there are two events that are unique to the data control that we need to discuss – the **`Validate`** event and the **`Reposition`** event – and both are triggered, among other things, by the user's interaction with the data control navigation buttons."

I started by explaining about the **`Validate`** event.

### *The Validate Event*

"The **`Validate`** event," I continued, "is an event that occurs just before the record pointer changes and moves you to a different record in the recordset. In other words, if your record pointer is currently on record number 4, and you use the data control's navigation button to move to another record in the recordset, the **`Validate`** event is triggered *just before* that movement occurs. Because this event occurs *before* the actual movement takes place, the programmer has a chance to stop this movement of the record pointer from taking place. I should also mention that the **`Validate`** event can be triggered by Visual Basic code you write – in addition to clicking on the navigation buttons."

I stopped our demonstration program, and double-clicked on the data control to open up the code window for the data control's **`Validate`** event:

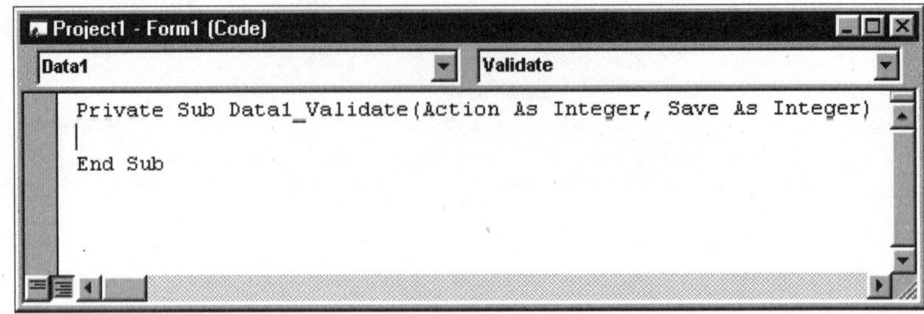

"Notice from the event procedure header," I said, "that there are two arguments being passed to the `Validate` event – the `Action` argument and the `Save` argument. The `Action` argument provides us with information about *why* the record pointer is being moved. The `Save` argument allows us to *cancel* whatever action made the record pointer move in the first place."

"I'm afraid I'm a little confused," Rhonda said.

"Let me show you the possible values for the `Action` argument," I continued, "and maybe that will help make a little more sense out of this."

I displayed this summary chart on the classroom projector:

| Constant | Value | Description |
|---|---|---|
| vbDataActionCancel | 0 | Cancel the operation when the Sub exits |
| vbDataActionMoveFirst | 1 | MoveFirst method |
| vbDataActionMovePrevious | 2 | MovePrevious method |
| vbDataActionMoveNext | 3 | MoveNext method |
| vbDataActionMoveLast | 4 | MoveLast method |
| vbDataActionAddNew | 5 | AddNew method |
| vbDataActionUpdate | 6 | Update operation (not UpdateRecord) |
| vbDataActionDelete | 7 | Delete method |
| vbDataActionFind | 8 | Find method |
| vbDataActionBookmark | 9 | The Bookmark property has been set |
| vbDataActionClose | 10 | The Close method |
| vbDataActionUnload | 11 | The form is being unloaded |

"There are twelve possible values for the `Action` argument," I continued, "and one of those values is passed to the `Validate` event whenever the record pointer changes. For instance, if the user clicks on the 'next' button on the data control, a value of `3` is passed to the `Validate` event."

"And it looks like a value of `11` is passed," Dave said, "if the form is unloaded."

"That's right," I said. "Notice the value **7** – that's the value passed to the **Validate** event if the user attempts to delete an existing record in the recordset."

"Does that mean that we could use the **Validate** event to stop the user from deleting a record?" Peter asked.

"Yes we could," I answered, "or we could use the Validate event to pop up that confirmation dialog box Ward asked about a few minutes ago – just by checking for a value of **7** in the **Action** argument. Let's place some code in the **Validate** event to display the **Action** argument."

I entered the following code into the data control's **Validate** event:

```
Private Sub Data1_Validate(Action As Integer, Save As Integer)

MsgBox "The Action argument is " & Action

End Sub
```

"If we run the program and move the record pointer using the navigation buttons," I said, "we'll get a chance to see what the **Action** argument is that is being passed to the **Validate** event."

I then ran the program, and clicked on the 'next record' button on the data control, with the following result:

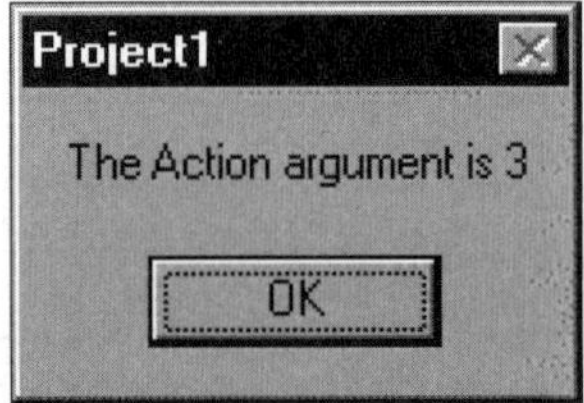


"I see now," Chuck said. "When you pressed the 'next record' button on the data control, the **Action** argument passed to the **Validate** event was 3 – indicating that a **MoveNext** method was executing. But we didn't actually execute a **MoveNext** method, did we?"

"That's an astute observation, Chuck," I said. "**MoveNext** is a recordset method, and something we'll talk about in a few weeks. And you're right, we didn't *explicitly* code a **MoveNext** method – it was the data control that executed the **MoveNext** method of the recordset in order to advance the record pointer."

"That's interesting," Kate said. "So the data control really executes recordset methods in order to perform record navigation. Are the other methods mentioned in your chart – **MoveFirst**, **AddNew**, **Delete** – all recordset methods?"

"Yes they are," I said. "Now you're getting the idea. The data control is doing all of the hard work by executing recordset methods in order to move the record pointer around in the underlying recordset. Later in the course, you'll see that we can execute these methods directly ourselves if we want – in fact, there are some programmers who routinely do this."

"I think I would rather have the data control do all of the hard work for me," Rhonda said.

"That's a perfectly natural and valid approach to take until you've gained in experience and confidence," I said.

Turning my attention back to the running program, I clicked on the 'first record' button, with the following effect:

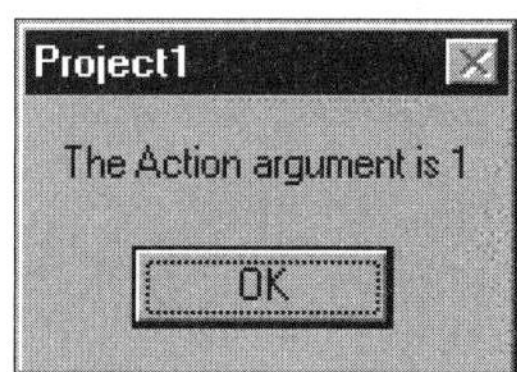


"That makes sense," Ward said. "The **MoveFirst** method of the underlying recordset was executed, and the **Action** argument passed to the **Validate** event is **1**. I recall you saying that because the **Validate** event fires *before* the **Action** takes place there's is a way to prevent the **Action** from executing? For instance, could we place code in the **Validate** event to stop the user from deleting a record?"

"Yes we can," I said. "Take a look at this code..."

I modified the **Validate** event of the data control to look like this:

```
Private Sub Data1_Validate(Action As Integer, Save As Integer)

If Action = vbDataActionDelete Then
    MsgBox "You may not delete a record!"
    Save = False
End If

End Sub
```

... and ran the program.

"Let's try to delete a record in the DBGrid," I said, as I tried to delete the first record in the **Users** table. After selecting record number **1**, and pressing the *Delete* key, the following message box appeared:

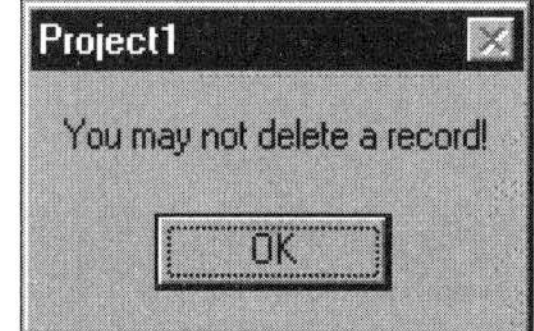

The record remained in the recordset.

"That's great," I heard Kathy say. "Being able to do this will come in very handy at my place!"

"Why did you check for **vbDataActionDelete** in your **If** statement instead of the number 7?" Rachel asked:

```
If Action = vbDataActionDelete Then
```

"**vbDataActionDelete** is the Visual Basic **Intrinsic Constant** value that's equal to **7**," I said "Visual Basic intrinsic constants can be used in place of numeric literals to make your code more readable."

"What stopped the *Delete* from taking place?" Rhonda asked.

"Setting the **Save** argument to False," I said:

```
Save = False
```

"In effect, it's as if the **Action** that triggered the Validate event in the first place never took place."

"I see," Rhonda said. "This is beginning to make more sense to me now."

"Excellent," I replied. "Now that we have a basic understanding of the **Validate** event, that should make understanding the **Reposition** event a little easier."

### *The Reposition Event*

"In contrast to the Validate event, which is triggered *before* the record pointer in the recordset moves, the **Reposition** event takes place *after* the record pointer moves. By the way, the **Reposition** event has no arguments."

"Isn't the **Reposition** event a case of closing the barn door after the horse has left?" Ward asked. "What good is it?"

"Well, Ward," I answered, "you're right, in the sense that by the time the **Reposition** event is triggered, it's too late to cancel whatever action it was that moved the record pointer – after all, the record pointer has already changed. But then again, the **Reposition** event procedure wasn't designed for that purpose. Typically, programmers place code in the **Reposition** event to display a message of some kind to the user – for example, you might want to let the user know that they've successfully deleted a record. Another example is where you might want to change the look of the form in response to a particular movement of the record pointer."

I waited a moment to see if there were any questions. There were none, and it was time to move on to a discussion of the data control's **methods**. But first, we took another break – today's lesson had a lot of detailed and difficult (but very necessary) material in it.

## Data Control Methods

"There are three data control methods I want to discuss today," I said. "`Refresh`, `UpdateControls`, and `UpdateRecords`."

"Aren't you going to discuss the other methods you mentioned earlier," Rhonda said, "`MoveFirst`, `MoveNext`, and the others?"

"`MoveFirst` and `MoveNext` are *recordset* methods," I answered, "rather than *data control* methods. We'll be discussing recordset methods in more detail next week and the following week. *Recordset* methods operate directly on the recordset items – that is, the data records in the recordset. *Data control* methods tend to operate on the recordset as a whole – that is, they change the state of the whole recordset, or make some change to the way that it's being used..."

### The Refresh Method

"For instance," I continued, "the `Refresh` method of the data control rebuilds the recordset from scratch. We discussed this a few minutes ago when we changed the `Options` property of the data control in code. We needed to execute the `Refresh` method of the data control to make the changes to the recordset take effect."

### The UpdateControls Method

"The `UpdateControls` method of the data control is an interesting method," I said. "When you are making changes to a row in a DBGrid, for example, the changes you make to the record are not immediately transferred to the underlying database. It isn't until the user moves the record pointer off the record that the changes are made to the database. Now suppose that the user makes all sorts of changes to a record in the `DBGrid`, and then changes their mind? If you execute the `UpdateControls` method of the data control, the original values for the current record will return."

"That sounds like an 'undo' command of sorts," Dave said.

"Exactly," I said.

## *The UpdateRecord Method*

"The final data control method I want to discuss today," I said, "is the **UpdateRecord** method. It's the exact opposite of the **UpdateControls** method. When you execute the **UpdateRecord** method of the data control, the values in the current record's bound controls immediately update the underlying database. The intriguing thing about the **UpdateRecord** method is that these updates take place without triggering the **Validate** event."

"That's kind of interesting, isn't it?" Dave pondered. "A data control method that doesn't trigger the **Validate** event? Theoretically, wouldn't that allow a programmer to bypass code that might be present in the **Validate** event procedure?"

"That's right, Dave," I agreed, "and that's typically why the **UpdateRecord** method of the data control is executed – the programmer might have code in the **Validate** event that they simply want to circumvent."

There were no further questions.

Some of the students were starting to look a little weary – which was understandable, as we'd covered a lot of technical material today. In fact, we were running late, so I decided to give the class a choice about finishing up for the day.

"We've got a choice to make now, folks," I began. "There's still some practical work scheduled in today's lesson, but I know that we've already been here a long time, and I want you to say if you think we should call it a day and carry today's exercises forward to next week's lesson?"

Everyone was silent for a moment, and I could see a few pairs of eyes glance up at the clock.

"Well," said Rhonda, "if the exercises are related to the China Shop..." – I nodded vigorously to confirm that they were – "...then I'd like to stay and do them today."

"Me too," agreed Ward, "I'm really keen to start enhancing the China Shop program."

Many other heads nodded, and no-one dissented.

"Thanks," I said, "I think your commitment to this is great!"

I had the series of detailed exercises right there, ready on the desk, but this had been a tough lesson, and I wanted everyone to be as fresh as possible for the exercises that followed. I asked the class to take a quick refreshment break, saying: "Let's take five minutes, and then let's bend the rules a little and bring our coffees and snacks back here into the lab. After the break we'll leave the theory work behind for the day and concentrate on getting to grips with enhancing the China Shop program. See you after the break."

## Modifying the China Shop Project

"Welcome back," I said after we had reassembled. "During the last part of our class today," I said, "we'll be starting the modifications to the China Shop project that will give it the database capabilities that Joe Bullina has agreed with us. In our first exercise, I'm going to ask you to create a second form in the China Shop project – the **`Users`** form. This form will permit the China Shop staff to view and update records in the **`Users`** table. Unlike the programs that I created and demonstrated for you today, where we used Label controls and then a DBGrid control to view and edit records in a database table, we'll be using text box controls for the display and update of the two fields in the **`Users`** table. Our first step is to do something that most of you have never done before – and that's to add a second form to a project."

Amid the slurping of coffee and the rustle of candy wrappers, I distributed the following exercise for everyone to complete.

### Exercise – Creating the Users Form

In this exercise, you'll add a second form to the China Shop project and save it in your **`C:\VBFILES\China`** directory.

1. Start up the China Shop project in Visual Basic (if you haven't already installed the China Shop project on your PC, please refer to Appendix B, which describes how to do this).
2. Select Project | Add Form from the Visual Basic menu bar:

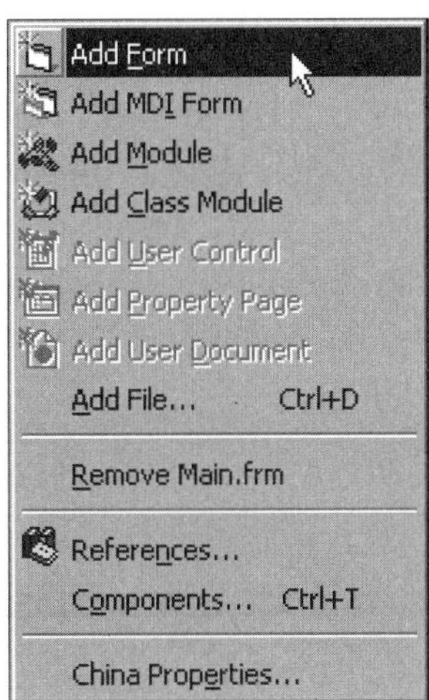

3. The following screen will appear (the exact contents of the screen will vary depending upon which version of VB you're running):

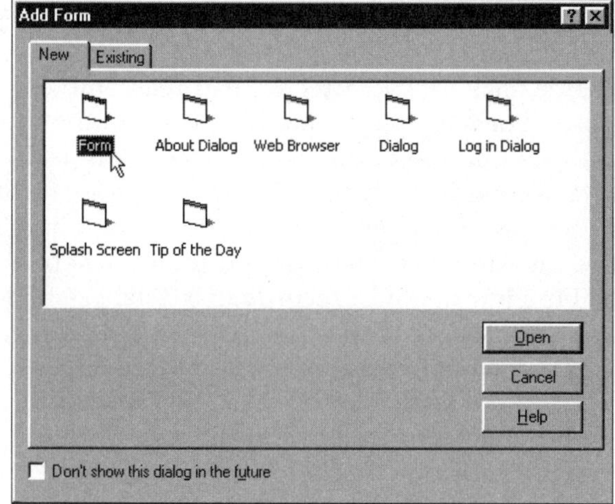


4. Make sure the New tab is selected, and then either double-click on Form or, select Form and click on the Open button. Visual Basic will then display a new form for you, with a caption reading Form1:

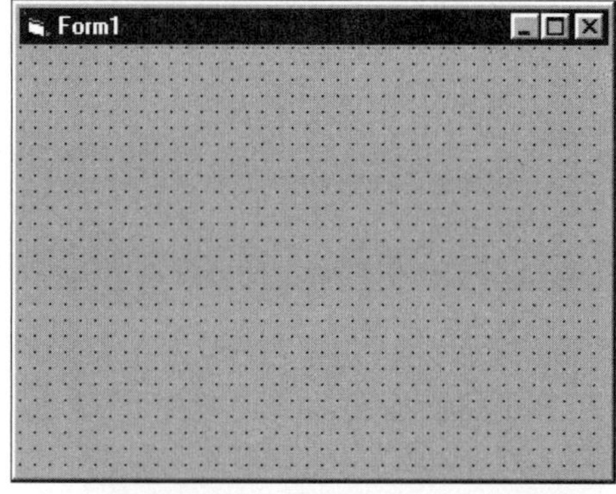


5. Select the form by clicking on it with your mouse, and bring up its Properties window. Find the **Name** property, and change it from **Form1** to **frmUsers**:

**6.** Click on the 'save' button on the toolbar:

Visual Basic will immediately prompt you to save the new form with a disk file name of **`frmUsers`**. **Do not** save the form with that name. Instead, after ensuring that the form will be saved in the correct folder or directory (**`C:\VBFILES\CHINA`**), change the File name to **`Users`**:

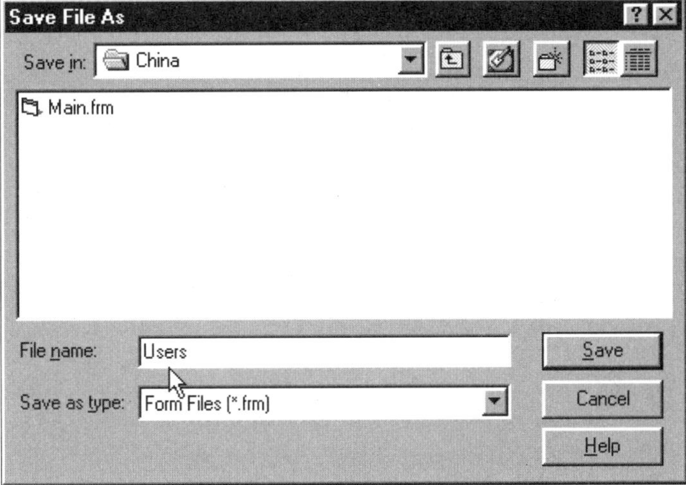


... and then click on the Save button.

**7.** Bring up the Visual Basic Project Explorer window. You should now see two forms: **`Main`** (with a **`Name`** property of **`frmMain`**), and **`Users`** (with a **`Name`** property of **`frmUsers`**):

***Discussion***

This exercise didn't seem like a big deal to most of the students, but it was an extremely important one. Adding a second form to a Visual Basic project was something that most of them had never done before, and it showed in the little details. Saving projects and forms is always an adventure in Visual Basic – and it's important to do it right the first time.

Despite my warnings, several students too quickly clicked on the Save button before changing the disk file name of the form from **frmUsers** to **Users**. This mistake meant that we needed to use Windows Explorer to rename the form disk file name. Another student inadvertently saved the new form in the wrong folder, and still another accidentally selected Add MDI Form from the Visual Basic Project menu bar instead of Add Form. As a result, the exercise that I had thought would take us about two minutes to complete took well over fifteen minutes – but in the end everything was fine.

"I'm sure you probably covered this in the introductory class," Rachel said, "but I wasn't here for that. How is the **Name** property of the form different from the file name that we specified when we saved the form?"

"The **Name** property," I replied, "is an *internal* name that Visual Basic uses to identify the form when referring to it in Visual Basic code. The disk file name that we specified in the Save File As dialog box is the name of the form file that is saved on your hard drive."

"I have a question," Valerie said. "When we clicked on the 'save' button on the toolbar, why weren't we prompted to save the project and the other form in the project?"

"Visual Basic," I said, "automatically saved both the **Main** form and the project when we clicked on the 'save' button. Visual Basic displayed the Save File As dialog box only because we had never saved our new form before. The first time you save a new form, Visual Basic wants to know both the name of the form *and* the location where you wish to save it. Once you have saved the form the first time, then the next time you click on the 'save' button, the form and project file will be saved for you automatically. Visual Basic knows to save the file to the location that you originally specified – you'll never be prompted for a name or a location again (unless the file has been marked as read-only!)."

I waited a moment to see if there were any questions.

"Aside from creating the **Users** form, and adding it to our project," Ward said, "we haven't really done anything with it. Will we be completing it today?"

"Yes we will," I answered. "In fact, here's an exercise to do exactly that."

I then distributed the following exercise:

## Exercise – Adding Controls to the Users Form

In this exercise, you'll add the controls that complete the **`Users`** form's interface.

1. Continue working with the China Shop project and the **`Users`** form.
2. Add two labels, two textboxes and a data control to the **`Users`** form. Size the form and position the controls, roughly according to the screenshot below. Remember, this is your project, and you may feel free to vary from my suggestions where you deem fit:

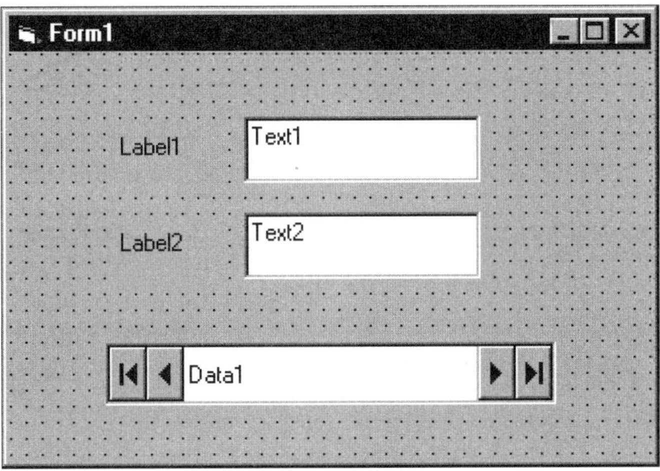


3. Use the following table to make changes to the label control currently named **`Label1`**:

| Property | Value | Comment |
|---|---|---|
| Name | lblUserID | Hungarian notation |
| Caption | User ID: | Don't forget the colon! |

4. Use the following table to make changes to the label control currently named **`Label2`**:

| Property | Value | Comment |
|---|---|---|
| Name | lblPassword | Hungarian notation |
| Caption | Password: | Don't forget the colon! |

5. Use the following table to make changes to the text box control currently named `Text1`:

| Property | Value | Comment |
|---|---|---|
| Name | txtUserID | Hungarian notation |
| Text | (blank) | Clear the property by selecting it and pressing the *Backspace* or *Delete* key |

6. Use the following table to make changes to the text box control currently named `Text2`:

| Property | Value | Comment |
|---|---|---|
| Name | txtPassword | Hungarian notation |
| Text | (blank) | Clear the property by selecting it and pressing the *Backspace* or *Delete* key |

7. Use the following table to make changes to the properties of the **`frmUsers`** form itself:

| Property | Value | Comment |
|---|---|---|
| Name | frmUsers | You did this in the *Create the Users Form* exercise earlier – double check! |
| BorderStyle | 1-Fixed Single | Prevents the user from resizing the form |
| Caption | China Shop Users | |
| Height | 3450 | Just a suggestion |
| MaxButton | False | We don't want the user maximizing the form |
| MinButton | False | We don't want the user minimizing the form either! |
| Moveable | False | We don't want the user to be able to move the form |
| StartUpPosition | 2-Center Screen | Will center the form within the Screen Object at startup |
| Width | 5055 | Just a suggestion |

Your form should now look similar to this screenshot:

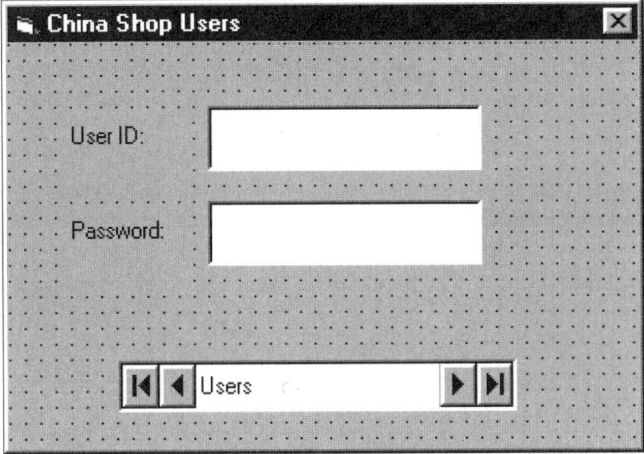


8. Save the China Shop Project by clicking on the 'save' icon on the toolbar. Remember that you won't be prompted in any way for a location to save the file to.

9. At the moment, there's no way to test the behavior of the `Users` form, as the China Shop Project's `Main` form is currently the startup form, and we haven't yet coded a way to make the `Users` form visible. However, we'll do that in the next exercise – so hang on!

#### *Discussion*

Unlike the previous exercise, where there were a number of small problems, no one seemed to have any problems with this exercise – just questions, starting with Ward: "I noticed that we haven't done anything with the data control yet," Ward said, "shouldn't we have modified some of its properties?"

"We'll do that in our final exercise of the day, Ward," I answered. "We need to take this process a step at a time. There's a lot to building a form that connects to a database – I want to make sure we don't miss anything."

"You mentioned that there's no way to test what we just did, and you're right," Steve said. "For the heck of it, I just ran the program – all that shows up is the main form – there's no way to even view the `Users` form."

"You're absolutely right, Steve," I said, "and that's the next stage in enhancing the project. We're about to modify the China Shop menu so that we can view the `Users` form."

"Didn't we say in our requirements statement that only the administrator should be able to see the `Users` form?" Melissa asked. "After all, it's the administrator who maintains the records in the `Users` table."

"That's right," I agreed, "but we won't be programming the logic into the China Shop program that allows the program to identify an administrator, for a few weeks. For now, we'll permit the Users form to be visible to everyone."

There were no other questions, and so I distributed the next exercise.

## Exercise – Modifying the China Shop's Menu

In this exercise, you'll modify the China Shop's main menu to include the menu modifications specified in the requirements statement. If you need more help in working with Visual Basic menus, check out Chapter 7 of my book, *Learn To Program With Visual Basic*.

1. Continue working with the China Shop project.
2. From the Project Explorer window, select the Main form and double-click on it to open it.
3. Select the displayed form by clicking on it with the mouse. You won't be able to open the Menu Editor if the form is not displayed and selected. Make sure the code window is **not** open.
4. Open the Menu Editor by either clicking the Menu Editor icon on the Visual Basic toolbar, or by selecting Tools| Menu Editor from the Visual Basic menu bar, or by pressing `Ctrl+E`.
5. When the Menu Editor is opened for you, you should see the China Shop's existing menu structure.
6. We need to add a top-level menu item right after the existing Preferences menu item. To add a new menu item, use your mouse to select a 'blank' menu item directly after the last one (Default) in the Menu Editor. When you do this, your screen should look like this:

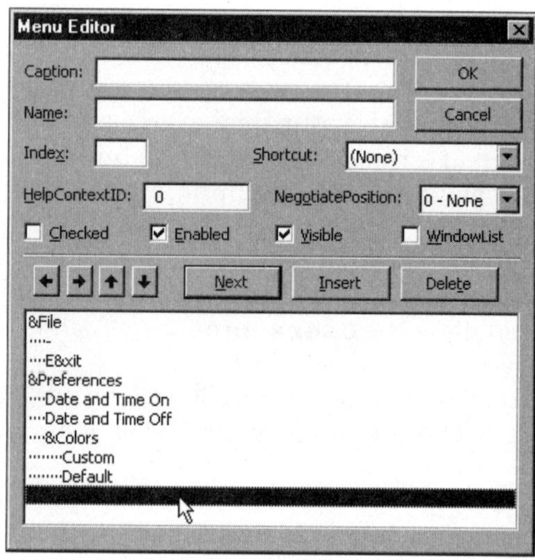

7. Use the following table as a guide to making the rest of the menu changes. A menu item listed as a **Submenu** should be indented from its parent menu item. Do this by selecting the submenu item in the Menu Editor, and then click on the Menu Editor's right arrow key.

| **Caption** | **Name** | **Submenu?** | **Parent** |
|---|---|---|---|
| Staff Functions | mnuStaff | No | |
| View/Update Users | mnuUsers | Yes | mnuStaff |
| View/Update Customers | mnuCustomers | Yes | mnuStaff |
| View/Update Inventory | mnuInventory | Yes | mnuStaff |
| View Transactions | mnuTransactions | Yes | mnuStaff |

8. When you have finished making the menu changes, your menu hierarchy should be **identical** to the screenshot. If anything is wrong, select the menu item in the menu control list box and correct it to match the settings shown here:

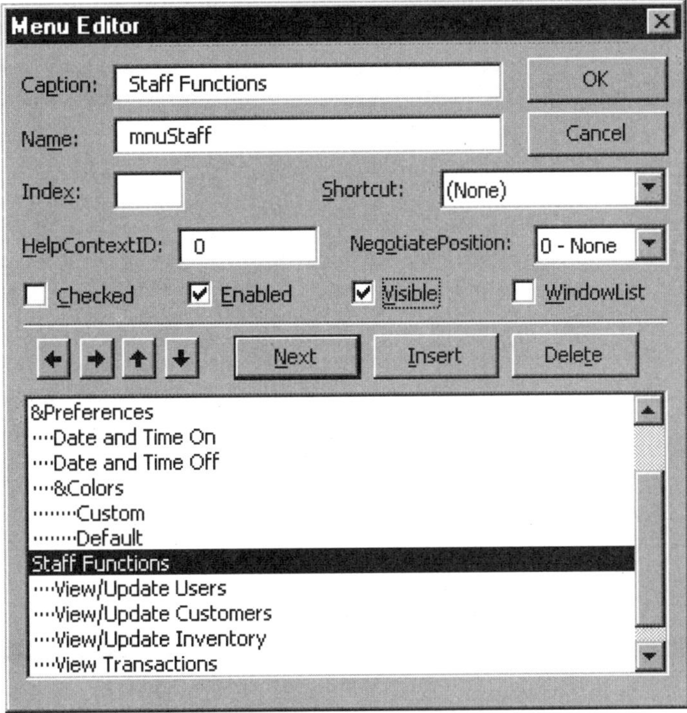


9. Click on the OK button to save your changes (if you don't, your changes will be lost!). This will close the Menu Editor.

10. Save the China Shop project by clicking on the 'save' button on the toolbar.
11. Run the program now to verify the menu structure. At this point, if you click on any of the new menu items, nothing will happen. Don't worry – it won't be long before we add code to remedy that!

***Discussion***

This was a rather tedious exercise for the class to do – it had been some time since most of them had worked with the **`Menu Editor`**, and they needed time to get themselves comfortable with it again. But it wasn't too long before everyone had the new menu structure in place. One student made the mistake of invoking the **`Menu Editor`** with the new **`Users`** form selected, and was about halfway through the process of creating a menu for the **`Users`** form before I noticed it. While I was attending to that student, the rest of the class was running the China Shop program and discovering for themselves exactly what I had warned them about: without code in the **`Click`** event procedures of the new menu items, clicking on them would do nothing!

There were no further questions, and so I distributed the following exercise:

## Exercise – Adding Code to the mnuUsers Click Event

In this exercise, you'll add code to the **`Click`** event procedure of **`mnuUsers`**. This will result in the **`Users`** form being displayed when the user clicks on the Staff/Functions | View/Update Users menu options.

1. If the China Shop project is running, stop it by clicking on the 'end' button.
2. Double-click the **`Main`** form in the Project Explorer window to open it up.
3. In design mode, click on the **`Main`** form's Staff Functions | View/Update Users menu item: the code window for the **`Click`** event procedure of **`mnuUsers`** will open.
4. Add the following highlighted code into the **`Click`** event procedure:

```
Private Sub mnuUsers_Click()

Me.Hide
frmUsers.Show

End Sub
```

5. Save the China Shop project.
6. Run the program and select Staff Functions | View/Update Users from the China Shop's menu bar. You should see the **Users** form displayed. There's only one problem now. The **Users** form, at this point anyway, doesn't really permit you to do anything useful. Worse still, when you close the **Users** form, the **Main** form doesn't reappear, and the program is just left running. Hang on – we'll take care of that next! For now, click on the 'end' button on the Visual Basic toolbar to stop the program.

***Discussion***

After completing this exercise, everyone was pretty impressed when they clicked on the View/Update Users menu item for the first time, and displayed the **Users** form – for most of them, this was something they had never done before.

"With two lines of code," I said, "we make the **Main** form invisible, and make the **Users** form appear."

"I know there are only two lines of code," Rachel said smiling, "but I have questions on both of them. What's that **Me.Hide** statement – I don't think I've ever seen that before:"

```
Me.Hide
```

"**Me** is a Visual Basic keyword that represents the name of the form from which this code is being run," I explained. "Some programmers use '**Me**' as a shortcut for the name of the current form. I like to introduce '**Me**' in my classes just so that you're aware the syntax exists. We could just as easily have written this code like this:"

```
frmMain.Hide
```

"May I presume that **Hide** is a method of the form?" Kevin asked. "I was wondering why you didn't use the **Unload** statement – I've seen that in some code at work."

"That's a fair point, Kevin," I said. "Some programmers might have used the **Unload** statement to unload the **Main** form prior to displaying the **Users** form. And you're correct – **Hide** *is* a method of the form. I prefer to use the **Hide** method over the **Unload** statement since it keeps the **Main** form loaded in memory – but *invisible*. Unloading the **Main** form doesn't make sense here, because as soon as the user closes the **Users** form, the **Main** form should be displayed again – and unloading and loading forms repeatedly is a bad idea – loading forms takes a second or two, and will make your program run slower. The rule of thumb is that if the form is likely to be used again – as our **Main** form is – don't **Unload** it, just **Hide** it. This will make your program will run faster."

"I have a question similar to Kevin's," Peter said. "I've seen code where a second form is loaded using the **Load** statement. Here you used the **Show** method instead."

"That's right, Peter," I said, "and you're also right about using the **Load** statement. We could have used the **Load** statement, like this..."

```
Load frmUsers
```

"... and the **Users** form would have been loaded into memory. But unfortunately, just by using the **Load** statement by itself, we wouldn't have been able to see it. All the **Load** statement does is load the form into memory. But unless you then either use the **Show** method of the form, or set the form's **Visible** property to **True** like this..."

```
Load frmUsers
frmUsers.Visible = True
```

"... you won't be able to see the second form."

"I can attest to that," Kevin said. "I wrote a Visual Basic project at work a while ago where I needed to load up a second form. I decided to use the **Load** statement to load up the second form, but I couldn't see it. I then spent the next two days trying to figure out what I was doing wrong. Was that frustrating! As you said, the form was loaded into memory, but I just couldn't *see* it. Finally, I set the **Visible** property of the second form to **True** by chance, and there it was!"

"So you're saying that by executing only the **Show** method of the form, in effect you are both loading the form *and* making it visible?" Valerie asked.

"That's exactly right, Valerie," I said. "One line of code is doing the work of two."

"I'm going to have to write that one down," I heard Tom say.

"Can we get back to that **Hide** method?" Rhonda asked. "Rather than use the **Hide** method on the **Main** form, could we have just set its **Visible** property to **False**?"

"Right again, Rhonda," I said. "Yes, we could have done that – functionally, there's no difference."

"Why then," Ward asked, "did you choose to execute the **Hide** method rather than set the property value?"

"If you can achieve the same end result by setting a property's value or by executing a method," I said, "the Microsoft recommendation has always been to execute the *method*. The assumption is that it will make your program more efficient, and run faster."

There were no more questions – everyone seemed anxious to get going with the remainder of the modifications to the **Users** form. I distributed the penultimate exercise of the day for them to complete.

## Exercise – Adding Code to the QueryUnload Event Procedure of frmUsers

In this exercise, you'll add code to the **QueryUnload** event procedure of **frmUsers** so that the **Main** form is redisplayed when the **Users** form is closed.

1. Make sure that the China Shop program is not running.
2. Double-click on the **Users** form in the Project Explorer window to open it up in design mode.
3. Double-click on the **Users** form to bring up the code window and key the following highlighted code into the form's **QueryUnload** event procedure. Be careful to place the code into the correct event procedure:

```
Private Sub Form_QueryUnload(Cancel As Integer, UnloadMode As Integer)

frmMain.Show

End Sub
```

4. Save the China Shop Project.
5. Run the program and select Staff Functions | View/Update Users from the China Shop's menu bar. The **Users** form should be displayed. Now close the **Users** form: this time when it closes, the **Main** China Form should reappear.

### Discussion

The only problem completing this exercise was the accidental placing of the code in the **Load** event of the **Users** form.

"The **QueryUnload** event," I explained, "is triggered whenever the user closes the form. This event procedure is the recommended place to put code that you want to execute as the form is being unloaded."

"Is the **Users** form automatically unloaded from memory whenever the user closes it?" Linda asked. "Is that why we don't need to code an **Unload** statement in the **QueryUnload** event procedure?"

"That's a good point, Linda," I said. "You're right. As soon as this event procedure ends, the form's **Unload** event is triggered, and then the form is unloaded and removed from memory."

"Did you say that the **Unload** event occurs *after* the **QueryUnload** event?" Steve asked.

"That's right," I said. "When the user closes the form, the **QueryUnload** event is triggered first. The **QueryUnload** event procedure, as you could probably see from its header, is a little like the **Validate** event of the data control: it tells us *why* the form is being unloaded. Just like the **Validate** event of the data control, the **QueryUnload** event procedure provides us with a way to cancel the **Unload** of the form by setting its **Cancel** argument to **True**."

"And the **Main** form becomes visible once again because of its **Show** method?" Melissa added.

"That's perfect, Melissa," I said. "We made the **Main** form invisible by executing its **Hide** method, and we make it visible again by using it's **Show** method."

"Not to be a nag about this," Ward said, "but what about the **Users** form? It *still* isn't doing anything. Are we going to be able to use the **Users** form to view and update **Users** in the China Shop database today – or is that something we'll do next week?"

"That's the goal of our final exercise for the day," I said. "In just a few minutes, you'll have officially 'database enabled' the China Shop project."

With that, I distributed the final exercise of the day for the class to complete.

## Exercise – Modifying frmUsers for Database Access

In this exercise, you'll modify the properties of the controls on the **Users** form to permit access to the China Shop database's **Users** table.

1. Make sure that the China Shop program is not running.
2. Open up the **Users** form in design view.
3. Use the following table to make changes to the properties of the **Data1** data control:

| Property | Value | Comment |
|---|---|---|
| Name | datUsers | Hungarian notation |
| Caption | Users | |
| DatabaseName | C:\VBFiles\China\China.mdb | Use the dialog box to select this |
| EOFAction | 2-AddNew | In order to be able to add a new record |
| RecordsetType | 0-Table | |
| RecordSource | Users | Select from the drop-down list box |

4. Save the project. Now use the following table to make changes to the properties of **txtUserID**. Be sure to make them in this order!

| Property | Value | Comment |
|---|---|---|
| DataSource | datUsers | Select from the drop-down list box |
| DataField | UserID | Select from the drop-down list box |
| MaxLength | 13 | The FieldLength for this field in the Users table |
| ToolTipText | The User's UserID | |

5. Use the following table to make changes to the properties of `txtPassword`. Be sure to make them in this order!

| Property | Value | Comment |
|---|---|---|
| DataSource | datUsers | Select from the drop-down list box |
| DataField | Password | Select from the drop-down list box |
| MaxLength | 8 | The FieldLength for this field in the Users table |
| ToolTipText | The User's Password | |

6. Save the China Shop project.
7. Run the program and select Staff Functions | View/Update Users from the China Shop's menu bar. The `Users` form should be displayed, and you should now be able to view and edit the records in the `Users` table. In fact, if you wish, you can even add a new record to the `Users` table.

#### *Discussion*

To say that everyone in the class was impressed with what they had just done would be a gross understatement. For many of the students, database enabling a Visual Basic project was the reason they had signed up for my Introductory Visual Basic class in the first place – and now they had finally done it.

"There's only one problem that I see," Ward said, "I just added a bunch of new records to the `Users` table, but there's no way to delete them. Am I missing something?"

"Don't worry, Ward," I said, "we'll take care of that in the coming weeks. The data control has no built-in support for deleting records from the recordset. We'll either need to remove the text boxes, and replace them with a DBGrid, or we'll need to provide that functionality ourselves by executing the `Delete` method of the underlying recordset – and that's a topic for next week's class."

"Ward, did you say that you were able to add records?" Rhonda said. "How did you do that?"

"Click on the 'last record' button on the data control, then click on the 'next record' button," Ward explained. "When you do that, you should see an empty record appear, with vacant text boxes for you to fill in with the information for a new record."

"That's right, Rhonda," I said, "if you click on the 'last record' button, then click on the 'next record' button, you should see something that looks like this:"

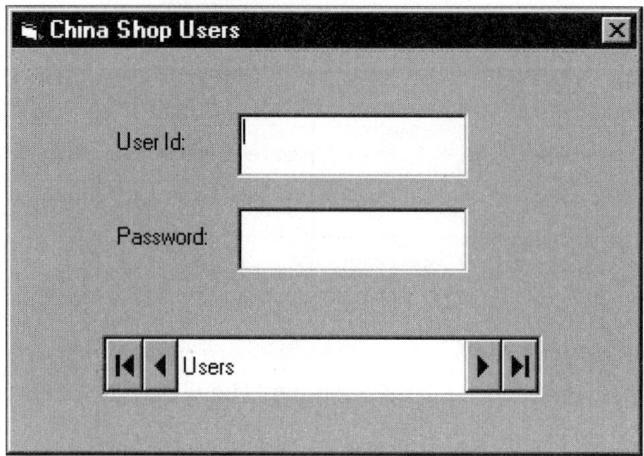


"That doesn't seem to be working for me," Rhonda said. "I don't see any empty record. I have two records, and when I click on the 'last record' button on the data control, my record pointer is still on the last record – CUSTOMERS."

I walked over to Rhonda's workstation, and watched her do exactly as Ward and I had instructed. But no luck.

I took a quick look at Rhonda's project – specifically, at the data control properties: as I had suspected, she had forgotten to set the `EOFAction` property of the data control to `2-AddNew`. It was still set on `0-Move Last`, which is why she couldn't add a new record. As soon as she changed it, she was able to successfully add new records to the `Users` table.

Rhonda was happy – and the rest of the class looked happy as well, but a bit tired. It had been a long, demanding class, and everyone had done really well to stick with it. In fact, we had gone well over our time. I thanked everyone for their great work, and dismissed the class for the day.

## Chapter Summary

In this chapter we set about 'database enabling' the China Shop project by starting to integrate the existing program with the `China` database that we created in Chapter 3. In doing this, we followed my class as they learnt about the Visual Basic controls and features we'll use to let our program work with the database. Specifically, we saw that:

- The **data control** connects our program to the database and the tables that it contains
- The data control creates a **recordset**. This is a 'virtual table' that exists in the computer's memory, and which contains the records from the underlying database table(s) that we want to view and update
- Our program reads and updates the recordset directly, and any changes to the recordset get passed through to the underlying physical tables
- We can add **bound controls** to our program's forms. These controls are linked to the database and its tables by the data control, and they allow us to display and update database data right there on the form
- The data control and the recordset each have their own properties, methods and events that our program can interact with. This gives us a rich array of functions to choose from when manipulating database data with our program

We also added a new form and menus to the China Shop program: these will enable the China Shop staff to update and maintain the data in the `China` database's `Users` table.

In this chapter, we concentrated on the properties, methods and events of the data control. In the next chapter, we're going to explore methods, events and properties of the recordset. Doing this will enrich our understanding of how the program and the database interact, and this knowledge will prepare us for further enhancement of the China Shop program.

See you in next week's class!

isual Basic Learn to Program Databas
with Visual Basic Learn to Progra
atabases with Visual Basic Learn
rogram Databases with Visual Basic Lea
o Program Databases with Visual Bas
earn to Program Databases with Visu
asic Learn to Program Databases wi
isual Basic Learn to Program Databas
with Visual Basic Learn to Progra
atabases with Visual Basic Learn
rogram Databases with Visual Basic Lea
o Program Databases with Visual Bas
earn to Program Databases with Visu
asic Learn to Program Databases wi
isual Basic Learn to Program Databas
with Visual Basic Learn to Progra
atabases with Visual Basic Learn

# Chapter 5

# More on Data Access – the Recordset

In the previous chapter we used the Visual Basic data control to gain access to the `Users` table of the China Shop's database. In this chapter, you'll learn more about the recordset that the data control generates when it connects to a database. When our program interacts with the recordset we gain amazing power and flexibility beyond the use of the data control.

A recordset is a 'virtual table' created in memory when the data control connects to a database. The recordset can be based on fields from a single table or from multiple tables, and can be viewed and updated (depending on the type of recordset used). Once the recordset has been created, your program can interact with the recordset's properties and methods, and thereby manipulate the data in the underlying tables. The recordset is a powerful mediator and messenger between our program and the database.

Here's a preview of what we'll cover in this lesson:

- We'll review the relationship between the data control and the different types of recordset
- We'll look in detail at some of the most important properties of the recordset. Specifically, we'll look at:
- Properties that help us see where we are in the recordset
- Properties that let us mark a position in the recordset and return to it
- Properties that help find specific records swiftly
- Finally, we'll continue building our enhanced China Shop project

Covering all of this ground will help us understand the recordset better – all great preparation for when we start using the recordset in conjunction with our VB program. Let's begin.

## The Recordset

When I arrived at the classroom for our fifth class, the students were all there before me, looking alert and keen. That was good: I knew that we had a lot of material to cover. I also knew from previous courses that working our way through the properties of the recordset would provide my students with an important foundation for their future learning.

"I know you're all in a hurry to get going with the China Shop project," I said, "but we still have a lot of work ahead of us. Don't forget, not only do we need to modify the China Shop project for database access, be we also need to understand the reasons behind what we're doing. In today's class, we're going to discuss the recordset that is generated when the data control connects to a database. In fact, we're going to spend the bulk of the session discussing recordset properties, and towards the end of the class, we'll make a few more modifications to the China Shop project that will set us up nicely for completing the `Login` form next week."

"It's going to take us two weeks to code the `Login` form?" Ward asked. "Is it that complicated a process?"

"The recordset is a pretty complicated object," I said. "It will take us two weeks to discuss its properties and methods, and we need to have an understanding of both of those before we write code for the `Login` form."

## DAO and ADO

Peter raised his hand with a question.

"When I arrived at work last Monday, I was really excited," he said. "I immediately went down the hall to see a Visual Basic programmer friend of mine who works in the Information Technology department to tell her about the database work we had done last Saturday with the China Shop project. But as soon as I mentioned that we had used the built-in Visual Basic data control, she cringed. She told me that she never uses the data control to connect to a database – instead, she uses something called **Data Access Objects (DAO)**. Furthermore, she said that if you were teaching us to use any type of data control, it should be the **ActiveX Data Objects (ADO)** data control – **not** the DAO data control, which she said was the standard data control that we were using."

"Your friend in the IT department," I said, "undoubtedly has more experience using Visual Basic than anyone in this class – besides me of course – and she's expressing an opinion about using the data control that many experienced programmers share."

"Why is that?" Kate asked.

"Well," I replied, "some experienced programmers – especially those who started programming with Visual Basic using its early versions – tend to shy away from using the data control. Early Visual Basic versions came with a data control that really dragged down the performance of a program, and so programmers did just about anything they could do to avoid using it."

"I thought you *needed* to use the data control to connect to a database?" Rhonda asked.

"There are alternative ways of connecting to the database," I said. "As we saw last week, when the data control connects to a database it creates a recordset. It's also possible to create a recordset without using a data control, and this is what Peter's friend is alluding to."

"Isn't that what you mentioned we'll be doing later on in the course?" Dave asked.

"Exactly," I answered. "It's possible to bypass the use of the data control by using DAO – but before we get to that point, we need to learn more about recordsets. I'm sure even Peter's friend would admit that she learned to use the data control first – and then learned how to bypass it by using DAO."

"What about the issue of the **ActiveX Data Object (ADO)** data control?" Blaine said. "Is that data control better to use than the one we're using?"

"Whether the ADO data control is better is arguable," I said. "We're using the DAO data control in this class, and it's the older of the two data controls. I prefer to teach Visual Basic database techniques using this data control because it's very simple to use – which is what's important when you are first learning – and it currently has a larger established user base than the ADO data control."

"That could be important if we go looking for a Visual Basic programming job after this class," Valerie said. "There are probably more companies with existing applications written using the DAO data control – at least at the moment."

"That may well be true," I said. "But regardless, the great thing about the DAO data control is that everything you learn about it is applicable to the ADO data control as well."

"So if we're hired by a company using the ADO data control," Dave said, "what we've learned about the DAO data control is pretty portable."

"That's right, Dave," I said.

## The Data Control and the Recordset – Revisited

Rhonda had a question.

"The data control and recordsets – I know I keep getting these two confused," she said. "But aren't the data control and the recordset the same thing?"

"I'm confused too," Blaine interjected, "It seems to me that you're going out of your way to make a distinction between the data control and the recordset, and between the recordset and the underlying database."

"I can understand your confusion," I said. "especially when you're relatively new to database programming and haven't yet internalized the ideas. The data control and the recordset *are* different. The data control is something that you place on your Visual Basic form. When you start your Visual Basic program and the form is loaded, the data control connects to a database, based on the values specified in the data control's `DatabaseName`, `RecordsetType`, and `RecordSource` properties. This connection then creates a recordset – a virtual database table of sorts, based on the physical tables in the physical database – in the computer's memory. And the bound controls display the data from the recordset."

I redisplayed a picture that I'd shown in a previous lesson:

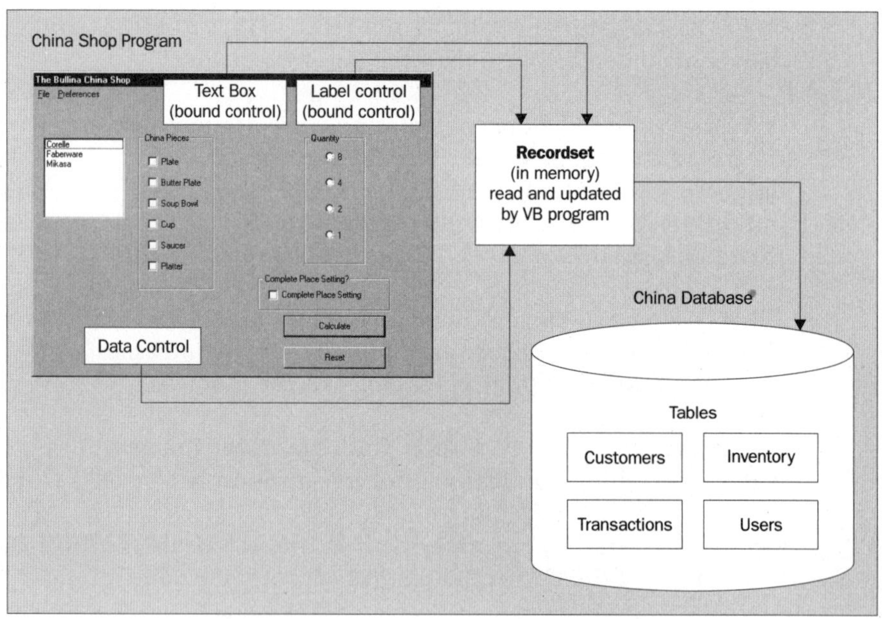


"I believe I remember reading," Dave said, "that depending upon the type of recordset created, the values we see in the bound fields may or may not be the current values in the database. Is that right?"

"That's absolutely right, Dave," I said. "The up-to-dateness – or otherwise – of the records in the recordset depends on the type of recordset that we create."

## Recordset Types – a quick Review

"Many beginners," I went on, "make the mistake of believing that the values they see in the bound controls on the form are always the *current* values in the database."

"Wait a minute," Rhonda said, perturbed. "Are you saying that the values in the bound controls are not necessarily current?"

"That's right, Rhonda," I said. "In some cases, the recordset created from the data control is just a 'frozen in time picture' of the database at the time the connection was made to the database."

"Ah, yes!" Mary said. "You mentioned that type of recordset last week. That would be the `Snapshot` kind of `RecordsetType`, wouldn't it?"

"Excellent," I said. "If you create a `Snapshot` type of recordset, the records in the recordset created from the `Snapshot` could be changed *seconds* after you make the connection to the database – and you would never know it."

"That's not very comforting," Rhonda said. "But who in the world would be changing the records in the database after we build a recordset?"

"Other users," I answered.

"How so?" Chuck asked.

"Don't forget," I said, "the China Shop program is a stand-alone application – that means just **one** user is expected to use it at one time: there's just a single PC in the China Shop. But you never know – Joe Bullina could call us a few months from now and tell us that he'd like to have an additional PC set up in the shop to provide price quotes to his customer. All at once, a stand-alone application becomes a multi-user application – one in which more than one user may be accessing the China Shop database simultaneously."

"That's right," Kathy said. "Most of our major applications at work are installed on our Local Area Network, and are multi-user programs."

"I guess I developed tunnel vision," Rhonda said. "After programming the China Shop program for just a single user, I had never considered multi-user access. I see what you mean now – whether just one user or multiple users will be accessing the program does impact your decision as to the type of recordset you will create."

"That's right," I said. "As soon as you start to add database functionality to your program, you need to start to think about the possibility of multi-user access. With more than one person using the program simultaneously, it's very possible that your program may create a recordset based on the current view of the database – and then another user might change data in the underlying database. This can have a severe impact on your program."

"Can you give us an example?" Steve asked.

"Sure thing, Steve," I said. "Let's say you write a program that allows User A, working on PC number 1, to make decisions based on the current quantity of inventory in a database. Your program builds a recordset that informs User A that the current quantity of Part ABC is 3 – but while User A is viewing this recordset, User B at PC number 2 processes a telephone sale for the last 3 pieces of Part ABC. A properly-written program should alert User A that Part ABC has just gone out of stock."

"I see," Steve said. "Can we do that in Visual Basic? That is, alert the user that something along these lines has happened?"

"We can," I said, "provided we create a recordset that is kept informed as things change."

"That isn't always the case?" Rachel asked.

"No, not always," I said. "For instance, once the `Snapshot` recordset is built, you could delete every record from the table on which the recordset is based, and the user viewing the `Snapshot` would never know it."

"So there's no update of the `Snapshot` recordset if the underlying table changes." Tom said. "What good is this type of recordset, then?"

"A `Snapshot` recordset is fine for retrieving certain types of data," I said. "For instance, data that you know for certain won't change while the user is viewing the recordset is a perfect candidate for a `Snapshot` type recordset. For example, we'll use a `Snapshot` recordset in a few weeks to retrieve the names of the brands of china from the `Inventory` table in the `China` database. Once we have those brand names in the recordset, we'll use those names to populate the china brands list box on the user interface."

"If I recall," Kevin said, "at the moment those brands are being read from the `Prices.txt` disk file. That file is rarely changed– and if it is changed, it's done when the program isn't running."

"That's right, Kevin," I said. "We'll modify the code in the `Load` procedure of the `Main` form to read the china brands from the `China` database instead of the disk file – and it makes perfect sense to use a `Snapshot` recordset in this instance."

"You implied that there's another reason we would use a `Snapshot` recordset," Ward said.

"That's right," I said. "And that's to ensure that any changes made to the underlying database while your program is using the `Snapshot` recordset have no impact on any decision the program or the user may make."

"Are all the recordset types like this?" Valerie asked. "Do *any* of them reflect the current values in the database?'

"I think it may be best if I just display a summary chart on the projector," I said. "Take a look at this:"

| | Dynaset | Snapshot | Table |
|---|---|---|---|
| Updatable? | Yes | No | Yes |
| Retrieve data from more than one table? | Yes | Yes | No |
| See other user's additions? | Only if Requery Method is executed | No | Yes – as soon as you move the record pointer |
| See other user's updates? | Yes – as soon as you move the record pointer | No | Yes – as soon as you move the record pointer |
| See other user's deletions? | Notified if you try to access the deleted record | No | Yes – as soon as you move the record pointer |

"To interpret this chart properly," I said, "we need to bear in mind the types of actions that can be performed against the underlying database while our program is working with a recordset built from it. First, records can be added to the database. Secondly, records can be updated. And finally, records can be deleted."

"I guess that ideally," Dave said, "we'd like to be told – using a message box, for example – whether any one of those actions has taken place against the records we are viewing in the recordset."

"That's well put, Dave," I said. "That would be the ideal, but as you can see from the chart I've prepared for you, that's only the case with the `Table` type recordset. And even then, the records in the recordset are updated only when the record pointer is moved."

"Does that mean," Melissa said, "that if we are viewing records in a DBGrid using a `Table` type recordset in the data control (like we did last week), then any changes made to the database will be reflected in the DBGrid?"

"That's right, Melissa," I said, "but you'll only see the changes when you move your record pointer."

"The `Table` type recordset appears to be good at keeping us abreast of changes in the underlying database," Kevin said, " the `Snapshot` seems to be the weakest."

"You're right, Kevin," I said, "the `Table` type recordset automatically provides you with updated information about the underlying database whereas the `Snapshot` gives you none! In between the two, we have the `Dynaset` – which automatically displays changes to records that have been edited in the underlying database as soon as you move your record pointer. However, the `Dynaset` doesn't automatically show you any new records that may have been added to the database, and only lets you know that records appearing in the recordset have been deleted from the underlying database if you try and access them."

"All of this talk of multi-user access is scaring me," Rhonda said. "Do we really need to be concerned about this for the China Shop project?"

"No, we don't," I said. "The China Shop project is strictly a single user application – for now. It isn't likely that a beginner will write a database program that is anything but a single user program. But remember this: in the fast-paced world of Visual Basic, beginners don't stay beginners very long. The next logical step forward is to write multi-user database programs where many people are updating the database at any given time – so you should be aware of the strengths and limitations of each type of recordset."

I paused, waiting for any further questions. There were none, so I continued.

"Last week," I said, "we discussed the data control's properties, methods and events. Today we'll be concentrating on recordset **properties**, and next week we'll discuss recordset **methods**."

"Did you forget about recordset events?" Linda asked.

"Actually, Linda," I said, "there are no recordset events – recordsets have properties and methods, but there are no events to which a recordset responds."

## The Recordset's Properties

"We won't be examining *every* property of the recordset," I said, "but we will be looking at quite a few. Remember, when we talk about a recordset, we can be talking about any one of three different types – `Dynaset`, `Snapshot` or `Table` type. Not all of the properties that we will discuss today apply to all three types of recordsets. Not only that, but there are some properties of the recordset that can only be used when the recordset is opened using a Data Access Object – and **not** when using the data control. I hope this chart will help keep things straight for you."

I displayed the following chart on the classroom projector and distributed a copy to everyone in the class:

### *Recordset Properties*

| Property | Dynaset? | Snapshot? | Table? | Comments |
|---|---|---|---|---|
| AbsolutePosition | | | No | |
| BOF | | | | |
| BookMark | | | | |
| Bookmarkable | | | | |
| DateCreated | No | No | | Returns a date and time |
| EOF | | | | |
| Index | No | No | | |
| LastModified | | No | | Returns a bookmark |
| LastUpdated | No | No | | Returns a date and time |
| NoMatch | | | | |
| PercentPosition | | | | |
| RecordCount | | | | For a Dynaset or recordset, this value is only accurate if you have moved to the end of the recordset. |
| Updatable | | | | |

"Let's use this chart as our guide," I said, "as we discuss the properties of the recordset."

"So why aren't we going to discuss all recordset properties?" asked Melissa. "Are you holding out on us?"

"No, Melissa," I laughed. "Some of those extra properties are way beyond the introductory nature of this course – and remember, some of them don't apply to recordsets created using the data control."

"And the other kinds of recordsets that those properties **do** apply to," Tom said, "are those the ones created using data access objects?"

"Exactly, Tom," I agreed, "and that's a topic we'll look at a little towards the end of the course."

I waited a moment to see if anyone else had any questions or comments.

"Last week," I said, "we developed a demonstration program to illustrate the data control by placing a data control and a DBGrid on a form, and using the data control to connect to the `Users` table in the `China` database. Let's do something similar this week – but this time, instead of using the China Shop database, let's connect to the `Titles` table of the `Biblio` database – it has significantly more records in it, which will make today's demonstrations more effective."

To get the demonstration underway, I created a new VB project and placed a data control on the form, along with a DBGrid.

> **Don't forget that some versions of Visual Basic don't supply you with the DBGrid control. If you have the control, then feel free to run these demonstrations yourself. If you don't have it, you can just follow along with the demonstrations as I run through them.**

I continued by setting the `DatabaseName` property of the data control to access the `Biblio` database: we saw how to do this in Chapter 2. Next, I set the `RecordsetType` property of the data control to `Dynaset`, the `RecordSource` property to access the `Titles` table, and the `EOFAction` property to `2-Add New`. I then set the `DataSource` property of the `DBGrid` to `Data1` and the `AllowAddNew` property to `True`,and then ran the program. The following screen was displayed:

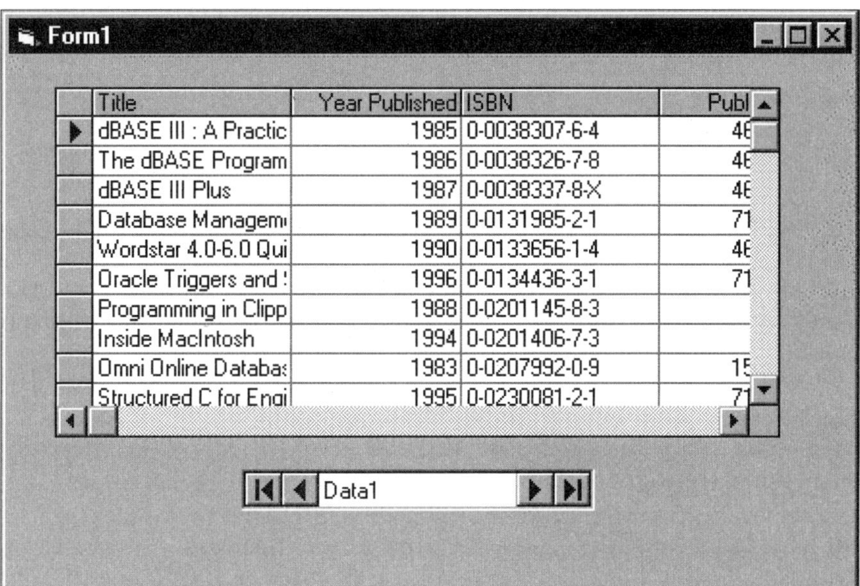


"Consider what's happened," I said, "when I've clicked on the 'run' button. The form containing the data control was loaded, and at that point a connection to the database was made, resulting in a **Dynaset** recordset being created. This recordset contains all of the records in the underlying **Titles** table of the **Biblio** database. We'll continue to work with this form and grid throughout the rest of the day as we discuss the properties of the recordset. Let's start with these three – **AbsolutePosition**, **RecordCount**, and **PercentPosition**."

## *The AbsolutePosition, RecordCount, and PercentPosition Properties*

"These first three properties of the recordset are pretty interesting," I began. "The **AbsolutePosition**, **RecordCount**, and **PercentPosition** properties give your program basic information about the record pointer, and the position of the current record within the recordset. But I must warn you – not all of these properties operate on every type of recordset. We'll get to that in a minute."

"Did you say *current record*?" Rachel asked.

"Yes, Rachel," I said. "A few weeks ago we were viewing records in Access using the datasheet view. Do you remember the icon in the left hand column of the datasheet grid?"

"Yes, I think so," Rachel answered. "Didn't it look like an arrowhead?"

"That right," I said:

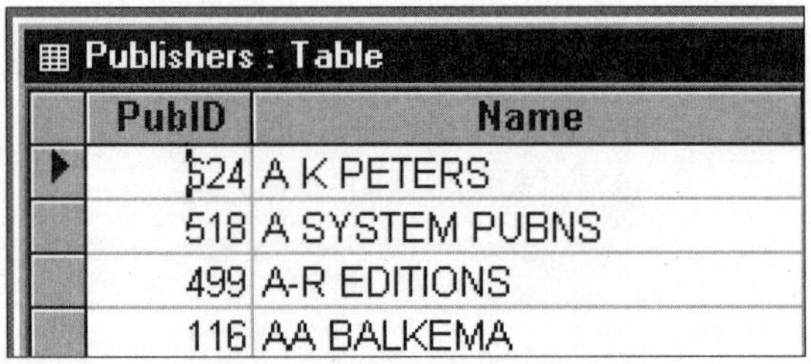

Publishers : Table

| | PubID | Name |
|---|---|---|
| ▶ | 524 | A K PETERS |
| | 518 | A SYSTEM PUBNS |
| | 499 | A-R EDITIONS |
| | 116 | AA BALKEMA |

"That icon," I went on, "indicates the row that contains the current record. In the same way, a recordset can also have a current record, even though the recordset is a transient object maintained in the computer's memory."

"What's the significance of the current record?" Ward asked.

"With recordsets," I answered, "the idea of the current record is highly significant, because we can perform operations on the current record through code, without actually having to see the record in front of us on the screen. The concept of the current record is vitally important, because so many recordset operations take place on it. For instance, next week we'll examine the `Delete` method of the recordset, which operates on the current record. It's important, therefore, to have a good understanding of the current record, and those properties and methods which operate on it."

I waited to see if I had lost anyone before I continued.

"The recordset's `AbsolutePosition` property sets or returns the **relative record number** of a recordset object's current record. However, this property will **not** operate on a `Table` type recordset."

"When you say it won't operate, what does that mean in practice?" Ward asked.

"Unfortunately, Ward," I answered, "if you try to refer to it in a `Table` type recordset, your program will bomb – so you must be careful."

"You mentioned the *relative record* in your definition of `AbsolutePosition`," Peter said, "what exactly do you mean by relative record number?"

"**Relative record number** just means that the record number is zero-based," I replied. "The first record in the recordset has an `AbsolutePosition` value of 0, the second record 1 and so forth. We can easily use the Immediate window to illustrate the `AbsolutePosition` property."

I paused the still-running program by clicking on the 'break' button on the Visual Basic toolbar, and typed '? Data1.' into the Immediate window:

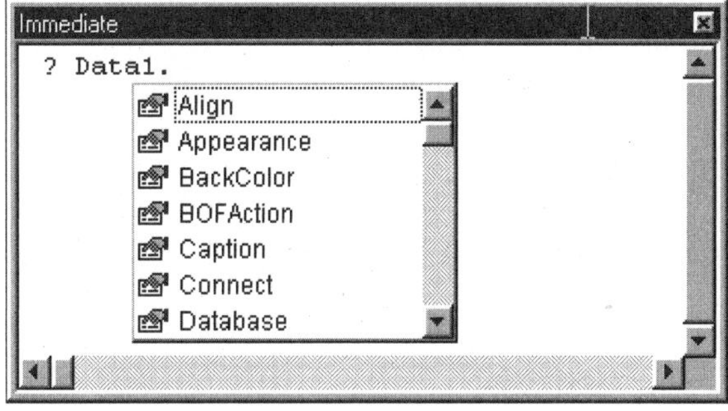


As soon as I typed ? Data1. into the Immediate window, I paused to let the class see what was happening.

"Can anyone tell me what these names are," I asked, "that have shown up in the `AutoList` members drop-down list box?"

"They look like the properties of the data control," Mary said. "At least I think so."

"You're right, Mary," I said. "We talked about some of them last week. Now everyone watch carefully when I scroll down through the list a little bit."

I did exactly that, scrolling through the members in the list box until the following screenshot was displayed on the classroom projector:

"There's that recordset you keep talking about," Rhonda said. "It looks like it's a property of the data control, doesn't it?"

"It may look that way," I said, "but watch what happens if I now hit the *tab* key to accept Recordset, and then type a period."

I did exactly that, with the following result:

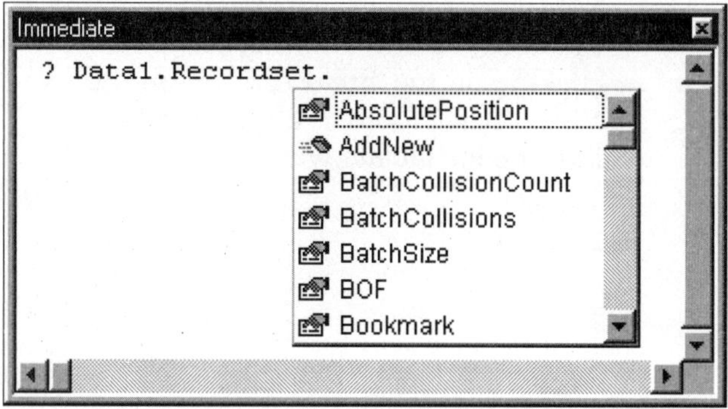


"Wow," Peter said. "You pressed the period and a whole bunch of other properties and methods showed up. I don't think I've ever seen anything like that before."

"What is happening," I said, "is that the `AutoList` members drop-down list box is confirming what I've been saying all along: the recordset is a separate 'object' that is generated by the data control. That's the significance of the **two dots** here. In the course I'm teaching next semester on Visual Basic objects, you'll see that what we have here is an **Object hierarchy**: that is, the data control is an object that creates another object – the recordset, which itself has properties and methods. That's why when I typed the period after the word Recordset, a list of properties and methods pertaining to the recordset object was displayed."

"So the `AbsolutePosition` property," Dave said, "is a property of the **recordset** object, which itself is like a 'child' of the data control object?"

"Right you are, Dave," I answered.

"Can you show us that again," Valerie asked, referring to the display of the `AutoList` members in the Immediate window. "I think you went a little too fast for me."

"I'd be glad to," I said as I repeated the process again in the Immediate window, one character at a time, allowing Visual Basic to `AutoList` first the properties and methods of the data control, and then the recordset.

Valerie and the others seemed to catch on better the second time through.

"Are there other object hierarchies like this in Visual Basic?" Ward asked.

"Yes," I replied, "there are some that we'll discuss when we cover DAO later in the course."

"I'm anxious," Rhonda said, "to see what the value of the `AbsolutePosition` property actually is. Can you please hit the *Enter* key?"

"Sorry, I almost forgot about that," I said, and pressed the *Enter* key. Here's what happened:

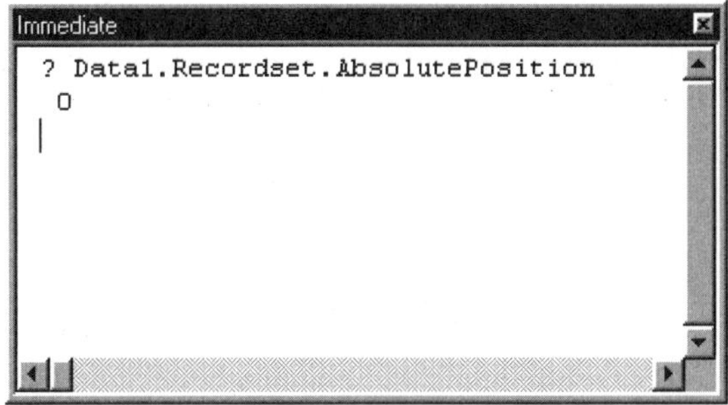


"Zero," Mary asked. "Our record pointer is positioned on the first record in the `DBGrid`. Shouldn't the `AbsolutePosition` property be `1`?"

"Don't forget, Mary," I said, "that the `AbsolutePosition` property is **zero-based**. The first record in the recordset will always have an `AbsolutePosition` property of 0."

"That's right," Rhonda said, "just about everything in a computer begins with zero, doesn't it?"

"For the most part, yes," I said. "Let's try this out on another record in the recordset."

I then resumed the program by clicking on the 'run' button, clicked on the 'last record' navigation button on the data control and then, after pausing the program again, typed the identical statement into the Immediate window: this time, the `AbsolutePosition` property showed up as 8568:

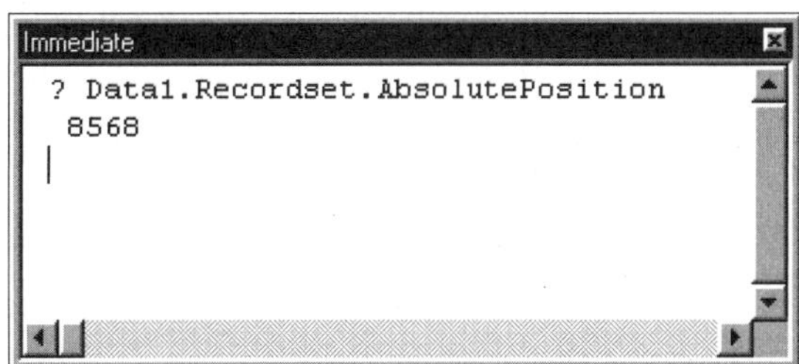


"That means that there are 8,569 records in the table, doesn't it?" Steve asked. "If the last record in the recordset has an `AbsolutePosition` property of 8,568 then, since we started with 0, there must be 8,569 records in the recordset."

> **Don't fret if the number of records in your version of the Biblio database doesn't match mine – there are different versions of the Biblio database in existence, with subtle differences between them.**

"That's exactly right, Steve," I said. "Even better, there's a property of the recordset that can tell us the **exact** number of records in a recordset – it's the `RecordCount` property. Watch this."

I then typed another statement into the Immediate window: ? Data1.Recordset.RecordCount. This returned the following result:

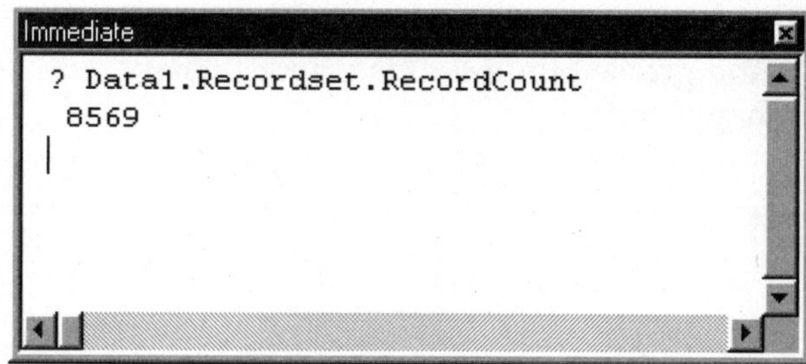


"Is the **RecordCount** property off-limits to the **Table** type recordset, like the **AbsolutePosition** property?" Rachel asked.

"No," I answered, " it's perfectly OK to use the **RecordCount** property with a **Table** type recordset. In fact, of all the properties of the recordset we'll discuss today, *only* the **AbsolutePosition** property may **not** be used on a **Table** type recordset."

"It's a shame," Kevin said, "that the data control doesn't display the total number of records in the recordset, and the current record pointer value like Access does in the datasheet view."

"You raise a good point, Kevin," I said. "Even though the data control *itself* doesn't display that information by default, there's no reason that we can't display that information ourselves. All we need to do is place code in the **Reposition** event procedure of the data control. The **Reposition** event is fired when the record pointer gets moved. Here's the code..."

I then stopped the program and typed the following code into the **Reposition** event procedure of the data control:

```
Private Sub Data1_Reposition()

Data1.Caption = Data1.Recordset.AbsolutePosition + 1 & " of " &
      ↳Data1.Recordset.RecordCount

End Sub
```

"This code," I said, "should display the current values for the **AbsolutePosition** and **RecordCount** properties via the data control's **Caption** property. Watch this..."

I then ran the program, with the following result:

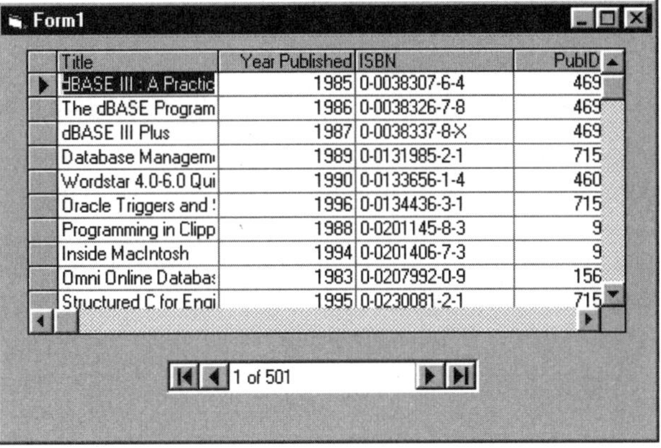


"Oops," Ward said. "I'd say there's something wrong there. It looks like the current record number is correct, but that record count is definitely wrong. We don't have 501 records in the recordset – we have 8,569!"

"You're correct, Ward," I said. "In fact, if you check the recordset properties chart that distributed a little earlier, you'll notice that I have a comment about the accuracy of the `RecordCount` property included in the comments column."

"I see it," Tom said. "The comments say that for a `Dynaset` or `Snapshot`, the `RecordCount` property is accurate only if you have first navigated to the **end** of the recordset."

"You're absolutely right, Tom," I said. "For a `Dynaset` or a `Snapshot`, the `RecordCount` property is only accurate if you have first moved to the *very* end of the recordset. The easiest way to do that is to use the `MoveLast` method of the recordset, something we'll look at in more detail next week. Take a look at this code."

I stopped the program again and placed this code into the `Initialize` event procedure of the form. Placing the code here would mean that it would be executed straight away when the program started:

```
Private Sub Form_Initialize()

Data1.Recordset.MoveLast
Data1.Recordset.MoveFirst

End Sub
```

"We'll look at both of these recordset methods next week," I said. "Executing them is the code equivalent of clicking on the 'last record' navigation button on the data control, and then on the 'first record' button. Once we move to the end of the recordset, we establish an accurate value for the **RecordCount** property. Then we execute the **MoveFirst** method to position the record pointer back to the first record in the recordset – which is what the user would expect to happen when the DBGrid is first displayed."

I re-ran the program, and this time the values displayed in the **Caption** property of the data control were correct:

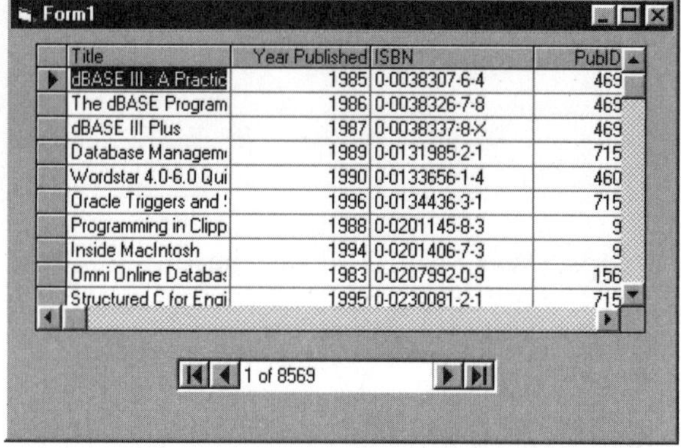


As I clicked my way through the records in the **DBGrid**, I could see from the looks on the faces of my students that the recordset properties were already popular.

"I love the dynamic way the data control's caption is changing," Blaine said. "Does the **Reposition** event procedure take place each time the record pointer changes?"

"Not quite, Blaine," I said. "To be really precise, the **Reposition** event procedure is triggered **after** the record pointer moves."

"Aha," said Melissa, "that's why the **Reposition** event procedure is a better choice than the **Validate** event procedure. I just placed your code in the **Validate** procedure, and I can see that the record pointer is always '1 behind'."

"Yes," I agreed, "that's because – as you imply – the **Validate** procedure runs *before* the record pointer changes position. Another point to note is that the display in the data control's caption only changes when you *click* your way through the records: you'll find that the display doesn't change if you use the vertical scroll bar. That's because using the scroll bar doesn't move the record pointer, meaning that the **Reposition** event doesn't get fired."

I waited to see if there were any other questions.

"I may be missing something here," Rachel said, "but why are we adding 1 to the value of the **AbsolutePosition** property of the recordset?"

"That's because the first record is record number 0," Rhonda interjected.

"Excellent, Rhonda," I replied. "That's exactly right. We need to add 1 to the value of `AbsolutePosition` because the `AbsolutePosition` property is zero-based. But notice that we didn't add 1 to the `RecordCount` property: as that property is not zero-based we can just display its value in the data control's caption."

"Will we be able to do this with our data controls in the China Shop project?" Lou asked.

"Yes, Lou," I confirmed, "provided that our recordset type is **not** a `Table` type recordset. Unfortunately, if you check the properties chart I distributed earlier, you'll see that the `AbsolutePosition` property is not a valid property of the `Table` type recordset. In fact, let me show you what happens if you change the data control's `RecordsetType` from a `Dynaset` to a `Table` type recordset."

Top demonstrate this, I stopped the program, brought up the data control's properties window, and changed the `RecordsetType` from `Dynaset` to `Table`.

"Let's run the program now," I said, "and see what happens."

I clicked on the run button, and:

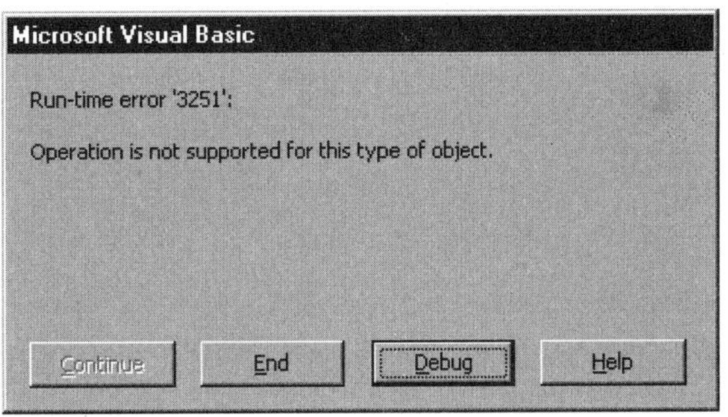


"Oops!" I heard Kathy say. "Bad news. All because the recordset type is `Table`?"

"That's right, Kathy," I said. "This is something that you'll need to bear in mind if you ever want to work with the `AbsolutePosition` property of a recordset."

"So we may not be able to display the current record number in the data control's `Caption`?" Lou asked.

"Correct," I answered, " unless the recordset is either a `Dynaset` or a `Snapshot`."

"Are most recordsets `Table` types?" Peter asked.

"I would bet, Peter," I replied, "that most recordsets are actually `Dynasets`. When we choose our recordset type, we should do so with a good reason. The main advantage of a `Table` type recordset is the ability to use the `Seek` method of a recordset. The `Seek` method is a very fast method for locating an individual record in a recordset, and only the `Table` type recordset supports it."

"But," Kevin said, "I remember from last week that we can still locate records in a recordset if it's `Dynaset` or `Snapshot`, by using `Find` instead of `Seek`. It's just slower, right?"

"Absolutely right," I said, "we discussed this in the previous lesson."

"In the China Shop project, will we be using many `Table` type recordsets?" Valerie asked.

"I believe we'll only have one `Table` type recordset," I answered, "and that will be associated with the data control we place on the `Login` form. Most of the other recordsets will be `Dynasets`, with one `Snapshot` thrown in for good measure. That means we should be able to display a caption similar to this one in the data controls of the China Shop project."

"That's great!" Mary said, "I don't know about anyone else, but I think the display of the current record number and record count is pretty cool – it looks really professional."

"Is it possible," Ward asked, "to use the `AbsolutePosition` property to return to a record once the user has left it and moved on somewhere else in the recordset?"

"That's a good question, Ward," I said, "and I think I know what you're getting at. In other words, if you want to move to record number 4,000 in the recordset, can you position the record pointer to that record quickly?"

"That's exactly what I mean," Ward replied.

"The answer," I said, "is yes. If you know the specific record number of the record that you wish to move to, all you need to do is set the value of the recordset's `AbsolutePosition` property to equal that record number – and the record pointer will move directly to that record. Let me demonstrate."

I changed the `RecordsetType` of the data control back to a `Dynaset` (remember, I had changed it to `Table` to cause the program to bomb in the previous demonstration) – and added a command button to the form. I change the command button's `Caption` property to `Move to record #`, and then placed the following code in the command button's `Click` event procedure:

```
Private Sub Command1_Click()

Dim varRecordNumber As Variant

varRecordNumber = InputBox("To which record do you wish to move?")

Data1.Recordset.AbsolutePosition = varRecordNumber - 1

End Sub
```

"This code," I said, "will prompt the user for a record number in an input box and assign that number to the variable `varRecordNumber`..."

```
varRecordNumber = InputBox("To which record do you wish to move?")
```

"...then the code will subtract 1 from the value that's entered and set the recordset's `AbsolutePosition` property to equal to that number:"

```
Data1.Recordset.AbsolutePosition = varRecordNumber - 1
```

"Let's see what happens when we tell this program we want to move to record number 4,000."

I ran the program, clicked on the command button, and entered the value 4000 into the input box:

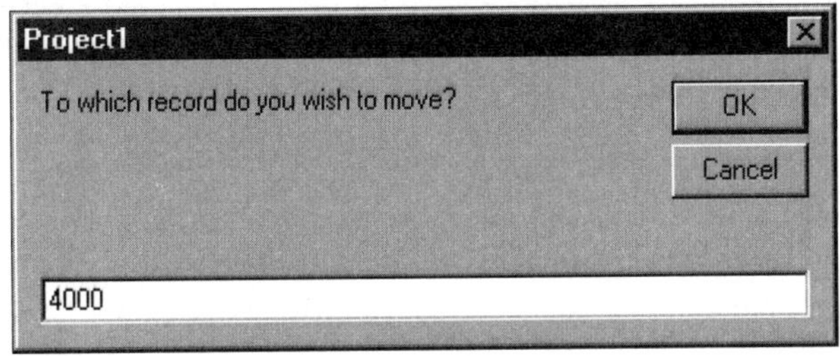

Then I clicked on the OK button and – hey presto! – the record pointer moved immediately to record number 4,000:

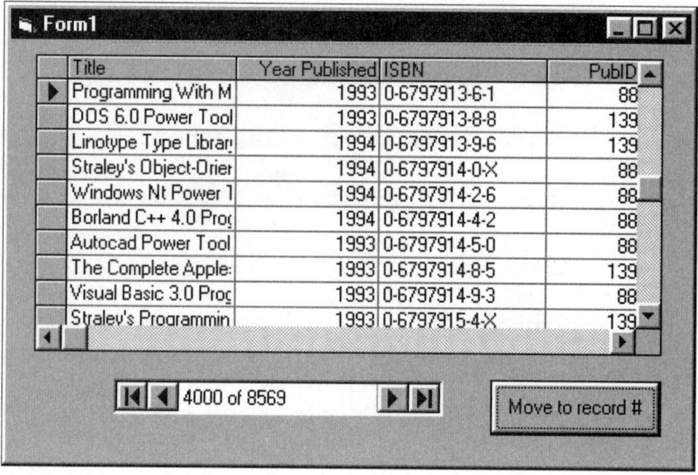

"I'm impressed!" Rhonda said. "But this time, instead of just *reading* the value of the **AbsolutePosition** property, we're *setting* it, causing the recordset's record pointer to move directly to that record. That's great."

"That's a fine analysis, Rhonda," I said.

"What about those **Table** recordsets?" Steve asked. "Does the fact that a **Table** type recordset doesn't support the **AbsolutePosition** property prevent us from doing something similar with them?"

"That's a great question, Steve," I replied. "Since the **Table** type recordset doesn't have the **AbsolutePosition** property, we can't use this technique to move to a particular record. However, there is *another* technique that we can use that will work with every type of recordset – and that's to use the recordset's **BookMark** property: as the name suggests, this allows you to mark a particular record and come back to it later. We'll examine that technique in just a few minutes. First, let's take a look at the **PercentPosition** property."

Steve nodded.

"OK then," I continued. "The **PercentPosition** property will give us an approximate percentage figure for the location of the current record based on the total number of records in the recordset. For instance, if a recordset contains 100 records, and the current record pointer is on record number 5, the value of the **PercentPosition** property will be 5. I should mention here that the vertical scrollbar on the DBGrid in the program I've been demonstrating gives you the same kind of information visually. Let's display the value of the **PercentPosition** property in the Immediate window."

I then dragged the `DBGrid`'s scrollbar until it was about halfway through the recordset (actually, record number 4,042), then paused the program and entered the following statement into the Immediate window:

```
? Data1.Recordset.PercentPosition
```

When I pressed *Enter*, we saw this result:

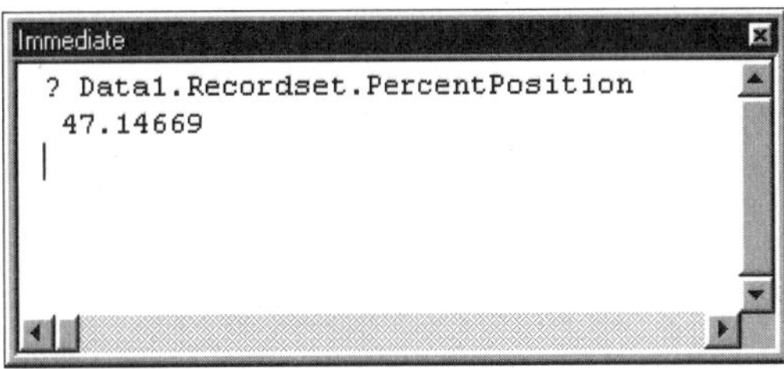


"That's pretty close to halfway through the recordset," Ward said.

"So this means this record – number 4,042 – is just over 47% of the way through the recordset?" Kathy asked.

"That's right, Kathy," I said.

With that, I concluded our discussion of properties that indicate to us where we are in the recordset, and moved on to the recordset's `BOF` and `EOF` properties.

### *The BOF and EOF Properties*

"Does anyone remember what the `BOF` and `EOF` properties of the recordset represent?" I asked.

"I think," Rhonda said, "that the **BOF** and **EOF** are those invisible 'records' at the beginning and end of a recordset that we discussed last week in connection with the `BOFAction` and `EOFAction` properties."

"And I bet that the `BOF` and `EOF` properties of a recordset," Mary added, "let us know if our record pointer is at the BOF or EOF respectively."

"Excellent, both of you," I said. "That's exactly right. BOF and EOF are Boolean properties, and `BOF` is `True` if the record pointer of the recordset is at the invisible BOF record, and `EOF` is `True` if the record pointer of the recordset is at the invisible EOF record. By the way, if both the `BOF` and `EOF` properties of the recordset are `True`, that means that the recordset is empty."

**If the values of the BOF and EOF properties are both True, the recordset is empty.**

"Is it possible to create an empty recordset?" Dave asked.

"By all means it is," I said. "For instance, if a table exists, but has no records, and we connect to it using the data control, the resultant recordset will have no records."

I waited to see if there were any questions before proceeding.

"Let's use the Immediate Window," I said, "to work with these properties a little bit."

I reran the existing demonstration program, and clicked on the 'last record' button on the data control:

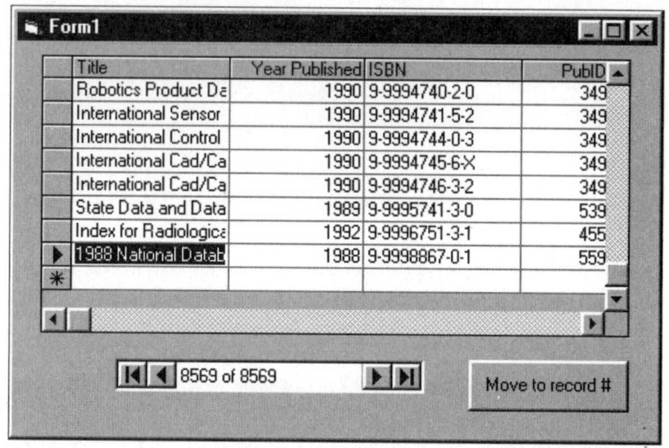


"Are we at the end of the file?" I asked.

"No," Ward answered, "right now our record pointer is positioned at the last record in the file – but that's not the same as being at the EOF."

"That's a good answer, Ward," I said. "Many beginners mistakenly believe that if the record pointer is positioned at the last record in the recordset they are at the EOF – but the EOF is actually the invisible record *after* the last data record in the recordset."

"Can the record pointer be positioned at the BOF or EOF?" Kathy asked.

"Yes it can, Kathy," I said. "If you remember, last week we discussed the `BOFAction` and `EOFAction` properties. These are the data control properties that determine what action to take if the record pointer should happen to move into either the BOF or EOF. So it's definitely possible for it to happen."

"That rings some bells now," Kathy said.

"Let's use the Immediate window to determine the current value of the recordset's `EOF` property," I said. "Remember, right now our record pointer is positioned on the *last record* of the recordset."

I clicked on the 'break' button, and entered this statement into the Immediate window:

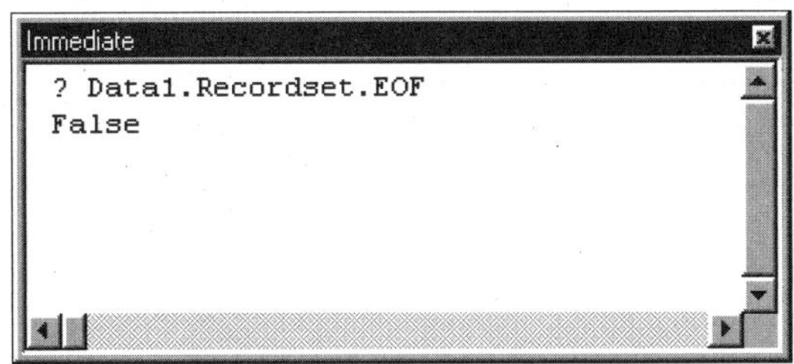


"**EOF** is **False**," I said, "indicating that we are **not** at the EOF."

"What would happen," Kathy asked, "if we were to try to add a new record to the recordset by clicking on that last row in the DBGrid – you know, the one that contains the asterisk?"

"My guess," Lou said, "is that the **EOF** property will be **True**."

"Let's see," I said, and I resumed the program by clicking on the 'run' button before clicking on the last row in the DBGrid:

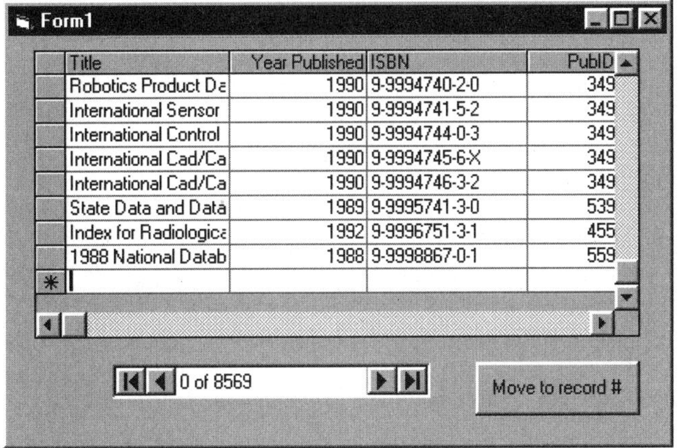


"Hang on," Steve said. "The record pointer in the data control's caption indicates that we are on record number 0. How can that be right?"

"That's because," I answered, "the recordset's **AbsolutePosition** property is set to -1 when the record pointer is at either the BOF or EOF. Since the code we put in the data control's **Reposition** event adds 1 to the **AbsolutePosition** property before displaying it, the current record is being displayed as 0."

I clicked on the 'break' button and entered another statement into the Immediate window:

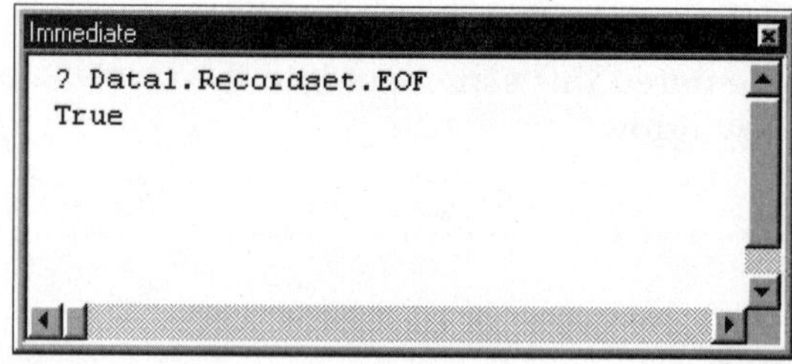


"**EOF** is **True**," I said, "and that's not surprising. The row with the asterisk is really positioned at the EOF."

"This is beginning to make more sense to me now," Rhonda said, "it's a shame we won't be writing our programs in the Immediate window. Can we use these statements in our code?"

"Yes we can," I said, "and we *will*. We'll actually be writing code like this next week when we add code to the **Login** form."

I paused and checked that everyone looked OK to continue. "Our next property is one that I mentioned a few moments ago – the **BookMark** property."

## The BookMark Property

"The **BookMark** property," I said, "provides an alternative way to move to a particular record in a recordset – remember, we used the **AbsolutePosition** property to do this earlier. Now, each and every record in a recordset – whatever the recordset's type – has a unique **BookMark** property assigned to it when the recordset is created. When the record pointer is positioned on a given record, then the recordset's **BookMark** property is set to match that individual record's **BookMark**."

"So you're saying that each record has a **BookMark**," Ward said, "but that at any given time only **one** record's **BookMark** value will be found in the recordset's **BookMark** property?"

"That's perfect, Ward," I said.

"Can the **BookMark** property be used just like the **AbsolutePosition** property?" Kathy asked.

"Not quite," I said. "The end result – moving to a particular record in the recordset – is the same, but the **BookMark** property is a little more complicated to work with than the **AbsolutePosition** property. You can't just set the **BookMark** property of a recordset to equal a specific record *number* the way we did with **AbsolutePosition**. Rather, using the **BookMark** property of the recordset to move to a particular record is a three-step process.

**First**, you need to position the record pointer on the record that you wish to return to later. **Second**, you need to read the `BookMark` property of the recordset to determine that particular record's `BookMark` value and store that value in a `Variant` variable. **Finally**, to move back to that record, you need to set the recordset's `BookMark` property to the value stored in that Variant variable. This final step will move the record pointer to the record you want to return to."

"You did say," Valerie asked, "that we can't just set the `BookMark` property equal to a record number, is that right?"

"That's right Valerie," I said. "Each record in a recordset has a **unique** `BookMark` value, and these values are arbitrarily assigned and not consecutive. There's no way of knowing what an individual record's `BookMark` property is, unless you first read it and store it in a `Variant` variable."

"Can we use the Immediate window to see a record's `BookMark` property?" Linda asked.

"We can," I replied, "but it won't look very intelligible! Bookmarks are arrays of `Byte` data types."

To demonstrate, I ran the demonstration program again and clicked on a record, then paused the program and typed another statement into the Immediate window:

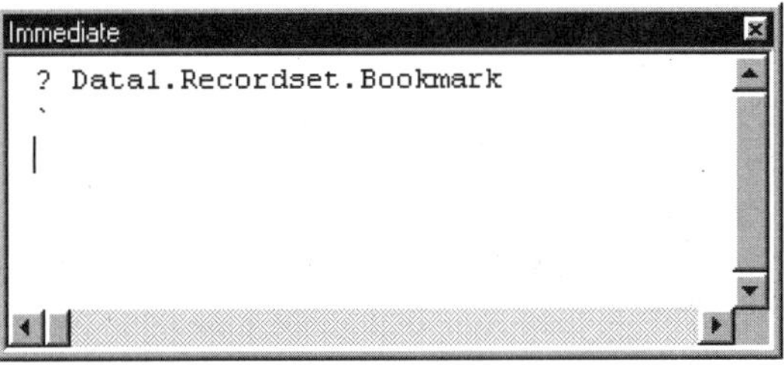


"Is that an apostrophe on the second line down?" Kate asked, having to squint a little to make out the image on the projector screen.

"Yes," I confirmed. "The apostrophe is Visual Basic's way of displaying a value that can't reasonably be shown in the Immediate window. Because the `BookMark` property is defined as an array of `Byte` data, trying to display it is pretty futile. The recordset's `BookMark` value is really only useful if you store it in a `Variant` variable and then assign that variable's value to the `BookMark` property of the recordset – remember that doing so will move your record pointer back to that record."

"Will a given record in a recordset – for instance, the first record – *always* have the same `BookMark` value?" Dave asked. "For instance, if we run our program tomorrow, will the `BookMark` for the first record be identical to what it is today?"

"That's a good question, Dave," I said, "and the answer is **no**. The `BookMark` properties for the records in a recordset change every time the recordset is built. If you were thinking of saving the `BookMark` values from one session of the program to another, that simply won't work."

"I'm still having a little problem conceptualizing all of this," Lou said, "Can you give us a demonstration of the `BookMark` property?"

"I'd be glad to, Lou," I said. "Let's modify the project we've been working on today. First, let's change the `RecordsetType` of the data control from a `Dynaset` to a `Table` type...just to prove that the `BookMark` technique I'm about to demonstrate will also work for a `Table` type recordset." That said, I changed the data control's `RecordsetType` property to `0-Table`:

"In a moment I'll add two command buttons to the form," I continued, "one whose `Click` event procedure reads the current value of the `BookMark` property and stores it in a Variant variable, and another whose `Click` event procedure sets the `BookMark` property of the recordset to equal the value of that Variant variable. Now, because the `Click` event procedures of each of those command buttons will need to read the value stored in the same Variant variable, we'll need to declare that variable in the General Declarations section of the form..."

I added a line of code to the form's General Declarations section:

```
Dim varBookmark As Variant
```

"...like this:"

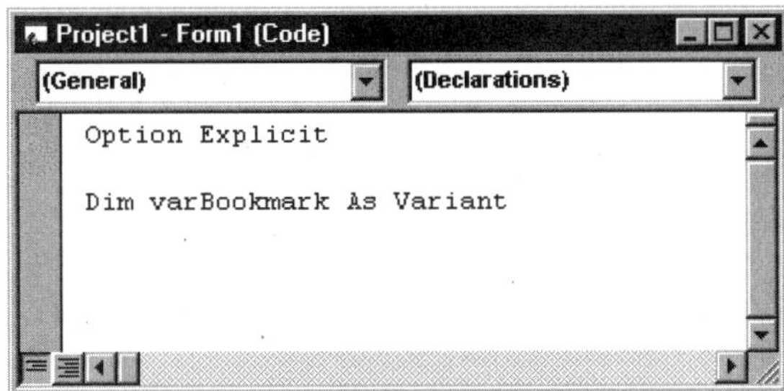


I deleted the existing command button from the form and deleted all the existing code in the `Command1_Click` event procedure before enlarging the form a bit to accommodate two new command buttons.

Once I had placed these on the form, I changed the `Caption` property of the first command button to `Save BookMark` and keyed the following code into its `Click` event procedure:

```
Private Sub Command1_Click()

varBookmark = Data1.Recordset.Bookmark

End Sub
```

Then I changed the `Caption` property of the second command button to `Goto BookMark`, and entered this code into its `Click` event procedure:

```
Private Sub Command2_Click()

Data1.Recordset.Bookmark = varBookmark

End Sub
```

"Notice," I said, "that in the `Click` event procedure of the first command button we take the value of the recordset's `BookMark` property and store it in our form-level `Variant` variable called `varBookmark`:"

```
varBookmark = Data1.Recordset.Bookmark
```

"The code in the `Click` event procedure of the second command button will be used to move back to the original record by setting the **recordset's** `BookMark` property equal to the value of our `Variant` variable:"

```
Data1.Recordset.Bookmark = varBookmark
```

"Like this..."

I was about to run the program when I realized that I still had code in the **Reposition** event procedure that would cause the program to bomb. I had changed the **RecordsetType** from **Dynaset** to **Table** type, and had almost forgotten that I had code in the **Reposition** event procedure referencing the **AbsolutePosition** property of the recordset – a property not supported by the **Table** type recordset.

"For now," I said, "let me comment out the code in the **Reposition** event procedure of the data control."

I then placed an apostrophe – the comment character – in front of the single line of code in the data control's **Reposition** event procedure.

"I may have missed this since I wasn't in the Intro class," Rachel said, "but what do you mean by 'comment out'?"

I explained that if you place the comment character – the apostrophe – in front of a line of code, Visual Basic will ignore the entire line. For now, it's easier to tell Visual Basic to ignore that line of code by doing this rather than to delete the line and have to reinsert it later:

```
'Data1.Caption = Data1.Recordset.AbsolutePosition + 1 & " of " &
    ↳Data1.Recordset.RecordCount
```

"I see now," Rachel said.

I ran the program and moved the record pointer to about halfway through the recordset.

"Let's select this record," I said, and I clicked on the row containing a record whose **Title** began with the words Computer Performance. I asked everyone to record the name of the **Title** and the **ISBN** for later verification:

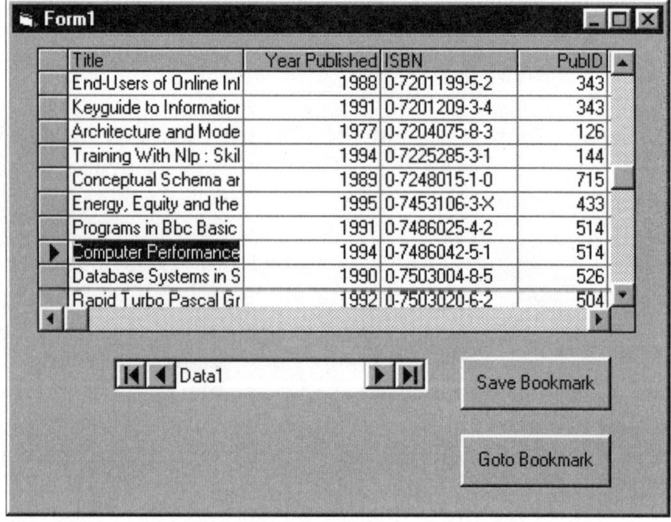

Next, I clicked on the Save Bookmark command button, triggering the **Click** event procedure that saved the current value of the recordset's **BookMark** property to the variant variable **varBookmark**.

"If we now move to the end of the recordset," I said, "we can test how well that **BookMark** property works."

I then clicked on the 'last record' navigation button on the data control:

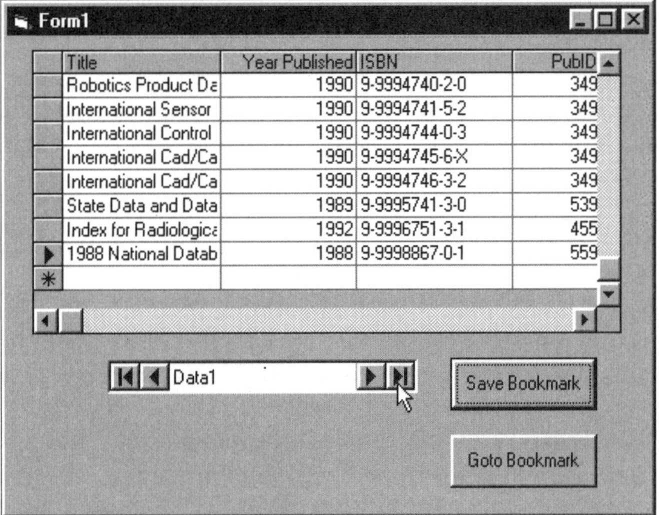

"Now that we've moved off the original record," I said, "if we click on the Goto BookMark button, the record pointer should be set back to that record we were on prior to moving to the end of the recordset. Let's see..."

I clicked on the Goto BookMark button, and the following screen shot was displayed:

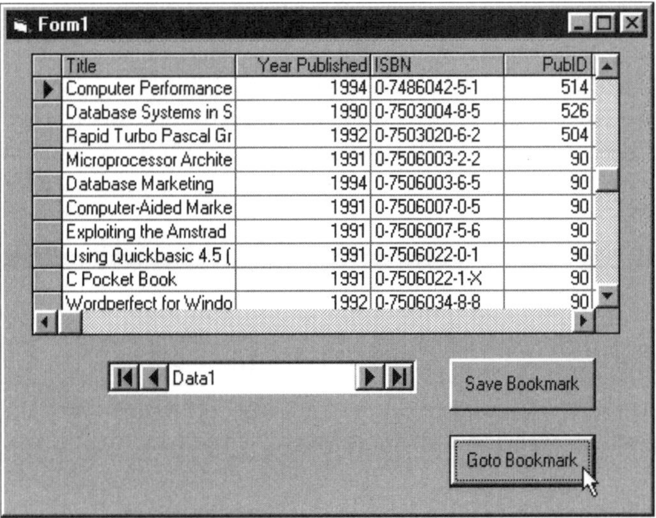

"Is that the correct record?" I asked.

"That's it," chorused several people in the class.

"That `BookMark` property worked beautifully," I heard Chuck say.

I waited to see if there were any questions.

"Is there any limit on the number of bookmarks you can keep track of?" Peter asked.

"No, there isn't," I said, "although you'll need to declare a separate `Variant` variable for each record's `BookMark` you wish to store. You could also create an array of `Variant` variables to hold the bookmarks."

"What happened to our display of the record number and record count in the data control's `Caption`?" Peter asked.

"We commented out the code in the `Reposition` event which displays that," I said. "Remember, we can't refer to the `AbsolutePosition` property of a `Table` type recordset."

"That's right," Peter answered, "I forgot all about that."

"We've spent quite a bit of time," Ward remarked, "discussing two recordset properties that permit us to quickly move from one record to another in a recordset – `AbsolutePosition` and `BookMark`. Is this type of movement something that's used frequently? Are these properties all that practical?"

I answered as follows: "I would say that permitting the user to move quickly from one record to another, and allowing them to mark a record and return to it very quickly later on, are both features that are incorporated quite often – particularly in forms containing the DBGrid. You won't see these features so much in the China Shop project – at least not at first – since there simply aren't that many records in the tables of the database. But it wouldn't surprise me if somewhere down the line we don't build something like this into the program – particularly as the number of records in the `Transactions` table grows."

"When you say 'somewhere down the line'," Rachel said, "do you mean after the course is over?"

"That's right, Rachel," I said. "Part of the Systems Development Life Cycle that I introduced in our introductory class was the notion of feedback and maintenance. Even after we had completed the China Shop project in the Introductory class, members of the class still kept in contact with Joe Bullina to see how well the program was meeting his expectations."

There were no more questions about the `BookMark` property, and so I continued on to the `Bookmarkable` property.

### The Bookmarkable Property

"The `Bookmarkable` property," I said, "returns a value indicating whether a recordset supports bookmarks. It's a good idea, prior to reading or setting a recordset's `BookMark` property, to check the recordset's `Bookmarkable` property first to make sure that this particular recordset supports bookmarks."

"Didn't you say that **all** recordsets support the `BookMark` property?" Kate asked.

"I should have made it clearer earlier that all *Microsoft Access* database recordsets support bookmarks," I replied. "Other databases you connect to may or may not support bookmarks – and for that reason, you really should check the `Bookmarkable` property prior to working with the `BookMark` property."

"I presume the `Bookmarkable` property is a Boolean property, isn't it?" Tom asked.

"Yes it is, Tom," I said. "Let's check the `Bookmarkable` property by using the Immediate window."

I paused the demonstration program again and entered yet another statement into the Immediate window:

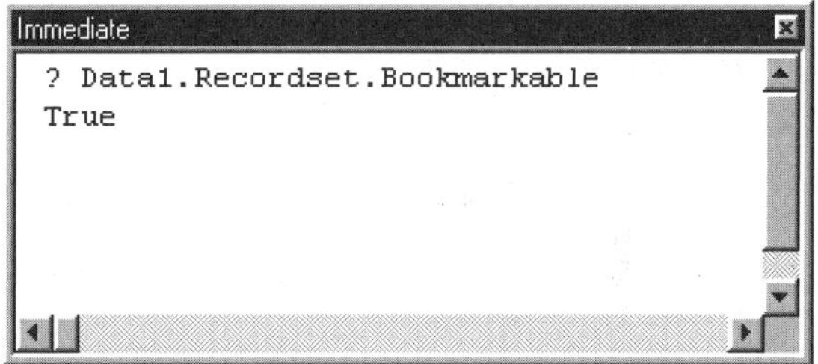


"Just what I would expect," I said. "As we're dealing with a Microsoft Access database which supports bookmarks, we'd expect to see this return a value of `True`. Next," I went on, "let's take a look at a group of properties that tell us something about the database and the records that we're dealing with."

### The DateCreated, LastModified,and LastUpdated Properties

"The `DateCreated`, `LastModified`, and `LastUpdated` properties," I said, "are pretty interesting, and I think you'll find them useful."

"I can see from the handout you gave us," Rachel said, "that the `DateCreated` property is another one of those 'gotcha' properties – it's only supported by the `Table` type recordset."

"'You're right, Rachel," I said. "That makes sense since, only one of the three recordset types is 'real' as opposed to 'virtual' – and that's the **Table** type recordset. Both **Dynasets** and **Snapshots** are virtual representations of tables, and so neither one supports the **DateCreated** property."

"Why would we use the **DateCreated** property?" Ward asked. "Is it just an informational type of property?"

"That's right, Ward," I said. "The value of the **DateCreated** property lies in the information it provides us – knowing the date and time that a table was created can come in handy. Let's use the Immediate window to check the date and time that the **Titles** table of the **Biblio** database was created."

I then entered the following statement into the Immediate window:

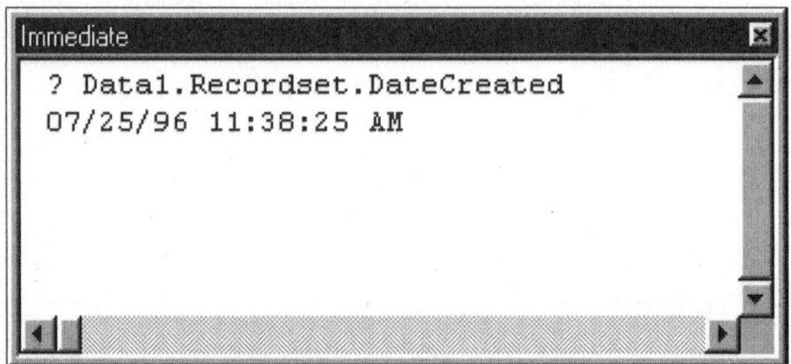


"Is that the creation date for the **Titles** table that's displayed here," Mary asked, "or does it refer to the entire **Biblio** database?"

"No, it's just for the **Titles** table," I said. "Each table in the underlying database maintains its own information about when it was created."

"Can we see what happens," Linda said, "if you change the **RecordsetType** from **Table** to **Dynaset** – I know you said the property is not supported."

"OK, fair enough," I said, as I changed the **RecordsetType** from **Table** to **Dynaset**, ran the program, paused it, and then re-typed the statement to display the **DateCreated** property in the Immediate window. This was what we saw next:

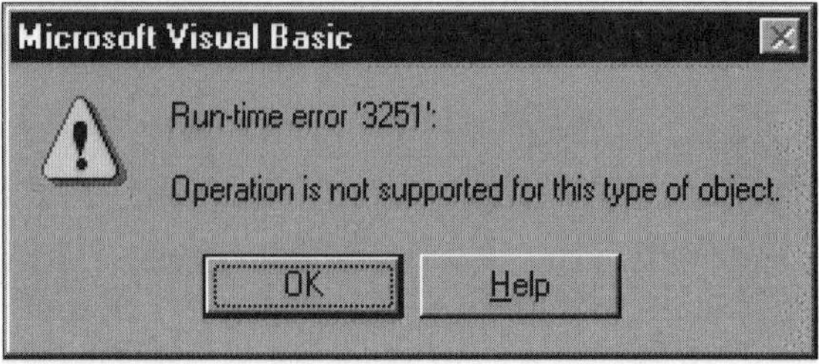


"There's that 'gotcha' message," Rachel said. "I wish it were a bit more explanatory."

I grinned. "Me too," I agreed, "This error message just means that the `DateCreated` property is not supported by the `Dynaset` recordset type – I personally think that it would be better for all concerned if that's what the error message actually said."

"How does the `LastUpdated` property of the recordset fit in here?" Dave asked.

"The `LastUpdated` property," I said, "like the `DateCreated` property, applies only to a `Table` recordset, and it returns the date and time of the most recent change made to the recordset – in this case, that really means the date and time that a record in the table was last updated."

"Is that the date and time that **any** record in the table was last updated," Mary asked, "not the particular record that the record pointer happens to be on?"

"That's a great point, Mary," I said, "the `LastUpdated` property tells us when the recordset – the table – was last updated, **not** a particular record. There is no built-in facility to determine the modification dates and time of individual records–only to the table as a whole."

"So there's no way of knowing when a *particular* record in a recordset was last modified," Ward asked. "I could see that being useful."

"There's no property of the recordset that will give us that information," I said, "but that doesn't mean we couldn't create a field in the table called 'LastUpdated' and programmatically update it whenever the record is changed. In fact, I typically create a field like that in all of my multi-user programs, along with a field to identify the name of the user who made the last change to the record."

"Will we be doing something like this in the China Shop project?" Mary asked. "I know creating fields like that would make my boss very happy – he's constantly talking about the need for something my company calls an **audit trail**."

"That's a good point," I said. "Theoretically an audit trail is a way of determining when and by whom a database record was changed – and a 'LastUpdated' and a 'UpdatedBy' field would do that. However, providing that kind of functionality is not in our plans for the China Shop as yet."

"Uh huh," said Mary.

"Let's see how the `LastUpdated` property of the recordset works," I said, "by changing one of the records in our recordset and then displaying the `LastUpdated` property of the recordset in the Immediate window."

I then changed the **`RecordsetType`** property back to **`Table`** – having previously changed it to **`Dynaset`** – and ran the program. I went to the very last record in the recordset, and changed the date from 1988 to 2000:

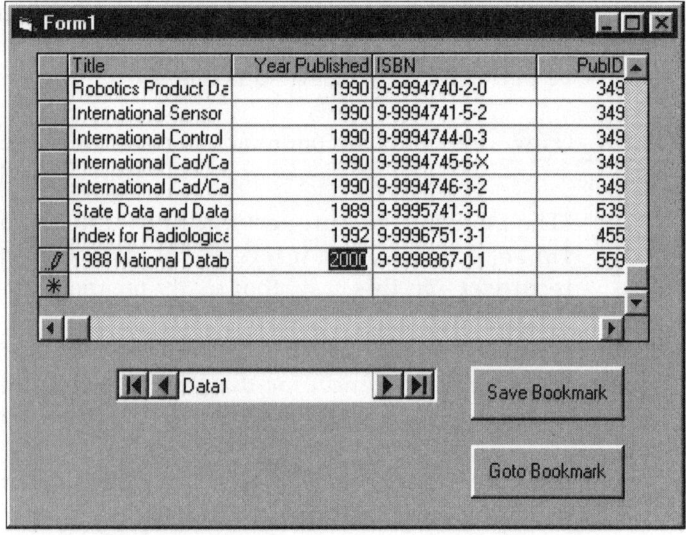


...then typed this statement into the Immediate window:

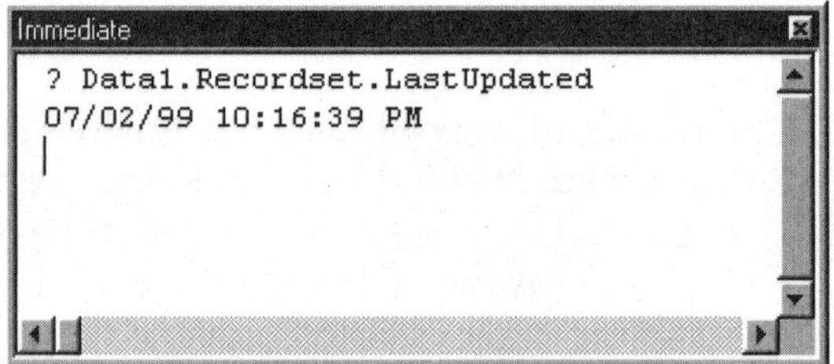


"As you can see," I said, "the value for **`LastUpdated`** property of the recordset is today's date, and the time is just a few seconds or so ago."

"I'm starting to get a little confused," Ward said. "How is the **`LastUpdated`** property different from the **`LastModified`** property?"

"These two **can** be confusing," I said. "The **`LastUpdated`** property returns a date and time, but the **`LastModified`** property returns a **`BookMark`**. In addition, unlike the **`LastUpdated`** property – which only applies to **`Table`** recordsets – the **`LastModified`** property applies to both **`Table`** and **`Dynaset`** type recordsets."

"When you say **`BookMark`**, you mean a **`BookMark`** value, just like the **`BookMark`** property?" Kevin asked.

"That's right, Kevin," I replied. "The **`LastModified`** property returns a **`BookMark`** value, which can then be used to move directly to the record in the recordset that was last modified."

"I can see some value in this property," Dave interjected. "A user might want to be able to quickly move to the record in a recordset that they had last modified."

"Or in a multi-user application, the record that *another* user had last modified," Blaine added.

"You need to be careful with the terminology, Blaine," I said, "the **`LastModified`** property returns the **`BookMark`** value of the record in the user's recordset that they last modified – **not** the record in the underlying table that was last modified (potentially by someone else)."

"I see," Blaine said. "This property is local to the recordset the user is working with."

"That's one way of thinking about it," I said. "To use the **`LastModified`** property to move to the record last modified in the recordset, what you need to do is set the **`BookMark`** property of the recordset to equal the **`LastModified`** property of the recordset, like this..."

I stopped the program, and placed a third command button on the form. I changed its **`Caption`** property from **`Command3`** to **`Goto Last Modified`** and keyed the following code into the command button's **`Click`** event procedure:

```
Private Sub Command3_Click()

Data1.Recordset.Bookmark = Data1.Recordset.LastModified

End Sub
```

"Remember," I warned the class. "The **`LastModified`** property only works with the **`Table`** or **`Dynaset`** recordsets – **`Snapshots`** don't want to know about this property."

I ran the program and clicked on the GoTo Last Modified button:

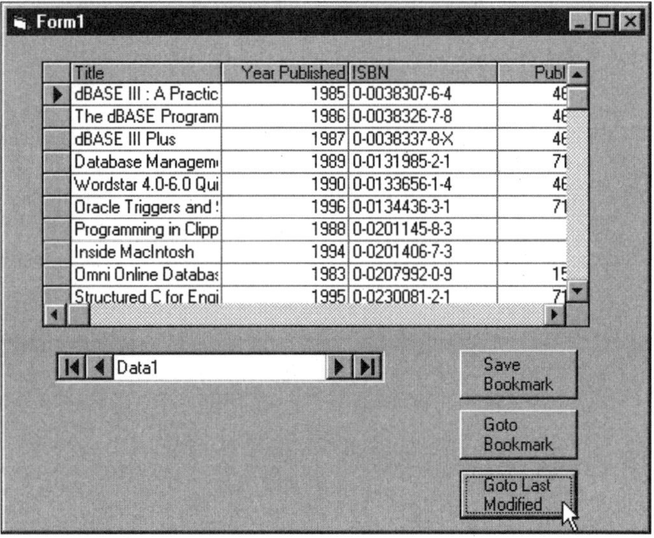

"Nothing happened," Linda said. "The record pointer is still on the first record. How come we didn't move to the last record in the recordset? We just changed its Year Published from 1988 to 2000."

"That's true, Linda," I replied. "We did just change that record in the *table*, but we changed that record in another *temporary* recordset – the recordset only lives for as long as the program is running and the data control has a connection with the database. Remember that I stopped the program to place a third command button on the form, and that when we re-ran the program we created a brand new recordset. Because we haven't modified a record in this recordset yet, there *is* no value in the `LastModified` property. It isn't until we change a record in **this** recordset that the `LastModified` property will have a value in it."

I then scrolled through the recordset and, about half way through, changed the `Year Published` field of a record to 2001:

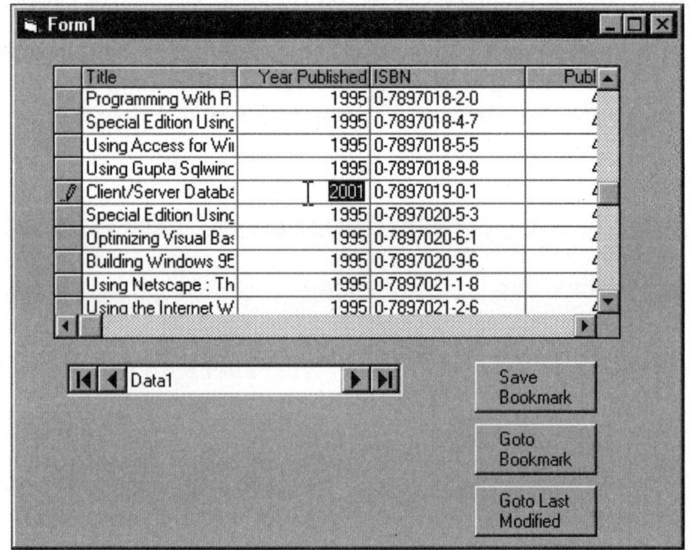


"OK, now we've modified a record in the recordset," I said. "Let's move to another."

I then clicked on the 'last record' navigation button on the data control to move to the last record in the recordset:

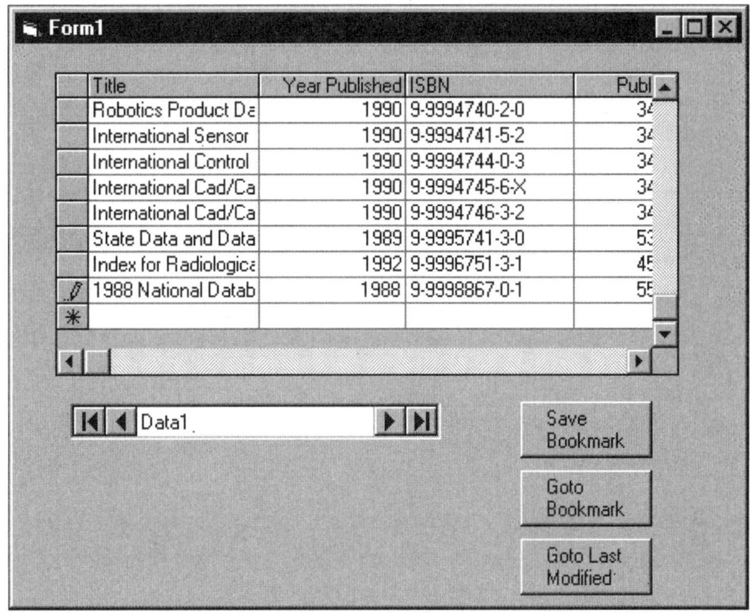


"...and then return to it."

I clicked on the Goto Last Modified command button again. This time, the record pointer moved to the record whose `Year Published` field I had just changed:

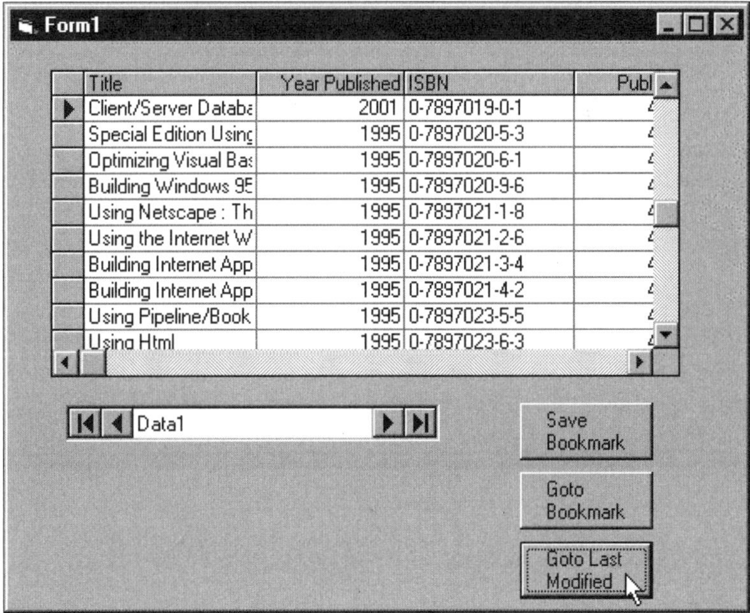

"I see now," Linda said, "that's better. That's the record we just changed."

"A lot of beginners," I said, "make the mistake of thinking that setting the recordset's `BookMark` to equal the `BookMark` value stored in the `LastModified` property will move the record pointer to the record in the **table** that was last modified. However, that's not the case – instead, you'll move the record pointer to the record in the **current recordset** that was last modified. This means that if you open a recordset and immediately click on the Goto Last Modified button before making any changes, your record pointer will stay exactly where it is. Since there have been no modifications to the recordset, the `LastModified BookMark` value is empty."

At this point, I got the class to take a short refreshment break, as they had done a lot of hard listening. When we reconvened, I started to talk about another very useful property – the `Index` property.

## *The Index Property*

"The recordset's `Index` property," I began, "when used in conjunction with the recordset's `Seek` method, is an extremely powerful feature which allows us to quickly find a record in a `Table` type recordset. We'll see next week that before we can use the `Seek` method of the recordset, we need to set the recordset's `Index` property to equal the name of an index that's already been created on the Access table that we're referencing in our data control. This means that we can use the predefined index to speed up our search. And there's another benefit of using the `Index` property."

"What's that?" Dave asked.

"I've been surprised that no one has asked about the order of the records displayed in the DBGrid," I said.

"I *was* wondering about that," Melissa said. "How *are* those records sequenced?"

"In general," I said, "records in a recordset are ordered into sequence by the primary key in the underlying Access table – for example, by the Customer ID number. Next week, when we discuss **SQL**, we'll see that we can use the SQL `order by` statement to change the default order of the recordset. However, for a `Table` type recordset, we can also change the `Index` property of the recordset to the name of an index associated with the table specified in the `RecordSource` property."

"So what **is** an index exactly?" Mary asked. "Is it the same as the primary key?"

"The primary key **is** an index," I said. "In Access, you can create as many indexes as you want and need. In Access, an index is used to help you find and sort records faster. Access uses an index as you would use an index in a book, and you can take advantage of these capabilities in Visual Basic by setting the `Index` property of the recordset to an index that you have previously created in Access."

"So in addition to the primary key," Ward said, "we can specify additional indexes on other fields in a table?"

"That's right," I said. "If you predict that the user of your program will need to quickly locate records in a table based on a particular field or see records in sequence based on a particular field (say, names in alphabetical order), you should create an index for that field or fields in Access."

"And then you'll be able to use that index from within Visual Basic?" Kathy asked.

"Exactly," I said. "All you need to do is set the `Index` property of the recordset to the name of the Access index. Doing so will sequence the recordset in order based on that index, and also allow you to use the super-fast `Seek` method of the recordset. Here, let me show you..."

I stopped the program (which was still running), started Access and opened the `Biblio` database, and then opened up the `Titles` table in design mode.

"If we select View | Indexes from the Access menu bar," I said:

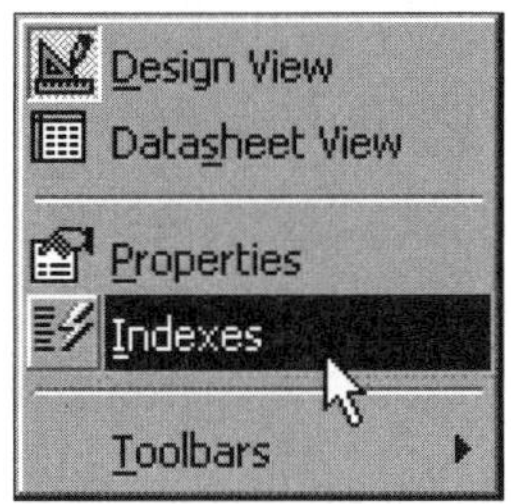

"...the Indexes window will be displayed, and you'll then be able to see all of the indexes associated with the **Titles** table:"

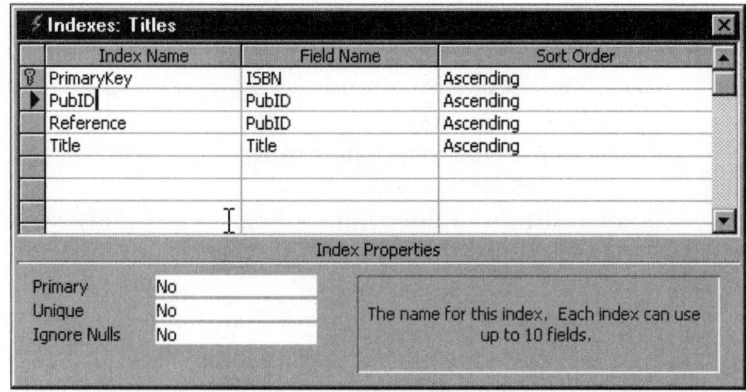


"The first column displays the name of the index, the second column displays the field or fields upon which the index is built, and the third column shows whether the Sort Order of the index is ascending or descending. As you can see, the **Titles** table has four indexes associated with it – PrimaryKey (based on the **ISBN** field sorted in ascending order), PubID (The **PubID** field in ascending order), Reference (again, the **PubID** field), and Title (the **Title** field, again in ascending order). These indexes give us the facility to search quickly for a variety of data."

"Am I right," Dave said, "that there are two indexes – **PubID** and **Reference** – that are both based on the same field?"

"Microsoft should know better than to try to put one over on you, Dave," I said, "Yes, I've noticed that myself, but I've never been able to figure out why that is. We'll just have to take it as read."

I then closed Access, confirmed that the **RecordsetType** of the data control was set to **Table**, and then ran our demonstration program again before immediately pausing it.

"Notice that the records in the DBGrid are now sequenced by **ISBN**," I said, "which is the field that the **PrimaryKey** index is based on. We can use the Immediate window to change the **Index** property of the recordset."

I then entered the following statement into the Immediate window:

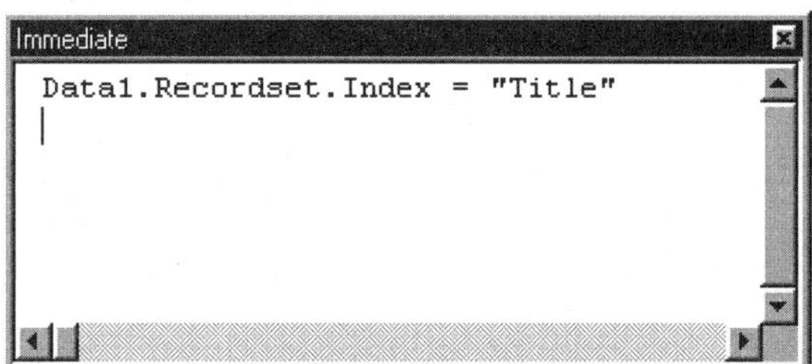


As soon as I pressed the *Enter* key, the records in the DBGrid were reordered. I clicked on the 'run' button to resume the program, and the records were now displayed in sequence, ordered by the `Title` field:

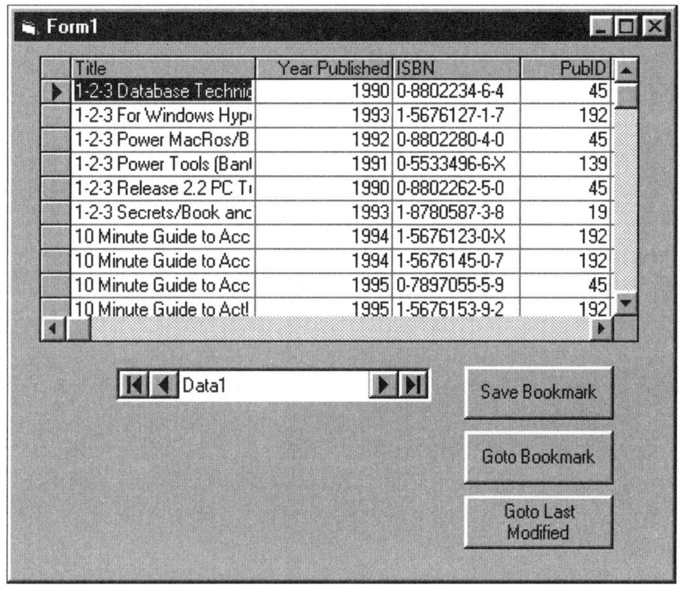


| Title | Year Published | ISBN | PubID |
|---|---|---|---|
| 1-2-3 Database Technic | 1990 | 0-8802234-6-4 | 45 |
| 1-2-3 For Windows Hyp | 1993 | 1-5676127-1-7 | 192 |
| 1-2-3 Power MacRos/B | 1992 | 0-8802280-4-0 | 45 |
| 1-2-3 Power Tools (Ban | 1991 | 0-5533496-6-X | 139 |
| 1-2-3 Release 2.2 PC T | 1990 | 0-8802262-5-0 | 45 |
| 1-2-3 Secrets/Book anc | 1993 | 1-8780587-3-8 | 19 |
| 10 Minute Guide to Acc | 1994 | 1-5676123-0-X | 192 |
| 10 Minute Guide to Acc | 1994 | 1-5676145-0-7 | 192 |
| 10 Minute Guide to Acc | 1995 | 0-7897055-5-9 | 45 |
| 10 Minute Guide to Act! | 1995 | 1-5676153-9-2 | 192 |

"Wow, the order of the records changed immediately," Linda said.

"That's pretty impressive," Ward said. "I can see that this feature might come in pretty handy for Joe Bullina when he's viewing records in the `Transactions` table."

"You're right, Ward," I said. "Joe might want to be able to view the records in the `Transactions` table by something other than the `TransID` field of the table – which is the field associated with the primary key. Later on in the course, I'll show you how to build this functionality into the DBGrid so that if the user clicks on a column heading in the DBGrid, the records in the DBGrid will be re-sequenced by that field."

"Are you going to show us how to use the `Seek` method to locate a record in the recordset?" Linda asked.

"Yes I am," I answered, "but before I do that, I want to first discuss the **NoMatch** property."

## The NoMatch Property

"The **NoMatch** property," I continued, "is a Boolean property that reports the result of the execution of either the **Seek** or **Find** methods of the recordset. In other words, it tells us whether the **Seek** or **Find** methods found the record they were looking for."

"I know you said the **Seek** method can only be used with a **Table** type recordset," Bob said, "but what about the **Find** method?"

"The **Find** method," I replied, "can be used with all three types of recordsets – **Dynaset**, **Snapshot**, or **Table**."

"So if **NoMatch** returns **True**," Kate said, "that means that the record **was not** found. If **NoMatch** returns **False**, that means the record **was** found?"

"That's right, Kate," I said. "If you set the **Index** property of the recordset to the name of any valid Access-created index name and then execute the **Seek** method to locate a record, then if the record is not found, the **NoMatch** property will be set to **True**."

"Don't you mean to say **False**?" Rhonda asked.

"It's confusing I know, Rhonda," I replied, "but the **NoMatch** property is **True** if the record is not located in the recordset – and **NoMatch** is **False** if the record is located. I think it's time for a demo now – that might help us quite a bit."

I added a fourth command button on the form, changed its **Caption** property to **Seek a Record**, and keyed the next piece of code into the command button's **Click** event procedure:

```
Private Sub Command4_Click()

Dim strISBN As String

Data1.Recordset.Index = "PrimaryKey"

strISBN = InputBox("Enter an ISBN")

Data1.Recordset.Seek "=", strISBN

If Data1.Recordset.NoMatch = True Then
   MsgBox "Sorry, no match - try again"
End If

End Sub
```

"Let's assume," I continued, "that we want to give our user a way to locate records in the recordset containing a particular ISBN. The first thing we do is use a `Dim` statement to declare a variable that will hold the string that we want to search for:"

```
Dim strISBN As String
```

"Next, we set the `Index` property of the recordset to the particular index we want to use with the `Seek` method – in this instance, the `PrimaryKey` index of the `Titles` table:"

```
Data1.Recordset.Index = "PrimaryKey"
```

"Then, using the `InputBox` function, we can prompt the user to enter an `ISBN`. Once we have that value, we can then pass that value as an argument to the recordset's `Seek` method:"

```
strISBN = InputBox("Enter an ISBN")

Data1.Recordset.Seek "=", strISBN
```

"If, when we execute the `Seek` method, a record with that `ISBN` is **not** located, the value of the `NoMatch` property will be set to `True`, and we use the message box function to display a warning message to the user:"

```
If Data1.Recordset.NoMatch = True Then
   MsgBox "Sorry, no match - try again"
```

"If, however, a record with that ISBN is located in the recordset, the record pointer will move directly to that record. Let's run the program now, and see this in action."

I ran the program and clicked on the Seek a Record command button. When the input box appeared, I entered the `ISBN` of a record located about halfway through the recordset:

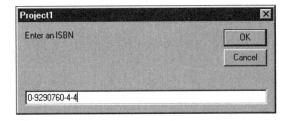

After clicking on the OK button in the input box, the **Seek** method of the recordset was executed and the record pointer in the grid was positioned to the record with the matching **ISBN**:

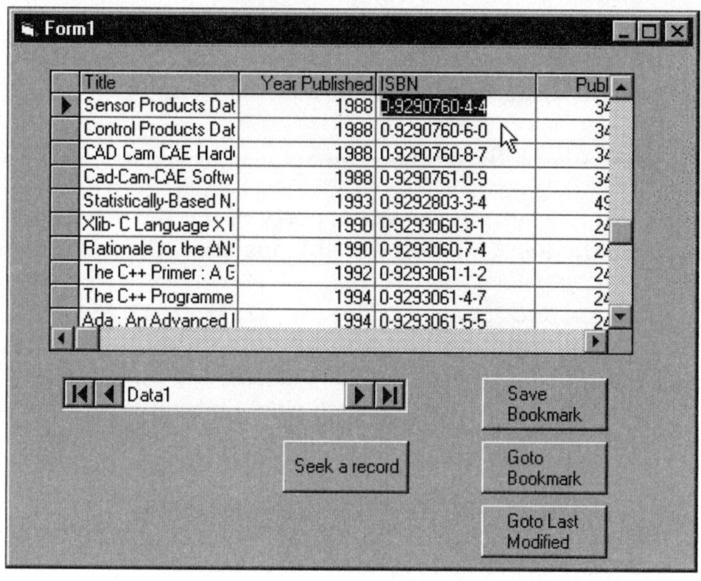


"I can see a lot of applications for the **Seek** method." Ward said. That was really fast."

"Can we use the Immediate window to display the current value of the **NoMatch** property?" Rhonda asked.

"Sure thing, Rhonda," I said, as I paused the program and typed the appropriate statement into the Immediate window:

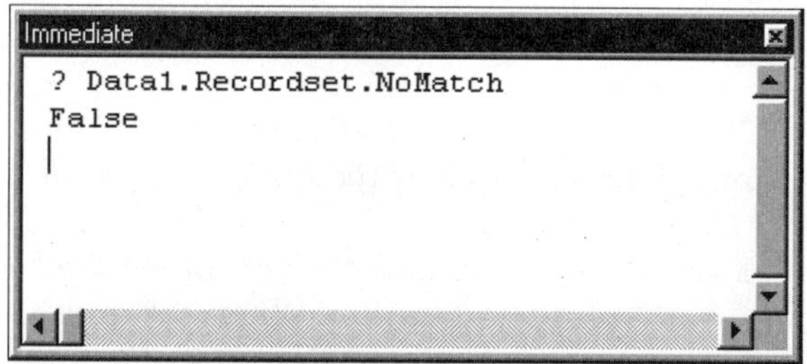


"As you can see," I said, "since the record we were seeking *was* located in the recordset, the **NoMatch** property was set to **False**. If, on the other hand, we had entered an **ISBN** that did not exist in the recordset, then the **NoMatch** property would be set to **True**."

"Can we try that, too?" Rhonda asked.

"No problem," I said.

I ran the program once more, again clicked on the Seek a record button, and this time intentionally typed the `ISBN` of an excellent book I happen to own that does not appear in the `Biblio` database's `Titles` table:

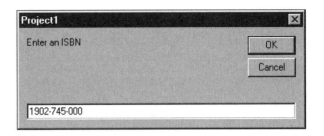

When I clicked on the OK button, the recordset's `Seek` method was executed. However, since no record was found in the recordset matching that particular `ISBN`, the following message box was displayed:

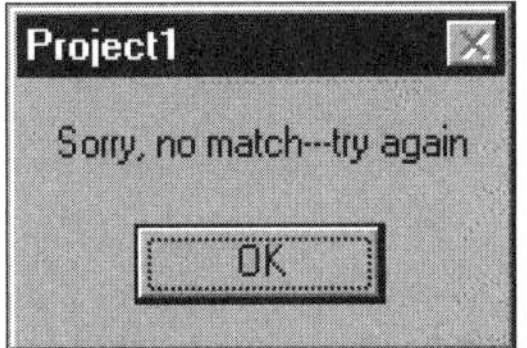


"Let's see what the value of the `NoMatch` property is by using the Immediate window," I said, as I paused the program and typed my latest statement into the Immediate window:

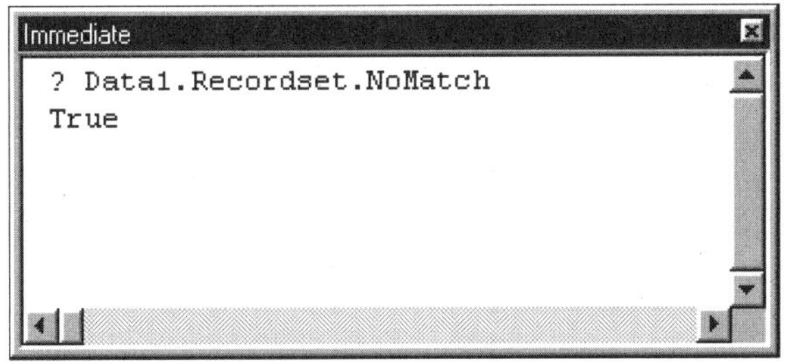


"I don't know whether anyone noticed," Dave said, "but when the `Seek` method failed to locate that record, our record pointer was set to the first record in the recordset." Sure enough, Dave was right:

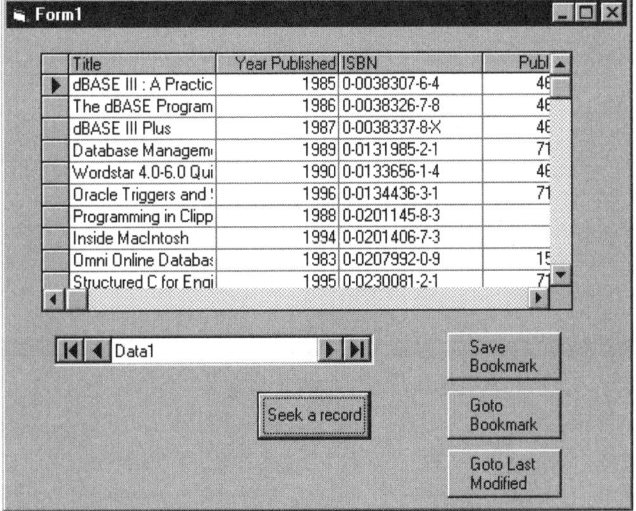

"That's right," Mary said, "the record pointer *did* move to the beginning of the recordset. Is there anything we can do about that?"

"Well," I said, "one of the default behaviors of both the **Seek** and the **Find** methods of the recordset is that if the record can't be located in the recordset, the record pointer is positioned at the beginning of the recordset. But we can take care of that little problem by using the **BookMark** property of the recordset to mark our place, like this..."

I then modified the code in the **Click** event procedure of the command button as follows. Modified code is highlighted:

```
Private Sub Command4_Click()

Dim strISBN As String
Dim varBookmark As Variant

varBookmark = Data1.Recordset.Bookmark

Data1.recordset.Index = "PrimaryKey"

strISBN = InputBox("Enter an ISBN")

Data1.recordset.Seek "=", strISBN

If Data1.recordset.NoMatch = True Then
   Data1.Recordset.Bookmark = varBookmark
   MsgBox "Sorry, no match-try again"
End If

End Sub
```

"I see what you're doing," Chuck said. "Before executing the **Seek** method, you declare a **Variant** variable and set it to equal the current value of the recordset's **BookMark** property:"

```
Dim varBookmark As Variant

varBookmark = Data1.Recordset.Bookmark
```

"...and then if the record can't be located by the **Seek** method, you position the record pointer back to that original record by setting the **Bookmark** value back to the value that's stored in the variable:"

```
If Data1.recordset.NoMatch = True Then
   Data1.Recordset.Bookmark = varBookmark
   MsgBox "Sorry, no match-try again"
End If
```

"Excellent analysis, Chuck. Does everyone see what's going on here?" I said, as I ran the program, positioned the record pointer to roughly halfway through the recordset, and then attempted to locate that beloved book of mine again. After failing to locate the record using the **Seek** method, this time the record pointer stayed put:

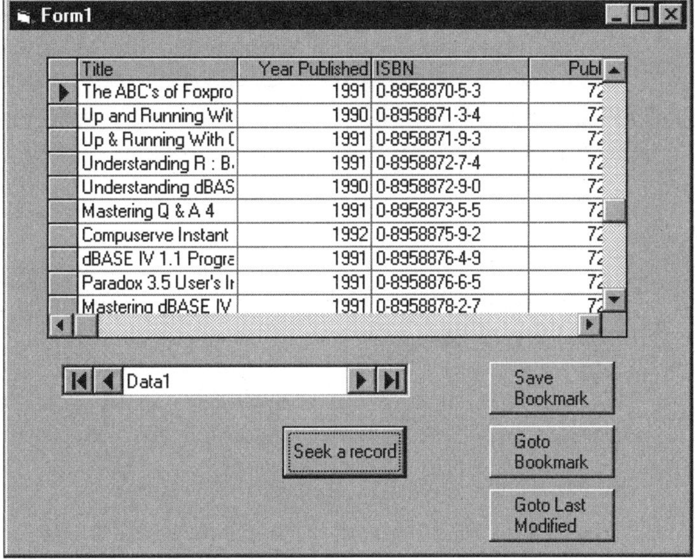


"That's great," Rhonda said. "This demo has really solidified things in my mind. Now I can see a practical use for the **BookMark** property."

"I'm glad that helped, Rhonda," I said. "By the way, we'll look at the **Seek** method in more detail next week when we discuss recordset methods. Right now, we have just one more property to discuss, and then we'll continue our work with the China Shop modifications. Let's acquaint ourselves with the **Updatable** property."

## The Updatable Property

"The last property of the recordset I want to discuss is the **Updatable** property," I said. "This is a Boolean property that tells us whether we can *change* the data in the recordset."

"Why wouldn't we be able to?" Dave asked. "With the exception of the **Snapshot**, aren't **all** recordsets always updatable?"

"Not necessarily, Dave," I said. "It's possible that you may write Visual Basic programs that connect to databases that have update restrictions placed on them."

"I remember that from the Access class I took," Kate said. "As I recall, when you define a database, you can specify permission levels for different users based on the tables they attempt to access. I believe you can even specify permissions down to the field level."

"That's right, Kate," I replied. "We must remember that the database programs we write in Visual Basic will sometimes be interacting with databases and tables that have been designed by other people. Our privileges to use the data in those databases may be determined by someone else. Even when we can successfully **connect** to a database, and perhaps even view records in one or more of its tables, it's quite possible that we won't be able to **update** the data in the database."

"I guess I never considered that possibility," Dave said.

"For that reason," I continued, "it's possible that the `Updatable` property of the recordset might be `False` – which means that the data in the recordset may not update the underlying database."

"Is this one of those properties that we really don't need to worry about if we're using the data control? Doesn't using the data control mean that our recordset will *always* be updatable?" Kathy asked.

"You're right to a degree, Kathy," I answered. "But it certainly doesn't *hurt* to check this, especially if you are writing a program that connects to a database that you didn't design yourself. Microsoft recommends that you routinely check the `Updatable` property for every recordset you build. This can come in quite handy when you have a data control and a DBGrid on your form and, for whatever reason, the updates the user is making in the DBGrid don't seem to be 'taking'."

"Just for the heck of it," Rhonda said, "can we see what the `Updatable` value is for our recordset?"

"Sounds like a good idea," I said, as I entered this statement into the Immediate window:

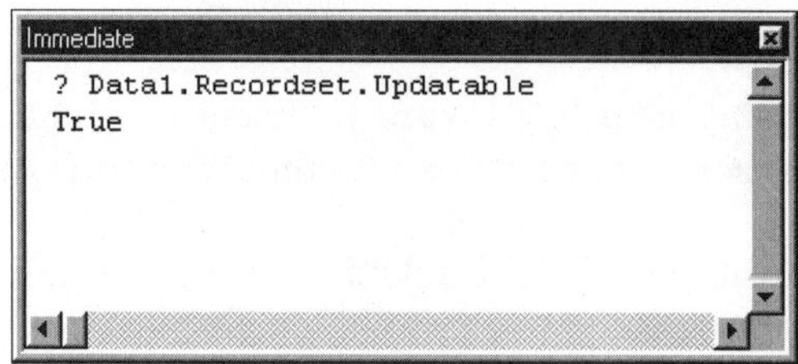


"That's pretty much as we would expect," I said.

"Suppose we change the `RecordsetType` to a `Snapshot`?" Lou asked.

"Let's try it," I said, as I brought up the Properties window for the data control and changed the **RecordsetType** to a snapshot. Running the program again, I paused it and keyed my next statement into the Immediate window:

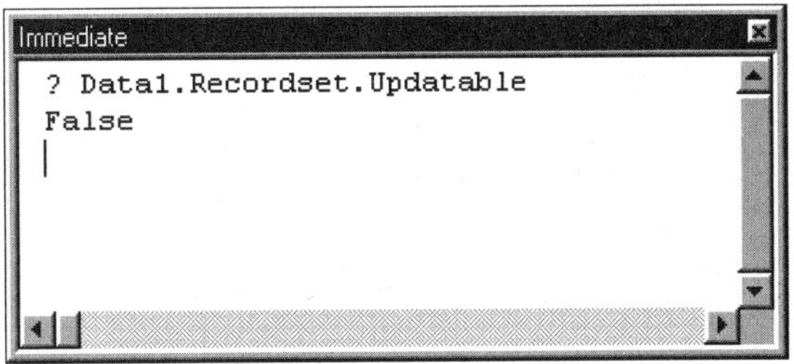


"Again, that's about what we would expect," I said. "A **Snapshot** recordset is a read-only recordset – and that's what the **False** value for the **Updatable** property is telling us."

I asked if there were any questions about any of the properties that we had covered this morning. We had gone through a bunch of them – and discussed some recordset methods along the way also. There were no questions, and so I asked everyone to take a fifteen-minute break.

After break, I explained that I had a few exercises for everyone to complete that would modify the China Shop project.

"Today," I said, "we'll do some preliminary work on the **Login** form, and by the end of next week's class, we'll have a working **Login** form. Before we get to that point, we need to learn more about recordset methods."

I then distributed our first exercise for the day.

## Exercise – Creating the Login Form

In this exercise, you'll add a third form to the China Shop project (the **Login** form) and save it in your usual **China** directory. If you're not completely comfortable with adding a new form, please refer back to the ***Creating the Users Form*** exercise in Chapter 4.

1. Load up the China Shop project and add another new form to it.Select the new form and bring up its properties window. Find the **Name** property, and change it from **Form1** to **frmLogin**.

2. Now click on the 'save' button on the toolbar. Remember that Visual Basic will immediately prompt you to save the new form with a disk file name of `frmLogin`. As in previous examples, **do not save it with this name**. Instead, first make sure that the form will be saved in the correct folder (`C:\VBFILES\CHINA`), then change the name in the file name box to `Login`:

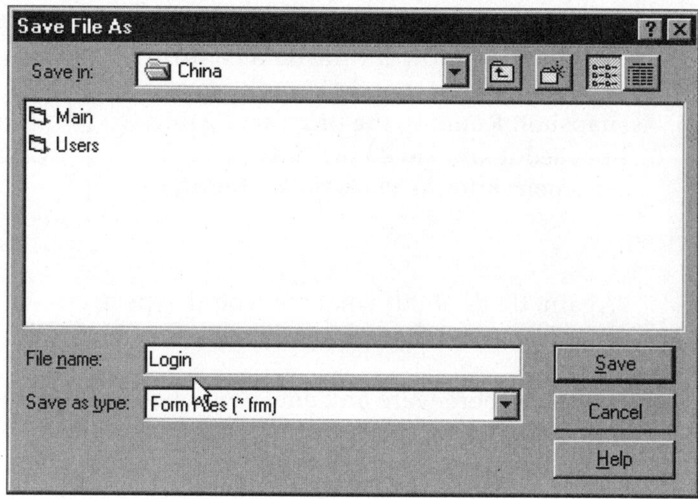


... and click on the Save button.

3. In the Visual Basic project explorer window, you should now see three forms – `Main` (with a `Name` propertyof `frmMain`), `Login` (with a `Name` property of `frmLogin`), and `Users` (with a `Name` property of `frmUsers`):

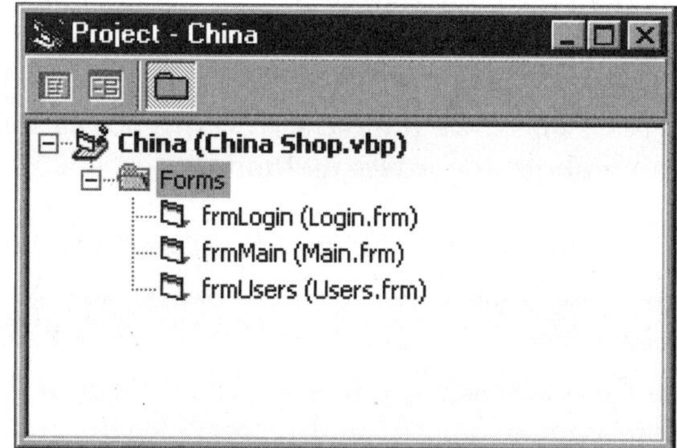


### *Discussion*

In this exercise, there were two students who had too quickly clicked on the Save button before changing the name of the form from `frmLogin` to `Login`. As we had done the previous week, we used Windows Explorer to rename the file that the form was stored in.

We moved on to the next exercise.

## Exercise – Adding Controls to the Login Form

In this exercise, you'll add controls to the `Login` form. These will let the China Shop staff enter a User ID and password when they start up the program.

1. Continue working with the China Shop project.

2. Add two labels, two text boxes, and two command buttons to the `Login` form. Size the form and position the controls roughly according to the screenshot below. Remember, this is *your* project!

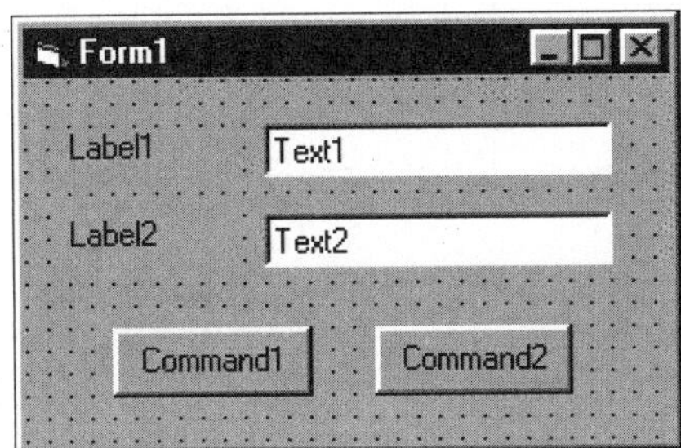


3. Use the following table to make changes to the properties of the label control currently named `Label1`:

| Property | Value |
|---|---|
| Name | lblUserID |
| Caption | &User Name: |

4. Use the next table to alter the properties of the label control currently named `Label2`:

| Property | Value |
|---|---|
| Name | lblPassword |
| Caption | &Password: |

5. Use this table to make the amendments to the properties of the text box control currently named `Text1`:

| Property | Value |
|---|---|
| Name | txtUserID |
| Text | (blank) |

Remember, to clear the `Text` property just select it and press the *Backspace* or *Delete* key.

6. Use the following table to make changes to the properties of the text box control currently named `Text2`:

| Property | Value |
|---|---|
| Name | txtPassword |
| Text | |
| PasswordChar | * |

Setting the `PasswordChar` property like this will mask whatever's typed into the text box and display asterisks instead.

7. Follow the guidelines in the next table to make changes to the properties of the command button currently named `Command1`:

| Property | Value |
|---|---|
| Name | cmdOK |
| Caption | OK |
| Default | True |

8. Use the following table to make changes to the properties of the command button currently named `Command2`:

| Property | Value |
|---|---|
| Name | cmdCancel |
| Cancel | True |
| Caption | Cancel |

9. Now change the properties of `frmLogin` to match the following chart:

| Property | Value |
|---|---|
| Name | frmLogin |
| BorderStyle | 3-Fixed Dialog |
| Caption | Bullina China Shop Login |
| Moveable | False |
| StartUpPosition | 2-Center Screen |

10. Your form should now look similar to this screenshot:

11. Now add a data control to the form. The data control will not be visible to the user when the program runs, so don't worry too much about the placement or size of the data control:

**12.** Use the following table to change the properties of the **data control (currently called `Data1`):**

| Property | Value | Comment |
|---|---|---|
| Name | datUsers | Hungarian notation: this data control will link to the Users table |
| DatabaseName | C:\VBFILES\CHINA\CHINA.MDB | Use the File dialog box to specify this property - **do not** type this into the property box! |
| RecordsetType | 0-Table | Will permit us to use the Index property |
| RecordSource | Users | Select from the drop-down list box |
| Visible | False | We don't want the user to see the data control |

**13.** Save the China Shop project. Remember that, because you have already saved this form, you won't be prompted for a file name.

At the moment, there's no way to test the behavior of the `Login` form, because the China Shop's `Main` form is still the **startup object** for the China Shop project. However, in our next exercise we'll make the `Login` form the startup object so that it appears immediately when the China Shop staff start the program.

### *Discussion*

"The controls that we've just placed on the `Login` form," I said "will allow the user of the program to enter their name and password, and to have those values checked against the `Users` table of the `China` database. In our next exercise, we'll make this form the startup object for the project, so that this is the form the user sees by default."

"Placing that data control in the middle of the form bothers me a little," Rhonda said.

"Don't worry too much about it, Rhonda," I said. "It doesn't look great in design mode, but when the program runs the data control will be invisible: the user will never see it and have their aesthetic sense insulted."

"Why are we making the data control invisible in the first place?" Lou asked. "Doesn't the user need to see it?"

"In this case," I said, "the user will **not** be directly interacting with the `Users` table – it will be the code in the `Click` event procedure of the command button that initiates the interaction. As long as the data control is on the form, and regardless of whether it is visible or not, we'll be able to use it to connect to the `Users` table of the `China` database."

"I notice," Rachel remarked, "that the two text boxes are not bound to the data control. Did we forget something?"

"That's a good question," I said. "We won't be binding any controls to the data control on the `Login` form. If we did that (and I've seen beginners do this quite a bit), when the `Login` form appears, the data from the first record in the `Users` table would appear in the two text boxes, and that's really not what we want. The text boxes are present just so the user can tell us their `UserID` and `Password`. Then, once the user has entered values into these text boxes, and clicked on the OK button, we will use those values to locate a matching record in the `Users` table. You'll see the code for that next week."

Having dealt with these questions, I distributed our third exercise.

## Exercise – Change the Startup Object of the China Shop project

In this exercise, you'll change the startup object of the China Shop project from `frmMain` to `frmLogin`. As we've seen, this will take the user directly to the `Login` form when the program starts up.

1. With the China Shop project in design view, select Project | China Properties from the Visual Basic menu bar. The following screen will be displayed:

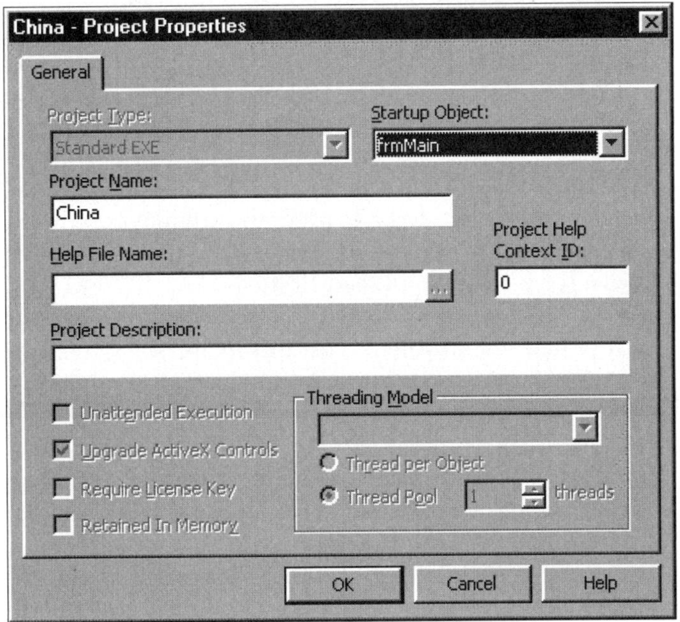

2. Click on the Startup Object drop-down list box, and select **`frmLogin`** as the Startup Object:

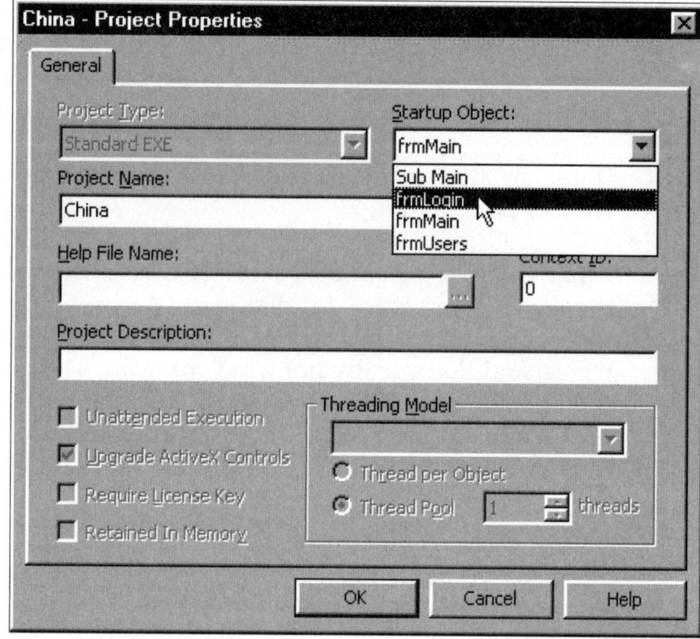


3. Click on the OK button, and then save the China Shop project.
4. Now run the China Shop program. As the **`Login`** form is now the startup object for the China Shop project, the **`Login`** form will be displayed immediately. At this point, however, with no code in the **`Click`** event procedures of the command buttons, we can't get very far! Close the **`Login`** form by clicking on its control menu box.

### *Discussion*

"The **Startup Object** property of the project," I said, "allows us to designate a particular form that we want to be loaded and displayed when the project starts up. In our case, since we now want to be able to identify the user of the China Shop program, we now want the **`Login`** form to be displayed first."

"I only had one problem with this exercise," Chuck said. "I was confused when I saw something called **`Sub Main`** in the drop-down list box for the startup object. We don't have a form by that name, do we?"

"**`Sub Main`**," I said, "refers to a subprocedure called **`Main`** in a **Standard Module**. When specifying the startup object for a Visual Basic project, you can either designate a form, or create a standard module and write a procedure (essentially, a self-contained chunk of code) called **Main** which can then be named as the startup object for your program. In fact, you're about to create a standard module of your own, although we won't be creating a **`Main`** subprocedure."

"What's a standard module?" Rhonda asked. "I know we discussed them briefly in the Introductory class, but beyond that, I don't remember any details."

"You can think of it as a repository for code," I said. "A standard module has no visual interface, and is used to declare variables, and to hold subprocedures and functions that need to be accessible from one or more forms in your project. This facility allows us to separate out code that serves more than one form, for example, and lets us create variables that can be shared by a number of forms. We'll be declaring two variables in a standard module that will need to be visible from more than one form in our China Shop project."

There were no further questions, so I handed out this exercise for the class to complete.

## Exercise – Creating a Standard Module

One of the things that we'll be doing in the modified China Shop project is keeping track of who has logged into the program. Because the user's identity must span more than one form in the China Shop project, we will need to create a **global** variable – and global variables in Visual Basic must be declared in a standard module. It's now time to create our first standard module.

1. Continue working with the China Shop project.

2. Select Project | Add Module from the Visual Basic menu bar:

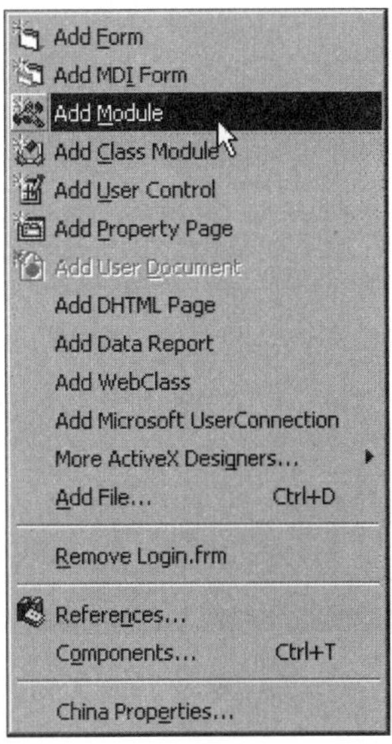

3. The following screen will appear:

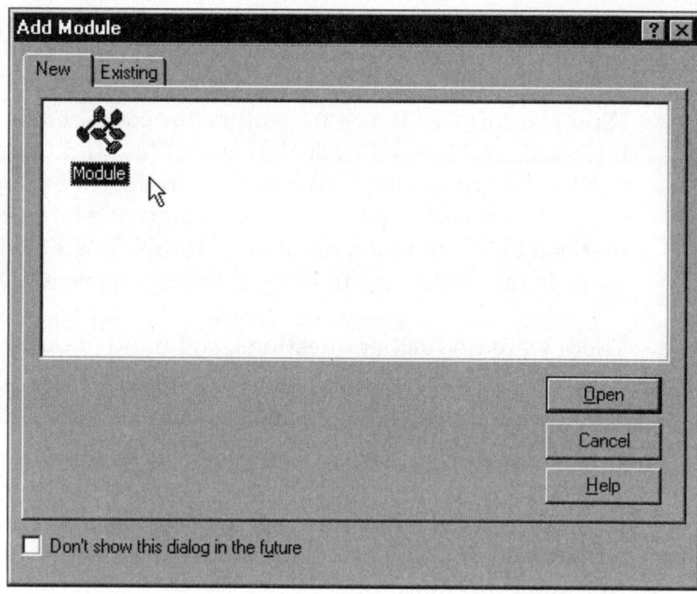


4. Make sure the New tab is selected, and then double click on Module. Visual Basic will then display what appears to be a code window for you – this is actually your new module – `Module1`:

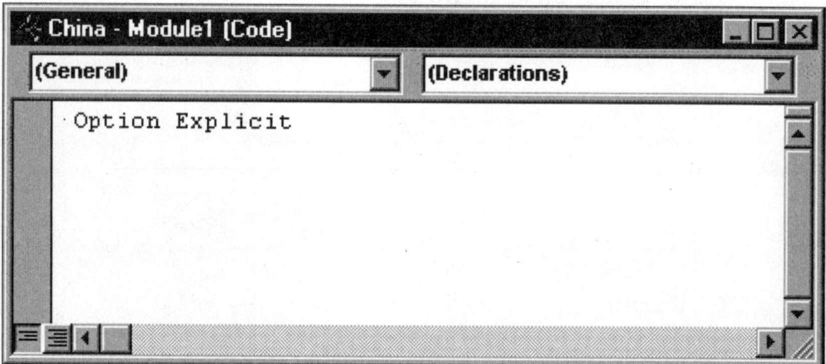

5. Bring up the Project Explorer window by selecting View | Project Explorer. In addition to the three forms in the China Shop project, you should now also see `Module1` in the Project Explorer window:

6. Now click on the 'save' button on the toolbar. Visual Basic will immediately prompt you to save the new standard module with a disk file name of `Module1`. Remember – **don't save it with this name**. Instead, first make sure that the standard module will be saved in the correct folder (`C:\VBFILES\CHINA`) and then change the name in the Save File As dialog box to `China`:

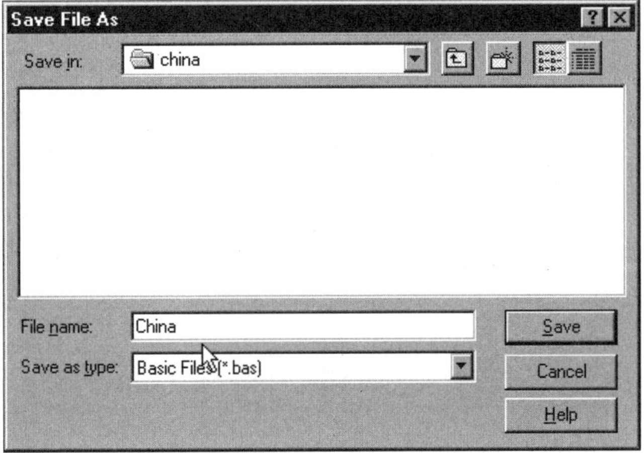


... and then click on the Save button.

7. In the Project Explorer window, you should now see a standard module whose `Name` property is `Module1` – but whose external disk file name is `China.Bas`:

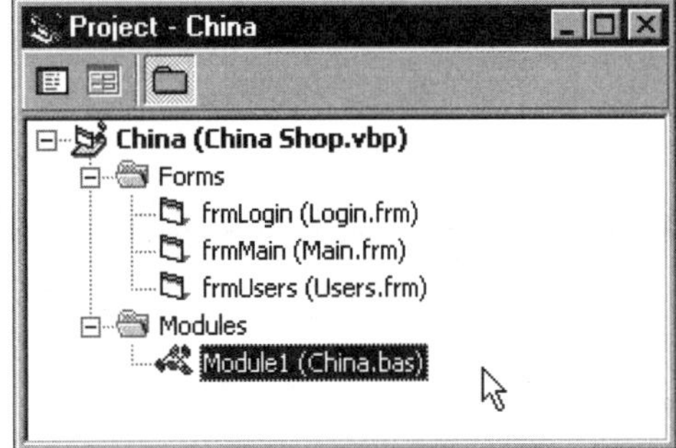

#### Discussion

Aside from the fact that no one in the class had ever created a standard module before, there were no major problems completing this exercise.

I then distributed the final exercise for the day.

## Exercise – Declaring a Global Variable in the Standard Module

In this exercise, you'll declare two **global variables** in the `General Declarations` section of the standard module. These global variables will then be available to all the forms in our project.

1. Continue working with the China Shop project.
2. Bring up the Project Explorer window and select the standard module by double-clicking on it. This will bring up the module's Code window.
3. Type the following variable declarations into the `General Declarations` section of the module (If you have the Require Variable Declaration box checked in the Tools | Options | Editor menu options, then `Option Explicit` should already be showing up in the code window):

```
Option Explicit
Public g_intCustomerNumber As Integer
Public g_strUser As String
```

Your code window will now look like this:

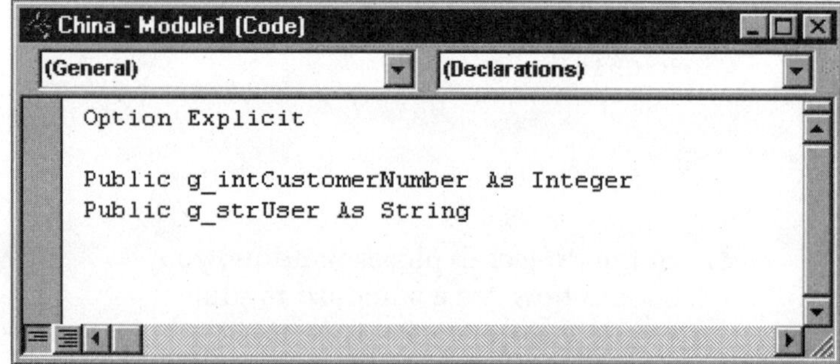


4. Save the China Shop project.

#### Discussion

"The two variables that we have declared here," I said, "are global variables, which means they can be accessed from more than one form in our project. Notice that I have prefixed the variable names with the letter 'g' and an underscore: these characters identify these variables as **global**."

"I also noticed," Ward said, "that you've declared them as `Public`."

"That's right, Ward," I answered, "in a standard module we have two choices as far as variable declarations are concerned – `Private`, which is the module equivalent of the `Dim` statement, or `Public`. A `Public` variable can be seen from any form in the project. A variable declared as `Private` in a standard module can only be seen by other code within that standard module."

"I'm guessing," Dave said "that `g_strUser` is the variable you mentioned that will enable us to know who has logged into the China Shop project? But what about `g_intCustomerNumber`?"

"You're right, Dave," I said. "`g_strUser` is a variable that will contain the name of the person who has logged in. Something else that we might need to know is the individual customer who is using the China Shop program. I know it's been a while, but if you think back to our requirements statement, we're also asking the customer who is purchasing china to identify themselves. The customer will either supply us with a Customer ID, or our program will automatically assign them one – either way, that Customer ID will need to be accessible from more than one form in the project: to achieve this, we'll assign it to the variable `g_intCustomerNumber`."

I waited to see if there were any more questions.

"Next week," I said, "we'll finish up our discussion of the recordset by looking at the methods of the recordset. Then we'll finish coding the login form."

I then dismissed class for the day. It had been a long class once again, and we had covered a lot of properties. But I knew that talking about the recordset and the properties that help us interact with it would be extremely useful knowledge to have later on: all the time, the students were learning more and more about the recordset, and building up their database-interaction toolkit.

## Chapter Summary

In this chapter we examined the recordset's properties, and began to develop the China Shop's `Login` form. Among the important things we covered in this chapter, we saw that:

- The recordset has an array of properties that we can use to interact with the recordset
- The `AbsolutePosition`, `RecordCount`, and `PercentPosition` properties let us see where our record pointer is in the recordset – we can use this information to help the user and to aid navigation
- We can bookmark records in the recordset and move quickly back to them
- We can set properties that enable us to use Access indexes to move swiftly to the records that we're interested in

Finally, we did some work to continue enhancing the China Shop project:

- We built up the `Login` form
- We made the `Login` form the **startup object** for the project so that it would appear on the screen when the program started
- We created a module that to house the **global variables** that will be shared by our project's forms

In the next lesson, we'll explore the recordset further by looking at its **methods**. We'll also take a look at Structured Query Language (**SQL**), the universal language of databases, before we implement some more enhancements to the China Shop project.

# More on Data Access – the Recordset

isual Basic Learn to Program Databas

vith Visual Basic Learn to Progra

atabases with Visual Basic Learn

rogram Databases with Visual Basic Lea

o Program Databases with Visual Bas

earn to Program Databases with Visu

asic Learn to Program Databases wi

isual Basic Learn to Program Databas

vith Visual Basic Learn to Progra

atabases with Visual Basic Learn

rogram Databases with Visual Basic Lea

o Program Databases with Visual Bas

earn to Program Databases with Visu

asic Learn to Program Databases wi

isual Basic Learn to Program Databas

vith Visual Basic Learn to Progra

atabases with Visual Basic Learn

## Chapter 6

# More on the Recordset

Following on from the previous lesson, in this session we'll be examining the properties of the recordset in more depth. We'll be learning about ways to locate information within a database and to manipulate our data so we get the results we want quickly and efficiently; to do this we'll carry on looking at the `Biblio` database. We'll also touch on using **SQL** statements in Visual Basic: if you've never heard this term before, don't worry – we'll explain as much as you need to know. Additionally we'll take a quick look at ways of using Access queries to enhance the functionality of the data control.

Here's a summary of what we'll be looking at this week:

- Creating command buttons on a form as a shortcut for jumping straight to specific locations in the recordset
- Learning how to use the `Find` and `Seek` methods for locating the exact information we want
- Understanding what SQL is and how it can aid our work with databases
- Using Access to generate the SQL statements we need

We'll end up by completing the `Login` form of the China Shop project, and making an alteration to the `Main` form.

So now we join my class as they prepare to carry on from last week...

## More on the Recordset

We began our sixth class by continuing with our discussion of the recordset generated by the database connection of the data control.

"Last week," I said, "we discussed recordset properties. In today's class, we'll conclude our formal discussion of the recordset by discussing recordset **methods**."

"Don't recordsets have *events* that we can write code for?' Steve asked.

"That's a good question, Steve," I said. "**DAO** recordsets – which is the type that our data control creates – have no events, although **ADO** recordsets do have some events that you can write code for. Coding for ADO events makes the ADO recordset a good deal more complicated than the DAO recordset, which is one reason we're using the DAO data control in this database course."

"What about the `Reposition` event?" Rhonda asked. "We've already seen how to put code in that, haven't we? So that's definitely an event."

"Yes it is, Rhonda," I answered, "but the `Reposition` event is an event of the data control, **not** the recordset. Both of the events that we discussed two weeks ago – the `Reposition` and `Validation` event – belong to the data control. The underlying DAO recordset has no events."

"Before we go any further, could you clarify the differences between properties, methods and events?" Rhonda requested. "I'm worried about confusing them."

"Certainly," I responded. "A good way to explain the differences between a property and a method is to use an analogy. If you were talking about a car, and you were referring to its color or shape, you would be discussing one of its **properties**. Properties describe some aspect of the car. If, however, you were talking about the cars ability to turn left or to switch on its lights, then you'd be talking a bout **methods**. These are things that the car can do: to switch on the lights, we'd invoke the car's `TurnLightsOn` method. An **event** is something that which happens outside of or around the car, but which the car can respond to. Does that help?"

"Yes," Rhonda affirmed. "Thanks – these little reminders really help me to keep things straight."

As there were no recordset events to discuss, I moved on to recordset **methods**.

## Recordset Methods

"As was the case when we talked about recordset properties," I began, "we're not going to discuss every single recordset method. There are more recordset methods than there are recordset properties, and many of them are way beyond the introductory nature of our database course. Furthermore, some of these methods only apply to recordsets created by data access objects – something we'll look at in week 9 of the course."

"Definitely," I said, as I displayed this chart of recordset methods on the classroom projector. "Anything marked with a comment that reads 'Later' is a recordset method that we'll discuss in a future lesson:"

***Recordset Methods Summary Chart***

| Method | Dynaset? | Snapshot? | Table? | Comments |
|---|---|---|---|---|
| AddNew | | | | Later |
| Cancel | | | | Later |
| CancelUpdate | | | | Later |
| Close | | | | Later |
| Delete | | | | Later |
| Edit | | | | Later |
| FindFirst | | | No | |
| FindLast | | | No | |
| FindNext | | | No | |
| FindPrevious | | | No | |
| Move | | | | |
| MoveFirst | | | | |
| MoveLast | | | | |
| MoveNext | | | | |
| MovePrevious | | | | |
| NextRecordset | | | | |
| OpenRecordset | | | | Later |
| Seek | No | No | | |
| Update | | | | Later |

## *The MoveFirst, MoveLast, MoveNext,and MovePrevious Methods*

"Let's begin our discussion," I said, "by examining the **Move** family of recordset methods. Each one of these methods – **MoveFirst**, **MoveLast**, **MoveNext** and **MovePrevious** – equates to one of the four navigation buttons found on the data control. In fact, when you click on one of those navigation buttons on the data control, internally the data control is really executing one of these recordset methods."

"That's interesting," Kate said, "I didn't realize that."

I brought up the DBGrid demonstration project from the previous week, and displayed it on the classroom projector:

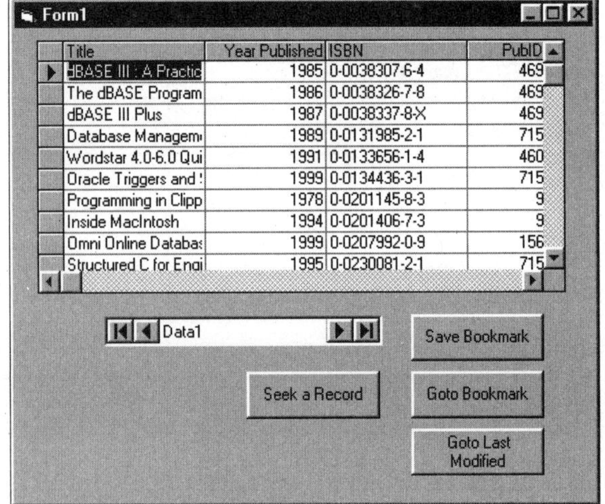


"Our form is getting pretty cluttered with all of these command buttons," I said, "but I think we have room for some more if I rearrange things a bit."

I then placed four new command buttons on the form and changed their **Name** properties to **cmdMoveFirst**, **cmdMoveLast**, **cmdMoveNext** and **cmdMovePrevious**. I also changed their **Caption** properties to: **MoveFirst**, **MoveLast**, **MoveNext** and **MovePrevious** respectively:

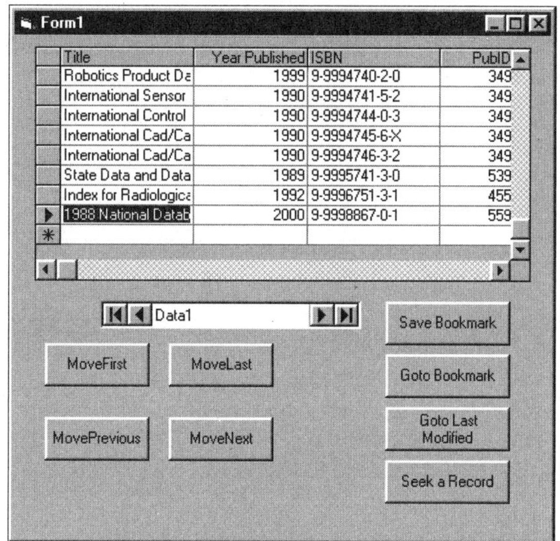


"Today's demonstrations," I said, "will focus very much on record counts and record pointers. Last week we commented out the line of code in the `Reposition` event procedure of the data control because it referred to properties of the recordset not supported by the `Table` type recordset. Today, for the most part, we'll be using the `Dynaset` recordset type, so let's remove the comment character from the `Reposition` event's code and change the `RecordsetType` property from `Table` to `Dynaset`."

I made these two important changes before continuing.

"We can now place the following code in the `Click` event procedure of the command button captioned MoveFirst:"

```
Private Sub cmdMoveFirst_Click()

Data1.Recordset.MoveFirst

End Sub
```

"This code just executes the **MoveFirst** method of the recordset," I said. "Let's test this code now by clicking on the 'last record' button on the data control, and move the record pointer to the end of the recordset:"

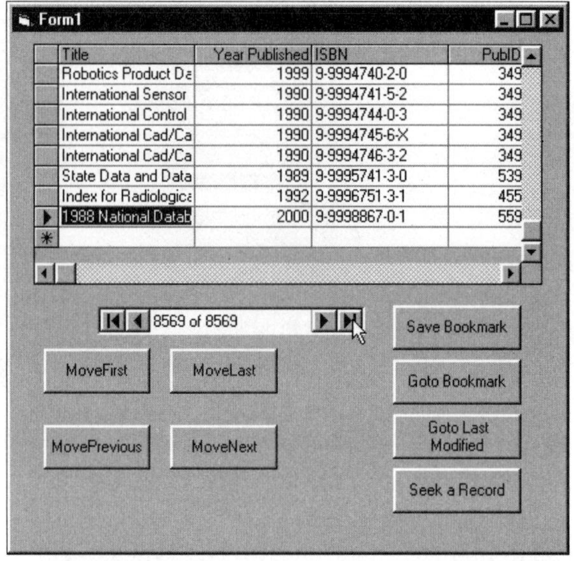


"... and then we'll click on the new MoveFirst button. That should move the record pointer to the first record in the recordset:"

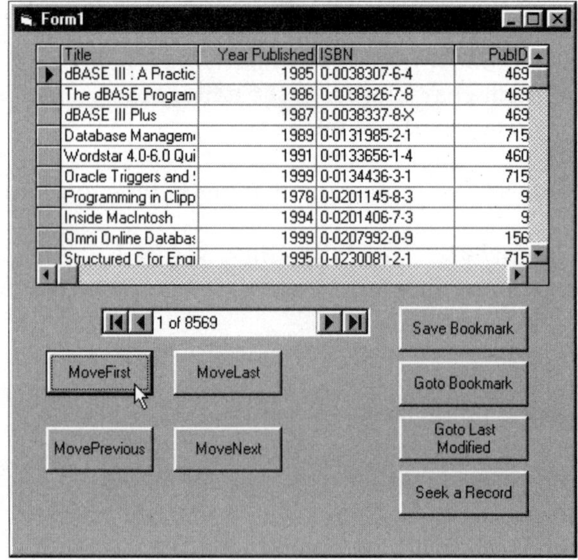


"What we've seen here," I said, "is that executing the **MoveFirst** method of the recordset moves the record pointer to the first record in the recordset. Similarly, we can place code in the `Click` event procedure of a command button to move to the last record in a recordset."

To demonstrate this, I keyed the following code into the `Click` event procedure of the command button captioned MoveLast...

```
Private Sub cmdMoveLast_Click()

Data1.Recordset.MoveLast

End Sub
```

... and ran the program. When I clicked on the MoveLast command button, the record pointer immediately moved to the final record:

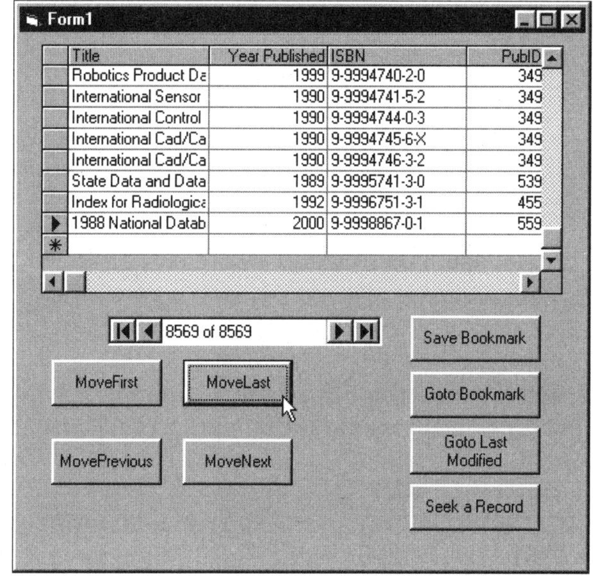


"Now we've seen `MoveLast` in action," I said, "let's carry on and write some code that uses the `MoveNext` method."

I typed this code into the MoveNext command button's `Click` event procedure:

```
Private Sub cmdMoveNext_Click()

Data1.Recordset.MoveNext

End Sub
```

... and ran the program. With the record pointer on the first record, I clicked on the MoveNext button, and the record pointer advanced to the second record:

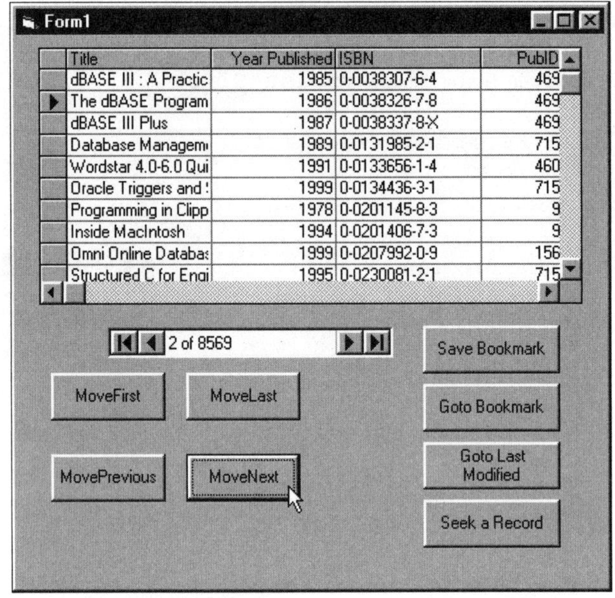


"This seems pretty straightforward," Rhonda said. "What we're doing here is using the command buttons to mimic the behavior that's already built into the navigation buttons of the data control, is that right?"

"That's right," I said, "but we need to do a bit more beyond that. The data control provides some built-in safety features that we don't get automatically when we perform the recordset navigation ourselves. I'll just finish adding the code for the final button, MovePrevious, and then I'll show you what I mean. Let's place this code into MovePrevious..."

```
Private Sub cmdMovePrevious_Click()

Data1.Recordset.MovePrevious

End Sub
```

"...and see how it works."

I used the MoveLast button to move the record pointer to the end of the recordset, and then clicked on the MovePrevious button:

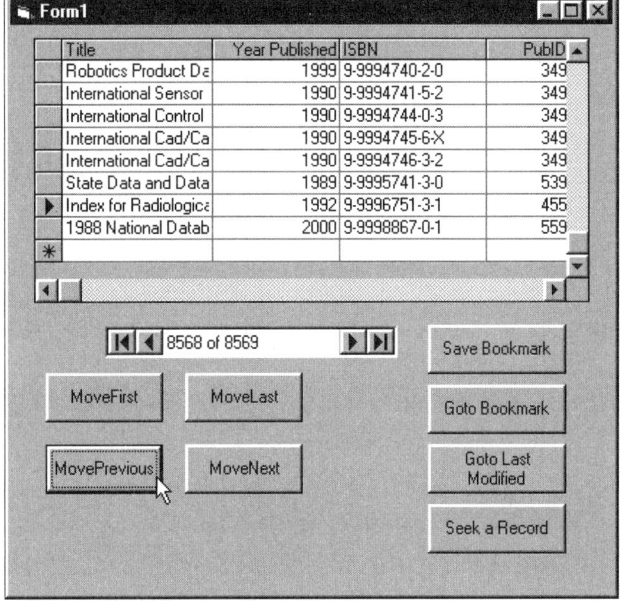


"Now we've finished creating the buttons," I said, "I'll demonstrate one of those safety methods. I'll use MoveLast to position the record pointer to the final record:

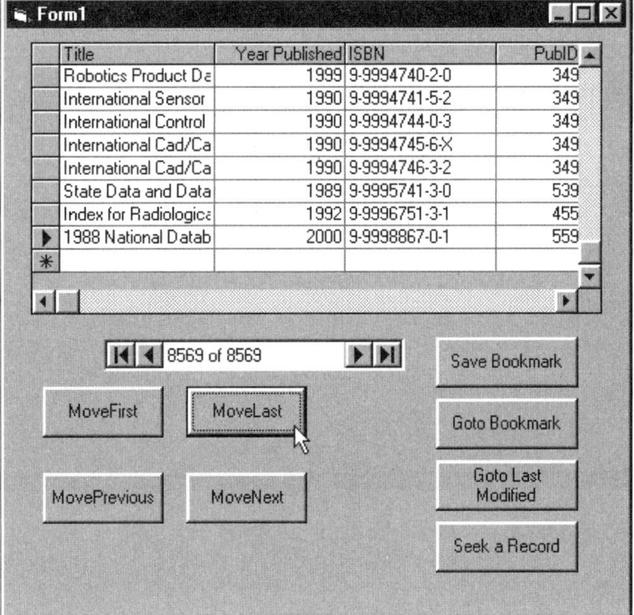

... and then clicked on the MoveNext command button:

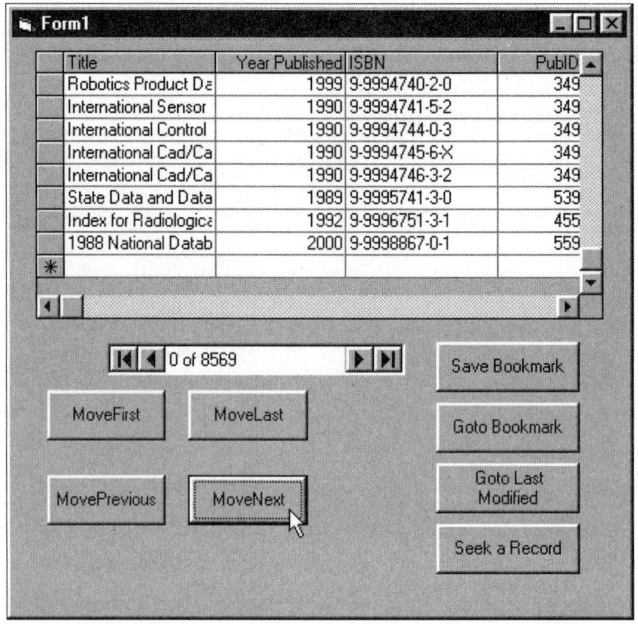


"That's peculiar," Melissa said. "The record number in the data control's caption now reads 0, and the record pointer seems to have disappeared. It's no longer displayed in the DBGrid. What happened?"

"I bet we've 'gone off the edge' of the recordset," Rachel said. "Is the record pointer now at the `EOF`?"

"That's good thinking, Rachel," I said, "but we haven't quite fallen off the 'edge' yet, although the record pointer *is* now positioned in the `EOF`. When we clicked on the MoveLast button, the record pointer advanced to the last record in the recordset. Then, when we clicked on the MoveNext button, the record pointer advanced one 'record' beyond the last record, which is the `EOF`. Any guesses as to what will happen if I click on the MoveNext button again?"

No one ventured any guesses, and so I clicked on MoveNext once more:

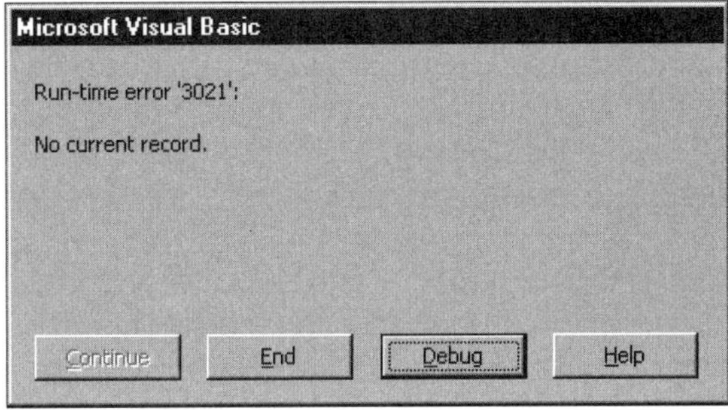


"What happened?" Rhonda asked. "What does this mean?"

"Now we really have fallen off the edge of the recordset, as Rachel put it earlier," I said. "Our record pointer was already positioned at the `EOF`, and when we clicked on the MoveNext button, our record pointer went beyond the boundary of the recordset, and Visual Basic generated this error message telling us that we could no longer move in that direction."

"I thought," Chuck said, "that the `EOFAction` property of the data control specified a value of `Add New`. Shouldn't that value prevent this from happening?"

"You're right, Chuck," I said, "the `EOFAction` property of the data control is set to `Add New`. However, that's a property of the data control, **not** the recordset. Remember that our button is invoking the **recordset's** `MoveLast` method:"

```
Data1.Recordset.MoveLast
```

"Getting back to our Run-time error message," Ward said, "I see that the `EOFAction` property of the data control prevents our record pointer from falling off the edge when we use the data control's navigation buttons to move through the recordset, but *not* when we use our own code."

"That's right, Ward," I said, "when you execute recordset methods in code, you're on your own, so to speak, and you really need to consider the `BOF` and `EOF` properties, and cater for them in your code."

"Is it really necessary to execute these recordset methods directly, like we're doing here?" Rachel asked. "Can't everything we need to do be done using data control?"

"Not quite," I said, "The data control is really a control for the user to interact with, rather than a tool for the programmer."

"What do you mean?" Mary asked.

"Later on today," I said, "we'll be completing the **Login** form of the China Shop. During the login process, the user will enter a **UserID** and a P**assword** in text boxes on the **Login** form, and then click on the OK button. At that point, we need to execute code that locates and validates the **UserID** and **password** in the **Users** table of the **China** database. We can't do that in our code by using data control methods and properties; we need to use recordset methods and properties instead."

"Why can't we use data control methods to do that?" Steve asked.

"Data control methods don't have the functionality we need to locate a record in the **Users** table," I said. "The only way to locate a record in the **Users** table is to use either the **Seek** method or one of the **Find** methods of the recordset. Later on, we'll also need to be able to add records to the **Transactions** table, and that's something we can't do using data control methods. Instead we'll need to use a recordset method called **AddNew**."

"I guess," Rhonda said, "that I'm still confused by the fact that on one hand you say we won't be using the data control methods or properties for the **Login** form, but on the other hand the data control is still on the form, even if it's invisible. If we don't need the data control, why did we place it on the form in the first place?"

"We need the data control to create the recordset," I answered. "It's the data control that connects to the database and then generates the recordset that we'll access via recordset methods and properties. Without the data control, we'd have no records to work with!"

"Ah, I see!" Rhonda said. "I think I get it. For the **Login** form, we need the data control to give us access to the records in the **Users** table, but since we're using those records 'behind the scenes' to perform user validation, the user doesn't need to see them; that's why we made the data control invisible."

"That's right, Rhonda," I said, "and that's also why we don't have any bound controls. The recordset that we are building is strictly for our use – the user doesn't need to see it."

"Is the data control the only way to generate a recordset?" Chuck asked.

"There is one other way," I said, "and that's to use data access objects, which we'll cover later on in the course. Data access objects allow you to create recordsets without the data control."

"That means no navigation buttons then?" Ward asked.

"That's right," I said. "In my commercial work, I use data access objects when no visual interface is required for the user. Essentially, the work we're doing here is 'behind the scenes' as far as the user is concerned. We'll see this later when we work with the `Login` form, or in the next few weeks when we write the code to read china brands from the `Inventory` table."

"That sounds complicated," Rhonda said. "Will we have to use data access objects for our work in the China Shop project?"

"We don't *have* to," I said. "Everything we need to do for the China Shop project can be done using the data control to generate our recordsets. But I will introduce you to data access objects later in the course."

I waited a moment to see if there were any more questions.

"Getting back to that error message," Lou said, "is there anything we can do to prevent the user from falling off the edge of the recordset?"

"Yes there is, Lou," I said. "There are a couple of ways we could approach this. We could permit the user to position their record pointer to the `EOF` record, and if they attempt to move beyond it, move them back to the `EOF`. Or we could take the approach I'm going to use here, which is to prevent the user from getting to the `EOF` at all when they click on the `MoveNext` button. Like this:"

I then modified the `cmdMoveNext` button's `Click` event procedure to look like this (modified code is highlighted):

```
Private Sub cmdMoveNext_Click()

Data1.Recordset.MoveNext

If Data1.Recordset.EOF Then
    Data1.Recordset.MovePrevious
End If

End Sub
```

"As you can see," I said, "here we're executing the `MoveNext` method of the recordset. We then immediately determine if that movement has positioned the record pointer to the `EOF`:"

```
If Data1.Recordset.EOF Then
```

"If the record pointer **is** at **EOF**, we execute the **MovePrevious** method to move back one record:"

```
Data1.Recordset.MovePrevious
```

"As I mentioned, we could use similar code to permit the user to advance to the **EOF**, but not beyond it."

I then ran the program, used the MoveLast button to go to the last record in the recordset, and then clicked on MoveNext. This time, the record pointer did **not** advance beyond the last record in the recordset:

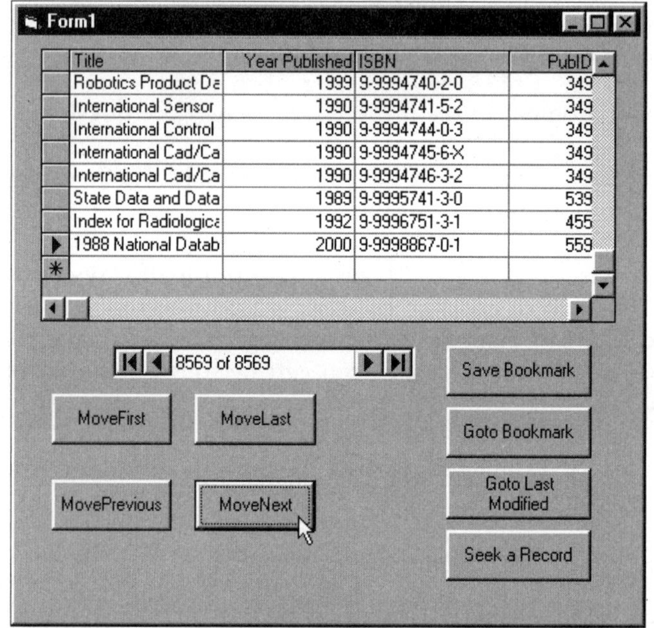


"In effect," said Dave, "what you've done is add your own **EOFAction** property to the **MoveLast** method."

"That's exactly right, Dave," I said. "This code moves the record pointer to the last record in the recordset if the user moves to the **EOF. This is** exactly what the **EOFAction** property specifies should happen when its value is set to **MoveLast**."

"Will we need to do something similar for the code in the MovePrevious button?" Kate asked.

"That's a good point, Kate," I said, "yes, we will. Here's the code for the MovePrevious button's **Click** event procedure."

I then typed the following code into the `Click` event procedure of the command button captioned MovePrevious (again, the changed code is highlighted):

```
Private Sub cmdMovePrevious_Click()

Data1.Recordset.MovePrevious

If Data1.Recordset.BOF Then
   Data1.Recordset.MoveNext
End If

End Sub
```

I clicked on the MoveFirst button to move the record pointer to the first record in the recordset, and then clicked on the MovePrevious button.

"No problem there," Dave said, as the record pointer remained on the first data record in the recordset.

"That's right, Dave," I said, "without the check for the **BOF**, our program would have bombed when we attempted to move beyond the **BOF**. By checking for the **BOF** and then executing the **MoveNext** method, we've ensured that the user doesn't move beyond the **BOF** and into 'no man's land'."

I asked if there were any questions about any of the family of **Move** methods we had just covered. There were none, and so I moved onto a discussion of the generic **Move** method.

### *The Move Method*

"There's one more **Move** method of the recordset to discuss," I said, "and it's what I call the **generic** **Move** method. The generic **Move** method accepts a single argument, which is either a positive or a negative number. It uses this argument to move the record pointer either up or down from its current position in the recordset."

I placed a new command button on the form, changed its **Name** property to **cmdMoveHowMany** and its **Caption** property to **Move how many Records?**. Then I added the following code into its **Click** event procedure:

```
Private Sub cmdMoveHowMany_Click()

Dim lngHowManyRecords As Long

lngHowManyRecords = Val(InputBox("Enter a number"))

If lngHowManyRecords <> 0 Then
    Data1.Recordset.Move lngHowManyRecords
End If

If Data1.Recordset.EOF Then
    Data1.Recordset.MovePrevious
End If

If Data1.Recordset.BOF Then
    Data1.Recordset.MoveNext
End If

End Sub
```

"As you can see," I said, "this code displays an input box, and asks the user to enter a number representing the number of records to move either forward or backward in the recordset:"

```
lngHowManyRecords = Val(InputBox("Enter a number"))
```

"I'll talk you through the rest of the code when we've seen it in action," I said, before running the program, clicked on the Move how many Record button, and the input box prompting me to enter a number to move the record pointer was displayed.

"Let's enter the number 4," I said. "Since our record pointer is currently positioned on the first record of the recordset, our record pointer should move forward 4 records, to record number 5:"

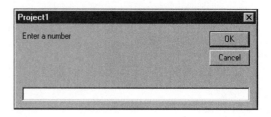

...I clicked on the OK button, and in an instant the record pointer was positioned to record number 5:

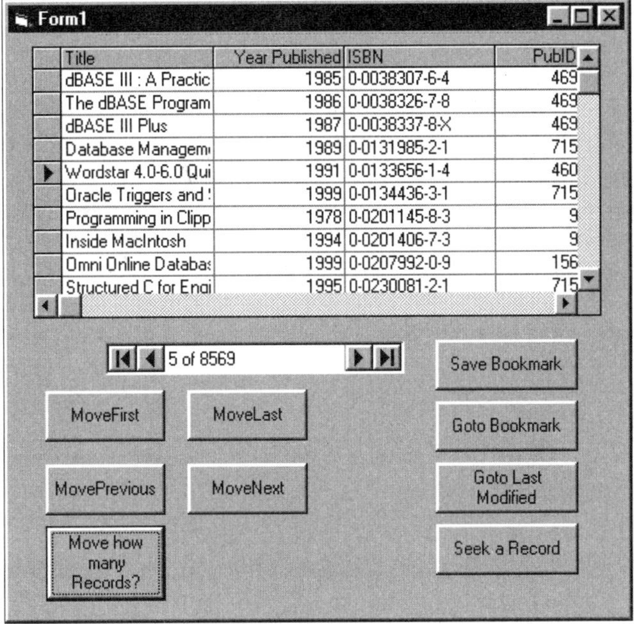


"The code in this **Click** event procedure," I said, "accepts a value from the user via the input box function, stores that value into a long type variable, and then uses that variable as an argument to the **Move** method of the recordset. If the user enters a positive number, the record pointer is moved forward. If the user enters a negative number, the record pointer is moved backward in the recordset."

I waited to see if anyone had a question.

"I just coded this myself," Dave said, "and I must say I was surprised to see that if I enter a very large value into the input box – one that exceeds the size of the recordset – then the record pointer seems to move to the **EOF**, then to the last proper record in the recordset. I figured that the program would bomb if we tried to move beyond the **BOF** or **EOF**."

"You're right, Dave," I said, "one of the characteristics of the **Move** method of the recordset is that it won't permit you to supply it with an argument that causes the record pointer to move beyond the boundary of the recordset. For instance, if the user enters 999999 in the input box, and the recordset contains only 100 records, the **Move** method will position the record pointer to the **EOF**."

"And at that point," Dave interjected, "if **EOF** is **True**, the record pointer is moved to the last record in the file."

"That's right," I agreed.

"And the same goes for a large *negative* value?" Kathy asked.

"Correct, Kathy," I agreed, "the behavior of the **Move** method with respect to the **BOF** is identical; it won't allow you to move off that 'edge' of the recordset either."

"I can see a lot of practical value in the **Move** method," Ward said. "For instance, we could create command buttons with code that allows the user to move through the recordset in increments of 50, 100 or 500 records."

"I've seen that in some programs," Valerie chimed in. "It's great when you're dealing with a lot of records in a DBGrid."

There were no more questions, and so we moved to the **Seek** method.

## The Seek Method

"We've just spent some time," I said, "seeing how we can move the record pointer forwards and backwards through a recordset. With the family of **Move** methods, you need to know exactly where you want to go in the recordset. Now we start to look at methods that allow us to locate records in a recordset even when we don't know exactly where they are."

"In the next few minutes," I continued, "we'll be discussing the **Find** family of methods. Last week we took a quick look at the **Seek** method when we discussed the **Index** property of the recordset. Using the **Seek** method, you can quickly locate a record in a **Table** type recordset, after first having set the **Index** property of the recordset to a valid Access index name. The keyword here is 'quickly', as the **Seek** method utilizes an Access table's index to quickly find the record in a recordset. So the **Seek** method only works on a **Table** type recordset because, unlike **Dynasets and Snapshots** , a **Table** type recordset can have an index. The **Seek** statement has the following syntax," I said, displaying this slide:

*Recordset.***Seek** *comparison, key1, key2...etc*

where the comparison operators are: <, <=, =, >=, or >.

> and the key values are one or more values corresponding to fields in the **Recordset** current index, as specified by its **Index** property setting. You can use up to 13 *key* arguments.

"Let me try and clarify this a little," I said, sensing that this syntax wasn't completely transparent. "Let's pretend," I went on, "that we have a table in a database called **Players** that keeps track of statistics for the players in an ice hockey league. Let's pretend further that we have created an index in that table based on the **GoalsScored** field, which stores data on the number of goals scored by players in the league. If we wanted to quickly locate the first record in the table which has a value of 30 in the **GoalsScored** field, this code would do it:"

```
Data1.Recordset.Index = "GoalsScored"
Data1.Recordset.Seek "=",30
```

"That's peculiar-looking," Lou said. "By that, I mean the equals sign inside the quotation marks, separated from the number by a comma. It looks odd!"

"That's the syntax of the **Seek** method," I said. "Beginners in Visual Basic are often tripped up by this, and I'll admit that it does take some getting used to. You can choose to use any of the six comparison operators, but each operator must be specified within quotation marks. Also, the key value you are seeking must be separated by a comma."

I waited to see if everyone was following me.

"Suppose there's more than one player in the league," Dave asked, "who has scored 30 goals. Will the **Seek** method only locate the *first* record?"

"That's right, Dave," I replied. "The **Seek** method will locate the first record. But, as you may remember from last week, as soon as you set the **Index** property of the recordset equal to a particular index, the records in the recordset are sequenced in that order. That means as soon as you locate the first record you are looking for, if there are any others with the same value they'll be next in line in the display, since we're ordering the records using the **GoalsScored** index."

"That makes sense," Rhonda said. "Can you show us an example of the **Seek** method using another operator?"

"Sure thing," I said, "here's some code that will locate the first record in the **Players** table where the value in the **GoalsScored** field is *greater* than 50."

```
Data1.Recordset.Index = "GoalsScored"
Data1.Recordset.Seek ">",50
```

"I think I'm OK with this," Kathy said. "I somehow thought this would be more difficult."

"Using the **Seek** method can get a little complicated," I said, "especially if you are dealing with an **index** that's based on more than one field. That's why, in the syntax I displayed on the classroom projector, it showed how you need to separate key values by commas."

"I must be missing something," Rhonda said. "How can you have more than one key value?"

"If you have an Index that is based on more than one field in the table." I said. "For instance, again using that mythical **Players** table, suppose you have an index called **Name** which is based on the **FirstName** and **LastName** fields in the table. If you wanted to locate a record in the table where the name was Eric Lindros, here's what the code would look like:"

```
Data1.Recordset.Index = "Name"
Data1.Recordset.Seek "=","Eric","Lindros"
```

"You're right," Linda said, "this is getting a little more complicated. I notice that this time the values are enclosed within quotation marks. Is that because both of those fields are defined as **Text** fields in the table?"

"That's a good point, Linda," I said, "the values you supply as arguments to the **Seek** method must match the data types of the fields in the table. So if the field is a number, then you must supply a number as an argument. It's important to remember that, in Visual Basic, numbers do not have quotation marks around them. As soon as you sandwich a number between quotation marks, it becomes a **String Literal**."

"That's right," Chuck said, "I remember that from the intro class."

"I think it's time now," I said, "to display the code we wrote last week for the **Click** event of the command button labeled Seek. I promised last week to discuss it in more detail today." I then displayed the code from the **cmdSeek** button:

```
Private Sub cmdSeek_Click()

Dim strISBN As String

strISBN = InputBox("Enter an ISBN")
Data1.Recordset.Index = "PrimaryKey"
Data1.Recordset.Seek "=", strISBN
```

```
If Data1.Recordset.NoMatch = True Then
   MsgBox "Sorry, no match---try again"
End If

End Sub
```

"This is pretty straightforward," I said. "As you can see, we accept a value from the user via the input box function:"

```
strISBN = InputBox("Enter an ISBN")
```

"We then set the recordset's `Index` property equal to the primary key of the table, which happens to be based on the field `ISBN` in the `Titles` table:"

```
Data1.Recordset.Index = "PrimaryKey"
```

"`ISBN`, by the way, is defined as a *number* in the `Titles` table. At that point, we execute the `Seek` method of the recordset, supplying it a single argument, the value of the variable `strISBN`:"

```
Data1.Recordset.Seek "=", strISBN
```

"I know I shouldn't still be getting confused over this," Rhonda said, "but supplying a variable as an argument instead of using a literal still puzzles me a bit."

"That's understandable, Rhonda," I said, "that abstraction takes a bit of getting used to. Just do what Visual Basic does, which is evaluate the line of code in two steps. When Visual Basic sees a line of code that looks like this..."

```
Data1.Recordset.Seek "=", strISBN
```

"...it makes the same kind of substitution that you should mentally. That is, it looks in RAM, locates the current value of the variable `strISBN` – let's say it's 1902-745-000 – and makes this substitution:"

```
Data1.Recordset.Seek "=", 1902-745-000
```

"That helps," Rhonda said.

"You did say the `Seek` method can only be used for a `Table` type recordset, didn't you?" Linda asked.

"That's right, Linda," I said, "if you need to locate a record in either a `Dynaset` or `Snapshot` recordset, you must use one of the four `Find` methods. We'll look at those methods right now."

## The FindFirst, FindLast, FindNext, FindPrevious Methods

"The `Find` methods of the recordset," I said, "are fairly similar to the `Seek` method, but I think you'll find the syntax is different. The `Find` methods use a syntax similar to an SQL statement, which is something we'll look at later on today."

"How many `Find` methods are there?" Peter asked.

"There are four," I replied, "`FindFirst`, `FindLast`, `FindNext`, and `FindPrevious`. The difference between these methods and the `Seek` method is how they locate the records in a recordset. The `Seek` method, as we discussed just now, uses a table's index. The `Find` methods are slower; they start at the beginning of the recordset and work their way record by record to the end until they locate the record they're looking for. If the recordset is very large, the `Find` methods will take longer to locate a record than `Seek will`."

"Similar to the difference between using an index to find a reference in a book," Rachel said, "and thumbing through each one of the pages?"

"Exactly," I answered.

"Can you use the `Find` methods with `Table` type recordsets?" asked Melissa.

"No you can't," I answered, "the `Find` methods apply only to the `Dynaset` and `Snapshot` recordsets, just like the `Seek` method only applies to the `Table` type recordset."

"What's the difference between the four different `Find` methods?" Linda asked.
"`FindFirst` locates the first matching record in the recordset," I said. "Once a record is located, then `FindNext` can be used to locate the next record with the criteria you're looking for, and `FindPrevious` is used to locate the previous matching record. Remember, in a `Dynaset` or `Snapshot` type recordset, the records will not be in sequence as they are when you are locating a record using the `Seek` method. The `FindLast` method will, as its name suggests, find the last record which matches your request."

"Are there any other differences between them?" Kevin asked.

"Yes." I replied. There are variations as to where in the recordset the search begins, as well as in the direction of the search. Here's a chart that summarizes the four **Find** methods:"

| Find method | Begins searching at | Search direction |
|---|---|---|
| FindFirst | Beginning of Recordset | End of Recordset |
| FindLast | End of Recordset | Beginning of Recordset |
| FindNext | Current record | End of Recordset |
| FindPrevious | Current record | Beginning of Recordset |

"As you can see," I continued, "**FindFirst** starts at the beginning of the recordset, and searches to the end. **FindLast** starts at the end of the recordset, and searches to the beginning. **FindNext** starts at the current record and moves towards the end. **FindPrevious** starts at the current record and moves towards the beginning. In all cases, as soon as the relevant record is located the search ends and the record pointer is placed on that record."

I waited a moment for questions before continuing.

"As I mentioned, the syntax for the **Find** method is different from that of the **Seek** method," I said. "It's very similar to the SQL syntax I'll be discussing with you in just a few minutes. Let me place one more command button on the form, and we'll write some code to illustrate the **FindFirst** method."

I then positioned a new command button and changed its **Name** property to **cmdFindFirst**. I then changed its **Caption** property to **FindFirst** and keyed the following code into its **Click** event procedure:

```
Private Sub cmdFindFirst_Click()

Dim strISBN As String

strISBN = InputBox("Enter an ISBN")
```

*continued on following page*

```
Data1.Recordset.FindFirst "ISBN = '" & strISBN & "'"

If Data1.Recordset.NoMatch = True Then
    MsgBox "Sorry, no match---try again"
End If

End Sub
```

I then ran the program and clicked on the FindFirst button. When the input box appeared, I entered the same ISBN of the record I had located using the **Seek** method the previous week:

When I clicked on the OK button the **FindFirst** method of the recordset was executed, and the record pointer in the DBGrid was positioned to the record with this matching ISBN:

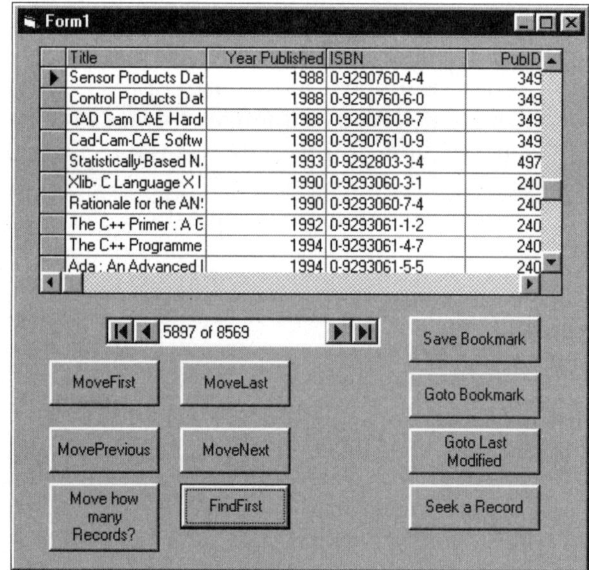


"Was it my imagination," Chuck said, "or did the **FindFirst** method seem slower in locating that record than the **Seek** method did?"

"No, I don't think that was your imagination, Chuck," I said. "The **Seek** method is much faster than any of the **Find** methods. This becomes more apparent in larger recordset, and also depends on how far down the recordset the record is located."

"I think you mentioned," Rhonda added, "that the syntax for the **Find** methods would be a more complicated than that of the **Seek** method. I'm a little confused. Why are we mixing quotation marks and apostrophes here? And what about the concatenation characters? The syntax of the **Seek** method seemed a bit more straightforward."

"The confusion," I think, "lies in the fact that the argument to the **Find** methods is itself a string, and therefore must be enclosed within quotation marks. More confusing is the fact that if we are executing the **Find** method on a field which is defined as a **Text** field in the recordset – in this case ISBN – the criteria we need to specify to locate the record in the recordset must also be enclosed within quotation marks."

"If I heard you right," Ward said, "you really need quotation marks *within* quotation marks."

"That's right, Ward," I said, "but there are two problems there. For one, Visual Basic gets a bit confused by the syntax, and you need to code quotation marks within quotation marks in a special way. That leads me to our second problem – this syntax is extremely confusing to beginners, and so – initially – I code the syntax for the **Find** methods of the record set using apostrophes, which for the most part is fine."

I looked around the classroom and saw some confusion.

"I think it will help if I show you what I mean," I continued. "The statement we ultimately want Visual Basic to see is this one..." I quickly wrote this statement on the wipeboard:

```
Data1.Recordset.FindFirst "ISBN = '0-9290760-4-4'"
```

"That statement," I said, "tells Visual Basic to locate the first record in the recordset where the ISBN is equal to **0-9290760-4-4**. Now here's the problem: how do we format a string so that Visual Basic interprets our statement this way? The problem is further complicated by the fact that we are using a string variable, not a string literal, in the argument to the **FindFirst** method. That means that Visual Basic must look to RAM to find the value of the string variable. And then somehow we need to enclose the value of that string variable within apostrophes."

"The 'sandwich' effect, right?" Steve asked.

"That's right," I agreed. "That 'sandwich' effect, as you rightly describe it, is just what we need. Let's take a look at the code in the **Click** event procedure of the command button, and I'll try to explain how we go from this..."

```
Data1.Recordset.FindFirst "ISBN = '" & strISBN & "'"
```

"...to this:"

```
Data1.Recordset.FindFirst "ISBN = '0-9290760-4-4'"
```

"First of all," I said, "the value of the variable `strISBN` is `0-9290760-4-4`. Visual Basic then interprets the line of code like this, substituting the value of the variable `strISBN` in the expression:"

```
Data1.Recordset.FindFirst "ISBN = '" & 0-9290760-4-4 & "'"
```

"We're closer to what we need," I continued, "but we need to 'sandwich' apostrophes around the string literal. That's what the concatenation characters are used for, so that, finally, the expression is interpreted by Visual Basic as:"

```
Data1.Recordset.FindFirst "ISBN = '0-9290760-4-4'"
```

"I think that's better," Lou said.

"That helped me a lot." Rhonda smiled.

"I hate to throw a monkey wrench into the works," I said, "but using apostrophes to sandwich the value of the string variable is not ideal. It can pose some problems when the string variable itself contains an apostrophe as it confuses Visual Basic. For instance, suppose instead of looking for a particular ISBN, we were instead looking for a last name, perhaps an Irish last name such as O'Malley?"

"That will confuse Visual Basic?" Melissa asked.

"That's right," I said. "Quotation marks and apostrophes are key symbols in what is known in computer science as **parsing**; that's a technical term for how Visual Basic interprets the characters that comprise its commands, statements, methods, and arguments. The apostrophe in the string variable will lead to an expression that will confuse Visual Basic and ultimately result in a syntax error.

I originally wrote the code in the FindFirst button's `Click` event procedure using apostrophes to make it easier to explain it to you. Although that syntax works, it really should look like this..."

I then re-wrote the code in the `Click` **event** procedure to look like this. Changed code is highlighted as usual:

```
Private Sub cmdFindFirst_Click()

Dim strISBN As String

strISBN = InputBox("Enter an ISBN")

Data1.Recordset.FindFirst "ISBN = """ & strISBN & """"

If Data1.Recordset.NoMatch = True Then
    MsgBox "Sorry, no match - try again"
End If

End Sub
```

I then ran the program, clicked on FindFirst, entered the same **ISBN** into the input box as before, and clicked on the OK button. The record pointer immediately moved to that record.

"The program works the same as it did before," I said, "we've just replaced each apostrophe in the expression with two quotation marks. I know this code looks peculiar, but this syntax is the better choice."

```
Data1.Recordset.FindFirst "ISBN = """ & strISBN & """"
```

"Whenever Visual Basic sees a pair of quotation marks within a string," I said, "it interprets the pair of quotation marks as just a single quotation mark. Therefore, this statement:"

ISBN = """0-9290760-4-4"""

"...is *really* interpreted like this:"

ISBN = "0-9290760-4-4"

"That also means that this expression:"

Data1.Recordset.FindFirst "ISBN = """ & 0-9290760-4-4 & """"

"...is interpreted by Visual Basic as:"

Data1.Recordset.FindFirst "ISBN = "0-9290760-4-4""

"Ultimately," I concluded, "this is the string argument that is finally passed to the `FindFirst` method."

"I don't know about anyone else," Rhonda said, "but this is all pretty confusing."

"This is confusing to everyone at first, Rhonda," I said. "Here are some tips which I think will make composing the argument to the `Find` methods easier for you:"

**1. First write the statement using apostrophes. Sandwich apostrophes around the literal or variable of the string using the Visual Basic concatenation characters. Work from the inside to the outside when formatting the expression.**

**2. Ensure that you have an even number of apostrophes in the statement**

**3. Ensure that you have four apostrophes at the end of the statement.**

**4. Rewrite the statement, replacing each apostrophe with two quotation marks.**

"OK, that concludes our discussion of recordset methods," I said. "The syntax for the `FindLast`, `FindNext` and `FindPrevious` methods are just about identical to the `FindFirst`. I'd like to take a fifteen-minute break now. When we return, our next topic will be the Structured Query Language – SQL. We'll be taking a look at how SQL can help us find and retrieve records, and this is a natural continuation of the kind of processes we've been examining so far today. See you after the break."

## A SQL Primer

"Structured Query Language, or SQL," I began, straight after the break, "is a standard language for accessing data in a database. We've spent the last few weeks specifying properties of the data control to produce recordsets containing records. So far, it's been an 'all or nothing' proposition. By that I mean we've retrieved *all* of the records from the `Titles` table, or *all* of the records from the `Users` table. We'll see in a few moments that SQL provides you with a lot more flexibility for retrieving records."

"Do we need to do to do anything special to be able to use SQL in a Visual Basic program?" Peter asked.

"Let me preface my answer," I said, "by saying that you can use SQL either with the data control or with data access objects. As you know, we'll touch upon data access objects later on in the course, and I'll discuss the use of SQL with data access objects at that point. As far as the data control is concerned, SQL can only be used with a recordset type of `Dynaset`, and the SQL statement must be assigned to the `RecordSource` property of the data control."

"I guess I just don't see how that can be easier than specifying a table name for the `RecordSource` property," Tom said.

"It's not really *easier*," I said, "the SQL statement is much more difficult to work with than merely selecting a table name from a drop-down list box. However, there are many advantages to using SQL, and the three that I think you will find most useful are: (1) using a SQL statement, you can restrict the **fields** that are returned in the recordset (2) you can also restrict the **records** that are returned in the recordset (3) you can return fields from more than one table and display them as if all the fields were in a **single** table."

"You mean that when we use SQL, we don't need to display every field in a record or every record in a table?" Rhonda asked.

"That's right, Rhonda," I said. "By specifying an SQL statement in the data control's `RecordSource` property, we can restrict the records that are returned in the recordset based on some condition in the record, such as `Date of Birth`, `Date Hired`, or `Salary`, for instance. An example would be where you only wanted to see records for people above a certain level of salary. This kind of feature can be very useful when you have a table with a large number of records, and the user is interested only in a subset of them."

"That sounds extremely flexible," Chuck said.

"Yes, Chuck," I replied. "We can restrict both the records **and** the fields that are returned in the recordset. For example, you might have a table with a large number of fields. Perhaps the user simply doesn't need to see data from all of them. Or perhaps the user is not permitted – due to company rules or policy – to see the data in every field in the database. SQL gives you the ability to restrict the fields in the recordset to only the fields the user is entitled to see. A knowledge of SQL gives us tremendous possibilities for filtering and retrieving records."

### The SQL Select Statement

"Let's start our demonstration of SQL with a simple `Select` statement," I said. "Let's start out with a fresh Visual Basic project."

I then created a new `Standard.EXE` project and placed a data control on the form, along with a DBGrid. I set the `DatabaseName` property of the data control to the `Biblio` database and left the `RecordsetType` property of the data control as `Dynaset`, which is the default value. I then changed the `EOFAction` property to `Add New` and set the `DataSource` property of the DBGrid to `Data1` and the `AllowAddNew` property to `True`.

"Let's now place that code we had in the **Reposition event** procedure from the previous project," I said. "That way, we'll be able to see the number of records we're returning in the recordset:"

```
Private Sub Data1_Reposition()

Data1.Caption = Data1.Recordset.AbsolutePosition + 1 & " of " &
Data1.Recordset.RecordCount

End Sub
```

"Can anyone tell me," I said, "what property I haven't specified that I had placed a value in earlier this morning?"

"The **RecordSource** property?" Rachel asked.

"That's right, Rachel," I said. " I've already specified a **RecordSource** property of **Titles** to tell Visual Basic that I wanted to retrieve *every* record from the **Titles** table of the **Biblio** database. What I'm going to do now, instead of selecting **Titles** from the drop-down list box of the **RecordSource** property, is to enter SQL code directly into the **RecordSource** property. This will have the same effect as selecting the table name **Titles** from the list box."

I entered the following SQL statement into the data control's **RecordSource** property:

**SELECT * FROM TITLES**

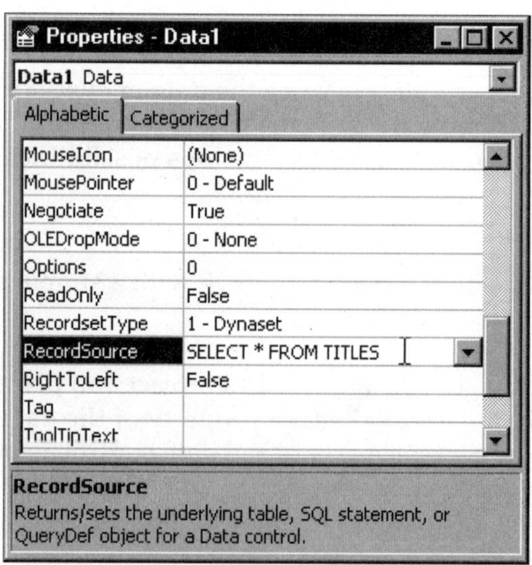


"Did I just see you type that statement straight into the **RecordSource** property?" Rhonda asked. "Isn't there usually a drop-down list box there containing the **Table** names in the **Biblio** database?"

"That's right, Rhonda," I said, "and, ordinarily, we would choose from one of the tables in that drop-down list box. However, the data control also gives us the option of specifying a SQL statement for the `RecordSource` property instead of selecting a table name. Let me run the program now and show you what happens:"

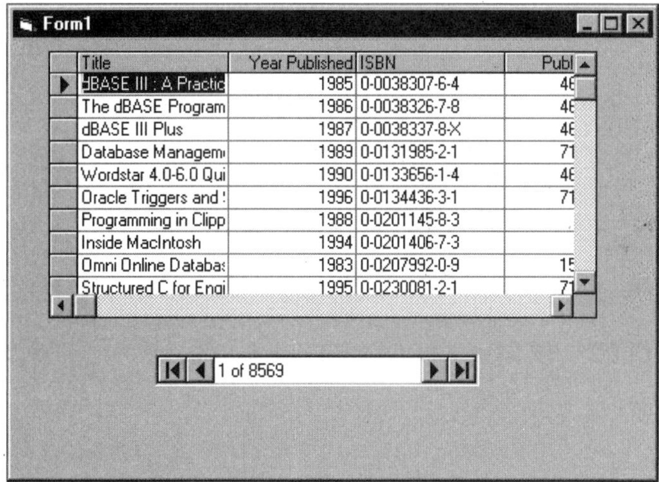


"As you can see," I said, "the SQL statement returned every field and every record in the `Titles` table of the `Biblio` database."

> **Remember that you'll need to add code to the form's `Initialize` event to get the correct number of records displayed in the data control's caption. We added similar code to a demonstration project in Chapter 5**

"Let me get back to that SQL statement now:"

**SELECT * FROM TITLES**

"The heart of the SQL statement is the `Select` statement," I said. "The `Select` statement is the SQL verb that tells Access to retrieve records. The basic format of the `Select` statement is this:"

**SELECT *fields* FROM *table***

"What does the asterisk mean in the statement you used in the program?" Rhonda asked. "That's not a field name in the `Titles` table."

"Well observed, Rhonda," I said. "When you specify an asterisk following the `Select` keyword, it tells Visual Basic to retrieve *every* field from the specified table. In this instance, that means every field in the `Titles` table. As was the case when we specified a table name in the `RecordSource` property, once the data control makes the connection to the database using the SQL statement in the `RecordSource` property, a `Dynaset` recordset type is created, and any controls bound to the data control are then populated with the data from the recordset."

## *The SQL Select Statement for a Single Field*

"May I presume," Dave said, "that if we coded a statement something like..."

```
SELECT TITLE FROM TITLES
```

"...then we would see only *one* field in the `DBGrid`: the `Title` field?"

"Great thinking, Dave," I said. "Let's try that and see."

I then stopped the program, and changed the `RecordSource` property to...

```
SELECT [TITLE] FROM TITLES
```

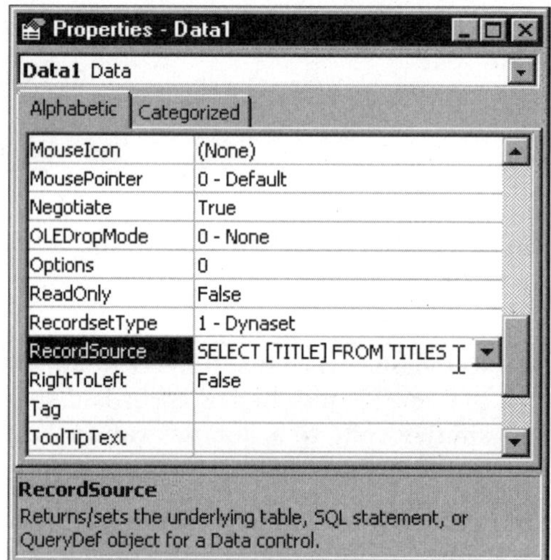


"Why the brackets around the `TITLE` field name?" Kate asked.

"Just experience," I responded. "I've worked with quite a few Access databases where the field names contained spaces. If they do, you need to enclose the field name within brackets in an SQL statement. Out of habit, I just place brackets around them, regardless."

"Why is it capitalized?" Melissa wondered.

"That's my way of clearly denoting this as a SQL statement," I responded. "Let's run this program now and see if Dave is right about what's displayed in the DBGrid:"

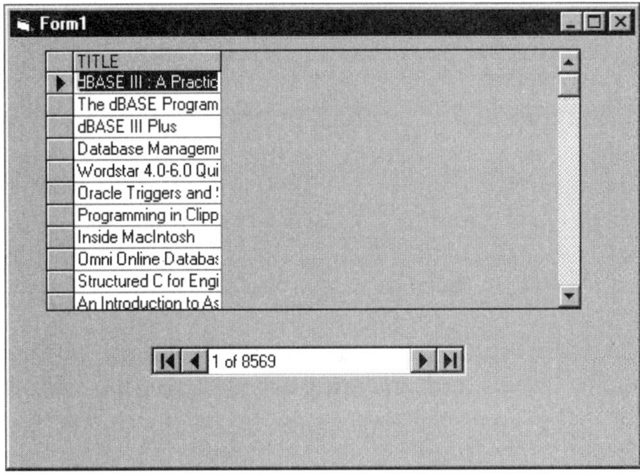


"Dave was right," I said to the class, "only one field is in the recordset."

"And that was because only one field was specified in the SQL statement?" Bob asked.

"That's right," I said.

"What about the other fields in the table," Melissa said. "Are they in the recordset somewhere behind the scenes?"

"No, Melissa," I replied, "because we specified just a single field in the `Select` statement, that's the only field contained in the recordset."

"The DBGrid looks pretty gawky," Rachel said, "is there any way to resize the column so that we can see more of the data in the `Title` field?"

"Yes there is," I said. "One of the characteristics of the DBGrid is that the user can resize any of the columns just by clicking and dragging the right boundary of the first row – the DBGrid's header – like this:"

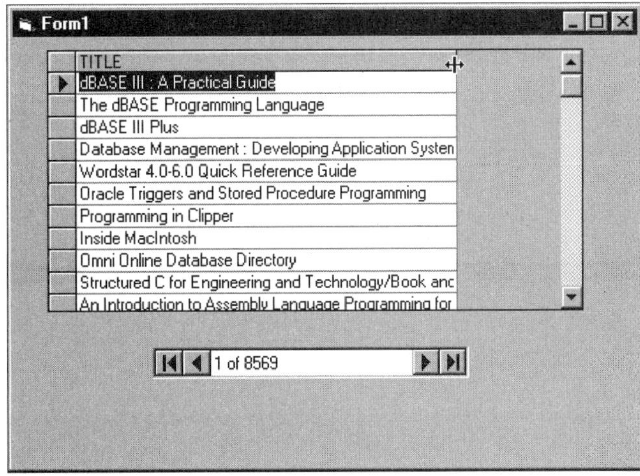

"Unfortunately," I continued, "when this program ends, the user's preference for column size is lost, and the DBGrid columns will be set back to their defaults."

"Couldn't we store the user's preferred column settings in the Windows registry?" Dave asked.

"Later on in the course," I replied, "we'll do exactly that, so that the user's preferred column settings can be retained after the program ends."

"Can't we store them in Visual Basic?" asked Melissa.

"No," I replied. "If you wanted to make an alteration in Visual Basic you would need to make it in design view and, for our purposes, we don't want users having access to this."

I waited to see if any one had any questions about using a `Select` statement to retrieve a single field into a recordset. No one did.

## *The SQL Select Statement for more than One Field*

"Suppose we want to display two fields from the table in the DBGrid," Valerie asked, "how can we do that?"

"To select more than one field," I said, "all we need to do is specify the fields we want returned in the recordset, and separate them with commas. Like this:"

```
SELECT [TITLE],[PUBID] FROM TITLES
```

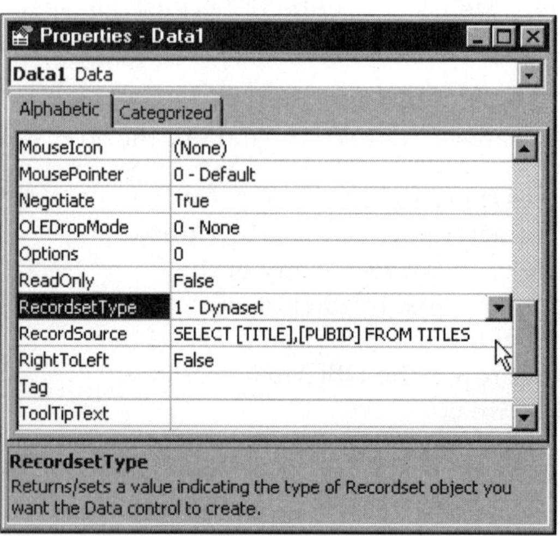

I ran the program, with the following result:

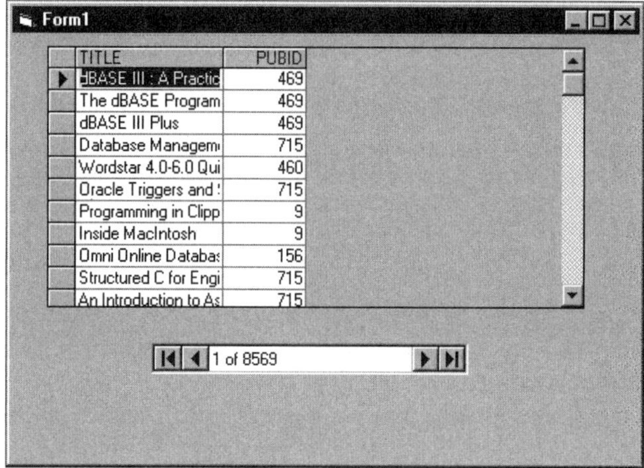


"Notice that we now have *two* fields returned in our recordset," I said, "**Title** and **PubID**."

"You were right about the column size of **Title** reverting back to its default width," Valerie said.

"Don't worry about that," I reassured her, "I'll show you how to take care of that later."

### The SQL Where Clause

"You said that you can use an SQL statement to restrict the number of records returned based on some condition," Dave said. "Can you show us how to do that? How about returning those records that have a **PubID** equal to a particular value, like 469?"

"Sounds good, Dave," I said. "To do that, all we need to do is use the SQL **Where** clause, like this:"

```
SELECT [TITLE],[PUBID] FROM TITLES WHERE
[PUBID] = 469
```

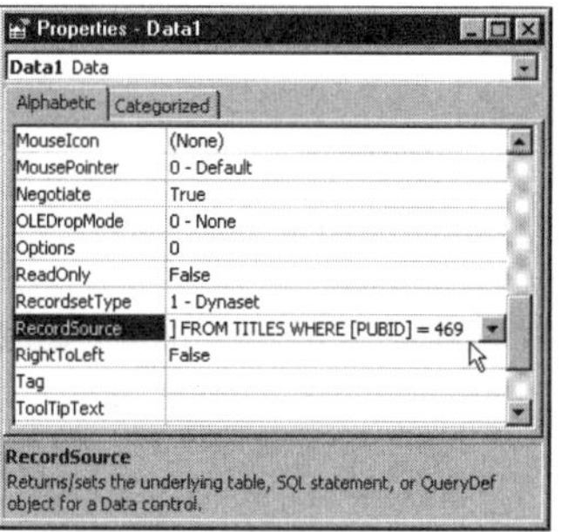


"This SQL statement will return only the records whose **PubID** field is equal to **469**." I said.

I was about to run the program when Ward commented, "That Properties window is getting a bit cramped," he said. "Is there any way that we can set the entire `RecordSource` property value without resizing the Properties window?"

"Ward's right," Kate said, "it is hard to see what you're typing in the `RecordSource` property. In Microsoft Access, I know there's something called a Zoom feature, which allows you to edit a property value like this in a full screen. Does Visual Basic have something similar?"

"I know exactly what you mean, Kate," I said. "Unfortunately, Visual Basic doesn't have a Zoom feature. I agree that not being able to see the entire SQL statement as you enter it into the `RecordSource` property is a source of frustration. It's often the source of errors as well! The best workaround for this is to use an editor like Notepad. Code the statement in Notepad, get the syntax just the way you want it, and then copy and paste it into the `RecordSource` property."

"I suppose it's possible to set the `RecordSource` property in code, isn't it?" Dave suggested.

"Yes, that is possible, Dave." I said. " We'll be doing exactly that before the course is over."

I then ran the program, and the following screen shot was displayed on the classroom projector:

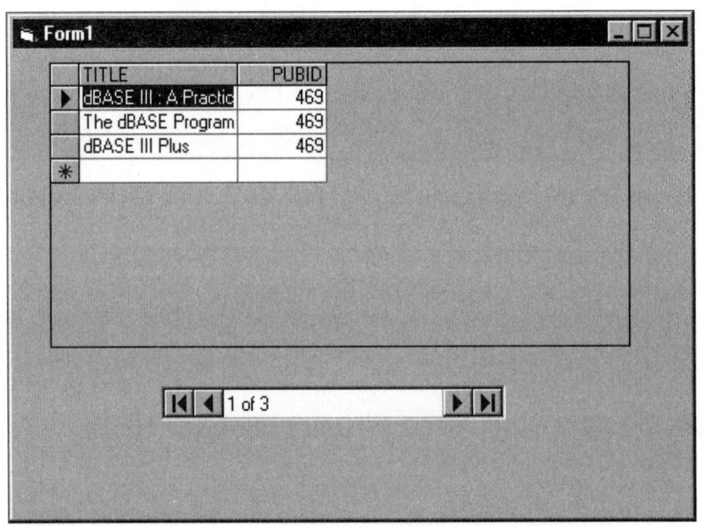


"As you can see, I observed, "The SQL statement returned a recordset containing just those records in the `Titles` table that contained a `PubID` field equal to `469`. And if you needed to retrieve records based on some compound condition – for instance, using the `And` or `Or` operators – all you need to do is use code like this…"

```
SELECT [TITLE],[PUBID] FROM TITLES WHERE [PUBID] = 469 AND [TITLE] =
"Dbase III Plus"
```

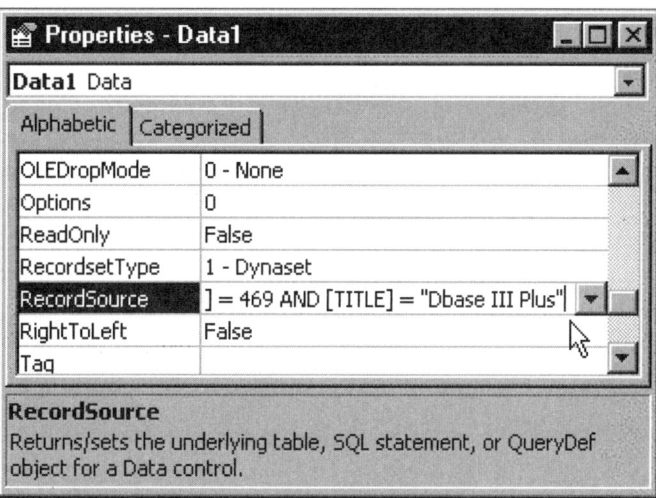


I then ran the program, and the following screen appeared:

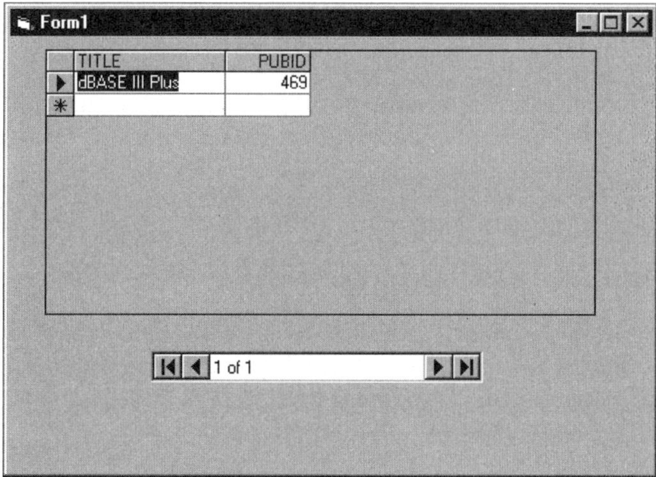


"This recordset contains just a single record," I said, "where the `Title` field is equal to `dBase III Plus` and the `PubID` = `469`."

"I'm really beginning to get a sense of SQL's power and flexibility," Kathy said. "I notice that the data control's caption is smart enough to realize that there is only one record in the recordset."

"I'm curious about something," Rhonda said. "Why, in the SQL statement, didn't you enclose the number **469** in either apostrophes or quotation marks? This SQL statement looks very similar to the **Find** statement you used a little earlier in the class, and you made it clear then that we needed to enclose the value within either apostrophes or quotation marks. Yet you *did* enclose the value for the **Title** field within apostrophes."

"That's a good observation, Rhonda," I said. "When you formulate your SQL statement, you need to be aware of the data type of the fields for which you are specifying values. **PubID** is a numeric field, and therefore the value 469 is not a string value but a numeric value. This means that it must **not** be enclosed within quotation marks or apostrophes, as that action would tell Visual Basic that it is a string value, and cause the SQL statement to fail (or at least not to perform in the way we would expect). But the **Title** field is a different story. **Title** is defined as a **Text** field in Access. This means that any comparison of a value with this field must be done using a string value – which must be enclosed either within quotation marks or apostrophes."

## The SQL Join Clause

"It seems like SQL can do just about anything," Ward said. "It sure would be nice to know the actual name of the **Publisher instead** of some arcane **Publisher ID** code. I know when you first introduced the **Biblio** database a few weeks ago, you said there would be a way of using the **PubID** field in the **Titles** table to 'look up' the actual name of the **Publisher** in the **Publishers** table. Can SQL do this?"

"That's a great point, Ward," I said. "Yes, there is a way to do that. We can use something called the SQL **Join** clause to connect or relate the two tables – **Titles** and **Publishers** – based on their common field, **PubID**. The **PubID** field in the **Titles** table is a foreign key to the **Publishers** table."

I waited a moment to see if this was sinking in.

"Does anyone remember what a foreign key is?" I asked.

"A foreign key," Melissa volunteered, "is a field in one table which is a primary key in another table. In this case, the **PubID** field in the **Titles** table is the primary key in the **Publishers** table. That means that **PubID** is a foreign key in the **Titles** table. Is that right?"

"That's perfect, Melissa," I said. "If two tables each share a key field like this then, using the SQL **Join** clause, we can tell Visual Basic to display the **Title** field from the **Titles** table, and the **Publishers Name** field from the **Publishers** table using the **PubID** field in each table to 'join' or match on. Like this..."

I then changed the SQL statement in the **RecordSource** property to read as follows:

```
SELECT [TITLES].[TITLE], [PUBLISHERS].[NAME] FROM TITLES INNER JOIN
PUBLISHERS ON [TITLES].[PUBID] = [PUBLISHERS].[PUBID]
```

...and ran the program:

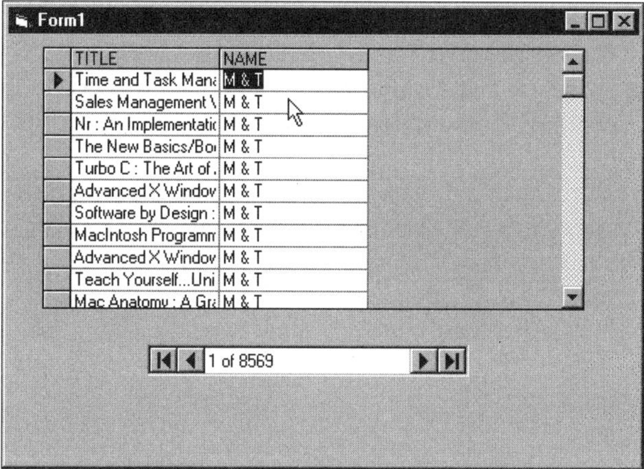


"As you can see," I said, "using the **Join** clause of the SQL Statement, both **Title** and **Name** appear to come from just a single table, although we know that **Title** is in the **Titles** table, and **Name** is in the **Publishers** table."

"That's great," Blaine said, "it really is. My only question is, what is the significance of the phrase **Inner Join**?"

"There are three types of **Join** statements in SQL," I said. "Probably the most common of the three is the **Inner Join**. With an **Inner Join**, only records from the **Titles** table that have a matching **PubID** in the **Publishers** table are returned to the recordset."

There was a moment of silence in the classroom.

"What other possibility could there be?" Dave asked. "Won't *every* record in the **Titles** table have a **PubID** field with a value contained in the **Publishers** table?"

"It's possible, but not likely," I said, "that there could be a record in the **Titles** table containing a **PubID** value not found in the **Publishers** table. More likely, there may be records in the Publishers table containing **PubID** values that are not found in the **Titles** table. When you specify an **Inner Join** in your SQL statement, you tell Visual Basic not to return records of either of these types in your recordset."

"Suppose," Linda said, "for the sake of argument, that we also wanted to see records in the **Titles** table that have no matching **PubID** in the **Publishers** table. Could we do that?"

"That's known as a `Left Outer Join`," I said. "In a `Left Outer Join`, records from the first table – the `Titles` table in this case – are returned in the recordset even if they do not have related records in the second table (the `Publishers` table). With a `Right Outer Join`, all records in the second table are returned in the recordset, and only related records from the first table are returned. Finally, there's a `Full Outer Join` where all records from both tables are returned in the recordset, whether they can be related on the matching field or not."

"This is getting to be pretty confusing," Lou said. "We started off pretty simple with the SQL statements. Now the SQL statements are starting to get much more complex. Is there much call to use `Joins`, other than the `Inner Join`?"

"By far, the most common join is the `Inner Join`," I said.

"I don't know how I'm ever going to keep this syntax straight," Peter said.

"Try to relax, everyone," I said. "Learning SQL takes some time, but I have a shortcut that I'd like to show you now that can actually help to generate SQL statements for you."

"That would be great," Rhonda said. "I'm all for the easy approach. What is it?"

"The shortcut is to use Access to generate your SQL statements for you." I said, "Let me show you how we can use Access to generate the same SQL statement we just coded manually to join of the `Titles` and `Publishers` table."

## *Using Access to Generate your SQL statements*

I stopped the demonstration program and started up Access. From the Database window, I selected the Queries tab:

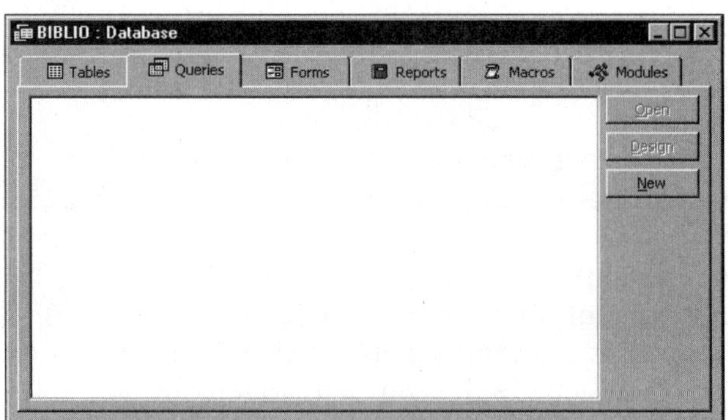

"Access," I said, "can be used to generate the SQL code we need for the `RecordSource` property. To do this, we use Access's `Query By Example` designer. A `Query` is nothing more than a question asked of the database;it just so happens that Access permits you to ask this question visually. It then translates the question into SQL code. We should now select the New button, to create a new query. Now we select Design View..."

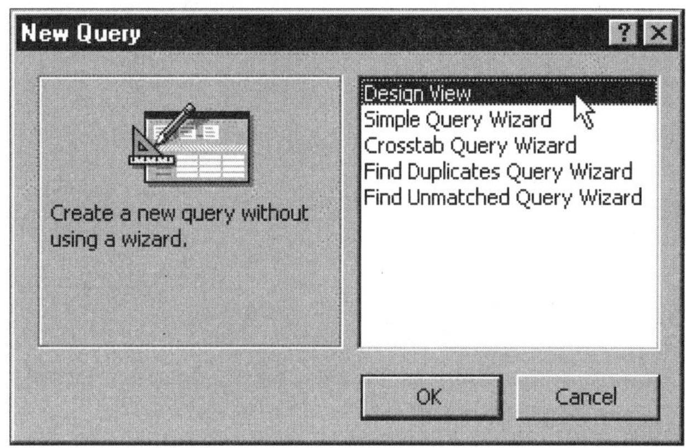


"...and click on the OK button. "A Show Table window will now appear, prompting us to name the tables whose fields will appear in our `Query`. First, we'll select the Titles table and click on the Add button:"

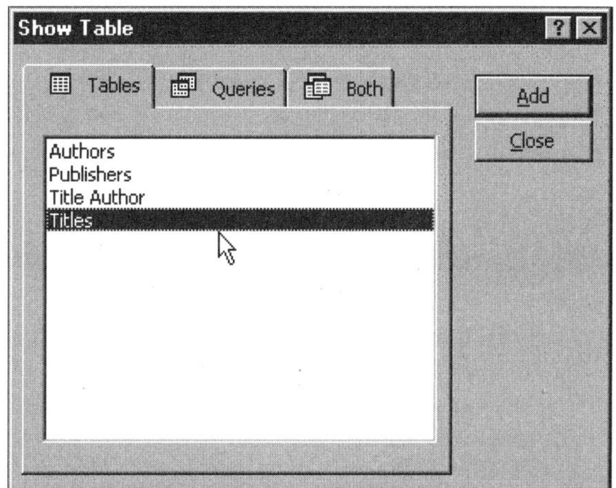


"Once we've closed the Add Table window, this is what we'll see:"

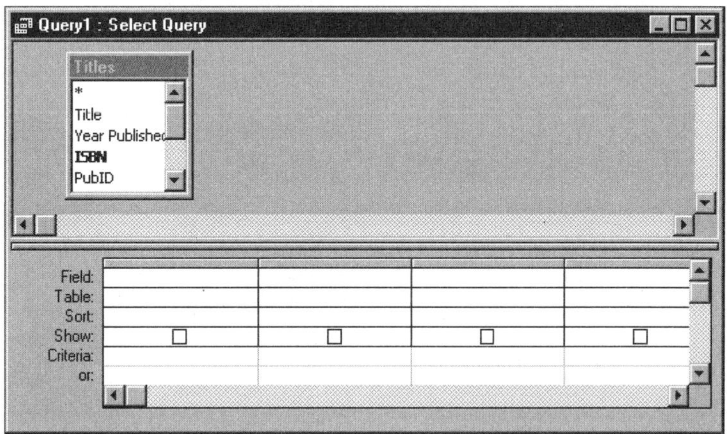

"Notice," I said, "that when I selected the Titles table from the Show Table window, the Titles table was automatically placed in the Select Query window. Now we need to select the Publishers table in the same way, and it too will be placed in the Select Query window." I did just that, with the following result:

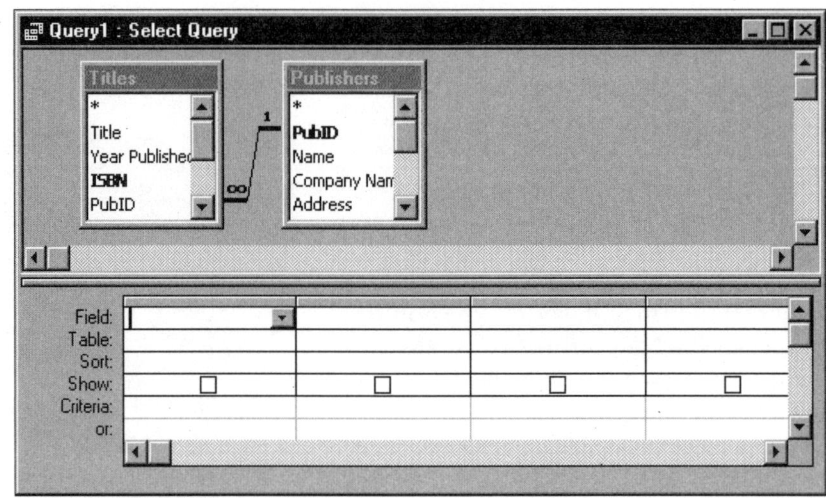


"Did you see that?" Dave asked. "It appears that Access has automatically recognized the relationship between the two tables, Titles and Publishers, and has drawn the relationship. Can completing the query be as easy as selecting the fields to appear in the recordset from each table?"

"The one thing to note, Dave," I said, "Is that this could only happen because a relationship between these tables had already been specified. And since we have already established those relationships when we built the database, Access does make it easy for us. All we need to do at this point is select the two fields we want included in the recordset by selecting one each from the drop-down list box in the Field row of each column. Alternatively, you could drag the field from the table list box into the grid. Let's start with the Title field from the Titles table:"

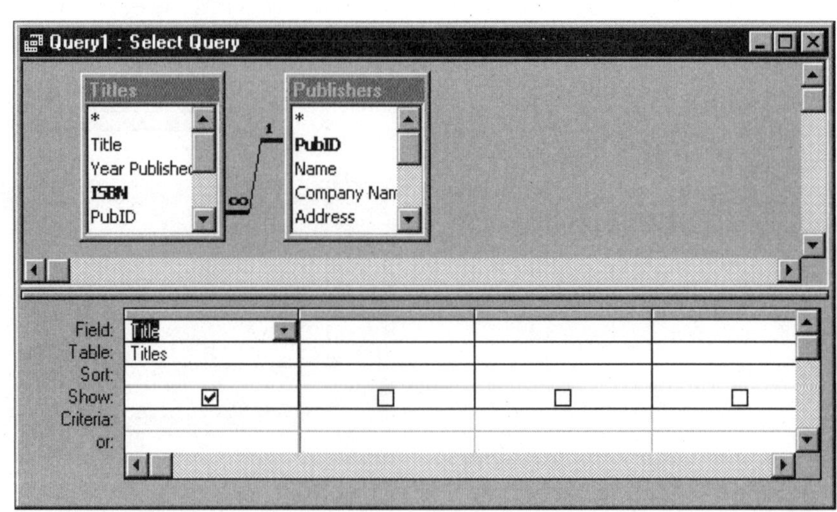


"...and now the Name field from the Publishers table. The actual process of *joining* the tables is taken care of by Access:"

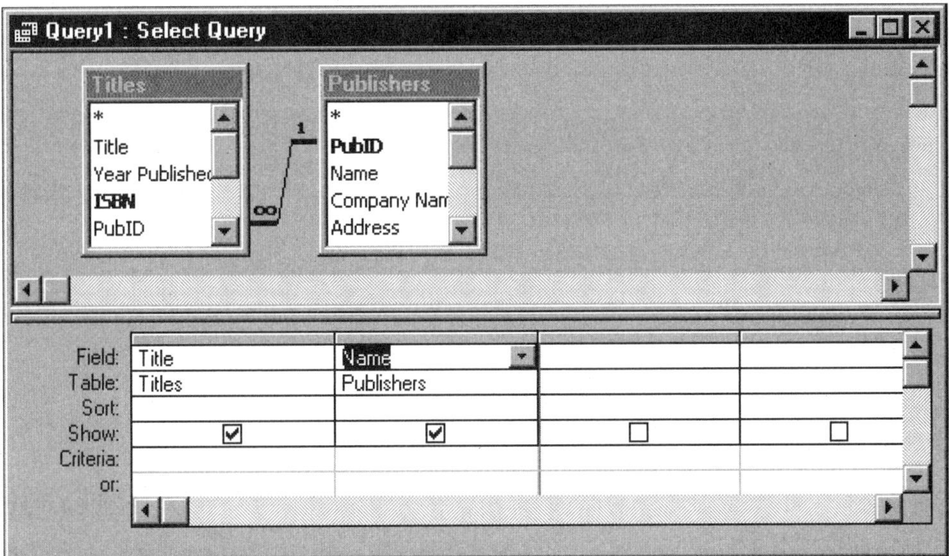


"Now that the selection of the **Query** is complete," I said, "we can run the query by clicking on the 'run' button on the Access toolbar – it looks like an exclamation point:"

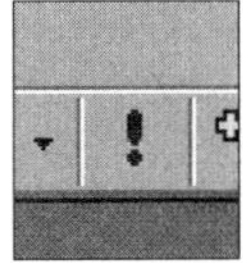

"When we run this query," I continued, "the results of the query will be displayed in something resembling the Datasheet view we saw several weeks ago in Access."

I then clicked on the **Run** button on the Access toolbar, and the following screen shot was displayed:

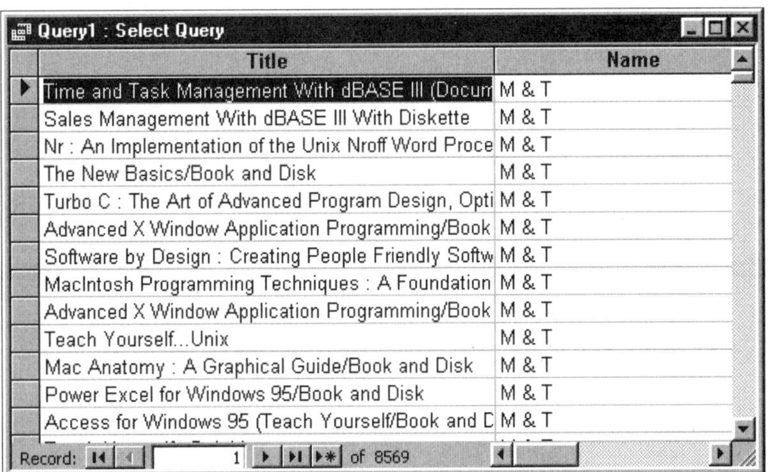

"This view of the recordset," Rachel said, "is virtually identical to what we saw with the DBGrid in Visual Basic just a few minutes ago. This is so straightforward!"

"That's right, Rachel," I said, "these are the same records that we returned in the recordset in our Visual Basic program, except this time Access did all the work for us so we didn't need to write any SQL at all. A word of caution, though. Because it is so easy to generate a query in Access, sometimes people don't bother to validate the results. You should make sure that the records you see in the grid are correct and that they're what you expected."

"SQL was generated somewhere to return this recordset, wasn't it?" Dave asked. "Ultimately, isn't that the way Access generates this recordset – using SQL?"

"And didn't you say earlier that there's a way to use the query created here in Access to generate a SQL statement to do the same thing in Visual Basic?" Rachel asked.

"You're both right," I said, "even though Access has made our work easier by giving us a user friendly interface to develop the query and create the recordset, in the final analysis, everything is really done using SQL in the background. And we can 'borrow' the SQL that Access generates for use in our own Visual Basic program by selecting View | SQL View from the Access menu bar:"

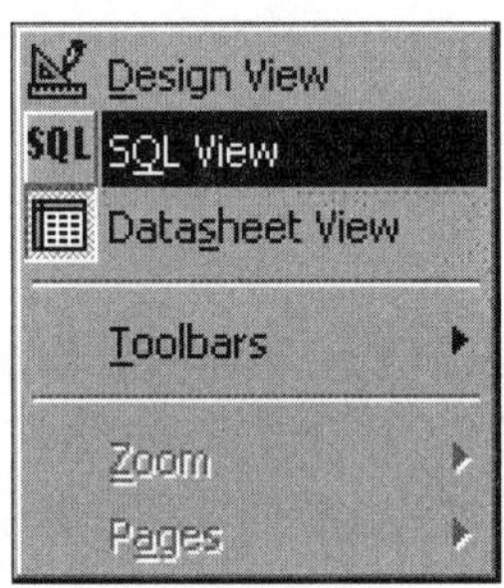


"...and there you'll have your SQL statement:"

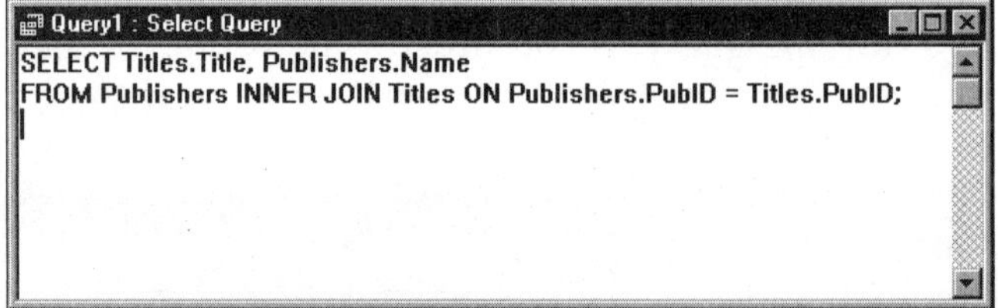


"...which you can then copy and paste directly into the `RecordSource` property of the data control back in Visual Basic:"

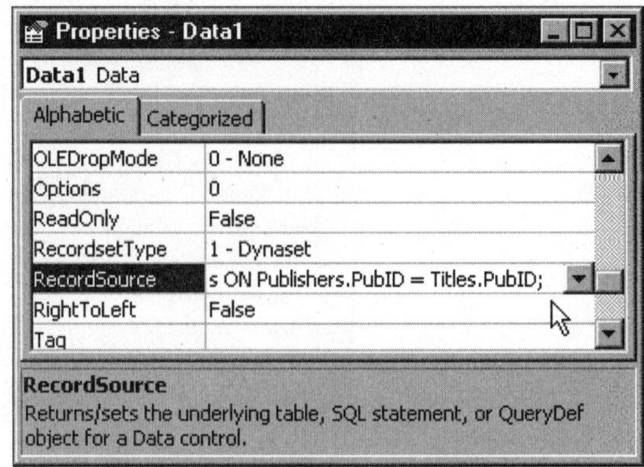

> **You may find when you copy and paste the SQL statement from Access into Visual Basic that there is a carriage return between the two lines of the SQL Statement. Before you copy and paste, join the two lines together in Access, removing the carriage return.**

"If we now run the program with the SQL generated by Access," I said, "we'll see the same results as before, but this time with a lot less work!"

"I notice that the SQL statement that Access generated for us isn't identical to yours," Bob said. "I presume there's some latitude in the syntax of the SQL statement. For example, Access ended the statement with a semicolon."

"Good point, Bob," I said. "You're right; there is some flexibility in the SQL syntax. The semicolon isn't required when interacting with Access databases, although you can see Access that generated one itself. Some other databases – such as Oracle – may actually require it."

I then ran the program using the Access-generated SQL, with this result:

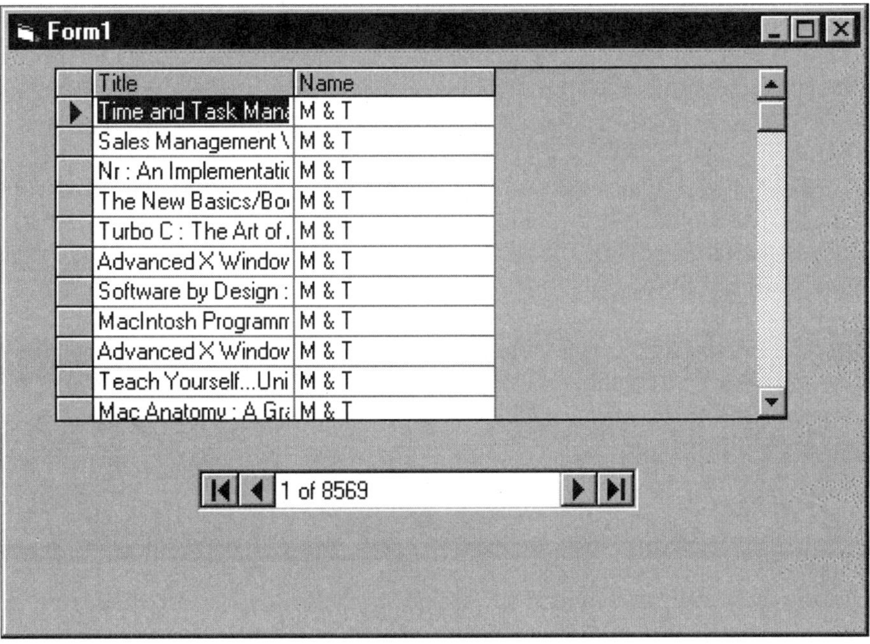


"I guess," said Ward, "that it would be a good idea for us to get comfortable creating queries within Access so that we can take advantage of its ability to generate SQL statements?"

"That wouldn't be a bad idea, Ward," I said, "especially for complex SQL statements. There's nothing easier than using Access to generate the recordset, and then copying and pasting the SQL code into your program. Still, after a while, some programmers just get comfortable with SQL, and code all of their SQL statements themselves from scratch. Still, at least you know the facility is there if you need it."

There were no more questions and our brief discussion of SQL was completed.

> **There are some excellent SQL Reference books on the market – I recommend Wrox Press's *Instant SQL Programming.***

### *Using an Access Query as the RecordSource in a Data Control*

"There is just one more thing I want to show you," I said, "and that's how to save this query in Access, so that instead of creating it from scratch the next time you need it, you can just reference it and run it."

"That could certainly come in handy," Kate said. "So, the next time you need to run the query, it's already there!"

"That's right, Kate," I said. "But there's another great benefit – and that's the fact that a saved Access query can also serve as the `RecordSource` property in the data control."

"Can you repeat that?" Rhonda said. "I'm not sure I understand. So far we've seen that we can specify a table name for the `RecordSource` property of the data control, and we just learned that we can place SQL statements in the `RecordSource` property also. Now you're saying we can also specify this query by name?"

"That's exactly what I'm saying, Rhonda," I said, as I switched back to Access, and attempted to close the Query window by clicking on its close button:

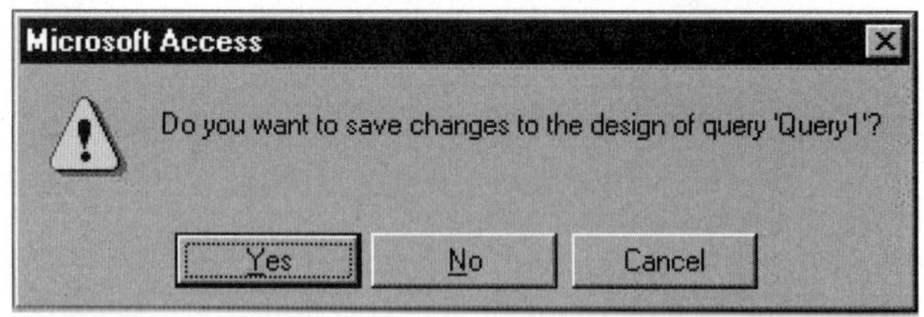


"When we close the Query window," I said, "Access gives us the option of saving the query with a name that we can then use later to execute the query. Let's click on the Yes button now, and name the Query QTitlePubname."

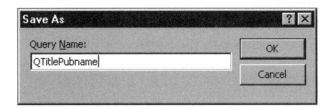

"Now that we've given our query a name, if we now click on the OK button," I continued, "we'll see it as a saved query in the Database window:"

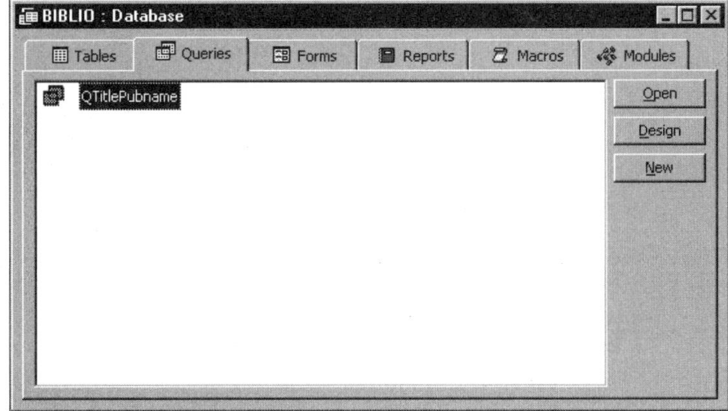


No one had any questions about saving the query in Access, so I continued.

"Now let's switch back to Visual Basic," I said. "If we select the drop-down list box in the **RecordSource** property of the data control, in addition to the four tables in the **Biblio** database, we should also see the query that we've just saved:"

"There it is," I heard Rhonda say.

I selected QTitlePubname from the drop-down list box and ran the program:

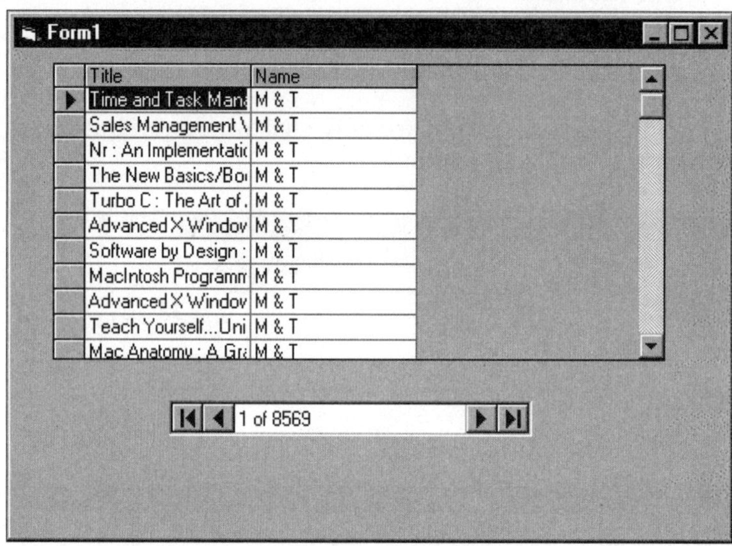


"Once again, I'm impressed," Ward said. "Now we don't need to manually write any SQL at all – we can directly use the query in the `RecordSource` property."

"That's certainly an option, Ward," I said.

"Do other databases such as Oracle and SQLServer permit you to do this?" Linda asked.

"Yes they do," I said, "although Oracle and SQLServer call their queries **stored procedures**."

"Let me make sure I understand this," Rhonda said. "We created a query in Access, saved it with a unique name, and now we're able to specify it here in Visual Basic."

"That's right, Rhonda," I said. "So you see you really have three choices for the `RecordSource` property of the data control. You can (1) specify a table name (2) write your own SQL statement or copy and paste it from Access (3) create a query in Access, save it there, and then specify it in the drop-down list box of the `RecordSource` property. Before we begin to work on finishing the `Login` form we began last week, I just want to tell you that the power of Access, SQL, and Visual Basic is virtually unlimited."

### *SQL and Beyond*

"There are many other features of SQL that are beyond the scope of this course. For instance, it's possible within Access to create something called a **Parameterized Query**."

"If I remember correctly," Mary said, "a parameterized Access query is a query that prompts the user for the answer to a question. That answer is then used as a search value in the query. Is that right? Is it possible to do this from within Visual Basic?"

"Yes it is," I said, "but it can get pretty complicated, and as I suggested, it's a bit beyond the scope of our course."

"What else can we do with SQL?" Dave pressed. "You implied there's more."

"There most certainly is," I said. "Through the use of SQL statements, we can add, edit, and delete records in tables. It may also interest you to know that it's possible to *create* the entire database structure using special SQL statements, all from within Visual Basic."

"Wow, I think that's *definitely* beyond the scope of this course, or at least I hope it is!" Rhonda said nervously.

"Don't worry, Rhonda," I said, "It is. But I wanted to let you know the very powerful capabilities of SQL that are available to you after you get just a little more experience working with Visual Basic and databases."

## Back to the China Shop

It had been a long class, but we still needed to write code for the `Login` form that we had created the previous week. I distributed the first exercise for the day.

### Exercise – Adding Code to the Cancel Button

In this exercise, you'll create some code in the `Click event` procedure of the Cancel button to make the interface more user-friendly and intuitive.

1. Load up the China Shop project.
2. Bring up the Project Explorer window by selecting View | Project Explorer, and select the `Login` form in the Project explorer by double-clicking on it. Once the `Login` form becomes visible, double-click on the Cancel button to bring up its Code window.

3. Enter the following code into the **cmdCancel** button's **Click** event procedure:

```
Private Sub cmdCancel_Click()

If vbOK = MsgBox("Are you sure you want to exit?", vbOKCancel) Then
  Unload Me
  End
Else
  txtUserID.SetFocus
End If

End Sub
```

4. Save the China Shop project.
5. Run the China Shop program, and when the **Login** form appears, click on the Cancel button. A message box should appear asking you if you are sure you want to exit. Click on Cancel and focus should then be set to the **UserID** text box.
6. Click on the Cancel button again. Once again, a message box should appear asking you if you are sure you want to exit. Click on the OK button and the program should end.

***Discussion***

"We started with the Cancel button's **Click** event procedure," I said, "since it's by far the easier code of the two command buttons to write. When the user clicks on the command button, we display a message box asking them if they are sure. If they click on the OK button, we end the program. If they click on Cancel, we set focus to the **UserID** text box, and the program continues to run.

"What's that piece of code saying **Unload Me** for?" Rachel asked. "What's **Me**?"

```
Unload Me
```

"**Me**," I said, "is a Visual Basic keyword representing the current form. **Unload Me** is the same as saying **Unload frmLogin**, and causes the **QueryUnload** and **Unload** events of the form to take place. Experienced programmers frequently use **Me** in place of form names and I want you to become familiar with the syntax."

There were no more questions, so I distributed this second exercise for everyone to complete.

## Exercise – Adding Code to the OK Command Button

In this exercise, you'll work on the `Login` form and place code in the OK command button's `Click` event procedure.

1. If the China Shop program is still running, end the program.
2. Bring up Project Explorer and select the `Login` form by double-clicking on it. Once the `Login` form becomes visible in design view, double-click on the OK button to bring up its Code window.
3. Enter the following code into the `Click` event procedure of OK command button:

```
Private Sub cmdOK_Click()

Static intBadLogins As Integer

'Set variable equal to Text value of txtUserID Textbox
g_strUser = UCase(txtUserID.Text)

'Set Index Property of Recordset to Primary Key---necessary for Seek
'Operation
datUsers.Recordset.Index = "PrimaryKey"

'Seek a record in the Users table with that UserID
datUsers.Recordset.Seek "=", UCase(txtUserID.Text)
If datUsers.Recordset.NoMatch = True Then
    MsgBox "You are not an authorized user..."
    Unload Me
    End
End If

'If found, check the value of the Password in the Recordset
If UCase(txtPassword.Text) =
      ⇘UCase(datUsers.Recordset("password").Value) Then
    MsgBox g_strUser & ", you are successfully logged on.
         ⇘ Please proceed..."
    Unload Me
    frmMain.Show
Else
  intBadLogins = intBadLogins + 1
  If intBadLogins = 3 Then
    MsgBox "Oops---three tries and you're out!"
    Unload Me
    End
```

```
   Else
      txtPassword.Text = ""
      txtPassword.SetFocus
      MsgBox "Your password is incorrect. Please Try Again..."
   End If
End If

End Sub
```

4. Save the China Shop project.

### Discussion

This was a pretty time-consuming exercise for the students to complete but, aside from a few typos and some difficulty in finding the correct form in the Project Explorer window, there weren't many problems.

"Let me explain what we're doing here," I said. "This code is executed when the user has entered a value for `UserID` and `Password` into the text boxes on the form. When they click on the OK button, the user believes that they have entered a valid user ID and password in these text boxes. There are three possibilities that we need to account for in our code:"

1. **Both the UserID and the Password match a record found in the Users table of the China database. In this eventuality, the user is authorized to use the China Shop program**

2. **The UserID exists in the Users table, but the password does not match. The possibility exists that they have simply mistyped or forgotten their password. Most login programs permit them two more attempts to login properly before telling them to 'call it a day'**

3. **The UserID does not exist in the Users table**

"There's also a slight caveat here," Dave said. "Is the user logging in as a customer or as an administrator?"

"That's a good point, Dave," I said. "If the user is an authorized user of the program, we'll then give them access to the China Shop program, and store their `UserID` in the global variable `g_strUser` we created last week. This will allow the program to know who the user is for the duration of the session."

I waited to see if there were any questions before I continued.

"Because we'll be keeping count of the number of times the user attempts to login," I said, "the first thing we do is declare a **Static Integer** variable:"

```
Static intBadLogins As Integer
```

"For those of you who took my Intro course, you'll recall that a static variable retains its value even after the event procedure in which it is declared ends. A static variable is a great way to keep track of the number of times a procedure is executed. In this case, we want to know how many times the user clicks on the OK button in when attempting to log in to the China Shop program. Next, we take the value of the text property of `txtUserID`, and store it in the global variable `g_strUser`."

```
'Set variable equal to Text value of txtUserID Textbox
g_strUser = UCase(txtUserID.Text)
```

"The text value of this text box is the user's `UserID`," I said, "and we'll use it as an argument to the `Seek` method of the recordset created by the data control on the form. Next, prior to executing the `Seek` method of the recordset, we first need to set the `Index` property of the recordset equal to the primary key index of the `Users` table. Just as a reminder, the primary key to the `Users` table is the `UserID`:"

```
'Set Index Property of Recordset to Primary Key - necessary for Seek
'Operation
datUsers.Recordset.Index = "PrimaryKey"
```

"Once the `Index` property is set," I continue, "we use the `Seek` method of the recordset with an argument of the uppercase value of `txtUserID`'s `Text` property of to locate the record in the `Users` table:"

```
'Seek a record in the Users table with that UserID
datUsers.Recordset.Seek "=", UCase(txtUserID.Text)
```

"Why did you use the `UCase` function on the `Text` property of the text box?" Melissa asked.

"Just to ensure that the value is passed in all upper case," I said. "The user may enter their `UserID` in any combination of upper and lower case letters," I said. "Since we entered both users in the `UserID` in all upper case letters, it makes sense to first take the value that the user has entered into the text box, and then convert that into upper case letters prior to using the `Seek` method."

"I see," Melissa said, "that does make sense."

"I suppose you could also have placed some code in the **KeyPress** event procedure to convert the letters the user enters into upper case?" Ward asked.

"Yes, that would have been another alternative," I agreed.

I paused briefly to take a sip of water before proceeding.

"When we execute the **Seek** method using the **UserID** to locate the record," I said, "if the **NoMatch** property of the recordset is **True**, that means we couldn't find a matching record in the **Users** table. We display a message box informing the user that they are not authorized to use the program, then unload the **Login** form and execute the **End** statement, thereby ending the program."

```
If datUsers.Recordset.NoMatch = True Then
    MsgBox "You are not an authorized user..."
    Unload Me
    End
End If
```

"That's a bit harsh, isn't it?" Valerie said. "Shouldn't we have given them another chance?"

"It's a tough call," I said. "Some programs give you another chance, and some just bounce you out immediately, as we are doing here. In any event, the user can just start the program over again, and log in with the correct **UserID** the next time around."

"If we have reached this far into our code," I went on, "that means that a record has been located in the **Users** table with a matching **UserID**. Now it's a matter of determining whether the password the user has entered is correct. That's what the next section of code does by using an **If** statement to see if the value of the **Password** field in the recordset is equal to the text property of **txtPassword**."

```
'If found, check the value of the Password in the recordset
If UCase(txtPassword.Text) =
    ↳UCase(datUsers.Recordset("Password").Value) Then
```

"That term **Value** near the end of the second line here," Dave said, "is that a property of the recordset?"

"Actually, no," I said, "**Value** here is a property of the **Field** object of the recordset which, in this case, is **Password**. To put it another way: when the recordset is created and loaded with data, each field is represented in the object hierarchy that we discussed in a previous lesson. Remember that our hierarchy was the data control, then the recordset. There's another layer in the hierarchy, and one of the objects in that layer is the **Field** object. We can see this by typing a statement into the Immediate window..."

```
? datUsers.Recordset.UserID
```

"Here, we're asking VB to show us the current value of the `UserID` field in the recordset. Let's take a look at what happens if I type this into the Immediate window and hit the *Enter* key..."

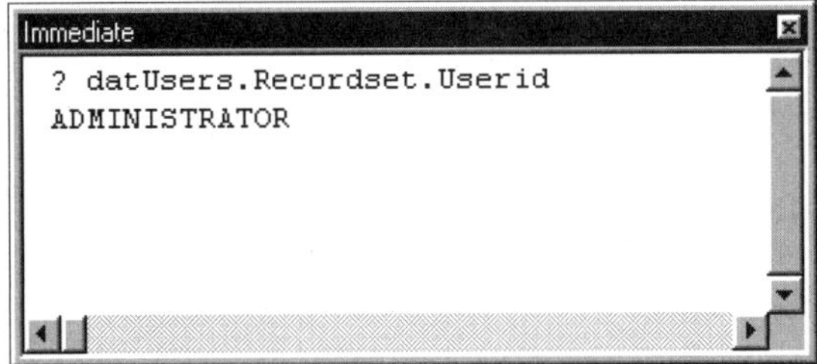


"So in other words," Ward said, "the argument that we pass to the `UCase` function in our code..."

```
If UCase(txtPassword.Text) =
UCase(datUsers.Recordset("Password").Value) Then
```

"...is the way to determine in code what the value of field in a recordset is?"
"Exactly," I said. "Just place the name of the field within parenthesis and quotation marks as we've done here, and Visual Basic will return the value of the field to you."

I paused for a moment and then carried on.

"If the value of the `Password` field is equal to the text property of `txtPassword`," I explained, "then we display a message informing the user that they are successfully logged on..."

```
MsgBox g_strUser & ", you are successfuly logged on.
↳ Please proceed..."
```

"... unload `frmLogin`, and then display the `Main` China form using its `Show` method."

```
Unload Me
frmMain.Show
```

"If, however, the value of the `Password` field is **not** equal to the text property of `txtPassword`, that means that the user has entered an incorrect password. We then increment the value of `intBadLogins` , which started at 0, by 1:"

```
Else
  intBadLogins = intBadLogins + 1
```

"Next, we determine if they have entered an incorrect password three times. If they *have*, we display a warning message, unload the form, and end the program."

```
  If intBadLogins = 3 Then
    MsgBox "Oops---three tries and you're out!"
    Unload Me
    End
```

"If the value of **intBadLogins** is *less* than 3, we give them another chance by clearing the value of **txtPassword**'s **Text** property, set focus to it using the **SetFocus** method, and then display a warning message prompting the user to try again:"

```
  Else
    txtPassword.Text = ""
    txtPassword.SetFocus
    MsgBox "Your password is incorrect. Please Try Again..."
  End If
End If
```

"That's really it, as far as coding the **Login** form is concerned," I said, "I have three exercises to assist you in testing the **Login** process, and one final exercise to modify the **Load** event of the main form to properly display menu items based on the identify of the user. Here's the next exercise..."

## Exercise – Testing the Login Form: Log in as an Unauthorized User

1. Run the China Shop program.
2. When the **Login** form appears, enter Bill Gates (or any other unauthorized identity) into the User Name text box and click on the OK button:

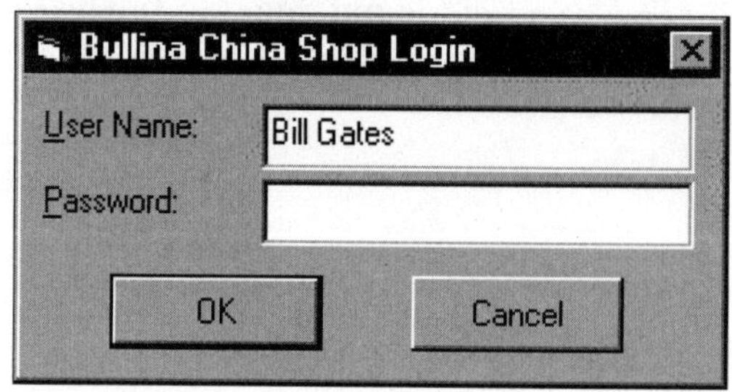

You should see this error message:

3. When you click on the OK button, the China Shop program will end.

***Discussion***

A number of people had the same problem in completing this exercise.

"I'm receiving an error message when I click on the OK button," Rhonda said. "Look:"

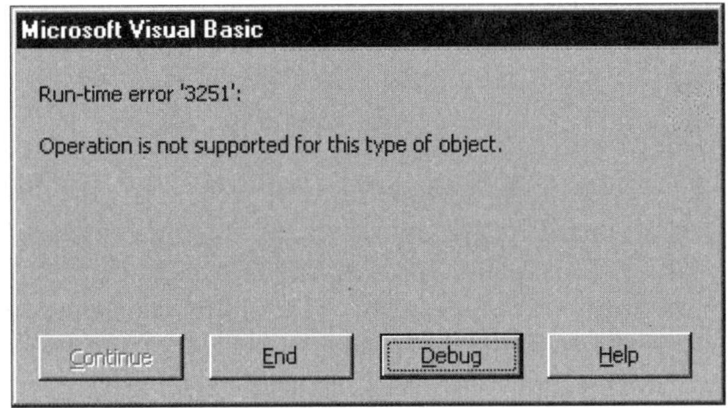


"And when I click on the Debug button," she continued, "the line of code where I set the `Index` property is highlighted in yellow. I must have done something wrong."

"I think I know what the problem is," I answered. "Check the `RecordsetType` property of the data control. I bet it says `Dynaset`, not `Table`."

I waited a moment while Rhonda checked.

"How did you know?" she marveled. "Should I change that from `Dynaset` to `Table`?"

"Yes, you should," I said. "Remember, you can only set the `Index` property of a recordset for a `Table` type recordset, not a `Dynaset`."

With that, I distributed our next exercise of the day.

## Exercise – Testing the Login Form: Log in as an Authorized User who Forgets their Password

1. Run the China Shop program again. This time, when the `Login` form appears, enter a valid `UserID` – Administrator – but enter an incorrect password of 123199. Notice how the characters typed into the Password textbox are 'masked' because of the asterisk we placed in the `PasswordChar` property:

When you click on the OK button you should see this error message:

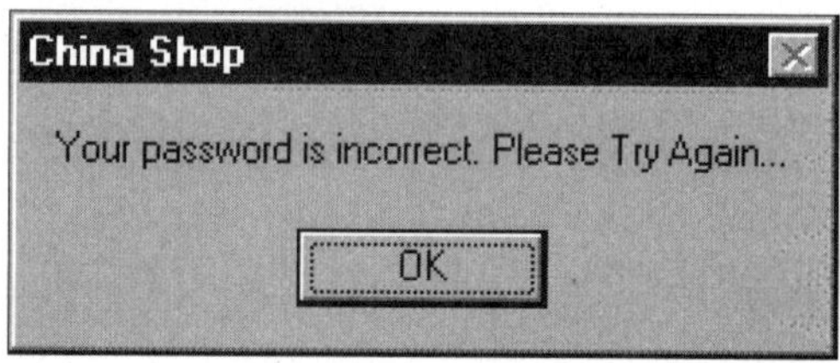


2. Click on the OK button; the Password text box will be cleared, and you'll be returned to the `Login` form. Enter an incorrect password once more, and the error message will be redisplayed, once again giving you a chance to enter the correct password.

3. Enter the incorrect password for the *third* time, and click on the OK button. You should now see *this* error message:

4. When you click on the OK button, the China Shop program will end.

Again, this exercise passed without any problems, so I distributed the next one to the class.

## Exercise – Testing the Login Form: Log in as an Authorized User

1. Run the China Shop program once again.
2. When the `Login` form appears, enter Administrator into the User Name text box.
3. Enter 061883 into the Password text box and click on the OK button. You should see this message:

4. Click on the OK button. The Login form will disappear, and the China Shop's main form will appear. Congratulations! You've successfully logged into the China Shop program. Notice that the Staff Functions menu is visible:
5. End the program.
6. Log in again, this time as CUSTOMER with a password of 030655. Once again, you will receive a message indicating that you are successfully logged on, and when you click the OK button, the `Login` form will disappear and the main form of the China Shop project will appear. There's only one problem, thought, which is that the Staff menu functions are still visible. Don't worry; we'll take care of that shortly.

#### *Discussion*

No one had any trouble completing this exercise, and I sensed a feeling of great accomplishment among many of the students.

"We have just one more exercise to complete today," I said, "and that's to modify the code in the `Load procedure` of the `Main` form to display the Staff Functions menu **only** if the user of the program is `ADMINISTRATOR`."

And so to the final exercise of the day.

## Exercise – Modifying the Load Event of frmMain

In this exercise, you'll modify the `Load event` procedure of the `Main` form to display the Staff Functions menu only if the user is the Administrator.

1. Stop the China Shop program.
2. Bring up the Project Explorer window and select the Main form by double-clicking on it. Once the `Main` form is visible in design view, double-click on it to bring up the Code window.
3. Modify the code in the `Load` event procedure of the `Main` form to look like this (amended code is highlighted):

```
Private Sub Form_Load()

Call ReadTheRegistry
Call ReadPrices

If m_blnDateDisplay Then
   Call mnuPreferencesDateandTimeOn_Click
Else
   Call mnuPreferencesDateandTimeOff_Click
End If

frmMain.BackColor = m_lngBackColor

If g_strUser = "ADMINISTRATOR" Then
    mnuStaff.Visible = True
Else
    mnuStaff.Visible = False
End If

End Sub
```

4. Save the China Shop project.
5. Run the China Shop program again.
6. Log in using the `UserID` of ADMINISTRATOR with a `Password` of 061883. You will receive a message indicating that you are successfully logged on, and when you click the OK button, the `Login` form will disappear, and the `Main` form of the China Shop project will appear, complete with the Staff Functions menu.

**7.** Shut down the China Shop project and restart it. Now log in using CUSTOMER as the `UserID`, and 030655 as your password. Again, you will receive a message indicating that you are successfully logged on and, when you click the OK button, the `Login` form will disappear, to be replaced by the China Shop project's `Main` form, but this time without the Staff Functions menu.

#### *Discussion*

"That's just great," Rhonda said, "I really can't believe we've come so far with this."

Everyone else was equally impressed, even Ward! No one had any questions, and so I dismissed class for the day.

"Next week," I said, "we'll examine some of those other recordset methods I told you we would cover, such as `AddNew` and `Delete`, plus we'll create the `Customers` and `Inventory` forms, and rework the `Users` form. Make sure you're well rested!"

# Chapter Summary

In this chapter we learned how to navigate our way around a recordset using a variety of techniques. This is important because, having created the China Shop database, we need to know how to move around the data and retrieve the information from it that Joe wants. Specifically, we saw that:

- The recordset has methods that help us to navigate to precise locations in the recordset
- We can create command buttons that use these recordset methods to move around the recordset. Particularly, we looked at the recordset's `MoveFirst`, `MoveLast`, `MoveNext`, and `MovePrevious` methods in this context
- The `Seek` and `Find` families of recordset methods are used for locating for locating the individual bits of data that we're interested in
- Understanding what SQL is and how it works gives us increased flexibility in working with our database
- We can use Access's query-building facilities to write our SQL statements for us

We ended the lesson by making some important changes to the China Shop's `Login` form. Firstly, a user can only have three attempts to log in; after the third unsuccessful attempt the program will end. Secondly, we altered the `Main` form so that if a user is logged on as a customer they can't see the Staff Functions menu.

In the next lesson we'll do some more work with the recordset: this time, we'll see how we go about *updating* the recordset. We'll use the knowledge we've gained so far to continue building up the database capabilities of the China Shop project: in doing so, we'll create forms that let us add data to the `China` database, and see how to create robust data-entry forms. Join us next week!

Learn to Program Databases with Visual Basic

## Chapter 7

# Updating the Recordset

In the last lesson, we finished up our discussion of the basic recordset methods and properties, and continued our modifications to the China Shop program by completing its **`Login`** form.

This chapter is all about expanding our knowledge of the recordset, and using that knowledge to create more dynamic Visual Basic forms that can interact with our database. The focus in this chapter is on how we can update the recordset and its underlying database using the controls and code attached to our Visual Basic forms. This is important ground to cover, and it will help us to understand the recordset in more depth, as well as allowing us to create data entry forms for the China Shop project.

The first half of the chapter looks at more recordset methods in detail, and in the second half we continue building our enhanced China Shop program.

In this chapter, we'll look at:

- The recordset methods that let us create, update, and delete records
- Error handling when using the recordset and the data control
- Creating and modifying the data entry forms for the **`Users`** and **`Inventory`** tables in the China Shop database
- Adding buttons and code to the data entry forms so that they are easy to use

By the end of this chapter, you'll have a firmer grasp of the data control's intricacies, and you'll have made substantial additions to the China Shop project.

Let's join the class...

## More on the Recordset

"At the conclusion of today's lesson," I said as I began our seventh class, "you'll have completed the **`Users`** and **`Inventory`** forms for the China Shop project, and seen how to integrate our forms and the database for data entry purposes. Should be an exciting class!"

"I thought we already completed the **`Users`** form," Chuck said. "Didn't we work on the **`Users`** form back in week 4?"

"I thought so too," said Rhonda.

"You're both right," I confirmed. "We did work on the **Users** form already, but it wasn't really intended to be a permanent solution to the China Shop's requirements. The form we created back then to interact with the **Users** table of the China Shop database is not nearly as user-friendly as we'll be able to make it by the end of today's class. Three weeks ago, we simply didn't have the knowledge or experience necessary to design and code a very user-friendly form, but we've learned an awful lot in the last two weeks about interacting with databases through Visual Basic. The other thing is that right now there's no way to **delete** records using the existing form, nor is there an easy way for Joe Bullina or any of his China Shop staff to **add** records. For review purposes, let's take a look at the current **Users** form."

I then loaded up the China Shop program, ran it, logged in and displayed the **Users** form on the classroom projector:

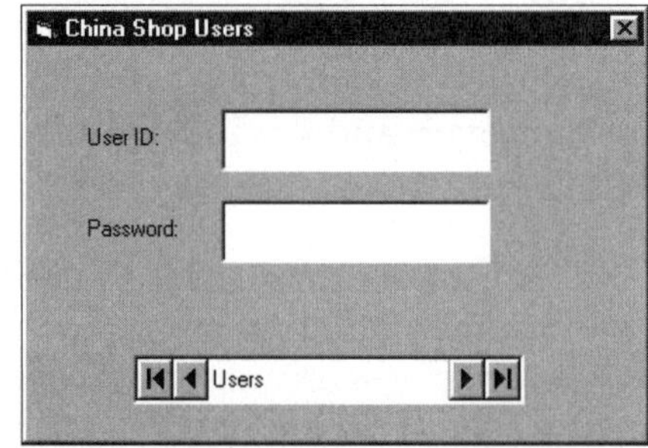


I saw Dave fidgeting. "Something the matter, Dave?" I asked.

"I was pretty sure you had said that we were going to modify this form at some point, so I didn't say anything before," he said. "But I did think this form looked pretty weak myself."

"Fair comment, Dave," I said, "but I wanted to give the class the chance to create a data entry form quite early on in the class – and that just means that today we'll need to improve upon what we did a few weeks ago."

"What types of improvements will we be making to the **Users** form?" Rachel asked.

"We'll take some of the built-in functionality of the data control," I said, "and replace it with command buttons."

I could see that Rachel, and some others, weren't sure exactly what I meant.

"For instance," I said, "we'll place command buttons on the form that, if clicked, allow the user of the form to add, update or delete a record more easily – and also change their mind more easily if they so desire."

"Add, update and delete – aren't those are the major functions of data entry forms?" Valerie asked.

"You hit the nail on the head there, Valerie," I agreed.

"But can't the user add, update and delete using the existing **`Users`** form right now?" Rhonda asked.

"At the moment," I said, "the user can add or update a record in the **`Users`** table. But they can't delete records, and I think you would agree that the current form is hardly user-friendly."

"I agree with that," Kate said. "Adding a record to the **`Users`** table isn't user-friendly *at all* at the moment."

"How so?" Rhonda inquired.

"For one thing," Kate continued, "in order to add a record to the **`Users`** table, the user needs to first click on the 'last record' navigation button on the data control – then they need to click on the 'next record' navigation button. At that point, the bound controls on the form are displayed with nothing in them – I can just imagine Joe Bullina or a member of the China Shop Staff trying to work their way around this form."

"I see what you mean, Kate," Rhonda said. "I guess I'm just having trouble visualizing what a more user-friendly data entry form will look like."

"Don't worry, Kate," I replied, "with the enhanced design of the **`Users`** form, data entry should be a snap. And Rhonda, I can certainly understand your plight. Visualizing a user-friendly data entry form can be difficult unless you've seen one in action. But it won't be long before we get to that point."

"Are we going to start redesigning the **`Users`** form right now?" Tom asked.

"Not quite," I said. "Before we can begin, we need to spend a few minutes discussing some recordset methods that we didn't cover last week – specifically, the methods designed to facilitate **updates** to the recordset. After that, we'll spend the majority of today's class modifying the China Shop program."

## The Recordset's Update Methods

"Today," I continued, "we'll discuss four recordset methods and one data control method that will let us to build a dynamic and user-friendly data entry form. The recordset methods are: **`AddNew`**, **`CancelUpdate`**, **`Delete`**, and **`Update`**; and the single data control method is **`UpdateControls`**."

"Isn't there an **Edit** method of the recordset?" Dave asked. "I thought you said we would be covering that sometime in the future."

"The **Edit** method," I said, "is a recordset method that we'll discuss in more detail during the last week of class. Executing the **Edit** method essentially means that it is OK to change the recordset, but when using the data control on a form, it's really not necessary: the data control *automatically* executes an implicit **Edit** method every time the record pointer changes."

"However, as we'll see a little later on, there's one case where we *do* need to use the **Edit** method, because of some unhelpful behavior that occurs if we don't."

I paused for a moment before resuming.

"As we've been doing during the last few weeks with the other recordset properties and methods," I said, "let's use the **Biblio** database to examine the recordset's 'update' methods. First, let's create a form, similar to our current **Users** form, that will permit us to view and edit the **Authors** table of the **Biblio** database."

True to my word, I created a new **Standard.EXE** project, and placed a data control on the form, along with three labels and three text box controls. I changed the captions of the three labels to Au_ID, Author and Year Born respectively:

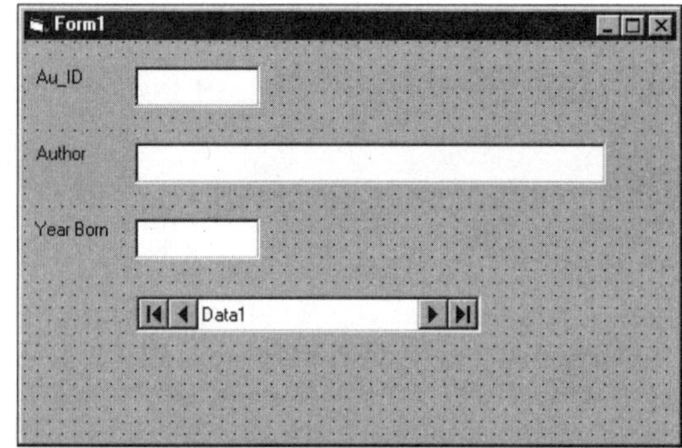


...and named the text boxes **txtAuID**, **txtAuthor** and **txtYearBorn**.

"Because the **Au_ID** of the **Authors** table is an **AutoNumber** field," I continued, "we'll set the **Locked** property of **txtAuID** to **True**. That will prevent us from accidentally trying to change its value – something that we don't want to do, and in fact *can't* do in the underlying database (it just throws out an error). So we might as well lock the user out of this field from the start. We'll also set its **TabStop** property to **False**:"

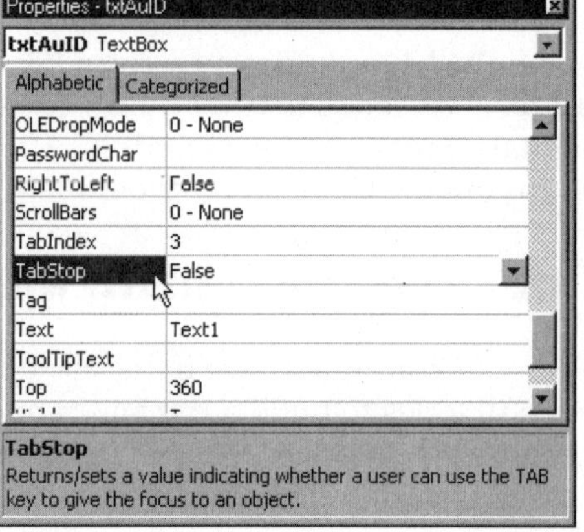

"...which will prevent the text box from receiving focus. To the user, it will be obvious that this field cannot be updated."

"Why did you do that again?" Rachel asked.

"**Au_ID**," I said, "is the primary key to the **Authors** table – it's also an **AutoNumber** field – and because of that, Access will automatically set the value for this field. Setting the **Locked** property ensures that the user can't make an entry in the text box, and setting the **TabStop** property to **False** ensures that the user can't even tab into it."

"I see now," Rachel said. "Will we be doing something similar for the forms we design? We have several tables with **AutoNumber** fields, don't we?"

"That's right," I said. "Every form we design that connects to a table with an **AutoNumber** field will need to have these two properties set for its bound text box control."

I then set the **DatabaseName** property of the data control to the **Biblio** database and the **EOFAction** property to **Add New.** The **RecordsetType** property remained on its default value of **Dynaset**, while the **RecordSource** property became the **Authors** table:

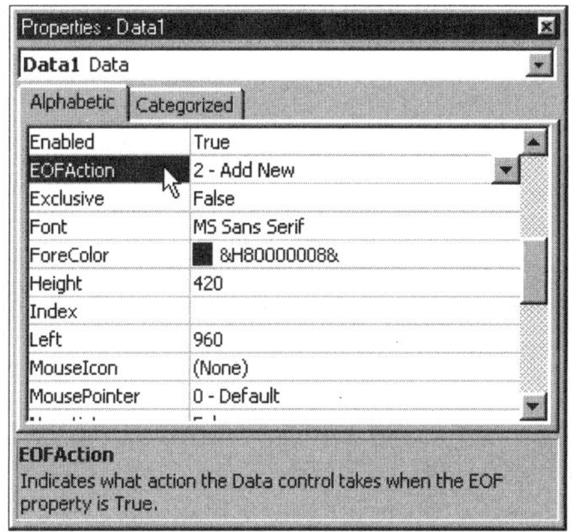


"By setting the **EOFAction** property to **AddNew**," I said, "we ensure that when the user reaches the EOF in the recordset, the data control will automatically execute an **AddNew** method – which will clear the bound text box controls in preparation for the user entering data for a new record."

"I thought," Ward said, "that we were going to write code to add new records ourselves. Shouldn't the **EOFAction** property be set to **MoveLast**?"

"That's a good point, Ward," I said. "When we write our own code to add new records to the recordset, we will set the **EOFAction** property to **MoveLast**. We'll do that a little later on in the demo."

I then set the **DataSource** property of each of the three text box controls to **Data1**, and then set their **DataField** properties to **Au_ID**, **Author** and **Year Born** respectively:

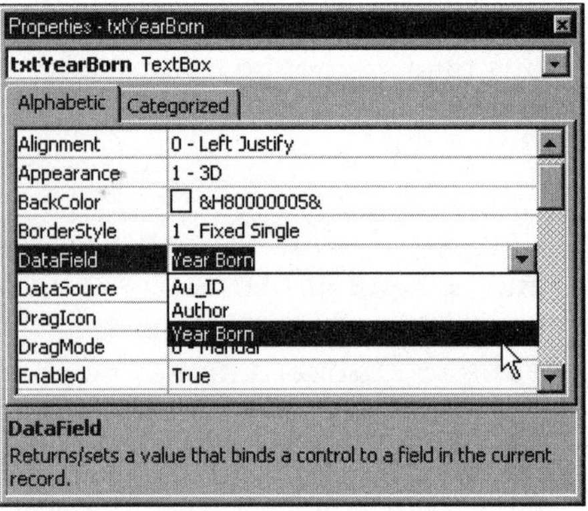


"Remember," I said, "that setting the **DataSource** and **DataField** properties of the text box binds the control to a field in the underlying recordset."

Next, I opened up the Visual Basic code window and placed the following code in the **Activate** event procedure of the form:

```
Private Sub Form_Activate()

Data1.Recordset.MoveLast
Data1.Recordset.MoveFirst

End Sub
```

...and this code in the **Reposition** event procedure of the data control:

```
Private Sub Data1_Reposition()

Data1.Caption = Data1.Recordset.AbsolutePosition + 1 & " of " &
Data1.Recordset.RecordCount

End Sub
```

"I remember what the code in the **Reposition** event procedure does," Lou said, "but refresh my memory on the other piece of code. What's the purpose of the code in the **Activate** event?"

"We execute the **MoveLast** and **MoveFirst** methods," I said, "so that we get an accurate record count. Otherwise the record count we display in the **Caption** property of the data control won't be right. Just a little quirk of the recordset!"

I then ran the program...

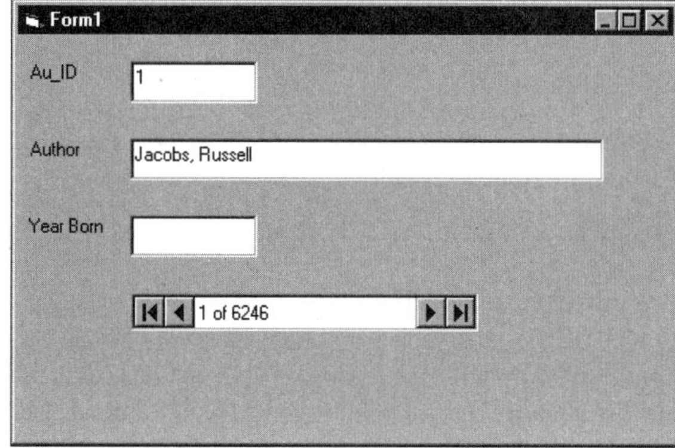


"What we see here for the **Authors** table," I said, "isn't that different from what's in the current **Users** form – some labels, some text boxes, and a data control. It's pretty easy for the user to edit records. All they need to do is locate the record, move the record pointer to that record, and just type their amendments into the text box."

I then changed the name of the **Author** in the first record from 'Jacobs, Russell' to 'Smith, John':

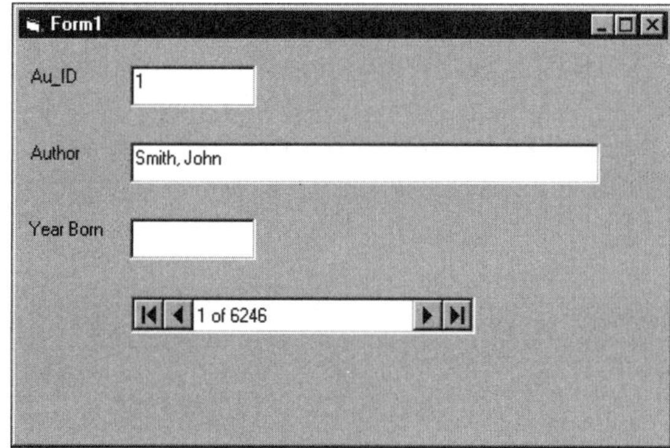


I clicked on the 'next record' navigation button on the data control, and the record pointer moved to record number 2. I then moved back to record number 1 – to show everyone that the changes I made to the first record were permanent.

"That's what you meant when you said the data control executes an implicit **Edit** method, isn't it?" Kevin asked.

"That's right, Kevin," I said. "As soon as we use one of the data control's navigation buttons to move around in the recordset, the data control executes an (implicit) **Edit** method, which means that whatever the user types into the text box replaces the current value of that field as soon as..."

"...as soon as the record pointer moves off the record," Valerie interjected.

"That's excellent, Valerie," I said. "That's exactly right. As soon as the record pointer moves off the record, any changes made in the bound controls are written to the underlying recordset."

"I don't think that editing records using the data control and bound text boxes is all that unfriendly," Dave said, "but perhaps a Save or an Update button would make the form a little easier to use."

"You raise a good point, Dave," I said. "We, the designers of the program, know that moving the record pointer off a changed record will save the changes the user has just made, but the user doesn't necessarily know that, and a button explicitly marked Save or Update would probably make most users more comfortable."

I waited to see if there were any questions. There were none, so I continued.

"**Adding** records to the `Authors` table using this form," I said, "is much more of an adventure."

"You're not kidding," Rhonda said. "We only did it a few weeks ago, and already I can't remember how to do it. I can't believe a user who only needs to add a record or two every few weeks or so is ever going to remember how to do it."

"You're right, Rhonda," I agreed, "it's hardly obvious or intuitive. To refresh your memory: to add a record to the recordset using a data control, first we need to click on the 'last record' navigation button on the data control, then on the 'next record' button. When we do that, the bound text boxes on the form are emptied, and we then have the opportunity to enter values for the new record..."

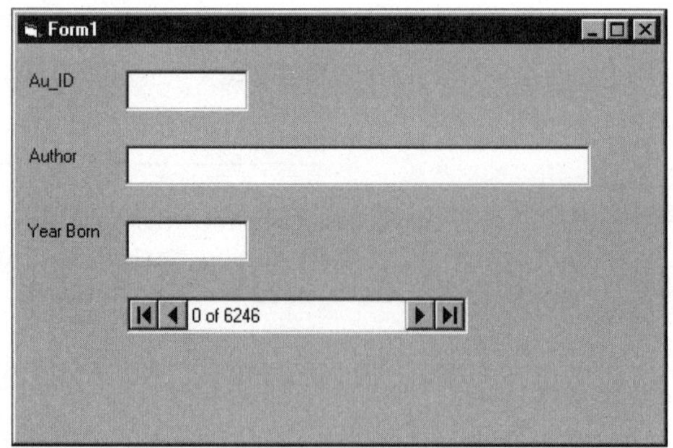


"Notice that the three bound text boxes have been cleared," I said, "indicating that a new record is ready to be added to the underlying `Authors` table."

"Indicating to whom?" Kate said. "This is really pretty bad. Asking the user to click on two navigation buttons on the data control in order to be able to add a new record isn't very user-friendly at all. And then to present an empty form to them is even worse. Finally, after they've had to deal with all of this, we must then rely on them to move the record pointer in order for the new record to actually be added to the table."

"I agree, Kate," I said, "it's not very intuitive or helpful. But don't worry, I have no intention of leaving Joe Bullina with something like this. I feel confident that we can improve upon it. For now, let's add a new record to the **`Authors`** table:"

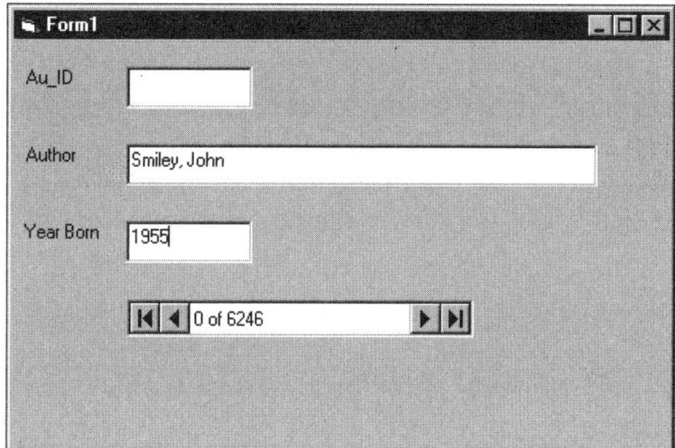


I filled in the empty bound text box controls with information about one of my favorite authors. I was about to click on the data control's 'previous record' navigation button to move the record pointer when Blaine spoke...

"I was about to say that you forgot to make an entry in the **`Au_ID`** field," he said. "But then I remembered what you said about that field being an **`AutoNumber`** field."

"That's right, Blaine," I said, "because **`Au_ID`** is an **`AutoNumber`** field, we'll see that Access will *automatically* assign a value to the field when the record is added to the **`Authors`** table. Let's add this record now by moving the record pointer."

I did so by clicking on the 'previous record' button, with this result:

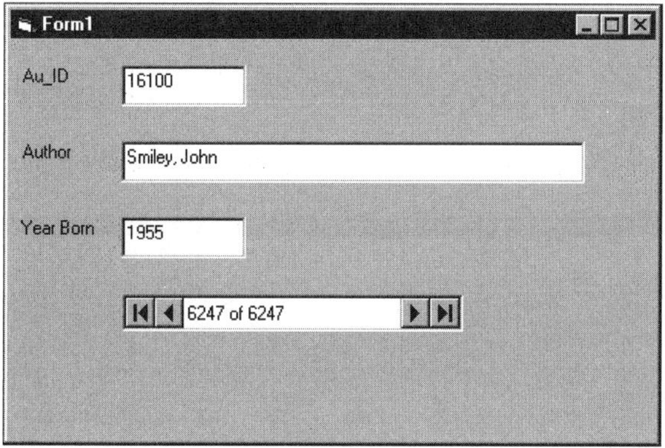

"As you can see," I commented, "once we enter data into the empty text box controls and move the record pointer, a new record is added to the **Authors** table. Also, notice that Access has automatically created the record with an **Au_ID** field equal to 16100 – which is a value one greater than the previous record's value of 16,099."

"That's great," Rhonda said. "If you know what you're doing, it's not all that difficult."

"That's the problem, Rhonda," I said, "as designers of programs, we need to make our programs as intuitive to use as possible. Unfortunately, this form is not nearly user-friendly enough for the China Shop staff. We'll be fielding phone calls every other week from users who've forgotten how to add records."

"And what about deleting records?" said Steve. "Didn't you say that it's **not** possible to delete a record from the recordset using this form?"

"That's right, Steve," I replied. "There's absolutely no way to delete a record from the recordset using this form – but we now know what we need to do. First, we need to make the process of adding a record to the recordset a little more user-friendly and intuitive. And secondly, we need to provide a way for the user to delete a record from the recordset. Let's take a few minutes now to reconstruct this form – and in the process, we'll discuss those remaining update recordset methods I mentioned earlier. The first one we need to look at is the **AddNew** method which – not surprisingly – is the recordset's method for creating new records."

## The AddNew Method

"Let's begin," I said, "by adding a command button to this form called 'Add', which will allow the user to add a record to the recordset. The difference this time is that they'll no longer need to click on the data control's navigation buttons to initiate the **Add** action."

I then added a command button to the form, changed its **Name** property to **cmdAdd**, and its **Caption** property to Add:

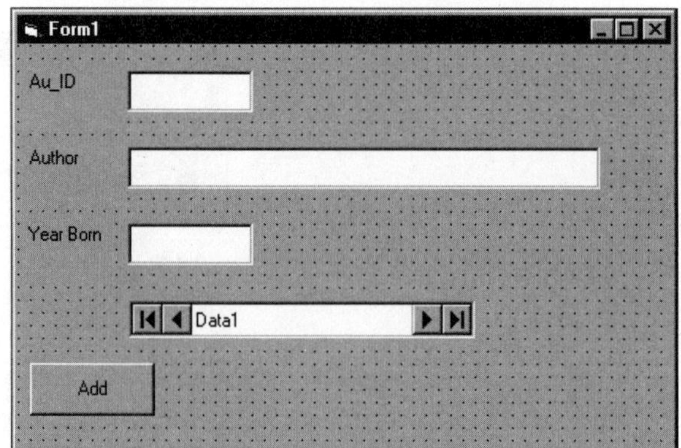

"In this command button's **Click** event procedure," I continued, "we'll insert some code that will execute the recordset's **AddNew** method. Executing the **AddNew** method in code will have the same effect as clicking in succession on the data control's 'last record' and 'next record' navigation buttons. Let's not forget to change the data control's **EOFAction** property to **LastRecord** – now that we're adding this code to the form, we no longer want the user clicking on the data control's navigation buttons to add a new record anymore..."

So saying, I changed the **EOFAction** property of the data control from **2-AddNew** to **0-Move Last**, and then keyed the following chunk of code into **cmdAdd**'s **Click** event procedure:

```
Private Sub cmdAdd_Click()

Data1.Recordset.AddNew

End Sub
```

"Remember," I said, "**AddNew** is a recordset method, not a data control method. If we now run this program, and click on the Add button, we should see the same effect as clicking on those two data control navigation buttons..."

I then ran the program, and clicked on the Add command button...

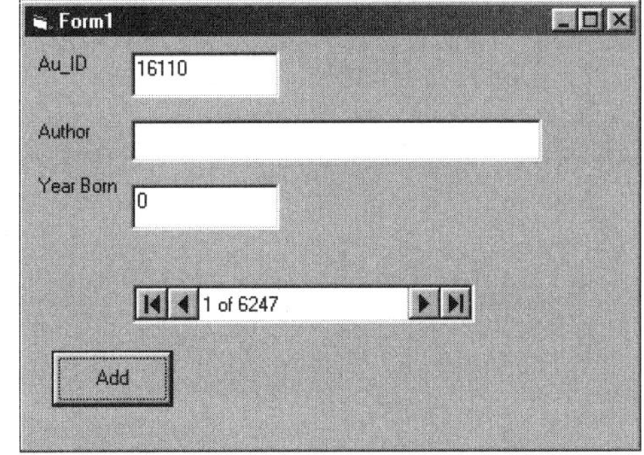


"This form looks a little different from when we used the data control to add a record," Ward said. "Two of the fields – **Au_ID** and **Year Born**, already have values in them. Why is that?"

"Good observation, Ward," I said. "The behavior of the **AddNew** method is similar to that of using the data control, but not *identical*. When we execute the **AddNew** method of the recordset, values for any **AutoNumber** fields are automatically calculated and displayed. That's why **Au_ID** already has the value **16101** in it, which is the next **Au_ID** number in sequence. In the same way, any fields that contain default values – such as **Year Born** – will also be displayed. Aside from that, we are basically at the same point as when we used the data control by clicking on the 'last record' and 'next record' navigation buttons – except I think this is a lot more user-friendly."

## The Update Method

"How will the user actually add this record to the recordset then?" Kathy asked. "Do they still need to move the record pointer as they did before, or does the **`AddNew`** method somehow do that for them also?"

"Well, Kathy, that's a fine question," I said. "Unfortunately, there's no magic to the **`AddNew`** method that allows it to know when the user has finished entering data into the bound controls. The user still needs to 'finalize' the addition of the new record, and they can do that in one of two ways. They can either move the recordset's record pointer as they did before, which will result in the new record being added to the recordset. Alternatively, we can place a second command button on the form called Update whose **`Click`** event procedure executes the recordset's **`Update`** method, and have the user click on it when they are done entering the data for the new record. Let's take a look at that second method now by placing a second command button on the form."

I then ended the program by closing the form *without* moving the record pointer.

"Was that record with the **`Au_ID`** of 16101 added to the **`Authors`** table?" Rhonda asked. "I know you only had the two default fields completed on the form – we had 6,247 records. Do we now have 6,248 records in the **`Authors`** table?"

"I'm afraid I don't quite understand Rhonda's question," Chuck said.

"Rhonda's question is a good one, Chuck," I said. "What she's saying is that I clicked on the Add button, but never moved the record pointer prior to clicking on the close button of the form. Rhonda's wondering if the record was added to the underlying table."

"I'm betting the record wasn't added," Dave said, "since you said that the only way the record can be added to the recordset (and thereby to the table that the recordset represents) is to move the record pointer."

"You're right, Dave," I said. "And the answer is no – as we never moved the record pointer, the new record was **not** added to the recordset. Let me show you."

To prove my point, I ran the program again, and the following screen appeared:

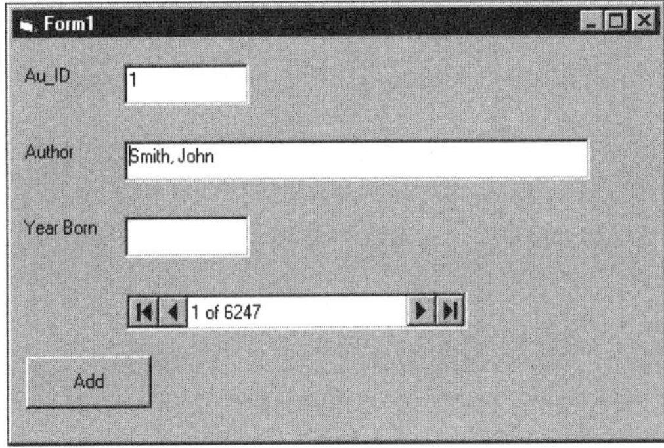


"See, everyone? We still have 6,247 records," I said. "The new record was never added to the **Authors** table."

"Might it be a good idea to warn the user that they were in the middle of adding a record to the recordset prior to closing the form?" Melissa asked, "like Microsoft Word does if you try to exit without saving your document?"

"That's a good idea, Melissa," I said. "And in the final analysis, that's a decision only you can make. Some programmers do, and some don't. Either way, you can easily determine if the user is in the middle of adding a record by checking the **EditMode** property of the recordset prior to permitting the user to unload the form."

"**EditMode**?" Rhonda asked. "Is that a property we've discussed already?"

"We haven't looked at it yet," I said, "but we'll see it quite a bit later on today. Speaking of the **EditMode** property," I continued, "let me show you something. Suppose we run the program again, and then click on the Add button *twice*."

I then ran the program, clicked on the Add button once, which opened up an empty record on the form:

"Now let's see what happens if we click on the Add button again," I said.

"But why would a user ever do that?" Rhonda said puzzled.

"Most likely a user wouldn't do this *intentionally*," I said, "but when we write programs that access databases, we need to try to anticipate everything that a user *might* do in the program. In this case, clicking on the Add button a second time executes the **AddNew** method of the recordset again, even while we are in the midst of adding the first record..."

I then clicked on the Add button again, with this result:

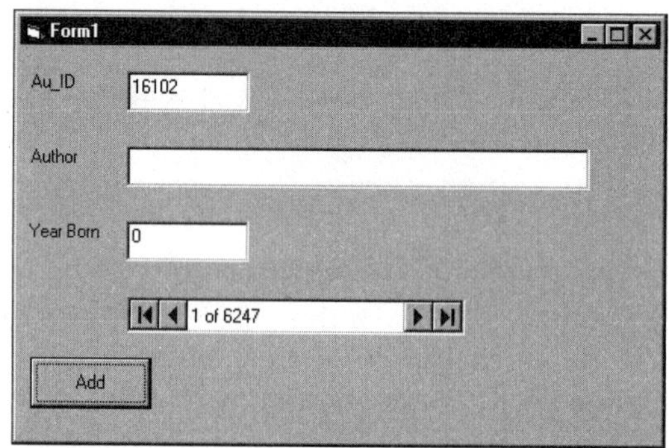


"That's strange," Peter said. "It looks like the **Au_ID** field has been incremented by one – however, the record count still appears to be the same. Was that first record added?"

"This is similar to the case when we began to add a record but then closed the form before completing it: since we didn't advance the record pointer, the new record wasn't added. However, executing the **AddNew** method of the recordset again during the existing 'add' operation caused the bound controls to be re-emptied, and any **AutoNumber** fields were incremented by 1. But that's all that happened – remember, unless the record pointer is moved, or the **Update** method of the recordset is executed, no new record is added to the recordset. And if it's not added to the recordset, it's not added to the table."

"That incrementing of the **Au_ID** field is really going to bother me," Ward said. "We've used up those **AutoNumber** values, but they don't appear in any physical records, do they? Is there any way to get the **Au_ID** reset back to the what would have been the next number in sequence if we hadn't wasted all the others?"

"I'm afraid not," I said. "Once an **AutoNumber** field has advanced (even if the record isn't added to the recordset) there's no way to reset it – it really is gone forever. But remember, when you create an **AutoNumber** field, you are telling Access that there's no real significance in the actual *value* of the automatically generated number anyway – so it shouldn't be a big deal if for some reason there *are* numbers that are skipped."

"I hear you," Ward said, "I guess it's just my personality – I hate to waste anything! But what about this case where we were able to click on the Add button twice in succession? Isn't there a way to prevent that?"

"Yes, Ward," I said, "there *is* something we can do. My preference is to check the **EditMode** property of the recordset – this will give us an indication of what the user was doing when they clicked the Add button. Some other developers I know would choose to disable the Add button when it was clicked by the user the first time – and not enable it again until the user had either added the record to the recordset or cancelled the addition operation."

"You say that you prefer checking the **EditMode** property," Linda said. "Is there a particular reason for that?"

"My philosophy is to keep things as simple as possible," I said. "I think checking the **EditMode** property is simpler – especially for my beginner students. Let me show you how I would use the **EditMode** property to affect the behavior of the Add button."

I stopped the program, opened up the code window, and modified the code in the **Click** event procedure of **cmdAdd** to look like this (changed code is highlighted as usual):

```
Private Sub cmdAdd_Click()

If Data1.Recordset.EditMode <> dbEditNone Then
   MsgBox "Please finish your current updates before adding
      ↳another new record"
   Exit Sub
End If

Data1.Recordset.AddNew

End Sub
```

"The **EditMode** property has three possible values: **dbEditNone** (numeric value = 0), **dbEditInProgress** (1) and **dbEditAdd** (2). What's weird is that the **dbEditInProgress** mode *only* occurs if an explicit **Edit** method is used; it doesn't happen in the control's *implicit* **Edit** method is invoked by clicking on a navigation button.

"What we're doing here is checking the **EditMode** property of the recordset for one of those values: **dbEditNone**," I said. "If the **EditMode** property of the recordset **is** **dbEditNone**, then we know that the user hasn't started to edit the recored. If the **EditMode** property **is not equal** to **dbEditNone**:"

```
If Data1.Recordset.EditMode <> dbEditNone Then
```

"...that means that some type of update is in progress – either a new record is being added, or an existing record is being edited. If that's the case, we then display a message to the user, and bypass the rest of the code in the procedure that executes the **AddNew** method of the recordset by exiting the subprocedure."

```
    MsgBox "Please finish your current updates before adding
        ↳another new record"
    Exit Sub
End If
```

I waited to see if anyone had any questions.

"Let's run the program," I said, "and once again, click on the Add button twice."

I then ran the program, clicked on the Add button once, then clicked on it again. This time, our message box appeared:

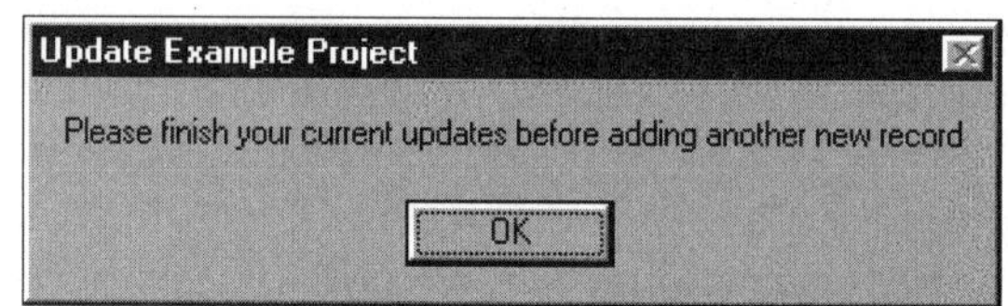


"That's better," I heard Ward say.

"As you can see," I said, "the first time we clicked on the Add button, the now familiar form with empty bound controls was displayed. But when we clicked on the Add button a second time, instead of initiating the addition of a second new record, this time a warning message was displayed to the user."

Again I waited a moment to see if anyone had a problem with what we had just done.

"OK," Valerie said, "we've taken care of this little problem with the click of the Add button. Now what?"

"In a few moments," I said, "we'll place two command buttons on the form. One will be called Update which, when clicked, will add a new record to the recordset by executing the recordset's **Update** method. The second button will be called Cancel: when it's clicked, this button will execute the **CancelUpdate** method of the recordset. This Cancel button will let the user to change their mind about adding a record and retreat with dignity in a clean manner."

"Change their mind?" Rachel asked.

"Yes, that's right, Rachel," I said. "If the user is in the process of adding a record, executing the **CancelUpdate** will cancel that addition."

"That sounds great," Peter said, "I can't wait to see that in action."

"Before we do that, Peter," I said, "we still have a little work to do with this form."

"What kind of work?" Linda asked.

"Well," I answered, "Before we add a record to the recordset we should ensure that the user has supplied us with all the information that we need."

"So we're doing some **validation**, in other words?" Mary said.

"That's right, Mary," I said. "For instance, on this form, I think it makes sense that both **`Author`** and **`Year Born`** are filled in – even though neither one is a required field in the **`Authors`** table. Besides, it will be a good learning experience."

"How can we do this?" Chuck queried.

"Do you remember our discussion on the **`Validate`** event procedure of the data control from a few weeks back?" I asked. "We can place code in the **`Validate`** event to perform **field-level** validation – that is, we can check that each field has been correctly processed. Since the **`Validate`** event takes place **before** the record pointer changes, that's the perfect place to put code that checks the information in any controls that are bound to a specific database field. Here, take a look at this code..."

I stopped the program, and typed the following lines of code into the data control's **`Validate`** event procedure:

```
Private Sub Data1_Validate(Action As Integer, Save As Integer)

If Data1.Recordset.EditMode = dbEditNone Then Exit Sub

If txtAuthor.Text = "" Then
   MsgBox "Author cannot be blank"
   txtAuthor.SetFocus
   Save = False
   Action = vbDataActionCancel
   Exit Sub
End If

If txtYearBorn.Text = "" Then
   MsgBox "Year Born cannot be blank"
   txtYearBorn.SetFocus
   Save = False
```

*Continued on following page*

```
        Action = vbDataActionCancel
        Exit Sub
    End If

    If Val(txtYearBorn.Text) <= 1900 Then
        MsgBox "Year Born must be greater than 1900"
        txtYearBorn.SetFocus
        Save = False
        Action = vbDataActionCancel
        Exit Sub
    End If

    End Sub
```

I looked around and saw some puzzled faces.

"I know we discussed this a few weeks ago," Ward said, "but what causes the **Validate** event of the data control to trigger?"

"Essentially," I said, "the **Validate** event is invoked by any action that causes the recordset's record pointer to move. That means: any click of the data control's navigation buttons, the execution of any of the **Move** methods of the recordset, or any of the **AddNew**, **Update** or **Delete** methods that we'll examine later today. Even the **Find** or **Close** methods of the recordset, or setting a **Bookmark** property like we did a few weeks ago will **also** trigger the **Validate** event. Just remember, the **Validate** event procedure fires before the record pointer moves – meaning that we can intervene and tell the record pointer not to move at all, just by setting the **Action** argument equal to **vbDataActionCancel**."

"Yes, I see that you're doing that here in the code," Steve said, "can you explain this in a little more detail?"

"I'd be glad to, Steve," I answered. "The first thing we do is check to see if the **EditMode** of the recordset is equal to **dbEditNone**. If it is, we just bypass the rest of the code by executing an **Exit Sub** statement – there's no need to perform validation if we're not adding records or editing them:"

```
    If Data1.Recordset.EditMode = dbEditNone Then Exit Sub
```

"After the check for the **EditMode** property of the recordset," I continued, "we then look at the **Text** property of every bound text box control on the form that we consider to be a required field and ensure that the user has keyed some data into it:"

```
If txtAuthor.Text = "" Then
...
If txtYearBorn.Text = "" Then
```

"We also check to see if the **`Text`** property of the **`Year Born`** text box contains a value less than or equal to 1900:"

```
If Val(txtYearBorn.Text) <= 1900 Then
```

"If any of these three conditions are true, we display an error message to the user, and set focus to the text box control that has broken our validation rules. Most importantly, we then set the **`Save`** argument of the **`Validate`** event procedure to **`False`**. This ensures that no records in the underlying recordset are changed. Finally, we set the **`Action`** argument of the **`Validate`** event procedure to **`vbDataActionCancel`** – in essence, canceling whatever action the user took, which triggered the **`Validate`** event procedure of the data control in the first place:"

```
Save = False
   Action = vbDataActionCancel
```

"In other words," Dave said, "if the user has clicked on the Next button on the data control, then setting the **`Action`** argument to **`vbDataActionCancel`** means that the result is the same as if they had **never** clicked on the button?"

"That's exactly right, Dave," I said. "Let's see this in action."

I ran the program, clicked on the Add button to execute the **`AddNew`** method of the recordset, and then immediately clicked on the data control's 'next record' button to trigger the **`Validate`** event procedure. Here's what happened...

"Notice how the code in the **`Validation`** event procedure," I said, "has detected that the **`Author`** text box is empty, displayed this error message, and also stopped the record pointer from advancing."

Since I was still in 'add' mode, I completed the **Author** field with some information and then clicked on the 'next record' button on the data control again:

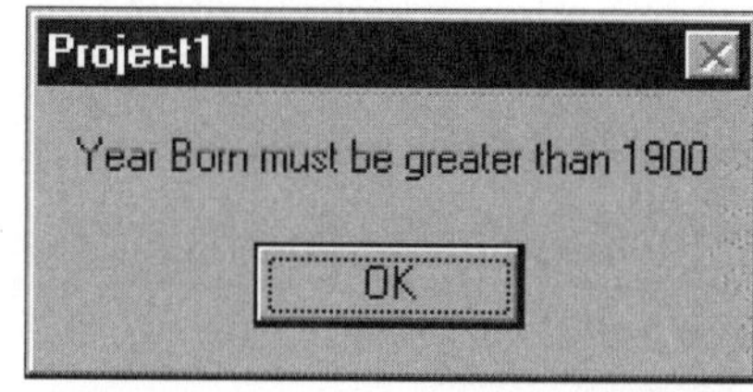


"Because the default value for **txtYearBorn** is 0, and since the program had automatically placed this value in the field," I said, "we didn't receive a message saying a value for **txtYearBorn** is required. But obviously, since 0 is less than 1900, we received this error message."

Finally, I entered a year greater than 1900 into the **Year Born** field, clicked on the data control's 'next record' button, and the record was successfully added to the recordset. However, it seemed to immediately disappear.

"Where did the new record go?" Mary asked.

"Aha!" I said, mysteriously. I clicked on the 'last record' button – and there was that elusive record:

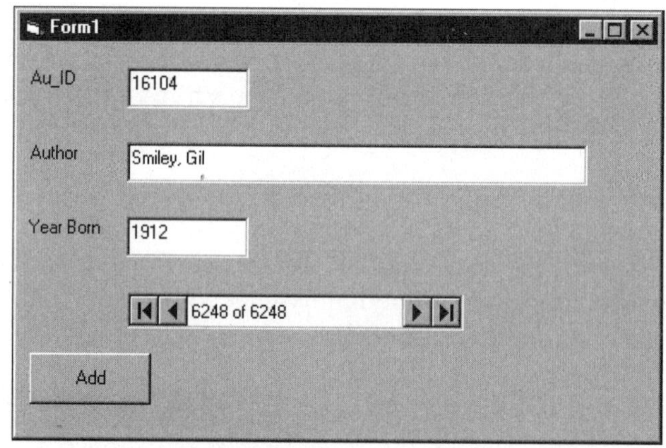


"New records are placed at the **end** of the recordset," I explained.

"Notice that the **Au_ID** is 16104," I said, and looked at Ward with a smile. "That reflects several aborted attempts at adding new records to the recordset."

Again I waited to see if there were any questions.

"Let's look at coding the **Update** method in the **Click** event procedure of a command button," I said. "I think you'll find that it's a little more user-friendly than expecting the user to use the navigation buttons."

I added a second command button to the form, changing its **Name** property to **cmdUpdate** and its **Caption** property to Update:

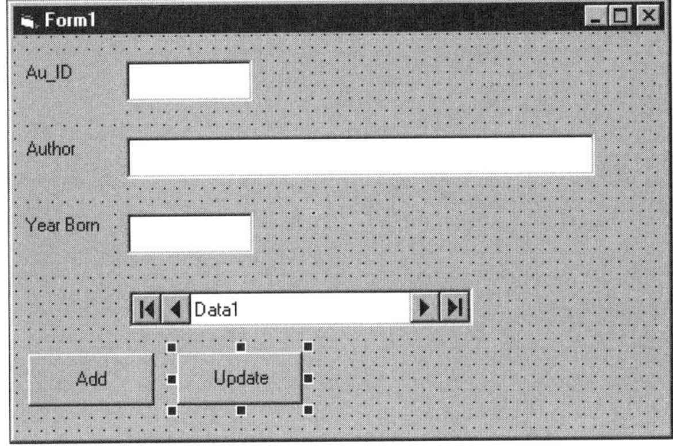


I then placed the following code into **cmdUpdate**'s **Click** event procedure:

```
Private Sub cmdUpdate_Click()

Data1.Recordset.Update

End Sub
```

"This code just executes the recordset's **Update** method," I said. "In Visual Basic, you should execute this method at some time *after* you execute either the **AddNew** or **Edit** methods. Basically, the **Update** method updates the recordset with any changed values, just as if the user clicked on a navigation button on the data control."

After restarting the demonstration program, I immediately clicked on the Add button. I filled in the **Author** and **Year Born** fields on the form, and then clicked on the Update button.

As was the case with the previous record, the new record appeared to vanish, and we needed to navigate to the end of the recordset to find it:

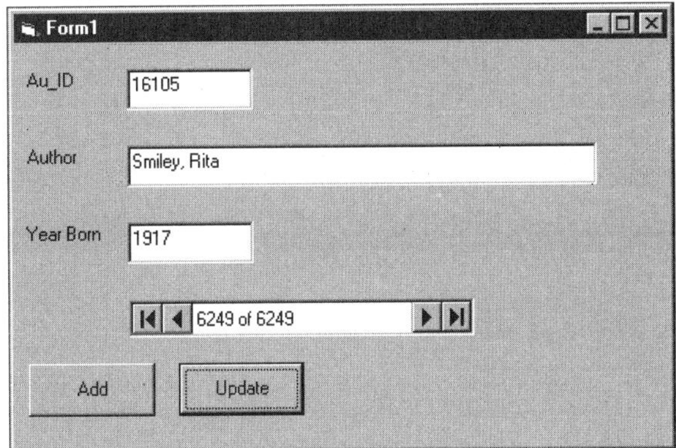

"There's the new record," I said. "I think you'll agree that providing the user with an Update button is a step forward in making this form easy for them to use."

"Overall," Valerie said, "I think this code is working well, and I think the idea of an Update button is a good one."

"I agree, Valerie," I said, "but working with database controls can be a little tricky, and there are nuances that you need to be aware of. For instance, you can't execute the **`Update`** method without first having executed either the **`AddNew`** or the **`Edit`** method of the recordset.

Let me show you by stopping the program...if I then start it again, and immediately click on the Update button:"

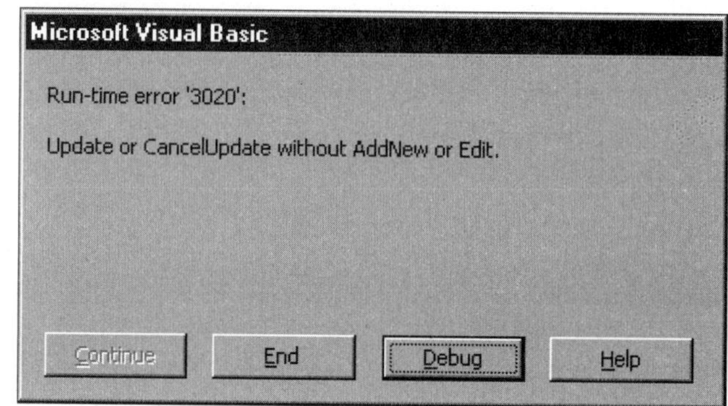


"What happened?" Rhonda asked.

"By clicking on the Update button," I said, "we executed the **`Update`** method of the recordset, and Visual Basic recognized that we hadn't previously executed either the **`AddNew`** or **`Edit`** methods of the recordset. As no editing activity had taken place, executing the **`Update`** method made our program bomb."

"Is there a way to check for update-type activity before we execute the **`Update`** method?" Peter asked.

"Yes there is," I said, "we can check the **`EditMode`** property of the recordset prior to executing the **`Update`** method. The **`EditMode`** property will reflect what's going on. Like this:"

```
Private Sub cmdUpdate_Click()

If Data1.Recordset.EditMode = dbEditAdd Then
   Data1.Recordset.Update
Else
   Data1.Recordset.Edit
   Data1.Recordset.Update
```

```
End If

End Sub
```

I then ran the program, and immediately clicked on the **Update** button.

"No problem now," I said.

"I'm totally confused about what's going on with this code," Rachel said. "I see that you are checking the **EditMode** property of the recordset to see if a record is being added – in which case you execute the **Update** method of the recordset. But why are you executing the **Edit** and **Update** methods if the EditMode is **not dbEditAdd**?

"That's a good question, Rachel," I said, "I've tried to put myself in the mindset of the user of the program. They will click on the Update button for one of two reasons: first, because they've clicked on the Add button, and they want to save the new record; or secondly, because they've made changes to a record on the form, and they want to *save* the amended record. The problem is that (because of the way **Update** works) an error is thrown in the second case if we don't execute the **Edit** method first, so we make sure that an error *doesn't* occur by executing the **Edit** method just before we use the **Update** method:"

```
Else
   Data1.Recordset.Edit
   Data1.Recordset.Update
End If
```

"I see," she said, "you figure that something on the form has changed, and for that reason you're going to execute the **Edit** method followed by the **Update** method to avoid that weird error."

"Exactly," I said.

"Makes sense to me," Ward said.

"OK, now let's see about **deleting** a record," I said. "To delete a record, all we need to do is execute the **Delete** method of the recordset. It's really pretty straightforward."

### The Delete Method

I added another command button to the form, changed its **Name** property to **cmdDelete**, and its **Caption** property to Delete:

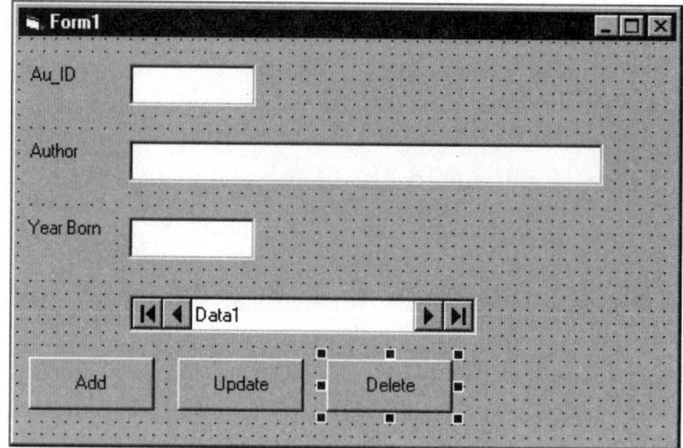


I then keyed the following code into the **cmdDelete** button's **Click** event procedure:

```
Private Sub cmdDelete_Click()

Dim intResult As Integer

If Data1.Recordset.EditMode <> dbEditNone Then
 MsgBox "If you're currently adding a record, please use the
     ↳Cancel button to cancel the addition"
   Exit Sub
End If

intResult = MsgBox("Are you sure you want to delete
     ↳this record?", vbYesNo, "Delete an Author")

If intResult = vbYes Then
   Data1.Recordset.Delete
   Data1.Recordset.MoveNext
   If Data1.Recordset.EOF Then
      Data1.Recordset.MovePrevious
   End If
End If

End Sub
```

"Let me explain this code before we try running it," I said. " The first thing we do here is to ensure that we aren't in the process of adding or editing a record by checking the **EditMode** property of the recordset. If its value is anything other than **dbEditNone**, then we display a message to the user and exit the procedure using the **Exit Sub** statement:"

```
If Data1.Recordset.EditMode <> dbEditNone Then
 MsgBox "If you're currently adding a record, please use the
     ↳Cancel button to cancel the addition"
   Exit Sub
End If
```

"I'm not sure I get that," said Rhonda.

"Well," I explained, "what I'm really doing here is checking to make sure that the user isn't adding a record at the time they hit the Delete button. This message box ensures that the user has completed their process properly – we'll add the Cancel button shortly, by the way."

"What's the second **message box** function for?" Rachel asked. "I don't believe I'm familiar with this format:"

```
intResult = MsgBox("Are you sure you want to delete
     ↳this record?", vbYesNo, "Delete an Author")
```

I explained that because the **Delete** method of the recordset will delete the current record without warning or prompting the user for a confirmation, it's a good idea to ask the user if they are *really* sure they want to delete the record. That's what we're doing with the second message box function – and that we're using the 'Buttons' argument value of **vbYesNo** to tell Visual Basic to display Yes and No buttons in the message box.

"That's why we need to check the return value from the message box function, right?" Tom asked, " – so that we know which of the two buttons the user selected?"

"Yes, that's excellent, Tom," I said. "Whenever you display a message box with more than one button, you need to handle the return value of the message box function in some way. In this case, we do that by assigning the return value of the **message box** function to a variable, and we then check whether its value is **Yes** or **No**. If the user's response to the question of deleting the record is 'Yes', we then execute the **Delete** method of the recordset, which deletes the current record."

"I'm OK with that," Mary said. "What I don't understand is why you are executing the **MoveNext** method of the recordset after deleting the record:"

```
If intResult = vbYes Then
   Data1.Recordset.Delete
   Data1.Recordset.MoveNext
```

"That's because of a quirk with the **Delete** method of the recordset," I said. "When we execute the **Delete** method, the record itself is immediately deleted in the recordset – but its old values remain visible in the bound controls of the form. We need to execute a **Move** method of some kind – I chose **MoveNext** – in order to make another record in the recordset current."

"And because of the possibility that the **MoveNext** method may take the record pointer into the **EOF**," Linda said, "you need to check the **EOF** property of the recordset – and move backward one record if you are there:"

```
If Data1.Recordset.EOF Then
      Data1.Recordset.MovePrevious
```

"Excellent, Linda," I said. "That's exactly what we're doing."

"I'm sure I've asked this before," Rhonda said, "but if the data control's **EOFAction** is set to **MoveLast**, how can we move to the **EOF** by executing the **MoveNext** method?"

Almost as soon as Rhonda said it, I knew she had the answer, but I replied anyway.

"That's because," I said, "the **EOFAction** is a property of the data control. Using these recordset methods, you can move past the last record of the recordset and to the **EOF** quite easily. The **EOFAction** property of the data control cannot protect us from ourselves!"

"That's right," Rhonda said, "I remember you saying that before."

As a demonstration, I ran the program, added an new record to the recordset using the Add and Update buttons, and then made it the current record by clicking on the 'last record' navigation button (remember, new records are added to the end of the recordset):

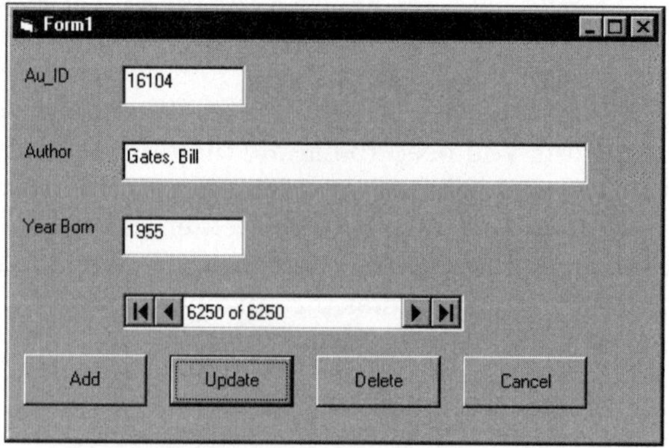

...and then clicked on the Delete button, with the following result:

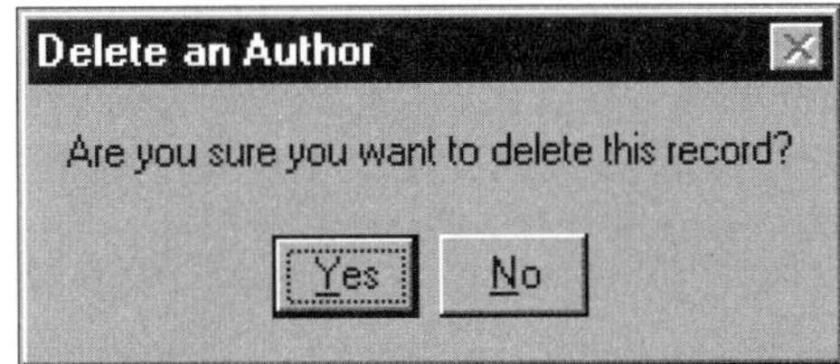


I answered No (I didn't really want to delete the record – not yet, anyway), and the record remained in the recordset. Finally, I clicked on the Delete button again, and this time answered Yes to confirm the deletion. The record was then deleted...

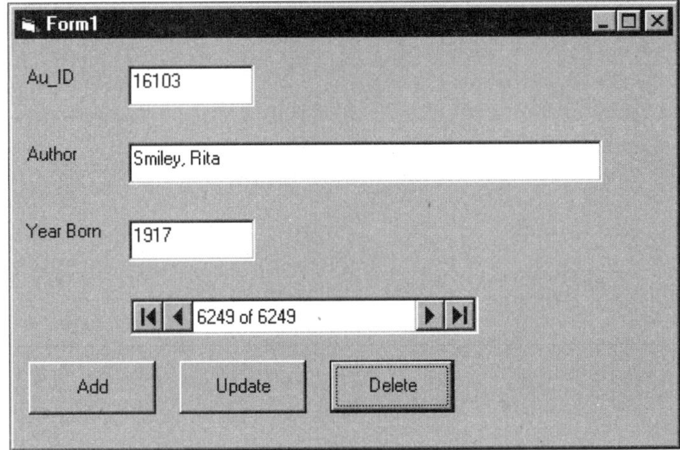


"Notice that our record count has gone down by 1," I said, "and the record is now gone."

"That's impressive," Blaine said. "We can now perform all of the major functions on a recordset – add, delete, edit and view records. That's just about it, isn't it?"

"Just about," I said, "but there is one more function that I think we should add to the form."

"What's that?" Rachel asked. "I thought we had coded them all."

"We need to handle one more possibility," I said. "Suppose the user clicks on the Add button – but then changes their mind. As it stands right now, once the user clicks on the Add button, they're committed to adding the record. We need to provide a way for them to change their mind."

"Good point," Bob said, "I never really thought about that."

"Fortunately," I went on, "there are two methods that fit the bill here – `CancelUpdate` and `UpdateControls`."

## The CancelUpdate and UpdateControls Methods

"**CancelUpdate** can be used to cancel a pending **AddNew** or **Edit** method. And **UpdateControls** is just a quick way of refreshing the bound controls on a form with the current data in the underlying recordset. Here, let me show you."

I added another command button to our form. Then I changed its **Name** property to **cmdCancel**, and its **Caption** property to Cancel:

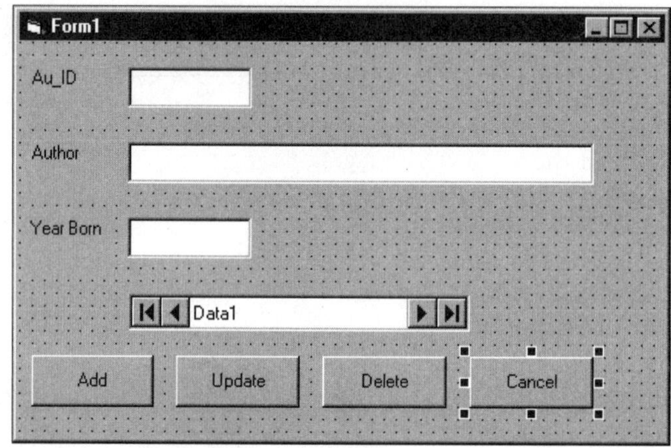


I then typed the next chunk of code into **cmdCancel**'s **Click** event procedure:

```
Private Sub cmdCancel_Click()

If Data1.Recordset.EditMode = dbEditNone Then
   Data1.UpdateControls
Else
   Data1.Recordset.CancelUpdate
End If

End Sub
```

"If you followed our discussion of the **Update** method," I said, "I think you'll be OK with this code. If you think about it, there are really only two types of updates that the user can cancel – an addition of a record, and an edit of an existing record."

I waited a moment before continuing.

"Essentially, the **dbEditNone** value of the recordset's **EditMode** property indicates that the user hasn't yet made any entries or updates:"

```
If Data1.Recordset.EditMode = dbEditNone Then
   Data1.UpdateControls
```

"In this instance, we just use the **UpdateControls** method to refresh the values in the values displayed in the bound controls.

"However," I said, "if the user is in the process of adding a record and then changes their mind, the **CancelUpdate** method can be used to override the **AddNew** method:"

```
Else
   Data1.Recordset.CancelUpdate
```

"If the user is in 'add' mode, the blank record disappears and the display reverts back to the previously displayed record.

"In a similar way, if the user has just spent some time making changes to one or more bound controls and then changes their mind, the data control's **UpdateControls** method will reset those values back to their original values by refreshing them from the values in the underlying recordset."

"In other words," Dave said, "since the changes the user has made to the bound text box controls haven't yet been written to the recordset – because the record pointer hasn't been moved – the **UpdateControls** method just refreshes the controls?"

"That's exactly right, Dave," I said. "As was the case with the code in the **Click** event of **cmdUpdate**, first we check the **EditMode** property of the recordset to determine if we're currently in the process of adding a record. Remember that because of the way the data control works, the **EditMode** will **not** be **dbEditNone** **only** if we're adding a record. If we are adding a record, we execute the **CancelUpdate** method of the recordset to cancel it."

"If we're *not* in the process of adding a new record, then we just execute the **UpdateControls** method of the data control to refresh the bound controls with the original version of the data."

I ran the program and clicked on the Add button to initiate the addition of a new record:

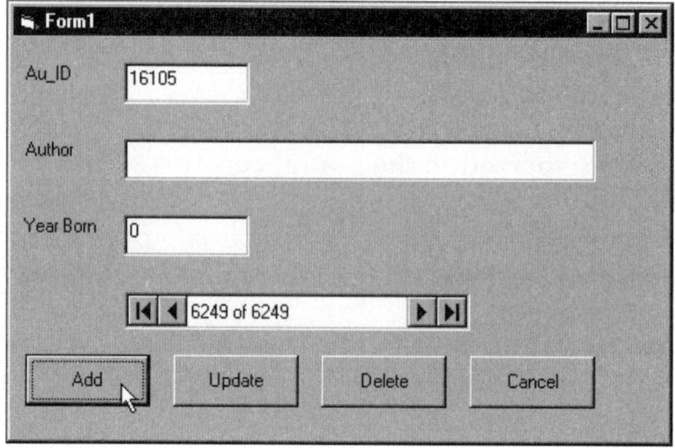


"If I now decide that I don't really want to add this record," I said, "I can then change my mind by clicking on the Cancel button."

I did just that:

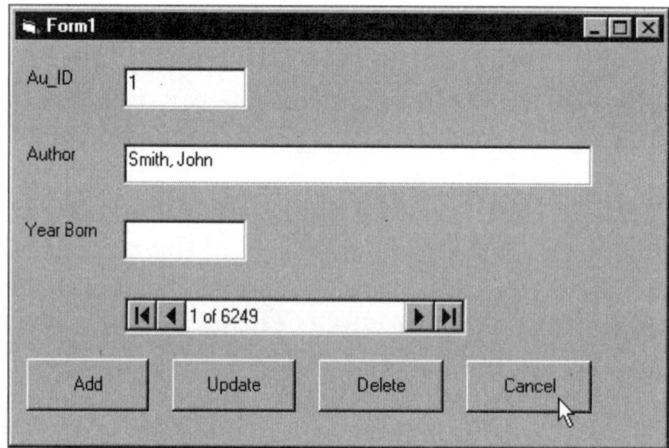


...and when I did, the addition of the new record to the recordset was cancelled, and the record pointer was moved to the first record in the recordset.

I waited to see if there were any more questions.

"You mentioned a little while ago," Steve said, "that we'll also be able to cancel an update of the record. For instance, if we begin to edit a record, and then change our mind, can you show us how that would work?"

"Sure thing, Steve," I said. "In the same way, if we begin to *edit* a record – then change our mind – all we need to do is click on the Cancel button and we can then set the current record back to the way it was before we started making changes."

"As long as we haven't moved the record pointer," Dave interjected.

"That's right, Dave," I agreed, "as long as we haven't moved the record pointer. Once we've moved the record pointer the changes will have been made to the recordset and thereby to the underlying table. Let me show you."

I then moved the record pointer to record number 6 – and began to change the name from Thiel, James R. to Gates, Bill:

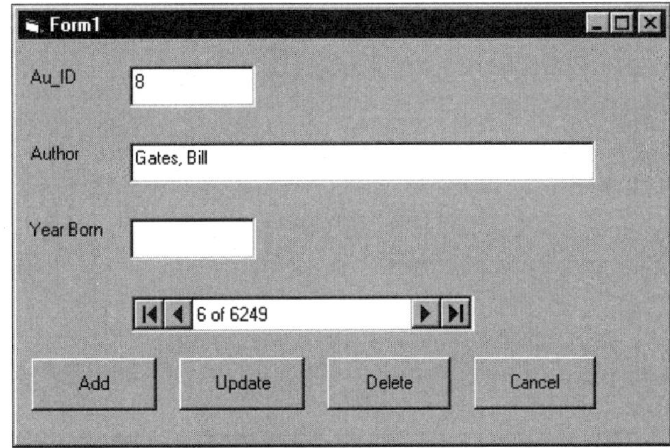


I then clicked on the Cancel button:

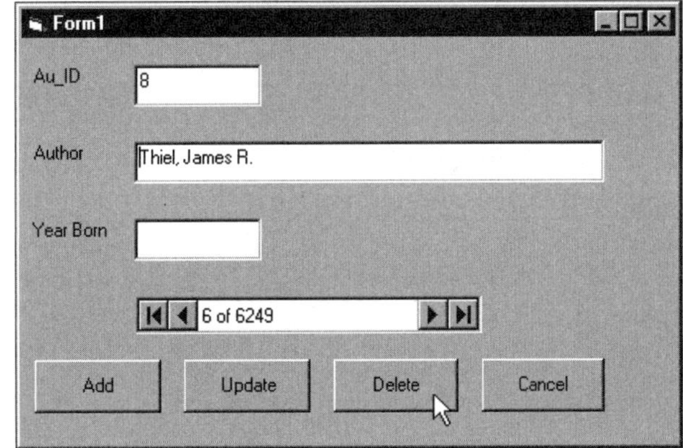


"See how the value in the **`Author`** field reverted back to its original value?" I asked the class.

"That's great," Blaine said. "That feature can come in handy, I'm sure. Is that about it for this demonstration form then? We're all anxious to start coding the China Shop program."

"Try to be patient just a few minutes longer," I laughed. "Before we begin working with the China Shop program, I just want to talk about error handling when using the data control and recordset methods."

## *Error Handling*

"A moment ago," I said, "we began to modify record number 6 by changing the author's name to Bill Gates. Now let's see what happens if we delete the record."

I then selected record number 6, clicked on the Delete command button, and answered Yes to the confirmation message box. This was the result...

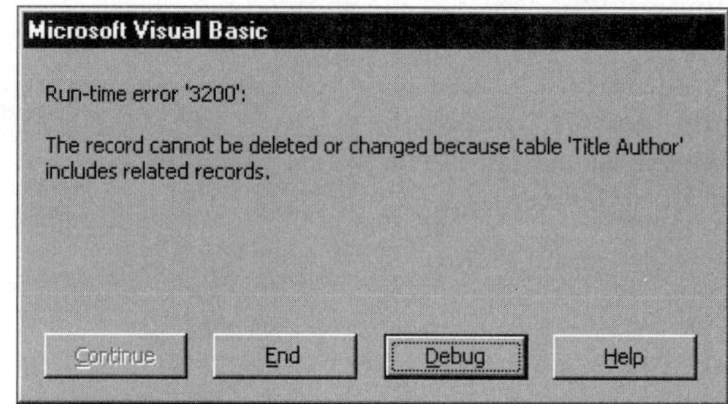


"Yikes!" exclaimed Rhonda. "What does that message mean?"

"Basically," I said, "this is a **Referential Integrity Error**. When we tried to delete this record, the underlying `Biblio` database protested by issuing this message. This is because when the database was designed, the relationships that were established between the **`Authors`** and **`Title Author`** tables specified that a record in the Authors table **cannot** be deleted if there is a matching record in the **`Title Author`** table with that **`author ID`**."

"That's right," Kevin said. "I hadn't fully realized what checking on 'Enforce Referential Integrity' in the Database Design window would do for us."

"This is a prime example," I said. "Relationships can enforce rules in your database – and as you can see, neither the user nor our Visual Basic code can violate those rules once they are established in Access. The result here is a '3200' error."

"But what do we do now?" Chuck asked, smiling. "The program has bombed – if that happens in the China Shop, it could ruin our growing reputations!"

"We can take care of this particular problem pretty easily by using standard Visual Basic error handling," I said, "the kind we learned about in the Intro class. Since we know the error number that the referential integrity error generates, we can code an error handler to trap for it. Like this."

I then modified the highlighted lines of code shown here in the **`cmdDelete`** button's **`Click`** event procedure:

```
Private Sub cmdDelete_Click()

On Error GoTo ErrorHandler

Dim intResult As Integer

If Data1.Recordset.EditMode <> dbEditNone Then
   MsgBox "Please finish your updates before deleting this record"
   Exit Sub
End If

intResult = MsgBox("Are you sure you want to delete
     ↳this record?", vbYesNo, "Delete an Author")

If intResult = vbYes Then
   Data1.Recordset.Delete
   Data1.Recordset.MoveNext
   If Data1.Recordset.EOF Then
      Data1.Recordset.MovePrevious
   End If
End If

Exit Sub

ErrorHandler:

Select Case Err.Number
   Case 3200
      MsgBox Err.Description
      Exit Sub
   Case Else
      MsgBox Err.Description
      Resume Next
End Select

End Sub
```

"For those of you who were students in my Intro class," I said, "you'll recognize this code as a standard error handler, that uses a **`Select Case`** structure to evaluate the **`Number`** property of the **`Err`** object. As soon as we attempt to delete this record, because of the referential integrity constraint, our error handler will kick in – notifying the user of the problem via a message box. However, instead of the program coming to a grinding halt, we'll just exit the **`Click`** event procedure without deleting the record. All in all, this is a much more graceful way of handling the problem. Watch this..."

I reran the program and navigated to the sixth record in the recordset once more. I clicked on the Delete button, and when the program asked me to confirm my intention to delete the record, I clicked on the Yes button. This time, instead of the program falling over gracelessly with a scary 3200 Error message, the following message was displayed:

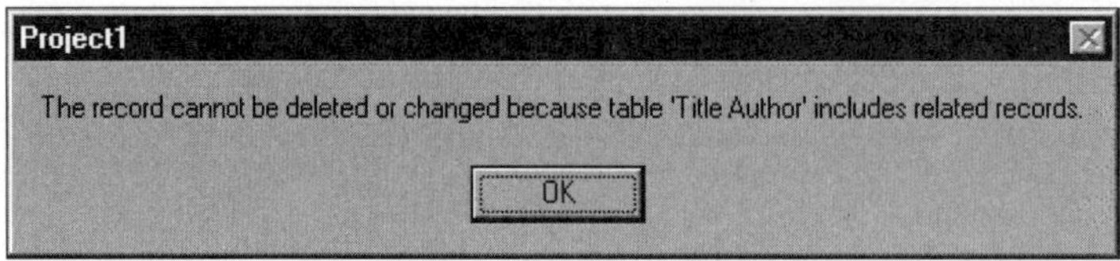


I clicked on the OK button, and the program smoothly resumed running.

"That's better," I said. "By the way, if we wanted to, we could customize the error message."

"I'm having a problem," said Rhonda, who had been following along by coding the demo on her classroom PC. "I placed the error handler code in the `Click` event procedure of the Delete button just like you did – but my program is still bombing with the 3200 error. I must be doing something wrong."

"I think I know what may be happening," I said, as I walked over to her PC. "I bet you have the Error Trapping option set to Break on All Errors instead of Break on Unhandled Errors. The Visual Basic default is Break on Unhandled Errors, which means that you only see errors where there is no error handler coded to deal with them. If, for some reason, you have Break on All Errors specified as your Error Trapping option, then **every** error, regardless of whether you have an error handler coded to deal with it, will cause the program to bomb."

Sure enough, when I checked Rhonda's Error Trapping options, Break on All Errors *was* selected.

"There," I said as I corrected the setting for her, "your Error Trapping options now read Break on Unhandled Errors..."

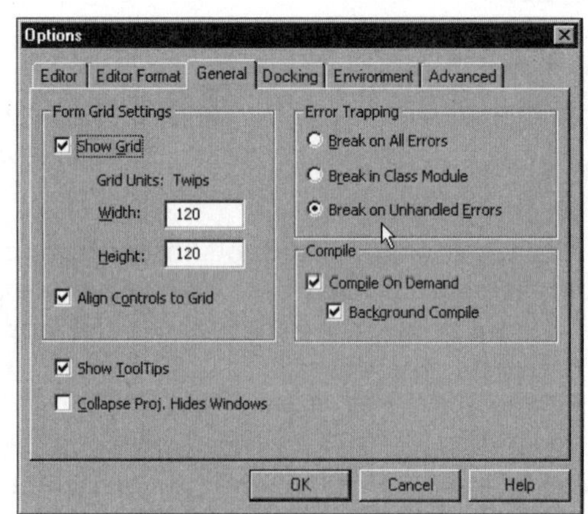

Rhonda then re-ran the program, and everything now worked properly.

"While you were attending to Rhonda's problem," said Ward, "I noticed that the data control has an **Error** event procedure. Can we use that in our program to handle errors like this?"

"That's a great question, Ward," I said. "The **Error** event procedure of the data control confuses a lot of beginners. It seems like the perfect place to put code to detect errors like this, but the problem is that the **Error** event procedure is only triggered when an error occurs as a result of the data control. In other words, errors like the one we just saw which are triggered by code that we write ourselves will not trigger the data control's **Error** event. Only errors that occur as the result of the action of the data control itself will trigger the **Error** event."

"Can you give us an example of the type of error that the data control could cause?" Kate asked.

"Sure, Kate," I said. "Here's a pretty common example. Suppose that the database specified in the **DatabaseName** property of the data control is not found when the form is first loaded – for whatever reason. This will cause the **Error** event of the data control to be triggered. We can place code in the **Error** event procedure that will be executed when the **Error** event is triggered. Like this..."

I quickly typed some code into the data control's **Error** event procedure:

```
Private Sub Data1_Error(DataErr As Integer, Response As Integer)

MsgBox "System Error - please contact John Smiley"
Unload Me

End Sub
```

"This code should look pretty familiar to the students who were in my Intro class," I said. "This is virtually identical to code we execute in the event that one of the crucial text files we need for the China Shop program is not being found when the program starts up."

"Can we test this?" Mary asked.

"Sure thing, Mary," I said. "Let's move the **Biblio.mdb** file from its current location to a new one, and then run the program. When the program runs, and attempts to initialize the data control, the **Error** event of the data control should be triggered."

I moved the **Biblio.mdb** file to a new location on my PC's hard drive and reran the program. As I anticipated, the message box was invoked:

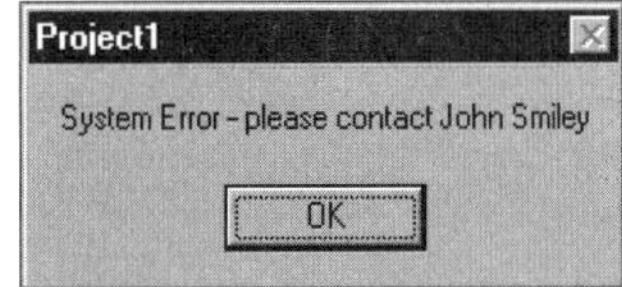

"I'm beginning to see now," Kate said. "Any error generated as a result of some action by the data control will trigger the data control's `Error` event. All errors that are the result of code that we write will **not** trigger the data control's `Error` Event – but **will** trigger errors of their own for which we need to write our own error handlers."

"I couldn't have said it better myself, Kate," I said.

I waited to see if there were any other questions. There were none, and so I asked the class to take a fifteen-minute break before starting on today's exercises for modifying the China Shop Program.

## Modifying the China Shop Program

"In the second half of today's class," I said, after returning from break, "we'll start to make some of the modifications to the China Shop program that will database-enable it. Let's start with the `Users` form – the form we began a few weeks ago. Remember, we need to enhance this quite a bit to make it more user-friendly for Joe Bullina and the China Shop staff."

### *Modifying the Users Form*

I then distributed the following exercise for the class to complete.

#### Exercise – Modifying the Users Form

1. Load up the China Shop project.
2. Open the `Users` form. Currently, the `Users` form looks something like this:

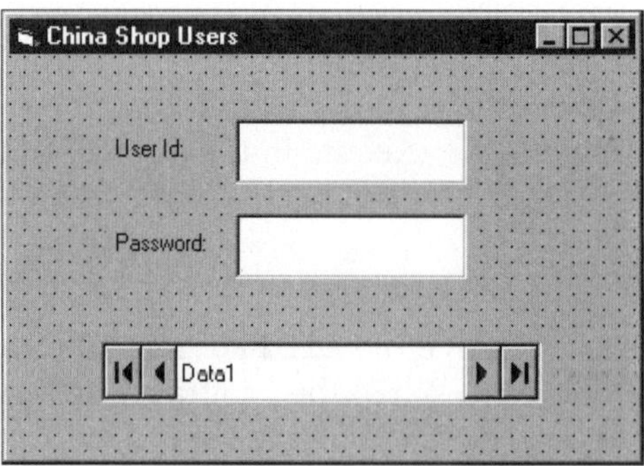


3. We'll be making major modifications to the `Users` form. Start by deleting the existing five controls on it and proceed to Step 4.
4. Place a single frame control on the form, and then place a second frame control within the first, sizing it roughly according to the screenshot below.

Although the frames are included for purely aesthetic purposes, remember that it's important that you do not create the second frame control by double-clicking the frame control in the toolbox. The second frame must be explicitly 'drawn' within the first frame by clicking on the Frame control in the toolbox and then using the mouse and cross-hairs to draw the second frame. To verify this has been done successfully, select the first frame and drag it. If the second frame is properly contained within the first frame, the second frame should move when you drag the first:

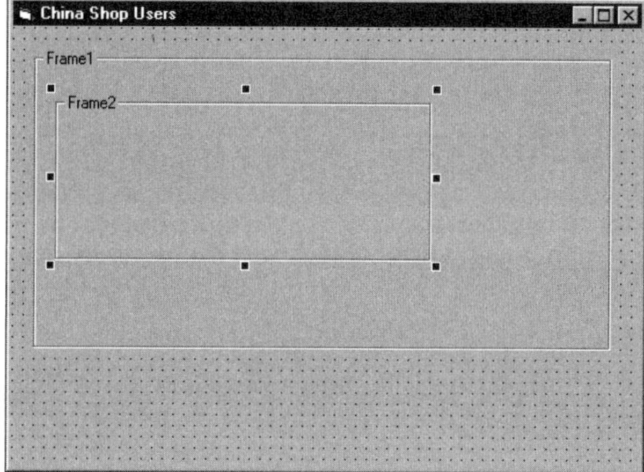


5. Draw two labels and two text box controls within **`Frame2`**, roughly in line with the screenshot below.

**Please note:** in order to preserve the correct **`TabIndex`** order, place **`Label1`** first, followed by **`Text1`**, then **`Label2`** followed by **`Text2`**. Be sure to *explicitly draw* these controls within **`Frame2:`**

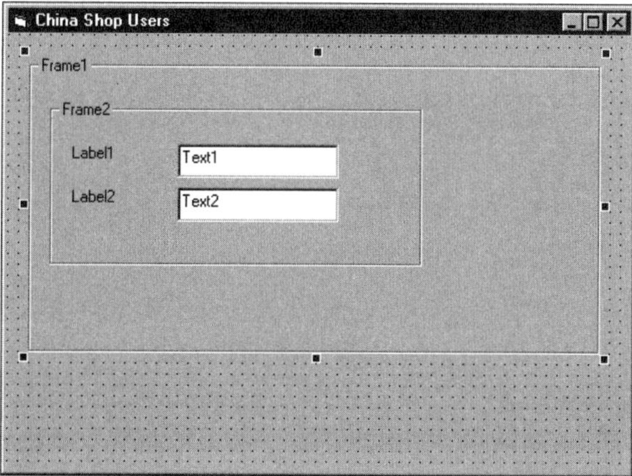

6. Now draw a data control and four command buttons within **`Frame1`**, along the lines of the screen shot. As was the case in Step 5, be sure that all of these controls are contained within the **`Frame`**...

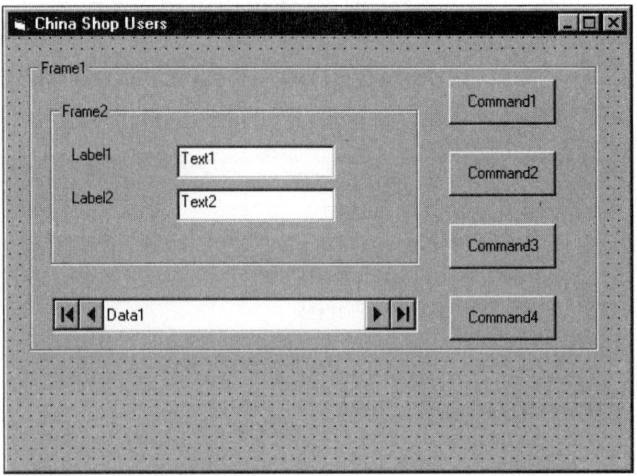


7. Finally, place a single command button on the form, outside of both frames, similar to the screenshot below:

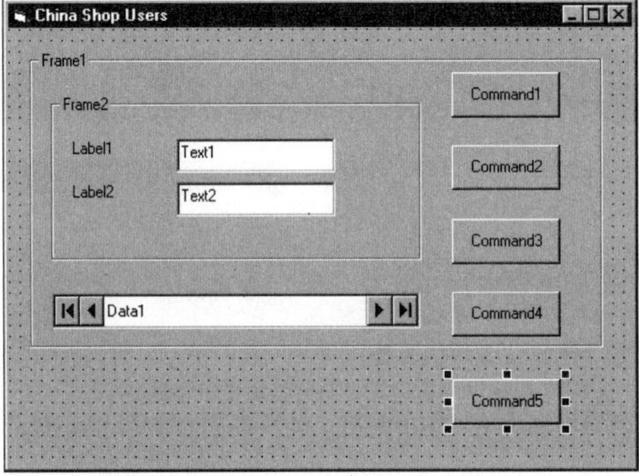


8. Now we need to set the appropriate property values for all of these controls. There's a lot of keying involved here, but it's important to do it all and do it right. Firstly, use the following table to make changes to the properties of the data control currently named **`Data1`**:

| **Property** | **Value** |
|---|---|
| Name | **`datUsers`** |

*Table continued on following page*

| Property | Value |
|---|---|
| Caption | China Shop Users |
| DatabaseName | `C:\VBFiles\China\China.mdb` |
| EOFAction | 0-MoveLast |
| RecordsetType | 1-Dynaset |
| RecordSource | Users |

The EOFAction property setting means that the user will only be able to add records by clicking on the Add button.

**9.** Now modify the frame control currently named **`Frame1`**:

| Property | Value |
|---|---|
| Name | fraOutside |
| Caption | (None) |
| TabIndex | 0 |

**10.** And now **`Frame2`**:

| Property | Value |
|---|---|
| Name | fraInside |
| Caption | Users |
| TabIndex | 1 |

**11.** Now update the properties for the label control currently named **`Label1`**:

| Property | Value |
|---|---|
| Name | lblUserID |
| Caption | User &ID: |
| TabIndex | 2 |

12. And `Label2`:

| Property | Value |
|---|---|
| Name | lblPassword |
| Caption | &Password: |
| TabIndex | 4 |

13. Next, modify the properties of the text box control currently named `Text1`:

| Property | Value |
|---|---|
| Name | txtUserID |
| DataSource | datUsers |
| DataField | UserID |
| MaxLength | 13 |
| TabIndex | 3 |
| Text | (blank) |

14. Now `Text2`:

| Property | Value |
|---|---|
| Name | txtPassword |
| DataSource | datUsers |
| DataField | Password |
| MaxLength | 8 |
| TabIndex | 5 |
| Text | (Blank) |

15. And now the command button currently named `Command1`:

| Property | Value |
|---|---|
| Name | cmdAdd |
| Caption | &Add |
| TabIndex | 6 |

**16.** And **Command2**:

| Property | Value |
|---|---|
| Name | cmdUpdate |
| Caption | &Update |
| TabIndex | 7 |

**17.** Next, **Command3**:

| Property | Value |
|---|---|
| Name | cmdDelete |
| Caption | &Delete |
| TabIndex | 8 |

**18.** How about **Command4**?

| Property | Value |
|---|---|
| Name | cmdCancel |
| Caption | &Cancel |
| TabIndex | 9 |

**19.** And **Command5**:

| Property | Value |
|---|---|
| Name | cmdExit |
| Cancel | True |
| Caption | E&xit |
| TabIndex | 10 |

The **Cancel** property setting means that if the user presses the *Esc* key, this has the same effect as clicking on this command button.

**20.** Now use the next table to confirm these properties of **frmUsers**:

| Property | Value |
|---|---|
| Name | frmUsers |
| BorderStyle | 1-Fixed Single |

*Table continued on following page*

| Caption | China Shop Users |
|---|---|
| Moveable | False |
| StartUpPosition | 2-Center Screen |
| Width | 6465 |

**21.** Your form should now look *similar* to this screenshot:

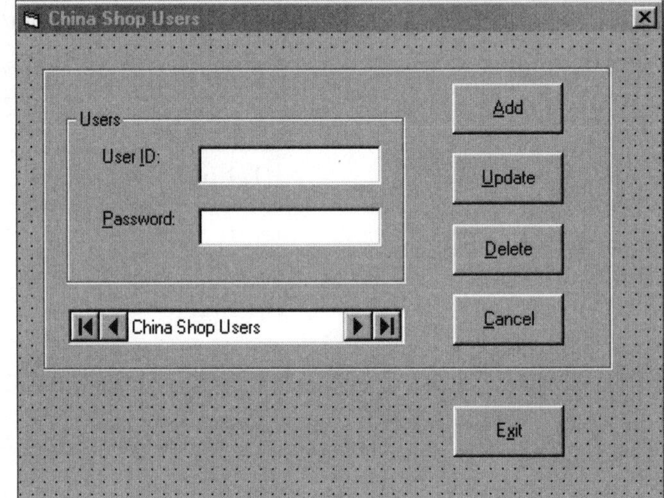


**22.** Save the China Shop project by clicking on the 'save' icon on the toolbar.

***Discussion***

I can't deny that this exercise was kind of tedious – and it took us about half an hour to complete.

The biggest problem we had, as had been the case in the Intro class, was the placement of the controls within the frames on the form. Complicating things even more was my design to have a frame contained within a frame. Chuck became pretty frustrated with the process, and I suggested that he might want to place a Shape control on the form, setting the **`Shape`** property to **`Rectangular`**, to simulate the look of the frame within a frame instead. But Chuck persevered, and eventually he had all the controls in place correctly.

"I have a question," Rhonda said. "I noticed that we've assigned a hot key to the label captions. What's the significance of that – labels can't receive focus, can they?"

"That's a very good question, Rhonda," I said. "You're right – labels can't receive focus. However, when we set a hot key – or access key – on a label's caption, the control with the **`TabIndex`** property *next in sequence* after that label receives the focus."

"In other words," Dave said, "if we press the *Alt+I* combination, focus will be set to the **txtUserID** textbox."

"That's right, Dave, assuming that our **TabIndex** properties are set correctly, of course!" I said. "This is a little trick of the trade – assigning an access key to the label control adjacent to a text box. Since there's no way of assigning an access key to a text box control – as it has no **Caption** property – this technique is a way of 'fooling' Visual Basic into simulating that behavior."

"I'm sort of curious," Kate said, "as to why we're assigning access keys on this form. We didn't make much use, if any, of access keys on the main form of the China Shop project, did we?"

"That was an oversight on my part," I said. "Windows design standards dictate that we assign access keys to all of our controls. One of your classmates reminded me how important this feature is for users of the program who may not have the ability to use a mouse. In fact, during the last week of class, one of the final modifications we'll make to the main form of the China Shop program is to assign access keys to all of the controls on the main form."

"I noticed," Rachel added, "that you have set the **Cancel** property of **cmdExit** to **True**. Doesn't that mean that if the user presses the *Esc* key, it's the same as clicking on that button?"

"That's right, Rachel," I said. "The Exit command button is typically set with a **Cancel** property equal to **True**. In this case, there really is no command button that we can categorize as the **Default** button (where pressing Enter should have the same effect as clicking on it) – so we haven't designated one."

I waited to see if there were any questions.

"Now," I said, "we're going to start coding the event procedures for the **Users** form. Of course there are many ways to paint a picture – the code that I'm asking you to write here is by no means the only way to do this – but the code does work, and it will provide a good interface for Joe Bullina and his staff. As you complete the remainder of these exercises, you'll recognize that the code we are using here on the **Users** form is identical, for the most part, to the code I demonstrated for you in the first half of today's class. If we use a new technique, I'll be sure to point it out. For the **Users** form, I'll ask you to complete a separate exercise for each event procedure on the form. As we complete the remainder of the forms in the China Shop project, I'll condense the exercises a bit."

There were no questions, and so I distributed this exercise:

## Exercise – Coding the Activate Event Procedure of the Users Form

1. Continue working with the China Shop project's **Users** form.
2. Double-click on the form, and key the following code into its **Activate** event procedure:

```
Private Sub Form_Activate()

datUsers.Recordset.MoveLast
datUsers.Recordset.MoveFirst

End Sub
```

3. Save the China Shop project by clicking on the 'save' icon on the toolbar.

### *Discussion*

No one had any problems completing this exercise. The code in the **Activate** event procedure was identical to the code I had demonstrated earlier that morning.

"All we're doing here," I said, "is moving to the end of the recordset and then back to the beginning in order to obtain an accurate record count for the data control's **Caption**."

I then distributed the following exercise to the class:

## Exercise – Coding the QueryUnload Event Procedure of the Users Form

1. Continue working with the **Users** form.
2. This code should already be in the **QueryUnload** event procedure of the **Users** form – you should just need to verify it.

```
Private Sub Form_QueryUnload(Cancel As Integer,
    ↳UnloadMode As Integer)

frmMain.Show

End Sub
```

3. Save the China Shop project again.

### *Discussion*

There were no problems completing this exercise – we had seen it all before.

"We actually coded this in week 4," I said. "Because we 'hide' the **Main** form of the China Shop program when we display the **Users** form, we mirror that process when we close the **Users** form, by 'showing' the **Main** form again."

"Don't we need to code an **Unload** statement here?" Kathy asked.

"No we don't, Kathy," I said. "The implicit behavior of the **QueryUnload** event procedure is to unload the form – so there's no need for to us to *explicitly* unload the form. Let's move on to the next exercise with the China Shop."

## Exercise – Coding the the Data Control's Reposition Event Procedure

In this exercise, you'll add code to the **Reposition** event procedure of the **datUsers** control on the **Users** form.

1. Once more, continue working with the **Users** form.
2. Place the following code into the **datUsers_Reposition** event procedure:

```
Private Sub datUsers_Reposition()

datUsers.Caption = "Users record " &
datUsers.Recordset.AbsolutePosition + 1
   ↳& " of " & datUsers.Recordset.RecordCount

End Sub
```

3. Save the China Shop project.

### *Discussion*

Again, there were no problems with this simple exercise.

"This code," I said, "displays the current record number and record count of the recordset in the data control's **Caption**..."

Everyone nodded – they were getting familiar with this code, now.

"...and so, on to the next exercise, where we add some more code to the data control."

## Exercise – Coding the Data Control's Validate Event Procedure

1. Again, continue working with the **Users** form.
2. Add the following code to the **datUsers_Validate** event procedure:

```
Private Sub datUsers_Validate(Action As Integer, Save As Integer)

If datUsers.Recordset.EditMode <> dbEditNone Then
   If txtUserID.Text = "" Then
      MsgBox "UserID must be entered"
      txtUserID.SetFocus
      Save = False
      Action = vbDataActionCancel
      Exit Sub
   End If
```

```
    If txtPassword.Text = "" Then
       MsgBox "Password must be entered"
       txtPassword.SetFocus
       Save = False
       Action = vbDataActionCancel
       Exit Sub
    End If
End If

End Sub
```

3. Save the China Shop project.

### Discussion

"This code is extremely important," I said, "and forms the basis of the validation of the data that the user enters into the bound text box controls. What we're doing here, essentially, is ensuring that the user keys data into the table's 'required fields'."

We had discussed the **Validation** event procedure quite a bit earlier, and none of the students had any problems with it, and so I handed out the next exercise.

## Exercise – Coding the KeyPress Event Procedure for txtPassword

In this exercise, you'll add code to the **KeyPress** event procedure of the **txtPassword** control. This code will ensure that all of the user's keyed input is in the correct case.

1. Carry on working with the **Users** form.
2. Key the next section of code into the **txtPassword_KeyPress** event procedure:

```
Private Sub txtPassword_KeyPress(KeyAscii As Integer)

If KeyAscii >= 97 And KeyAscii <= 122 Then
   KeyAscii = KeyAscii - 32
End If

End Sub
```

3. Save the China Shop project.

### Discussion

"I'm perplexed," Rhonda said immediately. "We haven't seen this code before, have we? What's going on?"

"We're executing this code," I said, "because we want all of the data in the **Users** table to be in upper case. This code, in the **KeyPress** event procedure of the **txtPassword** text box, causes whatever letter the user enters into the text box to appear in upper case – and that's the way we want the data to be either added or edited in the **Users** table."
"Do you mean to say," Chuck said, "that if the user types the lower case letter 'a' into the text box, the capital letter 'A' will automatically appear in the text box?"

"That's exactly right," I said.

"I thought the **KeyPress** event procedure sounded familiar from the Intro class," Kevin said. "Can you explain how that conversion happens?"

"I'd be glad to, Kevin," I replied. "Whenever a text box has focus and the user types a character into the text box, the **KeyPress** event of that text box is triggered. As you can see, an argument, called the **KeyAscii** argument, is passed to the **KeyPress** event procedure. The **KeyAscii** argument is the numeric equivalent of the key on the keyboard that the user pressed."

"Numeric equivalent?" Tom asked.

"That's right," I said. "Each key on the keyboard has a numeric equivalent ASCII character. For instance, the lower case letter 'a' has a numeric ASCII equivalent of 97. The lower case letter 'b' is 98, and so forth."

"So you're saying," Dave said, "that we can intercept the character that the user enters and replace it with another?"

"You're following this well, Dave," I said. "That's exactly what we are doing with this code – intercepting lower case letters and converting them into upper case letters even before they are displayed in the text box."

"And that's what you're doing when you assign **KeyAscii** a value equal to itself minus 32?" Tom said.

"Exactly, Tom," I replied. "The lower case letters have ASCII values beginning with 97 and ending at 122. The upper case letters have ASCII values beginning with 65 and ending at 90. So you see, the range of upper case letters is exactly 32 less than the range of lower case letters. To 'convert' a lower case letter to an upper case letter, all we need to do is subtract 32 from the value of **KeyAscii**."

"That's really smart," Melissa said.

"Another trick of the trade, Melissa," I said. "And in the next exercise, you'll place the same code into the **KeyPress** event procedure of **txtUserID**."

"I just ran my program," Steve said, "and I'm afraid that the characters I enter into my text box control aren't being converted into upper case. I must have done something wrong." "I'm almost certain, Steve," I said, "that you placed the code that should have gone into the **KeyPress** event procedure into the **Change** event procedure of the text box instead. Check that out."

After a few seconds, Steve confirmed that I was correct.

"How the heck did you know that?" he asked.

"When you double click on the text box control to open up the Code window," I answered, "by default, it's the **Change** event procedure of the text box that appears. You would be surprised at the number of students who enter code into the **Change** event procedure by accident for exactly that reason."

Steve cut and pasted the code from the **Change** event procedure into the **KeyPress** event procedure – ran the program (remember, we had already placed code in **mnuUsers** to load up the **Users** form) – and reported that everything was now working fine.

There were no further queries, so I distributed the next exercise:

## Exercise – Coding the KeyPress Event Procedure of txtUserID

1. Continue working with our old friend, the **Users** form.
2. This time, insert the following code into the **txtUserID_KeyPress** event procedure:

```
Private Sub txtUserID_KeyPress(KeyAscii As Integer)

If KeyAscii >= 97 And KeyAscii <= 122 Then
    KeyAscii = KeyAscii - 32
End If

End Sub
```

3. Save the project.

### Discussion

"Let's move on," I said. "We're nearly done with the coding for the **Users** form."

I then distributed this next exercise.

## Exercise – Coding the Click Event Procedure for cmdAdd

1. Continue working with the (now very familiar) **Users** form.
2. Place the following code into the **cmdAdd_Click** event procedure.

```
Private Sub cmdAdd_Click()

'Is the user adding a record already?
If datUsers.Recordset.EditMode <> dbEditNone Then
   MsgBox "Please finish your updates before adding a new record"
   Exit Sub
End If

'Implicit Save Operation may be taking place
'So, we need to Edit and then Update
'To avoid Error 3426 - See Microsoft Knowledgebase Article KBQ189851
datUsers.Recordset.Edit
datUsers.UpdateRecord

datUsers.Recordset.AddNew
txtUserID.SetFocus

End Sub
```

**3.** Save the China Shop project.

#### *Discussion*

"This code is similar to what we saw in one of the demonstrations earlier," I explained. "Here, we're ensuring that the user can only add records in an appropriate way."

"I'm a little puzzled," Steve said. "You have a comment in here concerning `Error 3426`. What is that? I don't remember seeing that error in the demonstration program."

"We didn't see it," I said, "but I did allude to a little 'bug' in the relationship between the data control and directly coding the recordset methods. It turns out that if you execute the **`AddNew`** method of the recordset, then the **`CancelUpdate`** recordset method, the program will bomb if the user begins to edit a field and then executes the **`AddNew`** method again. The error is numbered 3426, and the text reads 'Action cancelled by associated object'. We can get around this by executing an **`Edit`** followed by an **`Update`**."

"That's some combination of events," Rhonda said. "How did you ever discover that?"

"Lots of experience," I said smiling. "*Bad* experience."

"That's a really vague error message, what does it mean?" Kathy asked.

"According to the Microsoft Knowledgebase article," I explained, "that combination of events creates something which Microsoft calls an 'implied save in the bound controls' – and the execution of the **`AddNew`** recordset method in code will cause the 3426 error to occur."

"And you say that error can be avoided by first executing the **Edit** method of the recordset followed by **UpdateRecord** method of the data control?" Dave asked.

"Exactly," I said. "That's why we're executing this combination of methods just prior to executing the **AddNew** method."

I waited to see if there were any other questions or comments.

"I noticed," Mary said, "that we also execute the **SetFocus** method of the **txtUserID** textbox in this procedure. I think that's a nice feature."

With no other questions, I distributed another exercise.

## Exercise – Coding the Click Event Procedure for cmdCancel

1. Resume working with the **Users** form.
2. Add the following code to the **cmdCancel_Click** event procedure:

```
Private Sub cmdCancel_Click()

If datUsers.Recordset.EditMode = dbEditNone Then
    datUsers.UpdateControls
Else
    datUsers.Recordset.CancelUpdate
End If

End Sub
```

3. Save the China Shop project.

### *Discussion*

"Can you explain to me once more," Rhonda said, "the difference between **CancelUpdate** and **UpdateControls** methods?"

"Sure, Rhonda," I said, "The **CancelUpdate** recordset method can only be used after an **AddNew** or **Edit** method has been executed. **CancelUpdate** is used to cancel a pending addition or explicit edit of a record in a recordset."

"What about the **UpdateControls** then?" Chuck asked. "How is that different? Does the **UpdateControls** method refresh the values in the bound controls from the underlying recordset?"

"That's an excellent analysis, Chuck," I said. "That's exactly what the **UpdateControls** method does – it refreshes the values in the bound controls from the current values in the underlying recordset.

For instance, if the user makes changes to the bound text box controls on the **Users** form, executing this method 'resets' them back to the values they had before the user changed anything – and that can be extremely useful. We use it when no explicit **AddNew** or **Edit** method has been used, for example when the user has simply navigated to a record and started changing values."

There were no more questions, and so we moved on to another exercise (the tenth in the lesson).

## Exercise – Coding the Click Event Procedure for cmdDelete

1. Continue working with the China Shop project's **Users** form.
2. Key up the following section of code into the **cmdDelete_Click** event procedure:

```
Private Sub cmdDelete_Click()

On Error GoTo ErrorHandler

Dim intResult As Integer

If datUsers.Recordset.EditMode <> dbEditNone Then
  MsgBox "If you're currently adding a record, please use the
      ↳ Cancel button to cancel the addition"
Exit Sub
End If

intResult = MsgBox("Are you sure you want to delete a User record?",
     ↳vbYesNo, "Delete User Record")

If intResult = vbYes Then
   datUsers.Recordset.Delete
   datUsers.Recordset.MoveNext
   If datUsers.Recordset.EOF Then
      datUsers.Recordset.MovePrevious
   End If
End If

Exit Sub

ErrorHandler:

Select Case Err.Number
   Case 3200                  'Referential Integrity Check
      MsgBox Err.Description
```

*Continued on following page*

```
        Exit Sub
    Case Else
        MsgBox Err.Description
        Resume Next
End Select

End Sub
```

3. Save the China Shop project.

***Discussion***

No one had any major problems with this exercise (we had covered similar code earlier in the lesson already) – although the coding of the nested **If...Then** statement always requires care when typing it into an event procedure.

"Can you refresh my memory?" Valerie asked. "Why do we need to move the record pointer after executing the **Delete** method?"

"When a record is deleted," I said, "although it's no longer physically in the recordset, it leaves its values in the bound controls of the form. That's why we need to move the record pointer in order to clear the bound controls of the values of the deleted record."

"That's right," Valerie said. "I just forgot – thanks."

"We're moving right along here," I said. "It won't be long before we have a chance to test the **Users** form. But before we get into any more exercises, let's take a five-minute refreshment break and give our mouse-fingers a stretch."

After the break, I distributed the next exercise:

## Exercise – Coding the Click Event Procedure for cmdExit

Continue working with that old **Users** form.

1. Type the following code into the **cmdExitClick** event procedure:

```
Private Sub cmdExit_Click()

If datUsers.Recordset.EditMode <> dbEditNone Then
   MsgBox "Please finish your updates before closing the form"
   Exit Sub
End If

Unload Me

End Sub
```

2. Save the China Shop project.

### *Discussion*

"I didn't show an Exit button on the demo program," I explained, "because its code is relatively simple. We first check the **EditMode** property of the recordset to make sure the user isn't in the middle of adding a record – and if the user *isn't* adding a record, we execute the **Unload Me** statement, which ultimately results in the **QueryUnload** event procedure firing."

"Is it really necessary to have an Exit button?" Steve asked. "Can't the user just close the form in the usual way – by clicking on the control menu icon or the control button?"

"It's true, they can, Steve," I agreed. "But, in keeping with the theme of making this form as user-friendly as possible, another nice big command button reading Exit will go a long way toward preventing us from fielding a phone call from the China Shop asking us how to exit the **Users** form!"

"You're right," Steve said. "I see what you mean. It can't hurt!"

"This next exercise is the last one for the **Users** form," I said handing out the following exercise. "At the conclusion of this exercise, you'll be able to test the **Users** form to see how well it behaves. Have fun!"

## Exercise – Coding the Click Event Procedure for cmdUpdate

1. Continue working with that old favorite, the **Users** form.
2. Key the following code into the **cmdUpdate_Click** event procedure:

```
Private Sub cmdUpdate_Click()

If datUsers.Recordset.EditMode = dbEditAdd Then
    datUsers.Recordset.Update
Else
    datUsers.Recordset.Edit
    datUsers.Recordset.Update
End If

End Sub
```

3. Save the China Shop project.
4. Run the program and log in as ADMINISTRATOR using the 061883 password. Next, select Staff Functions | View/Update Users from the China Shop's menu bar. You should see the **Users** form displayed. Spend a few minutes performing the four basic database operations – **viewing** records, **adding** records, **editing** existing records, and **deleting** records. Do your best to make the program fall over – this is a good opportunity to discover if there are any errors or problems that we've missed.

### Discussion

It was all I could do to pry the students loose from the **Users** form. It had taken us nearly an hour to modify the form, and all of the students in the class were truly intrigued by its capabilities.

"The great news," I said, "is that the code we've written for the **Users** form by and large can be copied and pasted into the other data entry forms that we'll be coding this week and next. Of course, there will be some customization required, but for the most part, the code will be nearly identical."

"I'm having a great time with this, "Rhonda said, "so far, so good – no problems."

"I don't think you'll find many problems with the behavior of the form," I said, "it's been tried and tested many times. We have one more form to design and code today – the **Inventory** form..."

## Creating the Inventory Form

"...I think you'll find that with the **Users** form under your belts, the next form will be much easier."

With that, I distributed this exercise for the class to complete – the design of the **Inventory** form.

## Exercise– Creating the Inventory Form

In this exercise, you'll add a fourth form to the China Shop project, the **Inventory** form, and then save it in your **C:\VBFILES\China** directory.

1. Load up the China Shop project.
2. Select Project | Add Form from the Visual Basic menu bar.
3. From the next screen...

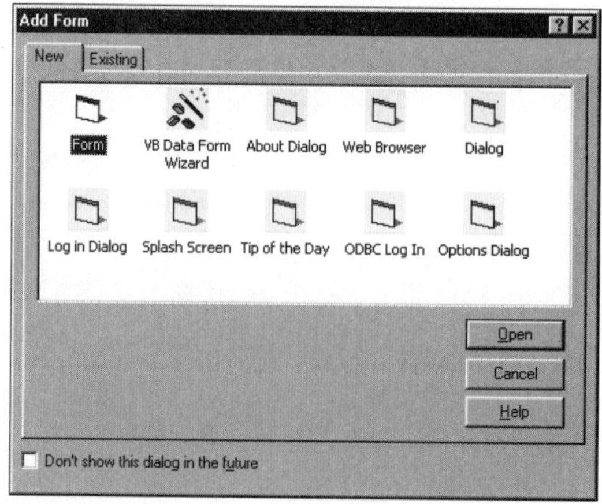

...make sure the New tab is selected and then double-click on Form. Visual Basic will then display a new form in the IDE for you, with a caption reading Form1.

4. Select the form, and bring up its Properties window. Find the **`Name`** property, and change it from **`Form1`** to **`frmInventory`**.
5. Now click on the 'save' button on the toolbar. Visual Basic will immediately prompt you to save the new form with a disk file name of 'frmInventory.' As ever, **don't save it with that default name**. Instead, first make sure that the form will be saved in the correct folder (**`C:\VBFILES\CHINA`**), then change the name in the File name box to Inventory:

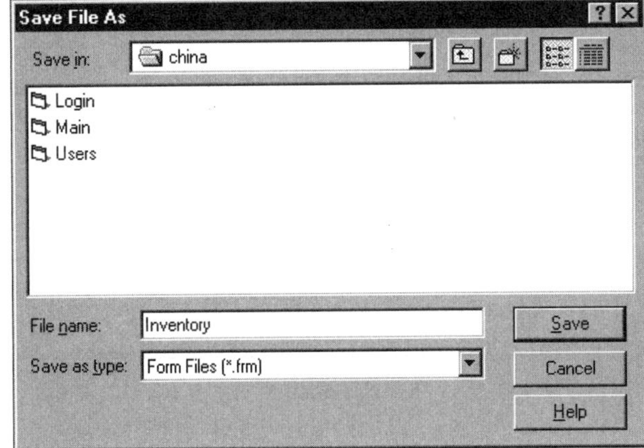


... and click on the Save button.

In the Visual Basic Project Explorer window, you should now see four forms as listed below:

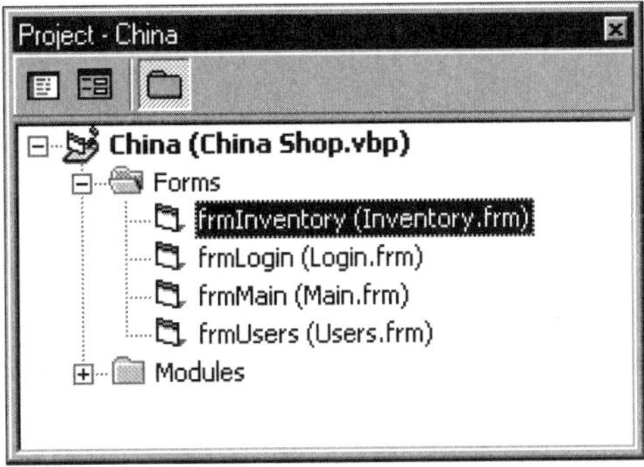

#### *Discussion*

By now, adding new forms to the China Shop project was becoming less and less of a big deal. Moving swiftly along, I distributed this exercise to the class:

### Exercise – Adding Controls to the Inventory Form

1. Continue working with the China Shop project.
2. Add two frames, four labels, four text boxes, a data control and five command buttons to the **Inventory** form. Size the form and position the controls roughly as in the screenshot.

   Be careful about the placement of the controls within the frame: to preserve the correct **TabIndex** order, place **Label1** first, followed by **Text1**, then **Label2** followed by **Text2**, then **Label3** followed by **Text3** and then **Label4** followed by **Text4**:

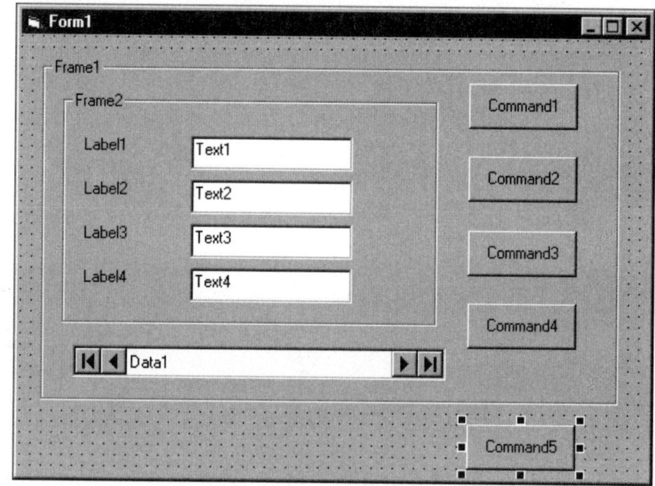


3. Use the following table to make changes to the properties of the data control currently named **Data1**:

| **Property** | **Value** |
|---|---|
| Name | datInventory |
| Caption | China Shop Inventory |
| DatabaseName | C:\VBFiles\China\China.mdb |
| EOFAction | 0-MoveLast |
| RecordsetType | 1-Dynaset |
| RecordSource | Inventory |

4. Now adapt the frame control currently called **`Frame1`**:

| Property | Value |
|---|---|
| Name | fraOutside |
| Caption | |
| TabIndex | 0 |

5. Now for **`Frame2`**:

| Property | Value |
|---|---|
| Name | fraInside |
| Caption | Inventory |
| TabIndex | 1 |

6. Next, change the properties of the label control currently named **`Label1`**:

| Property | Value |
|---|---|
| Name | lblItemID |
| Caption | &Item ID: |
| TabIndex | 2 |

7. Now **`Label2`**:

| Property | Value |
|---|---|
| Name | lblBrand |
| Caption | &Brand: |
| TabIndex | 4 |

8. Next, **`Label3`**:

| Property | Value |
|---|---|
| Name | lblItemName |
| Caption | Item &Name: |
| TabIndex | 6 |

9. And `Label4`...

| Property | Value |
|---|---|
| Name | lblPrice |
| Caption | &Price: |
| TabIndex | 8 |

10. Now alter the properties for the text box control currently named `Text1`:

| Property | Value |
|---|---|
| Name | txtItemID |
| DataSource | datInventory |
| DataField | ItemID |
| Locked | True |
| TabStop | False |
| TabIndex | 3 |
| Text | (Blank) |

11. And `Text2`...

| Property | Value |
|---|---|
| Name | txtBrand |
| DataSource | datInventory |
| DataField | Brand |
| MaxLength | 20 |
| TabIndex | 5 |
| Text | (Blank) |

**12.** Now, your friend and mine – `Text3`:

| Property | Value |
|---|---|
| Name | txtItemName |
| DataSource | datInventory |
| DataField | ItemName |
| MaxLength | 20 |
| TabIndex | 7 |
| Text | (Blank) |

**13.** And `Text4`:

| Property | Value |
|---|---|
| Name | txtPrice |
| DataSource | datInventory |
| DataField | Price |
| MaxLength | 7 |
| TabIndex | 9 |
| Text | (Blank) |

**14.** Use the following table to make changes to the properties of the command button currently named `Command1`:

| Property | Value |
|---|---|
| Name | cmdAdd |
| Caption | &Add |
| TabIndex | 10 |

**15.** Now modify `Command2`:

| Property | Value |
|---|---|
| Name | cmdUpdate |
| Caption | &Update |
| TabIndex | 11 |

**16.** And `Command3`:

| Property | Value |
|---|---|
| Name | cmdDelete |
| Caption | &Delete |
| TabIndex | 12 |

**17.** Wow – `Command4:`

| Property | Value |
|---|---|
| Name | cmdCancel |
| Cancel | True |
| Caption | &Cancel |
| TabIndex | 13 |

**18.** Next... `Command5`.

| Property | Value |
|---|---|
| Name | cmdExit |
| Cancel | True |
| Caption | E&xit |
| TabIndex | 14 |

**19.** Finally, use this table to make changes to the properties of the form itself:

| Property | Value |
|---|---|
| Name | frmInventory |
| BorderStyle | 1-Fixed Single |
| Caption | China Shop Inventory |
| MaxButton | False |
| MinButton | False |
| Moveable | False |
| StartUpPosition | 2-Center Screen |

**20.** Your form should look similar to the screen shot below...

**21.** Save the China Shop project.

***Discussion***

Having created a form very similar to this just a short while ago, the students had few problems completing this one.

"Notice," I said, "how we have set the **`Locked`** property of **`txtItemID`** to **`False`** in order to prevent the field from being updated, and the **`TabStop`** property to **`False`** so that the user won't be confused by being allowed to tab to it. Remember, **`txtItemID`** is bound to the **`ItemID`** field in the **`Inventory`** table – and that's an **`AutoNumber`** field that we shouldn't be updating directly."

Dave pointed out that he had discovered that setting the **`BorderStyle`** of the form to **`3-Fixed Dialog`** had the same effect as setting the **`BorderStyle`** to **`1-Fixed Single`** *and* setting both the **`MinButton`** and **`MaxButton`** properties to **`False`**.

After acknowledging Dave's comment, I then asked the class to take five and stretch their legs. When we resumed, I said "OK, get your typing fingers ready – there's a lot of code in the next exercise: but be of good cheer – you'll soon see the fruits of your labors in action."

I then distributed a further exercise for the class to complete.

## Exercise – Adding Code to the Inventory Form

In this exercise, you'll add code to the controls you just placed on the **Inventory** form.

1. Continue working with the China Shop's **Inventory** form.
2. Double-click on the form, and type the following code into its **Activate** event procedure:

```
Private Sub Form_Activate()

datInventory.Recordset.MoveLast
datInventory.Recordset.MoveFirst

End Sub
```

3. Now place the following code in the **QueryUnload** event procedure of the **Inventory** form:

```
Private Sub Form_QueryUnload(Cancel As Integer, UnloadMode As
    ↳Integer)

frmMain.Show

End Sub
```

4. Next, add this next section of code to the **datInventory_Reposition** event procedure:

```
Private Sub datInventory_Reposition()

datInventory.Caption = "Inventory record " &
    ↳datInventory.Recordset.AbsolutePosition + 1
        ↳& " of " & datInventory.Recordset.RecordCount

End Sub
```

5. Now key in this code in the **Validate** event procedure of **datInventory**:

```
Private Sub datInventory_Validate(Action As Integer, Save As Integer)

If datInventory.Recordset.EditMode <> dbEditNone Then
   If txtBrand.Text = "" Then
      MsgBox "Brand must be entered"
      txtBrand.SetFocus
      Save = False
      Action = vbDataActionCancel
```

```
      Exit Sub
   End If

   If txtItemName.Text = "" Then
      MsgBox "Item Name must be entered"
      txtItemName.SetFocus
      Save = False
      Action = vbDataActionCancel
      Exit Sub
   End If

   If txtPrice.Text = "" Then
      MsgBox "Price must be entered"
      txtPrice.SetFocus
      Save = False
      Action = vbDataActionCancel
      Exit Sub
   End If

   If Val(txtPrice.Text) <= 0 Then
      MsgBox "Price must be greater than 0"
      txtPrice.SetFocus
      Save = False
      Action = vbDataActionCancel
      Exit Sub
   End If

End If

End Sub
```

**6.** Place the following code in the `txtPrice_KeyPress` event procedure:

```
Private Sub txtPrice_KeyPress(KeyAscii As Integer)

If Chr(KeyAscii) = vbBack Then Exit Sub

If KeyAscii < 48 Or KeyAscii > 57 Then
   KeyAscii = 0
End If

End Sub
```

**7.** Key the following code into the **cmdAdd_Click** event procedure:

```
Private Sub cmdAdd_Click()

'Is the user adding a record already?
If datInventory.Recordset.EditMode <> dbEditNone Then
   MsgBox "Please finish your updates before adding a new record"
   Exit Sub
End If

'Implicit Save Operation may be taking place
'So, we need to Edit and then Update
'To avoid Error 3426--See KBQ189851
datInventory.Recordset.Edit
datInventory.UpdateRecord

datInventory.Recordset.AddNew
txtBrand.SetFocus

End Sub
```

**8.** This next batch of code goes in the **cmdCancel_Click** event procedure:

```
Private Sub cmdCancel_Click()

If datInventory.Recordset.EditMode = dbEditNone Then
   datInventory.UpdateControls
Else
   datInventory.Recordset.CancelUpdate
End If

End Sub
```

**9.** Now type this code into the **cmdDelete_Click** event procedure:

```
Private Sub cmdDelete_Click()

On Error GoTo ErrorHandler

Dim intResult As Integer

If datInventory.Recordset.EditMode <> dbEditNone Then
MsgBox "If you're currently adding a record, please use the Cancel
      ↳button to cancel the addition"
```

```
Exit Sub

End If

intResult = MsgBox("Are you sure you want to delete
     ➥an Inventory record?", vbYesNo, "Delete Inventory Record")

If intResult = vbYes Then
   datInventory.Recordset.Delete
   datInventory.Recordset.MoveNext
   If datInventory.Recordset.EOF Then
      datInventory.Recordset.MovePrevious
   End If
End If

Exit Sub

ErrorHandler:

Select Case Err.Number
   Case 3200           'Referential Integrity Check
      MsgBox Err.Description
      Exit Sub
   Case Else
      MsgBox Err.Description
      Resume Next
End Select

End Sub
```

**10.** Place the following code into the **cmdExit_Click** event procedure:

```
Private Sub cmdExit_Click()

If datInventory.Recordset.EditMode <> dbEditNone Then
   MsgBox "Please finish your updates before closing the form"
   Exit Sub
End If

Unload Me

End Sub
```

**11.** Finally, type this section of code into the **cmdUpdate_Click** event procedure:

```
Private Sub cmdUpdate_Click()

If datInventory.EditMode = dbEditAdd Then
   datInventory.Recordset.Update
Else
   datInventory.Recordset.Edit
   datInventory.Recordset.Update
End If

End Sub
```

**12.** Save the China Shop project.

### *Discussion*

There were no major problems with this exercise, although with more bound controls there was more to code with the **Inventory** form than there had been with the **Users** form, and it was time-consuming to key in. Still, it was essential stuff.

I could sense that the class was anxious to test the form – something they couldn't do until we coded the **mnuInventory Click** event procedure. However, there were a couple of questions, as I had anticipated.

"I must confess," Steve said, "I was a little confused as I went through the exercise and didn't find code to be inserted into the **KeyPress** event procedures of either **txtItemName** or **txtBrand**. Then I checked the database, and found that we had entered that data in mixed case. Is that why we're not 'upper casing' what the user enters into these text boxes?"

"That's a good observation, Steve," I said. "Ordinarily, I like to see the data in a table be entered uniformly in upper case. However, we've always been pretty particular in the China Shop program about mixing case with the brands and item names of the china – for that reason, we entered the data in mixed case, and you're right – that's why we're not uppercasing the value that the user enters into these text boxes."

"Can you explain what we're doing in the **KeyPress** event procedure of **txtPrice**?" Chuck asked. "The code in there is a little different from the code in the **KeyPress** event procedures of the text boxes on the **Users** form."

"Sure thing, Chuck," I said as I redisplayed the code on the classroom projector:

```
Private Sub txtPrice_KeyPress(KeyAscii As Integer)

If Chr(KeyAscii) = vbBack Then Exit Sub

If KeyAscii < 48 Or KeyAscii > 57 Then
   KeyAscii = 0
End If

End Sub
```

"The difference," I continued, "is that the **txtPrice** text box should have only *numbers* entered into it. That's why we're checking to make sure that the range of ASCII characters entered into this text box fall between 48 and 57 – the values for the characters 0 through 9."

"I'm OK with that," Chuck said, "but if the numbers are outside of that range, then why are we setting the value of **KeyAscii** to 0?"

"Setting the value of **KeyAscii** equal to 0," I said, "is the same as 'nulling' the user's entry into the text box. In other words, it's as if they never entered a character into the text box at all. This code ensures that only numeric characters will appear in the text box."

"What's that first line of code doing?" Mary asked.

```
If Chr(KeyAscii) = vbBack Then Exit Sub
```

"It's a check to determine if the user has pressed the *Backspace* key," I said. "We want them to be able to use the *Backspace* key as normal, so we don't want to block it out like we do with other keystrokes. That's what the intrinsic constant of **vbBack** means. Because the *Backspace* key has an ASCII value of 8, we need to determine if the *Backspace* key has been pressed – if it has, we bypass the rest of the code in the event procedure – which results in the *Backspace* key being passed as normal to the text box."

"I have only one question," Rhonda said, "why aren't we performing validation on the **txtItemID** text box? We have no code in either the **Validate** event procedure of the data control or in the **KeyPress** event procedure of the text box. Why is that?"

"That's because the user can't make an entry into that text box," I explained. "Remember, we set the **Locked** property of the **txtItemID** text box to **True**, and set the **TabStop** property to **False**. There's no way the user can make an entry into the text box – and neither would we want them to, since the value for the **ItemID** field in the Inventory table is assigned by Access."

"That's right," Rhonda said. "I had forgotten all about that."

There were no more questions, and it was time to modify the **Click** event procedure of **mnuInventory** so that we could finally access the **Inventory** form through the China Shop program...

## Exercise – Adding Code to the Click Event Procedure for mnuInventory

In this exercise, you'll add code to the **Click** event procedure of **mnuInventory** which will result in the **Inventory** form being displayed when the user clicks on Staff Functions | View/Update Inventory.

1. If the China Shop project is running, stop it by clicking on the 'end' button.
2. Select the **Main** form in the Project Explorer window.
3. In design mode, click on the main form's Staff Functions | View/Update Inventory menu item, and the code window for the **Click** event procedure of **mnuInventory** will open.
4. Place the following code in the **Click** event procedure of **mnuUsers**:

```
Private Sub mnuInventory_Click()

Me.Hide
frmInventory.Show

End Sub
```

5. Save the China Shop project.
6. Run the program and select Staff Functions | View/Update Inventory from the China Shop's menu bar. You should see the Inventory form displayed. At this point, spend a few minutes again performing the four basic database operations – **viewing** records, **adding** records, **editing** existing records, and **deleting** records. Do your best to 'break' the program – now's the time to discover if there are any errors!

***Discussion***

Designing and coding the Inventory form had taken us less time to complete than the Users form – about 20 minutes but our class time was way over.

"Next week," I said, "we'll design and code the `Customers` and `Transactions` forms, and along the way discuss the DBGrid in more detail. In fact, by the end of next week, all of the main China Shop forms will be completed."

I then dismissed class for the day.

# Chapter Summary

In this chapter, we saw how to use recordset methods to add, update, and delete data in our database – this is critical stuff to learn when thinking about database access. We also learned how to integrate these methods with command buttons and code on our Visual Basic forms.

In summary:

- We discussed the **`AddNew`**, **`Update`**, and **`Delete`** methods of the recordset, and saw them in action
- We saw how we can use the **`UpdateControls`** and **`CancelUpdate`** methods to abort changes that the user has changed their mind about
- We created two data entry forms for the China Shop project – the **`Users`** and **`Inventory`** forms. These forms allow the China Shop staff to add, edit, and delete records from the underlying tables
- We added buttons and code to these forms to create intuitive, user-friendly interfaces for the China Shop staff

This was quite a grueling lesson – there was a lot of theory and a lot of code. However, my class learned a great deal more about the recordset, and we began to see how we can use its facilities to tie our program and our database together. These are really important techniques, with wide applicability across a range of database access situations.

In the next lesson, we'll spend the bulk of our time doing practical work – creating the remaining `Customers` and `Transactions` forms for the China Shop project. This will complete the data access foundation, and we can then turn to integrating these components with the existing price quotation functionality of the China shop project.

isual Basic Learn to Program Databas
vith Visual Basic Learn to Progra
atabases with Visual Basic Learn
rogram Databases with Visual Basic Lea
o Program Databases with Visual Ba
earn to Program Databases with Visu
asic Learn to Program Databases w
isual Basic Learn to Program Databas
vith Visual Basic Learn to Progra
atabases with Visual Basic Learn
rogram Databases with Visual Basic Lea
o Program Databases with Visual Bas
earn to Program Databases with Visu
asic Learn to Program Databases wi
isual Basic Learn to Program Databas
vith Visual Basic Learn to Progra
atabases with Visual Basic Learn

## Chapter 8

# Completing the Staff Functions

The last chapter concentrated on recordset update methods, and we saw how we could improve our interface with a little behind-the-scenes recordset manipulation. Specifically, we designed and coded the `Users` and `Inventory` forms, using the data control and bound text boxes to let the China Shop staff display and modify data in the `Users` and `Inventory` tables of the China Shop database.

We need to concentrate for one more chapter on the staff functions of the database and program. After that, we can move on to enhancing the 'customer-end' of the project – letting the customer enjoy the benefits of the database functions that we've added to the program so far.

In this chapter, we'll be:

- Taking a look at a control that lets us format data on the form in special ways – the **Masked Edit** control
- Creating the `Customers` form and adding the code to it that will allow the China Shop staff to view and amend details of the store's customers
- Revisiting the DBGrid control and exploring its customizable properties
- Building the `Transactions` form that the China Shop staff will use to view records of the purchases that customers have made

There'll be a lot of detailed work in this chapter, as we need to set the correct properties for all the controls we'll be adding to our two new forms. This will be good experience for us, though, as attention to detail is important if we want our database and program to work together smoothly. At the end of this chapter we'll have added another substantial chunk of functionality to our project. We're getting there!

# We Meet Again

We began Week 8 of our Visual Basic Database class with a great deal of anticipation. At the end of our seventh class, we had finished designing and coding the **Inventory** form. By the end of today's class, all of my students would be done building the four forms that comprised the Staff Functions submenu of the China Shop project's menu bar:

- ❑ The **Users** form
- ❑ The **Inventory** form
- ❑ The **Customers** form
- ❑ The **Transactions** form

In completing these forms, we'll finish building the database 'back-end' that the China Shop staff and the customers will interact with in their different ways.

# Today's Agenda

"Today we're going to code both the **Customers** and **Transactions** forms," I said. "You'll find the **Customers** form very similar to the **Users** and **Inventory** forms, in that it lets the China Shop's staff view, amend, add, and delete records from the relevant tables in the **China** database. However, for the **Customers** form, I'd like to introduce you to another bound control – the **Masked Edit** control. I think that you'll find this very useful whenever you have data that has special formatting needs."

"Special formatting needs?" Rhonda asked. "What do you mean by that?"

"I think Professor Smiley means things like the **Phone** and **Zip** fields of the **Customers** table," Dave said. "The information stored in both of these fields tends to be displayed with special formatting. For example, the **Phone** field usually has parentheses around the area code, and a dash between the first three and last four digits of the phone number. Likewise, the **Zip** field is usually displayed with a dash between its first five and last four characters."

"Oh, I see what you mean now, Dave," said Rhonda. "I remember we defined the **Phone** field in Access with 10 characters, and the **Zip** field with 9. Didn't we decide not to store those special formatting characters in the database?"

"Yes, we did choose not to inflate the size of the **Customers** table by storing those extra characters," I answered her. "It's just as easy to store the data in the **Customers** table *without* the formatting characters, and use the Masked Edit control to make sure that the formatting characters *are* displayed on the user interface – that is, on the form."

"Can't we do that using the text box control?" Bob asked.

"Unfortunately, Bob, we can't – at least, not as easily. The text box control, when bound to a recordset, displays the data from the bound field exactly the way it appears in the underlying recordset. If we want to display the field in a formatted manner, we need to use another control."

"And that's where the Masked Edit control comes into play?" Lou asked.

"That's right," I said.

## The Masked Edit Control

"The Masked Edit control," I continued, "looks just like a text box control on the form, except that it permits you to display the data in a bound field in a formatted manner. The Masked Edit control is supplied with most versions of Visual Basic, but not all."

"Do we have the Masked Edit control here in the classroom?" Melissa asked.

"I think so," I answered. "If you find yourself working with a version of Visual Basic that does not have the Masked Edit control, don't panic – you can always use the text box control instead. But remember, the Masked Edit control gives you more flexibility in controlling the way that your data looks."

"How so?" Tom asked.

"The Masked Edit control has a `Format` property," I said, "and this property's value can be set to display the data from the bound recordset field in particular ways. For instance, even though the stored data for the `Phone` field in the China Shop's `Customers` table contains no parentheses or dashes, we can instruct the Masked Edit control to display the data so that it appears with those formatting characters on the user interface."

"Is there anything special we need to do to use the Masked Edit control?" Melissa asked. "I don't see it in my Toolbox."

"The Masked Edit control," I replied, "isn't part of the Visual Basic Intrinsic Control set, which means that we need to add it to the Toolbox before we can use it. Let me show you."

I then started a new Visual Basic project, selected Projects | Components from the Visual Basic menu bar, and searched for the Masked Edit control.

"Maybe the hardest part of using the Masked Edit control is finding it in the Project | Components tab," I laughed, as I scrolled through the list of available components. "Ah, there it is," I said, when I found it. I selected it from the list box...

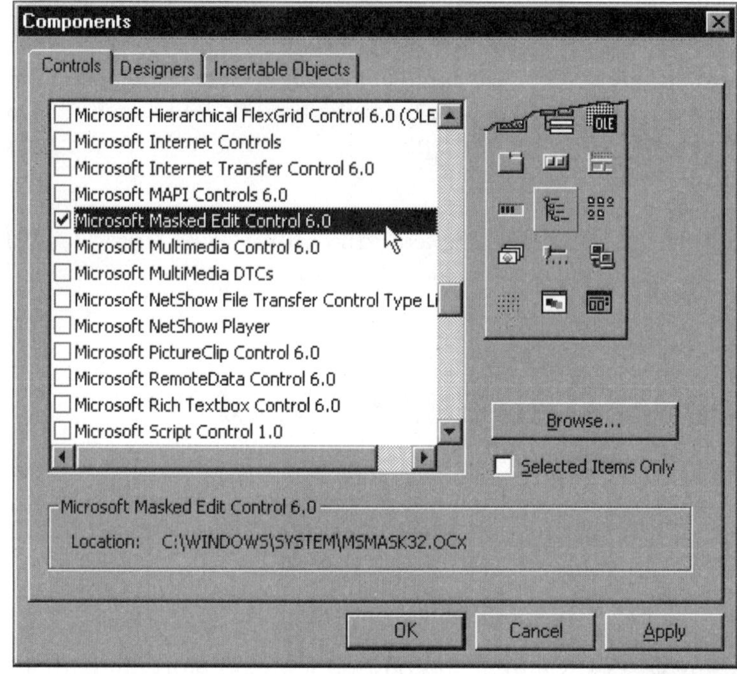


...and then clicked on the OK button. As soon as I clicked on the OK button, the Masked Edit control appeared in my Visual Basic toolbox:

"There it is," I said. "The Masked Edit control is the control at the bottom of the toolbox: its icon consists of two pound signs followed by the vertical line. Now let me show you what it can do for us."

## The Masked Edit Control in Action

To demonstrate the Masked Edit control's capabilities, I placed a data control on the form, along with a text box control on the left and a Masked Edit control on the right:

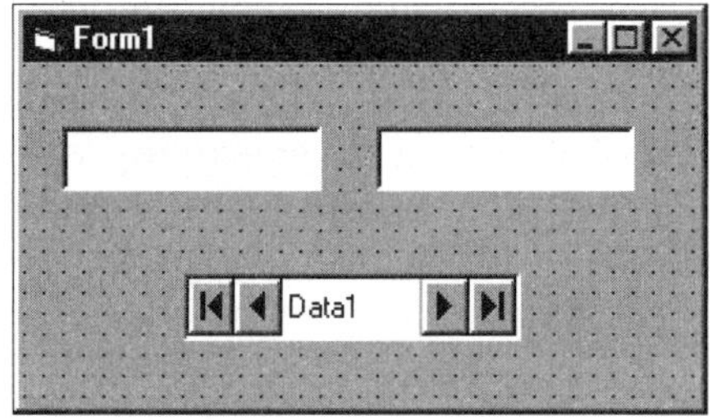


I set the **DatabaseName** property of the data control to point to the **China** database, specified its **RecordsetType** as **1-Dynaset**, and its **RecordSource** property as the **Customers** table. For the text box control, I specified a **DataSource** property of **Data1** and the **DataField** property to access the **Customers** table's **Zip** field. In the Masked Edit control, I also set the **DataSource** property to **Data1**, and the **DataField** property to **Zip**.

"Can you do that?" Mary said. "I mean, set two different controls to point to the same field in the recordset? I guess I didn't realize that."

"You can, Mary," I said, "although it's not usually a very practical thing to do in the real world. But it will illustrate my point here nicely: I want to show you the **Zip** field's value in a raw, unformatted state (in the text box control), and then show you how it can be formatted using the Masked Edit control."

I then set the Masked Edit control's **Format** property by typing the following into the property's setting box: **#####-####**. (That's five pound signs, a dash, and then four more pound signs):

"What does that **Format** value mean?" Lou asked.

"I *sort of* recognize that from the Visual Basic **Format** function," Valerie said.

"That's right, Valerie," I said, "if you are familiar with the Visual Basi **Format** function, you can probably relate to specifying values for the **Format** property of the Masked Edit control pretty easily. In this case, the pound signs specify that these character positions will be numbers, and the dash is a literal value that tells Visual Basic to insert a dash between the fifth and sixth characters of the data."

I waited to see if there were any other questions. There were none, and so I ran the program:

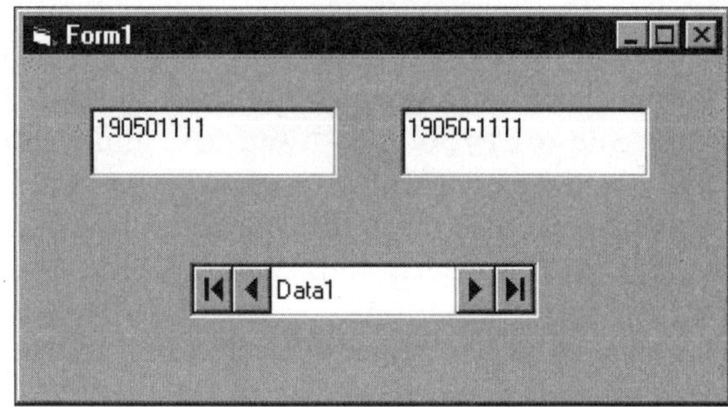


"I don't know if you remember," I said, "but earlier in the course, when we first created the **Customers** table, we added one test record, whose zip code was equal to 190501111. As you can see, the text box control on the left is displaying that data in an unformatted manner – but the Masked Edit control on the right is displaying the data in a more familiar, user-friendly manner."

"That's really all I need to tell you about the Masked Edit control before you create the **Customers** form in the next exercise," I said. "You'll see as you complete the exercise that you'll place two Masked Edit controls on the form in place of the more generic text box controls, then bind them to the **Phone** and **Zip** fields of the **Customer** table. Then all you'll need to do is set the **Format** property to display those two fields in a formatted manner. I think you'll be impressed!"

# Creating the Customers Form

To move us along in enhancing the China Shop project, I distributed the first exercise of the day, which focused on creating the **Customers** form.

## Exercise – Creating the Customers Form

1. Add a new form to the China Shop project as you've now done a number of times before. Bring up the new form's Properties window and change its **Name** property to **frmCustomers**. Save the form in your **China** directory as **Customers.frm**.

2. You should now see five forms in the Project Explorer window – Customers (with a Name property of frmCustomers), Inventory (Name property of frmInventory), Login (frmLogin), Main (frmMain), and Users (frmUsers):

After this now familiar exercise, I distributed an exercise that covered adding controls to the `Customers` form. In a matter of seconds, I knew we had a problem – just about everyone raised their hands at the same time.

## A Problem for the Class

"In Step 2 of this exercise," Dave said, "you've asked us to select the Masked Edit control from the Project | Components menu – but I don't see it anywhere. I know for a fact that it was here last week, because I was experimenting with it."

"Dave's right," Valerie said, "there *is* no Masked Edit control in the list of available components. And I just noticed something else – last week we had the Professional Edition of Visual Basic loaded to our PCs – this week, it looks like we have the Learning Edition on the machines instead. What's going on?"

I asked everyone to hold on while I chased down the university lab assistant. When I found her, what she told me made me unhappy. Apparently, there had been a misunderstanding with the Visual Basic licenses in the lab: whereas last week *all* of the PCs in the computer lab had the Professional Version of Visual Basic loaded, now only the *instructor's* PC had the Professional Version installed – all of the student PCs had been reconfigured with the Learning Edition.

When I re-entered the classroom, I explained the situation to the class.

"That explains why you are not seeing the Masked Edit control," I said. "It's not supplied with the Visual Basic 6 Learning Edition."

"What can we do?" Rachel asked. "Will this affect our ability to complete the China Shop project?"

"Not at all," I said. "We can design and code the `Customers` form using regular text box controls – the Masked Edit control would have been nice to use – but we can comfortably live without it."

> If your version of Visual Basic does include the Masked Edit control, feel free to use it in your version of the China Shop project. If not, it won't matter too much because the only functionality we'll lose is the slightly more professional feel of the application.

"What about the exercise?" Steve said.

"Let me amend the exercise and reprint it," I replied. "It'll only take a few minutes, as we were only going to use the Masked Edit control on a couple of fields. Why don't you all take an early ten-minute break while I make those changes?"

After a few hectic minutes keying the changes and reprinting the exercise, I handed out the new version as the class reassembled after their unscheduled caffeine-fix.

# Building up the Customers Form

"This is the version of the exercise *without* the Masked Edit control," I said. "Now it'll work on all of our machines. Let's give it a try."

## Exercise – Adding Controls to the Customers Form

1. Take a deep breath and add two frames, ten labels, ten text boxes, one data control and five command buttons to the `Customers` form. Size the form and position the controls roughly according to the screenshot below.

   **Please note:** it's important that you add the controls in the correct order so that the `TabIndex` properties are correct – this will ensure that the form behaves as advertised. Start with Frame1, followed by Frame2, taking care to draw the second frame explicitly rather than double-clicking on the frame control in the toolbox (likewise, ensure that all the other controls are properly *drawn* inside the relevant frames).

After the frames, add the labels and text boxes to Frame2: to preserve the correct **`TabIndex`** order, make sure that you place **`Label1`** first, followed by **`Text1`**, then **`Label2`** followed by **`Text2`**, then **`Label3`** followed by **`Text3`**, and so on. Once you've added the labels and text boxes in the correct order, add the command buttons in sequence, and then the data control:

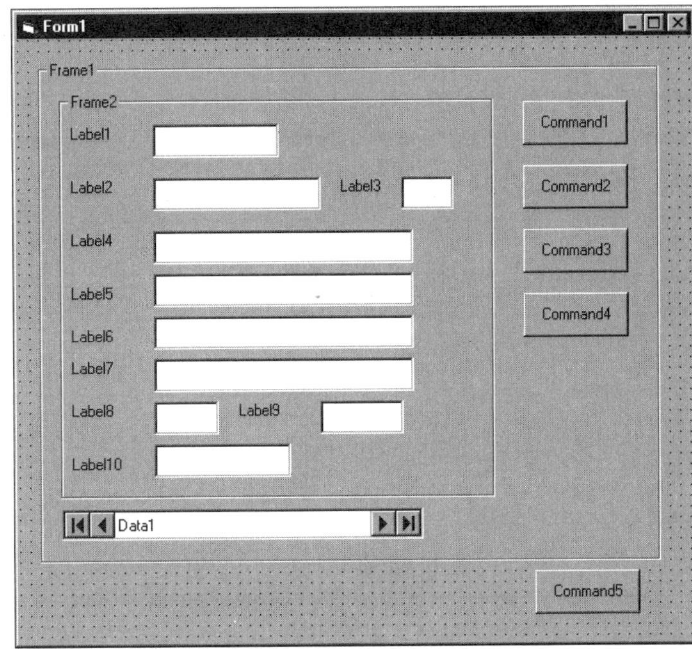


**2.** Now we need to set all of the controls' properties. Start by using the following table to make changes to the properties of the data control currently named **`Data1`**:

| **Property** | **Value** |
|---|---|
| Name | datCustomers |
| Caption | China Shop Customers |
| DatabaseName | C:\VBFiles\China\China.mdb |
| EOFAction | 0-MoveLast |
| RecordsetType | 1-Dynaset |
| RecordSource | Customers |

**3.** Now make these changes to the properties of the Frame control currently named **`Frame1`**:

| **Property** | **Value** |
|---|---|
| Name | fraOutside |
| Caption | (blank) |
| TabIndex | 0 |

4. `Frame2` will need these alterations:

| Property | Value |
|---|---|
| Name | fraInside |
| Caption | Customers |
| TabIndex | 1 |

5. These are the properties needed by the label control currently named `Label1`:

| Property | Value |
|---|---|
| Name | lblCustID |
| Caption | CustID: |
| TabIndex | 2 |

6. Use the following table to make changes to the properties of `Label2`:

| Property | Value |
|---|---|
| Name | lblFirstName |
| Caption | &First Name: |
| TabIndex | 4 |

7. Make these changes to the properties of `Label3`:

| Property | Value |
|---|---|
| Name | lblMI |
| Caption | &MI: |
| TabIndex | 6 |

8. Assign the properties below to `Label4`:

| Property | Value |
|---|---|
| Name | lblLastName |
| Caption | &Last Name: |
| TabIndex | 8 |

**9.** `Label5` will require these amendments:

| Property | Value |
|---|---|
| Name | lblAddress1 |
| Caption | Add&ress: |
| TabIndex | 10 |

**10.** Use the following table to make changes to the properties of `Label6`:

| Property | Value |
|---|---|
| Name | lblAddress2 |
| Caption | Su&ite/Apt: |
| TabIndex | 12 |

**11.** Make these alterations to the properties of `Label7`:

| Property | Value |
|---|---|
| Name | lblCity |
| Caption | Ci&ty |
| TabIndex | 14 |

**12.** Change the properties of `Label8` as shown below:

| Property | Value |
|---|---|
| Name | lblState |
| Caption | &State: |
| TabIndex | 16 |

**13.** Alter the properties of **`Label9`** in the following way:

| **Property** | **Value** |
|---|---|
| Name | lblZipCode |
| Caption | &Zip Code: |
| TabIndex | 18 |

**14.** Now modify **`Label10`**:

| **Property** | **Value** |
|---|---|
| Name | lblPhone |
| Caption | &Phone: |
| TabIndex | 20 |

**15.** Use the following table to make changes to the properties of the text box control currently named **`Text1`**:

| **Property** | **Value** |
|---|---|
| Name | txtCustID |
| DataSource | datCustomers |
| DataField | CustID |
| Locked | True |
| TabIndex | 3 |
| TabStop | False |
| Text | (blank) |

Notice that we set this text box's **`Locked`** property to **`True`** and its **`TabStop`** property to **`False`**. These property settings mean that the user can't tab to this box or change its contents – we don't want them to amend this field because it's an **`AutoNumber`** field, generated internally in the database.

**16.** Make the following amendments to `Text2`:

| Property | Value |
|---|---|
| Name | txtFirstName |
| DataSource | datCustomers |
| DataField | FirstName |
| MaxLength | 20 |
| TabIndex | 5 |
| Text | (blank) |

**17.** `Text3` will need these alterations:

| Property | Value |
|---|---|
| Name | txtMI |
| DataSource | datCustomers |
| DataField | MI |
| MaxLength | 1 |
| TabIndex | 7 |
| Text | (blank) |

**18.** Change the properties of `Text4` as shown here:

| Property | Value |
|---|---|
| Name | txtLastName |
| DataSource | datCustomers |
| DataField | LastName |
| MaxLength | 20 |
| TabIndex | 9 |
| Text | (blank) |

**19.** And `Text5`:

| **Property** | **Value** |
|---|---|
| Name | txtAddress1 |
| DataSource | datCustomers |
| DataField | Address1 |
| MaxLength | 30 |
| TabIndex | 11 |
| Text | (blank) |

**20.** Now `Text6`:

| **Property** | **Value** |
|---|---|
| Name | txtAddress2 |
| DataSource | datCustomers |
| DataField | Address2 |
| MaxLength | 30 |
| TabIndex | 13 |
| Text | (blank) |

**21.** Next, `Text7`:

| **Property** | **Value** |
|---|---|
| Name | txtCity |
| DataSource | datCustomers |
| DataField | City |
| MaxLength | 30 |
| TabIndex | 15 |
| Text | (blank) |

**22.** And, of course, who could forget `Text8`...

| Property | Value |
|---|---|
| Name | txtState |
| DataSource | datCustomers |
| DataField | State |
| MaxLength | 2 |
| TabIndex | 17 |
| Text | (blank) |

**23.** Now alter the properties of the text box control currently named `Text9`:

| Property | Value |
|---|---|
| Name | txtZipCode |
| DataSource | datCustomers |
| DataField | Zip |
| MaxLength | 9 |
| TabIndex | 19 |
| Text | (blank) |

**24.** And the final text box, `Text10`:

| Property | Value |
|---|---|
| Name | txtPhone |
| DataSource | datCustomers |
| DataField | Phone |
| MaxLength | 10 |
| TabIndex | 21 |
| Text | (blank) |

**25.** Now it's time to move onto the command buttons. Let's be logical and start with the command button currently named `Command1`:

| Property | Value |
|---|---|
| Name | cmdAdd |
| Caption | &Add |
| TabIndex | 22 |

**26.** Followed by `Command2`:

| Property | Value |
|---|---|
| Name | cmdUpdate |
| Caption | &Update |
| TabIndex | 23 |

**27.** Not forgetting `Command3`...

| Property | Value |
|---|---|
| Name | cmdDelete |
| Caption | &Delete |
| TabIndex | 24 |

**28.** Or `Command4`:

| Property | Value |
|---|---|
| Name | cmdCancel |
| Cancel | True |
| Caption | &Cancel |
| TabIndex | 25 |

**29.** And finally in the command button section, `Command5`:

| Property | Value |
|---|---|
| Name | cmdExit |
| Cancel | True |
| Caption | E&xit |
| TabIndex | 26 |

**30.** And now, at last, the final step; make these changes to the properties of the form itself:

| Property | Value |
|---|---|
| Name | frmCustomers |
| BorderStyle | 3-Fixed Dialog |
| Caption | China Shop Customers |
| Moveable | False |
| StartUpPosition | 2-Center Screen |

**31.** Your form should look similar to the screen shot shown here:

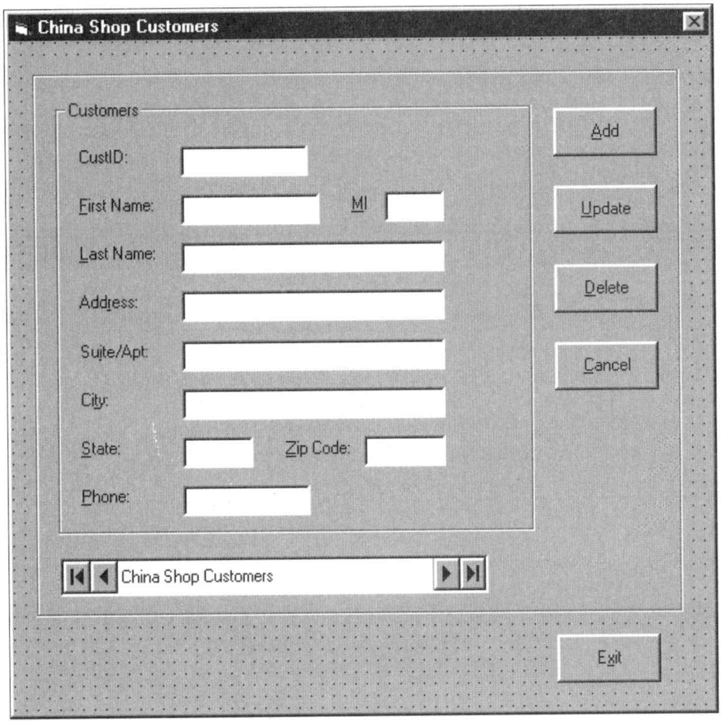

**32.** Save the China Shop project.

The only real problem we had completing this exercise was overcoming the shock of the missing Masked Edit control. However, everyone breathed a sigh of relief at the end of the exercise – this was a time-consuming form to build, with a lot of controls.

Dave said, " I think I'll have to consider employing a trainee programmer to handle all of this detail work for me – it takes a lot of time, doesn't it?"

"Yes, it does," I agreed, "but remember that that this is all good practice: every time you go through the process of adding controls and setting property values, you're reinforcing your knowledge of Visual Basic and how it interacts with databases. It's only with practice and more practice that these things will become second nature to you."

"I guess you're right," said Ward. "Sometimes the only way to learn is to keep doing the same things over."

"In that case," laughed Melissa, "I'd better get to work on my golf swing!"

"OK," I said, "let's put in some more practice – here's the next exercise..."

# Coding up the Customers Form

In this exercise, you'll add code to the controls you just placed on the **Customers** form. This is all pretty familiar code, similar to what we've added to previous forms. In fact, you could find similar sections from other forms and copy and paste them here – just make sure that you change the relevant sections!

## Exercise – Adding Code to the Customers Form

1. First, add the following code to the form's **Activate** event procedure:

```
Private Sub Form_Activate()

datCustomers.Recordset.MoveLast
datCustomers.Recordset.MoveFirst

End Sub
```

2. Now add these lines of code to **Customers** form's **QueryUnload** event procedure:

```
Private Sub Form_QueryUnload(Cancel As Integer, UnloadMode As Integer)

frmMain.Show

End Sub
```

3. Now populate the **datCustomers** data control's **Reposition** event procedure:

```
Private Sub datCustomers_Reposition()

datCustomers.Caption = "Customer record " &
datCustomers.Recordset.AbsolutePosition
   ↳ + 1 & " of " & datCustomers.Recordset.RecordCount

End Sub
```

4. This code is for the **Validate** event procedure of **datCustomers**:

```
Private Sub datCustomers_Validate(Action As Integer, Save As Integer)

If datCustomers.Recordset.EditMode <> dbEditNone Then
   If txtFirstName.Text = "" Then
      MsgBox "First Name must be entered"
      txtFirstName.SetFocus
      Save = False
      Action = vbDataActionCancel
      Exit Sub
```

```
    End If

    If txtLastName.Text = "" Then
       MsgBox "Last Name must be entered"
       txtLastName.SetFocus
       Save = False
       Action = vbDataActionCancel
       Exit Sub
    End If

    If txtAddress1.Text = "" Then
       MsgBox "Address must be entered"
       txtAddress1.SetFocus
       Save = False
       Action = vbDataActionCancel
       Exit Sub
    End If

    If txtCity.Text = "" Then
       MsgBox "City must be entered"
       txtCity.SetFocus
       Save = False
       Action = vbDataActionCancel
       Exit Sub
    End If

    If txtState.Text = "" Then
       MsgBox "State must be entered"
       txtState.SetFocus
       Save = False
       Action = vbDataActionCancel
       Exit Sub
    End If

    If txtZipCode.Text = "" Then
       MsgBox "Zip Code must be entered"
       txtZipCode.SetFocus
       Save = False
       Action = vbDataActionCancel
       Exit Sub
    End If

End If

End Sub
```

5. This next batch of code is for the **txtFirstName_KeyPress** event procedure, and will convert lowercase letters to uppercase:

```
Private Sub txtFirstName_KeyPress(KeyAscii As Integer)

If KeyAscii >= 97 And KeyAscii <= 122 Then
   KeyAscii = KeyAscii - 32
End If

End Sub
```

6. The same code, but this time it's for the **txtLastName_KeyPress** event procedure:

```
Private Sub txtLastName_KeyPress(KeyAscii As Integer)

If KeyAscii >= 97 And KeyAscii <= 122 Then
   KeyAscii = KeyAscii - 32
End If

End Sub
```

7. Now use the same code again for the **txtMI_KeyPress** event procedure:

```
Private Sub txtMI_KeyPress(KeyAscii As Integer)

If KeyAscii >= 97 And KeyAscii <= 122 Then
   KeyAscii = KeyAscii - 32
End If

End Sub
```

8. We also use this same code for the **KeyPress** event procedure of **txtAddress1**:

```
Private Sub txtAddress1_KeyPress(KeyAscii As Integer)

If KeyAscii >= 97 And KeyAscii <= 122 Then
   KeyAscii = KeyAscii - 32
End If

End Sub
```

**9.** And the same again for the **`txtAddress2_KeyPress`** event procedure:

```
Private Sub txtAddress2_KeyPress(KeyAscii As Integer)

If KeyAscii >= 97 And KeyAscii <= 122 Then
   KeyAscii = KeyAscii - 32
End If

End Sub
```

**10.** Not to mention the **`txtCity_KeyPress`** event procedure...

```
Private Sub txtCity_KeyPress(KeyAscii As Integer)

If KeyAscii >= 97 And KeyAscii <= 122 Then
   KeyAscii = KeyAscii - 32
End If

End Sub
```

**11.** And, finally, the good old **`txtState_KeyPress`** event procedure:

```
Private Sub txtState_KeyPress(KeyAscii As Integer)

If KeyAscii >= 97 And KeyAscii <= 122 Then
   KeyAscii = KeyAscii - 32
End If

End Sub
```

**12.** Next, key this chunk of code into the **`KeyPress`** event procedure of the **`txtPhone`** text box:

```
Private Sub txtPhone_KeyPress(KeyAscii As Integer)

If KeyAscii = 8 Then Exit Sub

If KeyAscii < 48 Or KeyAscii > 57 Then
   KeyAscii = 0
End If

End Sub
```

This code will ensure that we only get numeric values entered into this text box.

**13.** Repeat the same code in the **txtZipCode_KeyPress** event procedure:

```
Private Sub txtZipCode_KeyPress(KeyAscii As Integer)

If KeyAscii = 8 Then Exit Sub

If KeyAscii < 48 Or KeyAscii > 57 Then
   KeyAscii = 0
End If

End Sub
```

**14.** Now add the next code selection to the **cmdAdd_Click** event procedure:

```
Private Sub cmdAdd_Click()

'Is the user adding a record already?
If datCustomers.Recordset.EditMode <> dbEditNone Then
   MsgBox "Please finish your updates before adding a new record"
   Exit Sub
End If

'Implicit Save Operation may be taking place
'So, we need to Edit and then Update
'To avoid Error 3426-See KBQ189851
datCustomers.Recordset.Edit
datCustomers.UpdateRecord

datCustomers.Recordset.AddNew
txtFirstName.SetFocus

End Sub
```

**15.** We also need to create the **cmdCancel_Click** event procedure. Here's the code for that:

```
Private Sub cmdCancel_Click()

If datCustomers.Recordset.EditMode = dbEditNone Then
   datCustomers.UpdateControls
Else
   datCustomers.Recordset.CancelUpdate
End If

End Sub
```

**16.** And here's the code for the `cmdDelete_Click` event procedure:

```
Private Sub cmdDelete_Click()

On Error GoTo ErrorHandler

Dim intResult As Integer

If datCustomers.Recordset.EditMode <> dbEditNone Then
 MsgBox "If you're currently adding a record, please use the Cancel
      ↪button to cancel the addition"
 Exit Sub
End If

intResult = MsgBox("Are you sure you want to delete a Customer
      ↪ record?", vbYesNo, "Delete Customer Record")

If intResult = vbYes Then
   datCustomers.Recordset.Delete
   datCustomers.Recordset.MoveNext
   If datCustomers.Recordset.EOF Then
      datCustomers.Recordset.MovePrevious
   End If
End If

Exit Sub

ErrorHandler:

Select Case Err.Number
   Case 3200            'Referental Integrity Check
      MsgBox Err.Description
      Exit Sub
   Case Else
      MsgBox Err.Description
      Resume Next
End Select

End Sub
```

**17.** Now type the following code into the **cmdExit_Click** event procedure:

```
Private Sub cmdExit_Click()

If datCustomers.Recordset.EditMode <> dbEditNone Then
   MsgBox "Please finish your updates before closing the form"
   Exit Sub
End If

Unload Me

End Sub
```

**18.** And, finally, add this code to the **cmdUpdate_Click** event procedure:

```
Private Sub cmdUpdate_Click()

If datCustomers.EditMode = dbEditAdd Then
   datCustomers.Recordset.Update
Else
   datCustomers.Recordset.Edit
   datCustomers.Recordset.Update
End If

End Sub
```

**19.** Save the China Shop project.

### *Discussion*

Except for a student or two who placed code intended for the **KeyPress** event procedure into the **Change** event procedure of the text boxes, this exercise went very smoothly.

"Everything we've just coded," I said, "we've seen before with the forms we created last week. That's the great thing about getting a methodology into place – if it works on one form, it should work on others."

"I only have one question," Rhonda said. "Why don't we validate the contents of the **txtPhone** text box in the data control's **Validation** event procedure? Shouldn't we be checking to make sure that the phone number is there?"

"Well," I explained, "that's because the **Phone** field, according to Joe Bullina's directions, is an *optional* field – he doesn't want the user of the program to be forced to enter their phone number. The same applies to the customer's **MI** (middle initial) and **Address2** fields."

"I don't know about anyone else," Ward said, "but I'm beginning to feel like I'm getting the hang of this. I can't wait to see this form in action."

"In that case, Ward," I said, "let's place some code in the `Click` event procedure of the `mnuCustomers` menu item so that we can view the single test record we currently have in the `Customers` table."

So saying, I handed out this next exercise.

## Exercise – Adding Code to the Click Event Procedure of mnuCustomers

In this exercise, you'll add code to the `Click` event procedure of `mnuCustomers` that will result in the `Customers` form being displayed when the user clicks on the Staff Functions | View/Update Customers menu option on the `Main` form.

1. If the China Shop project is running, stop it by clicking on the **End** button.
2. Select the **Main** form in the Project Explorer window.
3. In Design mode, click on the Main form's Staff Functions | View/Update Customers menu item, and the code window for the **Click** event procedure of **mnuCustomers** will open.
4. Key the following code into the Click event procedure of mnuCustomers:

```
Private Sub mnuCustomers_Click()

Me.Hide
frmCustomers.Show

End Sub
```

5. Save the China Shop project.
6. Run the program and select Staff Functions | View/Update Customers from the China Shop's menu bar. You should see the Customers form displayed. At this point, spend a few minutes performing the four basic database operations – viewing, adding, editing, and deleting records. See if you can find any problems, and fix anything that goes wrong!

### *Discussion*

Before anyone had a chance to ask any questions, I ran the program and clicked on the Staff Functions | View/Update Customers menu item, with this result:

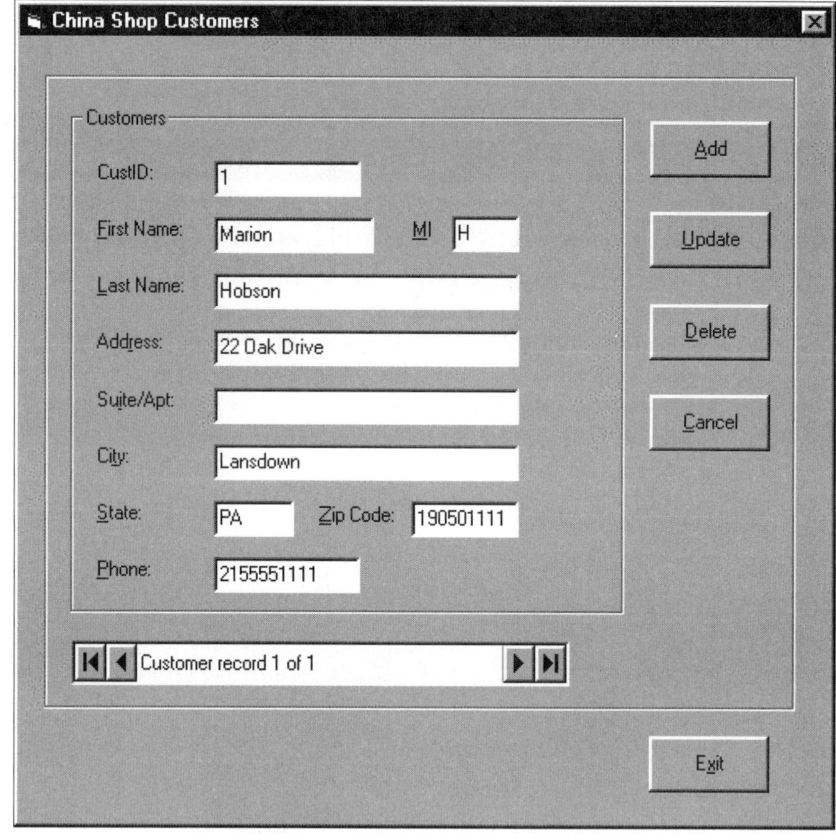


"Why isn't the data in the fields in uppercase?" Rhonda asked.

"It looks the same as it did when I entered this record several weeks ago," I said, "I must have entered it in mixed case. Remember that we entered our test record directly using Access – so we had no validation rules applied to any of the fields. I can correct that now either by editing the record – simply by typing into the fields. In fact, that would be a good test of our `KeyPress` event procedures."

I then re-edited the record via the customers form and clicked on the Update button so that it looked like this:

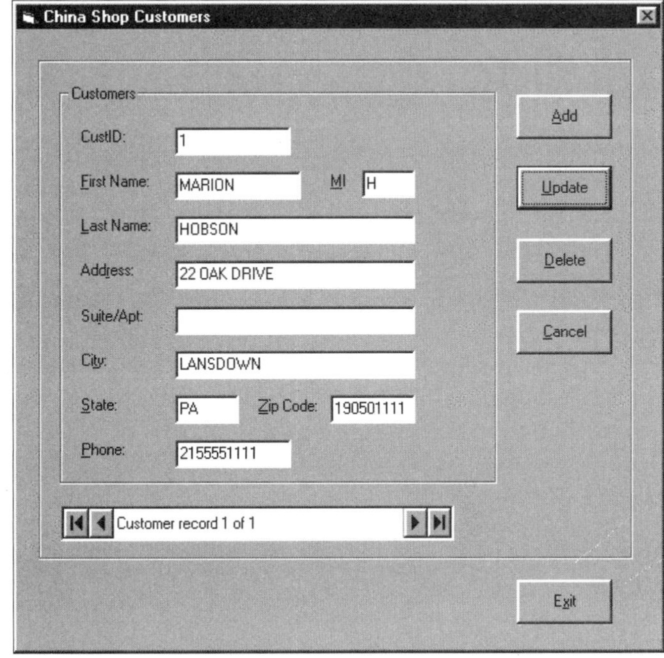


I waited a moment to see if there were any other questions.

Dave said, "Um...it looks kind of clunky in all upper case, doesn't it?"

"Well," I conceded, "maybe a little. But we have to try and walk a line here between code simplicity and usability. In this context, we're *learning* rather than building a full-blown professional application, so I think that our form is an acceptable compromise."

"I can see that," agreed Dave. " I didn't mean to be critical – I guess I'm just a perfectionist."

"No need to apologize for that!" I laughed. "The thing is, you can experiment with these kind of details on your own version of the project, and get the project looking just the way that you want it. For instance, you might add some string manipulation code to the validation code – this could capitalize only the first letter of a word, for example."

"Hey," said Ward, "I might just do that."

"Good luck, Ward," I said encouragingly. "OK folks, we're just about through coding the forms for the Staff Functions menu," I continued. "We have just one more form – the `Transactions` form – to complete. But before we begin coding that form, I want to take a few minutes to discuss the DBGrid in a little more detail."

## The DBGrid Control Revisited

"You spent a good deal of time using sing the DBGrid to demonstrate recordset methods and properties the last few weeks," Valerie said. "I was wondering if we were going to have a chance to use it ourselves. Will we be using it to view the transaction records in the **`Transactions`** table?"

"That's my plan," I said. "As you've found out for yourselves, designing forms using a data control and bound text boxes can be pretty onerous, especially as the number of fields in the record grows. Using the DBGrid makes creating a form to display records in a recordset a snap – all you need to do is place a data control on the form, then the DBGrid, and set a few properties for each control. I particularly like using the DBGrid if the recordset I'm dealing with is read-only, as the **`Transactions`** table is: that way, we don't need to worry about the unfriendly characteristics of the DBGrid. Remember, adding records and deleting records can be done using the DBGrid, but it *can* be a pain. I still have customers who call me asking me how to delete a record using the DBGrid."

"What do you mean when you say that the **`Transactions`** table is read-only?" Steve asked.

"Remember," I explained, "Joe Bullina has asked that we don't allow anyone to be able to update transactions records in the **`China`** database."

"Suppose a mistake occurs when creating one of the transaction records?" Rhonda asked.

"The likelihood of that happening is pretty remote if we do our job right," I said, "as it's the program itself that will be creating the records in the **`Transactions`** table. Since there's no user interaction, there won't be any user errors. Of course, there's always the possibility Joe will ask for this capability in the future. If that's the case, we can either modify the program slightly, or show him how to edit the records directly using Access."

"So the **`Transactions`** form," Dave said, "does look like a good candidate for the DBGrid..."

"I think so, Dave," I said. "That's not to say that we couldn't use bound text box controls on the **`Transactions`** form as we did with the **`Users`**, **`Inventory`** and **`Customers`** forms. In fact, depending upon the version of Visual Basic you are using, you may *have* to. Some versions of Visual Basic don't include the DBGrid control that we've been using in this class, in which case the only way to design the form is to use bound text boxes, or perhaps label controls."

Even as I said this, I realized that we might well have the same problem with the DBGrid as we had earlier with the Masked Edit control. I continued the discussion, though, as I knew that it would still be useful for the students to have a better understanding of the DBGrid.

"From what we saw while you were running through those demos earlier," Rachel said, "it seems to me that the DBGrid control is a little quicker and easier to work."

"That's right, Rachel," I said. "All you need to do is place a data control and a single DBGrid on your form, and in no time you have database records displayed. However, there's a little more to the DBGrid than I've shown you in the demonstrations, and I'd like to take a few minutes to show you some of its more sophisticated features."

I created a new **`Standard.EXE`** project and placed a data control on the form. I then set the **`DatabaseName`** property of the data control to target the **`Biblio`** database and set the **`EOFAction`** property to **`2-Add New`**. I left the **`RecordsetType`** property on its default value of **`Dynaset`** and changed the **`RecordSource`** property to read the **`Titles`** table.

"Now I'll place a DBGrid control on the form," I said, "and set its **`DataSource`** property to **`Data1`**."

Having done this I ran the program, with this result:

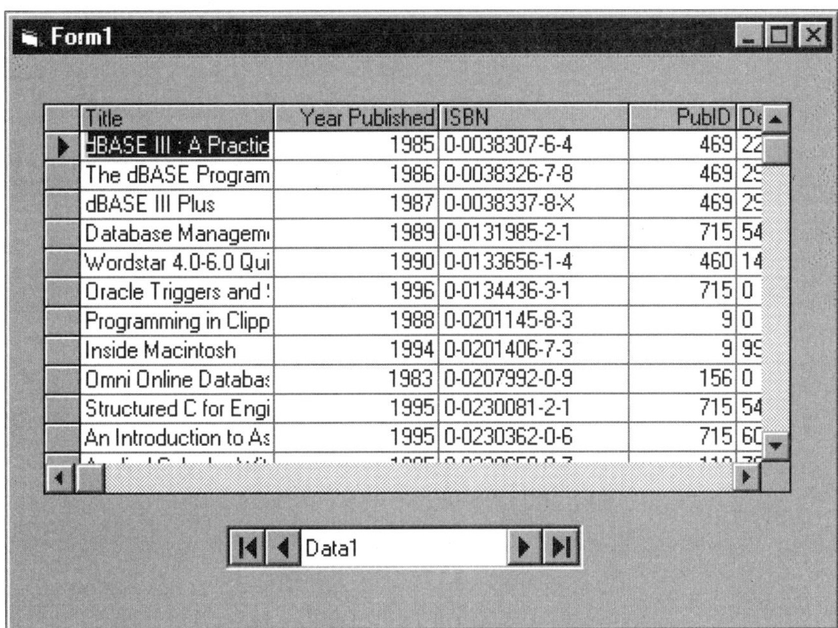


"This is the default look and feel of the DBGrid," I said. "In the default view, each and every field in the underlying recordset is displayed from left to right, in sequence, across the columns of the DBGrid. The heading displayed for each column is the full name of the field in the recordset. Although the data in the DBGrid is *updateable* in this default view, which means that we can change the values in existing records, we *can't* add new records by default, and we can't delete existing records."

"How do you know what the defaults are?" Mary asked. "Can we see these in the DBGrid's Properties window?"

"Yes we can," I answered. "The values for these defaults can be changed individually in the Properties window or, if you like, you can select the DBGrid's **`Custom`** property..."

"...and if you click on the **`Custom`** property's ellipsis, you'll see what's known as the DBGrid's Property Pages:"

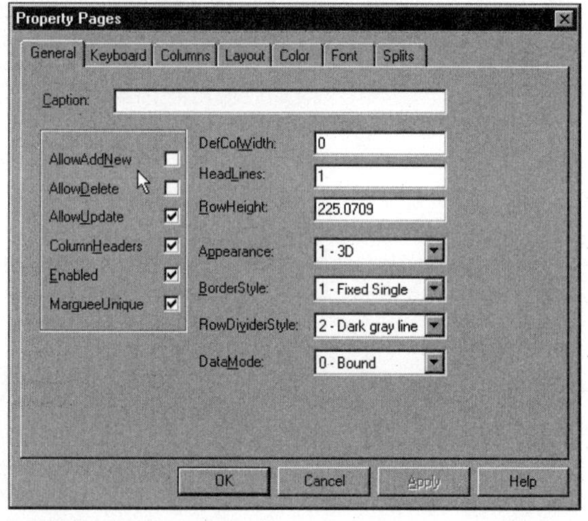


"Property Pages?" Lou asked.

"That's right, Lou," I said. "A **Property Page** is essentially a dialog box that lets you customize a control's properties. The Property Page gives you a tighter grip on a control's properties than if you just used the regular **`Properties`** window."

"So," Ward said, "there are properties listed here that might not appear in the standard Properties window?"

"Yes there are, Ward," I said. "As you start to work with more complex controls, you're likely to see the `Custom` properties in the Properties window more and more. If you do see the `Custom` property, make sure you select it and take a look so that you gain access to all of the properties of the control."

"I just checked some of the standard controls in the toolbox," Melissa said. "They don't have Property Pages, do they?

"You're right, Melissa," I said, "they don't. You won't find any Property Pages for the Visual Basic Intrinsic Controls such as the text box control or option buttons. It's only more specialized controls like the DBGrid – controls usually shipped with the Professional Edition of Visual Basic and upwards – that provide you with a Property Page – usually because the control is so complex."

"I see the options for **`AllowAddNew`**, **`AllowDelete`** and **`AllowUpdate`**," Mary said. "Is that how the defaults you spoke of earlier are established?"

"Yes, Mary," I said, "and we can modify those properties to permit the user of the DBGrid to add new records to the recordset or to delete existing ones."

"What does that Columns tab do for us?" Kathy asked. "Does it give us more control over the appearance of the columns in the DBGrid display?"

"That's a good question, Kathy," I said. "Let's take a peek. If we click on the Columns tab we can alter the default behavior of the DBGrid. For example, we can tell the DBGrid not to display every field in the recordset – that is, we can choose to display only a selection of the fields in the recordset. We can also vary the order in which the fields are displayed, and change the field's caption as it appears in the heading of the column. For instance, if we select Column0 in the Column drop-down list box, enter a descriptive caption in the Caption box, and then select a field name from the Data Field drop-down list box... "

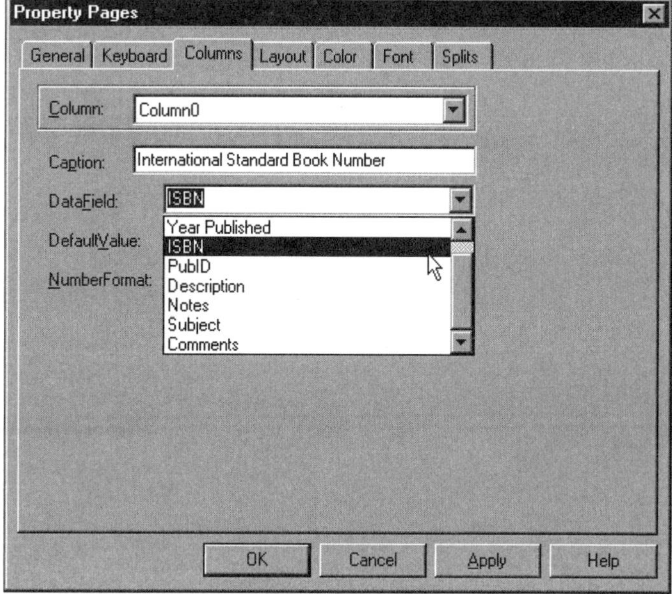


"...and then click on the OK button..."

"Notice how the DBGrid has changed appearance," I said, "even in the design-time environment. We're now displaying part of our custom Column Heading."

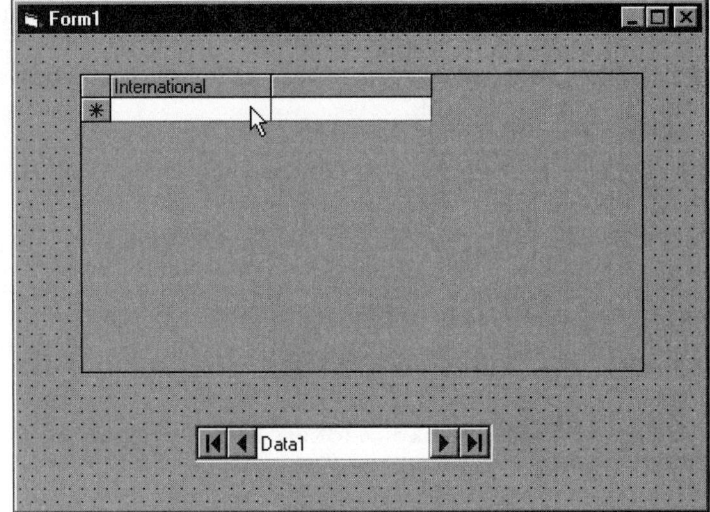


"If we now run the program and drag the line that lets us change the column widths," I said, "we'll see the DBGrid displaying data from just a single field, with the complete custom caption that we specified in the Columns tab of the Property Page:"

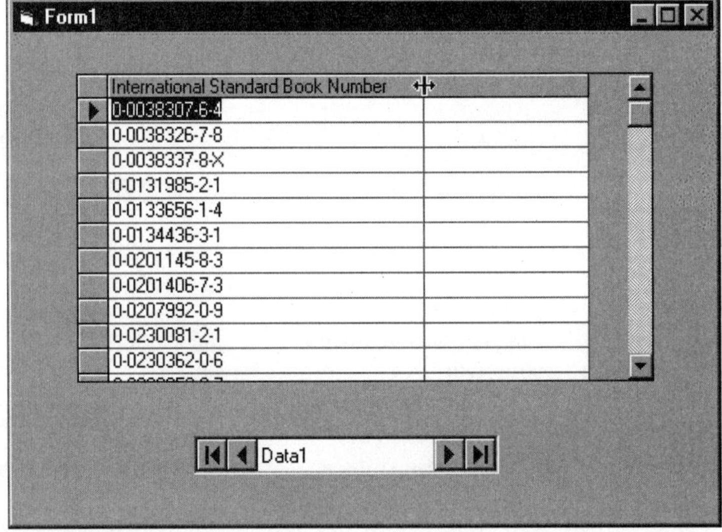


"Just a second," said Dave, "I'm feeling all perfectionist again. How can we change the display so that we don't see the empty column on the right?"

"Good question," I replied. "What you need to do is go the DBGrid's Property Pages and click on the Layout tab. Next, select the 'blank' column (Column1) in the Columns list box, and then uncheck the Visible check box..."

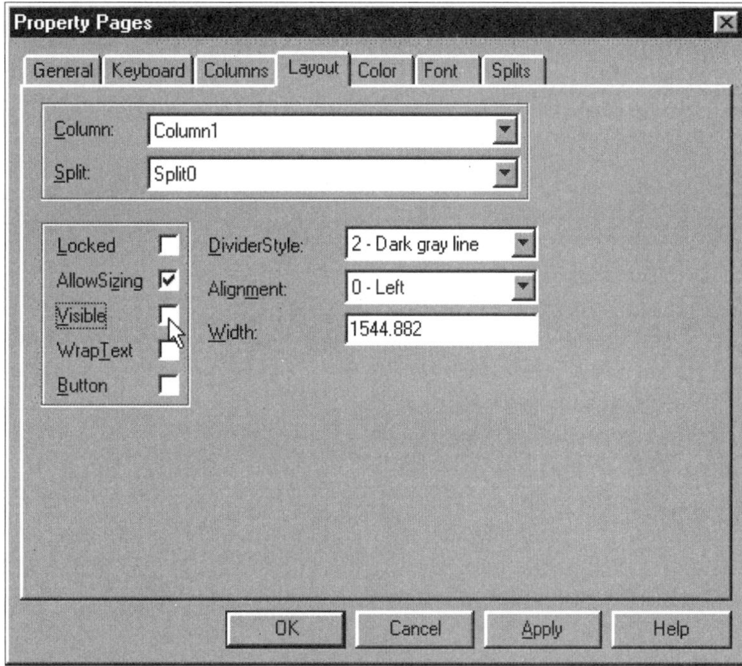


"Now, if we click on OK and run the program again..."

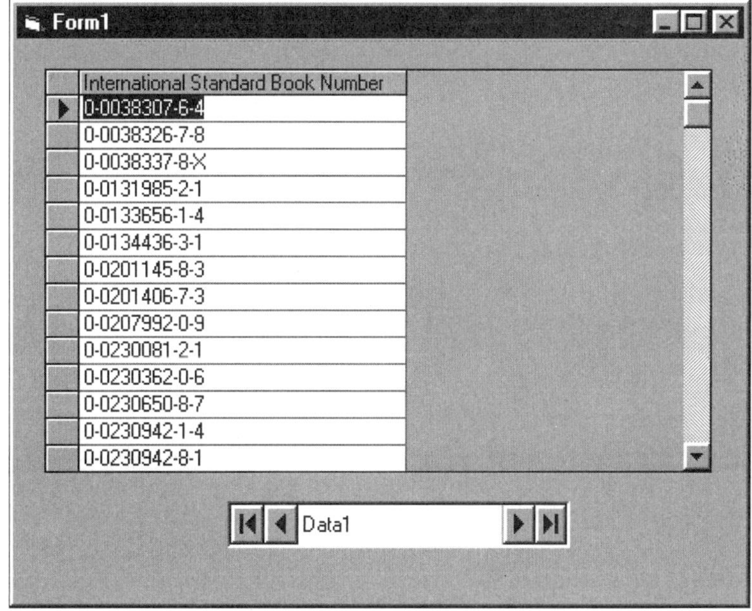


"Great," said Dave. "Thanks, John."

"I've done some frustrating experimentation with the DBGrid at work." Kate said. "I say frustrating, because I've managed to use the DBGrid to display *every* field from the recordset (using the DBGrid normally), and I've been able to include one or two (using the Property Pages) – but nothing in between those two extremes. Do you know what I mean?"

"Yes, Kate," I answered, "I know exactly what you mean. You're referring to the fact that if you click on the Column drop-down list box it displays, by default, Column0 and Column1 – but nothing beyond that. The question is – how can you customize any other columns from the recordset using the Property Pages if you can only see two here..."

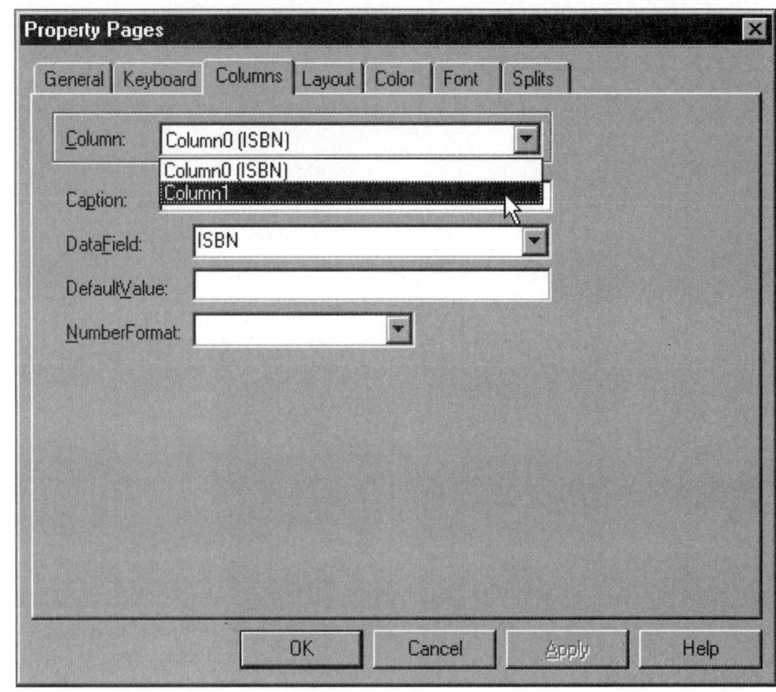


"...after all, we know that there are more than two columns in the **`Titles`** table, don't we? Am I right – is that what you're asking about?"

"You read my mind!" Kate answered.

"That's something that confuses a lot of programmers," I said, "and not just beginners either! The problem is that you *can't* add any additional columns to this drop-down list box via the Property Page. Instead, you need to close the Property Page, select the DBGrid on the form, then right-click your mouse on it. Let me show you what I mean, and to make things a little cleaner, let's start with a new DBGrid."

I deleted the existing DBGrid from the form, added a new one to it, and specified **`Data1`** as its data source.

"Now let me select the DBGrid," I said, "and right-click on it, we'll bring up a popup menu..."

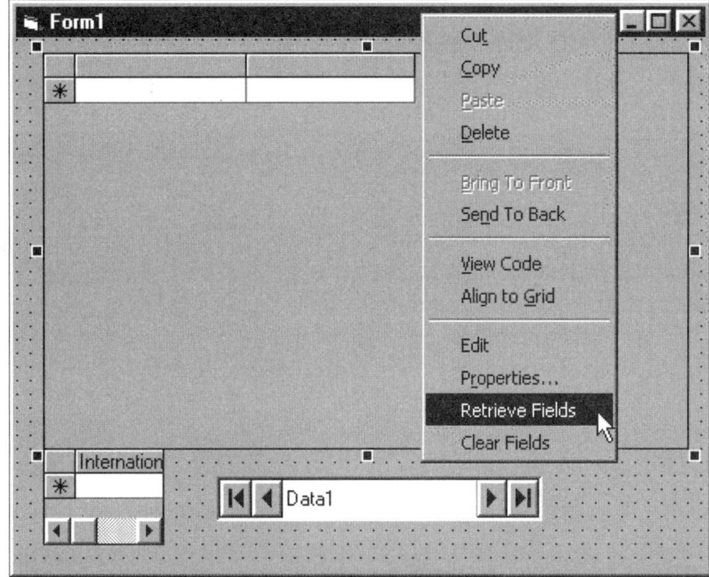


"This popup menu," I said, "is how you can customize the Columns in the DBGrid so that you can choose which ones from the recordset are displayed. Let's choose the Retrieve Fields menu option, and then go straight back to the Property Pages for the DBGrid. If we *now* click on the Columns tab and select the Column drop-down list box, we'll see that every field in the recordset has been assigned to a Column, and is now available for you to customize:"

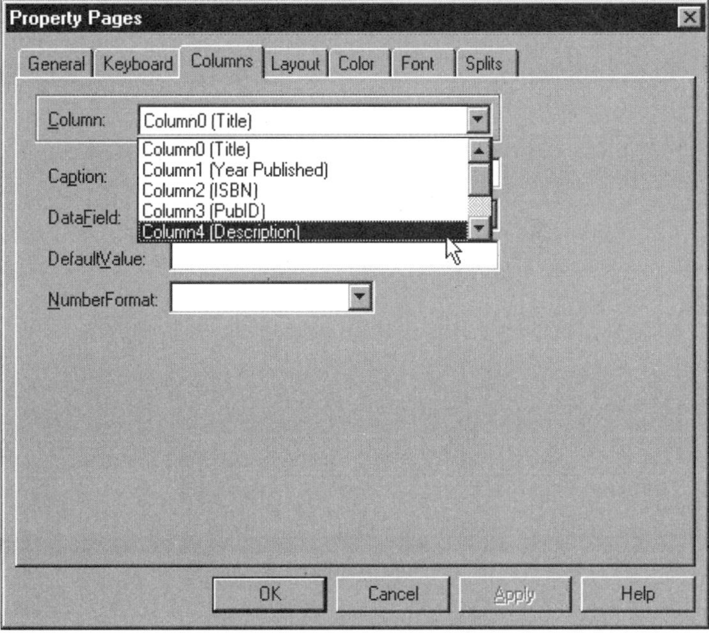


"Terrific," said Kate, "you don't know how long I've been trying to figure that out. From now on, I'll be able to change the caption and default values for *every* column in the DBGrid as well."

"But at this point," Kathy said, "don't you have every field in the DBGrid? Suppose you don't want to display the **ISBN** field – how should we do that? At work I've tried to select the column header and pressed the *Delete* key, but the entire DBGrid disappears!"

"That *is* frustrating, I know," I commiserated. "To delete columns from the DBGrid and rearrange them, we first need to put the DBGrid into 'edit' mode. To do that, we need to select the DBGrid with our mouse..."

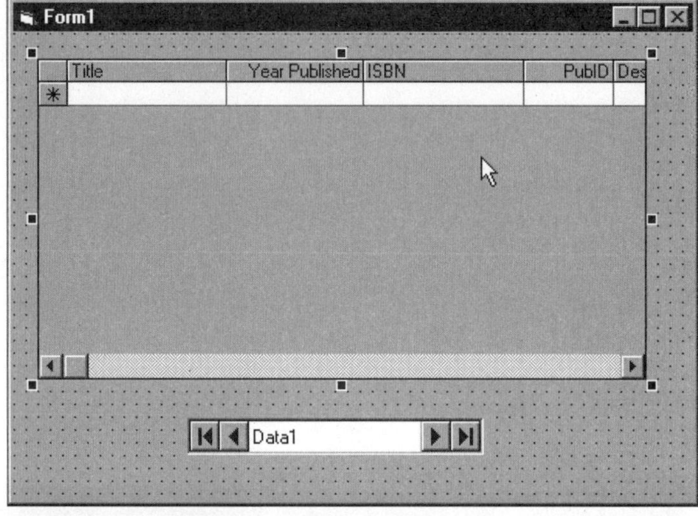


"...then right-click on it. The same popup menu that we saw earlier will appear, and we need to choose the Edit option:"

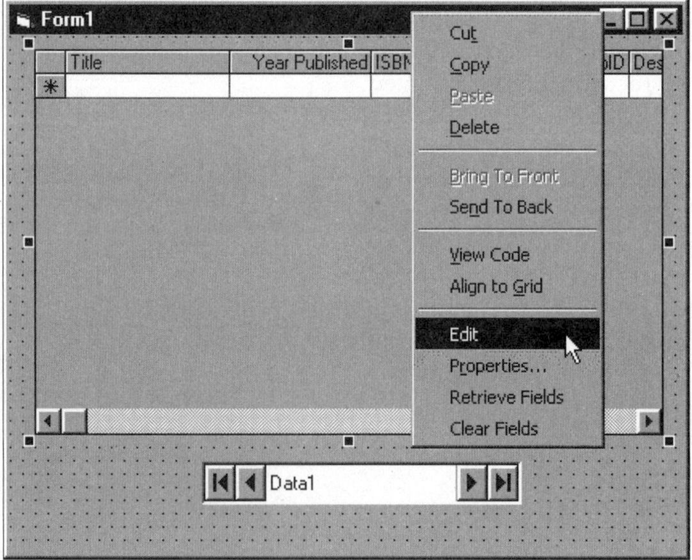

"When you select Edit from the popup menu, the DBGrid is put into 'edit' mode, and you can now work with the individual columns, very much like we can in an Excel worksheet. If we want to delete the **`ISBN`** field from the DBGrid, we can just select the **`ISBN`** column..."

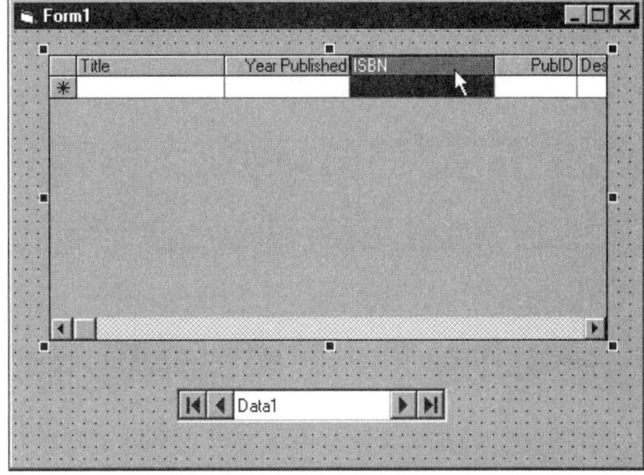


"... and right click the mouse again – one of the menu options that pops up is Delete, which allows you to – surprise! – delete the selected column. Notice that there's also an Insert option. Let's select Delete:"

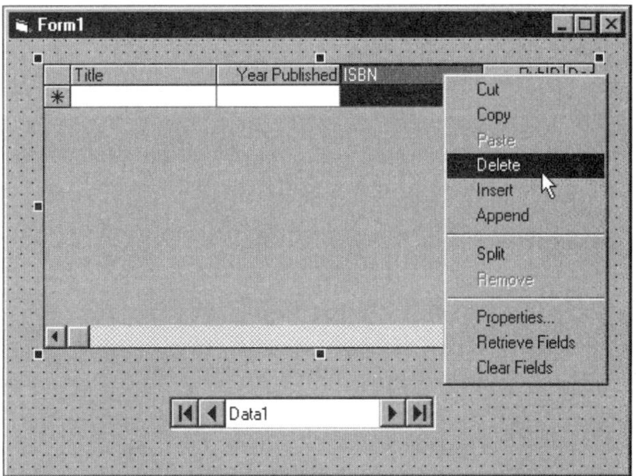


"... and the **`ISBN`** column has now gone:"

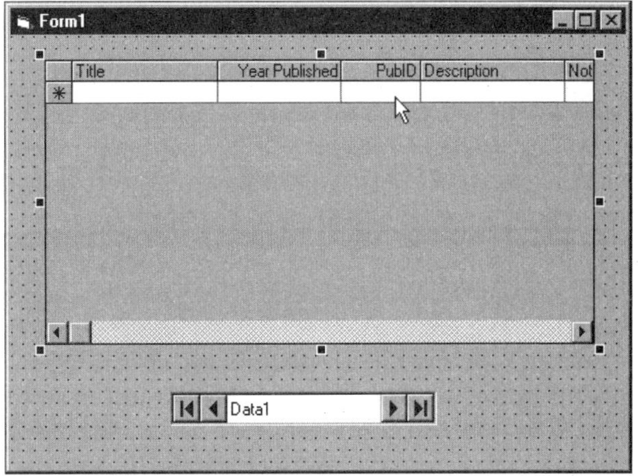

"You've answered a lot of questions I had about working with the DBGrid." said Kate.

"I'm glad I was able to help," I demurred.

"When you come back from our next break," I briefed the class, "we'll work on the design and coding of the **Transactions** form. Let's take fifteen minutes to freshen ourselves up." I knew that I had to work fast to head off the potential problem we had – the DBGrid control wouldn't be on the student's PCs! This meant that I had another exercise to amend.

# Creating the Transactions Form

The next stage in developing our project (as I'd already indicated to the class) was to complete the last of the forms that would be seen by the China Shop staff alone – the **Transactions** form.

When we resumed after the break I handed around the next exercise for the class.

### Exercise – Creating the Transactions Form

1. Add another new form to the China Shop project. Change the new form's **Name** property to **frmTransactions**, and save it away in the **China** directory with a file name of **Transactions.frm**.

2. In the Project Explorer window you should now see **six** forms:

# A Problem with the DBGrid

The next step that I'd planned was to have added a DBGrid to the **Transactions** form: this would have enabled us to display the records from the **Transactions** table in a single control. However, I'd realized earlier in the lesson that I wouldn't be able to do this now that the students machines were only running the Learning Edition of Visual Basic – the DBGrid isn't supplied with that edition, nor with others such as the Working Model Edition.

I explained the situation to the class: the change in Visual Basic versions precluded them from using the DBGrid in their projects.

"What about the Microsoft **Data Grid** control?" Steve asked. "Won't that work?"

"That Grid only works with the ActiveX data control," I said, "on this course we're only using the standard DAO data control."

"I'm puzzled," said Mary. "I have the DBGrid on my machine at home, and I know that I'm running the Learning Edition of Visual Basic there too. So why isn't on the PCs *here*?"

"The DBGrid is shipped with the Visual Basic 5 Learning Edition," I said, "but not with the Visual Basic 6 Learning Edition. I'm afraid we're not going to be able to use it in the China Shop project."

> For those readers whose version of Visual Basic includes the DBGrid, feel free to use it in your version of the China Shop project

"Will this hurt the program?" Rhonda asked.

"Not at all," I said. "We were only going to use the DBGrid on the `Transactions` form anyway. We'll just need to design the form using bound text box controls instead. In fact, I have a copy of the exercise using bound text box controls with me."

## Building up the Transactions Form

"OK, let's get those controls rolling onto the Transactions form."

What I didn't tell the students was that the sweat on my brow was the result of feverishly amending and reprinting the exercise during the break to take account of the unavailability of the DBGrid control. However, I did see that Rhonda noticed that the paper the exercise was printed on was still warm from the printer, and she raised her eyebrow quizzically at me...

### Exercise – Adding Controls to the Transactions Form

1. Continue working with the China Shop project.
2. We need to add two frames, five labels, eight text boxes, one command button, and one data control to the `Transactions` form. We'll size the form accordingly and position the controls roughly in line with the screenshot below.

3. Start by adding Frame1, then draw Frame2 within Frame1. When you start adding the labels and text boxes within Frame2, again make sure that you draw the controls: you do this by clicking on the control's icon in the toolbox and then using the crosshairs and the mouse to size the control within the frame.

4. To guarantee the correct **`TabIndex`** order, follow the screenshot and add the labels and text boxes by working your through the first row from left to right, and then moving on to the next row of controls. That is, refer to the screenshot and add the controls in this sequence: **`Label1`** followed by **`Text1`**, then **`Label2`** followed by **`Text2`**, then **`Label3`** followed by **`Text3`** and **`Text4`**, then **`Label4`** – and so on. Finally, add the command button and the data control:

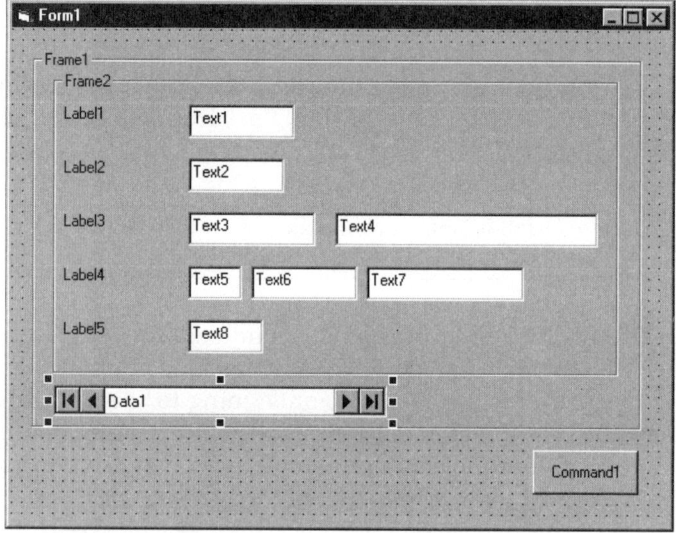


5. Next, we'll use Access to create a query that you'll use later to populate the data control's **`RecordSource`** property. This query will use a SQL statement to extract all of the fields that we need to display the correct data on the **`Transactions`** form. Unless you are very familiar with SQL, using Access to create the SQL for us is by far the easiest way to complete this part of the exercise, because the SQL syntax is quite complex.

> If you don't have Access on your machine to build this query, you'll find a copy of the China database that contains this pre-built query in the For Chapter 8 folder on the CD. You need to copy this version of the database into your `C:\VBFiles\China` folder to be able to use it (you'll also need to right-click on the `China.mdb` file in Windows Explorer and change its attributes so that the database file is not read-only).

At this stage in the exercise, Rhonda needed to ask a question: "There's something I'm not sure about here, Professor Smiley."

"What's that, Rhonda?"

"Well," she went on, "I don't see why we're having to use a SQL statement to retrieve the data that we want to display on the form – why can't we just use the data control to connect to the **`Transactions`** table and display what's in there? Why do we need a SQL statement at all?"

"That's a really good question, Rhonda," I said approvingly, "and it cuts to the heart of what we've been working on for these past few weeks. Let me explain. If you remember, the **`Transactions`** table stores information about which products customers have purchased, when they purchased them, and what price they paid for the items they purchased."

To clarify a little, I started up Access and opened up the **`Transactions`** table in design view:

Transactions : Table

| Field Name | Data Type | Description |
|---|---|---|
| TransID | AutoNumber | Transaction ID Number |
| CustID | Number | Customer Id Number |
| ItemID | Number | Inventory ID Number |
| Quantity | Number | Quantity of item purchased |
| Price | Currency | Price of item purchased |
| DateOfPurchase | Date/Time | Date of purchase |

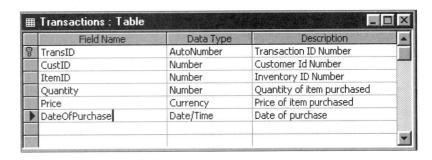

"If we look at an example transaction record as it's stored in the **`Transactions`** table..."

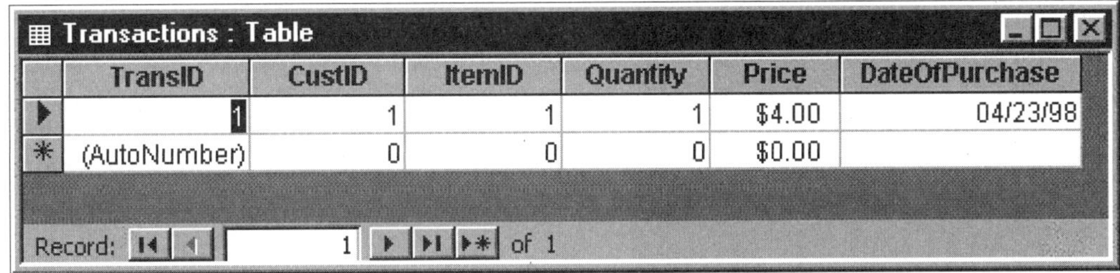

Transactions : Table

| TransID | CustID | ItemID | Quantity | Price | DateOfPurchase |
|---|---|---|---|---|---|
| 1 | 1 | 1 | 1 | $4.00 | 04/23/98 |
| (AutoNumber) | 0 | 0 | 0 | $0.00 | |

Record: 1 of 1

"...we can see that the actual data in the records is very minimal."

"I can see that," said Rhonda. "That's because we want to reduce 'bloat' in our database, isn't it?"

"Correct," I agreed. "Now, the problem here is that if we displayed just this information on a form for the China Shop staff, it wouldn't be very helpful. It would just look something like this:"

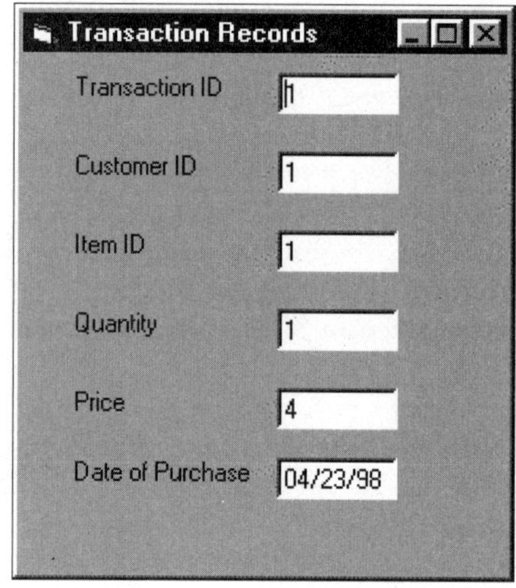


"Imagine," I continued, "that a customer telephones Joe's Bullina's store, asking a member of the China Shop staff to check up on a purchase that they'd previously made – this form wouldn't be very helpful, would it?"

"I should say not!" exclaimed Ward, "you can't see the customer's name, or the name of the pieces of China they bought! So, unless you swap backwards and forwards between different forms, cross-checking *who* the **`CustID`** refers to, and which piece of china the **`ItemID`** refers to, you wouldn't be able to check the customer's purchase at all!"

"Precisely," I agreed. "And that's where our SQL statement comes in. We can use SQL to do all of that cross-checking for us in the background. The SQL statement will use the **`CustID`** from the **`Transactions`** table to retrieve the *actual customer name* from the **`Customers`** table, and display it on the **`Transactions`** form – much more user-friendly than just showing **`CustID`**. Similarly, the SQL statement will use the **`Transaction`** table's **`ItemID`** value to retrieve the brand and name of the china pieces from the **`Inventory`** table, and display them on the **`Transactions`** form. This way, we get the best of both worlds – the data is stored efficiently in the database in separate tables, and we can display it clearly for the user on a form."

"I think," said Rhonda, "that the China Shop staff will really appreciate being able to see names rather than numbers!"

"Yes, I think you're right," I said. "Let's get back to the exercise and build the SQL statement that will make the lives of Joe's staff so much easier."

6. To build the query, open up the **China** database in Access, click on the Queries tab, then click on the New button. From the next screen, choose the Design View option and click on the OK button. You'll now be presented with the Show Table window, from which we can choose the tables that we want to base our query on:

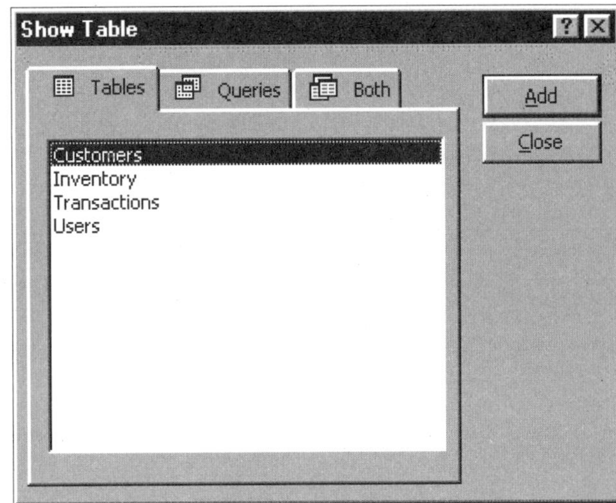


7. For the query that we want to create, add the **Customers**, **Transactions**, and **Inventory** tables, and click on the Close button. These three tables and their relationships will now be visible at the top of the query design window:

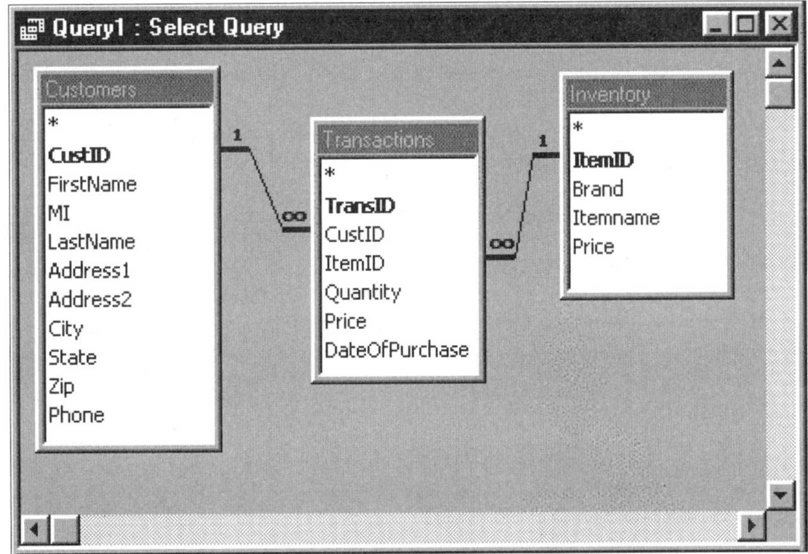

**8.** Next, we need to tell the query which fields we want to select from each table. On the `Transactions` form, we want to display the following fields from the relevant tables:

| Table | Field |
|---|---|
| Customers | FirstName |
| Customers | LastName |
| | |
| Transactions | TransID |
| Transactions | DateOfPurchase |
| Transactions | Quantity |
| | |
| Inventory | Brand |
| Inventory | ItemName |
| Inventory | Price |

**9.** Use this table to build the query by adding the table and field names to the query-building grid in the query design window. Remember, we built a query like this in Chapter 6: you can select the table and field names in the drop-down boxes, or drag the field names from the tables to the grid, or even double-click on the field in the relationships window at the top of the screen – all of these techniques will add the table and field names to the query design grid. When you've finished, your grid will look something like this:

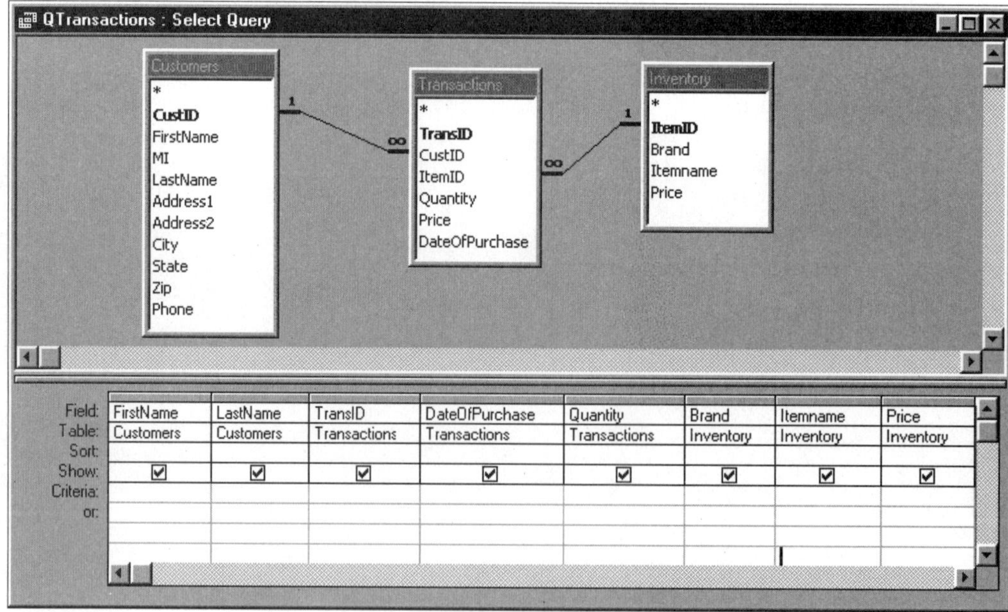

**10.** Save the query as QTransactions.

**11.** Remember that Access and SQL will use the relationships that we previously established to join together the related fields from the different tables. To see the SQL statement that this query has generated, you can click on the View | SQL View option from the Access menu bar:

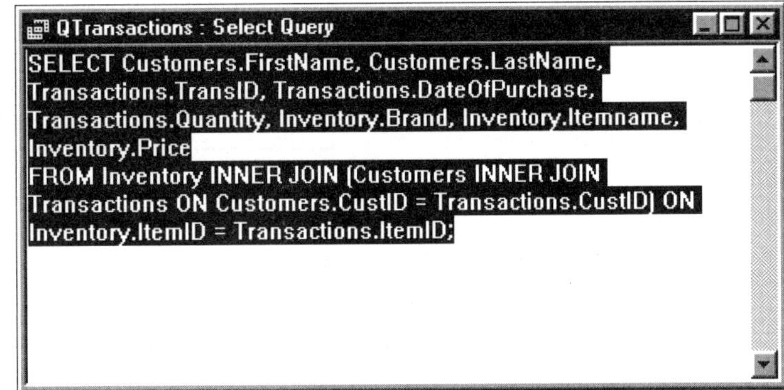


When my students got to this stage in the exercise, there were a few gasps.

"Ouch," said Lou, "that's scary stuff."

"It does look pretty horrible, doesn't it?" I replied. "As I've said a couple of times before, explaining SQL in-depth is really beyond the scope of this course, although I'll discuss this particular SQL statement shortly. The best thing to do at this stage in our careers is to trust Access to build and execute the SQL for us – this lets us concentrate on our program."

"Amen to that," said Ward, "I think maybe SQL is something that I'll look to explore in depth later in my learning program."

"Sure thing, Ward," I said. "Getting back to the exercise, note that you could cut and paste this SQL statement into the `RecordSource` property of the data control. However, when we come to set that `RecordSource` property in a moment, you'll see that our QTransactions is available as a choice in the drop-down list box – that's the way that we'll get the query and its underlying SQL statement into our program."

With that, I told my students to take a five-minute break before getting back to the body of the exercise, the next stage of which was to set the properties for the controls on the `Transactions` form.

**12.** Use the following table to make changes to the properties of the data control currently named **`Data1`**:

| Property | Value |
|---|---|
| Name | datTransactions |
| Caption | China Shop Transactions |
| DatabaseName | C:\VBFiles\China\China.mdb |
| EOFAction | 0-MoveLast |
| RecordsetType | 2-Snapshot |
| RecordSource | QTransactions |

Note that we populate the **`RecordSource`** property by selecting our pre-built **`QTransactions`** query from the drop-down list box:

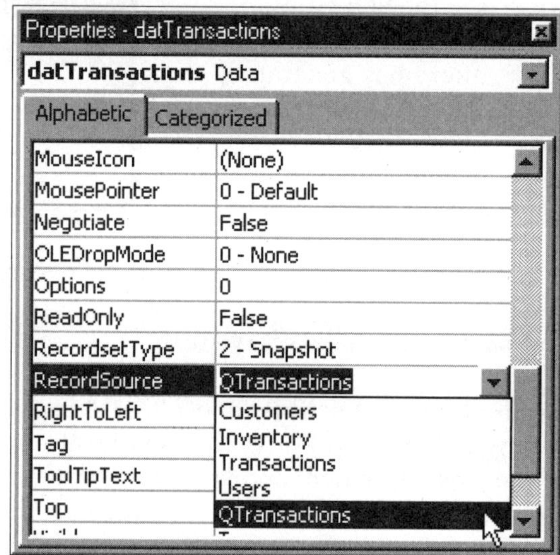


**13.** Now make these changes to **`Frame1`**:

| Property | Value |
|---|---|
| Name | fraOutside |
| Caption | (blank) |
| TabIndex | 0 |

**14.** Modify **`Frame2`** in the following ways:

| Property | Value |
|---|---|
| Name | fraInside |
| Caption | Transactions |
| TabIndex | 1 |

**15.** Now change `Label1`:

| Property | Value |
|---|---|
| Name | lblTransID |
| Caption | &Transaction ID: |
| TabIndex | 2 |

**16.** As well as `Label2`:

| Property | Value |
|---|---|
| Name | lblDateOfPurchase |
| Caption | &Date Of Purchase: |
| TabIndex | 4 |

**17.** Now `Label3` needs these amendments:

| Property | Value |
|---|---|
| Name | lblCustomerName |
| Caption | &Customer's Name: |
| TabIndex | 6 |

**18.** This is what you have to do to `Label4`:

| Property | Value |
|---|---|
| Name | lblItem |
| Caption | &Item Purchased: |
| TabIndex | 9 |

**19.** `Label5` requires these property settings changes:

| Property | Value |
|---|---|
| Name | lblPrice |
| Caption | &Price: |
| TabIndex | 13 |

20. Now for the text boxes that will display the results of our **`QTransactions`** query. First, use the following table to make changes to the properties of the text box currently named **`Text1`**:

| Property | Value |
|---|---|
| Name | txtTransID |
| DataSource | datTransactions |
| DataField | TransID |
| Locked | True |
| TabIndex | 3 |
| TabStop | False |
| Text | (blank) |

Note that all the text boxes on this form have their `Locked` property set to `True`: remember that the `Transactions` table is read-only as far as the user is concerned – we don't want anybody to make any updates to it except for the China Shop program itself.

21. These are the changes needed by **`Text2`**:

| Property | Value |
|---|---|
| Name | txtDate |
| DataSource | datTransactions |
| DataField | DateOfPurchase |
| Locked | True |
| TabIndex | 5 |
| TabStop | False |
| Text | (blank) |

22. And now **`Text3`**:

| Property | Value |
|---|---|
| Name | txtFirstName |
| DataSource | datTransactions |
| DataField | FirstName |
| Locked | True |
| TabIndex | 7 |
| TabStop | False |
| Text | (blank) |

**23.** And `Text4`:

| Property | Value |
|---|---|
| Name | txtLastName |
| DataSource | datTransactions |
| DataField | LastName |
| Locked | True |
| TabIndex | 8 |
| TabStop | False |
| Text | (blank) |

**24.** Et voila! `Text5`...

| Property | Value |
|---|---|
| Name | txtQuantity |
| DataSource | datTransactions |
| DataField | Quantity |
| Locked | True |
| TabIndex | 10 |
| TabStop | False |
| Text | (blank) |

**25.** Followed by `Text6`:

| Property | Value |
|---|---|
| Name | txtBrand |
| DataSource | datTransactions |
| DataField | Brand |
| Locked | True |
| TabIndex | 11 |
| TabStop | False |
| Text | (blank) |

**26.** We're up to `Text7` now, so we've nearly done with the text boxes:

| Property | Value |
|---|---|
| Name | txtItem |
| DataSource | datTransactions |
| DataField | ItemName |
| Locked | True |
| TabIndex | 12 |
| TabStop | False |
| Text | (blank) |

**27.** `Text8` – the final one:

| Property | Value |
|---|---|
| Name | txtPrice |
| DataSource | datTransactions |
| DataField | Price |
| Locked | True |
| TabIndex | 14 |
| TabStop | False |
| Text | (blank) |

**28.** Now we're onto the sole command button, `Command1`:

| Property | Value |
|---|---|
| Name | cmdExit |
| Cancel | True |
| Caption | E&xit |
| TabIndex | 15 |

**29.** And finally, these are the changes we have to make to the properties of the form itself:

| Property | Value |
|---|---|
| Name | frmTransactions |
| BorderStyle | 3-Fixed Dialog |
| Caption | China Shop Transactions |
| Moveable | False |
| StartUpPosition | 2-Center Screen |

**30.** Your form should look similar to the screen shot:

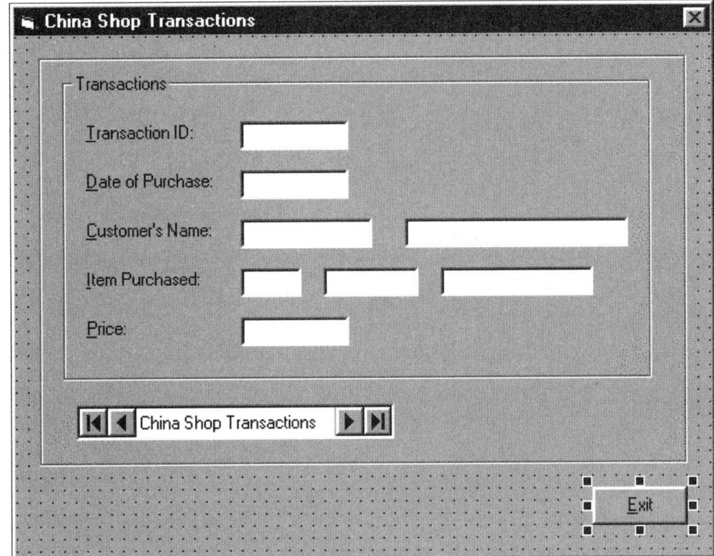


**31.** Save the China Shop project.

Well done – that was a long haul.

### *Discussion*

Some problems arose from people trying to manually type the SQL statement into the data control's `RecordSource` property.

"At first, using the SQL we'd built in Access as a guide, I tried to type that statement directly into the `RecordSource` property of the data control," Melissa said, "but I kept making small typos."

"That happens!" I said "If you want to compose the statement yourself, it's better to type it into Notepad and then copy and paste it into the **RecordSource** property. I'm not going to discourage you from practicing SQL, but I do think the Access method is far and away the best way for beginners to create SQL statements based on their related tables. After all, SQL is a specialized field that has a host of books dedicated to it – we can only scratch the surface here."

"Are there any disadvantages to using the Access method?" asked Linda.

"There are advantages and disadvantages to using the name of the query directly in the **RecordSource** property," I said. "One big advantage is that when you are more experienced in SQL, and if you find that your SQL statement needs a little fine tuning after you've written your program, you don't need to modify the program to tune up the SQL statement. Instead, you can go into Access and change the saved query there, and your program will pick up the changes dynamically without any modification to the program code or the properties of any controls."

"What about the disadvantages?" Chuck asked.

"The main disadvantage," I said, "is that a key component of your program is open to attack (as it were) by the end user. For instance, I once had a user find a program's underlying database, open it up in Access, and delete all of the queries I had saved there! When the end-user fired up the program, many of the database connections failed because the **RecordSource** values couldn't be found – they were referring to the saved queries that had been sabotaged!"

"So it sounds like you're saying 'it's up to us'," Ward said.

"That's a fair assessment," I replied, "feel free, if you're comfortable in SQL, to set the **RecordSource** property either way."

"Can you explain that SQL statement a little bit?" Rhonda said. "I still don't properly understand how the **DataField** properties of the different text box controls can refer to fields from more than one table. For example, the **txtTransID** text box's **DataField** property refers to the **TransID** field (from the **Transactions** table), and **txtFirstName**'s **DataField** property points to the **FirstName** field, which is in the **Customers** table. Can you just clarify how we're able to do that again?"

"Sure thing, Rhonda," I said. "Do you remember we said that **Dynaset** and **Snapshot** recordsets can contain information from more than one table? Well, the data control in our program connects to the **China** database and uses the SQL statement built into our **QTransactions** query to create a **Snapshot** recordset containing the fields from the different tables that we specified when we built the query. So SQL, combined with the table relationships that we've built, populate the recordset with the linked fields from the different tables to create the recordset."

"OK," said Rhonda, "I see that. Is it too much to ask to see how SQL does that?"

"Let's give it a shot," I replied. "Our SQL statement...

```
SELECT Customers.FirstName, Customers.LastName, Transactions.TransID,
  Transactions.DateOfPurchase, Transactions.Quantity, Inventory.Brand,
  Inventory.Itemname, Inventory.Price
FROM Inventory
INNER JOIN (Customers INNER JOIN Transactions
  ON Customers.CustID = Transactions.CustID)
  ON Inventory.ItemID = Transactions.ItemID;
```

"...requests all the fields that we're interested in from three separate tables (`Customers`, `Transactions`, and `Inventory`)..."

```
SELECT Customers.FirstName, Customers.LastName, Transactions.TransID,
  Transactions.DateOfPurchase, Transactions.Quantity, Inventory.Brand,
  Inventory.Itemname, Inventory.Price
```

"...and uses the two `Inner Join` clauses to 'link' the records from the different tables based on a common field – the foreign key. That's what the `ON` keywords specify..."

```
ON Customers.CustID = Transactions.CustID)
ON Inventory.ItemID = Transactions.ItemID;
```

"They determine which field from the first table will be used to link records from that table with the related records in the second table. In the first line here, SQL determines that the `CustID` field in the `Customers` table will link to records with a matching `CustID` in the `Transactions` table."

"And if I recall from early on in the class," Dave said, "a foreign key is a field in one table that happens to be the primary key in another."

"That's perfect, Dave," I said. "In this instance, the `Transactions` table contains two foreign keys – `CustID` which is the primary key of the `Customers` table, and `ItemID` which is the primary key of the `Inventory` table."

"I really had no idea you could do this," Ward said. "I know you talked about recordsets containing information from more than one table, but I guess a picture is worth a thousand words. When I originally envisioned building a `Transactions` form, I figured we would just display the `Transaction ID`, plus the `Customer ID` of the customer who made the purchase, plus the `Item ID` of the china pieces purchased. This is much better because it lets the China Staff know the customer's name, and the actual china purchased – not just some arcane codes."

"That's exactly why we did it," I said. "You can be sure if we didn't, a few weeks from now the China Shop staff would be requesting a change to the program."

"OK," I continued, "that was a heavy session. Let's take five before we get back to our Visual Basic code and finish up the **Transactions** form."

We took our break, and then got right down to it.

# Coding the Transactions Form

## Exercise – Adding Code to the Transactions Form

In this exercise, you'll add code to the controls you recently placed on the **Transactions** form.

1. Continue working with the **Transactions** form of the China Shop project.
2. Key this code into the form's **Activate** event procedure:

```
Private Sub Form_Activate()

datTransactions.Recordset.MoveLast
datTransactions.Recordset.MoveFirst

End Sub
```

3. Type this next lot of code into the **Transactions** form's **QueryUnload** event procedure:

```
Private Sub Form_QueryUnload(Cancel As Integer, UnloadMode As
Integer)

frmMain.Show

End Sub
```

4. Next, key this code into the data control's **datTransactions_Reposition** event procedure:

```
Private Sub datTransactions_Reposition()

datTransactions.Caption = "Transaction record " &
   ↳ datTransactions.Recordset.AbsolutePosition + 1 & " of " &
        ↳ datTransactions.Recordset.RecordCount

End Sub
```

5. Finally, add this code to the command button's **cmdExit_Click** event procedure:

```
Private Sub cmdExit_Click()

Unload Me

End Sub
```

6. Save the China Shop project.

All of the code we added in this exercise by now was 'old hat' – we'd seen similar code in the other forms in the project, so we moved swiftly along to the exercise.

## Exercise – Adding Code to the Click Event Procedure of mnuTransactions

In this exercise, you'll add code to the `Click` event procedure of `mnuTransactions`. This will mean that the `Transactions` form will be displayed when the user clicks on the Staff Functions | View Transactions menu option in the `Main` form.

1. If the China Shop project is running, stop it by clicking on the 'end' button.
2. Select the `Main` form in the Project Explorer window.
3. In design mode, click on the `Main` form's Staff Functions | View Transactions menu item, and the code window for the `mnuTransactions`'s `Click` event procedure will open.
4. Key the following code into the `Click` event procedure:

```
Private Sub mnuTransactions_Click()

Me.Hide
frmTransactions.Show

End Sub
```

5. Save the China Shop project.

6. Run the program, log on as Administrator, and select Staff Functions | View Transactions from the China Shop's menu bar. You should see the **Transactions** form displayed. You should find that you can do nothing more than view the **Transactions** records – exactly what we want:

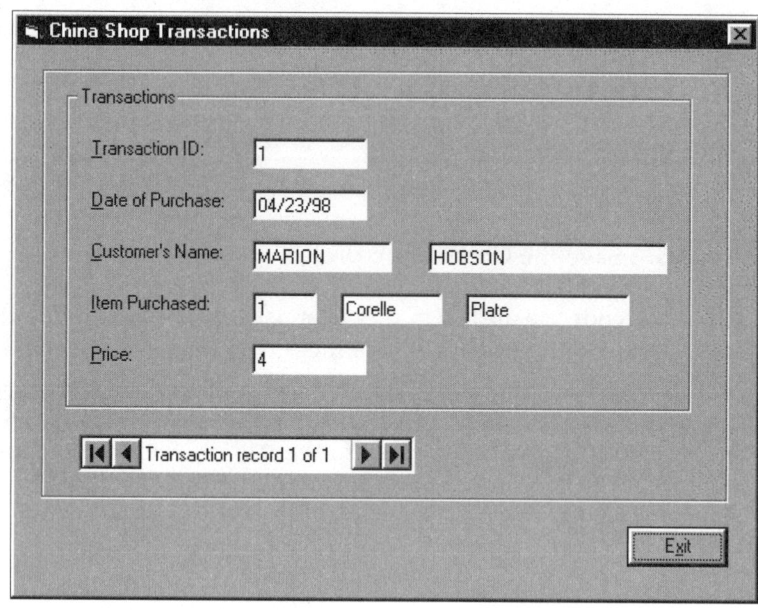


***Discussion***

"Working with a form that the user can't update," I said, "makes things a little simpler for us programmers – for instance, there are fewer command buttons to deal with, and less code to write. However, it's so easy to forget, after designing the form and coding it, that **no updates at all** may be performed on the **Transactions** form. For that reason, I can't emphasize enough the importance of verifying that each and every field on the form is read-only."

I could see a few nervous glances as I made this statement – and I also noticed that more than one person, after testing their form, stopped the program and made changes to a property or two.

"I hate to say this," Peter said, "but my program is bombing as soon as I select View Transactions from the menu bar."

I took a walk over to Peter's workstation and looked at his PC:

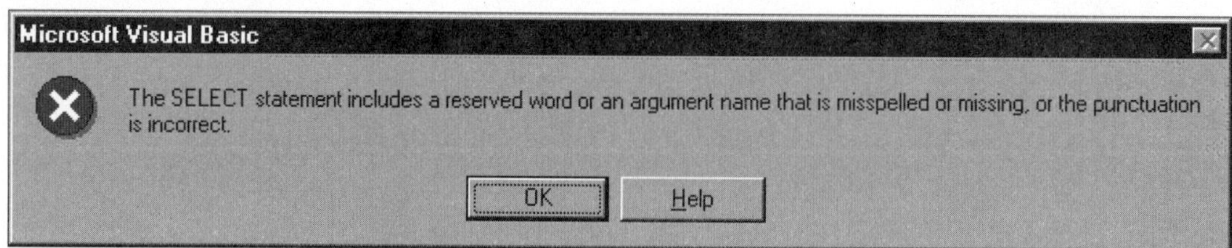

"What's the problem?" Peter asked.

"This message indicates an error with your SQL statement," I said. "When you code an SQL statement using Notepad, you mustn't break the statement onto multiple lines. If you do, you introduce carriage returns and line feeds into your SQL statement, and when you copy and paste that statement into the `RecordSource` property of the data control, you wind up truncating the SQL statement. I'm willing to bet if we look at your `RecordSource` property that it ends with '`LastName`'. Let's check."

I cleared the error message, then brought up Peter's data control and checked the `RecordSource` property. Sure enough, it was truncated as I had predicted:

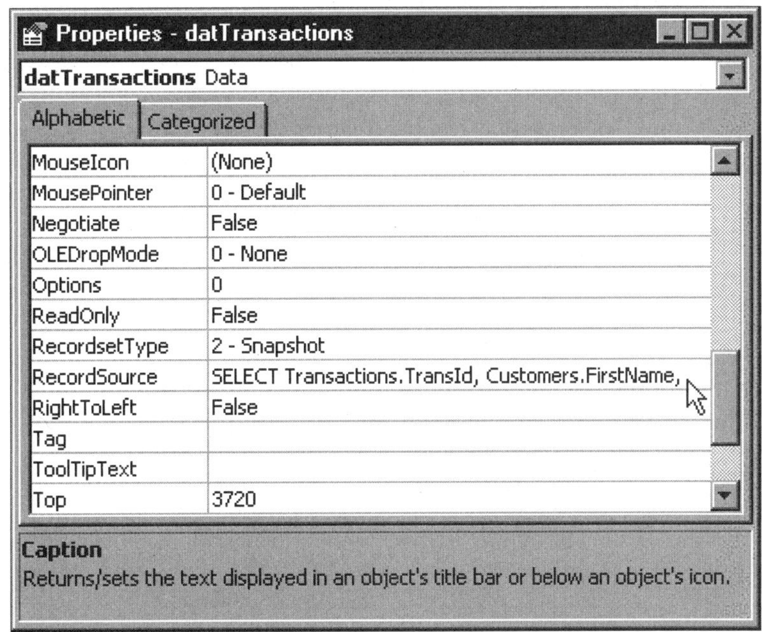


"I see," Peter nodded. "Let me re-key that SQL statement..."

"Either that," I said, "or you could try creating a query in Access and referencing that instead," I said.

"My only question," Rhonda said, "is where did that record come from in the `Transactions` table? I don't remember putting it there, and we know there's no way to enter a record via this form, so..."

"We added that record way back in Week 3," I answered. "And next week, we'll begin to write the code which will enable our program to create a transaction record automatically."

"That will be great," Ward said, "that's exactly what I've been waiting for – putting the database functions together with the original China Shop project."

"I think you'll find that the functionality we add in the final two weeks of class will be pretty extensive," I said. "But I'm afraid that will have to wait until next week – for today, we're all out of time."

I then dismissed the class for the day, and urged everyone to make sure they were well rested for next Saturday's class – we had a lot of important work to do!

# Chapter Summary

The new forms we have added to the China Shop has made our project more flexible and better-suited to Joe's needs. However, the actual work of creating the forms was quite time-consuming; we had to add a lot of controls and then make sure we gave them the properties they needed. All this hard work will pay off, though, when we deliver the project to Joe!

In this chapter, we've focused on the following topics:

- Seeing how the Masked Edit and DBGrid controls can be used to make our programs look more professional (provided, of course, that we have them in our version of Visual Basic!)
- Completing the staff functions of the China Shop project by building the `Customers` and `Transactions` forms. Joe's staff now have all of the tools that they need to view and update the `China` database
- Seeing how – in the `Transactions` form – we can use SQL to tie together fields from multiple tables and display them on a single form

# The Story so Far

In the eight lessons to date, my class has built up the `China` database and the components and code that the Joe's staff need to interact with it. Here's a summary of the functionality that we've added to the China Shop project so far:

We've built the China database that the China Shop program uses:

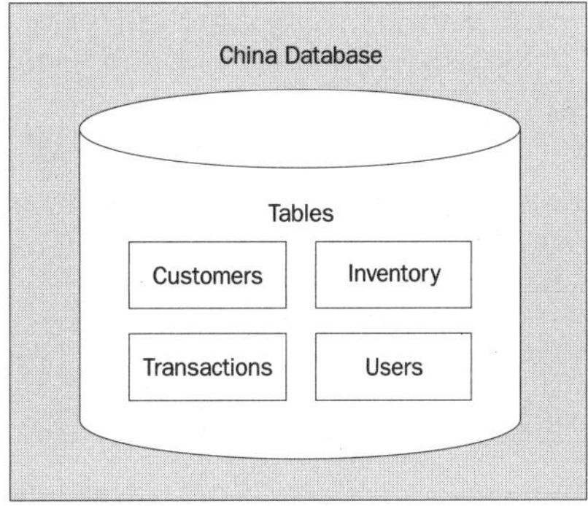


We've created and coded the forms that the China Shop staff use to view and administer the database:

### The Login Form

This is the form that opens when the program starts.

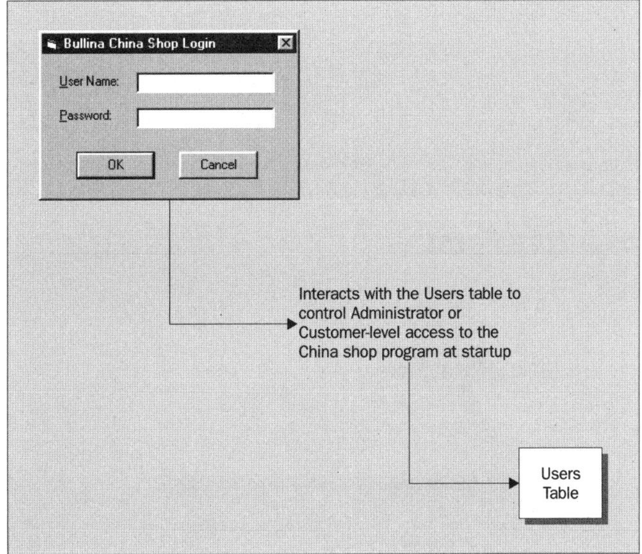


### Staff Functions Menu Options

We've also created the menu options that give the China shop staff access to the data stored in the database:

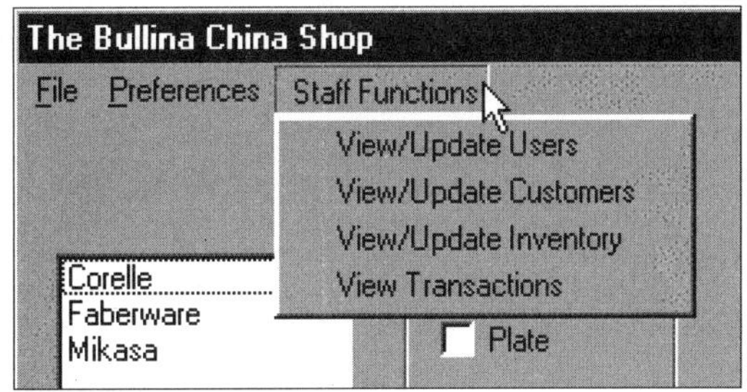

This menu provides Joe's staff with the doorway to the remaining forms:

## The Users Form

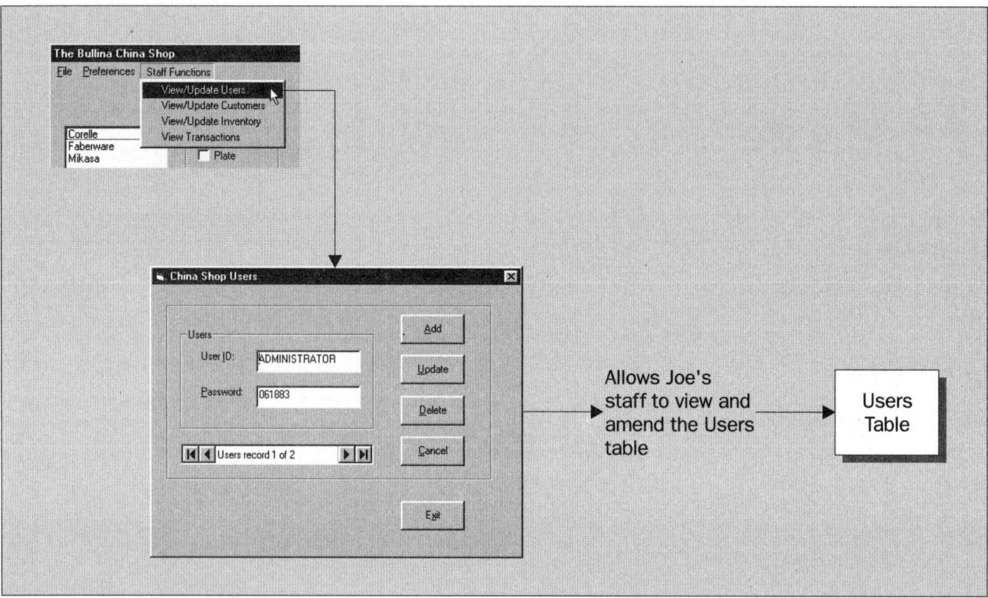


## The Inventory Form

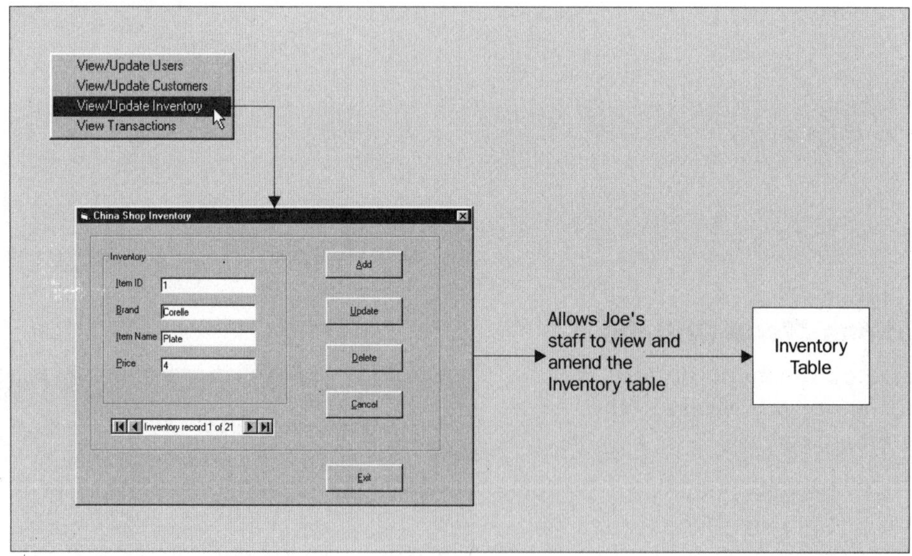

### The Customers Form

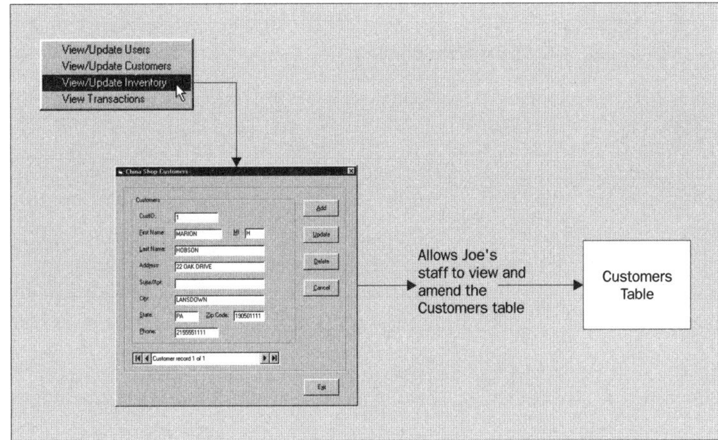


### The Transactions Form

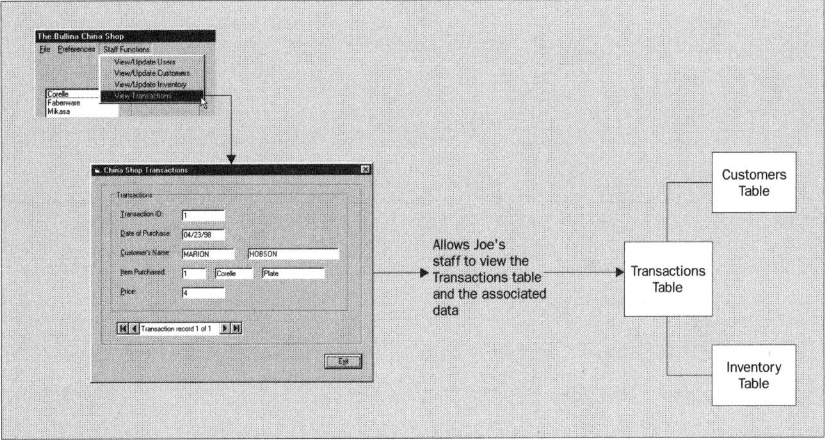


So that's where we've got to so far.

Next week we'll shift our focus from the staff functions of the project and look at the user interface instead – the **`Main`** form. We still need to add the new functionality that Joe has requested for the user interface of the China Shop program that his customers use. Currently, the customer can use the **`Main`** form to generate a price quotation for their potential purchases. What we need to do next is add code to the **`Main`** form that will satisfy Joe's requirements for gathering customer details from new customers, writing transaction records, and printing sales receipts.

That's what we'll start doing in the next lesson – altering the user interface to meet Joe's needs.

isual Basic Learn to Program Databa
vith Visual Basic Learn to Progr
Databases with Visual Basic Learn
Program Databases with Visual Basic Lea
o Program Databases with Visual Ba
earn to Program Databases with Vis
Basic Learn to Program Databases w
isual Basic Learn to Program Databa
vith Visual Basic Learn to Progr
Databases with Visual Basic Learn
Program Databases with Visual Basic Lea
o Program Databases with Visual Ba
earn to Program Databases with Vis
Basic Learn to Program Databases w
isual Basic Learn to Program Databa
vith Visual Basic Learn to Progr
Databases with Visual Basic Learn

# Chapter 9
# Enhancing the User Interface

In the previous chapter, we created the forms that will let the China Shop staff maintain and interrogate the `China` database. With the completion of those four forms, we are now done with the portion of the program that is intended only for the 'eyes' of the China Shop staff.

In this chapter we change direction just a bit. Up to now, the updates we've made to the China Shop project have had virtually no impact on the China Shop's original (single) `Main` form. Now, all of that changes, as we turn our attention to modifications which will impact that original main form, and therefore the user. This chapter, and the next, will be devoted to making those changes.

The specific changes that we'll make to the original program in *this* chapter will:

- Allow the customer to accept the price quotation generated by the program
- Let the program use stored details about *existing* customers, or request details from new customers
- Modify the China Shop program to read price information from the `China` database rather than from the `Prices.txt` disk file

We'll also take a few minutes to discuss how to use Data Objects instead of the data control – being able to do this can place you in good stead with potential employers, so listen up!

## Week 9's Class

Week 8's class had been one of some anticipation and excitement, and week 9 found my university class eagerly awaiting my arrival as I walked into the classroom.

"We have quite a lot of work ahead of us today," I said. "This class and next will be devoted to modifying the behavior of our program's single original form, `frmMain`. In today's class, we'll concentrate on what I call the **Customer Identification Process**."

## The Customer Identification Process

"Customer Identification?" Peter asked. "What do you mean by that?"

"In the previous version of the program," I said, "after the customer selected the china they wanted to buy on the program's user interface, they received a price quotation, and then walked to the sales counter. Now, Joe Bullina wants us to collect information about the customer for future mailing purposes, which means that before the customer makes their way to the sales counter, we need to know *exactly* who they are."

"So," I said, "when the customer clicks on the Calculate button of the **Main** form in the modified program, a button captioned I'll Take It will appear on the form. If the customer clicks on that button, our program will display a new form, the purpose of which will be to ask the customer if they have already been issued with a China Shop Customer ID. The customer will be able to answer in one of four ways..." Here, I displayed a slide on the projector, illustrating the four choices that the customer would be presented with:

- Yes
- No, I'm a new customer
- Yes, but I forgot it
- Cancel

"Depending on the customer's answer, we'll display other forms and prompts in order to process their information. It's this whole process that we'll be designing and coding during the first part of today's class."

"Sounds complicated..." Tom said.

"Don't worry, Tom," I said, "we'll take it a step at a time.

"What will we be doing in the second half of today's class?" Linda asked.

"We'll be modifying the **Load** event procedure of **frmMain** to load the list box of china brands from the **Inventory** table of the **China** database instead of from the **Prices.txt** disk file."

"Wow," Melissa said, "we really are making the China Shop project database-enabled. When do we start?"

"Right now!"

# Building up the China Shop Project

"The first thing we need to do," I said, "is to create that I'll Take It command button I referred to a minute ago. Let's do that now."

## Adding the I'll Take It Command Button

To take us through this process, I passed around the first exercise of the day. "Remember," I said, "this is giving the customer the chance to accept the price quotation the program's generated, and trigger the next part of the sales process."

### Exercise – Adding the I'll Take It Command Button to the Main Form

1. Load up the China Shop project and select `frmMain` from the Project Explorer window.
2. Add a command button to `frmMain` of the China Shop project. Name it `cmdIllTakeIt` (note that you can't use an apostrophe in the name, as VB would interpret it as the start of a comment). Next, set its `Caption` property to 'I'll Take It', and its `Visible` property to `False`. Place and size it roughly according to the screen shot below:

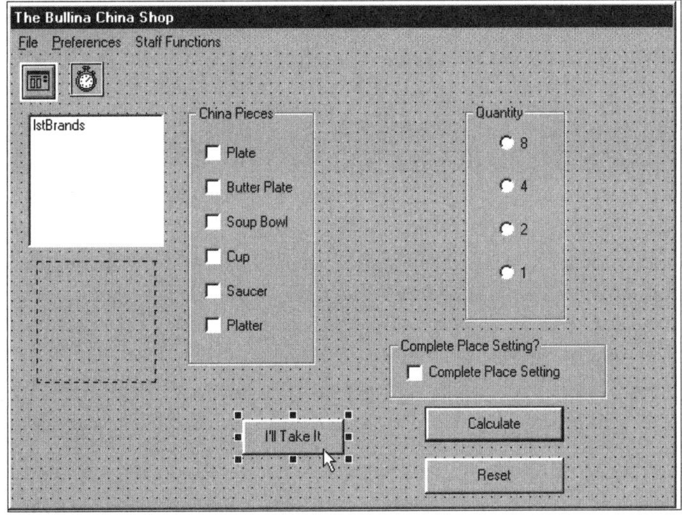


3. Place the following code in the `Click` event procedure of `cmdIllTakeIt`. Notice the apostrophes – they're not typos, but comment characters. For the moment, we don't want these lines of code to execute, so placing a comment character in front of them tells Visual Basic to ignore them. Later, these 'commented out' lines of code will be used to call the functions that take the sales process forward:

```
Private Sub cmdIllTakeIt_Click()

frmCustomerAsk.Show vbModal

If g_intCustomerNumber > 0 Then
'Call PrintSalesReceipt
'Call UpdateTrans
Else
   MsgBox "Sorry, we cannot process your order without a Customer ID"
End If

Call cmdReset_Click

End Sub
```

4. Save the China Shop project.

5. For the moment, there's no way to test this code. We'll be doing that shortly.

***Discussion***

"The code in this **Click** event procedure," I said, "is intended to display a form we'll be designing shortly – the **CustomerAsk** form – when the user clicks on the I'll Take It command button."

"Can you explain again why we placed a comment character in front of those two lines of code?" Chuck asked. "Won't we be executing them?"

"We'll execute those lines of code eventually," I said, "but we won't be writing the two subprocedures referred to in those two lines until next week. For today, it's best to comment them out so we don't accidentally try to execute them."

"I know we've seen the **Unload Me** statement before," Linda said, "and we've also discussed the **Show** method of the form before, but what is **vbModal**? Is that an argument to the **Show** method?"

```
frmCustomerAsk.Show vbModal
```

"Yes, Linda," I said, "that's exactly what it is. **vbModal** is an argument passed to the form's **Show** method, and it determines the **mode** that the form is displayed in."

"Mode?" Rhonda asked.

## *Non-Modal and Modal Forms*

"By default," I continued, "Visual Basic forms are displayed in a **non-modal** fashion, which means that while that form is displayed, the user of the application can still interact with other forms in the project. For instance, if we create a project that has two forms – `Form1` and `Form2` – it means that if we display `Form1`, and we then show `Form2` in a non-modal way, the user can swap between them and go back and interact with the controls on `Form1`."

"Is it a good idea to let this happen?" asked Kevin.

"Good question," I said, "and the answer is a resoundingly indeterminate 'not always'. We may want the user to finish interacting with `Form2` and close it before going back and working with `Form1`. Fortunately, Visual Basic gives us the ability to enforce this kind of behavior by showing the form **modally** – and the way to do that is to supply the `vbModal` argument to the `Show` method."

"Let me get this straight then," Melissa said, "`vbModal` means that while `Form2` is shown, the user won't be able to interact with any other forms in the application?"

"That's right," I said, "although I should point out that they *can* interact with other Windows applications – such as the Calculator, or Word or Excel."

"So `vbModal`," Dave said, "only affects forms in the same application or project."

"That's right, Dave," I said.

"Can you give us an example of a modal form in another Windows program?" Steve asked.

"Yes, I can think of several," I said. "For instance, if you are working in Microsoft Word and you select Tools | Options from the Word menu, a form is displayed which contains a variety of options – and this form is displayed in a modal fashion. By that, I mean that until the options form is closed, you can't go back and edit the document in the document window – if you try, the PC's bell will ring, alerting you to the fact that you can't work in the document until you first close the options form."

"So that's a practical example of a modal form..." Rachel added, "I never thought of it like that. How about a non-modal example?"

"Sure," I said. "How about VB Help? While working in Visual Basic, if you click on the Help menu, Visual Basic Help is displayed on a form – but it's a non-modal form. Even while Help is displayed, you can still continue to work in Visual Basic."

"I've noticed that myself," Rhonda said. "But getting back to our China Shop project, can you tell us why we'll be displaying this form – **frmCustomerAsk** – as a modal form?"

"Simply speaking," I said, "we don't want the customer to do anything else in the program until they identify themselves. Until that point, everything else is really on hold."

"I think I understand the concept of a modal form now," Bob said, "but if the I'll Take It button is invisible, how will the user ever see it?"

"In our next exercise," I said, "we're going to add code to make the **cmdIllTakeIt** button visible when the user clicks on the Calculate button and receives a valid sales quotation."

"I have a question about that **If** statement," Ward said. "What's going on there?"

```
If g_intCustomerNumber > 0 Then
'Call PrintSalesReceipt
'Call UpdateTrans
Else
   MsgBox "Sorry, we cannot process your order without a Customer ID"
End If
```

"Well, Ward," I said, "after we display the **frmCustomerAsk** form, the customer will interact with that form, the end result being that we expect a valid Customer ID to be assigned to the global variable **g_intCustomerNumber**, which we initialized in the standard module we created in week 5: remember, this is the variable that we use to make the customer's ID available to every form in the project. If, after interacting with the **frmCustomerAsk** form, the value of **g_intCustomerNumber** is not greater than 0, then we know that the customer has not properly identified themselves. At this point, we can go no further, so we display a warning message to the customer, and exit the subprocedure."

"What's that line of code," Linda asked, "where you appear to be calling the **Click** event procedure of **cmdReset**? I don't think I've never seen that syntax before."

```
Call cmdReset_Click
```

"You haven't? Oh, I thought I'd covered that in the introductory class last semester. Well, no matter. It's very simple: it's just like calling any other subprocedure. Once we've completed all of the China Shop's new code, when a customer clicks on the I'll Take It button, we'll write a record of the customer's sale to the **Transactions** table and print a sales receipt. At that point, it makes sense to reset the **Main** form for the next customer. Since we already have code written to do all that in the **Click** event procedure of **cmdReset**, all we need to do to execute that code is 'call' it using the **Call** statement."

There were no more questions, so I distributed this next exercise, which builds on the **cmdCalculate** button's functionality.

## Exercise – Adding New Code to the cmdCalculate Button

In this exercise, you'll add code to the `cmdCalculate` command button – this code will display the I'll Take It command button when the user generates a price quotation.

1. Continue working with the `Main` form of the China Shop project.
2. Modify the last few lines of `cmdCalculate_Click` to look like this (the changed line of code is highlighted):

```
'If the price is greater than 0, display the price and
'make the label visible
   If curTotalPrice > 0 Then
      lblPrice.Caption = "The price of your order is " &
         ↳Format(curTotalPrice, "$##,###.00")
      lblPrice.Visible = True
      cmdIllTakeIt.Visible = True
   End If

End Sub
```

3. Save the China Shop project.
4. At this point you can't test this, as we haven't finished updating the code for the Calculate button. Once we have finished that code, the I'll Take It command button will become visible once we click on the Calculate button and display the price quotation:

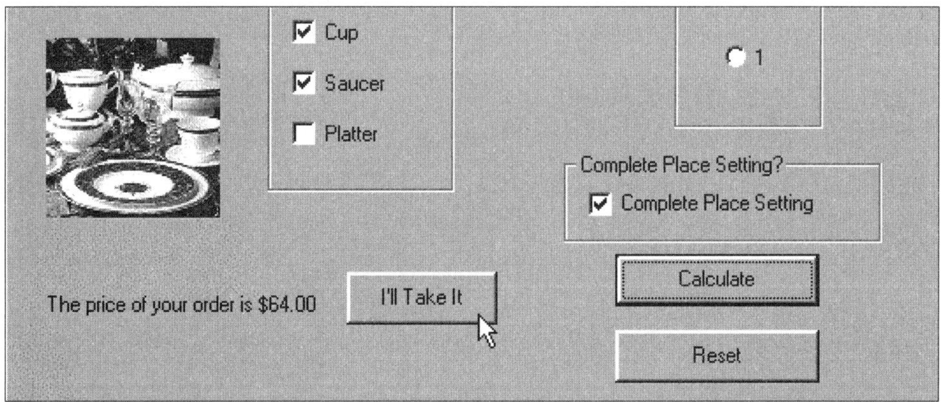


### *Discussion*

"All we're doing here," I said, "is making the I'll Take It button visible when we display a sales quotation to the customer. At that point, it's up to the customer to review the sales quotation, and to click on the I'll Take It button if they like. Any questions?"

"I have a question," said Chuck. "It's about the label control that displays the price quotation to the user. I know that the label is there, because it shows the price on the form..."

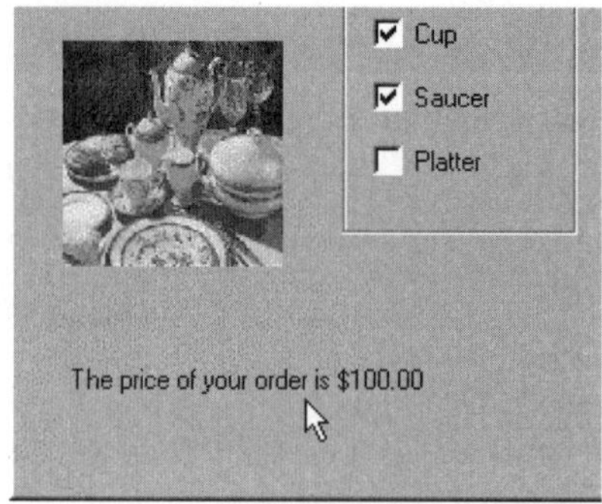


"...but I can't find the label control on the form in design view on the **Main** form. Can you help?"

"That's a good observation, Chuck," I answered. "We made the label small in the original project so that we could 'autosize' it to fit the generated text when the program filled it with the price quotation information. But you're right – this makes it tricky to find in design view."

"What's the solution, then?" asked Melissa.

"The simplest thing to do," I replied, "is to go to the Properties window for the **Main** form in design view and click on the drop-down list box that contains the names of all the controls..."

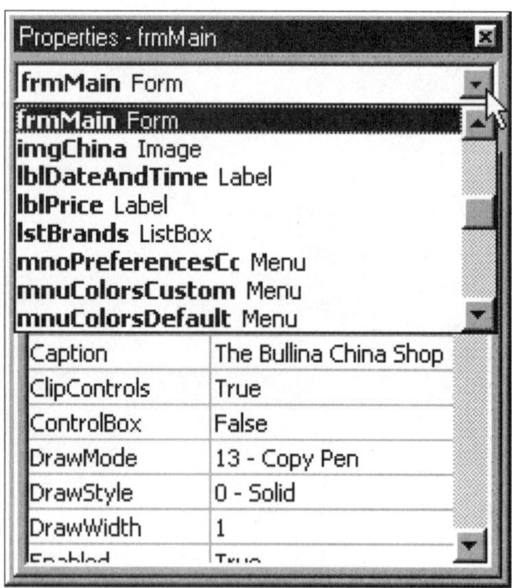

"...select the lblPrice label from the list..."

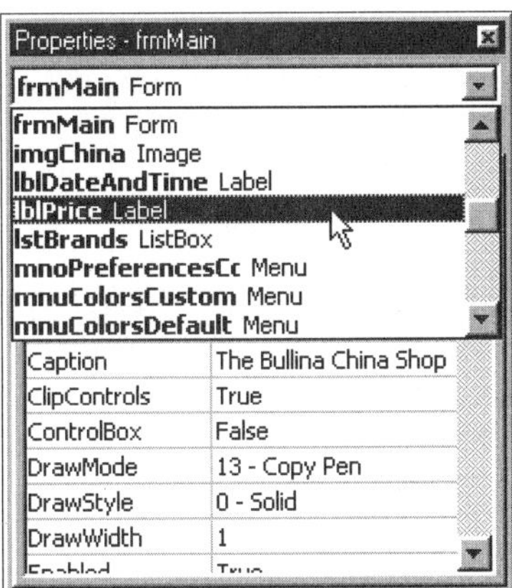


"...and the label will then be highlighted in design view:"

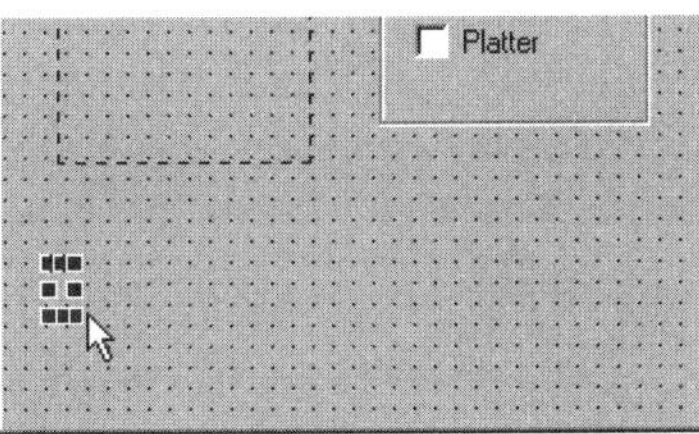


Chuck nodded, confirming that he'd now done this for himself.

"OK," I went on, "any more questions on this one?"

There were no more, so I moved on to creating the `CustomerAsk` form itself.

# Creating the CustomerAsk Form

In this next exercise, you'll add another form to the China Shop project – the `frmCustomerAsk` form. This form is used to determine whether or not the user already has a Customer ID, and to guide them through the next steps in the sales process as appropriate.

## Exercise – Creating the CustomerAsk Form

1. Use the Project | Add Form menu option to add another form to the China Shop project (you'll be familiar with doing this by now!).
2. Once you've created the form, bring up its Properties window and change its `Name` property from `Form1` to `frmCustomerAsk`.

3. Now save the file away with a file name of **CustomerAsk**. You should now see seven forms in the Project Explorer window:

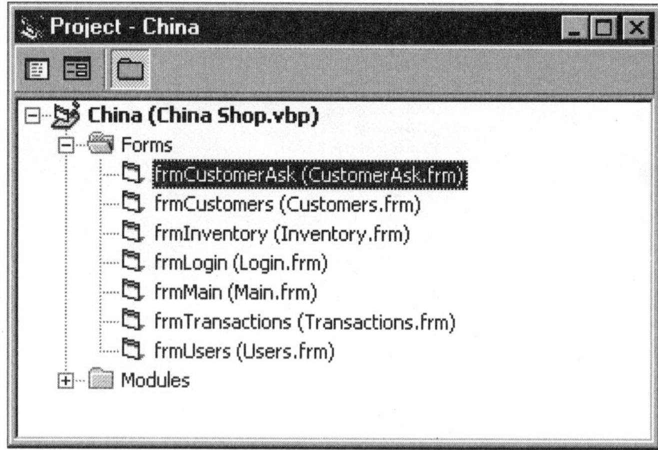


"It's now time to add controls to this form," I said as I distributed the next exercise.

## Exercise – Adding Controls to the CustomerAsk Form

1. Continue working with the `frmCustomerAsk` form of the China Shop project.
2. Add four command buttons and a data control to the `CustomerAsk` form. Size the form and position the controls roughly according to the screenshot below. To preserve the correct `TabIndex` order, place `Command1` first, followed by `Command2`, then `Command3` and `Command4`. Don't worry about the location of the data control – it will be invisible at run time, so the customer will never see it:

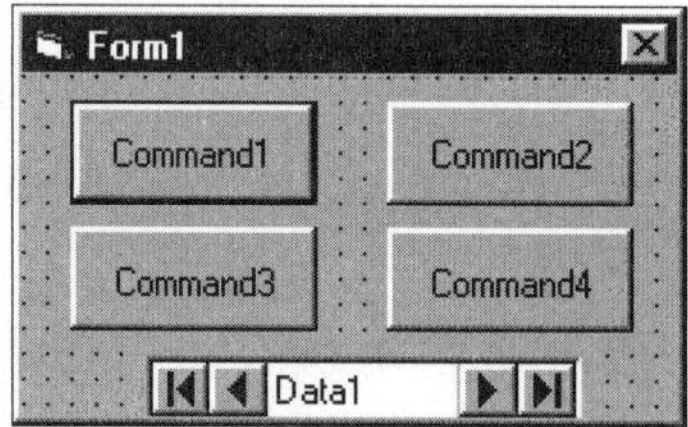


3. Use the following table to make changes to the properties of the data control currently named `Data1`. Don't forget the `Visible` property – we don't want the user to use the data control!

| Property | Value |
|---|---|
| Name | `datCustomers` |
| DatabaseName | C:\VBFiles\China\China.mdb |
| EOFAction | 0-MoveLast |
| RecordsetType | 0-Table |
| RecordSource | Customers |
| Visible | False |

**4.** Now change the properties of **`Command1`**:

| Property | Value |
|---|---|
| Name | cmdExisting |
| Caption | &Yes |
| Default | True |
| TabIndex | 0 |

**5.** Next, **`Command2`**:

| Property | Value |
|---|---|
| Name | `cmdNew` |
| Caption | &No, I'm a new customer |
| TabIndex | 1 |

**6.** Now do the same for **`Command3`**:

| Property | Value |
|---|---|
| Name | `cmdForgot` |
| Caption | Yes, but I &forgot it |
| TabIndex | 2 |

7. Continue with `Command4`:

| Property | Value |
|---|---|
| Name | cmdCancel |
| Cancel | True |
| Caption | &Cancel |
| TabIndex | 3 |

8. Now use this table to make changes to the properties of the form itself:

| Property | Value |
|---|---|
| Name | frmCustomerAsk |
| BorderStyle | 3-Fixed Dialog |
| Caption | Do you have a Customer ID? |
| Moveable | False |
| StartUpPosition | 2-Center Screen |

9. By now, your form should look similar to the one below:

10. Save the China Shop project.

11. At the moment, we have no code behind the buttons on this form, so there's no use testing it. But don't worry, we'll get there shortly!

### *Discussion*

"The design of this form," I said, "is much simpler than the others we've done lately – it really just consists of four command buttons."

"I don't mean to criticize the visual appeal of this form," Rhonda said, "but wouldn't you say we have the data control in an awkward position? I think it's going to look pretty bad to the user when they run the program."

"I suspect, Rhonda," I replied, "that you missed my instructions to set the `Visible` property of the data control to `False` – the user won't be seeing this control at run time. The data control is only there to enable the program to verify the user's Customer ID – the customer won't even know that the data control is on the form."

"You're right," said Rhonda, "I did miss that. Oops."

"I'm glad Rhonda asked that question," Steve said, "I totally missed that instruction too."

Apparently Steve and Rhonda weren't the only ones – I noticed more than one student bring up their forms, and change a property or two!

"Out of interest, Rhonda," I added, "before I deliver the project to Joe, I'll actually resize the form in design view so that there's no tell-tale gap at the bottom of the form, like this:"

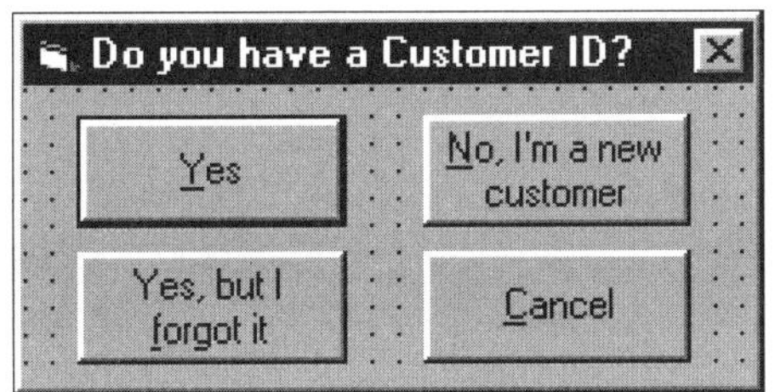


"So, the data control is still on the form, but it's dropped off the bottom, out of sight, is that right?" asked Dave.

"That's exactly right," I confirmed.

I paused a moment, and then continued on.

"Our next job is to put some code behind those buttons," I said, while handing out another exercise. "Again, don't worry about what the code does for the moment – I'll explain the details when you've worked your way through the exercise. Suffice to say – for the moment – that this code will cater for the choices that the user can make from the `CustomerAsk` form."

## Exercise –Adding Code to the CustomerAsk Form

1. Keep on working with the China Shop's **frmCustomerAsk** form.
2. Continue by keying the following code into the **cmdExisting_Click** event procedure:

```
Private Sub cmdExisting_Click()

Dim varResult As Variant

varResult = InputBox("Please enter your customer number",
   ↳"Customer Number?")

If Val(varResult) <= 0 Or Val(varResult) > 32767 Then
   MsgBox "I'm sorry, that's not a valid Customer ID"
   Exit Sub
End If

g_intCustomerNumber = varResult
datCustomers.Recordset.Index = "PrimaryKey"
datCustomers.Recordset.Seek "=", g_intCustomerNumber

If datCustomers.Recordset.NoMatch Then
   g_intCustomerNumber = 0
   MsgBox "I'm sorry, I can't find a matching Customer ID"
   Exit Sub
End If

varResult = MsgBox("Are you " &
datCustomers.Recordset.Fields("FirstName") &
   ↳ " " & datCustomers.Recordset.Fields("LastName") &
      ↳   "?", vbYesNo, "Customer Confirmation")

If varResult = vbYes Then
   MsgBox "Hi " & datCustomers.Recordset.Fields("FirstName") &
      ↳ ", thanks for your order!"
   Unload Me
Else
   g_intCustomerNumber = 0
   MsgBox "Please try again..."
End If

End Sub
```

3. Now type this code into the `cmdNew_Click` event procedure:

```
Private Sub cmdNew_Click()

Unload Me
frmCustomerNew.Show vbModal

End Sub
```

4. Next, key this batch of code into the `cmdForgot_Click` event procedure:

```
Private Sub CmdForgot_Click()

Unload Me
frmCustomerLookup.Show vbModal

End Sub
```

5. Finally, enter this code into the `cmdCancel_Click` event procedure:

```
Private Sub cmdCancel_Click()

Unload Me

End Sub
```

6. Save the China Shop project. Although you may be tempted to run the program at this point to test the functionality of the I'll Take It command button, my advice is to resist the temptation. We're not quite there yet – so please be patient and wait until I explain the code and demo it to the class.

### *Discussion*

"To make things easier to understand," I said, "I'm going to run the code and demonstrate the code we just wrote."

I ran the China Shop program, logged in, made a selection of china pieces and quantities, and then clicked on the Calculate button, with this result:

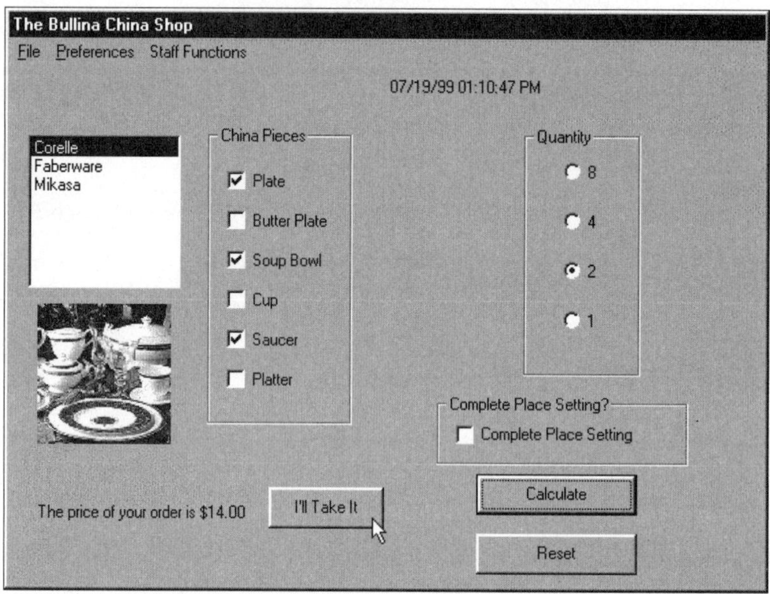


"As I mentioned a few minutes ago," I said, "after the customer makes a selection of china, and clicks on the Calculate button, the I'll Take It command button will be displayed. If the user then clicks on that button, this form will be displayed..."

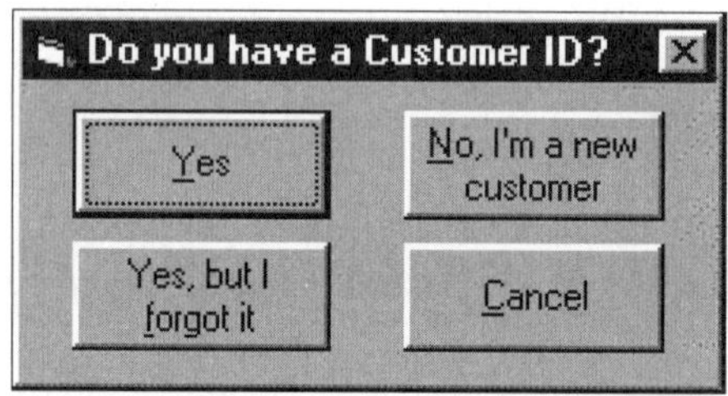


"...and the customer has the choice of clicking on any one of the four command buttons."

"OK," I went on, "let's start by examining the code which is executed when the user clicks on the No, I'm a new customer button, indicating that they do not yet have a China Shop Customer ID."

"What about the code in the Yes command button?" Peter asked.

"The code in there is a little more complicated than the others," I said, "so let's discuss that code last."

I then displayed the code for the **Click** event procedure of **cmdNew** on the classroom projector.

"As you can see," I continued, "the **frmCustomerAsk** form is first unloaded..."

```
Private Sub cmdNew_Click()

Unload Me
```

"... and then the **frmCustomerNew** form is displayed modally..."

```
frmCustomerNew.Show vbModal
```

"...we'll design that form – the **frmCustomerNew** form – and write its code in the next exercise, and the form will look very much like the **frmCustomers** form that we built last week. **frmCustomerNew** will permit the user to add a new customer record for themselves to the **Customers** table."

I waited to see if there were any questions.

"In a similar way," I continued, "if the customer believes they already have a Customer ID, but can't remember it, they click on the button captioned Yes, but I forgot it, and the following section of code is executed:"

```
Private Sub cmdForgot_Click()

Unload Me
frmCustomerLookup.Show vbModal

End Sub
```

"Again, as was the case with the code in **cmdNew**, we unload the form and display another form that we'll design and code shortly – the **frmCustomerLookup** form – in a modal way. The **CustomersLookup** form will let the user search a list of 'valid' customers to see if they can find themselves on it."

I waited to see if there were any other questions.

"Now, suppose the customer simply changes their mind when presented with this form and clicks on the Cancel button," I said. "In that case, we just unload the form:"

```
Private Sub cmdCancel_Click()

Unload Me

End Sub
```

"Finally, let's take a look at the code in the `Click` event procedure of `cmdExisting`," I said. "This is the code which is executed if the customer believes that they have a valid China Shop Customer ID and remember it."

"*Believes* that they do? What if they're wrong?" asked Tom.

"Well, we'll have to make sure that we can verify their choice of ID. We'll see how we do that later on. Now, since we'll be accepting input from the customer using an `InputBox` function, the first thing we do is to declare a variant variable to hold their response..."

```
Private Sub cmdExisting_Click()

Dim varResult As Variant
```

"Excuse me, Professor Smiley?" piped up Mary. "Why are we using a variant here? It seems like a pretty weird choice. Can't we declare it as an integer? That's what the `CustomerID` is, after all."

"Well, now, that's true, and I'll get to that in a second. It's to do with the input box, which is the next line of code. We execute the `InputBox` function to ask the user for their customer number..."

```
varResult = InputBox("Please enter your customer number",
   ↳"Customer Number?")
```

"One of the problems with input boxes," I said, "is that we can't validate what the user enters into them until they click on the OK button. Once they do this, the value they've entered into the input box is then assigned to the return value variable – `varResult` – which we declare for that purpose. We need to verify that a numeric value greater than 0 and less than 32,768 has been entered by the user into the input box. After all, a customer could just as easily type their name into the input box by accident..."

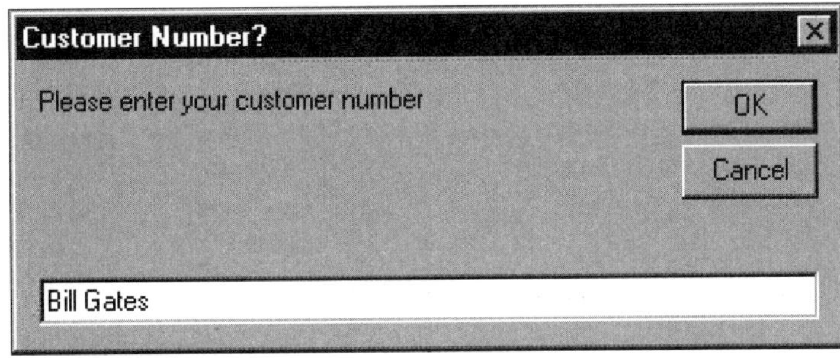


"For that reason, we use the `Val` function here. The `Val` function returns the numeric value of the value in the input box. The standard return value of an input box comes in the form of a string variable. "

"Suppose no number has been entered into the input box?" Kevin asked.

"In that case," I said, "the `Val` function returns a 0. Therefore, this line of code..."

```
If Val(varResult) <= 0 Or Val(varResult) > 32767 Then
```

"...can be used to determine if there's a valid number in the `InputBox`. If there is not, then we display a message to the user and exit the event procedure via the `Exit Sub` statement. Here's the relevant code..."

```
   MsgBox "I'm sorry, that's not a valid Customer ID"
   Exit Sub
End If
```

"..and here's the message box:"

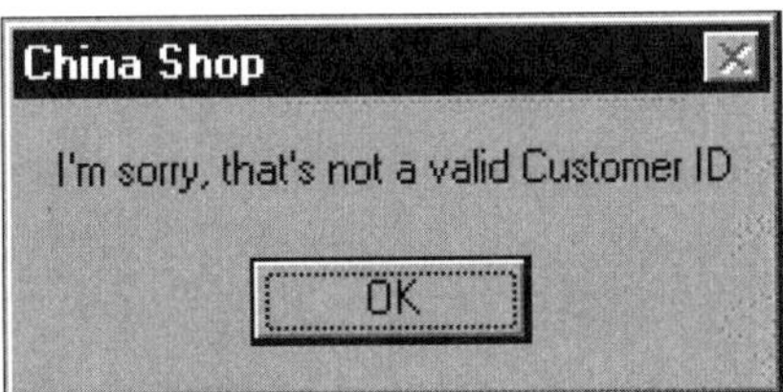


"When the user clicks on OK, the `frmCustomerAsk` form is redisplayed, ready for the user to try again."

I waited to see if I had lost anyone. So far, so good.

"If we've got this far in the `cmdExisting` event procedure," I said, "that means that the user has made a valid numeric entry into the input box, like this:"

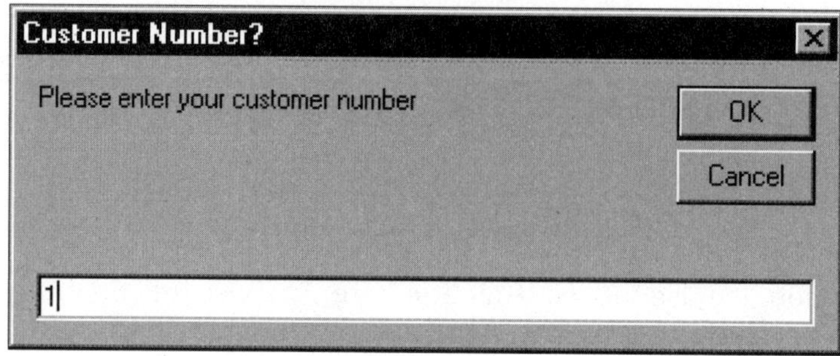


"Now it's time to see if a record with that Customer ID exists in the `Customers` table. Do you remember the global variable – `g_intCustomerNumber` – that we declared in the General Declarations section of our standard module a few weeks back, and which I mentioned at the start of the class? We now assign the number that the user has entered into the input box to that global variable..."

```
g_intCustomerNumber = varResult
```

"Then we set the `Index` property of the data control's recordset to the primary key of the `Customers` table..."

```
datCustomers.Recordset.Index = "PrimaryKey"
```

"This makes our search as efficient as possible. To conduct the search for a matching value, we use the `Seek` method of the recordset to locate that Customer ID in the `Customers` table..."

```
datCustomers.Recordset.Seek "=", g_intCustomerNumber
```

"Of course," I continued, "there are two possibilities – a record with a matching Customer ID *will* be found in the `Customers` table, or one *won't*. If the `Seek` method fails to locate a record with a matching Customer ID, then the `NoMatch` property of the recordset will be set to `True`. At that point, we then set the value of `g_intCustomerNumber` to 0 – which you may recall is a signal to our program that the customer has not been properly identified – then display a message box to the user, and exit the event procedure via the `Exit Sub` statement:"

```
If datCustomers.Recordset.NoMatch Then
   g_intCustomerNumber = 0
   MsgBox "I'm sorry, I can't find a matching Customer ID"
   Exit Sub
End If
```

"Now," I continued, "if we get beyond this point in our code, it means that the value of the **NoMatch** property is equal to **False** – or, in other words, a customer record with a Customer ID matching the number the customer has entered into the input box does exist. That sounds great, but the possibility exists that the user may have made a mistake entering the number."

"How so?" Ward asked.

"For instance," I said, "suppose the customer enters 1 into the input box when they meant to enter 11. We know that we have a customer record with a Customer ID of 1 – but in this instance, that's not the correct customer! That's why it's a good idea to verify that we have the right customer record selected, and we do that using a Yes/No message box ..."

```
varResult = MsgBox("Are you " &
datCustomers.Recordset.Fields("FirstName") &
   ↳ " " & datCustomers.Recordset.Fields("LastName") &
      ↳ "?", vbYesNo, "Customer Confirmation")
```

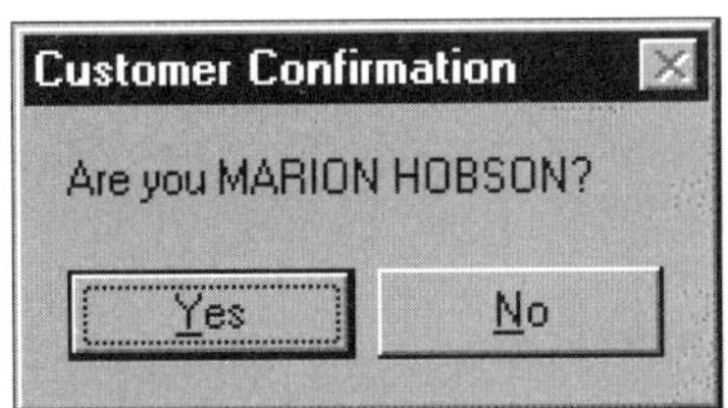


"What's going on here?" Kate asked. "This syntax – particularly the line referencing the **Recordset** – is confusing me."

"Let's all bear in mind," I said, "that at this point, we have just found a matching record in the recordset based on the **Customers** table and, as a result, the recordset's record pointer is now resting on that record. What we're doing here is displaying fields from the matching customer record, and asking the customer to verify them."

"How can we reference fields from the recordset?" Rhonda asked. "This form has no bound controls – in fact, the data control is even invisible."

"Even though we have no fields visible on the form," I replied, "the recordset exists nonetheless, which means that we have access to the values in every field of the recordset. That's how we're able to use the **`FirstName`** and **`LastName`** fields of the customer record in the message box. This syntax..."

```
datCustomers.Recordset.Fields("LastName")
```

"...is equivalent to telling Visual Basic to display the value of the current **`LastName`** field of the recordset, and in this instance, we use this expression as an argument to the **`MsgBox`** function."

"That's better," Rhonda said. "I think I understand now. We talked about this syntax before in a previous lesson, didn't we?"

"That's right," I confirmed, "back in lesson...five, it would have been."

I waited for any more questions.

"With a Yes/No message box displayed," I resumed, "we need to be able to react to the customer's answer. They're either going to tell us Yes, the first and last name do indeed belong to them, or No, the first and last name belong to someone else. If the customer confirms their identity by clicking on the Yes button in the message box..."

```
If varResult = vbYes Then
```

"... we then thank them for their order..."

```
   MsgBox "Hi " & datCustomers.Recordset.Fields("FirstName") &
      ↳ ", thanks for your order!"
```

"...by displaying the message box..."

"... and unload the form:"

```
Unload Me
```

"What happens now?" Kate asked.

"We now have their Customer ID stored in the global variable `g_intCustomerNumber`, and the rest of the code in the `cmdIllTakeIt` command button will execute, ultimately writing a record to the `Transactions` table and printing a sales receipt."

"And if they answer No?" Lou asked.

"If the customer answers No in the message box," I continued, "that means that they have entered an incorrect Customer ID in the input box. In this circumstance, the value of `g_intCustomerNumber` is set to 0 and a message asking them to try again is displayed:"

```
Else
   g_intCustomerNumber = 0
   MsgBox "Please try again..."
End If

End Sub
```

Much to my surprise, no one seemed to be having any problem following the code in these event procedures.

"In my opinion," I said, "the code on the `frmCustomerAsk` form is probably the most complicated in the project – so if you can follow this code pretty well, I think you're in pretty good shape."

"We have two more forms to build in the China Shop project," I said. "In the next exercise, we'll build the form that the customer will see if they believe they already have a China Shop Customer ID, but can't remember it."

## Creating the CustomerLookup Form

I distributed another exercise for the class to complete.

### Exercise – Creating the CustomerLookup Form

1. Continue working with the China Shop project.
2. Select our old friend, the Project | Add Form option from the Visual Basic menu bar and add another new form to the project.
3. Next, select the new form and, in its Properties window, change its **`Name`** property to **`frmCustomerLookup`**.
4. Now save this new form with the file name **`CustomerLookup`**.
5. You'll now have *eight* forms in the Project Explorer window:

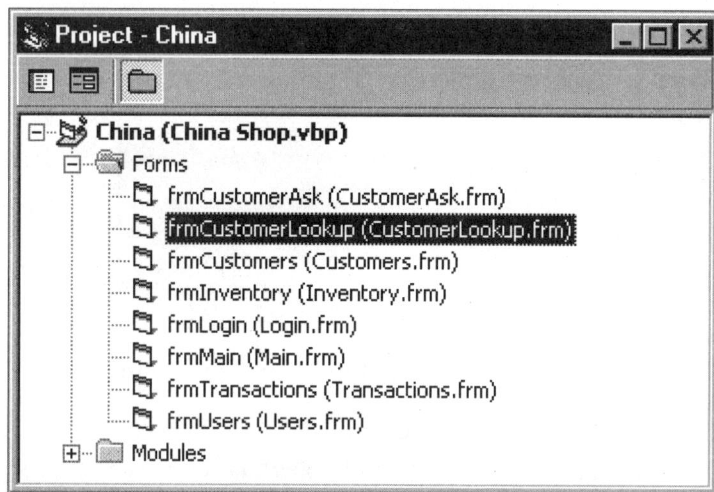


By now, creating a new form was no routine for the class. Moving right along, I handed out the next exercise for the students to complete.

### Exercise – Adding Controls to the CustomerLookup Form

1. Continue working with the **`frmCustomerLookup`** form.
2. Add, one list box, three command buttons, two labels and one data control to the **`frmCustomerLookup`** form, using the screenshot below as your guide. To make sure that the right **`TabIndex`** order is created, place the list box first, followed by **`Command1`**, **`Command2`** and **`Command3`**. Then add **`Label1`** followed by **`Label2`**, and finally add the data control:

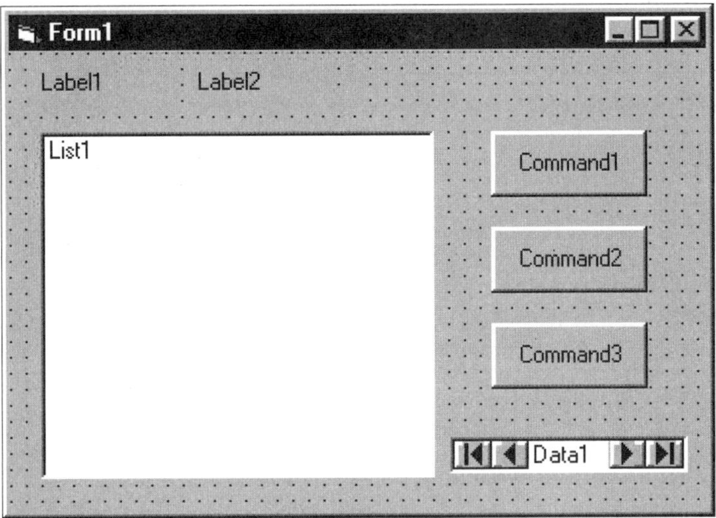


3. Now let's set the properties for these controls. Start by using the following table to make changes to the data control currently named `Data1`:

| Property | Value |
|---|---|
| Name | datCustomers |
| DatabaseName | C:\VBFiles\China\China.mdb |
| EOFAction | 0-MoveLast |
| RecordsetType | 2-Snapshot |
| RecordSource | Customers |
| Visible | False |

4. Now change the properties of `Label1`:

| Property | Value |
|---|---|
| Name | lblCustID |
| Caption | Customer ID: |

5. Similarly, change the properties of `Label2`:

| Property | Value |
|---|---|
| Name | lblLastName |
| Caption | Last Name: |

6. Here's the table to use to make changes to the list box currently named `List1`. Note that the first character in the `Name` property is a lowercase 'L', **not** the number '1':

| Property | Value |
|---|---|
| Name | lstCustomers |
| TabIndex | 0 |

7. Now change `Command1`:

| Property | Value |
|---|---|
| Name | cmdThatsMe |
| Caption | &That's me! |
| Default | True |
| TabIndex | 1 |

8. And `Command2`:

| Property | Value |
|---|---|
| Name | cmdImNotHere |
| Caption | &I'm not in the list, please add me... |
| TabIndex | 2 |

**9.** Now change `Command3`:

| Property | Value |
|---|---|
| Name | cmdCancel |
| Cancel | True |
| Caption | &Cancel |
| TabIndex | 3 |

**10.** Finally, make the changes necessary for the form itself:

| Property | Value |
|---|---|
| Name | frmCustomerLookup |
| BorderStyle | 3-Fixed Dialog |
| Caption | Let me help you... |
| Moveable | False |
| StartUpPosition | 2-Center Screen |

**11.** Right about now, your form should look something like this:

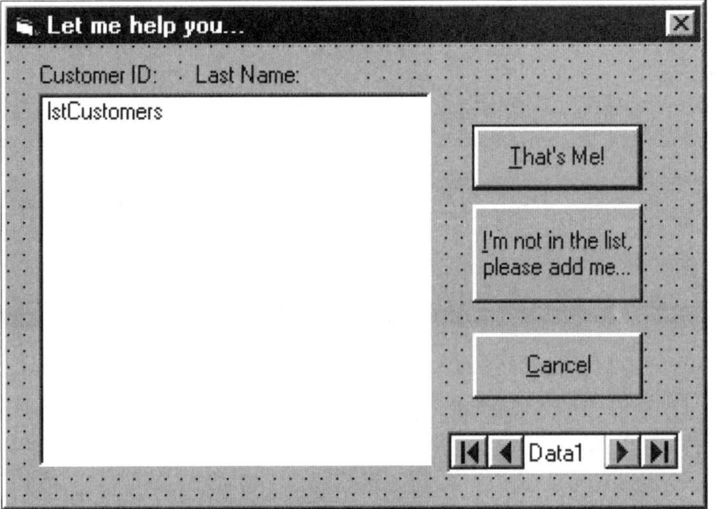

**12.** Save the China Shop project.

***Discussion***

Once again, I reminded the students that the data control's `Visible` property should be set to `False` – the user should never see it.

"When does this form appear again?" Rhonda asked. "I'm sorry, with all these forms flying around, I get all confused."

I smiled. "That's understandable, Rhonda. Here's a quick summary of what can be displayed from the `CustomerAsk` form, depending upon which buttons the user presses:"

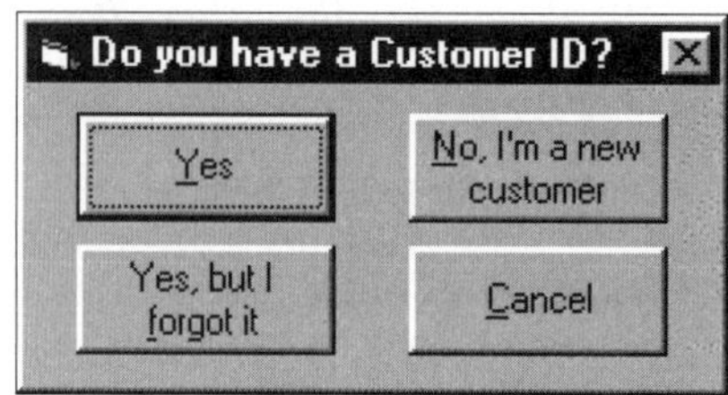


"So," I went on, "when the user clicks on the Yes, but I forgot it button on the `CustomerAsk` form," I said, "it's the `CustomerLookup` form that will be displayed. In the next exercise, we'll be writing code that will display the `CustomerID` and `LastName` of every record in the `Customers` table, in a list box. At that point, the user will be able to make a selection from the list."

"Suppose they don't see their record?" Ward asked.

"Good question, Ward," I said, "in that case, they can either click on a button which will enable them to enter a new customer record, or they can simply click on the Cancel button, and return to the `frmCustomerAsk` form. Let's code up the `CustomerLookup` form now."

## Exercise – Adding Code to the CustomerLookup Form

In this exercise, you'll add code to the controls you just placed on the `frmCustomerLookup` form.

1. Continue working with the `frmCustomerLookup` form.
2. Start by keying up this chunk of code into the `datCustomers_Reposition` event procedure:

```
Private Sub datCustomers_Reposition()

Do While Not datCustomers.Recordset.EOF
   lstCustomers.AddItem datCustomers.Recordset.Fields("CustID") &
```

```
     ↳ vbTab & vbTab & datCustomers.Recordset.Fields("LastName")
   datCustomers.Recordset.MoveNext
Loop

End Sub
```

3. Now place the following code in the `lstCustomers_DblClick` event procedure:

```
Private Sub lstCustomers_DblClick()

g_intCustomerNumber = Val(lstCustomers.Text)
Unload Me

End Sub
```

4. Type this code (or copy and paste it, since it's the same as the previous chunk) into the `cmdThatsMe_Click` event procedure:

```
Private Sub cmdThatsMe_Click()

g_intCustomerNumber = Val(lstCustomers.Text)
Unload Me

End Sub
```

5. Now add this code to the `cmdImNotHere_Click` event procedure:

```
Private Sub cmdImNotHere_Click()

Unload Me
frmCustomerNew.Show vbModal

End Sub
```

6. Type this next batch of code into the `cmdCancel_Click` event procedure:

```
Private Sub cmdCancel_Click()

g_intCustomerNumber = 0
Unload Me

End Sub
```

7. Save the China Shop project. Again, although you may be tempted to run the program at this point to test the functionality of the I'll Take It command button, you must resist! Be strong. Wait until I demonstrate and explain the code to the class.

***Discussion***

"Let's start our discussion of this code," I said, "by looking at the code in the data control's **Reposition** event procedure. When the **CustomersLookup** form is first displayed, it's this code that loads up the list box with every Customer ID and last name from the **Customers** table:"

```
Private Sub datCustomers_Reposition()

Do While Not datCustomers.Recordset.EOF
   lstCustomers.AddItem datCustomers.Recordset.Fields("CustID") &
       ↳ vbTab & vbTab & datCustomers.Recordset.Fields("LastName")
   datCustomers.Recordset.MoveNext
Loop

End Sub
```

"As you can see," I continued, "we use a **Do While...Loop** structure to access each record in the data control's recordset, and then use the **AddItem** method of the list box to add both the **CustID** and **LastName** field values to the **lstCustomers** list box."

"Why are you concatenating the tab characters using the ampersands?" Linda asked. "Is that for formatting purposes?"

"That's right, Linda," I said. "By using the tab character, in the form of the intrinsic constant **vbTab**, we can format the field values in the list box into nice neat columns."

I waited to see if anyone else had any questions.

"Let's run the China Shop program now and see what happens," I said. I ran the program and logged in, then selected some china, clicked on the Calculate button, and then on the I'll Take It button. The **CustomerAsk** form appeared:

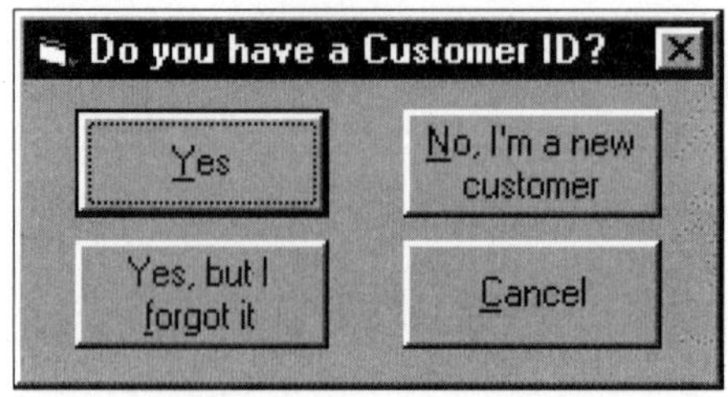

"Let's pretend that I have a Customer ID, but can't remember it," I said. "I'll click on the Yes, but I forgot it button and the `frmCustomerLookup` form should appear with a list box containing two columns – one for Customer ID, and the other for last name, and then I can check if I'm in on the list..."

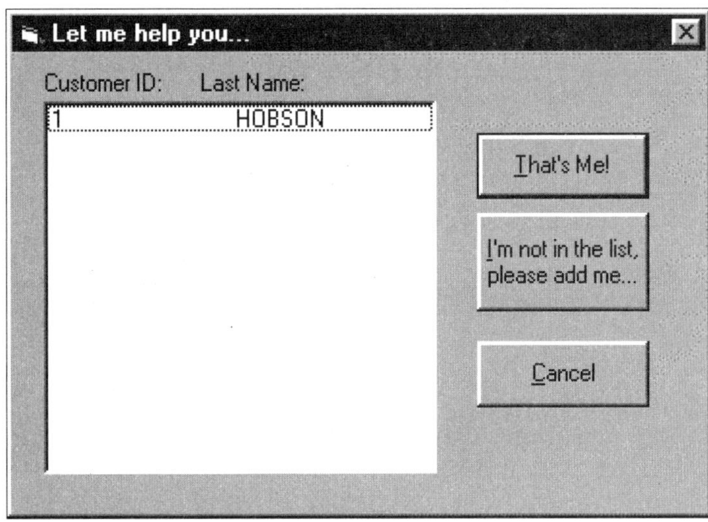


"Well, you can see that I'm not on the list. Anyway, it comes in quite handy to have some records in the database for test purposes – although we really should have entered a few more. At least we can see the program working."

"What happens now?" Steve asked.

"At this point," I said, "if the customer recognizes their last name in the list box, they have two choices – they can either double-click on their name in the list box, or select their name in the list box using their mouse and click on the That's me command button. Either way, the code they execute is the same, although it's in different event procedures. Here's the code again for the That's Me! Command button:"

```
Private Sub cmdThatsMe_Click()

g_intCustomerNumber = Val(lstCustomers.Text)
Unload Me

End Sub
```

"...and here's the code that executes if the user double-clicks on their name in the list box:"

```
Private Sub lstCustomers_DblClick()

g_intCustomerNumber = Val(lstCustomers.Text)
Unload Me

End Sub
```

"As you can see," I said, "in both event procedures, we execute the `Val` function to 'extract' the Customer ID of the currently selected item in the list box."

"How's that working?" Ward asked. "I thought the `Val` function only worked on numeric values, but the `Text` property of the list box contains both a number, and a string – the last name – as well. Can you do this? Shouldn't you use a string manipulation function like `Left` to extract the Customer ID from the `Text` property of the list box?"

"That's a good observation, Ward," I said. "However, one of the nice characteristics of the `Val` function is that it returns a numeric value from a string starting from the left and working its way right. Once it detects a non-numeric character in a string, it just stops. Therefore, if the user selects an item in the list box such as..."

**1 HOBSON**

"...the `Val` function executes and returns the number 1..."

"Which just happens to be their Customer ID," Dave said.

"That's right, Dave," I agreed. "Using the `Val` function in this way saves us from having to search through the `Text` property of the list box with a string manipulation function. Now, once we've extracted the Customer ID from the list box, we assign it to the global variable `g_intCustomerNumber` – which identifies the customer throughout the rest of the program."

"So *that's* why we made it a global variable!" said Ward.

"That's exactly right," I said. "Global variables can be seen from wherever you are in the program," I reminded them.

Everyone seemed to be following me.

"What about the I'm not in the list, please add me button," Rhonda asked. "How does that one work?"

"If the customer clicks on that button," I said, "it indicates that even though they were certain they already had a valid China Shop Customer ID they don't, in fact, have a customer record related to them in the database. At this point, we unload the `frmCustomerLookup` form..."

```
Private Sub cmdImNotHere_Click()

Unload Me
```

"... and then display the `frmCustomerNew` form – a form we'll design and code in the next series of exercises:"

```
frmCustomerNew.Show vbModal

End Sub
```

"That form will permit the customer to enter their full information into the `Customers` table of the `China` database."

I paused – everyone still seemed attentive and comfortable.

"Finally," I said, "this code ..."

```
Private Sub cmdCancel_Click()

g_intCustomerNumber = 0
Unload Me

End Sub
```

"...is executed if, for whatever reason, the customer simply changes their mind about proceeding with the sales process. Remember, it's always a good idea to permit the customer to change their mind at any point in the program. Once again, notice that we are setting the value of `g_intCustomerNumber` to 0 – which signals to our program that no valid customer identification has taken place."

As a reminder, I displayed the code for the `Click` event procedure of `cmdIllTakeIt` on the classroom projector..."

```
Private Sub cmdIllTakeIt_Click()

frmCustomerAsk.Show vbModal
```

*Continued on following page*

```
If g_intCustomerNumber > 0 Then
'Call PrintSalesReceipt
'Call UpdateTrans
Else
   MsgBox "Sorry, we cannot process your order without a customer ID"
End If

End Sub
```

"As you can see," I continued, "when `frmCustomerAsk` is displayed as a modal form, the code in the `Click` event procedure just sits there, waiting for the form to be unloaded. When the form is eventually unloaded, the next line of code in the `Click` event procedure examines the value of `g_intCustomerNumber` to see if it's greater than zero. If it is, that means that the customer has been identified, and we can go ahead with the process of printing a sales receipt and adding a record for this purchase to the `Transactions` table. If the value of `g_intCustomerNumber` is *not* greater than zero, that means that the customer was never identified, or the customer elected not to enter their information, in which case we display a message box informing the customer that we cannot process their order."

I waited to see if there were any further questions.

"OK folks, let's take a quick break before we continue," I said, and we did just that.

## Creating the CustomerNew Form

After the break, we got straight down to coding up the final form for the enhanced China Shop project – the `CustomerNew` form.

### Exercise – Creating the CustomerNew Form

1. Load up the China Shop project.
2. For the last time for this project, use the Project | Add Form menu option to create another new form.
3. Select the new form and bring up its Properties window. Change the `Name` property to `frmCustomerNew`.
4. Now click on the 'save' button and save the form with a file name of `CustomerNew`. You'll now see nine forms in the Project Explorer window:

And so, straight on to our next exercise, where we'll add the requisite controls to this new form.

## Exercise – Adding Controls to the CustomerNew Form

1. Continue working with the `frmCustomerNew` form.
2. Loosen up those fingers and add two frames, ten labels, ten text boxes, one data control, and two command buttons to the CustomerNew form. Size the form and position the controls similarly to the screenshot below, taking care to add the frames first. Remember to draw the frames explicitly, and to be careful about the placement of controls within the frames.

As in the last chapter, where we built the similar `Customers` form, make sure that you maintain the correct `TabIndex` order: work from the top of the form and from right to left; place `Label1` first followed by `Text1`, then `Label2` followed by `Text2`, then `Label3` followed by `Text3`, etc. Once you've added all the labels and text boxes, move on to the two command buttons and, finally, the data control:

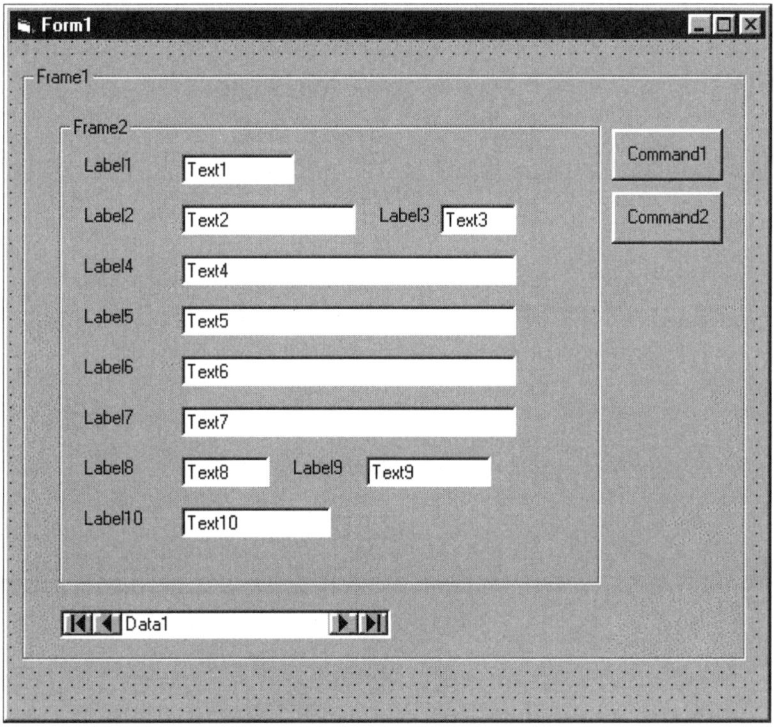

**3.** Now for the usual series of property changes. First, use the following table to make changes to the properties of the data control currently named `Data1`:

| Property | Value |
|---|---|
| Name | datCustomers |
| Caption | China Shop Customers |
| DatabaseName | C:\VBFiles\China\China.mdb |
| EOFAction | 0-MoveLast |
| RecordsetType | 1-Dynaset |
| RecordSource | Customers |
| Visible | False |

**4.** Now the properties of `Frame1`:

| Property | Value |
|---|---|
| Name | fraOutside |
| Caption | (blank) |
| TabIndex | 0 |

**5.** Next, change the properties of `Frame2`:

| Property | Value |
|---|---|
| Name | fraInside |
| Caption | Customers |
| TabIndex | 1 |

6. And now the labels. Here's the table of properties for `Label1`:

| Property | Value |
|---|---|
| Name | lblCustID |
| Caption | Cus&tID: |
| TabIndex | 2 |

7. And `Label2`:

| Property | Value |
|---|---|
| Name | lblFirstName |
| Caption | &First Name: |
| TabIndex | 4 |

8. Now `Label3`:

| Property | Value |
|---|---|
| Name | lblMI |
| Caption | &MI: |
| TabIndex | 6 |

9. Next, `Label4`:

| Property | Value |
|---|---|
| Name | lblLastName |
| Caption | &Last Name: |
| TabIndex | 8 |

**10.** Use this table for `Label5`:

| Property | Value |
|---|---|
| Name | lblAddress1 |
| Caption | Add&ress: |
| TabIndex | 10 |

**11.** But this one for `Label6`:

| Property | Value |
|---|---|
| Name | lblAddress2 |
| Caption | Su&ite/Apt: |
| TabIndex | 12 |

**12.** Not to be confused with this one, which is for `Label7`:

| Property | Value |
|---|---|
| Name | lblCity |
| Caption | Cit&y |
| TabIndex | 14 |

**13.** If you're thinking that the next table is for `Label8`, you're right...

| Property | Value |
|---|---|
| Name | lblState |
| Caption | &State: |
| TabIndex | 16 |

**14.** What used to be `Label9` needs to be changed thus:

| Property | Value |
|---|---|
| Name | lblZipCode |
| Caption | &Zip Code: |
| TabIndex | 18 |

**15.** And our final label, `Label10`:

| Property | Value |
|---|---|
| Name | lblPhone |
| Caption | &Phone: |
| TabIndex | 20 |

**16.** And now for those lovely text boxes. Use the following table to make changes to the properties of the text box control currently named `Text1`:

| Property | Value |
|---|---|
| Name | txtCustID |
| DataSource | datCustomers |
| DataField | CustID |
| Locked | True |
| TabIndex | 3 |
| TabStop | False |
| Text | (blank) |

Make sure you set the `Locked` property to `True` – we don't want the user trying to change this AutoNumber field!

**17.** Onwards to `Text2`:

| Property | Value |
|---|---|
| Name | txtFirstName |
| DataSource | datCustomers |
| DataField | FirstName |
| MaxLength | 20 |
| TabIndex | 5 |
| Text | (blank) |

**18.** And `Text3`:

| Property | Value |
|---|---|
| Name | txtMI |
| DataSource | datCustomers |
| DataField | MI |
| MaxLength | 1 |
| TabIndex | 7 |
| Text | (blank) |

**19.** Behold the fourth text box – `Text4`:

| Property | Value |
|---|---|
| Name | txtLastName |
| DataSource | datCustomers |
| DataField | LastName |
| MaxLength | 20 |
| TabIndex | 9 |
| Text | (blank) |

**20.** And `Text5`...

| Property | Value |
|---|---|
| Name | txtAddress1 |
| DataSource | datCustomers |
| DataField | Address1 |
| MaxLength | 30 |
| TabIndex | 11 |
| Text | (blank) |

**21.** Here's the one for `Text6`.

| Property | Value |
|---|---|
| Name | txtAddress2 |
| DataSource | datCustomers |
| DataField | Address2 |
| MaxLength | 30 |
| TabIndex | 13 |
| Text | (blank) |

**22.** Now let's work with `Text7`:

| Property | Value |
|---|---|
| Name | txtCity |
| DataSource | datCustomers |
| DataField | City |
| MaxLength | 30 |
| TabIndex | 15 |
| Text | (blank) |

**23.** Go make a sandwich while I do the next one for you. No, actually, I won't after all. *You'll* have to do `Text8`:

| Property | Value |
|---|---|
| Name | txtState |
| DataSource | datCustomers |
| DataField | State |
| MaxLength | 2 |
| TabIndex | 17 |
| Text | (blank) |

**24.** Here's `Text9`:

| Property | Value |
|---|---|
| Name | txtZipCode |
| DataSource | datCustomers |
| DataField | Zip |
| MaxLength | 9 |
| TabIndex | 19 |
| Text | (blank) |

**25.** At last, at last – the end of text boxes. Let's give a big hand to `Text10`:

| Property | Value |
|---|---|
| Name | txtPhone |
| DataSource | datCustomers |
| DataField | Phone |
| MaxLength | 10 |
| TabIndex | 21 |
| Text | (blank) |

**26.** Now we get to do buttons. Buttons are easy. Here's `Command1`:

| Property | Value |
|---|---|
| Name | cmdAddMe |
| Caption | &Add Me |
| TabIndex | 22 |

**27.** And `Command2`.

| Property | Value |
|---|---|
| Name | cmdCancel |
| Cancel | True |
| Caption | &Cancel |
| TabIndex | 23 |

**28.** What, only 2 buttons? Well, now we're almost done. Just check the properties of the form:

| Property | Value |
|---|---|
| Name | frmCustomerNew |
| BorderStyle | 3-Fixed Dialog |
| Caption | Welcome, New Customer! |
| Moveable | False |
| StartUpPosition | 2-Center Screen |

**29.** And your new form should look similar to the form shown here:

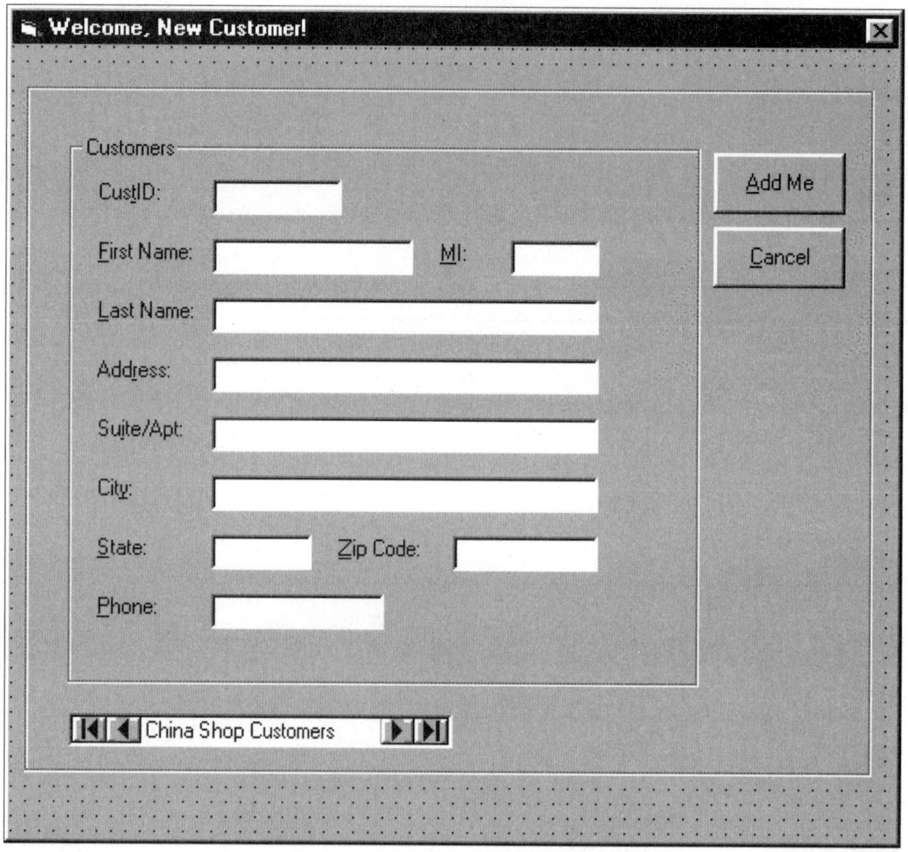

**30.** Save the China Shop project.

### *Discussion*

Again, no one had any real problems completing this exercise. "Constructing forms is one of the least interesting parts of VB programming once the novelty wears off, at least if you're following a set of instructions," I told the class, and there were some ironic nods of assent. "I can't deny that having to change all those properties is kind of boring. But it's a necessary part of programming, and when you're designing the interface and making decisions about the properties as you go, it's a little less tedious."

I then distributed the following exercise for the class to complete.

## Exercise – Adding Code to the CustomerNew Form

1. Continue working with the `frmCustomerNew` form.
2. Double-click on the form, and place the following code in its General Declarations section:

```
Option Explicit

Private m_blnAddSuccessful As Boolean
```

3. Next, add this code to the form's `Activate` event procedure:

```
Private Sub Form_Activate()

datCustomers.Recordset.AddNew
txtFirstName.SetFocus

End Sub
```

4. Now type this code into the form's `QueryUnload` event procedure:

```
Private Sub Form_QueryUnload(Cancel As Integer, UnloadMode As
     ↳Integer)

If g_intCustomerNumber > 0 Then
  MsgBox "Your record has been added - your new customer ID is " &
     ↳ g_intCustomerNumber & vbCrLf &
        ↳"Please make a note of it using the note paper provided next
            ↳to the PC."
End If

End Sub
```

5. Take a deep, deep breath, and then type the following code into the `Validate` event procedure of the `datCustomers` data control:

```
Private Sub datCustomers_Validate(Action As Integer, Save As Integer)

m_blnAddSuccessful = False

If txtFirstName.Text = "" Then
   MsgBox "First Name must be entered"
   txtFirstName.SetFocus
   Save = False
   Action = vbDataActionCancel
   Exit Sub
End If
```

*Continued on following page*

```
If txtLastName.Text = "" Then
   MsgBox "Last Name must be entered"
   txtLastName.SetFocus
   Save = False
   Action = vbDataActionCancel
   Exit Sub
End If

If txtAddress1.Text = "" Then
   MsgBox "Address must be entered"
   txtAddress1.SetFocus
   Save = False
   Action = vbDataActionCancel
   Exit Sub
End If

If txtCity.Text = "" Then
   MsgBox "City must be entered"
   txtCity.SetFocus
   Save = False
   Action = vbDataActionCancel
   Exit Sub
End If

If txtState.Text = "" Then
   MsgBox "State must be entered"
   txtState.SetFocus
   Save = False
   Action = vbDataActionCancel
   Exit Sub
End If

If txtZipCode.Text = "" Then
   MsgBox "Zip Code must be entered"
   txtZipCode.SetFocus
   Save = False
   Action = vbDataActionCancel
   Exit Sub
End If

m_blnAddSuccessful = True

End Sub
```

**6.** Now move on and add this code to the `txtFirstName_KeyPress` event procedure:

```
Private Sub txtFirstName_KeyPress(KeyAscii As Integer)

If KeyAscii >= 97 And KeyAscii <= 122 Then
   KeyAscii = KeyAscii - 32
End If

End Sub
```

**7.** Copy and paste the same code into the `txtLastName_KeyPress` event procedure:

```
Private Sub txtLastName_KeyPress(KeyAscii As Integer)

If KeyAscii >= 97 And KeyAscii <= 122 Then
   KeyAscii = KeyAscii - 32
End If

End Sub
```

**8.** And the same again for the `KeyPress` event procedure of `txtMI`:

```
Private Sub txtMI_KeyPress(KeyAscii As Integer)

If KeyAscii >= 97 And KeyAscii <= 122 Then
   KeyAscii = KeyAscii - 32
End If

End Sub
```

**9.** And the same code once more for the `txtAddress1 KeyPress` event procedure:

```
Private Sub txtAddress1_KeyPress(KeyAscii As Integer)

If KeyAscii >= 97 And KeyAscii <= 122 Then
   KeyAscii = KeyAscii - 32
End If

End Sub
```

**10.** Yep – you've guessed it: paste the self-same code into the **`KeyPress`** event procedure for **`txtAddress2`**:

```
Private Sub txtAddress2_KeyPress(KeyAscii As Integer)

If KeyAscii >= 97 And KeyAscii <= 122 Then
   KeyAscii = KeyAscii - 32
End If

End Sub
```

**11.** And, for the penultimate time, copy that same block of code into the **`txtCity_KeyPress`** event procedure:

```
Private Sub txtCity_KeyPress(KeyAscii As Integer)

If KeyAscii >= 97 And KeyAscii <= 122 Then
   KeyAscii = KeyAscii - 32
End If

End Sub
```

**12.** And finally, paste the same code into the **`txtState_KeyPress`** event procedure:

```
Private Sub txtState_KeyPress(KeyAscii As Integer)

If KeyAscii >= 97 And KeyAscii <= 122 Then
   KeyAscii = KeyAscii - 32
End If

End Sub
```

**13.** Now type this code into the **`KeyPress`** event procedure for **`txtPhone`**:

```
Private Sub txtPhone_KeyPress(KeyAscii As Integer)

If KeyAscii = 8 Then Exit Sub

If KeyAscii < 48 Or KeyAscii > 57 Then
    KeyAscii = 0
End If

End Sub
```

**14.** You can copy and paste that same code into the `txtZipCode_KeyPress` event procedure:

```
Private Sub txtZipCode_KeyPress(KeyAscii As Integer)

If KeyAscii = 8 Then Exit Sub

If KeyAscii < 48 Or KeyAscii > 57 Then
   KeyAscii = 0
End If

End Sub
```

**15.** Now move right along to the `cmdAddMe` command button and add this code to its `Click` event procedure:

```
Private Sub cmdAddMe_Click()

g_intCustomerNumber = txtCustID.Text
datCustomers.Recordset.Update
If m_blnAddSuccessful = True Then Unload Me

End Sub
```

**16.** Finally in this exercise, key the following code into the `cmdCancel_Click` event procedure:

```
Private Sub cmdCancel_Click()

datCustomers.Recordset.CancelUpdate
g_intCustomerNumber = 0
Unload Me

End Sub
```

**17.** Save the China Shop project.

***Discussion***

"I'm sure you noticed," I said, "that the code for this form is very similar to the code for the `Customers` form we created last week – in fact, the form itself is almost identical – with just a few exceptions."

"I did notice that," Kate said. "This form has just two command buttons whereas the `Customers` form has five, and the data control is invisible on this form."

"That's right," I agreed. "The forms are very similar, and their differences are attributable to the different audiences that will be using them. Unlike the `Customers` form, which will be used by the China Shop staff for customer information maintenance, this `CustomersNew` form will be used by the customer themselves to enter their own information. For that reason, we don't need a visible data control – we don't want the customer to be able to move through the `Customers` table. We also don't want them to be able to delete a record, and for that reason we have just the two command buttons – Add Me and Cancel."

"The code is similar as well," Dave observed, "but there are some significant differences. Can you explain them?"

"Sure thing, Dave," I said, "let's start with the `Activate` event procedure of the form...."

```
Private Sub Form_Activate()

datCustomers.Recordset.AddNew
txtFirstName.SetFocus

End Sub
```

"We need to remember how this form is displayed," I said. "Picture this – the customer has been interacting with the `CustomerLookup` form, and can't find a record belonging to them in the list box. If they want to make a purchase of china, they're going to have to enter their information – and they announce their intention to do that by clicking on the I'm not in the list, please add me button on `frmCustomerLookup`. When they do, our `CustomerNew` form is displayed. Since the sole intent of this form is to permit the customer to add a record to the `Customers` table with their own unique information, as soon as the form is displayed, we execute the `AddNew` method of the `Recordset`, and set the focus to the `txtFirstName` text box."

"That makes sense to me," Linda said. "And without a data control, all the customer sees is a blank form – is that right?"

"That's right, Linda," I said, "Actually, the Customer ID *will* have a value in it. Since **CustID** is an AutoNumber field, Access will assign a value for the new record, and place it in the text box bound to the **CustID** field:"

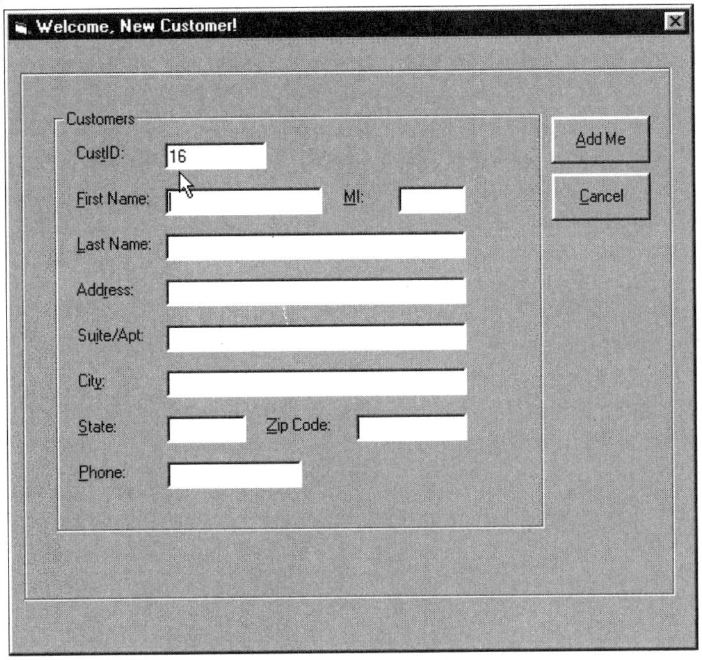

"Then as soon as the customer has completed the rest of the information," Kevin added, "they click on the Add Me button, and a new record with their information is created in the **Customers** table."

"That's right, Kevin," I said. "Let's take a look at the code in the **Click** event procedure of the **cmdAddMe** command button right now. As you can see, the first thing we do is take the value of the **Text** property of the **txtCustID** text box, and store it in the global variable **g_intCustomerNumber**, so that the rest of the program can now use the new customer's identifier:"

```
Private Sub cmdAddMe_Click()

g_intCustomerNumber = txtCustID.Text
```

"Where does the value for that **Text** property come from again?" Rhonda asked.

"Because the **CustID** field in the Customer table is an AutoNumber field," I said, "Access assigns that number on its own. As soon as we execute the **AddNew** method of the **Recordset**, the number appears in the **txtCustID** field on the form."

I paused to give the students an opportunity to ask questions. On this occasion, there were none, so I continued with my explanation.

"After that," I went on, "we execute the `Update` method of the recordset, which ensures that the new customer record is added to the `Customers` table. Remember, if you execute the `AddNew` method but forget to execute the `Update` method, the record is **never** added to the recordset:"

```
datCustomers.Recordset.Update
```

Tom had a question.

"What's going on with that `If` statement?" he asked.

```
If m_blnAddSuccessful = True Then Unload Me
```

"`m_blnAddSuccessful`," I said, "is a Boolean variable that we declared in the General Declarations section of the form..."

```
Option Explicit

Private m_blnAddSuccessful As Boolean
```

"...if its value is `True`, we then execute the `Unload` statement."

"How does the value of this variable become `True`?" Melissa asked, "and why do we need it at all? I just checked the code on `frmCustomers` – we didn't have a variable like this on *that* form."

"That's true, Melissa," I agreed. "We need the `m_blnAddSuccessful` variable because the `Click` event procedure `cmdAddMe` executes two statements – `Update` and `Unload` – consecutively. Each method triggers the `Validate` event of the data control."

"Is that a problem?" Kathy asked.

"It can be," I said. "For instance, it would be a problem where the customer fails to complete a mandatory piece of information – their `City`, for example. When the `Update` method is executed, the `Validate` event is triggered, and the customer receives an error message. The problem then is that immediately after doing that, we execute the `Unload` method."

"I'm beginning to see the potential problem," Dave said. "If we execute the `Unload` method immediately after the `Update` method, when we're still missing some field information, the `Validate` event of the data control is triggered again, and the customer will receive the same error message."

"That's right, Dave," I said. "For that reason, we need some way to determine if the `Update` method resulted in a record which can be added to the `Customers` table. That's where the variable `m_blnAddSuccessful` comes in. We initially set its value to `False` in the `Validate` event procedure of the data control – then, if the `Validate` event procedure agrees with all of the customer's information, the value of `m_blnAddSuccessful` is set to `True` in the last line of code in the event procedure."

"The `Validate` event..." Peter said, "is that the event procedure where we have all of our validation code?"

"That's right, Peter," I said. "As soon as the customer has completed their information, they click on the Add Me command button. The `Update` method of the recordset is then executed, which triggers the `Validate` event procedure of the data control. If anything is wrong, such as the customer failing to fill in information that is mandatory – we then display a warning message to the customer, set focus to the text box with the missing or invalid information, set the `Save` argument to false, the `Action` argument to `vbDataActionCancel`, and then exit the sub procedure using the `Exit Sub` statement. Like this..."

I then displayed a portion of the `Validate` event procedure that shows the relevant code:

```
Private Sub datCustomers_Validate(Action As Integer, Save As Integer)

m_blnAddSuccessful = False

If txtFirstName.Text = "" Then
   MsgBox "First Name must be entered"
   txtFirstName.SetFocus
   Save = False
   Action = vbDataActionCancel
   Exit Sub
End If
```

"There's that `m_blnAddSuccessful` variable again," Mary said.

"That's right, Mary," I said. "Notice that we immediately set its value to `False`. If the code in the `Validate` event procedure determines that any of the information on the form is incorrect, the value of `m_blnAddSuccessful` *remains* `False`. That's why we have the `If` statement in `cmdAddMe` – to check to see if `m_blnAddSuccessful` is `True`. If it is, we execute the `Unload` method of the form – if not, we leave the form displayed. "

"How does the value of `m_blnAddSuccessful` get set to `True`?" Blaine asked.

"At the very end of the **Validate** event procedure, and only then" I answered, "we set its value to **True**. This line of code will **only** be executed if all of the validation tests are passed."

I then displayed the last portion of the **Validate** event procedure on the classroom projector:

```
If txtZipCode.Text = "" Then
   MsgBox "Zip Code must be entered"
   txtZipCode.SetFocus
   Save = False
   Action = vbDataActionCancel
   Exit Sub
End If

m_blnAddSuccessful = True

End Sub
```

"But do we really need to bother with all of this?" Ward asked. "If we don't check for the value of **m_blnAddSuccessful**, we would just execute the **Validate** event procedure a second time – would that hurt?"

"Unfortunately," I said, "that would mean that the user would receive two messages every time they forgot to complete information in a text box."

"I see," Ward said, "that *would* be pretty annoying."

Valerie had a question.

"Can you explain the code in the **QueryUnload** event procedure?" Valerie said.

"I'd be glad to, Valerie," I said as I displayed it:

```
Private Sub Form_QueryUnload(Cancel As Integer, UnloadMode As Integer)

If g_intCustomerNumber > 0 Then
   MsgBox "Your record has been added - your new customer ID is " &
     ↪ g_intCustomerNumber & vbCrLf &
       ↪ "Please make a note of it using the note paper provided next
          ↪to the PC."
End If

End Sub
```

"Remember," I said, "the QueryUnload event is triggered just before the form is actually unloaded. The first thing we do is use an If statement to determine whether the user has successfully added their customer record: we do this by checking if the value of g_intCustomerNumber is greater than zero. If it is we display – as a courtesy – their new customer number along with a reminder to make a note of it on a slip of paper to be stocked near the China Shop PC. At that point, the form is unloaded, and the user is returned to the China Shop's Main form, where the remainder of the code in cmdIllTakeIt will then execute."

"How will the value of g_intCustomerNumber be set to zero?" Chuck asked. "If the user clicks on the Cancel button?"

"That's right, Chuck, that's the only way," I said, as I displayed the code for the cmdCancel event procedure on the classroom projector.

```
Private Sub cmdCancel_Click()

datCustomers.Recordset.CancelUpdate
g_intCustomerNumber = 0
Unload Me

End Sub
```

No one had any more questions, and I then spent some time verifying the process with the class by selecting china items, clicking on the I'll Take It command button, and trying all of the possibilities presented by the CustomerAsk form. (For my reader at home, now is a good time to do the same!) After a few minutes, the class seemed content that the program was working as advertised.

## What Remains to be Done

"The changes we have made to the program so far this morning," I said, "are the last of the visible changes we'll be making to the China Shop project. All of the remaining modifications will be invisible to the user."

"Such as?" Lou asked.

"Well, let's check the requirements statement and see what's left," I said, as I perused the remaining items that we still had to complete. "We'll need to modify the program to be able to..."

1. **Load the lstBrands list box from the database instead of from the Prices.txt disk file**
2. **Change the color of every form**
3. **Calculate Prices based on prices found in the database instead of from the Prices.txt disk file**
4. **Write a record of the Sales Transaction to the Transactions table**
5. **Print a Sales receipt**

"Will we be able to complete all of these today?" Mary asked.

"Unfortunately not," I said. "We'll only have time to complete item #1 on this list today – modifying the program to load items in the list box from the China database instead of from the `Prices.txt` disk file. Right now, I'd like you to take a break, and when you return, I'll ask you to complete an exercise that will do exactly that."

When the class returned from break, I distributed the following exercise for them to complete.

## Exercise – Adding two Data Controls to the Main Form

In this exercise, you'll add two data controls to the main form of the China Shop project. These data controls will provide the China Shop program with a connection to the `Inventory` and `Transaction` tables of the `China` database.

1. Go into Project Explorer and select the China Shop's `Main` form.
2. Add two data controls to the form. The data controls will not be visible when the program runs, so you may place them anywhere you wish, although I would advise placing them *roughly* according to the screen shot below:

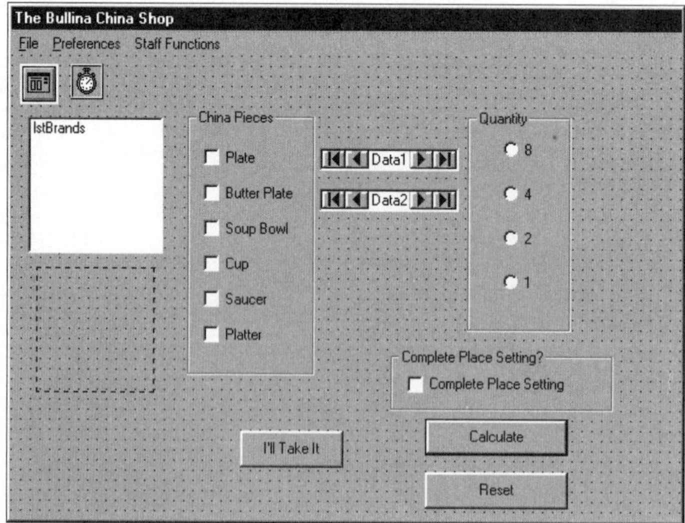

3. Use the following table to make changes to the properties of the data control currently named `Data1`:

| Property | Value |
|---|---|
| Name | `datInventory` |
| Caption | Inventory |
| DatabaseName | C:\VBFiles\China\China.mdb |
| EOFAction | 0-MoveLast |
| RecordsetType | 1-Dynaset |
| RecordSource | Inventory |
| Visible | False |

4. Now change the `Data2` data control to match this table:

| Property | Value |
|---|---|
| Name | datTransactions |
| Caption | Transactions |
| DatabaseName | C:\VBFiles\China\China.mdb |
| EOFAction | 0-MoveLast |
| RecordsetType | 1-Dynaset |
| RecordSource | Transactions |
| Visible | False |

5. Save the China Shop project.

***Discussion***

"These two data controls," I said, "will provide us with the connections to the `Inventory` and `Transactions` tables we'll need to implement the rest of our China Shop modifications. We'll use the `datInventory` data control to load up the `lstBrands` list box and to look up china item prices, and we'll use the `datTransactions` data control to write transaction records to the `Transactions` table. In the next series of exercises, we'll be using the `datInventory` data control. First, I'm going to ask you to write a procedure of your own that will load the `lstBrands` list box with unique china brands."

## Creating the LoadListBox Subprocedure

"Did you say write our own procedure?" Rachel asked. "I've never done that."

"That's OK, Rachel," I said, "we wrote our own procedures in last semester's intro course. Procedures allow you to streamline your code, and are especially useful when you have a piece of code that needs to be executed from various places within your program. I like to write my own procedures because it makes my code more readable. But don't worry, the instructions I have for you are pretty precise. I think you'll be able to handle it with no trouble."

No one had any questions, and so I handed out this next exercise.

### Exercise – Creating the LoadListBox Subprocedure

1. Continue working with the `Main` form of the China Shop project.
2. Make sure the code window is open, and then select Tools | Add Procedure from the Visual Basic main menu (if the code window is not open, this option will not be available).
3. A dialog box will be displayed. Complete the entries according to the screenshot below...

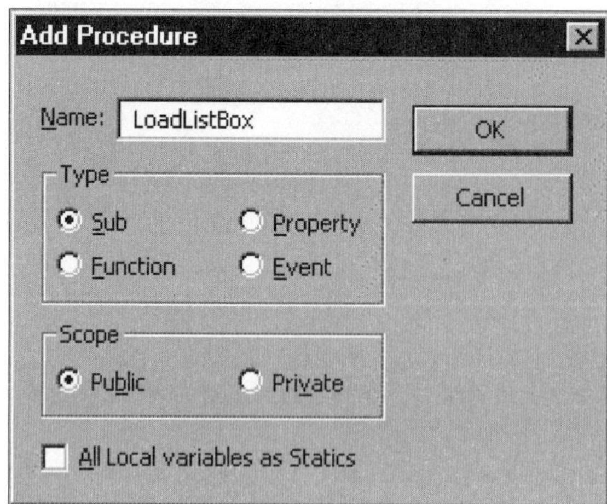

4. ...and click on the OK button. The code window for the **LoadListBox** subprocedure will now appear.
5. Enter the following code between the subprocedure header and the **End Sub** line.

```
Public Sub LoadListBox()

Dim strSQL As String

strSQL = "SELECT DISTINCT Inventory.Brand FROM Inventory"

datInventory.RecordSource = strSQL
datInventory.Refresh

Do While Not datInventory.Recordset.EOF
   lstBrands.AddItem datInventory.Recordset.Fields("Brand").Value
   datInventory.Recordset.MoveNext
Loop

End Sub
```

6. Save the China Shop project.
7. At this point, there's no way to test this subprocedure, but don't worry, we'll do that in the next exercise.

#### *Discussion*

"I'm not quite sure what we're doing here," Lou said. "It looks like we're modifying properties of the data control in code – can we do that?"

"You're right, Lou," I said, "that's exactly what we're doing – and yes, we can do that. We initialized the data control at design time with some initial values, but here at run time we're modifying the **RecordSource** property of the data control with a SQL statement to build an entirely different recordset from the one specified in the data control..."

"What is that **strSQL** variable?" Kathy asked.

"**strSQL**," I answered, "is just a plain old string variable that I use as a container for SQL statements whenever I'm writing SQL in code. I first declare a string variable..."

```
Dim strSQL As String
```

"... and then I assign the SQL statement I wish to write to the variable..."

```
strSQL = "SELECT DISTINCT Inventory.Brand FROM Inventory"
```

"...I think it makes writing the code a little easier. As you can see, in the next line of code I assign the **RecordSource** property of the data control the value of the variable **strSQL**..."

```
datInventory.RecordSource = strSQL
```

"... and then execute the **Refresh** method of the data control to rebuild the recordset...."

```
datInventory.Refresh
```

"...I could have just as easily assigned the **RecordSource** property the SQL literal itself, but I think this is a little more elegant."

"Can you explain what the word **DISTINCT** means in the SQL statement?" Ward asked.

"**SELECT DISTINCT Inventory.Brand**," I said, "tells Visual Basic to return a record for each unique brand in the **Inventory** table. Although we have 21 records in the **Inventory** table, we have only *three* unique brands – **Corelle**, **Faberware** and **Mikasa** – therefore, this SQL statement returns only three records in the recordset."

"And at that point," Dave said, "it looks like we're using a **Do...Loop** to loop through each of the three records, using the **AddItem** method to load the list box with the **Value** property of the **Brand** field of each record..."

```
Do While Not datInventory.Recordset.EOF
   lstBrands.AddItem datInventory.Recordset.Fields("Brand").Value
   datInventory.Recordset.MoveNext
Loop
```

"That's exactly right, Dave," I said.

"Suppose we hadn't specified '**SELECT DISTINCT**' in the SQL statement?" Rhonda asked. "What would have happened?"

"We would then have created a recordset containing 21 records," I replied, "and the list box would have duplicate brand names in it."

"That would be a catastrophe, wouldn't it?" Ward said. "I can't wait to see this code in action. Can we run the program now?"

"Before we do that, Ward," I said, "we need to modify the **Load** procedure of **frmMain** to populate the list box using our newly written **LoadListBox** subprocedure. Remember that we want to do it this way instead of loading up the list box using the contents of the **Prices.txt** file. You may recall that currently the **Load** procedure of **frmMain** executes the **ReadPrices** subprocedure, which opens the **Prices.txt** file, reads all of the records in the file into a variable array, and then loads the brand names into the list box. In the next exercise, we'll say goodbye to that subprocedure – we no longer need it, nor the **Prices.txt** file anymore."

No one had any further queries, so I distributed the exercise.

## Exercise – Modifying frmMain's Load Event Procedure

In this exercise, you'll modify the **Load** event procedure of **frmMain** so that the **LoadListBox** subprocedure executes when the **Main** form of the China Shop is loaded.

1. Continue working with the **Main** form.
2. Modify the **Load** event procedure of **frmMain** so that it looks like the snippet shown below (modified code is highlighted, as ever). **Be sure to delete the line of code reading `Call ReadPrices`** – we no longer need it.

```
Private Sub Form_Load()

Call ReadTheRegistry
Call LoadListBox

If m_blnDateDisplay Then
   Call mnuPreferencesDateandTimeOn_Click
Else
   Call mnuPreferencesDateandTimeOff_Click
End If

frmMain.BackColor = m_lngBackColor

If g_strUser = "ADMINISTRATOR" Then
   mnuStaff.Visible = True
Else
   mnuStaff.Visible = False
End If

End Sub
```

3. Save the project.
4. To ensure that the program is no longer dependent upon the `Prices.txt` file, use Windows Explorer to rename `Prices.txt` to `Prices.old` in your `C:\VBFfiles\China` directory.
5. Run the China Shop program. Log in, and when the `Main` form of the China Shop appears, verify that the `lstBrands` list box is being loaded from the database. At this point, don't try and use the program any further – otherwise it will 'fall over'. This is because, since we are no longer opening and reading the `Prices.txt` file (which contains both inventory and price information), the China Shop program currently has no way to calculate a sales price quotation. Don't worry, we'll take care of that problem next week!

### *Discussion*

Virtually no one had any trouble completing this exercise, and I noticed quite a bit of enjoyment on the faces of my students.

"This is pretty impressive," Ward said. "I don't think the impact of what we've done with the China Shop hit home until I realized that those list box items are now being retrieved from a database, not a disk file. We've totally database-enabled the China Shop!"

"I agree, Ward, this is all quite impressive," I answered, "but we still have some work ahead of us. Next week we'll need to modify the code in the `cmdCalculate` command button to calculate the sales quotation based on prices stored in the `Inventory` table. And we still need to write some code to write a transaction record of the customer's purchase to the `Transactions` table, and some code to print a Sales receipt. But we're nearly done. Complete those items, plus a few odds and ends next week, and we'll be able to deliver this program to Joe Bullina sometime next Saturday."

"We still have a half hour left," Melissa said, "we aren't done, are we? What tricks do you have up your sleeve for the last half hour of class?"

# A Digression on Data Objects

"You're right, Melissa, we're not done yet," I said. "The last thing I want to do today is to briefly discuss Data Access Objects – something I've been promising to talk to you about for the last few weeks. All I'll have time to do here is give you a 'taster' of what we can do with Data Objects – the details will have to wait for another course [and another book! – ed.]."

"You may recall," I continued, "that I had promised I'd show you how to access the `China` database without using a data control – I think you'll find this technique amazingly simple and flexible."

"Why would we want to do that?" Valerie asked. "What's wrong with the data control?"

"Nothing's *wrong* with the data control," I said, "but learning to connect to a database without using a data control is a good idea."

"Why is that?" Ward asked.

"There are probably three good reasons," I replied. "First, connecting to a database using Data Objects is faster than using the data control to make the same connection. Secondly, I think we've already seen that using the data control can be a bit 'buggy' at times. Third, employers find a knowledge of Data Objects to be a feather in your cap – a sign of your programming prowess and flexibility."

"How do we know when to use Data Objects?" Kathy asked. "Should we always use Data Objects instead of the data control?"

"Not at all," I said, "The data control is frequently preferable to using Data Objects. We've all seen that nothing is much easier than placing a data control on the form, setting a few properties, and then binding the recordset to some bound controls. But in my experience, whenever I find myself making a data control invisible, and writing a bunch of code that directly executes the underlying recordset's methods, that suggests to me that it might be a good idea to abandon the data control and use Data Objects directly.

"As a practical example, let's take the code in the `LoadListBox` subprocedure. What do we have there? We have a data control on a form. We then modify properties of the data control at run time, generate a recordset which the user never sees, and then loop through that recordset to populate the `lstBrands` list box with china brands."

"That's pretty invisible isn't it?" Dave said. "The user never even knows that a database connection created the list box items – sounds like a good reason to use Data Objects, doesn't it?"

"I agree," I said. "Instead of using the `datInventory` data control to make the connection to the database, we could use Data Objects in this instance."

"Is there anything special we need to do in order to use Data Objects?" Valerie asked.

"Yes there is," I answered. "First, we need to include the Data Access Objects library in our project. We do that by selecting Project | References from the Visual Basic menu bar..."

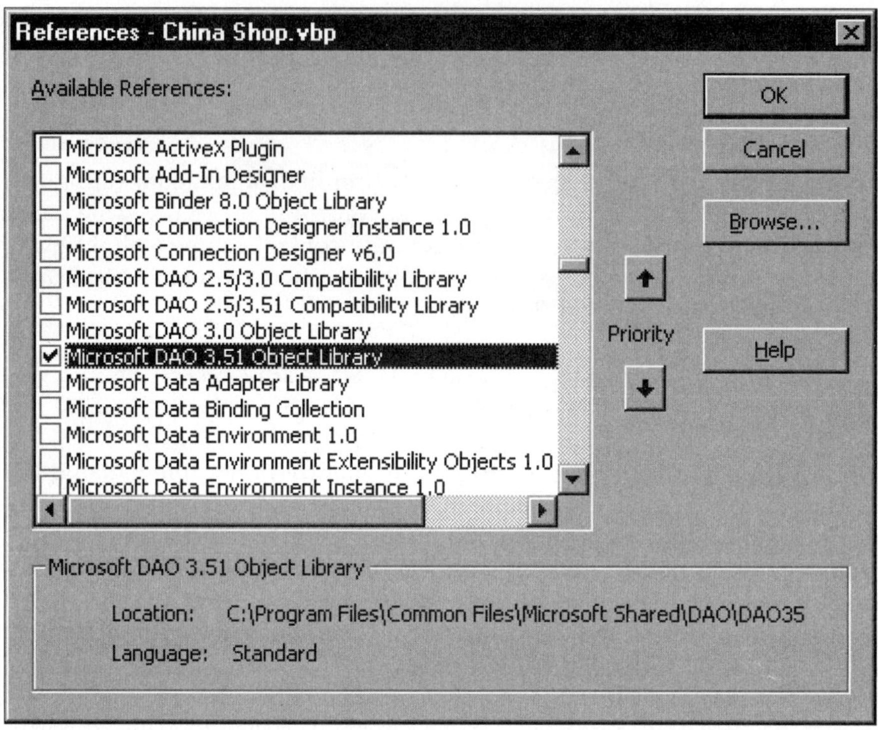


"There's more than one type of Data Object library; the newest is called ADO, just to confuse us, I'm sure! But we'll be using DAO," I said, "so we'll choose the Microsoft DAO 3.51 Object Library."

I then selected the Microsoft DAO 3.51 Object Library for inclusion within the project.

"Once we've done that," I continued, "we can then write some alternative code to the original `LoadListBox` subprocedure."

I then created another procedure called **`LoadListBoxDAO`**:

```
Public Sub LoadListBoxDAO()

Dim strSQL As String

Dim Ws As Workspace
Dim Db As Database
Dim Rs As Recordset

strSQL = "SELECT DISTINCT Inventory.Brand FROM Inventory"

Set Ws = DBEngine.Workspaces(0)
Set Db = Ws.OpenDatabase("c:\vbfiles\china\china.mdb")
Set Rs = Db.OpenRecordset(strSQL, dbOpenDynaset)

Do While Not Rs.EOF
   lstBrands.AddItem Rs.Fields("Brand").Value
   Rs.MoveNext
Loop

End Sub
```

"As you can see," I said, "all references to the data control are gone – in fact, if we wanted to, we could just delete it from the form. The connection to the China Database is achieved with just a few lines of code."

"What are those **`Dim`** statements?" Kevin asked. "**`Workspace`**, **`Database`**, and **`Recordset`**, are those data types? We haven't seen those before, have we?"

"Kevin's right," Rhonda said. "In the past, when I've typed the word **`Dim`** in my code window, I've never seen these pop up as possible data types before. What are those, and where did they come from?"

"You both raise good questions," I said. "Let me answer those by saying that not everything that follows the word **`As`** in a Visual Basic declaration statement is a data type."

"What are they then?" Lou asked.

"In addition to data types," I said, "some are **object types** – Visual Basic Objects – and that's what **`Workspace`**, **`Database`** and **`Recordset`** are. Using these names, we can create objects – such as recordset objects – 'on the fly'. We can create them by declaring them in our code and then use them in subsequent code. So we can just create a recordset..."

```
Dim Rs As Recordset
```

"...by declaring it as an **object variable**. This creates a recordset called `Rs` that we can then refer to by name in our code."

## Declaring Object Variables

"In answer to your question Rhonda, the reason why you haven't seen these before, is that you never had a project that included a reference to the DAO Object Library. Once we included the DAO Object Library in our project, these Variable types showed up in addition to the others that we're more familiar with."

I then brought up the code window, created a `Test` subprocedure, and typed a variable declaration statement like this. As soon as I typed the word `As` the following screen shot was displayed:

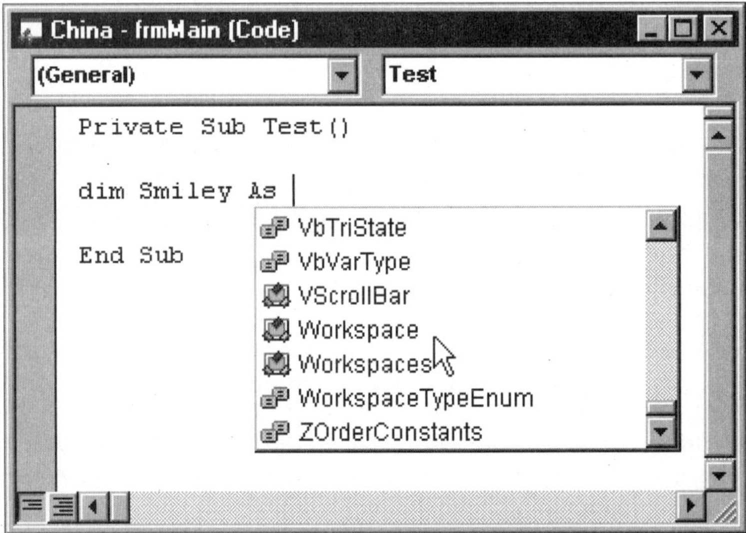


"Do you see the `Workspace` type?" I asked. "All in all, there are probably several hundred different variable types that you can declare. By the way, notice the symbol next to the word `Workspace` – it signifies that `Workspace` is an **Object** – something we'll talk about more in an upcoming Visual Basic course here at the university – and using that type in a variable declaration declares what is known as an **Object Variable**."

"That sounds confusing," Bob said.

"It doesn't have to be, Bob," I said. "If you think of object variables as references to something that exists elsewhere – like a `Database` or a `Recordset` – I think you'll find it easier to understand. Now, since in our case we're using data objects to connect to the China Shop database, we first need to declare an 'instance' of each object that we need to make that connection. In the case of DAO, this means declaring a `Workspace` object, a `Database` object and a `Recordset` object."

"That sounds very much like the hierarchy we see when we first start up Microsoft Access," Dave suggested, "except that I'm not familiar with a `Workspace` object."

"You're right, Dave," I said, "The actual object hierarchy in Microsoft Access is `DBEngine`, followed by `Workspace`, followed by `Database`, and `Recordset:`"

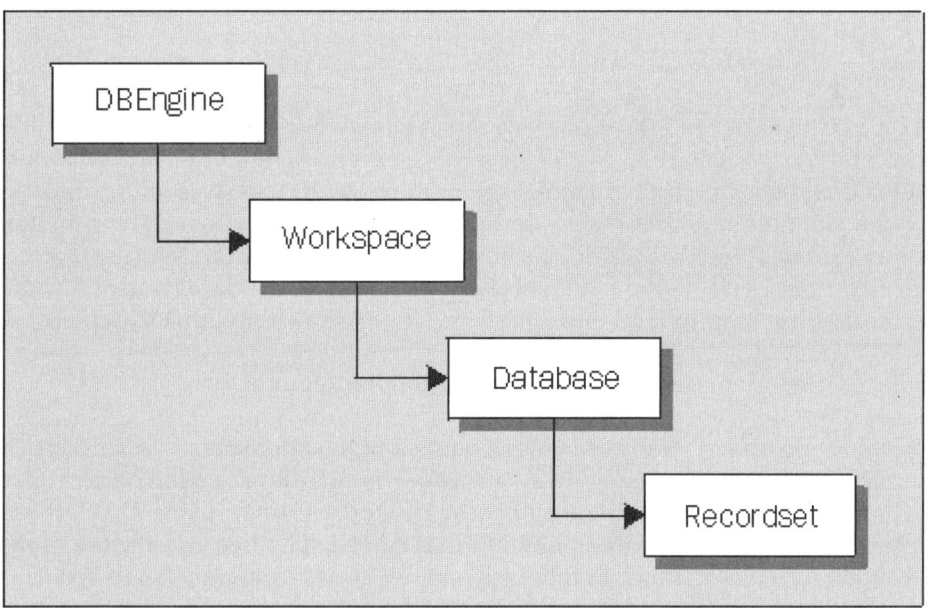


"You didn't declare an object variable for the `DBEngine`?" Dave asked. "Why not?"

"It's not required," I answered. "The rules for DAO state that we only need to declare an object variable for `Workspace`, `Database` and `Recordset`, the `DBEngine` object is implicit. Once we've declared all of these objects, we're in business, and we can start using them in conjunction with our code."

"I noticed," Ward said, "that after we declared an instance of the `Workspace`, `Database` and `Recordset` objects, we then executed `Set` statements. What exactly are those for?"

## The Set Statement

"The `Dim` statements declare a **type** for each of the objects that we need to declare," I said, "but beyond that, the `Dim` statements don't really do anything. For instance, they don't specify the name of the `Database`, or its location, or the name and type of the recordset. In order to provide Visual Basic with that information, we then need to execute a `Set` statement for each one of the object variables that we declare using the `Dim` statement. For instance, this statement..."

```
Set Ws = DBEngine.Workspaces(0)
```

"... creates a `Workspace` object within which our `Database` object can exist. This statement..."

```
Set Db = Ws.OpenDatabase("c:\vbfiles\china\china.mdb")
```

"...specifies the name and location of the `Database` we wish to open, within the `Workspace` that we previously declared. Notice that we're executing the `OpenDatabase` method of the `Workspace` and passing it the name of the path to our database as an argument. And again, notice the 'dot notation' that we use to refer to different objects and their methods. This all has a similar effect to what we do when we select a `Database` in Microsoft Access, or when we specify a `Database` in the `DatabaseName` property of the data control – we're telling the program that we want to read our data from. In the same way, this statement..."

```
Set Rs = Db.OpenRecordset(strSQL, dbOpenDynaset)
```

"... creates a recordset – in this instance, using a SQL statement to do so. This is really the same thing we do when we specify a `RecordsetType` and `RecordSource` property in the data control. And just as in the case of those properties, when using DAO, there are arguments to the `OpenRecordset` method that can be specified to vary the type of `Recordset` created. As I said, in this instance, we're creating a `Dynaset` type `Recordset` using the SQL statement stored in the variable `strSQL`. We could just as easily have specified a table name or a query name instead of the SQL statement."

"Can we see this in action?" Rachel asked.

"Sure thing, Rachel," I said. I then changed the `Load` event procedure of `frmMain` to execute `LoadListBoxDAO` instead of `LoadListBox`, and ran the program. I logged in, and the class watched as the `lstBrands` list box was loaded with china items just as before:

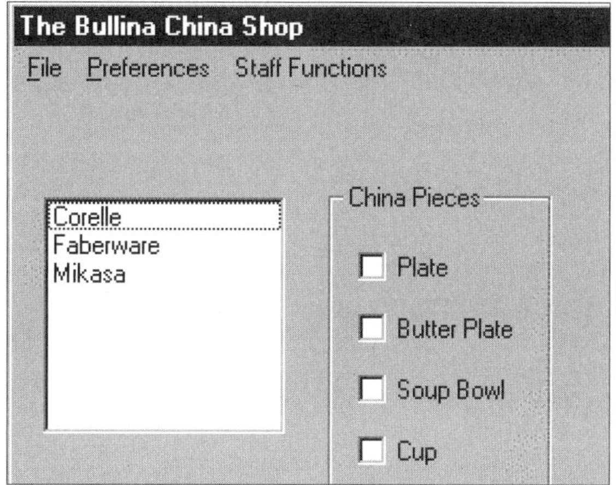


"I'm convinced," Ward said. "This works as well as using the data control. I'll need to consider using this."

"Data objects are just another skill to place in your bag of Visual Basic tricks," I said, "and it's one that some employers hold in some high regard – but don't abandon the data control either. I'll be focusing on using these object principles in your programs in a future course."

"Next week," I said, "we'll be finishing up with the modifications to the China Shop program – and don't forget, anyone who wants to travel out to the Bullina China Shop to install the program is more than welcome to do so. Joe Bullina's been known to throw a great party."

I then dismissed class for the day.

# Chapter Summary

In this chapter, we moved a long way towards integrating the China Shop's 'front-end' – the user interface – with the `China` database and the code that we created in chapters 1 thru' 9.

We started this chapter by ensuring that all customers would be able to get price quotations and proceed with the sales process once they had got their quotation. To achieve this, we created a series of forms for new and existing customers to work with, and tied these forms up with the existing China Shop program and the `China` database. We also looked a little at what Data Objects are, and how you can use them to work with data without the data control even being there.

Don't worry if you don't fully understand the implications of that brief section, as it does involve some new thinking. In a future Visual Basic Objects book, we'll go into more detail about how you work with objects, and how powerful they are. For now, just look on it as a little introduction to the wonder of objects.

Specifically, the key things we did were:

- Create the customer identification and verification processes
- Create the `CustomerAsk` form, which gives the user access to the other forms that they need to use
- Create the `CustomerLookup` form, which lets forgetful customers search for their Customer ID in a list box
- Create the `CustomerNew` form, which enables new customers to add their name and address details directly to the database

Together, these added features have substantially enhanced the elements of the program that the customer will use directly, in line with Joe Bullina's requirements.

In our final chapter, we'll add the final bits of functionality to the program that will database-enable the China Shop project. This will involve building the code to print sales receipts and automatically create transaction records, as well as a number of smaller changes that will finally integrate all of our enhancements with the original China Shop program.

Join my class next week, and let's put the project to bed!

# Enhancing the User Interface

Learn to Program Databases with Visual Basic

# Chapter 10

# Completing the China Shop Program

In last week's class, we completed all of the China Shop forms and finalized the customer identification process.

In this chapter, we'll put the finishing touches to the China Shop project and deliver the enhanced program to Joe Bullina at the China Shop. There are a number of things we need to do to make the program ready to ship:

- Add code that allows the user to change the background color of every form except the **`Login`** form
- Modify the project to read china item prices from the **`China`** database instead of from the **`Prices.txt`** disk file
- Build code that adds a transaction record to the **`Transactions`** table each time a customer makes a purchase
- Add code to print a sales receipt for the customer. This will contain details of their purchase and a reminder of their Customer ID

When we've done this, all that will remain is to test the code. When we're sure all versions work equally well, it'll be up to the class to decide which student's project will be installed in the China Shop's kiosk. Then we'll all go to Joe's for the last part of our assignment – delivering and installing our finished product. We've still got a fair amount of code to complete, so let's begin – we don't want to deliver the project late!

## Let's Finish the Program

We began our tenth and final class by discussing what needed to be done to complete our program.

"This list," I said, as I displayed it on the classroom projector, "is what remains for us to complete today. When we're done we're going to the China Shop to present the finished item to Joe Bullina and is staff. Here's the list:"

We Need to:

1. Change the color of every form based on a user's color preferences
2. Calculate a Sales Quotation using prices from the China database rather than from the Prices.txt disk file
3. Write a Transaction record of the Customer's purchase to the Transactions table
4. Print a Sales receipt

"The first thing we'll do is build the code that will 'globally' implement the user's color choices."

## Changing Form Colors Throughout the China Shop project

"Changing the color of every form in the China Shop project when the form is loaded," I said, "is probably the simplest of all the changes we have to make today. In order to do this, we need to slightly change the code already in place to change the color of **`frmMain`**, and then add some code to the **`Load`** event procedures of the other forms in the project."

"I know you mentioned this at the beginning of the course," Rachel said, "but for those of us who were not in the Introductory class, can you refresh our memory as to how the color of **`frmMain`** is changed right now?"

"I'd be glad to do that, Rachel," I replied. "Right now, whenever the user wants to change the **`BackColor`** of **`frmMain`**, they do this by selecting a menu item from the project's menu bar. A color dialog box is then displayed, and when the user selects a color, the value of that color preference is saved to a form-level **`Long`** type variable – **`m_lngBackColor`**. The **`BackColor`** property of **`frmMain`** is changed immediately to the value of that variable, and the value of the variable is then saved to the Windows Registry. Remember that saving the value in the registry means that the color choices are retained for when the program starts up the next time."

"I suspect," Dave said, "that since we now have multiple forms, we're going to need to save the user's preferred color in a global variable in our standard module – isn't that right?"

"Well said, Dave," I agreed. "Since the value of the user's selection needs to be available in every form throughout the project, a global variable declared in a standard module is the perfect place to store that value."

"As I recall," Melissa said, "we have two global variables declared already: **`g_intCustomer`** and **`g_strUser`**, and we chose to create them as global variables for exactly for that reason – they need to be accessed by code on more than one form."

"That's right, Melissa," I said. "Whenever you have a variable that needs to be accessed from more than one form, it's sensible to declare it in a standard module."

"I understand the need to declare the variable in a standard module," Linda said, "but what about all the code we already have that references the existing form-level variable? Will we have to change that code too? We must have a dozen references to it, I guess. Won't it be a real pain to find every reference and change them all?"

"Linda, you're right to an extent," I agreed. "We *will* need to declare a global variable called **`g_lngBackColor`**, and then change every instance of the existing form level variable **`m_lngBackColor`** to reference the new **`g_lngBackColor`** variable instead. But don't worry – we can do that pretty easily by using the code window's Search and Replace facility."

"Search and Replace in the code window?" Peter asked. "That's great – that could save us a lot of time."

"Yes, it will," I said. "It's a great time saver, and it will also ensure we don't miss changing any references to the variable that we're making redundant."

"Won't we also need to add code to the **`Load`** event procedures of every form?" Chuck asked. "In order to change the **`BackColor`** when the form is loaded – just as we do now with **`frmMain`**?"

"Well spotted, Chuck," I said. "We will need to do that also."

"I have a series of exercises here," I said, as there were no more questions, "that will lead us through this process. Let's start by declaring that global variable in our standard module."

## Exercise – Adding a Global Variable for Color Selection

In this exercise, you'll declare a third global variable in the China Shop project's standard module. This variable will give the program the ability to alter the **`BackColor`** properties of all the project's forms.

1. Select the China Shop program's existing **Module1** in the Project Explorer window...

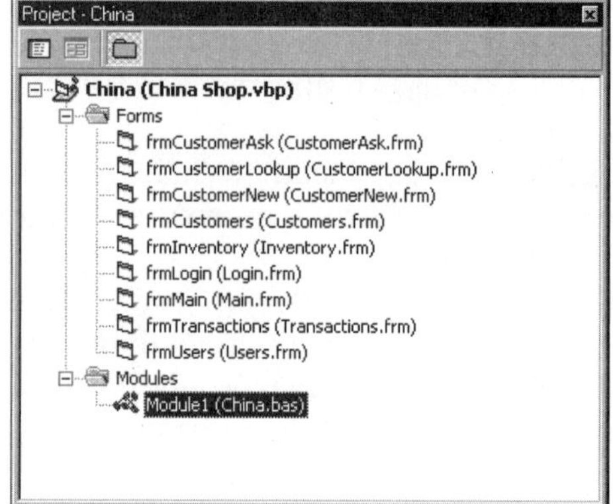


...and double-click on it to open it up.

2. This will bring up the code window for the standard module. You should already have two global variables declared, **g_intCustomerNumber** and **g_strUser**. Declare your third global variable, **g_lngBackColor**, as shown in the bottom line here:

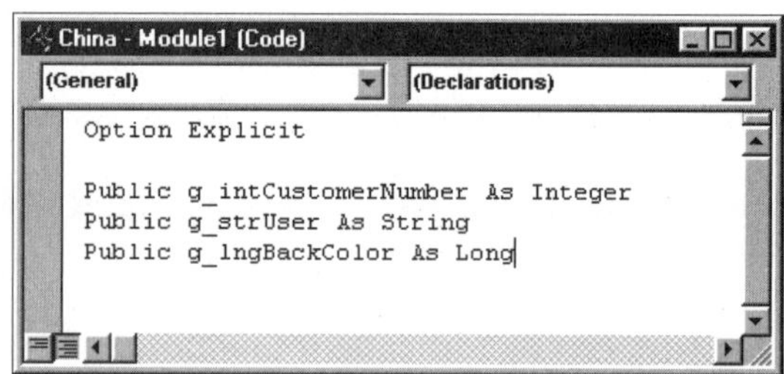


Note once again that the Hungarian notation for the **Long** variable type is **lng**, starting with a lower case 'L', and not the number '1'.

3. At this point, we should delete the declaration of the form-level variable **m_lngBackColor** from the General Declarations section of **frmMain**. To do that, find the declaration for **m_lngBackColor** in the General Declarations section of the form, select it, and delete it:

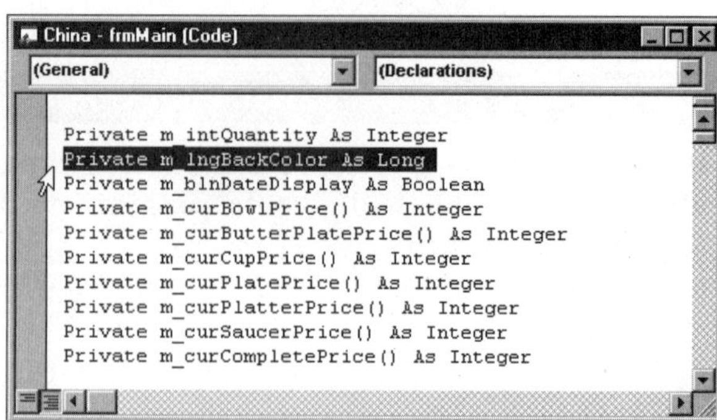

4. Save the China Shop project.

Aside from a little difficulty in finding the standard module in the Project Explorer window, everyone successfully completed this exercise.

"Now," I said, "let's see how easy it can be to change every reference from `m_lngBackColor` to `g_lngBackColor`."

I distributed an exercise to do just that.

## Exercise – Globally Replacing m_lngBackColor with g_lngBackColor

In this exercise, you'll replace every instance of `m_lngBackColor` in the China Shop project with `g_lngBackColor`.

1. Continue working with `frmMain`.
2. Make sure the code window is open, and then select Edit | Replace from the Visual Basic menu bar. Complete the Find What and Replace With text boxes according to the screenshot below. Make sure that you select Current Project as the Search type, **not** the default Current Module:

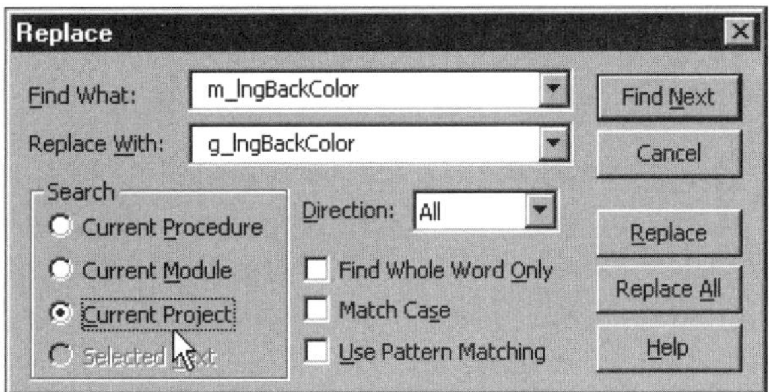


3. Now click on the Replace All button. You should see a message indicating that **six** replacements have been made.
4. Save the China Shop project.
5. At this stage, you can run the China Shop program and verify that the color change process for `frmMain` still works properly. However, at this point, only the color of `frmMain` will be changed: the other forms' colors will stay the default color until we place some code in their `Load` event procedures – we'll come to that soon.

Everyone was happy with what we'd done so far, so I handed out an exercise that would take us on to the next stage of the journey.

## Exercise – Altering several Forms' Load Event Procedure

In this exercise, you'll place code in the `Load` event procedure of every form **except** the `Login` form. This code will result in the `BackColor` property of those forms changing to the user's color preference when the form is loaded.

1. Add the code below to the **Load** event procedures of the following forms:
   - ❑ `frmCustomerAsk`
   - ❑ `frmCustomerLookup`
   - ❑ `frmCustomerNew`
   - ❑ `frmCustomers`
   - ❑ `frmInventory`
   - ❑ `frmTransactions`
   - ❑ `frmUsers`

Here's the code to add:

```
Me.BackColor = g_lngBackColor
```

There's one important thing to note here: **Do not** add this code to the `frmLogin` form.

2. Save the China Shop project.
3. Run the China Shop program and verify that the color change process works properly for each form accessed from the Staff Functions menu option. Remember that you won't be able to test out the forms that the customers use yet – we still have some code to write before we can get to them by clicking on the Calculate and I'll Take It buttons. The following screenshot will give you some idea of the areas of each form that you can expect to remain unchanged:

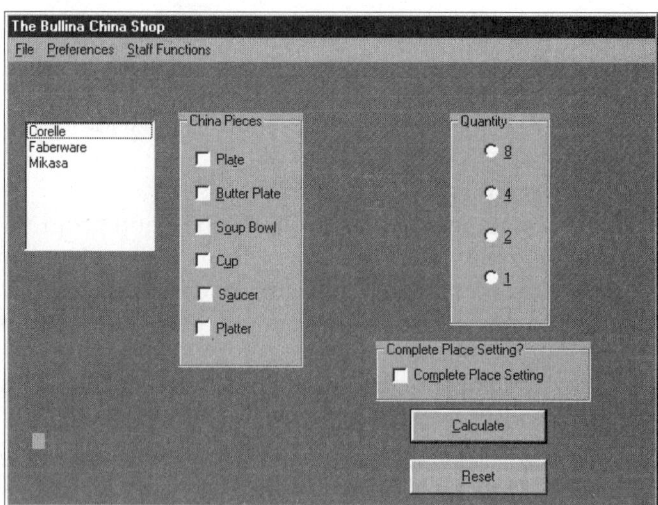

***Discussion***

I could see that Dave was frowning.

"What's up, Dave?" I asked.

"Well," he replied, "I just can't help thinking that I'd like the **BackColor**s of the frames and buttons to change too..."

"That's not unreasonable, Dave," I agreed, "but we only have so much time available to us here. Still, you do have the global variable stored now, so it could be an enhancement that you can work on for your own version of the project."

"That's a good idea," nodded Dave, "I think I'll try to do that at home."

"Let me know how you get on with that," I encouraged him. I looked at the class, and saw that Blaine had something to say.

"There's that **Me** keyword again," Blaine said...

```
Me.BackColor = g_lngBackColor
```

"...using that 'shortcut' syntax does make it easier to copy and paste into each form's **Load** event procedure."

"Yes it does," I concurred.

"I have a question," Rhonda said. "Why didn't we add code to the **Login** form to change its **BackColor** when it's loaded?"

"That's just a personal preference of mine," I said. "In my opinion, the **Login** form is the one form whose **BackColor** property should not change – it's just too vital an entry point into the China Shop program. If you think about it, it's possible for the user to change their preferred color scheme to something that may make a form virtually unreadable – and I don't want that change to impact the user's ability to be able to at least login to the program."

I waited to see if there were any more questions on this exercise. There were none, and so we continued.

# Calculating Prices using the Database

"Our next step," I said, "is to change the way the China Shop project calculates prices. Previously, we were reading the contents of the **Prices.txt** disk file into a variable array. Now that our inventory prices are contained in a database, we can use the more efficient recordset methods we learned about in previous weeks to quickly locate the prices of the items that the customer has selected. Modifying the program will be a three-step process. I have a list of what we need to do:"

> **We need to turn the form-level arrays we created in the original program into regular variables.**
>
> **Then we need to create a custom function called** PriceLookUp **to perform the price lookup on the** Inventory **table of the China database.**
>
> **Finally, we need to modify the code in the** Click **event procedure of** cmdCalculate **to call that function.**

"Here's the exercise that will set us on our way," I said.

## Exercise – Modifying Form-level Variables in frmMain

In this exercise, you'll change the declarations of seven variables in the General Declarations section of **frmMain** from dynamic **variable arrays** to **regular variables**. In the new program we'll be using recordset methods to dynamically 'look up' prices for the items that the user has selected. The look-up function will retrieve prices from the **Inventory** table of the China database, instead of reading them from the **Prices.txt** disk file. This means that we no longer need to read the price of every brand of inventory into a variable array.

1. Continue working with **frmMain**.
2. In the General Declarations section of **frmMain**, change all seven of the dynamic variable array declarations to regular variable declarations. Right now, the General Declarations section looks like this:

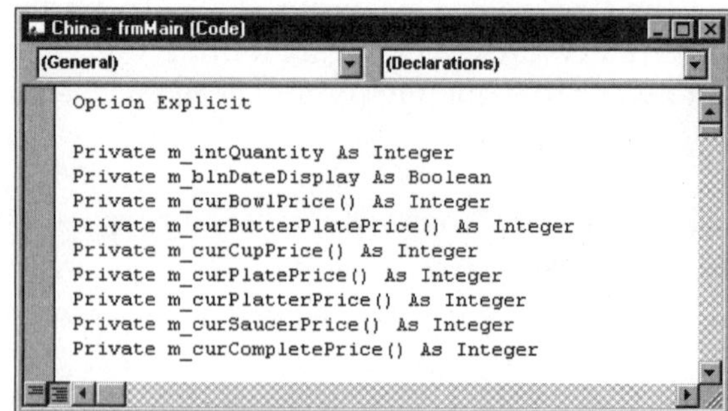
China - frmMain (Code)
(General)
(Declarations)
Option Explicit
Private m_intQuantity As Integer
Private m_blnDateDisplay As Boolean
Private m_curBowlPrice() As Integer
Private m_curButterPlatePrice() As Integer
Private m_curCupPrice() As Integer
Private m_curPlatePrice() As Integer
Private m_curPlatterPrice() As Integer
Private m_curSaucerPrice() As Integer
Private m_curCompletePrice() As Integer

**3.** Change it so that it looks like this next screenshot. Take care here: ensure that you erase the empty set of parentheses after the variable declarations, and be careful to change the appropriate data types from **`Integer`** to **`Currency`** as shown. Finally, don't forget to add the last line, which declares the **`m_curTotalPrice`** variable:

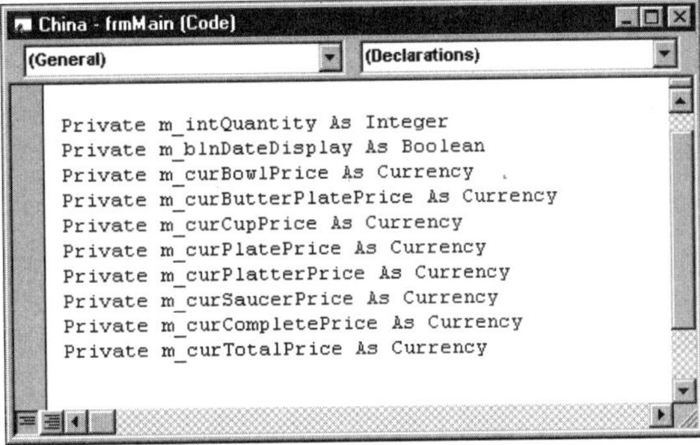
China - frmMain (Code)
(General)
(Declarations)
Private m_intQuantity As Integer
Private m_blnDateDisplay As Boolean
Private m_curBowlPrice As Currency
Private m_curButterPlatePrice As Currency
Private m_curCupPrice As Currency
Private m_curPlatePrice As Currency
Private m_curPlatterPrice As Currency
Private m_curSaucerPrice As Currency
Private m_curCompletePrice As Currency
Private m_curTotalPrice As Currency

**4.** Save the China Shop project.

### *Discussion*

"So what we did here," Rhonda asked, "was to remove the empty set of parentheses after the variable names?"

"That's right, Rhonda," I said, "that changes the variables from dynamic arrays to regular variables."

"Why," Tom asked, "have we changed the data type of the seven variables from **`Integer`** to **`Currency`** type?"

"Quite honestly, Tom," I said, "that's down to a mistake that I made in the original version of the China Shop program – one that I've only recently noticed. Those variables really should have been declared as **`Currency`** right from the start!"

"What kind of problems could that have caused if we hadn't caught it here?" Valerie asked.

"We were fortunate," I replied, "in that Joe Bullina's items were always priced in whole dollars. For instance, if he had charged $3.50 for a Corelle platter, the program would have erroneously rounded this down made all of its calculations based on a price of $3.00!"

"I guess we were pretty lucky on that one, weren't we?" Blaine said.

"Yes we were, Blaine," I answered. "This is a pretty good example of how long a program bug can exist in a program before someone notices it. In our case, we avoided getting egg on our face by catching it before our client did!"

I waited to see if there were any other questions.

"Before we modify the code in the **Click** event procedure of the **cmdCalculate** command button," I said, "we first need to write a function of our own which will perform the price lookup of the china items, using the **Inventory** table."

"A function of our own?" Steve asked.

"That's right, Steve," I said. "Last week we wrote a subprocedure of our own, so that's pretty fresh in your minds. Subprocedures and functions are almost identical – both execute program instructions. The difference between the two is that a function returns a **value** to the calling procedure, whereas a subprocedure does not. In the case of the **PriceLookUp** function we're about to write, it will execute recordset methods to locate a china item in the **Inventory** table, then return the price of that item to the calling procedure – the **cmdCalculate Click** event procedure."

I passed around the next exercise for the class to work through:

## Exercise – Creating the PriceLookUp Function

1. Continue working with the **Main** form of the China Shop project.
2. Make sure the code window is open, and then select Tools | Add Procedure from the Visual Basic main menu.
3. A dialog box will be displayed. Complete the entries according to the screenshot below:

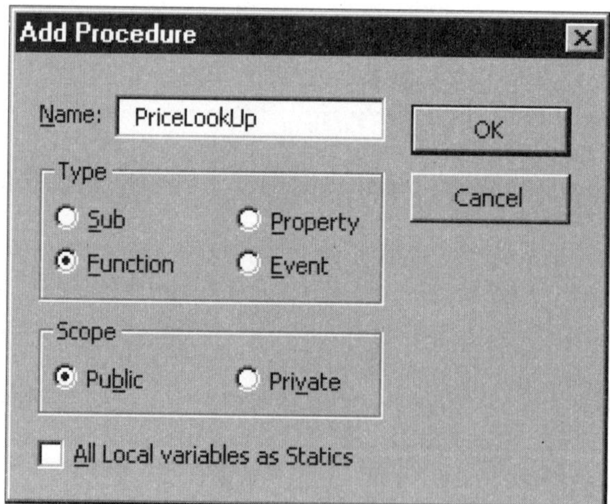

4. Click on the OK button, and the code window for the function **PriceLookUp** will appear. Change the function header to accept two arguments, **Brand** and **Item**, and to return a **Currency** type value, by changing the function header to look like this:

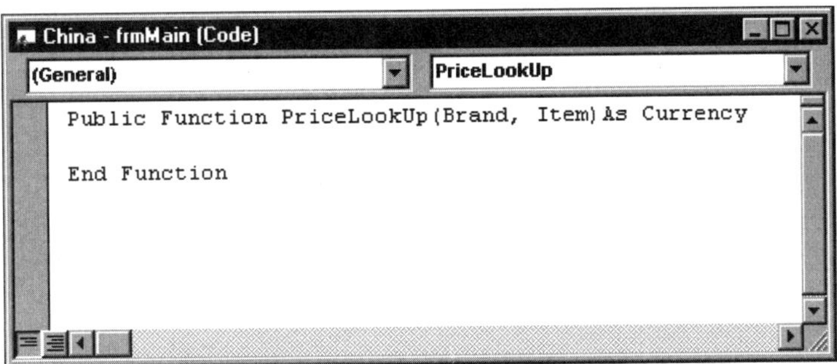


5. Now enter the following code between the function header and the **End Function** line:

```
Function PriceLookUp(Brand, Item) As Currency

datInventory.RecordsetType = vbRSTypeTable
datInventory.RecordSource = "Inventory"
datInventory.Refresh

datInventory.Recordset.Index = "BrandItemName"
datInventory.Recordset.Seek "=", Brand, Item

If datInventory.Recordset.NoMatch = True Then
    MsgBox "Inventory record not found! Contact John Smiley"
    PriceLookUp = 0
Else
    PriceLookUp = datInventory.Recordset("Price").Value
End If

End Function
```

6. Save the China Shop project.
7. At this point, we can't test this function, since we haven't written the code to call it yet. We'll do that in the next exercise.

### Discussion

"What we're doing with this function," I said, "is locating a china item in the **Inventory** table based on the china brand and china item passed to the function as arguments. That's why we specified two arguments in the function header. The first thing we do in the function is to change the values of both the **RecordsetType** and **RecordSource** properties of the data control:"

```
datInventory.RecordsetType = vbRSTypeTable
datInventory.RecordSource = "Inventory"
```

"After changing these data control properties, we then execute the **Refresh** method of the data control, which rebuilds the recordset:"

```
datInventory.Refresh
```

"Why did we need to change these data control values?" Rhonda asked. "They already had values in them, didn't they?"

"That's true, Rhonda, they did," I said, "but the initial values aren't the ones we need to be able to use the recordset's **Seek** method to quickly find a china item in the **Inventory** table. Since we're using the **Seek** method to locate china items in the Inventory table, we need to have a table-type recordset – but the initial value of the **RecordsetType** property is **Dynaset**. Furthermore, the initial value of the **RecordSource** property is a SQL statement that's used to load the **lstBrands** list box with unique china brands."

"Why couldn't we just initialize these property values at design time?" Rhonda asked. "Wouldn't that be easier?"

"I think I see why not," Kevin said. "The data control is really being used for two separate purposes at two different times. When the form is first loaded, the data control generates a recordset that's used to populate the list box. Then, after the form is loaded, we're using the data control for an entirely different purpose – to locate china items in the **Inventory** table. Isn't that right?"

"That's excellent, Kevin," I said. "Let me reiterate that to make sure everybody understands – it's important. We're using the same data control to generate different recordsets in the program. The initial values of the data control create a recordset that we use to populate the list of china brands in the **lstBrands** list box, but now we're using the data control to generate a recordset that we can use to locate items in the **Inventory** table."

"I think I see now," Rhonda said.

I waited to see if there were any other questions before continuing.

"The next two lines of code," I said, "are used to locate an individual record in the **Inventory** table. First, we set the **Index** property of the recordset to use the **BrandItemName** index of the **Inventory** table. Then we use the **Seek** method with the two key values required by that index, the china brand and the china item name:"

```
datInventory.Recordset.Index = "BrandItemName"
datInventory.Recordset.Seek "=", Brand, Item
```

"These two arguments are passed to the **PriceLookUp** function from the calling procedure – **cmdCalculate**."

"I don't remember creating an index in the **Inventory** table called **BrandItemName**," Ward said, "when did we do that?"

"According to my notes, Ward," I said, "we created that index way back in Week 3, when we were creating the **Inventory** table. You may have missed that exercise. But don't worry, if you did miss it somehow, you can always create the index now – it's based on both the **Brand** and **ItemName** fields in the **Inventory** table."

I paused for a moment before resuming.

"After the **Seek** method is executed," I continued, "if a matching record is **not** found in the recordset, then the **NoMatch** property of the recordset will be set to **True**. If that's the case, we display a warning message that the **Inventory** record has not been found…"

```
If datInventory.Recordset.NoMatch = True Then
   MsgBox "Inventory record not found! Contact John Smiley"
```

"… and return a value of 0 to the calling procedure by setting the function name equal to zero:"

```
PriceLookUp = 0
```

"I'm sorry to interrupt," Rhonda said, "but what's going on with that line of code again? Why are we assigning a value of zero to the **PriceLookUp**? Is that a variable of some kind?"

"That's a good question, Rhonda," I said. "**PriceLookUp** is not a variable – it's the name of the function. Remember, a Visual Basic function returns a **value** to its calling procedure. The way that a value is passed back to the calling procedure is by assigning the function name a value somewhere within the body of the function, and since the name of the function is **PriceLookUp**, this assignment statement returns a value of zero back to the calling procedure."

"I can see that," Bob said. "As the recordset's **Seek** method was unable to find an inventory item, it makes sense to return a value of zero. My question is this: How can this happen – I mean, how is it possible for a china item **not** to be in the **Inventory** table?"

"This condition shouldn't happen, Bob," I said, "but it's possible that a member of the China Shop staff could accidentally delete a record from the **Inventory** table – such as the Mikasa cup for instance. That accidental deletion could produce just this type of error condition."

"I see," Bob confirmed.

"On the other hand," I continued, "if the inventory record is found by the **Seek** method, the value of **NoMatch** is **False**, and we then return the value of the **Price** field in the inventory record to the calling procedure:"

```
Else
   PriceLookUp = datInventory.Recordset("Price").Value
End If
```

"That makes sense," Dave said. "That's beautifully efficient."

"I agree, Dave," I replied. "But then again, I would, wouldn't I?"

The class chuckled.

The next exercise was to modify the code in **cmdCalculate** button's **Click** event procedure:

## Exercise – Modifying the cmdCalculate Click Event Procedure

In this exercise, you'll modify the code in the **Click** event procedure of the **cmdCalculate** command button to make use of the **PriceLookUp** function you just wrote.

1. Continue working with the **Main** form.
2. Modify the code in the **cmdCalculate** button's **Click** event procedure to look like the code below. Be careful with this step – much of the code you already have in this event procedure will change. To help guide you, I've highlighted the sections where the changes have taken place. Take great care to ensure your code exactly matches what's shown below:

```
Private Sub cmdCalculate_Click()
'Declare our variables

m_curBowlPrice = 0
m_curButterPlatePrice = 0
m_curCupPrice = 0
m_curPlatePrice = 0
m_curPlatterPrice = 0
m_curSaucerPrice = 0
m_curCompletePrice = 0

'Has the customer selected a brand of china?
If lstBrands.Text = "" Then
    MsgBox "You must select a China brand"
    Exit Sub
End If

'Has the customer selected one or more china items?
If chkChinaItem(0).Value = 0 And
      ↳chkChinaItem(1).Value = 0 And
      ↳chkChinaItem(2).Value = 0 And
      ↳chkChinaItem(3).Value = 0 And
      ↳chkChinaItem(4).Value = 0 And
      ↳chkChinaItem(5).Value = 0 Then
   MsgBox "You must select one or more china items"
   Exit Sub
End If

'Has the customer selected a quantity?
If optQuantity(8).Value = False And
      ↳optQuantity(4).Value = False And
      ↳optQuantity(2).Value = False And
      ↳optQuantity(1).Value = False Then
   MsgBox "You must select a quantity"
   Exit Sub
End If

'If the customer has selected a platter
'warn them that there is only 1 permitted per sales
'quotation
If chkChinaItem(5).Value = 1 And m_intQuantity > 1 Then
   MsgBox "Customer is limited to 1 Platter per order" &
         ↳vbCrLf & "Adjusting price accordingly"
End If
```

*Continued on following page*

```
'All the pieces are here, let's calculate a price
'Calculate subtotal prices by item

If chkChinaItem(0).Value = 1 Then
   m_curPlatePrice = PriceLookUp(lstBrands.Text, "Plate")
End If

If chkChinaItem(1).Value = 1 Then
   m_curButterPlatePrice = PriceLookUp(lstBrands.Text, "ButterPlate")
End If

If chkChinaItem(2).Value = 1 Then
   m_curBowlPrice = PriceLookUp(lstBrands.Text, "Bowl")
End If

If chkChinaItem(3).Value = 1 Then
   m_curCupPrice = PriceLookUp(lstBrands.Text, "Cup")
End If

If chkChinaItem(4).Value = 1 Then
   m_curSaucerPrice = PriceLookUp(lstBrands.Text, "Saucer")
End If

If chkChinaItem(5).Value = 1 Then
   m_curPlatterPrice = PriceLookUp(lstBrands.Text, "Platter")
End If

m_curCompletePrice = PriceLookUp(lstBrands.Text, "Complete")

If chkChinaItem(0).Value = 1 And
   ↳chkChinaItem(1).Value = 1 And
   ↳chkChinaItem(2).Value = 1 And
   ↳chkChinaItem(3).Value = 1 And
   ↳chkChinaItem(4).Value = 1 Then

   MsgBox "Price includes a Complete Place Setting Discount"
   m_curTotalPrice = (m_curCompletePrice * m_intQuantity) +
   ↳m_curPlatterPrice
Else
   m_curTotalPrice = (((m_curBowlPrice +
                       ↳m_curButterPlatePrice +
                       ↳m_curCupPrice +
                       ↳m_curPlatePrice +
                       ↳m_curSaucerPrice) *
                       ↳m_intQuantity) +
                       ↳m_curPlatterPrice)
```

```
End If

'If the price is greater than 0, display the price and
'make the label visible
If m_curTotalPrice > 0 Then
   lblPrice.Caption = "The price of your order is " &
        ↳Format(m_curTotalPrice, "$##,###.00")
   lblPrice.Visible = True
   cmdIllTakeIt.Visible = True
End If

End Sub
```

3. Save the China Shop project.
4. Test the program now to ensure that prices are being properly calculated.

***Discussion***

This exercise had either a lot of typing (for those students who decided to start from scratch) or a lot of hunting around to see what to change – and I gave the class about twenty-five minutes to get through it all. As each member of the class finished up with the exercise and tested their modified code, they seemed very pleased with the progress they had made.

"Wow," Ward said, "it's so easy to dynamically locate and look up inventory prices in the database."

"Yes, it sure is faster, and easier, than reading prices from a disk file into a variable array," Lou said. "Can you explain what's going on?"

"Sure thing, Lou," I said. "This first section of code is a little different from what we saw in the previous version of this event procedure. In the old version, we declared a number of local variables in which to store the intermediate price calculations of each china component. In this version of the program, we don't need to access the values in those variables from procedures on this from, so we've changed the declaration of those variables from **local** variables to **form-level** variables. Because of this, whenever the event procedure is executed, we first need to set the values of all of them to zero:"

```
m_curBowlPrice = 0
m_curButterPlatePrice = 0
m_curCupPrice = 0
m_curPlatePrice = 0
m_curPlatterPrice = 0
m_curSaucerPrice = 0
m_curCompletePrice = 0
```

"Can you explain one more time why we are using form-level variables here instead of local variables?" Linda asked.

"We need to declare these variables as form-level variables," I said, "because we'll be accessing the values in these variables from several different procedures on this form. The values in these variables are initially updated by the code in this event procedure, which performs the actual price calculations. Later on, we'll create a subprocedure called **`UpdateTrans`**, which will create an **`Inventory`** record with the details of the customer's purchase – that subprocedure will read the values from these variables in order to store them in the inventory record. Finally, we'll print the customer's sales receipt, and the values in these variables will be read by another subprocedure we'll write, called **`PrintSalesReceipt`**."

"I see that it makes sense to declare these variables as form-level variables," Ward said, "but why are we setting their values to zero whenever we execute this event procedure? Is that really necessary, or is it just good programming practice? Aren't these values initialized to zero anyway?"

"Form-level variables are initialized to zero when the form is *first loaded*," I said. "Once values are stored in form-level variables, those values are retained for as long as the form is loaded in RAM, which in the case of **`frmMain`** is for as long as the program is running. Therefore, whenever the **`cmdCalculate`** event procedure is executed, these variables will still contain whatever values they had from the previous execution of the **`cmdCalculate`** event procedure. "

"Is that a problem?" Kevin asked.

"It can be a problem," I said. "For instance, we calculate the price of the customer's sales quotation as the total of the individual component prices of each item – **`m_curBowlPrice`**, **`m_curButterPlatePrice`**, **`m_curCupPrice`**, **`m_curPlatePrice`**, **`m_curPlatterPrice`** and **`m_curSaucerPrice`**. Because our algorithm is dependent on these individual prices, it's crucial that we set these individual variable values to zero each and every time we execute the code in this **`Click`** event procedure. Otherwise, we would have values from the previous execution of the event procedure in these variables – and our price calculation would be erroneous."

"Can you give us an example of that?" Lou asked.

"Here's one," I said. "If a customer selects a Mikasa plate and clicks on the Calculate command button, since the 'plate' check box has a checkmark in it, the **`PriceLookUp`** function is called in order to get the **`Plate`** component of the total sales price.

Once this price is retrieved from the database, the value of a Mikasa plate is stored in the variable **m_curPlatePrice**. Now, let's say that the customer changes their mind, unchecks the plate selection, and then selects a Mikasa bowl. This same **PriceLookUp** function is executed for a Mikasa bowl, and its value is then stored in the variable **m_curBowlPrice**. However, when the total price of the sales quotation is calculated, not only is the value of **m_curBowlPrice** factored into the equation, but also the residual value of **m_curPlatePrice** – since its value was retained from the customer's previous sales quotation."

I paused to see if there were any more questions about that section of code – there weren't.

"It looks like the next sequence of code is pretty much intact from the previous version," Blaine said. "Nothing has changed here."

"That's right Blaine," I said. "This next sequence of code verifies that the customer has made a selection from the list box..."

```
'Has the customer selected a brand of china?
If lstBrands.Text = "" Then
   MsgBox "You must select a China brand"
   Exit Sub
End If
```

"...and this sequence, that the customer has made a selection of at least one item of china..."

```
'Has the customer selected one or more china items?
If chkChinaItem(0).Value = 0 And
       ↳chkChinaItem(1).Value = 0 And
       ↳chkChinaItem(2).Value = 0 And
       ↳chkChinaItem(3).Value = 0 And
       ↳chkChinaItem(4).Value = 0 And
       ↳chkChinaItem(5).Value = 0 Then
   MsgBox "You must select one or more china items"
   Exit Sub
End If
```

"... and that the customer has selected a valid quantity."

```
'Has the customer selected a quantity?
If optQuantity(8).Value = False And
       ↳optQuantity(4).Value = False And
       ↳optQuantity(2).Value = False And
```

*Continued on following page*

```
       ↳optQuantity(1).Value = False Then
    MsgBox "You must select a quantity"
    Exit Sub
End If
```

"If the customer has not selected a china brand, one or more china items, and a valid quantity," I continued, "we simply don't have enough information to calculate a price, so we display a warning message to the user, and exit the sub procedure via an **`Exit Sub`** statement. This will return the customer to the **`Main`** form."

Again, I waited to see if there were any questions.

"This next section of code is also identical to the original," I said. "It checks to determine if the customer has made a selection of a platter. Since the customer is limited to only one platter per sale, we display an informational message informing them that they can only purchase a single platter – whatever quantities of the other items they have selected:"

```
'If the customer has selected a platter
'warn them that there is only 1 permitted per sales
'quotation
If chkChinaItem(5).Value = 1 And m_intQuantity > 1 Then
    MsgBox "Customer is limited to 1 Platter per order" &
           ↳vbCrLf & "Adjusting price accordingly"
End If
```

"The following section of code," I continued, "is where the major changes have taken place. In the previous version of this procedure, all of the inventory prices were loaded into several one-dimensional arrays, with each array representing an individual piece of china, and each array element representing a different brand of china. As you've already seen, we've eliminated those variable arrays. Instead, we'll execute the custom function **`PriceLookUp`** for each check box item whose **`Value`** property is equal to 1: in other words, for each check box that the customer has selected. Notice that we pass **`PriceLookUp`** two arguments – the brand of china in the form of the **`Text`** property of the **`lstBrands`** list box, and a string literal equating to the china item. Since **`PriceLookUp`** is a function, it returns a value, and we then assign that value to one of the seven form-level variables we declared for that purpose in the General Declarations section of **`frmMain:`**"

```
'All the pieces are here, let's calculate a price
'Calculate subtotal prices by item

If chkChinaItem(0).Value = 1 Then
    m_curPlatePrice = PriceLookUp(lstBrands.Text, "Plate")
End If
```

```
If chkChinaItem(1).Value = 1 Then
   m_curButterPlatePrice = PriceLookUp(lstBrands.Text, "ButterPlate")
End If

If chkChinaItem(2).Value = 1 Then
   m_curBowlPrice = PriceLookUp(lstBrands.Text, "Bowl")
End If

If chkChinaItem(3).Value = 1 Then
   m_curCupPrice = PriceLookUp(lstBrands.Text, "Cup")
End If

If chkChinaItem(4).Value = 1 Then
   m_curSaucerPrice = PriceLookUp(lstBrands.Text, "Saucer")
End If

If chkChinaItem(5).Value = 1 Then
   m_curPlatterPrice = PriceLookUp(lstBrands.Text, "Platter")
End If

m_curCompletePrice = PriceLookUp(lstBrands.Text, "Complete")
```

"I can't believe how compact this code is," Mary said. "It seemed a bit awkward to me before. Now we just execute the `PriceLookUp` function, and just like that, we have our item price. Amazing. I notice that we **always** perform the `PriceLookUp` function for the complete place setting price. "

"You're right, Mary," I agreed. "This code is efficient. All we need to do is pass the `PriceLookUp` function two arguments – the china brand and the item name – for each item of china selected, and the `PriceLookUp` function returns the price to us via its return value. Once the prices of the checked items are passed back to us and assigned to the appropriate form-level variable, it's just a matter of calculating the total price of the sales quotation, much as we did in the previous version of the code. Concerning the `PriceLookUp` for the complete place setting, you're right – we probably could have used an `If...Then` statement to execute the `PriceLookUp` function only if the component check boxes were selected – but it doesn't hurt."

"I notice," Rachel said, "that there are two ways to calculate the customer's total price in this code. Is that right?"

"You're right, Rachel," I said, "that's because of the 'Complete Place Setting' price discount the China Shop offers. If the customer selects **all** of the individual items that are considered to comprise a complete place setting – bowl, butter plate, cup, plate and saucer – then the total price is equal to the value of the complete place setting price, multiplied by the quantity the customer has selected, plus the cost of a platter, if the customer has selected one. That's what this code is doing here..."

```
If chkChinaItem(0).Value = 1 And
   ↳chkChinaItem(1).Value = 1 And
   ↳chkChinaItem(2).Value = 1 And
   ↳chkChinaItem(3).Value = 1 And
   ↳chkChinaItem(4).Value = 1 Then
     MsgBox "Price includes a Complete Place Setting Discount"
     m_curTotalPrice = (m_curCompletePrice * m_intQuantity) +
     ↳m_curPlatterPrice
Else
```

"...but if the customer does not select a complete place setting, the total price is calculated as equal to the cost of any selected bowl, butter plate, cup, plate or saucer, multiplied by the selected quantity, plus the cost of a platter (if selected). That's what *this* code is doing:"

```
   m_curTotalPrice = (((m_curBowlPrice +
                        ↳m_curButterPlatePrice +
                        ↳m_curCupPrice +
                        ↳m_curPlatePrice +
                        ↳m_curSaucerPrice) *
                        ↳m_intQuantity) +
                        ↳m_curPlatterPrice)
```

I waited to see if there were any questions before proceeding. Most of what the class was seeing here was similar to the way we had calculated prices in the previous version of this event procedure – the main difference was the introduction of the `PriceLookUp` function.

"Finally," I continued, "if the total price of the sales quotation is greater than zero, we format and display the price in the caption of the `lblPrice` label control, make the label control visible and, as we saw earlier, make the I'll Take It button visible as well:"

```
'If the price is greater than 0, display the price and
'make the label visible
If m_curTotalPrice > 0 Then
   lblPrice.Caption = "The price of your order is " &
         ↳Format(m_curTotalPrice, "$##,###.00")
   lblPrice.Visible = True
   cmdIllTakeIt.Visible = True
End If
```

"Maybe it's my imagination," Ward commented, "but I think this code is a little easier to follow now that we're using database processing."

"That's not unusual, Ward," I said. "Database processing can make your programming tasks much easier."

"Now that we've modified the way the program calculates prices," I said, "we need to make a minor adjustment to the code in **`Click`** event procedure of **`cmdReset`**. Here's a quick exercise that will help us do that."

## Exercise – Modifying cmdReset

This exercise will alter the **`cmdReset`** button's code so that the I'll Take It button is hidden if the user resets the program.

1. Continue working with **`frmMain`**.
2. Modify the code in the **`cmdReset`** button's **`Click`** event procedure to look like the following listing. Changed code is highlighted as usual:

```
Private Sub cmdReset_Click()

lstBrands.ListIndex = -1
chkChinaItem(0).Value = 0
chkChinaItem(1).Value = 0
chkChinaItem(2).Value = 0
chkChinaItem(3).Value = 0
chkChinaItem(4).Value = 0
chkChinaItem(5).Value = 0
optQuantity(8).Value = False
optQuantity(4).Value = False
optQuantity(2).Value = False
optQuantity(1).Value = False
chkCompletePlaceSetting.Value = 0
lblPrice.Visible = False
imgChina.Picture = LoadPicture()
cmdIlltakeIt.Visible = False

End Sub
```

3. Save the China Shop project.
4. Run the China Shop program. Select a price quotation, and then click on the Reset button. The I'll Take It button should disappear.

### *Discussion*

"All we're doing here," I said, "is ensuring that when the user clicks on the Reset command button, that the I'll Take It command button is made invisible."

"Um..." said Rhonda.

"Yes, Rhonda? What's up?"

"Oh, it's just that I can't remember what the first line of code does here..."

"Ah, I see," I said. "The `-1` value resets the list box so that none of it's items is selected," I reminded her.

She nodded. "Of course – I remember now!"

I waited to see if anyone had any questions. There were none, and I suggested that we adjourn for a fifteen minute break.

"We have just a few more exercises left before our work is complete," I said, "and then it will be time to head out to the China Shop to deliver our program."

I resumed class after break by explaining that our next step was to write the code that would record a transaction record for each item of china that the customer purchased.

# Writing Transaction Records

"To write transaction records," I said, "we'll first need to write both a function and a subprocedure of our own. The function, which we'll call **`ItemIDLookup`**, is designed to 'look up' the **`ItemID`** of the china item selected for purchase by the customer – we need to know the **`ItemID`** of the china item in order to add a transaction record to the database. This is because the name of the china item is not actually written to the transaction record of the **`Transactions`** table – only the **`ItemID`** is. The subprocedure we'll write, which we will call **`UpdateTrans`**, will add the transaction record to the **`Transactions`** table of the China Shop database."

"This sounds pretty complicated," Rhonda said.

"I don't think you'll have a problem with it, Rhonda," I said. "As with the code to calculate the sales quotation price, we'll take this a step at a time. One thing I forgot to mention is that before we do anything else, we need to modify the little-known **`Tag`** property of each element of the **`chkChinaItem`** control array with the name of its corresponding item name in the **`Inventory`** table. Doing so will make the code we write in the **`UpdateTrans`** subprocedure much more compact and streamlined."

I handed out the appropriate exercise to the class:

## Exercise – Updating the Tag Properties of the chkChinaItem Control Array

In this exercise, you'll update the **`Tag`** property of each member of the **`chkChinaItem`** control array. Be careful with your spelling!

1. Continue working with **`frmMain`**.

2. Change the **Tag** property of **chkChinaItem(0)** to **Plate**.
3. Change the **Tag** property of **chkChinaItem(1)** to **ButterPlate**. **Do not** insert a space between the words 'Butter' and 'Plate'.
4. Change the **Tag** property of **chkChinaItem(2)** to **Bowl**.
5. Change the **Tag** property of **chkChinaItem(3)** to **Cup**.
6. Change the **Tag** property of **chkChinaItem(4)** to **Saucer**.
7. Change the **Tag** property of **chkChinaItem(5)** to **Platter**.
8. Save the China Shop project.

"The **Tag** property," I explained, "is a control property that can be used for whatever purpose the programmer desires. Here, we'll put it to good use in just a few moments – it'll help us to write our transaction records to the **Transactions** table."

I then distributed this next exercise for the class to complete.

## Exercise – Creating the ItemIDLookup Function

In this exercise, you'll create the **ItemIDLookup** function. We'll use this function to look up the **ItemID** number for a selected china item in the **Inventory** table.

1. Continue working with the **Main** form.
2. Make sure the code window is open, and then select Tools | Add Procedure from the Visual Basic main menu.
3. Complete the entries in the resulting dialog box in line with the screenshot:

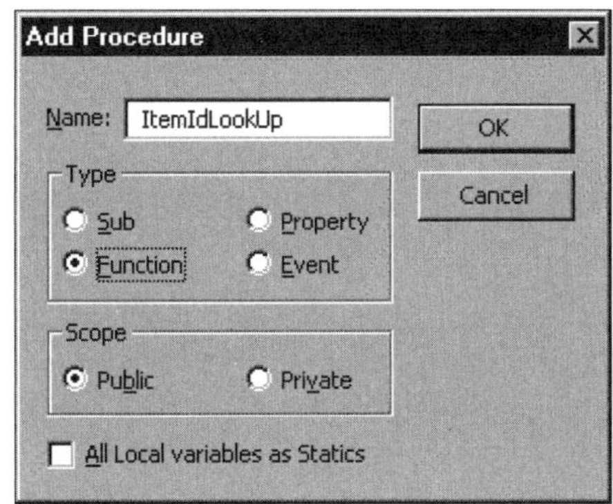


4. Click on the OK button, and the code window for the function **ItemIDLookUp** will appear. Change the function header to accept two arguments, **Brand** and **Item**, and to return an **Long** type value, like this...

5. Now enter the following code between the function name and the **`End Function`** line:

```
Public Function ItemIDLookup(Brand, Item) As Long

datInventory.RecordsetType = vbRSTypeTable
datInventory.RecordSource = "Inventory"
datInventory.Refresh

datInventory.Recordset.Index = "BrandItemName"
datInventory.Recordset.Seek "=", Brand, Item

If datInventory.Recordset.NoMatch Then
   MsgBox "Inventory record not found! Contact John Smiley"
   ItemIDLookup = 0
Else
   ItemIDLookup = datInventory.Recordset("ItemID").Value
End If

End Function
```

6. Save the China Shop project.

At this point, there's no way to test this function, but don't worry – we'll be doing that shortly.

### Discussion

"This function," Dave said, "looks very similar to the other function we wrote today – `PriceLookUp`."

"You're right, Dave," I said, "they are very similar, although the purpose of each function is slightly different. We previously designed the `PriceLookUp` function to look up and return the **price** of the china item the user has selected – the purpose of this new `ItemIDLookUp` function is to look up and return the `ItemID` number of the china item the user has selected."

"Why do we need to know the `ItemID`?" Melissa asked.

"Because," I explained, "it's a required field in the transactions record that we want to write to the `Transactions` table."

"That's right," Dave said, "that, plus the `CustID` – but we already know the `CustID` because of the customer identification process we programmed last week."

"Excellent, Dave," I said, "`CustID` and `ItemID`, along with the date of purchase and purchase price, are vital pieces of information that Joe Bullina requires in the `Transactions` table."

There was a momentary pause and then Chuck asked this question:

"Shouldn't we already know the `ItemID` of the user's selection?" he said. "After all, we do know the china brand and the item of china that the user has selected."

"Not really, Chuck," I said. "`ItemID`, although it's the primary key of the `Inventory` table, is **not** a piece of information that the China Shop program ever uses. We really have no way of knowing what the `ItemID` for a particular piece of inventory is unless we explicitly look it up in the `Inventory` table. And that, of course, is what what we're doing here in this function: using the `Seek` method of the recordset, together with the `Brand` and `ItemName`, to locate and retrieve the `ItemID`."

I waited briefly for questions before continuing.

"As Dave pointed out a minute ago," I continued, "the code in this function is almost identical to the code in the `PriceLookUp` function. The first difference is noticeable right from the start, in the function header itself: `ItemIDLookUp` returns a `Long` type return value, not the `Currency` type return value that `PriceLookUp` returned:"

```
Function ItemIDLookup(Brand, Item) As Long
```

"Like `PriceLookUp`, in `ItemIDLookUp` we also set the `RecordsetType` property of the data control to a `Table` type, and the `RecordSource` to the `Inventory` table:"

```
datInventory.RecordsetType = vbRSTypeTable
datInventory.RecordSource = "Inventory"
```

"We then execute the `Refresh` method of the data control to rebuild the recordset..."

```
datInventory.Refresh
```

"As was the case with the `PriceLookUp` function," I continued, "we then set the `Index` property of the `Recordset` to `"BrandItemName"`..."

```
datInventory.Recordset.Index = "BrandItemName"
```

"... and then execute the recordset's `Seek` method, using the arguments `Brand` and `Item` for the two key values. Remember, these two arguments will be passed to this function from the calling procedure – in this case the subprocedure we're about to code – `UpdateTrans`:"

```
datInventory.Recordset.Seek "=", Brand, Item
```

"If a matching record is **not** found in the `Inventory` table," I continued, "then the `NoMatch` property of the recordset will be set to `True`, and we'll display a warning message to the user that the inventory record was not found..."

```
If datInventory.Recordset.NoMatch Then
   MsgBox "Inventory record not found! Contact John Smiley"
```

"...and return a value of zero to the calling procedure by setting the function name equal to zero..."

```
   ItemIDLookup = 0
```

"As was the case with the `PriceLookUp` function, we don't like to think that this is something that can happen, but theoretically it is possible if a member of the China Shop staff accidentally deletes an inventory record. Finally, if the inventory record is found, we then return the value of the `ItemID` field in the inventory record to the calling procedure:"

```
Else
   ItemIDLookup = datInventory.Recordset("ItemID").Value
End If
```

"Let's write the `UpdateTrans` subprocedure now," I said. "That's the procedure that will call this function, and ultimately result in a transaction record being written to the `Transactions` table."

## Exercise – Creating the UpdateTrans Subprocedure

In this exercise, you'll create the `UpdateTrans` subprocedure that will store transaction records in the `Transactions` table of the `China` database.

1. Continue working with the `Main` form.
2. Make sure the code window is open and select Tools | Add Procedure from the Visual Basic main menu.
3. A dialog box will be displayed. Complete its entries to match the screenshot:

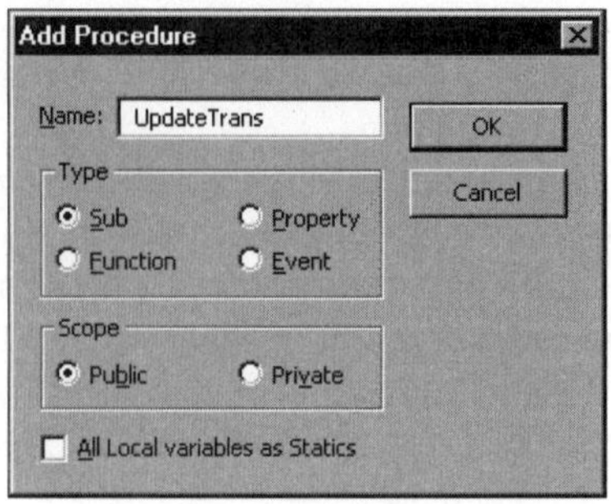

4. Click on the OK button, and the code window for the **UpdateTrans** subprocedure will appear. Unlike some of our other exercises, there is no need to change the subprocedure header – this subprocedure doesn't need any arguments:

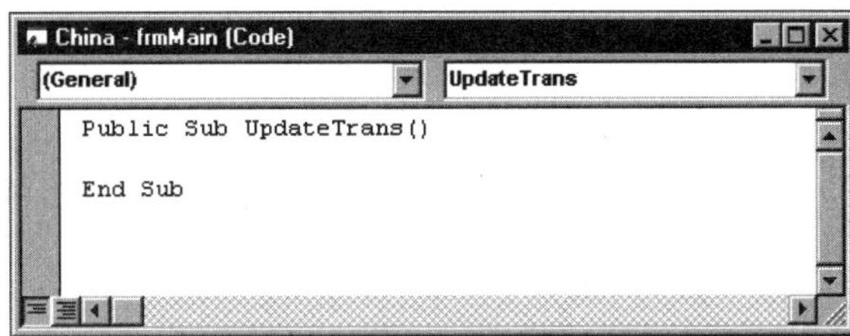


5. Eat some kind of energy-giving food, then enter the following code between the subprocedure name and the **End Sub** line:

```
Public Sub UpdateTrans()

Dim objChk As CheckBox

If chkChinaItem(0).Value = 1 And
   ↳chkChinaItem(1).Value = 1 And
   ↳chkChinaItem(2).Value = 1 And
   ↳chkChinaItem(3).Value = 1 And
   ↳chkChinaItem(4).Value = 1 Then
   datTransactions.Recordset.AddNew
   datTransactions.Recordset.Fields("CustID").Value =
                    ↳g_intCustomerNumber
   datTransactions.Recordset.Fields("ItemID").Value =
                    ↳ItemIDLookUp(lstBrands.Text, "Complete")
   datTransactions.Recordset.Fields("Quantity").Value =
                    ↳m_intQuantity
   datTransactions.Recordset.Fields("Price") =
                    ↳PriceLookUp(lstBrands.Text, "Complete")
   datTransactions.Recordset.Fields("DateOfPurchase").Value =
                    ↳Now
   datTransactions.Recordset.Update

   If chkChinaItem(5).Value = 1 Then
      datTransactions.Recordset.AddNew
      datTransactions.Recordset.Fields("CustID").Value =
                    ↳g_intCustomerNumber
      datTransactions.Recordset.Fields("ItemID").Value =
                    ↳ItemIDLookUp(lstBrands.Text, "Platter")
      datTransactions.Recordset.Fields("Quantity").Value = 1
      datTransactions.Recordset.Fields("Price") =
```

*Continued on following page*

```
                    ↳PriceLookUp(lstBrands.Text, "Platter")
      datTransactions.Recordset.Fields("DateOfPurchase").Value =
                    ↳Now
      datTransactions.Recordset.Update
   End If
   Exit Sub
End If

For Each objChk In chkChinaItem
   If objChk.Value = 1 Then
      datTransactions.Recordset.AddNew
      datTransactions.Recordset.Fields("CustID").Value =
                 ↳g_intCustomerNumber
      datTransactions.Recordset.Fields("ItemID").Value =
                 ↳ItemIDLookUp(lstBrands.Text, objChk.Tag)
      If objChk.Tag = "Platter" Then
         datTransactions.Recordset.Fields("Quantity").Value = 1
      Else
         datTransactions.Recordset.Fields("Quantity").Value =
                 ↳m_intQuantity
      End If
      datTransactions.Recordset.Fields("Price") =
                 ↳PriceLookUp(lstBrands.Text, objChk.Tag)
      datTransactions.Recordset.Fields("DateOfPurchase").Value =
                 ↳Now
      datTransactions.Recordset.Update
   End If
Next

End Sub
```

**6.** Save the China Shop project.

At this point, there's no way to test this subprocedure, but we'll soon fix that in the next exercise.

### *Discussion*

I saw quite a few puzzled looks on the faces of my students as they completed this exercise.

"I'm sure you all have questions about what's going on in this code," I said. "Don't worry – we'll examine each line of code in the procedure, starting with the – rather strange – very first line. This line of code..."

```
Dim objChk As CheckBox
```

"... is a declaration of an **object variable**."

"Is that similar to the object variable you showed us last week?" Lou asked, "when you showed us how to access data in a database using data objects instead of the data control?"

"That's exactly right, Lou," I said. "Just like last week, when we declared an object variable to 'point to' a `Workspace`, a `Database` and a `Recordset`, this line of code is the declaration of an object variable to be used to 'point to' one of the check boxes on the form."

Again I saw some puzzled faces.

"It's like this," I continued. "We can declare an object variable and then use it to refer to a series of specific objects of the same type – in this case, check boxes – that we have on our form. Instead of writing a bunch of repetitive code to check each and every one of the `chkChinaItem` check boxes by name to see if the customer has selected it, we'll use this `objChk` object variable as a shortcut to reference each individual member of the control array `chkChinaItems`. We'll do this with a special kind of loop structure called a `For Each` loop. We'll examine that code in just a minute or two."

"When we calculated sales quotation prices," I went on, " we used two different methods to calculate a price, and there are also two methods employed here to write transaction records to the `Transactions` table. Which of the methods we use is determined once again by the customer's selection of a complete place setting."

"That's a question I had before I saw this code," Dave said. "Would we write individual transaction records for each item of china purchased by the customer, or would we write a single transaction record for the entire purchase? It appears that we have a hybrid of both methods here."

"That's a good way of putting it, Dave," I replied. "If the customer purchases individual china items, then we want a separate transaction record for each item of china purchased. But if the customer selects a complete place setting, then we write a single transaction record representing the entire set."

"Can you give us an example of that?" Rachel asked.

"Yes, I can," I said. "For example, if the customer selects two Mikasa plates and two Mikasa cups for purchase, we'll write two transaction records to the `Transactions` table – one record for the plate transaction, and one record for the cup transaction."

"That makes sense to me," Melissa said. "Now suppose the customer instead selects a complete place setting of Faberware china – plate, butter plate, bowl, cup and saucer? Will we write five transaction records to the transactions table, one for each individual item comprising a complete place setting?"

"I think," Dave interjected, "that if we wrote a single transaction for each of the five china items comprising a complete place setting, the total value of the customer's purchase would be incorrect. Since we offer a complete place setting discount, the total of the individual items does **not** equal the complete place setting price as recorded in the `Inventory` table. Isn't that right? That's why we need to write a single transaction record representing the complete place setting transaction."

"That's excellent, Dave," I said, "and that's exactly what we're doing here."

"Would you mind translating what Dave just said?" Rhonda said, laughing. "I'm afraid that totally went over my head."

"I'd be glad to, Rhonda," I said. "What Dave is saying is this: if the customer purchased a complete place setting of Mikasa china – plate, butter plate, bowl, cup and saucer, then the prices for each of the individual pieces would look like this:"

| ItemID | Brand | Item | Price |
|---|---|---|---|
| 15 | Mikasa | Plate | $25 |
| 16 | Mikasa | Butter Plate | $10 |
| 17 | Mikasa | Soup Bowl | $10 |
| 18 | Mikasa | Cup | $5 |
| 19 | Mikasa | Saucer | $5 |

"... and total $55."

"OK," Rhonda said, "what's wrong with that?"

"The problem," I continued, "is that the China Shop offers a price discount for a complete place setting. If you look up the 'Complete Place Setting' inventory item for the Mikasa china brand in the `Inventory` table, you'll see that the customer should really only be charged $50."

I gave Rhonda and some of the others a chance to verify this for themselves.

"You're right," she said, "a discount is being applied. So if we did write five records to the **Transactions** table for this purchase, it would appear as though the customer paid $55 for the purchase, when really they only paid $50!"

"Absolutely right, Rhonda," I said. "Therefore, instead of adding five records to the **Transactions** table, we add just a single record reflecting the **ItemID** for a complete place setting, like this:"

| ItemID | Brand | Item | Price |
|---|---|---|---|
| 21 | Mikasa | Complete Place Setting | $50 |

"I think I see what you're talking about," Blaine said. "Is that what that next section of code is doing?"

"That's right, Blaine" I said, "here, we're using an **If...Then** statement to determine if the check box items which comprise a complete place setting are **all** selected:"

```
If chkChinaItem(0).Value = 1 And
   ↳chkChinaItem(1).Value = 1 And
   ↳chkChinaItem(2).Value = 1 And
   ↳chkChinaItem(3).Value = 1 And
   ↳chkChinaItem(4).Value = 1 Then
```

"If they are all selected, we execute the **AddNew** method of the recordset, which initiates the addition of a record to the underlying recordset..."

```
   datTransactions.Recordset.AddNew
```

"This next section of code confused me," Valerie said. "Is this how we complete the values for the fields in our new record – by assigning a setting to the **Value** property of the individual fields of the recordset?"

"Exactly, Valerie," I replied. "We need to update the **Value** property for each field of the transaction record. The first field, **CustID**, is the value of the global variable **g_intCustomerNumber**, like this:"

```
   datTransactions.Recordset.Fields("CustID").Value =
                 ↳g_intCustomerNumber
```

"However, the second field, **ItemID**, is a little more difficult to deal with."

"That's right," Chuck said, "this is the field whose value we don't know at the moment. That's why we wrote the **ItemIDLookUp** function, isn't that right?"

"That's right, Chuck," I said. "We don't know the correct value for the **ItemID** field, but we can look it up in the **Inventory** record by executing the **ItemIDLookUp** function we just wrote. We pass that function the brand of china in the form of the **Text** property of the list box, and a string literal corresponding to the item the customer has selected in the check box:"

```
datTransactions.Recordset.Fields("ItemID").Value =
                    ⇘ItemIDLookUp(lstBrands.Text, "Complete")
```

"Just a moment," said Rhonda, "I don't understand something."

"What's that, Rhonda?"

"Well, when we created the **ItemIDLookUp** function, I know we defined it with two arguments, but I didn't think we called them **lstBrands.txt**, and **"Complete"**, which are the arguments that we're passing to the function when we call it here:"

```
⇘ItemIDLookUp(lstBrands.Text, "Complete")
```

"That's a very interesting observation, Rhonda," I replied, "and it highlights a very common misconception about functions and their arguments. Let me digress for a moment and explain this. OK, here's the code that we used earlier to define our **ItemIDLookUp** function:"

```
Public Function ItemIDLookup(Brand, Item) As Long
```

"The fact that we have the two words in the parentheses, separated by a comma, indicates that whenever we run this function we will pass it two arguments. The arguments will contain the information that we want the function to process."

"Uh-huh," said Rhonda, "I'm with you so far."

"OK. Now, the actual names that we use here in the parentheses are kind of irrelevant to the work that the function actually does: all they really do is say to the function 'expect two pieces of information to be passed to you' – nothing more. So we could just as well call the arguments **(a, b)** and the function would still do its job. We call them **Brand** and **Item** here to make our code clearer for us when we come back to it – these names indicate to us exactly what's going in to our function."

"So," said Rhonda, "the names we use here are really just 'place-holders', right?"

"That's right, Rhonda," I confirmed. "When we come to use the function 'in anger', the function will expect to be passed two values, but it doesn't care what their actual names are when they're passed – it's their *position* that's important. That's part of what makes a function so flexible. Here, we pass the function the current contents of the **lstBrands.Text** property, and the string literal **"Complete"**:"

```
↳ItemIDLookUp(lstBrands.Text, "Complete")
```

"So, our function gets the two arguments it was expecting, separated by the comma, and it goes about its business, based on the input we've given it."

"I can see that now," said Rhonda, "thanks for explaining it."

"My pleasure," I replied.

"Moving back with our **UpdateTrans** code, we can see that the quantity field is just the value of the form-level variable **m_intQuantity**..."

```
   datTransactions.Recordset.Fields("Quantity").Value =
                   ↳m_intQuantity
```

"**Price** requires that we execute the **PriceLookUp** function:"

```
   datTransactions.Recordset.Fields("Price") =
                   ↳PriceLookUp(lstBrands.Text, "Complete")
```

"**DateOfPurchase** is today's date and time returned from the Visual Basic system function **Now:**"

```
   datTransactions.Recordset.Fields("DateOfPurchase").Value =
                   ↳Now
```

"Finally," I continued, "when all of the fields of the recordset have been completed with values, we execute the **Update** method of the recordset, which performs the actual addition of the record to the recordset..."

```
   datTransactions.Recordset.Update
```

I waited a minute to see if anyone had any further questions.

"Didn't we forget a field?" Rhonda asked. "What about **TransID** – we never completed a value for that field."

"The **TransID** field of the transaction record," I said, "is an AutoNumber field. When we execute the recordset's **AddNew** and **Update** methods, the Access database automatically takes care of completing that field for us with the next available value."

"That's great," Rhonda said. "That really is easy."

"I'm a little perplexed by that next section of code," Bob said, "Are we determining if the user has selected a platter?"

"That's right, Bob," I said. "Remember, a platter is not part of a complete place setting. We need to handle the possibility that the customer will select a complete place setting and either purchase, or not purchase, a platter to go along with it. That's why we check to see if the check box with an **Index** property of 5 has been selected:"

```
If chkChinaItem(5).Value = 1 Then
```

"If this checkbox *has* been selected, then we know that the customer has expressed a desire to purchase a platter, and we need to add a record to the **Transactions** table representing this purchase:"

```
      datTransactions.Recordset.AddNew
      datTransactions.Recordset.Fields("CustID").Value =
                    ↳g_intCustomerNumber
      datTransactions.Recordset.Fields("ItemID").Value =
                    ↳ItemIDLookUp(lstBrands.Text, "Platter")
      datTransactions.Recordset.Fields("Quantity").Value = 1
      datTransactions.Recordset.Fields("Price") =
                    ↳PriceLookUp(lstBrands.Text, "Platter")
      datTransactions.Recordset.Fields("DateOfPurchase").Value = Now
      datTransactions.Recordset.Update
   End If
```

"This code is nearly identical to what we used to add a transaction record for the complete place setting."

"Why did you specify a quantity of '**1**' for the **Quantity** field of this record?" Rachel asked. "Shouldn't we have used the value of **m_intQuantity** as we did for the complete place setting record?"

"That's a good question, Rachel," I said. "We specified a quantity of one for the platter because the customer is restricted to purchasing only one platter per order. If the customer elects to purchase a platter, they may only buy one."

"That's right," Rachel said, "I forgot that."

"No problem," I smiled, and waited to see if there were any other questions before proceeding.

"Finally," I said, "having taken care of the complete place setting logic, we exit the subprocedure by executing an **Exit Sub** statement:"

```
    Exit Sub
End If
```

"Am I right in saying," Dave asked, "that the next section of code is related to adding transaction records for items selected that *do not* comprise a complete place setting?"

"That's right, Dave," I said, "we've already executed the code to process transaction records if the customer has selected items comprising a complete place setting. If we've arrived at this point in the subprocedure, then the customer is choosing china items 'a la carte', and we need to add an individual record to the transaction table for each item of china selected. We *could* write a bunch of repetitive code for each china item selected by the customer, but instead we're going to use the **For Each** loop structure I mentioned earlier, in conjunction with the object variable we declared at the top of this subprocedure. Using these tools, we can check the value of each check box in the **chkChinaItem** control array. That's what this first line of code does:"

```
For Each objChk In chkChinaItem
```

"By using the **For Each** loop structure," I continued, "we tell Visual Basic to examine each check box in the **chkChinaItem** check box control array. As each one is examined, using the object variable name **objChk**, we can refer to the **Value** property of each check box in the control array using this syntax..."

```
    If objChk.Value = 1 Then
```

"So you're saying that the code in the **For Each** structure will be executed once for each member of the **chkChinaItem** control array?" Mary asked.

"That's exactly right, Mary," I said.

"So the first time through this **For Each** loop," Tom said, "the actual value of **objChk** would be **chkChinaItem(0)**, the second time **chkChinaItem(1)**, and so forth..."

"That's excellent, Tom," I said, "that's exactly the way to envision what is happening. As you can imagine, the flexibility that the **For Each** loop structure provides can allow us to write some very powerful generic code.

Instead of writing repetitive code that refers to individual check boxes on a form, we can write just a few lines of code that refer to the name of a single object variable instead. So if the **Value** property of the individual check box being examined in the **For Each** loop happens to be one..."

```
If objChk.Value = 1 Then
```

"...we execute this code:"

```
datTransactions.Recordset.AddNew
        datTransactions.Recordset.Fields("CustID").Value =
                    ↳g_intCustomerNumber
```

Melissa had a question: "What's up with the **Tag** property?" she asked. "I remember we set the **Tag** properties of the check boxes on the form. Here it looks like you are using the **Tag** property as an argument to both the **ItemIDLookUp** and **PriceLookUp** functions. I believe in the previous section of code you had used a string literal instead as an argument...."

```
        datTransactions.Recordset.Fields("ItemID").Value =
                    ↳ItemIDLookUp(lstBrands.Text, objChk.Tag)
```

"You're absolutely right, Melissa," I said, "we *are* using the value of the **Tag** property of each check box as an argument to both the **ItemIDLookUp** and **PriceLookUp** functions. Since the **Tag** property of each one of the check box controls contains the actual field name of the china item we wish to locate, we can use the **Tag** property as an argument to both **ItemIDLookUp** and **PriceLookUp**. If we hadn't used this technique, we would have had to write largely repetitive code for each check box in the **chkChinaItem** control array. The use of the **For Each** structure, plus the use of the **Tag** property as an argument to both of our custom functions, has made this code extremely flexible."

I waited to see if there were any questions before moving on.

"This next section of code," I continued, " determines, using the **For Each** loop structure, whether the check box we're dealing with represents a platter. We can check this just by looking at the **Tag** property of the object variable. If it *does* represent a platter, then since the customer is limited to the purchase of a single platter, we need to take care to add a transaction record with a quantity of 1 to the **Transactions** table:"

```
      If objChk.Tag = "Platter" Then
         datTransactions.Recordset.Fields("Quantity").Value = 1
      Else
         datTransactions.Recordset.Fields("Quantity").Value =
                ↳m_intQuantity
```

```
      End If
```

"The rest of this code," I said, "is very similar to the code in the previous section:"

```
      datTransactions.Recordset.Fields("Price") =
                ↳PriceLookUp(lstBrands.Text, objChk.Tag)
      datTransactions.Recordset.Fields("DateOfPurchase").Value =
                ↳Now
      datTransactions.Recordset.Update
   End If
Next
```

"...Notice that the `For Each` loop structure ends with the `Next` statement – this means 'now look at the next check box', and the loop will continue to execute until it has looped through all of the check boxes in the control array."

"I must confess," Blaine said, "that object variables are still a little confusing to me. Will we learn more about them in the Visual Basic Objects class that we'll be starting in a few weeks?"

"Yes, Blaine, we definitely will," I answered. "Don't forget: if you wish, you can always go back and rewrite this subprocedure so that it operates without the use of the object variable; the bottom line will be the same, but I think you'll find that you need to write a bunch of repetitive code to get that same result."

No one seemed anxious to take me up on my suggestion!

"When can we test these functions and procedures?" Kate asked. "I can hardly wait!"

"All we need in order to do that," I said, "is to make a small modification to the `Click` event procedure of `cmdIllTakeIt`. We can do that right now."

## Exercise – Modifying the cmdIllTakeIt Click Event Procedure

In this exercise, you'll modify the `cmdIllTakeIt Click` event procedure so that when this command button is clicked, the `UpdateTrans` subprocedure is executed.

1. Continue working with `frmMain`.
2. Modify the code in the `cmdIllTakeIt Click` event procedure so that it looks like the listing shown below. All we have to do here is remove the comment character from in front of the line reading `'Call UpdateTrans'`. Modified code is highlighted:

```
Private Sub cmdIllTakeIt_Click()

frmCustomerAsk.Show vbModal

If g_intCustomerNumber > 0 Then
'Call PrintSalesReceipt
Call UpdateTrans
Else
   MsgBox "Sorry, we cannot process your order without a customer ID"
End If

cmdReset.Value = True

End Sub
```

3. Save the China Shop project.
4. Run the program, and select some items of china to purchase. Click on the Calculate button, followed by the I'll Take It button, and enter a valid Customer ID. Then use the Staff Functions menu options to verify that records are being written to the **`Transactions`** table.

### *Discussion*

"Yes, it works!" I heard Rhonda say excitedly, as she verified that the transaction records were indeed being added to the **`Transactions`** table of the **`China`** database.

As I looked around the room, watching a bevy of activity as the students interacted with a Visual Basic database program they had programmed themselves, I was pretty happy. Students were busy running the China Shop program, selecting items of china, calculating a sales quotation, indicating that they wanted to make a purchase, and then watching as a record of their transaction was written to the **`Transactions`** table.

That's not to say everything went perfectly smoothly the first time through...

A few students had the same problem – a record of the customer's transaction was not being written to the **`Transactions`** table. A quick check of their code revealed that while they had executed the **`AddNew`** method of the recordset and properly stored values for each of the fields in the recordset, they had forgotten to execute the **`Update`** method of the recordset after doing so. As a result, their additions were lost, and weren't being committed to the underlying table in the database.

Ward pointed out to me and the rest of the class that it looked like the **`Date of Purchase`** text box on the **`Transactions`** form was just a bit too narrow to display the date that we were writing to the **`Transactions`** table. I double-checked, and discovered that he was right. I recommended to the class that everyone widen that text box just a bit to accommodate the field.

I glanced at the clock and saw that we were running short on time – we only had about an hour before it was time for everyone to leave for the Bullina China Shop. While I gave the class some more time to test the new features of the program, I quickly placed a phone call to Joe to make sure that he was ready for our arrival. Joe confirmed that he could hardly wait! He told me that his new printer was in place by the side of the China Shop PC, all powered up and ready to print the first Customer Sales Receipt! Joe also asked me if I knew anyone in Seattle who might be playing a trick on him. Someone, claiming to be a prospective customer from Seattle had called earlier in the day wanting to place a large order for china, and expressing dismay that the Bullina China Shop program was not yet web-enabled. While suspecting that I might know someone who would play such a trick, I promised Joe that my fall semester Visual Basic Web development course could always tackle that sort of requirement for him. In closing, I promised Joe that the class and I would be by to see him in a few hours, and that we'd be bringing the new program with us.

"We're not *quite* done yet," I said as I returned from making my phone call. "We now need to take the time to write the code that'll let us to print sales details when the customer accepts the price quotation."

# Printing a Sales Receipt

This is the exercise that I handed out to the class to achieve our next goal:

## Exercise – Creating the PrintSalesReceipt Subprocedure

In this exercise, you'll create the `PrintSalesReceipt` subprocedure, which will print a customer sales receipt to the China Shop's printer when the user clicks on the I'll Take It button.

1. Continue working with `frmMain`.
2. Make sure the code window is open, and then select Tools | Add Procedure from the Visual Basic main menu.
3. Complete the entries in the dialog box as follows:

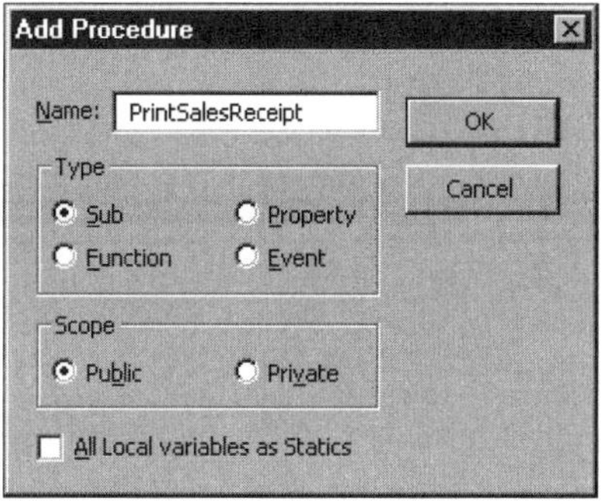

**4.** Click on the OK button, and the code window for the subprocedure `PrintSalesReceipt` will appear. Unlike some of our other exercises, there is no need to change the subprocedure header. Leave it as it is:

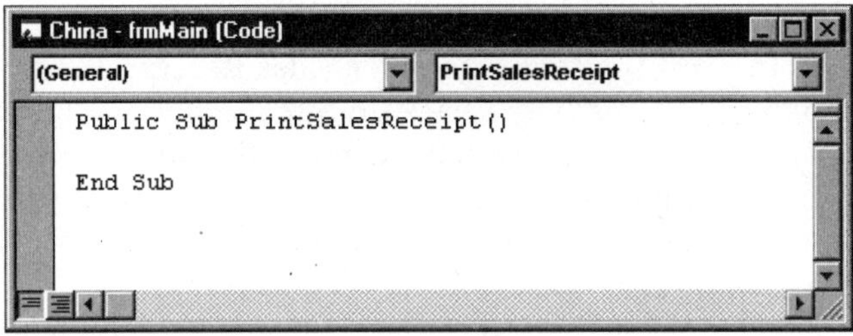


**5.** Now enter this final big batch of code between the subprocedure name and the `End Sub` line:

```
Sub PrintSalesReceipt()

Dim objChk As CheckBox

Printer.Print Format(Now, "mmmm d, yyyy hh:mm AMPM")
Printer.Print
Printer.Print
Printer.FontSize = "16"
Printer.FontBold = True
Printer.Print "The Bullina China Shop"
Printer.Print "22 Twain Drive"
Printer.Print "West Chester, PA 19380"
Printer.FontBold = False
Printer.Print
Printer.Print
Printer.Print "For future reference, your Customer ID is: " &
      ↳ g_intCustomerNumber
Printer.Print
Printer.Print
Printer.FontSize = "10"
Printer.Print "Dear Sir or Madam:"
Printer.Print
Printer.Print
Printer.Print "This is to confirm your order of the following ";
Printer.FontBold = True
Printer.Print lstBrands.Text;
Printer.FontBold = False
Printer.Print " components:"
Printer.Print
```

```
Printer.Print
Printer.Print "Item"; Tab(20); "Quantity"; Tab(40); "Unit Price";
      ↳Tab(60); "Total"
Printer.Print
Printer.Print
Printer.FontBold = True

For Each objChk In chkChinaItem
   If objChk.Value = 1 Then
      Printer.Print objChk.Tag;
   If objChk.Tag <> "Platter" Then
      Printer.Print Tab(20); (m_intQuantity);
   Else
      Printer.Print Tab(20); "1";
   End If
      Select Case objChk.Tag
         Case "Bowl"
            Printer.Print
            ↳Tab(40); Format(m_curBowlPrice, "currency");
            ↳Tab(60); Format((m_curBowlPrice * m_intQuantity),
            ↳"currency")

         Case "ButterPlate"
            Printer.Print
            ↳Tab(40); Format(m_curButterPlatePrice, "currency");
            ↳Tab(60); Format((m_curButterPlatePrice * m_intQuantity),
            ↳"currency")

         Case "Cup"
            Printer.Print
            ↳Tab(40); Format(m_curCupPrice, "currency");
            ↳Tab(60); Format((m_curCupPrice * m_intQuantity),
            ↳"currency")

         Case "Plate"
            Printer.Print
            ↳Tab(40); Format(m_curPlatePrice, "currency");
            ↳Tab(60); Format((m_curPlatePrice * m_intQuantity),
            ↳"currency")

         Case "Platter"
            Printer.Print
            ↳Tab(40); Format(m_curPlatterPrice, "currency");
            ↳Tab(60); Format(m_curPlatterPrice, "currency")
```

*Continued on following page*

```
            Case "Saucer"
                Printer.Print _
                ↳Tab(40); Format(m_curSaucerPrice, "currency");
                ↳Tab(60); Format((m_curSaucerPrice * m_intQuantity),
                ↳"currency")
        End Select
    End If
Next

Printer.Print String(80, "-")
Printer.Print
Printer.Print "Totals"; Tab(60); Format(m_curTotalPrice, "currency")

Printer.Font = "Times New Roman"
Printer.Print
Printer.Print
Printer.FontBold = True
Printer.Print "The total price of your order is ";
Printer.Print Format(m_curTotalPrice, "currency");
Printer.Print ". Thank you for your business!"
Printer.Print
Printer.Print
Printer.Print "Sincerely,"
Printer.Print
Printer.Print
Printer.Font.Name = "Script"
Printer.FontSize = 22
Printer.Print "Joe Bullina"
Printer.Font.Name = "Times New Roman"
Printer.FontSize = 10
Printer.Print
Printer.Print
Printer.Print "The Bullina China Shop"
Printer.Print
Printer.EndDoc

MsgBox "Sales Receipt Printing on Printer..."

End Sub
```

6. Save the China Shop project.
7. At this point, there's still no way of testing this subprocedure. We'll do that shortly, though.

### Discussion

"Some of this code looks familiar to me from the Introductory class," Chuck said.

"And it looks like we're using an object variable again," Mary added.

"Both of you are right," I replied, laughing, "we *did* cover how to print using the **Printer** object in our Introductory class and, once again, we're using an object variable – just as we did in the **UpdateTrans** subprocedure:"

```
Dim objChk As CheckBox
```

"For those of you unfamiliar with the **Printer** object that we covered in my Introductory class," I said, "the **Printer** object is an intrinsic part of Visual Basic. This means that we don't have to worry about the details of the actual printer being used – Windows will do all of that for us. What we're doing here is using the **Print** method of the **Printer** object to direct our readout to the printer – but it isn't until we execute the **EndDoc** method of the **Printer** object that what we have directed there actually begins to print."

I waited to see if there were any questions before continuing.

"This next section of code is pretty straightforward," I went on. "We're using the **Print** method to print the current date and time, plus the China Shop's address, in the top portion of the sales receipt. The **Print** method with no expression following it outputs a blank line to the printer. Notice that prior to printing the name and address of the China Shop we change the **Printer** object's **FontSize** property to 16, making the address very large..."

```
Printer.Print Format(Now, "mmmm d, yyyy hh:mm AMPM")
Printer.Print
Printer.Print
Printer.FontSize = "16"
Printer.FontBold = True
Printer.Print "The Bullina China Shop"
Printer.Print "22 Twain Drive"
Printer.Print "West Chester, PA 19380"
Printer.FontBold = False
Printer.Print
Printer.Print
```

"What does the '**Format**' part of the first line do?" asked Rachel.

"Sorry," I apologized, "I forgot to mention that – again, we discussed it last semester. In Visual Basic, the **Format** function lets you enhance your display: there are pre-defined formats, or you can create a format of your own. You need two arguments for the **Format** function: firstly, the expression to be formatted, and secondly, either a standard or a custom format. Here, the expression is the VB constant **Now**, and the format is what follows inside the quotes:"

```
Printer.Print Format(Now, "mmmm d, yyyy hh:mm AMPM")
```

"Does that explain everything?"

"Yes," Rachel nodded. "Thanks."

I paused again momentarily to allow further questions. None were forthcoming, so I returned to my explanation of the code.

"As a courtesy to the customer," I said, "we print their Customer ID on the sales receipt for future reference:"

```
Printer.Print "For future reference, your Customer ID is: " &
       ↳g_intCustomerNumber
Printer.Print
Printer.Print
```

"And next, we have a salutation to the customer," I continued. "Notice that first we change the `FontSize` of the printer object back to 10, then follow that up with a `Dear Sir or Madam` greeting:"

```
Printer.FontSize = "10"
Printer.Print "Dear Sir or Madam:"
Printer.Print
Printer.Print
```

"The following section confirms the customer's selection of brand…"

```
Printer.Print "This is to confirm your order of the following ";
Printer.FontBold = True
Printer.Print lstBrands.Text;
Printer.FontBold = False
Printer.Print " components:"
Printer.Print
Printer.Print
```

"…and the next segment prints a table of sorts," I said, "with headers for `Item`, `Quantity`, `Unit Price` and `Total Price`:"

```
Printer.Print "Item"; Tab(20); "Quantity"; Tab(40); "Unit Price";
       ↳Tab(60); "Total"
Printer.Print
Printer.Print
Printer.FontBold = True
```

"This next section of code," I continued, "uses the object variable, **objChk**, in conjunction with a **For Each** loop to print the individual items of china that the customer has purchased. Notice that we determine the customer's selection by checking if the **Value** property of the check box is set to **"1"**. Also, notice the special way we treat the platter's quantity, similarly to some of the other code we've written today:"

```
For Each objChk In chkChinaItem
   If objChk.Value = 1 Then
      Printer.Print objChk.Tag;
   If objChk.Tag <> "Platter" Then
      Printer.Print Tab(20); (m_intQuantity);
   Else
      Printer.Print Tab(20); "1";
   End If
```

"In the subsequent batch of code," I went on, "we use a **Select Case** structure, in conjunction with the object variable's **Tag** property, to determine how to properly format the item line of the sales receipt. Notice that the total price of the purchase is calculated as the price of the individual china items, using the appropriate form level variable, multiplied by the value of **m_intQuantity**, for every item *except* the platter. The **Format** function ensures that the prices are neatly displayed using a **Currency** format:"

```
      Select Case objChk.Tag
         Case "Bowl"
            Printer.Print
            ↳Tab(40); Format(m_curBowlPrice, "currency");
            ↳Tab(60); Format((m_curBowlPrice * m_intQuantity),
            ↳"currency")

         Case "ButterPlate"
            Printer.Print
            ↳Tab(40); Format(m_curButterPlatePrice, "currency");
            ↳Tab(60); Format((m_curButterPlatePrice * m_intQuantity),
            ↳"currency")

         Case "Cup"
            Printer.Print
            ↳Tab(40); Format(m_curCupPrice, "currency");
            ↳Tab(60); Format((m_curCupPrice * m_intQuantity),
            ↳"currency")

         Case "Plate"
            Printer.Print
            ↳Tab(40); Format(m_curPlatePrice, "currency");
```

*Continued on following page*

```
            ↳Tab(60); Format((m_curPlatePrice * m_intQuantity),
            ↳"currency")

        Case "Platter"
            Printer.Print
            ↳Tab(40); Format(m_curPlatterPrice, "currency");
            ↳Tab(60); Format(m_curPlatterPrice, "currency")

        Case "Saucer"
            Printer.Print
            ↳Tab(40); Format(m_curSaucerPrice, "currency");
            ↳Tab(60); Format((m_curSaucerPrice * m_intQuantity),
            ↳"currency")
        End Select
    End If
Next
```

"The **Tab** function of the **Printer** Object," I said, "for those of you unfamiliar with it, tells Visual Basic to align the print using the number in parentheses as a column number. **Tab(40)** tells Visual Basic to begin printing at the 40th column of the **Printer** object."

"I remember that from the Intro class," Rhonda said.

"Yes, we covered that in the Introductory class," I said, before continuing: "We conclude the printing of the sales receipt with some closing statements and information:"

```
Printer.Print String(80, "-")
Printer.Print
Printer.Print "Totals"; Tab(60); Format(m_curTotalPrice, "currency")

Printer.Font = "Times New Roman"
Printer.Print
Printer.Print
Printer.FontBold = True
Printer.Print "The total price of your order is ";
Printer.Print Format(m_curTotalPrice, "currency");
Printer.Print ". Thank you for your business!"
Printer.Print
Printer.Print
Printer.Print "Sincerely,"
Printer.Print
Printer.Print
```

"... including a 'scripted' signature from Joe Bullina:"

```
Printer.Font.Name = "Script"
Printer.FontSize = 22
Printer.Print "Joe Bullina"
Printer.Font.Name = "Times New Roman"
Printer.FontSize = 10
Printer.Print
Printer.Print
Printer.Print "The China Shop"
Printer.Print
```

"This next line of code," I said, "is perhaps the most important line of code in this subprocedure. The execution of the **EndDoc** method routes the sales receipt to the printer from the **Printer** object. If you forget to execute this line of code, nothing prints..."

```
Printer.EndDoc
```

"Finally," I concluded, "we display a message box informing the customer that their sales receipt is being printed..."

```
MsgBox "Sales Receipt Printing..."
```

I had expected some questions but there were none. Most of the students were familiar with the **Printer** object and **Print** method from the Introductory class – and the remainder of the students seemed pretty confident with its operation. Everyone seemed anxious to print their very own sales receipts.

"I know you're all anxious to see your own program print now," I said. "To do that, all we need to do is remove a comment character from the **cmdIllTakeIt Click** event procedure. Let's do that now."

## Exercise – Modifying the cmdIllTakeIt Click Event Procedure

In this exercise, you'll modify the **cmdIllTakeIt Click** event procedure to execute the **PrintSalesReceipt** subprocedure when the user accepts the price quotation.

1. Continue working with **frmMain**.
2. Modify the code in the **cmdIllTakeIt Click** event procedure so that it looks like the listing below. Again, all we're doing is removing a comment character, this time from in front of the line reading **Call PrintSalesReciept**. Modified code is highlighted:

```
Private Sub cmdIllTakeIt_Click()

frmCustomerAsk.Show vbModal
If g_intCustomerNumber > 0 Then
Call PrintSalesReceipt
Call UpdateTrans
Else
    MsgBox "Sorry, we cannot process your order without a Customer ID"
End If

cmdReset.Value = True

End Sub
```

3. Save the China Shop project.
4. Run the program, make select some china pieces and quantities, and then go through the price quotation and acceptance process to verify that the customer's sales receipt is printed when you click on the I'll Take It button.

### *Discussion*

This was one exercise where all I had to do was listen to see how everyone was doing. Almost immediately, I became aware of the sounds of the classroom laser printer as it clicked and whirred into life. However...

"I have a problem," said Dave, "come take a look."

I walked round to Dave's PC and, sure enough, when he accepted the price quotation and clicked through the customer verification process, his program generated the following error message:

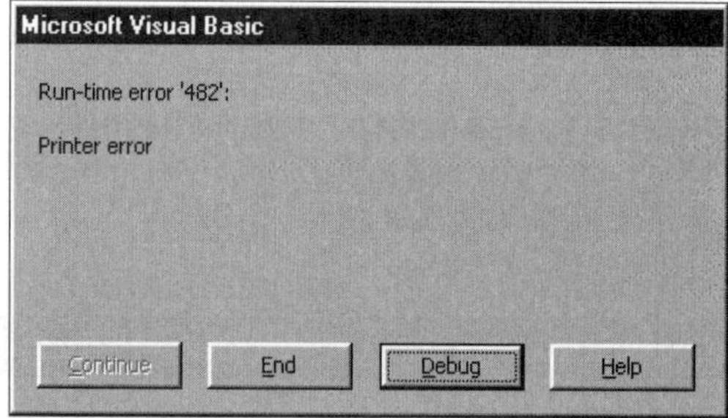


We did some checking, and it emerged that the reason for this failure was that Dave's PC hadn't been properly logged onto the classroom network, with the result that the program had been unable to connect to the printer.

"This shouldn't be a problem in Joe's store," I reassured the class, "as the printer is connected directly to the PC. However, if we had the time, I'd probably add some error-handling code so that the program doesn't fail if the printer is unavailable for some reason. We don't have time to do that today, but it's definitely something I'll look to do in the coming weeks."

Over the course of the next ten minutes, each and every student in the class had printed at least one sales receipt.

Time was running out – we had only a few minutes before we needed to pack up and travel to the China Shop. With just a hint of melancholy, I announced to the class:

"We have just one more exercise remaining in the course," I said. "If you recall, we had discovered that we failed to include access keys on the main form."

"That's right," Lou said, "you did say we should do that."

"True to my promise, Lou," I said, "here it is."

It was with some sadness that I then distributed the final exercise of the course for the students to complete – I always hate to see my classes drawing to a close:

## Exercise – Changing the Access Keys on frmMain

1. Continue working with `frmMain`.
2. Use the table below to change the `Caption` properties of the following controls on `frmMain`. Remember that to change the captions of the menu items you'll need to open up the Menu Editor:

| Control | Caption |
|---|---|
| chkChinaItem(0) | Pla&te |
| chkChinaItem(1) | &Butter Plate |
| chkChinaItem(2) | S&oup Bowl |
| chkChinaItem(3) | C&up |
| chkChinaItem(4) | S&aucer |
| chkChinaItem(5) | P&latter |
| chkCompletePlaceSetting | Co&mplete Place Setting |
| cmdCalculate | &Calculate |
| cmdIllTakeIt | &I'll Take It |

*Table continued on following page*

| Control | Caption |
|---|---|
| cmdReset | &Reset |
| optQuantity(8) | &8 |
| optQuantity(4) | &4 |
| optQuantity(2) | &2 |
| optQuantity(1) | &1 |
| MnuStaffFunctions | &Staff Functions |
| mnuCustomers | View/Update &Customers |
| mnuTransactions | View &Transactions |
| MnuInventory | View/Update &Inventory |
| MnuUsers | View/Update &Users |

Your form should now look similar to the screenshot:

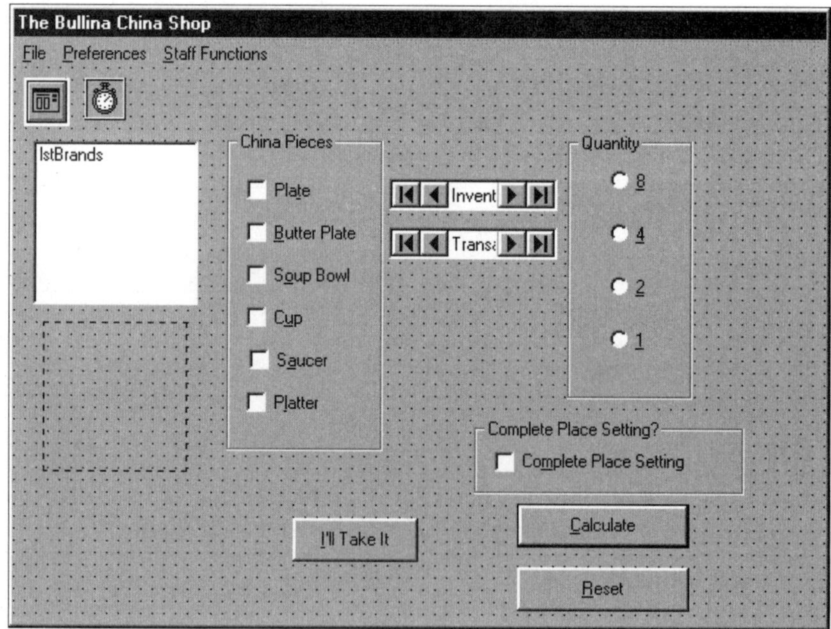


3. Save the China Shop project.

Well, we'd done it – we were finished with the modifications to the China Shop project.

## Testing the Program

"Those are all the changes we need to make to the program," I told the class.

"You mean we're really finished?" Rhonda said.

"That's right, Rhonda," I said, "if you check our requirements statement for the China Shop modifications, you'll see that there's nothing else that needs to be done with the program itself, although we do have some administrative details to take care of – and then it's off to the China Shop to deliver and install the program."

"What administrative details?" Melissa asked.

"Last semester," I said, "when we delivered the current version of the China Shop program to the China Shop, at Joe Bullina's insistence, we all voted for one student's program out of the nineteen developed in our class to be the program placed on the China Shop PC. We have the same dilemma here this semester – nineteen versions of the same basic program, with only one China Shop PC to install it on!"

"So how do we pick the program to be placed on the China Shop PC?" Tom asked.

"We'll do what we did last semester," I said. "I'm asking everyone to take a few moments to perform a final test of their program. When you're sure it's working as required, come to the front of the classroom and pick up a ballot, then take a quick walk around the classroom and vote for the top three projects. The project that receives the most first place votes will be the program that we install at the China Shop. As I did in the Intro class, I'm going to remove my project from eligibility, and Rhonda, whose project was the one chosen last semester, has also generously withdrawn her project from contention this semester. Remember everyone, this is your project – one of you deserves to have the place of honor in the China Shop."

"Speaking of testing," Rachel said, "can you give us some guidelines on testing our programs?"

"This version of the program is much more difficult to test than the original program," I said, "because there's so much more to it. At a minimum, you want to ensure that the program calculates the prices correctly, and for that you should have some kind of **price matrix** already calculated so that you know what the correct price should be for a variety of customer selections. In particular, you want to pay special attention to any selection involving a complete place setting and a platter."

"Anything else?" Kevin asked.

"We can't forget Joe Bullina's primary purpose in having us update this program," I said, "and that was to provide him and his China Shop staff with an easy way to update inventory prices. That's vitally important. Beyond that, we should ensure that all of the functionality that we identified in the requirements statement is present and working."

"I would think that most of the real bugs in the program would have been discovered by now," Kevin said.

"I'm not sure we can say that with 100% certainty, Kevin," I replied. "Remember, I discovered a hidden bug myself this week when I tried to add a new item of inventory with a price that contained a fraction and discovered that we had erroneously declared a variable in the Intro class as an `Integer` and not a `Currency` type. In fact, it's possible that there may be more of those types of bugs in this program – although I somehow doubt it."

"I would think," Ward said, "that the chances for a bug like that slipping through are even greater now than before. After all, we now have nine forms instead of one, and the amount of code in this program is probably triple what we had before."

"You're right, Ward," I said, "even more reason to spend as much time as possible testing your project one last time."

I then asked everyone to spend the next fifteen minutes or so giving their projects one final check, in playfully but respectfully reviewing their classmates' projects, and in voting for their three favorite projects. As I collected the ballots and secretly tallied the totals, I asked everyone to give me a disk with their copy of the China Shop project on it. I then provided everyone in the class with a map to the Bullina China Shop.

"Class is officially dismissed for today," I said, "I hope to see you all at the China Shop – and please drive safely."

I called Dave aside. As he had done during the Introductory class, Dave had volunteered to coordinate the installation of this version of the China Shop program at the Bullina China Shop. I handed Dave the diskette containing the project that had received the most first place votes.

"Dave, would you mind installing the program," I said, "you know how I drive – slowly!"

"I'll be glad to do the installation for you," he said, as he glanced at the student's name on the disk and smiled. "See you there."

## We Meet at the China Shop

No sooner had Dave left the classroom than I met a colleague in the hallway who was having a problem with a program she had written the previous week. Knowing that the delivery of the enhanced China Shop program was in Dave's capable hands, I then spent some time working with her. I arrived at the Bullina China Shop about two hours later, quite obviously the last one to arrive. Late afternoon business at the China Shop was brisk – the parking lot was jammed. As I walked through the door, a very pleasant sight soothed my eyes. As had been the case with the introduction of the inaugural China Shop program, the place was full of balloons and streamers – and there was a buffet table of food set up in the corner of the room. In addition, Joe had also hired the services of a small band that was playing soft music near the food table.

Joe caught sight of me.

"John," he said, "once again, you and your students have come through for me! This program is great – and I wouldn't have thought the original could have been improved on! I can't believe what a great job your students did with this. Everyone loves it, and even *I've* been able to update inventory prices – with ease! And those transaction records – fabulous! At last, I'll be able to know for sure exactly what I've sold. Here, have a sandwich!"

Amidst the hullabaloo and excitement, I glanced toward the middle of the China shop, and there on a kiosk in the middle of the sales floor was a computer running the enhanced China Shop program, with a brand new laser printer attached. Seated at the PC was Lou, training the sales staff.

"Well, Joe," I said, "as I said last semester, you really know how to throw a party. Thanks for everything."

"Lou's been demonstrating his version of the China Shop program to the sales staff now for the last ten minutes," Joe said. "And they haven't gotten up yet. Their attention has been riveted to the program since Lou started the demo. Your class really did a great job with it. I think Midge may reconsider her retirement plans!"

I wandered over to the kiosk and caught Lou's eye. He was busily watching Midge put the program through its paces, logging in using the Administrator UserID and password, and bringing up the Staff Functions on the menu.

"Going to stay on now, Midge?" I asked.

"It's very good," she smiled, "but no!"

"I'm stunned," Lou said, "that the class voted for my version of the project. I'm really honored."

"You did a great job with the program, Lou," I said, "I would say your Visual Basic future is very bright."

Joe Bullina motioned to a couple munching on some sandwiches at the buffet table to come over to the kiosk.

"I don't know whether you remember these folks from last year," Joe said, "but this is the couple who received the first sales quotation from the original China Shop program. For good luck, I invited them back to be the first to try out the new version of the program."

"Hi," I said, "I believe you're Rita and Gil – aren't you?"

"You have a good memory," Gil said, "you remind me a lot of our son."

"Last year Gil bought me china for our anniversary," Rita said. "This time Gil has promised to buy me new china for my birthday – 82 years young on June 7th."

"Congratulations!" Joe said.

As Midge and Lou vacated the area around the kiosk (after Lou had closed and restarted the program, and then logged in using the Customer UserID and password), Joe Bullina pulled up two chairs. Gil sat down beside Rita, and the two of them began to use the modified China Shop program. Lou and the rest of the students from the class watched the couple as they began to use the modified program.

Having used the previous version before, the two were pretty familiar with it. Gil seemed to know exactly what he wanted, and after making a selection of china...

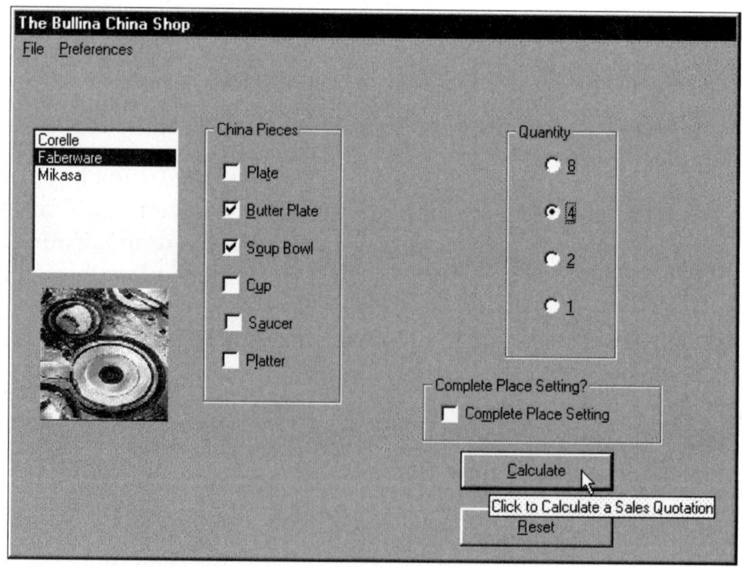

... and clicking the Calculate command button, the two of them were greeted with an unfamiliar – to them at least! – I'll Take It command button:

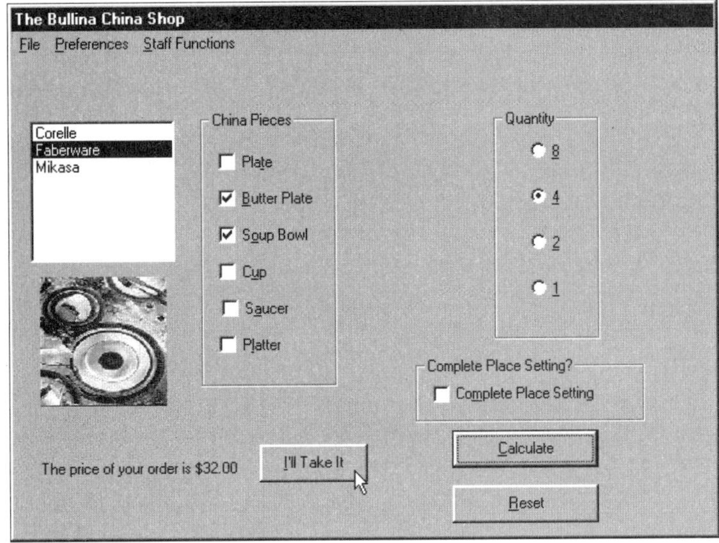


I overheard Gil say to Rita "the price looks good to me", and then he clicked on the I'll Take It command button. The program then asked him if he had a Customer ID...

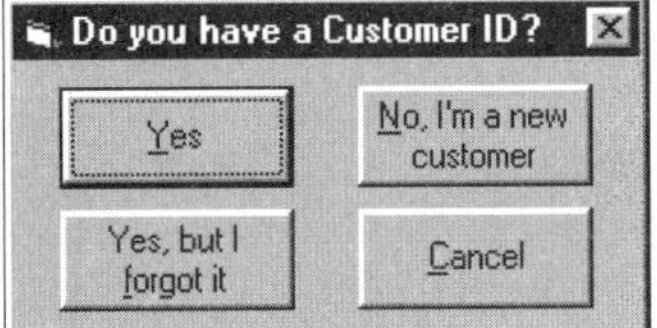


... to which he responded by clicking on the No, I'm a New Customer button. When the Welcome New Customer form appeared, he and Rita set about completing it:

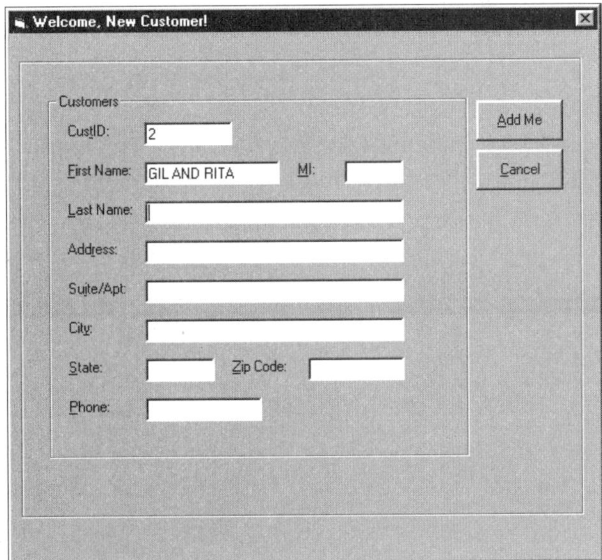

I noticed Gil hesitate slightly as he began to fill in the text boxes on the form, perhaps wondering whether he should make an entry in the Cust ID box. But, since focus was immediately placed on the First Name field, he made an entry in *that* field and then finished completing the rest of the boxes on the form.

After pausing a moment or two to check his input, Gil clicked on the Add Me button and the following screenshot was displayed:

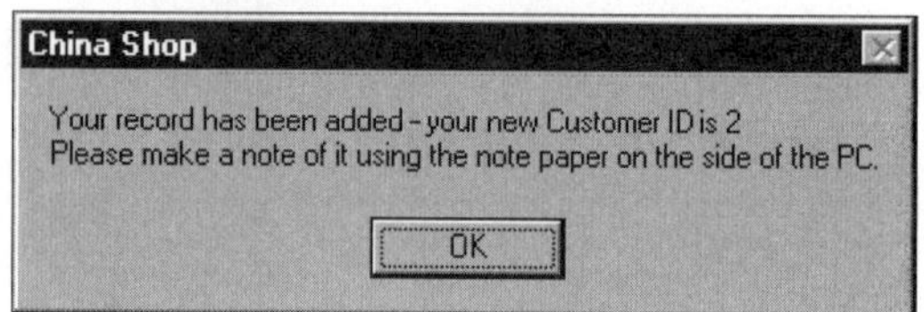


Gil picked up a sheet of notepaper arranged neatly by the PC and made a note of his new Customer ID. Gil then clicked on the OK button, and when he did, the following screenshot appeared:

Rita reached over to the laser printer, picked up the sales receipt from the printer, and the two of them proceeded to the sales counter at the front of the store to pick up their china. As Gil passed by me, he gave me a wink and said "Works great!"

As Rita and Gil walked to the counter, Joe addressed the assembled class.

"Hopefully they'll be back again and again," Joe said. "Can we view their transaction record?"

"Sure thing, Joe," I said. "First we need to exit the program, then log on again as an Administrator."

I did exactly that, and then selected Staff Functions | View Transactions from the menu bar…

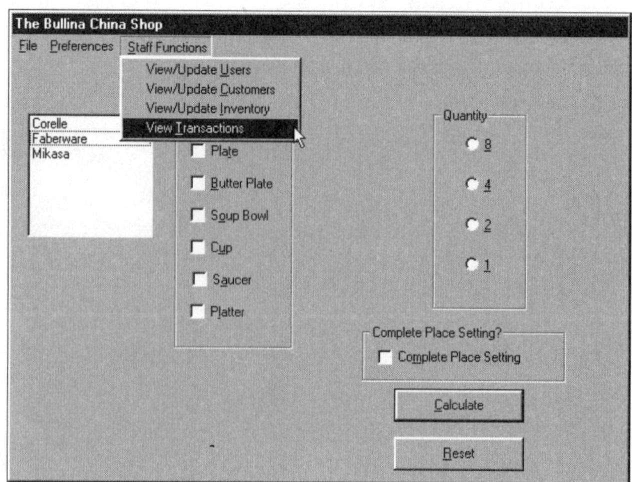

The Transactions form was displayed, and I moved to the second record in the table...

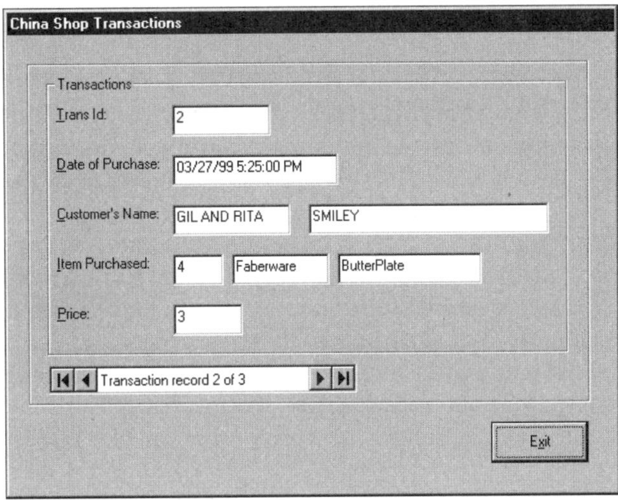


"There are Rita and Gil's transaction records," I said, "recorded permanently in the **`Transactions`** table. One record for the butter plate, and one record for the soup bowl. "

I turned to Joe Bullina.

"As we did last semester, Joe," I said, "pairs of students have volunteered to be on site to make observations and assist with any problems that might come up – they'll also be showing your sales staff how to update inventory prices, and some of the other staff functions."

"It's always great to have them here," Joe said, "and after seeing the wonderful work you've done on this project, I'm sure I'll have more work for your next class – that fellow who called me earlier this morning from Seattle gave me a few ideas!"

"Maybe we can tackle some of them in my upcoming Visual Basic Objects course or Web development course," I said. "I expect that some of these students will be in one or both of those classes. And Joe, on behalf of all the students in my class, I want to thank you for a wonderful learning opportunity. I'm sure we'll be in touch."

I then shouted across the room, "I've got to take off now. Everyone please be mindful of your coverage schedules, and if you have any problems, you all know where to find me. I hope to see you all in a few weeks."

I picked my way through the crowded parking lot and drove off into – well, not quite the sunset, but you know what I mean...

## Closing Thoughts

Congratulations! You've completed the class, and completed the database implementation of the China Shop project. I hope you felt the excitement of delivering and installing the China Shop project as much as the students in my class did, because you were a big part of it. But don't let this be the end of your learning experience with Visual Basic.

At this point, you should feel confident enough to tackle a variety of programs, including projects that have database implications. I hope that by following along with my Visual Basic Database programming class, you've seen how real-world database applications are developed. That's not to say that all projects go as smoothly as this one did, neither does every client meet us on delivery day with sandwiches, balloons and streamers. You can expect your share of mistakes, misinterpretations, and misunderstanding along the way. But it's always exciting, and if you love it like I do, it's always fun.

As I close, I just want to give you a few words of advice.

First, remember that in programming, there's rarely a single "correct" solution. There really is more than one way to paint a picture.

Secondly, always be your own best friend. Inevitably, while trying to work through a solution, there will be frustrating moments. Never doubt yourself, and never get "down" on yourself.

And finally, remember that there is always more to learn. The world of programming is an endless series of free-learning seminars. All you need to do is open up a manual, read a help file, surf the Internet, or pick up a Visual Basic book, and you are well on your way. You can never know it all, let alone master it all. But always move in that direction. Good luck, and I hope to see you in a future class of mine.

*John Smiley*

isual Basic Learn to Program Databas
ith Visual Basic Learn to Progra
atabases with Visual Basic Learn
rogram Databases with Visual Basic Lea
Program Databases with Visual Bas
earn to Program Databases with Visu
asic Learn to Program Databases w
isual Basic Learn to Program Databas
ith Visual Basic Learn to Progra
atabases with Visual Basic Learn
rogram Databases with Visual Basic Lea
Program Databases with Visual Bas
earn to Program Databases with Visu
asic Learn to Program Databases wi
isual Basic Learn to Program Databas
ith Visual Basic Learn to Progra
atabases with Visual Basic Learn

## Appendix A

# Student Biographies

On the evening of the first class I took home the biographies that the eighteen students had written about themselves. I'm always interested to know the mix of abilities and backgrounds of my students.

They turned out to be a varied bunch, who fell roughly into five categories.

**Some of the students were looking to have a new skill-set to use if their current job fell through:**

**Linda** wrote that she loved her Network Administration job, but was glad to have something to 'fall back' on in the future. She hoped that this course would give her a solid foundation in the database side of Visual Basic.

**Dave** reported that his job as a mid-level manager was still very much in jeopardy, and that he thought it was just a matter of time before he received 'bad news'. I knew that with his obviously outstanding abilities in Visual Basic he wouldn't have any trouble securing another job – particularly with this class under his belt too!

**Mary,** a statistical analyst for a railroad that was currently undergoing a merger, was also fearful for her job. She wrote that she hoped that this class in Visual Basic, along with the Introductory class, would enable her to obtain a new position if the worst did happen. I felt that after she heard the success stories from some other members of the class, her demeanor would perk up a bit.

**There were those who wanted to improve their current status at work:**

**Peter** wrote that he continued to enjoy his job as a COBOL programmer, and expressed hopes that after completing this class his company would finally let him tackle a Visual Basic project.

**Kathy**, a Microsoft Access programmer, reported that she was now working on a Visual Basic project at work – something she had been wanted to do for some time.

**Kate** happily reported that she was also writing Visual Basic programs back at the office. Kate, unlike Kathy, had no prior programming experience, so this was quite an accomplishment.

Working in a small office, Kate had taken advantage of her boss's offer to pay for a Visual Basic programming class, and in the few weeks between the end of the Introductory class and the beginning of this one, she had already designed, programmed and implemented a Visual Basic project! Needless to say, she was elated over the chance to do some more, and wrote that she was looking forward to 'database-enabling' her program.

**A few students wanted to use the skills they could gain on the course to help start a new career:**

**Valerie** was a stay at home mom looking to do some Visual Basic programming part time. Based on her performance in the introductory class, this class would make that desire achievable.

**Blaine** wrote that his greatest fears had been realized over the semester break – he had finally lost his job as a mainframe programmer. But, due in no small part to the Introductory Visual Basic course and the China Shop project, he had already been offered a new job, and would be starting work a week from Monday!

**We had two younger students and those that wanted to study for their own general interests:**

**Chuck,** the youngest student in the Introductory Visual Basic class, wrote that he had built a Visual Basic program for his mother's law firm over the semester break. He was joined by his friend Rachel. They were the youngest students in the class – both 16 years of age.

**Rachel** was a new student – both a friend and classmate of Chuck's. Chuck had told her how much he had enjoyed the introductory class. She wrote that she had done a lot of programming in C and C++, and had worked with Chuck on his Visual Basic programs during the Introductory class.

**Ward**, with his typically dry humor, wrote that, for a 78 year old senior citizen, he thought he was doing pretty well just getting up in the morning! That was a gross understatement; he made wonderful contributions to the Introductory class.

**Lou** wrote that his illness, which would one day totally disable him and leave him wheel chair bound, was slowly but gradually progressing. He wrote that he held high hopes for genetic research, and despite his worsening symptoms, reported that he had been able to write a Visual Basic program for his local florist during the semester break.

**Rhonda** reported that she had fulfilled her latest life's desire in the introductory class – to be able to keep up with her grandchildren! Not surprisingly, she told the class that she had taken her grandchildren to the China Shop to show them the program their grandmother wrote!

**That left five students who wanted to use visual basic within their workplace to either generally enhance procedures and speed up their work, or to use for a specific application:**

**Kevin**, new to the class, wrote that he had a Ph.D. in Microbiology, and that he was interested in using Visual Basic as a tool in his research.

**Tom**, also new to the class, wrote that he was both a civil engineer and an architect for a major construction firm in the Philadelphia area, and that he was interested in using Visual Basic to interface with a Computer Aided Design package he used for his job.

**Melissa** wrote that she was a physician currently doing research with a large pharmaceutical company, and that she was interested in using Visual Basic to assist her in genetic research.

**Steve** indicated that he had quite profitably used the Visual Basic techniques he learned in the Introductory class in his own computer consulting firm. He had invited everyone in the class to examining the brand new four-wheeled fruits of his Visual Basic labors in the parking lot after class!

**Bob,** a commercial plumber by trade, wrote that during the semester break he had written a Visual Basic program to automate his process of bidding on large construction jobs. According to Bob, the program had already saved him more money than the tuition for the Introductory Visual Basic course. He was definitely a happy camper!

That covered everyone, I was pleased to think that my class reflected a range of people who all had much to gain from this course.

isual Basic Learn to Program Databas
vith Visual Basic Learn to Progr
atabases with Visual Basic Learn
rogram Databases with Visual Basic Lea
o Program Databases with Visual Ba
earn to Program Databases with Vis
asic Learn to Program Databases w
isual Basic Learn to Program Databas
vith Visual Basic Learn to Progr
atabases with Visual Basic Learn
rogram Databases with Visual Basic Lea
o Program Databases with Visual Ba
earn to Program Databases with Visu
asic Learn to Program Databases wi
isual Basic Learn to Program Databas
vith Visual Basic Learn to Progra
atabases with Visual Basic Learn

# Appendix B

# Installing the China Shop Project

We've included the code for the existing China shop project (the one that was built in John Smiley's first book) on the CD that comes bundled in the back of *this* book.

If you haven't already got the completed version of the China shop program from *Learn to Program with Visual Basic 6* on your PC, you'll need to copy the relevant files from the CD before you can start work on enhancing it. (If you *do* already have a completed China Shop application on your machine, you can continue working with it.)

The following steps explain how to get a working version of the China Shop program up and running on your PC.

## Creating the Folders

Create a folder on your PC's hard drive called **`VBFiles`**. Note that all the references in the pre-built code supplied on the CD expect this folder to be on the PC's **`C:`** drive, so if you create the **`VBFiles`** folder elsewhere, you'll have to change the code accordingly.

Within the **`VBFiles`** folder, create a sub-folder called **`China`**. All of the China Shop's files will live in this **`C:\VBFiles\China`** folder. Your folder setup should look like this in Windows Explorer:

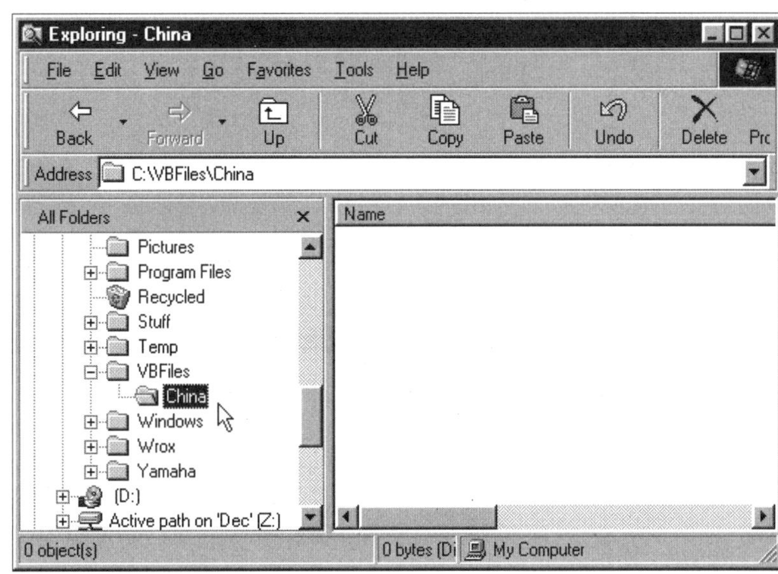

## Copying the Files

1. Open up the CD in Windows Explorer, navigate to the **For Chapter 1** folder, and select all of the files that you find there:

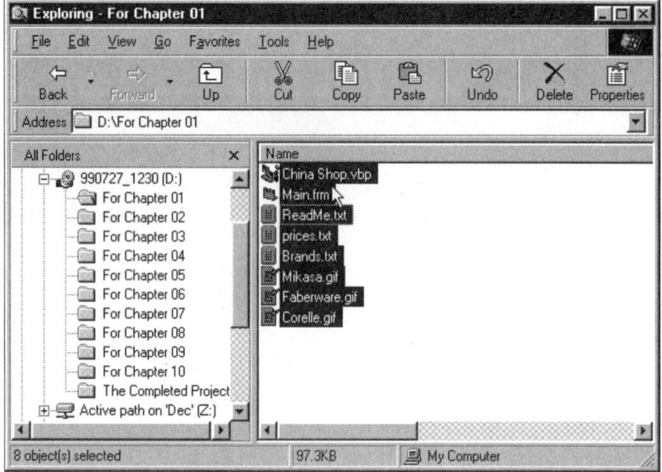


2. Drag these files across and drop them in the `C:\VBFiles\China` folder.
3. Next, make sure you've selected all the files in the `C:\VBFiles\China` folder, and then right-click on the multiple selection. From the pop-up menu…

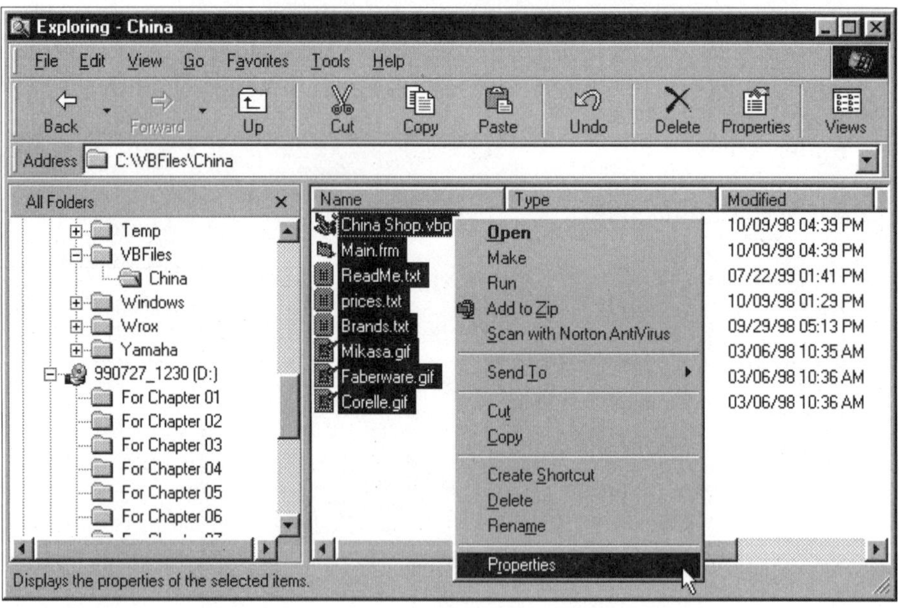


…select the Properties option.

4. Now make sure that the Read-only attribute box is **unchecked**, as shown below:

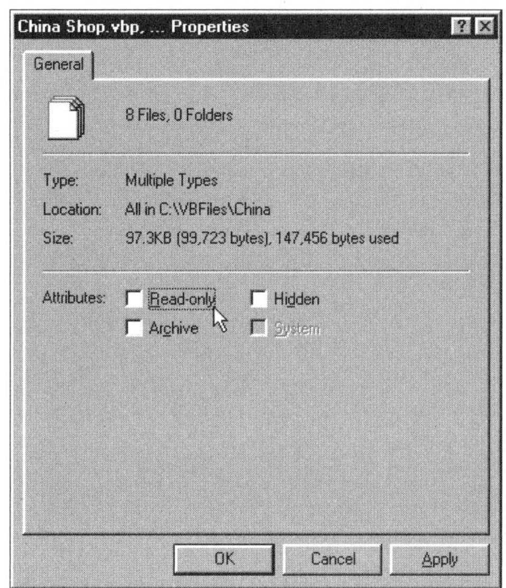


5. Click on the OK button, and the files for the initial version of the China Shop will be ready for you to use and update. You can now double-click on the **`China Shop.vbp`** file and the project will open up in design view in Visual Basic (assuming you have VB installed on your machine!)

This is what the files you've copied do: **`China Shop.vbp`** and **`Main.frm`** are the project file and single form file for the program; **`ReadMe.txt`** is information-only; **`Prices.txt`** and **`Brands.txt`** contain price and inventory information that the program uses; and the three **`.gif`** files are used to display images of china pieces on the project's user interface.

## Using the Built Versions of the Modified Code

The other folders on the CD contain the modified China Shop code at various stages of development through this book. Thus, the **`For Chapter 5`** folder contains the code as it appears at the end of Chapter 4, ready for input to Chapter 5, and so on.

If you need to replace your own code at any time, you can simply copy the relevant version from the appropriate folder on the CD and set the files' attributes so that they are not Read-only – just like you did in the steps described above. Note that if you don't have Microsoft Access, you can copy the completed **`China.mdb`** file – the file that contains the database that the modified project uses – from the **`For Chapter 4`** folder. However, we really really really do urge that you only use these built files as a last resort – building your skills and learning properly depend on practice and experience. Good luck!

isual Basic Learn to Program Databas

vith Visual Basic Learn to Progr

atabases with Visual Basic Learn

rogram Databases with Visual Basic Lea

o Program Databases with Visual Ba

earn to Program Databases with Visu

asic Learn to Program Databases w

isual Basic Learn to Program Databas

vith Visual Basic Learn to Progr

atabases with Visual Basic Learn

rogram Databases with Visual Basic Lea

o Program Databases with Visual Bas

earn to Program Databases with Visu

asic Learn to Program Databases wi

isual Basic Learn to Program Databas

vith Visual Basic Learn to Progr

atabases with Visual Basic Learn

# Index

## A



## B

# Index



## C

## D

# Index



# E

## Index

## M



## N

# Index

isual Basic Learn to Program Databas
ith Visual Basic Learn to Progr
atabases with Visual Basic Learn
rogram Databases with Visual Basic Lea
Program Databases with Visual Ba
earn to Program Databases with Vis
asic Learn to Program Databases w
isual Basic Learn to Program Databas
ith Visual Basic Learn to Progra
atabases with Visual Basic Learn
rogram Databases with Visual Basic Lea
Program Databases with Visual Bas
earn to Program Databases with Visu
asic Learn to Program Databases wi
isual Basic Learn to Program Databas
ith Visual Basic Learn to Progra

# *Can I Be an Author, Please?*

*Dear Sir or Madam,*

*I am writing to express my desire to contribute to your fine company's well-being by writing a book on Advanced Microwave Oven Programming. Large sums of money will, of course, have to change hands, for that is the nature of capitalist society, but I feel that it is my duty to pass on my accrued knowledge to the masses.*

*My previous short sample manuscripts on VCR timing skills and telephone keypad operation were never acknowledged by your good selves, but I feel that I have excelled the standard of even these works in the draft script 'LTP Microwaves' and am willing to overlook our previous lack of connection. I would be grateful if you would take the time to review my work as I feel that I have captured the very essence of Active Path material here. Not to boast, but I do feel that even John Smiley himself would be proud to share a book series with this title.*

*I look forward to hearing from you, and I hope that we can do business.*

*Yours sincerely,*

*Ethel Scrubdaisy*

Dear Ethel,

I regret to inform you that we cannot accept your manuscript, on the simple grounds that we are not in the business of publishing books on Microwave Programming. It is, unfortunately, an area into which we have not expanded as of yet. You have my sincerest pledge that on the day we break into that market, your name will be first on everyone's minds. I must, however, caution you that under no circumstances may this manuscript be published elsewhere: the title and style of presentation are so closely knitted to the Active Path brand (as you have said) and cannot, therefore, be used under any other guise.

I must stress here that we are only turning the work down on the basis of the subject matter. If you or anyone else you know is interested in writing a similar manuscript in the areas of Java, Access, VBA (all areas), C++, Visual Basic, or any form of web development, we would welcome your input. Don't hesitate to contact myself, Sarah Inston, on authors@activepath.com where we can discuss a suitable project.

Yours faithfully,

Sarah Inston

Learn to Program Databases with Visual Basic

# Forthcoming Titles from Active Path

We will continue to expand our output to teach you the programming skills that you need.

Our next publications are:

- **Learn to Program with HTML** by Chris Ullman
- **Learn to Program Objects with Visual Basic** by John Smiley
- **Learn to Program on the Web with Visual Basic** by John Smiley

sual Basic Learn to Program Databas
ith Visual Basic Learn to Progr
atabases with Visual Basic Learn
rogram Databases with Visual Basic Lea
Program Databases with Visual Ba
earn to Program Databases with Vis
asic Learn to Program Databases w
isual Basic Learn to Program Databas
ith Visual Basic Learn to Progr
atabases with Visual Basic Learn
rogram Databases with Visual Basic Lea
Program Databases with Visual Bas
earn to Program Databases with Visu
asic Learn to Program Databases wi
isual Basic Learn to Program Databas
ith Visual Basic Learn to Progra
atabases with Visual Basic Learn

## Learn To Program Databases with Visual Basic 6 Registration Card

Name ____________________

Address ____________________

____________________

____________________

____________________

City __________ State/Region __________

Country __________ Postcode/Zip __________

E-mail ____________________

Occupation ____________________

How did you hear about this book? ____________________

- ☐ Book review (name) ____________________
- ☐ Advertisement (name) ____________________
- ☐ Recommendation ____________________
- ☐ Catalog ____________________
- ☐ Other ____________________

Where did you buy this book? ____________________

- ☐ Bookstore (name) __________ City __________
- ☐ Computer Store (name) ____________________
- ☐ Mail Order ____________________
- ☐ Other ____________________

What influenced you in the purchase of this book?

- ☐ Cover Design
- ☐ Contents
- ☐ Other (please specify) ____________________

How did you rate the overall contents of this book?

- ☐ Excellent ☐ Good
- ☐ Average ☐ Poor

What did you find most useful about this book? ____________________

What did you find least useful about this book? ____________________

Please add any additional comments. ____________________

What other subjects will you buy a computer book on soon? ____________________

What is the best computer book you have used this year?

____________________

*Note: This information will only be used to keep you updated about new Active Path titles and will not be used for any other purpose or passed to any other third party.*

Active Path writes books for you. Any suggestions, or ideas about how you want information given in your ideal book will be studied by our team. Your comments are always valued at Active Path.

Free phone in USA 800-814-4527
Fax (312) 893 8001

UK Tel. (0121) 687 4100 Fax (0121) 687 4101

*Computer Book Publishers*

NB. If you post the bounce back card below in the UK, please send it to:
Active Path Ltd. Arden House, 1102 Warwick Road,
Acocks Green, Birmingham, B27 6BH. United Kingdom

NO POSTAGE NECESSARY IF MAILED IN THE UNITED STATES

**BUSINESS REPLY MAIL**

FIRST CLASS MAIL PERMIT#64 CHICAGO, IL

POSTAGE WILL BE PAID BY ADDRESSEE

WROX PRESS
29 S. LaSalle Street
SUITE 520
CHICAGO IL 60603